MASTERPLOTS II

POETRY SERIES
REVISED EDITION

MASTERPLOTS II

POETRY SERIES
REVISED EDITION

2

Briggflatts–Dreams of the Animals

Editor, Revised Edition
PHILIP K. JASON

Project Editor, Revised Edition
TRACY IRONS-GEORGES

Editors, Supplement
JOHN WILSON   **PHILIP K. JASON**

Editor, First Edition
FRANK N. MAGILL

SALEM PRESS

Pasadena, California   Hackensack, New Jersey

Editor in Chief: Dawn P. Dawson
Project Editor: Tracy Irons-Georges   *Research Supervisor:* Jeffry Jensen
Production Editor: Cynthia Beres   *Research Assistant:* Jeff Stephens
Copy Editor: Lauren Mitchell   *Acquisitions Editor:* Mark Rehn

Some of the essays in this work originally appeared in *Masterplots II, Poetry Series*, edited by Frank N. Magill (Pasadena, Calif.: Salem Press, Inc., 1992), and in *Masterplots II, Poetry Series Supplement*, edited by John Wilson and Philip K. Jason (Pasadena, Calif.: Salem Press, Inc., 1998).

∞ The paper used in these volumes conforms to the American National Standard for Permanence of Paper for Printed Library Materials, Z39.48-1992 (R1997).

Library of Congress Cataloging-in-Publication Data
Masterplots II. Poetry series.— Rev. ed. / editor, Philip K. Jason ; project editor, Tracy Irons-Georges
   p. ; cm.
  Rev. ed.: Masterplots two / Frank Northen Magill, 1992-1998.
  Includes bibliographical references and indexes.
  ISBN 1-58765-037-1 (set : alk. paper) — ISBN 1-58765-039-8 (vol. 2 : alk. paper) —
  1. Poetry — Themes, motives. I. Title: Masterplots two. II. Title: Masterplots 2. III. Jason, Philip K., 1941-   . IV. Irons-Georges, Tracy.

PN1110.5 .M37 2002
809.1—dc21

                      2001055059

First Printing

PRINTED IN THE UNITED STATES OF AMERICA

TABLE OF CONTENTS

TABLE OF CONTENTS

TABLE OF CONTENTS

MASTERPLOTS II

POETRY SERIES
REVISED EDITION

BRIGGFLATTS

Author: Basil Bunting (1900-1985)
Type of poem: Poetic sequence
First published: 1966

The Poem

   Briggflatts is a five-part poem of nearly seven hundred lines combining a celebration of the Northumbrian landscape of England with the poet's meditations on history, aesthetic reality, language, and his own participation in the events and incidents that give the poem its substance and emotional qualities. The title recalls the Quaker meeting house where Basil Bunting, as a young man, first experienced the illuminative insights that he came to believe were at the core of poetic possibility. The five-part structure of the poem is based on the sonata form of exposition/development and recapitulation that Bunting employs in each section and as an overarching frame for the entire work. Using sequences of action drawn imaginatively from personal experience and various mythologies, Bunting has composed a kind of "autobiography of feeling" that attempts to reconcile the poet's instinctive desire for adventurous mobility with his reflective recognition that some kind of home base is necessary to ground and organize the multiple images of a life's course.

   The poem begins as an echo of the traditional epic invocation to the gods or Muses, commanding (in this case) the spirit of the West Yorkshire fields, a "sweet tenor bull," to "Brag"—that is, to boast, or announce—the exuberant arrival of the spring season with its promise of passion and fertility. "Descant on Rawthey's madrigal," the poet continues, directing the song of the bull as a counterpoint to the melody of the river Rawthey and as a discourse upon the features of the land itself. This is the place where the poem begins and where the life of the poet who speaks—the narrative consciousness revealing itself as the poem progresses—begins to come into focus. As Herbert Read, a trenchant advocate for unconventional poetry, has pointed out, the poem operates as a series of impressions "recovered and evaluated," and the first section introduces the poet as a young man with a maid, a reprise of figures from classical ballads reaching into Anglo-Saxon antiquity who resonate with the sensual music of the earth coming into bloom.

   One of the ordering devices for the entire poem is an ongoing interchange between "then" and "now" as the poet's reflective intelligence shifts from a re-creation or recollection of action to a meditation on its ramifications through time. This pattern of transition is established initially in terms of a rock mason—the maid's father—who carves memorial words into stone, thus embedding ephemeral language into a more permanent medium. The mason is an emblem of the poet as craftsman, and his grave task sets up a counterpoint to the timeless present of the youth's intense moment. His work casts an ominous shadow of temporality and degeneration over the sexual union of the young people, and, as the first section concludes, the "sweet tenor" voice of the bull has been transformed into mere flesh ("the bull is beef"), love has been "murdered," and, accurately or not, the poet accepts blame for the loss. He recognizes that there is "No hope of going back" to an initial state of innocence and that a path for the rest of his life's journey has been opened, a journey launched with no destination in sight.

The guilt and even grief that the poet carries infects the wider world he enters as the second section begins. Surrounded by a debased society of "toadies, confidence men, kept boys," where he wanders aimlessly, "jailed, cleaned out by whores," the poet turns to the sea in a time-tested tactic for finding new horizons. There, he is transported not only away from the sordid urban wasteland but also further into a timeless realm that Bunting evokes by describing the ocean with the rhythms of old English alliterative verse: "Who sang, sea takes,/ brawn brine, bone grit./ Keener the kittiwake./ Fells forget him./ Fathoms dull the dale,/ gulfweed voices." Among other ports of call, the poet visits the Italian peninsula, and, in a series of crisp quatrains, Bunting calls forth the qualities of the landscape with a characteristic appeal to the senses: "It tastes good," "It sounds right," "It feels soft," and "It looks well" before adding "but never/ well enough." The seafarer has not been able to escape from himself, so the "wind, sun, sea upbraid/ justly an unconvinced deserter." The defect of character that the poet takes with him is explored in a kind of reverie on the violent death of the ninth century Norwegian king Eric Bloodaxe, who ruled Northumbria for a time and died (according to legend) at the battle of Stainmore. The king is offered as an allegorical parallel for the poet, his voyages to the British Isles depicted in terse, skaldic verses ("Scurvy gnaws, steading smell, hearth's crackle"), his downfall, at least partially, a result of his moral failure. Judgment is withheld, however, as the section closes with the poet making further inquiries: "But who will entune a bogged orchard,/ its blossom gone,/ fruit unformed, where hunger and/ damp hush the hive?" His queries are framed in terms of the natural world, recalling the springtime in Northumbria and suggesting that the summer of the second section is held in suspension while additional data is accumulated. This is preparation for the "hell-canto" of section 3, the center of the poem, a "different thing" that Bunting labeled "a nightmare or dream or whatever you fancy." Among other things, it is a version of the archetypal "Dark Night of the Soul" in which the innermost truth of being is (or can be) revealed.

In accordance with his plan to find semiautobiographical analogues for the poet's journey, Bunting uses the story of Alexander the Great's quest for wisdom, which he took from the Persian poet Firdusi's *Shahnamah* (c. 1010), as his model. In ninety-five lines dense with images of a vile and repugnant realm, the explorer climbs toward a mountain vision. Then, in a transformative dream, the nightmare world is replaced by a scene in which, as Bunting biographer Victoria Forde puts it, the poet is "delighted by the beauty and variety of nature which cleanses and renews." The surge of a beneficent life force suggests the possibility of living in harmony with the natural world: "Sycamore seed twirling,/ O, writhe to its measure!/ Dust swirling trims pleasure./ Thorns prance in a gale./ In air snow flickers,/ twigs tap,/ elms drip."

The fourth section, which was listed as "Autumn" in Bunting's original diagram, contains the ripening of this realization. To objectify it, Bunting uses the ancient Welsh poets Aneurin and Taliesin ("Clear Cymric voices," *cymru* being the Welsh-language name for Wales) as points of departure for a series of tales that encourage an acceptance of the landscape the poet left and to which he now returns. In the center of the section, the poet recalls, with poignant regret, the woman whose love he betrayed. His apostrophe to her ("My love is young but wise. Oak, applewood,/ her fire is banked with ashes till day./ The fells reek of her hearth's scent") is built on earthly images, and its tone of appreciation signals his readiness to reconcile his wanderlust with a fuller understanding of the value in his native ground. Impediments remain, however, as the poet still must overcome some psychic hurdle before he can rest content with his choices.

The fifth section is clearly set in a wintry vista: "Solstice past,/ years end crescendo," it declares, "Winter wrings pigment/ from petal and slough." There is a strong contrast with the verdant spring of the first part, but the winter landscape is alive with beauty since the poet/artist is able to see beyond the somewhat deceptive appeal of sheer sexual youth into a season of more subtle satisfactions. Pioneering British cultural commentator Eric Mottram calls this "a magnificently sustained pleasure in the particularities of music, sea-shore, the fells, and fishing boats on the water at night." The lyrical surge of these lines is Bunting's method for creating an ethos of awe that permits the joining of "Then is Now," his formulation for the fusion of the fading past and the ongoing present. When he states, near the poem's close, "She has been with me fifty years" in a line separated from the preceding and following lines, he is acknowledging his losses, but he is also accepting the inevitability of his wandering ("A strong song tows/ us") as the burden of his poetic insight. As he states in the beginning of section 2, "Poet appointed dare not decline." Now he is prepared to return to his community, the Quaker meeting place Briggflatts, and offer the poem as a summation of his life experiences. As Bunting told American poet and publisher Jonathan Williams, "My autobiography is *Briggflatts*," and the poem is a way of settling his debt to those he may have unwittingly hurt, including himself. The coda that follows the fifth section is appropriately open-ended, affirming the power of poetry to provide consolation for the trials of existence while continuing to question the meaning of all things: "Who,/ swinging his axe/ to fell kings, guesses/ where we go?"

Forms and Devices

Bunting, who wrote music criticism for *Outlook* and the *Musical Times* during the 1920's, regarded sound as the crucial core of all poetic expression. In a characteristic statement, he proclaimed, "Poetry, like music, is to be heard. It deals in sound. . . . Poetry lies dead on the page, until some voice brings it to life." His preparation for *Briggflatts* included not only a structural pattern based on the sonata but also a specific linking with sonatas by Italian composer Domenico Scarlatti. In a record he made of the poem, he placed selected Scarlatti sonatas before and after each part to emphasize the musical mood. Beyond this, Bunting suggested that an ideal reading would be in the voice of an inhabitant of the Northumbrian region of the British Isles so that the precise sound he had in mind would be accurately rendered. The epigraph he used for the entire poem, "The spuggies are fledged" (itself a translation from a thirteenth century life of Alexander the Great), must be spoken with a hard *g* in "spuggies," typical of what poet Donald Davie calls the "exceptionally tender care for its acoustic values" that Bunting brought to every syllable of the poem.

The sonic subtlety of Bunting's writing is a function of language and form. Bunting has fashioned, with intricate detail and exceptional invention, a demonstration of how musical principles can be applied to poetic form. Examples include the balance of the twelve thirteen-line stanzas in part 1; the accumulated pressure of the repetitive quatrains ("It tastes," "It sounds," "It feels," "It looks") in part 2; the ninety-five lines of dense, compressed descriptive detail of Alexander's ascent in part 3; the turn to the immediate and personal narrative ("I hear Aneurin," "I see Aneurin's pectoral muscle," "Where rats go go I") in part 4; and, as an epitome, the melding of word-sound and word-meaning in the evocation of the winter landscape in part 5. When he refers to "Rawthey's madrigal" at the start, he is establishing a musical style that interweaves numerous voices so that *Briggflatts* can contain examples of lyrical love poetry, elegiac recapitulation of heroic figures from antiquity, laments for various losses, caustic satiric dismissals of the ills of the modern world, numerous vividly descriptive passages that bring the locales of the poem to life, and extended narratives in the Bardic tradition that bring compelling tales of historical relevance to the poem's purpose. His success in unifying what are generally regarded as distinct subgenres depends on the extremely elaborate interlinkages of sound ("rich rhyming and chiming" in poet and literary theorist Charles Tomlinson's application of a phrase from nineteenth century English art critic and writer John Ruskin) that assume not only a skilled reader but also a very committed, attentive listener. The elemental coherence of the poem, however, depends not only on Bunting's extremely painstaking arrangement of sound patterns but also on the emerging narrative consciousness of the poet who is speaking. This is the mechanism that joins the poem's form to its essential themes, the evolving melodic strain around which Bunting's variations and inventions are played and into which they eventually coalesce.

Themes and Meanings

Briggflatts is a poem of departure and return, both in the musical sense and in terms of the poem's architecture. It includes more than five decades in the life of the poet and is structured as a journey from home ground into the world and then back to the poet's origins. The wide range of events and locales that it covers is ordered by the development of the distinctive sensibility of the poet. This central "character" is eager for experience, fascinated by phenomena, determined to confront moral conundrums, in love with learning, and deeply affected by his feeling for the countryside of his birth. He takes, as his task, the reconstruction of the crucial incidents of his formation as an artist and, in accordance with this goal, accepts the challenge of assessing the moral dimensions of the choices he made during that process.

To accomplish this, Bunting likens a person's life course to the progression of the seasons—a familiar and resonant comparison—calling spring a time of "Love and be-trayal," summer a period in which there is "no rest from ambition," autumn a season for "reflexion," and winter (or "Old age") the time when one "can see at last the loveli-ness of things overlooked." Throughout, there is an awareness of mortality, and the semiserenity of the poem's close is more a matter of a willingness to accept the ongo-ing mysteries of existence as a source of wonder and contemplative delight than any kind of answer to cosmic questions. The wild exuberance of the "sweet tenor bull" in the poem's first passages is eventually and gradually modified into the placidity of the "slowworm," Bunting's symbol for both the return of all living things to the soil and the renewal of the life force in the earth. In part 5, the Northumbrian landscape is cele-brated as if from within: Close to the earth, as if from the slowworm's furrow,

> The ewes are heavy with lamb.
> Snow lies bright on Hedgehope
> and tacky mud about Till
> where the fells have stepped aside
> and the river praises itself,
>
> . . . .
> Light lifts from the water.
> Frost has put rowan down,
> a russet blotch of bracken
> tousled about the trunk.

The distance from the bull in part 1, dancing on tiptoe, "ridiculous and lovely," chas-ing "hurdling shadows" but so consumed with its own energy that it cannot see the depth or totality of the land's richness, is a measure of the growth of the poet's mind. The transformation of language from words chiseled in stone that describe the cold sea to the song of harp and flute and the illuminations of starlight at the end of part 5 signifies the emotional fulfillment of the poet's heart. He has earned the right to live in Briggflatts—the special place where the Quaker community can speak to the spirit of God, the Creator of all things.

Leon Lewis

BROKEN BOAT

Author: Du Fu (712-770)
Type of poem: Lyric/meditation
First published: wr. c. 764, as "Po quan"; collected in *Zhuan Tang Shi*, early eighteenth century; English translation collected in *Travels of a Chinese Poet*, 1934

The Poem

In 757, Du Fu angered Emperor Su-tsung and was demoted to a minor position away from the capital. Widespread unrest and famine soon forced him to give up the post and travel in search of a livelihood. In 760, he managed to settle down in a "straw cottage" on the western suburbs of Ch'eng-tu (in Sichuan). The Straw Cottage became the focal point of interest in his poetry thereafter. Unfortunately, in 762, the uprising of Ch'eng-tu's Vice Prefect Hsü Chih-tao caused him to flee again. In 764, after turning down an offer of a minor position in the capital, Du Fu returned to the Straw Cottage. A year had scarcely passed when Yen Wu, a military friend, recommended him to serve under the Council of Military Advisors. He accepted and took office in the city of Ch'eng-tu. Soon, however, he gave up the post and returned to the Straw Cottage, where he stayed until 766. "Broken Boat" was probably written in 764 upon his first return. As the poem begins, the poet states that all his life he has had "a heart for rivers and lakes" and that he was early equipped with a tiny boat, which was not meant merely for cruising along the stream and traveling in the vicinity of his modest abode. The implication here is that the poet has had lofty aspirations but has always been frustrated. For example, he had to flee in haste from the horrendous revolt only recently. Even at a distance, however, he has longed for a return to the sanctuary that he cherishes as home. Written in the form of a couplet, lines 5 and 6 highlight the chaotic nature of Du Fu's times by accentuating his attachment to the Straw Cottage.

Upon his return, the poet discovers that his neighbors are gone and the place has been overgrown with wild bamboos. The boat itself, with "No one to rap its rim [while singing a song]," has sunk. The images of desolation in lines 7 and 8 carry the poignant hint that, in an age of turmoil and suffering, peace can be only a matter of nostalgia. The contrast between the past and present conditions of the homestead is so devastating that, in the couplet that follows, the nostalgia grows into an existential crisis:

> [I am] looking at the west-flying wings above;
> [I am] ashamed of the east-fleeting flow below.

The migration of the birds and the flow of the water seem to be the only constants in a world of tumultuous change. The spatio-temporal images here hint at a cosmic order that is not perturbed by human destiny. Such indifference renders one inconsequential and vulnerable. Feeling helpless and futile, the poet remarks that he is not saddened by the submerged boat—"The old one can perhaps be dug up;/ A new one is easy to be had" (lines 13 and 14)—but rather by the fact that, obliged to flee again and again, he cannot stay even in a humble house for long.

Forms and Devices

In the T'ang dynasty, poetry was written mainly in either the "recent" or the "ancient" style. All the lines in a recent-style poem follow a set pattern of tonal contrasts and harmonies. An ancient-style poem, however, does not have a predetermined length, and there is no rigid tonal arrangement. Because its format can be tailored to the needs of the poem itself, since it is free from prosodic constraints, the ancient style is an appropriate vehicle for narration and cursive expression.

T'ang poetry is also categorized according to whether each line has five or seven characters. The seven-character format is suitable for weighty and complex subjects because of its larger capacity and greater flexibility. The succinct five-character format, which has a longer tradition behind it, is ideal for essentialistic expression because the minimal language enhances a sense of immediacy through unadulterated concentration on thoughts and feelings.

"Broken Boat" is an ancient-style poem with sixteen five-character lines. Two important couplets are present in the poem.

The first couplet, which juxtaposes the hasty escape from the uprising (line 5) with the passionate yearning that materializes into the return visit (line 6), is characterized by a tension between the fragile order the poet once established and the disastrous disorder he has had to endure. This tension points up other tensions in the human condition: that between war and peace and that between the transience of tranquillity and the permanence of irremediable disruption.

The second couplet (lines 11 and 12), though deceptively simple, is meticulously constructed according to the principles of antithesis and incremental reinforcement. "Above" and "west" (line 11) are contrasted with "below" and "east" (line 12), but the directional antithesis also serves to underscore the insentient nature of the cosmic order exemplified by the migrating birds and the flowing water. The two lines are also incremental in emotional intensity—while line 11 describes an action (looking up at the birds), line 12 highlights a mental condition (feeling ashamed). In sum, this couplet dramatizes the poet's tragic sense of life by juxtaposing human nature in all its frailty with insensate Nature itself.

From a broader perspective, because its subject matter is a person returning home, "Broken Boat" also reminds one of "Returning to the Farm and the Fields to Stay," a poetic sequence by the recluse T'ao Ch'ien (365-427). One may even regard "Broken Boat" as a dialogue with *t'ien-yuan shih* (pastoral poetry). According to this genre, a rustic existence, which has pleasures of its own to offer, is definitely preferable to the anxieties and taboos of civil service. "Broken Boat" is both an outgrowth and an offshoot of this pastoral tradition. While Du Fu also tried to lead a private life, eulogizing it in the earlier, relatively complacent days of the Straw Cottage, this poem raises important questions about the validity and even possibility of security and serenity in rural life. Special circumstances in his times, it seems, have led him to write a poem that questions the validity of the pastoral genre itself.

Themes and Meanings

The poem begins with an allusion, in the phrase "a heart for rivers and lakes." The meaning of Du Fu's poem hinges on this phrase, which originally appears in the Taoist anthology *Chuang-tzu*. In a dialogue quoted in the essay "*Jang wang*" ("On Relinquishing the Throne"), a prince raises an existential question: "When a person's *body* is loitering about the rivers and lakes, and yet his *heart* is settled under the lofty portals [of the court], how does one handle this problem [of discrepancy]?" In other words, how can one reconcile the conflict between one's aspiration to be free (at the cost of deprivation) and one's desire to be a member of the court (at the cost of being free)? To this the interlocutor replies that one should regard life as more valuable than material gains. This dialogue sheds important light on the poem.

The allusion suggests primarily that Du Fu, like T'ao Ch'ien before him, may have eventually endorsed the Taoist position, feeling that the integrity of self is more precious than public life. The allusion does not, however, preclude the possibility that in Du Fu's case the Taoist position can still be accompanied by a desire to contribute to the well-being of the state. Does Du Fu, a diehard patriot, not wish to be doing something better? Has he, practically a refugee and vagrant, not had enough wandering? Because both conditions are sadly true, it would seem that in cataclysmic times the aspiration to be free and the desire to have a part to play are not meant to exclude each other but rather to be interwoven into an irresolvable conflict.

In the final analysis, the predicament of irreconciliation arises because a choice between aspiration and desire does not exist. Indeed, the absence of choice is the major theme of "Broken Boat," and it begins to develop after the opening allusion. The poet has chosen a home, but numerous social upheavals have rendered that choice null and void. A similar destiny also affects his neighbors (line 7). A boat would have kept him free at least in principle, but not even this option is left open. The realization that he is living through a social tragedy makes the poet conclude that his grief is not over a broken boat, but rather the perpetual condition of homelessness.

The boat can indeed be regarded as a thematic symbol of this homelessness. The east-flowing river may have put the poet to shame because of the factual vagabondage rather than the metaphysical liberation it symbolizes. Indeed, "Broken Boat" is emblematic of the last decade or so of Du Fu's life and career. Spending a large part of this period traveling by boat not in order to feel free but to take refuge, he wrote the last line of his poetry on the deck of a boat, which is also the place where he breathed the last breath of his life.

Balance Chow

THE BROKEN HOME

Author: James Merrill (1926-1995)
Type of poem: Poetic sequence
First published: 1965; collected in *Nights and Days*, 1966

The Poem

"The Broken Home" is a sequence of seven sonnets that are connected by imagery and themes, yet each is formally and narratively self-contained. The title refers to the poem's autobiographical subjects—the divorce of James Merrill's parents and his concern for the brokenness or incompleteness of his own childlessness.

The first sonnet begins with the poet outside, watching parents and a child framed by a window—a tableau he contrasts with his own "Sunless, cooler" room below. Thoughts of his childless ("Sunless") existence as a poet for whom "The flame quickens" and "The word stirs" prompt him to ask his "tongue of fire" (either his muse or his homosexual lover) whether "you and I are as real/ At least as the people upstairs."

The second sonnet focuses on the adult life of his father, Charles Merrill, founder of the brokerage firm Merrill Lynch, Pierce, Fenner and Smith. In the first two quatrains, Merrill discovers in his father the soul of a visionary "eclipsed" by a desire for business and sex that drove him to warm "up for a green bride" every thirteen years. "Too late now" the poet realizes that, as he did, his father could have "invested" in "cloud banks well above Wall Street and wife."

The third sonnet provides a historical backdrop for the particular breakdown of the marriage of the poet's parents. Merrill describes a set scene from the 1920's in which a veiled suffragette in "hobble skirt" attacks a famous man in a public place with insults: *"War mongerer! Pig! Give us the vote!"*

In the fourth and fifth sonnets, Merrill moves from outside, where at the poem's beginning he watched the idealized family "gleaming like fruit/ With evening's mild gold leaf," to inside the window to probe the harsh realities of two particular memories from his own childhood. The fourth sonnet presents an oedipal scene in which the young boy is led by his Irish setter to enter the bedroom of a sleeping woman—apparently his mother, "clad in taboos"—who awakens from a deathlike sleep to terrify dog and boy. Thinly veiled sexual images allow Merrill to explore troubling aspects of his own sexuality. In describing the bedroom that "throbbed like a bruise," Merrill creates an oedipal pun about "Blinds that beat sun from the bed." The phallic Irish setter Michael, "satyr-thighed" with "head/ Passionately lowered," penetrates the closed door but "slumps" "to the floor" at the possibility of a heterosexual encounter.

In the fifth sonnet of "The Broken Home," Merrill remembers overhearing his parents (who "love each other still") discussing their frenzied lifestyle outside his window after a party. The lead soldier guarding the boy's windowsill in the octave introduces a cluster of images the poet uses in the sestet to describe the gradual cooling of his parents' feelings, which were once intense "Like metal poured at the close of a proletarian novel,/ Refined and glowing from the crucible."

The sixth sonnet again focuses on the present status of Merrill as childless poet with which "The Broken Home" begins. In addition to defending his childlessness, this section of the poem introduces Merrill's justification for breaking with the examples of his parents by refusing to be political and rejecting a traditional family for himself. This sonnet also provides Merrill's rationale for his particular poetics by asserting the validity of the artifice of his apolitical poems—those rare avocados "gemmed with air" with "small gilt leaves."

The octave of the final sonnet presents Merrill's memories as a house in which "A child, a red dog roam the corridors,/ Still." The sestet describes the "real house" that Merrill's family occupied, which is now converted into a boarding school from which another child can watch a setting sun without the "stiflement" of the nightmares "The Broken Home" describes.

Forms and Devices

Throughout "The Broken Home," Merrill "confesses" through the "unstiflement" of his poetry his anxiety about his childlessness, his sadness over the rift in his family, and his discomfort over his strained relationships with his mother and father. Yet in the seventh sonnet, Merrill makes it clear that he is no "confessional" poet by carefully setting himself apart from those poets who, like Edgar in William Shakespeare's *King Lear* (c. 1605), expose their nakedness and madness to the elements, "Who on the heath impersonate Poor Tom/ Or on the barricades risk life and limb."

In "Broken Home," Merrill masks the painful issues he probes through his favorite device of wordplay. For example, in the second sonnet, he develops witty puns associated with his father—"had flown in World War I," "cloud banks," and "chilled wives/ In sable orbit—rings, cars, permanent waves"—to distract himself and the reader from the painful subject at hand (the philandering father's abandonment of Merrill's mother).

Merrill also uses puns and homophones to create multiple levels of meaning that operate simultaneously with the more obvious literal meaning often disguising more sensitive and volatile subjects. For example, he disguises his concerns for his own childlessness within his puns on his "Sunless, cooler" room in the first sonnet and "small gilt leaves" in the sixth sonnet (suggesting "guilt" over childlessness and homosexuality as well as "gold leaf" artifice). In the fourth sonnet, Merrill uses the homophones "satyr" and "setter" and the pun on "sun" in "Blinds beat sun from the bed" to mask his fairly explicit attempt to come to terms with his oedipal relationship with his mother.

The most significant pun in "The Broken Home," however, occurs in the final lines of the poem as the house is exorcised and Merrill himself gains relief from his confessions. Merrill develops puns on "cool," "story," and "setter" as he concludes that in the converted boarding school, "Someone at last" may "cool/ With the unstiflement of the entire story,/ Watch a red setter stretch and sink in cloud." On one level, the poet suggests that the house's new inhabitant may be able to watch a sunset cooled by the open window and the departure of Merrill's haunted family. At the same time, Merrill seems to be "Someone" who, having purged himself of "the entire story" of "broken home," can now with cool detachment watch the memories of the Irish setter (and its sexual baggage) disappear into his imagination.

Themes and Meanings

A central theme of "The Broken Home," as the title suggests, is the disintegration of a marriage. As he observes the "gold leaf" tableau of the ideal unbroken family in the first lines of the poem, Merrill is led to attempt to discover reasons for the breakup of his parents' marriage. In each of the next four sonnets, he explores potential explanations for his broken home: his father's being too absorbed in "sex/ And business," the conflict between the roles of men and women, the ghastliness of a mother-turned-corpse, his parents' indulgence in the aristocratic frenzy of the 1920's. By the end of the fifth sonnet, however, Merrill has no explanation, no certainties, and is forced to bury without judgment both mother and father and their once-glowing hearts "Cool here in the graveyard of good and evil."

A perhaps less obvious although no less important theme in "Broken Home" is childlessness. Just as the opening family tableau reminds Merrill of his parents' divorce, so it also contrasts with his childless life of art and homosexuality in the "room on the floor below." As he did with his parents' failed marriage, Merrill attempts to find explanations for his own choices in the sonnets that follow: a lack of connection with his father; his oedipal relationship with his mother; something in him growing "heavy, silver, pliable" as he observes his parents' deteriorating relationship; his reaction against his parents' world.

Once again left with no clear explanations for the phenomenon that troubles him, Merrill turns in the sestet of the sixth sonnet to look tenderly at the "offspring" he does produce—his poems. While in his poem "Childlessness" Merrill refers to his life as a garden in which "Nothing's been seeded," in "The Broken Home" he announces that he does not "try to keep a garden." Instead, he presents his poetry writing as another, more artificial form of gardening: the "rooting" in water of an exotic avocado "gemmed with air." He recognizes that his "offspring" poems—his "small gilt leaves"—are only provisional artifacts that grow "Fleshy and green." He knows he must again and again probe his past in an attempt to transform his painful memories into jeweled poems: "I let them die, yes, yes,/ And start another." When Merrill sadly concludes, "I am earth's no less," he means that he is no less a part of earth's fertility cycle than "the people upstairs" and also that producing his gilded "children" will neither assure his immortality nor prevent his death.

Janice Moore Fuller

THE BROKEN TOWER

Author: Hart Crane (1899-1932)
Type of poem: Lyric
First published: 1932; collected in *The Collected Poems of Hart Crane*, 1933

The Poem

"The Broken Tower" was the last poem that Hart Crane composed before committing suicide in 1932, and the poem does indeed have the eerie quality of a poetic last will and testament. Crane suffered from a chronic bent toward self-destructiveness, however, and much of his poetry explored the processes, purpose, and frustrations of the poetic sensibility confronting raw experience head-on in highly charged verbal arenas.

"The Broken Tower," whose title connotes a shattered or fractured vision, is composed in ten stanzas, each a perfect quatrain. In the very opening verse, the reader is asked to envision a bell tower and to hear the bells ringing at dawn; the speaker, however, is not in tune with these uplifting images. Rather, he has "dropped down the knell/ Of a spent day," his feet "chill on steps from hell."

The poem's central idea centers on this initial contrast between the power to make sounds that bespeak the godhead and the earthbound, or worse, condition of the maker of such sounds, who feels miserable in his inadequacy to write a poetry equal to his vision (the bells) and yet equally compelled to continue: "And I, their sexton slave!" The speaker engages the reader in his travail by the use of direct address: "Have you not heard, have you not seen . . . ?" While he has toiled and has in fact heard, it has been only from this worldly and imperfect end. The bells sound, but their source eludes him; the resulting poetry has become "my long-scattered score/ Of broken intervals."

After an intervening stanza rhapsodizing the power of that godly music that he has only imperfectly approximated in verse, the poet abandons the self-critical, confessional tone with which the poem opened in favor of an apologia. For if he entered the "broken world," it was only in an effort to "trace the visionary company of love." His aim was not wrong; the problem was, and is, that this sort of insubstantial vision does not linger long enough for anyone to limn its features. "Its voice/ An instant in the wind," there is not time enough "to hold each desperate choice." The poet questions whether the words which he "poured . . . [were] cognate, scored" of the Word Itself or were, instead, though "pledged to hope—cleft to despair." Was it, in other words, nothing more than self-deception?

The speaker admits that there is no answer, unless it is "she/ Whose sweet mortality stirs latent power." The surprise introduction of a beloved this late in the poem (the seventh stanza) may seem odd unless one realizes that the speaker has taken a necessary third step in his growth away from despair and toward acceptance. He abandons the solitude of the visionary quest and of self-critical evaluation in favor of a sharing of himself through physical union with a fellow, flawed creature like himself.

The new commitment made, the two lovers'—or at least sexual partners'—fleshly mortality evokes, through their heartbeats, an "angelus of wars" in his chest. It is from a different source, but it is no less music. He no longer needs to hear the sound of the mystical bells; he accepts himself and others as a part of the sound that the godhead makes. As his sights have been lowered to a wholly earthly level, so, too, the tower is itself internalized and, realized in his flesh, healed as it transforms finally into the male erection that, in the act of coitus, "Unseals her earth"; in the rhythms of the orgasmic climax, it "lifts love in its shower." What the speaker could not invoke, he evokes; what he could not bring down, he raises; what he could not repair, he reconstructs.

Forms and Devices

Though it is very much a twentieth century poem composed in the spirit of literary modernism, "The Broken Tower" utilizes a complex metaphorical technique that harks back to the so-called English Metaphysical poetry of the seventeenth century composed by poets such as John Donne and Andrew Marvell.

The conceit or extended metaphor is the foundation of such poetry. As the eighteenth century English critic Samuel Johnson once put it in rather disparaging terms, it is yoking two disparate things violently together; it is a farfetched comparison that, on balance and further consideration, actually does have the ring of truth. The twentieth century poet and critic T. S. Eliot was among the first to observe that Metaphysical poetry was actually a sort of precursor of the modern imagination, with its quest for up-to-date, startlingly fresh imagery within traditional themes and forms.

"The Broken Tower" is ostensibly relating a quasi-religious experience, but while biographical data suggests that the poem was inspired by Crane's attending a religious festival in Mexico while on a Guggenheim Fellowship in that country, one does both Crane and the poem an injustice if one fails to see that, in any real terms, religion has very little to do with it. The poem is structured around an extended metaphor for the visionary quest and the perils and frustrations that generally attend such a tenuous exercise. That metaphor is so layered and textured that it becomes the visionary quest itself, the striving to give voice to the inarticulate, and the effort to find entry into the spiritual through contact with another's flesh.

Without diminishing the validity of any of those readings, the poem ultimately comments on the creative process as an individual endeavor. The speaker/poet is first a sexton ringing bells he cannot see and can barely hear; then he is an acolyte hoping that his offerings might be found worthy by his God; and finally he is a lover who approaches the object of his passion as if she were herself a religious icon. That extended metaphor in each instance works best when its final reading is rendered wholly in terms of a poet trying to master the very substance, and duality, of his material: the word as it evokes the world.

Crane wishes to foster those other readings as well, however, so he subtly blends musical and religious terminology and references—"cathedral," "crucifix," "antiphonal carillons," "sexton," "encyclicals," "score," "intervals," and "angelus"—thus making the experience of the poem a richer one than if he had spoken only in terms of poems and verses, similes and metaphors, words and images. He is also able to glide from the ideal to the real by slipping through a virtually explicit description of male sexual arousal and penetration of the female without diminishing the spiritual tone of the verse or suggesting any less profound an intention.

Themes and Meanings

The image of the tower is the most outstanding signal of the poem's central theme. True, one can argue that it is indeed a bell tower. The Tower of Babel comes to mind as well; but when a poet talks about a tower, he invites his reader to think of the fabled ivory tower wherein he finds his necessary isolation and elevated point of view from which to contemplate and comment on the human condition.

Yet this is a "broken" tower. One cannot avoid the further implication that this poet believes that he has somehow lost his vision, perhaps even his talent. It is known, for example, that Crane did spend much of his Guggenheim grant in Mexico involved in alcoholic binges and other debaucheries, and he was much depressed by the relatively poor reception that his major poem, *The Bridge* (1930), had received.

The speaker/poet first carries on an argument with his readers. Life is hell, he tells them, and all humans are imperfect, limited creations. It is impossible to bring back from the edges of hope and despair words and images that will ring true. Then he finds the courage to admit that he nevertheless has tried to serve a cause larger than self, the cause of human love and enlightenment.

Finally, as if it were himself that he was arguing with and trying to assuage, he remembers that life after all is for the living, as is love. Where he had felt defeated, he now sees that transcendence unmindful of the human element is an empty triumph. Thus it is in another's embrace that he finds the proper expression of all the joy and all the meaning he has been seeking. The poem ends on the powerfully liberating insight that one has within oneself a creative force quite capable, if need be, of creating love where there had been nothing before.

Russell Elliott Murphy

BUCKDANCER'S CHOICE

Author: James Dickey (1923-1997)
Type of poem: Lyric
First published: 1965, in *Buckdancer's Choice*

The Poem

"Buckdancer's Choice" is a short poem written in an anapestic meter. The poem's narrator recalls that during his childhood, he would listen to his invalid mother whistle a song, which he now realizes represented the last assertions of her will and life force as she faced death. To highlight the human refusal to give in to death, the narrator develops an analogy between his mother's whistling and the dance of the buck-and-wing men who performed in minstrel shows.

The poem begins with the narrator remembering how his bedridden mother would "split" the air into "nine levels," as she continually whistled endless variations of the same song, "Buckdancer's Choice." The song originates from traveling minstrel shows, which were once popular but have almost died out since. Like the old minstrel shows, the narrator's mother is nearing the point when she will no longer exist. Though the disease from which she suffers affects her breathing by stripping the air from her lungs, the dying woman continues to whistle. Her whistling makes a profound impression on her son, who recalls creeping up to the closed door of her bedroom and intently listening to the countless versions of "Buckdancer's Choice" she could create. The narrator realizes that through her whistling, his mother was "Proclaiming what choices there are/ For the last dancers of their kind." In other words, he comes to see that she was doing the only thing she could in order to show that she was still alive and not ready to give in to death. Though his mother was not conscious of his listening to her whistling, the song makes the narrator aware of the power of the human will to survive. This realization culminates in the narrator imagining that such efforts in the face of death possess an almost magical or transcendental dimension.

Forms and Devices

James Dickey uses anapestic meter in "Buckdancer's Choice," giving the poem a strong rhythmic quality. Anapestic meter consists of three syllables, with two unaccented syllables followed by an accented one. The anapest's strong melodic quality is especially appropriate for a poem that involves music.

Dickey uses point of view both to relate how the child is drawn to his mother's whistling and to make a sophisticated assessment of the whistling's significance. The poem is narrated by an individual who recalls that as a child he would listen to his mother whistle. This perspective lets the narrator reflect and comment on the importance of this occurrence, and allows him to suggest how as a child he was almost magically attracted to the song, which related a message whose significance would not be clear until years later.

The use of an older and more experienced narrator also allows Dickey to develop convincingly the poem's central metaphor, which likens the mother's whistling to former slaves' performances in minstrel shows. The mother continues to whistle to herself, just as the minstrel show performers continue their acts despite the fact that their audience has practically disappeared. As the poem progresses, the narrator develops this metaphor, imagining the minstrel-show performers dancing to his mother's whistling; finally, he draws an analogy between his mother, the performers, and all of humanity. The music his mother makes and the performances of the ex-slaves become reflective of the human need to express emotion and live, even if no one else fully appreciates the value of that effort. Dickey's mature narrator is able to look back through time and develop the full implications of the analogy in a manner that he could not articulate or completely comprehend as a child.

Themes and Meanings

Like many of Dickey's poems, "Buckdancer's Choice" addresses the theme of the human will to exist when confronted with the inevitability of death. By comparing the narrator's mother to ex-slaves who continued to express themselves through their songs even as the minstrel-show tradition was nearing extinction, Dickey affirms the human will to celebrate life and shows how displays of the will to live provide people with a vital message.

In the final stanza, the narrator describes his mother's ability to whistle as a "gift of tongues." This description suggests the profound communication the mother's song holds for the listening child. A person who possesses the ability to speak in tongues is often regarded as a conduit who relays some essential message that emanates from a supernatural source. Similarly, the mother's message is not conveyed directly to the child but through a medium, the ex-slaves' song. Moreover, the mother whistles to herself and is not conscious of the child's presence, but the whistling enables the boy to gain greater insight into his mother's plight and, more generally, into the process of life and death.

The mother's whistling is also characterized as "The thousand variations of one song," with each variation symbolizing another continuing effort to ward off death by asserting her existence. Since her illness confines her to bed, her whistling becomes a way to declare that she is still in this world and not ready to give it up. Indeed, her whistling becomes a heroic act, something she continues to do despite the fact that she must battle "breathless angina."

Listening to the song conjures an image in the child's mind of a freed black who, "with cymbals at heel," forms a "one-man band" that dances to his mother's song. The narrator imagines that the buck-and-wing men's dance, in which the dancers flap their elbows, is an attempt to fly, to transcend the human and escape death. Like his mother's whistling, the dance becomes symbolic of the desire to live. This image is central to the poem because through it, the narrator expresses that seemingly trivial acts such as whistling or dancing can become deeply significant: Through them, people may be "Proclaiming what choices there are/ For the last dancers of their kind." A key word here, one that is echoed in the poem's title, is "choice." Having choice suggests that individuals retain some power of volition, some means to express themselves; it is a declaration that though their existence and autonomy may be slipping away, they can continue to fight for whatever life they still possess.

In the final three stanzas, the narrator widens the poem's frame of reference. Instead of referring to his dying mother, he speaks of "women"; instead of referring to his childhood, he speaks of "children." This broadening generalizes the significance of the exchange between the particular mother and child described in the poem to include all of humanity, for, as the poem declares, all are "slaves of death." The poem concludes with an image of "children enchanted at walls," listening to the song and imagining the dance. The children are "not dancing but nearly risen." The words "enchanting" and "risen" imply that the connection the song creates between people is magical, a revelation of the human spirit's insatiable appetite for life and significance. Though the word "nearly" modifies this optimistic vision, suggesting the impossibility of such a dream, what remains of uttermost importance is the human will to resist death, even if such an endeavor is inevitably futile.

Ernest Suarez

BUDDHA IN GLORY

Author: Rainer Maria Rilke (1875-1926)
Type of poem: Lyric
First published: 1908, "Buddha in der Glorie," in *Der neuen Gedichte anderer Teil*;
English translation collected in *Rainer Maria Rilke: Fifty Selected Poems*, 1940

The Poem

"Buddha in Glory" (or as one translator titles it, "The Buddha in the Glory") is a short poem of twelve lines divided into three stanzas of four lines each. The original poem is predominantly in trochaic meter (with alternating stressed and unstressed final syllables in each line); it begins in trochaic pentameter and ends in trochaic tetrameter. The original German rhymes *abab, cdcd, efef.*

The poem's title calls up visions of Eastern religion, mysticism, and meditation on the right path to Nirvana or salvation. Buddhism is a religion of eastern and central Asia that developed from the teachings of Gautama Buddha. The name Buddha is Sanskrit for "the enlightened"; the goal of the Buddhist is to arrive at a state of perfect spiritual fulfillment. This mental and moral self-purification is said to free one from the suffering that is inherent in life.

While Rilke undoubtedly had this religious history in mind as he wrote the poem in Paris in the summer of 1908, he was also probably working from a particular statue of Buddha that was located in the garden of the French sculptor Auguste Rodin, to whom Rilke was personal secretary for several years. Rilke described this sculpture in a letter to his wife Clara on September 20, 1905:

> Then the huge blossoming starry night is before me, and below, in front of the window, the gravel path goes up a little hill on which, in fanatic silence, a statue of Buddha rests, dispensing, with quiet discretion, the unutterable self-containedness of his gesture under all the skies of day and night. C'est le centre du monde [It is the center of the world], I said to Rodin.

Buddha is clearly a subject that fascinated Rilke, who wrote two earlier Buddha poems in the first part of the *Neue Gedichte* (1907; *New Poems*, 1964); "Buddha in Glory" is the closing poem of *New Poems, Part II.*

While the poem seems mystical in tone, speaking of the "center of all centers" and the "kernel of all kernels," one can follow the general movement of its imagery. In the first stanza, the persona of the poem acknowledges Buddha as the center of all being and compares this central position to an almond centered within its shell. Buddha is like a vital and dynamic almond, the fruit of which encompasses everything, including the heavens themselves. The persona clearly admires this spiritual accomplishment and salutes Buddha. The poem is addressed directly to the Buddha.

In stanza 2, Buddha's consciousness and the almond which serves as a metaphor for it continue to expand and to grow beyond time into infinity. The sap that fills the almond's fruit and Buddha's veins presses on infinity itself. The image of Buddha finally subsumes even the heavens, which are filled with Buddha's own suns that send their rays to assist the sap that drives through the almond's flesh. Having enveloped time and space, in stanza 3, Buddha participates in the heavenly realm itself as the rays of his own suns now burn and glow. Yet these external symbols are nothing compared to the intensity of consciousness that burns within the Buddha and that will long outlast the external glory of the sun: "But in you is already begun/ that which will outlive the sun." The spiritual growth of consciousness within Buddha is thus more crucial than any image of physical expansion.

Forms and Devices

Perhaps the most striking device Rilke uses in this poem is that of the double metaphor. Buddha himself is an image of spiritual perfection and expanded consciousness, but Rilke adds a second level of metaphor by comparing the statue of Buddha to the living system of the almond. The technique of embodying spiritual meaning in a specific physical object (often an artwork of some kind) is typical of many of the poems in *New Poems*. In this case, Rilke complicates matters further by using a metaphor from the natural world (the almond) to explicate the vital spiritual significance of the sculpture, which in turn symbolizes the perfected consciousness of Buddha himself. Sitting silently and self-contained at the center of time and space, Buddha resembles the seed or kernel at the center of the almond. This usually limited germ or nucleus expands along with Buddha's consciousness to encompass all of space, including the starry skies, as well as all of time as the almond's (and Buddha's) physical shell swells into infinity. The almond's casing (or Buddha's body) no longer serves to limit the consciousness it contains. The metaphors allow the spiritual world to subsume the physical world and thus to eliminate all physical boundaries. The idea of perfected spirituality is embodied in the perfectly taciturn statue but then linked to a natural image that can grow to include all of time and space. By describing the unfolding of his image, Rilke is able to symbolize a very complex and mystical spiritual development.

A second technique Rilke employs in this poem is that of constant expansion of his poetic vision. Rilke begins the poem at a single point of extreme concentration: "Center of centers, seed of seeds." From this single point, his image of the almond and of Buddha's spiritual perfection constantly expands until it envelops the heavens themselves. The image of Buddha thus unites many levels of existence. The Buddha statue is made of stone and embodies the inanimate world; the metaphor of the almond represents the natural world; Buddha as a historical figure brings in the human world; and finally, Buddha's spiritual perfection encompasses the transcendent realm of the heavens or the divine. Rilke thus accomplishes in his imagery his own unification of realms and of levels of consciousness. The poem itself becomes an act of spiritual unification and perfection.

To emphasize this unity, Rilke employs a rhyme scheme in German that links *Kerne* (seeds, kernels) and *Sterne* (stars) in lines 1 and 3 of stanza 1. His rhyme connects the concentrated point of the nucleus or seed to the stars, the infinitesimal to the infinite, just as his description does. In lines 2 and 4 of stanza 2, Rilke rhymes *Schale* (shell, husk) and *Gestrahle* (rays) to produce the same effect of breaking open the image so that it becomes boundless.

Themes and Meanings

"Buddha in Glory" is a poem about the triumph of the spiritual world over the physical world. Buddha himself symbolizes this triumph. Buddha's perfected and all-encompassing consciousness allows him to merge with all of existence. The suns are now his suns; the rays of the heavens are his. Rilke thus succeeds in embodying in his poem a very complex mystical experience of spiritual perfection, of the attainment of Buddhahood. While it would be extremely difficult for a poet to explain such an experience to a reader in discursive language, Rilke manages to capture this mystical fulfillment in a striking image (the almond) drawn from the natural realm more familiar to the reader.

The tone of the poem is one of admiration. The persona of the poem greets and celebrates Buddha and his spiritual accomplishments. The persona recognizes that Buddha has achieved the purification of consciousness that allows him to merge with all of existence, to burn with a spiritual intensity that will outlast the sun itself. The sculptor has captured this spirituality in his sculpture just as nature captures it in the perfection of its fruits. Rilke now attempts to do the same in his poem. In a gesture of unification reminiscent of German Romanticism, Rilke manages to merge the aesthetic world (the sculpture), the world of spirit (Buddha's consciousness), and the natural world (the almond) in a single image of metaphysical wholeness. Rilke creates in his poem something of the same experience that Buddha achieves in his unification with all of existence. Thus the poem, like Buddha, provides an example of perfected consciousness and reunified existence.

Although Rilke begins with a single point of concentration (perhaps akin to T. S. Eliot's "still point of the turning world" in the *Four Quartets*, 1943), his poem is about expansion of that center of centers into infinity—that is, about the elimination of all boundaries. Here Buddha (and the almond that symbolizes him) surpasses all dependencies, all limits of space and time, in order to become his own universe, his own suns. The apparent limitations of the shell or husk are overcome as the image encompasses all existence. The sap that flows in the almond's veins (and in Buddha's) is part of the system of the stars' rays. Yet the real growth and expansion is an inward one. Returning to that point of concentration within Buddha himself, the poem comes to rest on the internal rather than the expansive external universe it has opened up. Within, in the realm of the spiritual, is the source and beginning of an intensity that will outlive even the sun that symbolizes the life force of our ordinary universe. Consciousness, internal life, outstrips all external existence. Finally, Rilke suggests that the enlightenment signified by Buddha's name is to be found within.

Kathleen L. Komar

BUFFALO BILL 'S

Author: E. E. Cummings (1894-1962)
Type of poem: Satire
First published: 1920; collected in *Tulips and Chimneys*, 1923

The Poem

The poem announces that Buffalo Bill (William F. Cody, 1846-1917) is "defunct." Cody had made a name for himself in the wild west as a buffalo hunter and Indian fighter. He subsequently became a showman, hiring many of the Indians (among them was Sitting Bull) who had fought the U.S. Army and doing road tours that featured staged battles between cowboys and Indians, sharpshooting exhibitions, and other events associated with frontier America. Cody was more than a national phenomenon; his wild west show toured Europe, and he was received as an example of the vigorous American spirit that had conquered a continent. To say that he is defunct rather than simply dead is to imply that his example is outmoded and irrelevant.

E. E. Cummings does not limit his attention to the historical Buffalo Bill, however. The typography of the first line, "Buffalo Bill 's," with its space between the name and the apostrophe *s*, implies a pluralization. It is as if the poet is dismissing not a man but a symbol and all the copies of that symbol—all the men who think of themselves as Buffalo Bills. To be more precise, by separating the apostrophe *s* from Buffalo Bill, the poet conjures up an image of both the historical figure and his out-of-date followers or emulators, who trail after him leaving a gap (the space) between him and them. The America these wild west heroes thought they possessed no longer exists, and thus Buffalo Bill as America's representative is defunct.

Like many satires which poke at the pretensions of a subject by evoking and dramatizing it, the poem charges ahead like Buffalo Bill himself. The pigeons that Buffalo Bill is breaking "justlikethat" are most likely the clay pigeons used in shooting matches—in this case, in events contrived for the wild west shows. The pigeons break apart when shot. The show is impressive because Buffalo Bill hits his targets rapidly and easily. The show is also a kind of sham, however, because the birds are not real, and the show does not have much to do with the real wild west. That the poem has less than an admiring view of Buffalo Bill—while conceding his romantic appeal—is evident in the last five lines.

On one hand, the speaker pays tribute to Buffalo Bill's handsomeness, evoking what may be the wonder of an onlooker at a wild west show performance. On the other hand, Buffalo Bill, the "blueeyed boy," is subject to mortality, personified in the figure of "Mister Death." Buffalo Bill, the figure of youth, in other words, gives way to a rather grim reminder of the processes of time. Not even this true-blue American hero can defeat death.

Forms and Devices

Cummings is known as a poet who attacks conventional uses of grammar, and he turns capitalization, hyphens, apostrophes, and spaces between words to new uses. He runs words together. He separates words and lines in unique ways. Indeed, he employs no punctuation in places where most writers would favor a comma or period. His highly individualistic style is, by definition, a challenge to the way most people write and think. So it is not surprising that he would take an irreverent view of an American hero like Buffalo Bill.

The poem satirizes Bill as a idolatrous figure who can do miraculous things—like Jesus. His stallion is silver, gleaming no doubt like a precious metal, with the adjective "watersmooth" emphasizing how glossy and glittery Buffalo Bill's performance is. He is a shining symbol of American energy and know-how, and that easy efficiency of manner is combined with a romantic aura. The image of the "blueeyed boy" focuses on Buffalo Bill as a paragon of American innocence—as if showing off is comparable to conquering the world. Buffalo Bill's looks solve nothing, and over time they prove meaningless. He becomes not America's blue-eyed boy—analogous to someone like movie star Mary Pickford, once known as "America's sweetheart"—but Mister Death's victim.

The figure of Mister Death makes what has seemed a light-hearted poem much more sinister. Death often appears in medieval mystery plays as a character who reminds human beings that they will die and that they are subject to the corruption of the earth. In such mystery plays, people must be reminded that they will not live forever and that their gaudy shows and vanity will be overcome by death. In the poem, Mister Death appears to be the ultimate showman—the one who really controls Buffalo Bill's act. In other words, Buffalo Bill has not really been the master of his fate: He has been a tool of Mister Death.

Along with the shocking appearance of Mister Death comes a change of tone in the speaker's voice. In the first half of the poem, the speaker seems jocular—although he clearly foreshadows his darker tone in the poem's third word, "defunct." Nevertheless, the next six lines seem to indulge in a vivid memory of how pleasurable and exciting it was to watch Buffalo Bill. The words run together in line 6 in imitation of his sharpshooting. It is only with the single word in line 7—the mention of Jesus—that the poem slows down to contemplate the consequences of Buffalo Bill's behavior. The speaker concedes the hero's allure and then suddenly subverts that allure in the sobering last three lines, which form a question (the question mark itself is eliminated). Cummings usually omits end punctuation, as if refusing to come to a conclusion about life, which is, his poems imply, ceaseless, constantly reinventing itself and repeating the process of life and death.

Themes and Meanings

In the broadest sense, Cummings is both celebrating and attacking American optimism. The symbol of the wild west has become an essential part of the American identity. It expresses the American's quest to be an individual and the American worship of those who have created a heroic sense of themselves. On the one hand, Buffalo Bill was handsome, energetic, and successful. On the other hand, what does his fame amount to? What did he really accomplish?

Not only Buffalo Bill himself but also his kind of heroism is defunct, the poem announces. Cody died in 1917, so the poem, first published in 1920, is a kind of obituary for this fallen figure. He is remembered fondly by the speaker—almost as if the speaker is remembering his childhood pleasure in watching Buffalo Bill's wild west show. The adult speaker, however, is wondering what Buffalo Bill's legacy really is.

The poem implies that shows such as Buffalo Bill's are distractions from reality, from the knowledge of death. The idea of youth, of freshness and innocence, is worshipped in a kind of religion, and Buffalo Bill becomes a stand-in for Jesus. Ultimately such substitutes fade in importance. The American myth is that the United States is the New World and that Americans can escape from the tyranny of history, from the death and destruction that has struck Europe and other continents. Cummings insinuates that it is a little late in the day for Buffalo Bills—either for nostalgia about Buffalo Bill himself or for others who might try to pretend that they are "blueeyed" boys who can conquer the world. It is fun to remember this simpler past, the poem affirms, but dwelling on Buffalo Bill's exploits leaves one unprepared when death strikes—as it does abruptly in the poem, suddenly taking away the exciting images of the Buffalo Bill show.

This poem has a trajectory that is easily followed if the eye moves from the poem's first words "Buffalo Bill 's" to the single word Jesus on line 7 at the right-hand margin to Mister Death in the left-hand margin at the poem's end. The story of Buffalo Bill—his self-invention and fame—gives way to Jesus and Mister Death. Buffalo Bill cannot hold his own with these two figures; there is no hint of resurrection for him. He is "defunct."

Cummings, also a painter, provides a visual as well as a verbal demonstration of the promise as well as the demise of Buffalo Bill as a suitable American symbol. The tone of braggadocio in the first lines of the poem, which mimic the boisterous self-confidence of a wild west hero, gives way to a much more complex statement of the poem's theme in the last three lines. The speaker addresses Mister Death directly, acknowledging Buffalo Bill's demise but perhaps also feeling a little aggrieved that this symbol of the American go-getter has been cut down by death. There may be a bit of anger in the question addressed to Mister Death, a lingering lament for a hero and a way of life that had seemed so inspiring.

Carl Rollyson

THE BUILDING

Author: Philip Larkin (1922-1985)
Type of poem: Lyric
First published: 1974, in *High Windows*

The Poem

"The Building" is a poem of nine seven-line stanzas plus a single final line. It is written in Philip Larkin's characteristic rough iambic pentameter, with an equally characteristic subtle rhyme scheme. All the lines are not exactly ten syllables each; nevertheless, the pattern of stress is that of the iamb: a two-part (disyllabic), stressed-unstressed foot.

The poem is a description of a place that is never definitively named, although it is clearly a hospital or other health-care facility. The first stanza describes the building in contrast to what is around and outside it. The last lines of the first stanza, along with the entire second and third stanzas, describe the building's interior, including the inhabitants. The fourth and fifth stanzas describe what the building is like from the inside, from the point of view of the people waiting there: how being there is an interruption of their daily lives and what they are afraid will happen to them.

Stanza 6 returns to the exterior of the building, this time looking out from the inside. The outside world seems very far off; it goes on and on, out of sight. Further, in stanza 7, the world is addressed as a separate thing and is even said to be "beyond the stretch/ Of any hand from here." For a brief three-line sentence, the speaker of the poem is present and includes himself in the condition of the people in the building: The "loves" and "chances" of the world are only a "touching dream to which we are all lulled." Then he separates himself again in a way that he says is inevitable, because everyone will "wake from" that dream "separately." Awakening from that illusion of "self-protecting ignorance" is brought about by a more real confrontation with death in a building such as this.

Stanza 8 shifts back from speculation to more particulars about the experience of the people in the building. The sense of uncertainty remains, however, because the particulars of death are unknown on any level. So, continuing on to stanza 9, what is being said about the people in the building—"Each gets up and goes at last" and "All know they are going to die"—is being said about all humanity. The poem explains this when it says in the final lines, "That is what it means,/ this clean-sliced cliff; a struggle to transcend/ The thought of dying." The confrontation with death forced upon the people who arrive at this building is no different from that which faces those who have not arrived there yet, and what is done in the building of the poem is in a certain way no different from what is done in "cathedrals," because neither "contravenes . . ./ The coming dark" of death. The desire of all people to do so, to contravene both their own and others' coming dark, is poignantly represented by their offerings of "wasteful, weak propitiatory flowers."

Forms and Devices

Larkin's subtle rhyme scheme contributes significantly to the overall impact of the poem. While the stanzas run seven lines, the poem uses an eight-rhyme pattern: *abcbdcad*. This has two effects. First, because the rhyme carries over from one stanza to the next, the reader, too, is carried forward through the description by an imperceptible force; it is an experience akin to that which is being described. Second, through the middle stanzas of the poem this has the effect of disturbing the unity of each stanza. For example, the rhyme scheme begins at the second line of the third stanza, the third line of the fourth stanza, and so on, so that the reader is made to feel an unease and a lack of resolution, until the final stanza and the single final line.

This effect is further accomplished by a technique called enjambment, in which the sense of one line is carried over into the next. This occurs frequently within stanzas; more important, it occurs from one stanza to the next in every stanza except the first. The midsentence pause creates a momentary sense of meaninglessness. When that pause carries over across stanzas the sense of disorientation generated by the poem is more intense.

With the last eight lines of the poem, the beginning of the rhyme pattern and the beginning of the stanza coincide, as they did in the first stanza, and the pattern is allowed to complete itself with the final single line. This coincidence, the completion of the pattern and the end of the unrelenting enjambment, provides a sense of resolution for the reader, but it is an uneasy one, because the final line, standing alone, also breaks completely with the stanzaic form of the poem.

The absence of a first person, a narrative "I," in this poem contributes to its troubling sense of depersonalization. Not only is the first person absent, the only second-person reference is not to a singular "you" but to the whole "world" (stanza 7), after which there is a single reference to "we" (all of "us" in this world). All the other references to people are by category—"porters," "nurse," "kids," "girls"—or only as "humans" or "faces," lumped together in indefinite or plural third-person pronouns—"someone," "those who tamely sit," "some" who are young or old, "they" and "them," and even "all." The only exception occurs when the indistinct "they" see a singular "him" "wheeled past," in stanzas 5 and 6; that is, when someone is separated from the waiting mass and goes to face his fate alone.

The anonymity of the building, emphasized by all the indefinite pronouns as well as the poem's title, is reinforced by Larkin's repeated use of similes using the comparative word "like." The streets are "like a great sigh"; the waiting room is "[l]ike an airport lounge." Finally, in the ninth stanza, all that the waiting people know is that they will die in a place "somewhere like this."

Themes and Meanings

Larkin combines three themes that contribute to one another: Questions of health and sickness are hinted at in terms of bodily health but also in terms of mental and spiritual health. Outside the building is a living, normal world of "close-ribbed streets" that "rise and fall" in an image of breathing, "like a sigh," where people are "free" and go about their business. This everyday normalcy is belied by the later reappearance of images of the body in stanza 7. The dream of life occurs only when "conceits" (vanities) and "ignorance congeal" like blood within a vein, a vein which itself "collapses," taking that dream of life with it as death is confronted.

The confrontation with death is also sometimes cast in terms of crime and imprisonment. In stanzas 3 and 4, the presence of those "humans" in the waiting room is associated with something that "has gone wrong," with "error of a serious sort." In stanza 5, when someone is wheeled away, the "rooms, and rooms past those" into which they disappear and which are "hard to return from," carry a sinister implication of torture. At the same time, the references to confession and to a building of many rooms also has Christian connotations of the confessional and Christ's words about there being a place for everyone in heaven. This association is strengthened in later stanzas, with references such as the communionlike "Each gets up and goes," and "congregations" in "white rows." At the same time, however, that image of "white rows" could be prison cells and/or slabs of a morgue.

By mixing these three images, Larkin communicates the mixed attitudes society takes toward disease and death. The onslaught of fatal illness can be regarded as the result of moral failure, of "not living right," or, alternatively, as an opportunity to come to terms with things that are not of this world or as the beginning step toward eternal life. The cultural reluctance to name certain forms of terminal disease renders them even more mysterious and terrifying. Larkin reduplicates this effect by leaving the building and the plight of its inhabitants unnamed.

Finally, this poem has strong associations with Matthew Arnold's poem "Dover Beach" (1867). The image of the cliff appears in both, as does the lament that the world is a land of dreams. Most important, the "crowds" in "the coming dark" are the same as those clashing on Arnold's darkling plain. By this connection, Larkin's poem can be understood to be functioning at a level far beyond the immediate portrayal; it becomes a lament for the very nature of the human struggle.

Laurie Glover

THE BURIED LIFE

Author: Matthew Arnold (1822-1888)
Type of poem: Lyric
First published: 1852, in *Empedocles on Etna and Other Poems*

The Poem

"The Buried Life" is a ninety-eight-line poem divided into seven stanzas of varying length with an irregular rhyme scheme. A monologue in which a lover addresses his beloved, the poem yearns for the possibility of truthful communication with the self and with others.

The first line evokes the banter of a loving couple, but it is immediately checked by the deeply sad feelings of the speaker. Troubled by a sense of inner restlessness, he longs for complete intimacy and hopes to find it in his beloved's clear eyes, the window to her "inmost soul."

As the second stanza suggests, not even lovers can sustain an absolutely open relationship or break through the inhibitions and the masks that people assume in order to hide what they really feel. Yet the speaker senses the possibility of greater truth, since all human beings share basically the same feelings and ought to be able to share their most profound thoughts.

In a burst of emotion, expressed in two intense lines, the speaker wonders whether the same forces that prevent people from truly engaging each other must also divide him and his beloved.

The fourth stanza suggests that direct contact is possible only in fugitive moments, when human beings suddenly are aware of penetrating the distractions and struggles of life and realize that their apparently random actions are the result of the "buried stream," of those unconscious drives that motivate human behavior.

In the long meditative fifth stanza, the speaker advances the idea that there are occasions in the midst of busy lives when people are suddenly overwhelmed with the desire to understand their "buried life," the wellspring of all that they do. Yet no one ever seems to penetrate the origins of things and articulate what remains a mystery, what the speaker calls "nameless feelings." There is a "hidden" aspect of life, an underground sense that haunts people, that beckons to them, just as, in the sixth stanza, the lover beckons to his beloved, taking her hand and expressing—if only for a moment— a sense of complete communion between themselves and their emotions. It is at these times that people become aware of the deeper currents of their beings.

The final stanza expresses the utter peacefulness of this communion between lovers, when they feel at rest, when they are no longer bothered by the elusiveness of their beings' purpose and they comprehend the sources of their lives.

Forms and Devices

The poem is built around a central metaphor: the evocation of an individual's life and of life itself as a stream or river, ever flowing, ungraspable, and possessed of great depths. In the first line, for example, the lovers' conversation "flows"—a delightful and yet troubling metaphor because their words, like water, resist definition and do not reach the core of identity or meaning.

The poet uses the metaphor explicitly in the fourth stanza in referring to the "unregarded river of our life . . . eddying at large in blind uncertainty," because human beings usually ignore the true roots of their selves.

The fifth stanza is even more explicit, as the speaker uses the phrase "our buried life" to parallel his use of "buried stream" in the fourth stanza. To track the "mystery of this heart," to observe the "nameless feelings that course through our breast," again continues the metaphor of the stream, the watercourse that contains within it unanalyzed elements. When the speaker evokes the moment of communion in the sixth stanza, it is also in the terms of water, as "a man becomes aware of his life's flow." Knowing his life's basis is, as the last line of the poem suggests, similar to following the "sea where it goes."

Comparing human lives to a stream, to the flowing of water, is a traditional metaphorical conception of human life, which Matthew Arnold uses to capture both the enigma and the energy of life. Even the speaker's tears in the first stanza are an expression of this life flow—at once so soothing and troubling, so appealing and frustrating to human beings who wish to plumb the depths of their existence.

The poet also uses the device of a dramatic monologue, of a lover addressing his beloved, to generalize about human experience, to suggest that the lovers' feelings are a microcosm of the feelings that all human beings share. Beginning with a dramatic scene—the speaker moved to tears and wishing that he could see in his beloved her "inmost soul"—the poem gradually, stanza by stanza, develops the universal import of the speaker's feelings, showing how all human beings partake of this quest for self-knowledge and communion with one another.

Arnold also achieves an impressive unity in the poem by repeating certain key words—particularly those with which he evokes a "benumbed" and "jaded" world. This world is blind to the depths of things and distracted and deafened by its own surface affairs—by all the sounds and sights that obscure the quieter, softer, cooler forces at play in human nature, which are observed only at those rare moments of self-awareness. By implication, nature itself, its buried streams and its rising hills, evoke in the poem's last lines a sense of life's peaks and valleys, its origins and outcomes, that become apparent only in the lovers' momentary transcendence of daily cares and expressions.

In the poem's shift from first to third person, Arnold effectively transforms a personal, individual experience into a universal experience as well. For example, in the fifth and sixth stanzas, he moves from the speaker's address to his beloved to a hypothetical situation in which "a beloved hand is laid in ours," thus making his appeal to the human heart which, earlier in the poem (line 23), is described as beating "in every human breast." When the tones of a lover's voice suddenly open the beloved's heart, "a bolt is shot back somewhere in our breast" (line 84)—a line of shocking visual force that describes a moment of unlocking the heart that the speaker had yearned for earlier in the poem (line 13).

Themes and Meanings

A poem of great frustration and sadness, "The Buried Life" yearns for an openness which the poet fears that he will never achieve. Saddened by his own inability to express his deepest, truest self, he turns to his beloved, thinking that in her "limpid" eyes he can find true communion with another soul. He knows that people fear to reveal themselves, suspecting that they will be ignored or, worse, criticized for what they expose of themselves. Yet, his counterargument is that all human beings contain essentially the same feelings and thus should be able to bare their souls more freely than they do.

It has been pointed out that there may be a slight confusion in the poem, perhaps explained by the poet's shifting use of metaphor. On the one hand, lines 38-40 and 55-56 suggest that the river of life is subterranean and only rarely accessible. On the other hand, the river of life in lines 43-44 is treated as a surface flow interrupted or broken by eddies, emanations of a "genuine self" referred to in line 36. Evidently, Arnold is identifying the discrepancy between the self who thinks that he is determining his fate, who thinks he can "well-nigh change his own identity" (line 34), and the self who seems to pursue life with "blind uncertainty" (line 43) while actually "driving on with it [the buried life] eternally."

Thus, the poem raises but does not resolve disturbing questions about fate and free will. Human beings clearly deceive themselves—that much is clear from the fourth stanza—yet the poet just as clearly entertains the possibility that the lovers, and indeed all human beings, at least have the capacity to see truly and to understand the ultimate reasons for their actions.

Although the poem does not settle the "fate versus free will" conundrum, its use of metaphor does suppose that, as in nature where all rivers have their source, so in human nature all lives have their origin, which a man can glimpse, who "thinks he knows/ The hills where his life rose,/ And the sea where it goes." The ending is tentative because it refers to what the man "thinks he knows," yet it is positively rendered in the simple declarative rhymes of the last words, mimicking the "unwonted calm," of the knowledge that the speaker has acquired.

Carl Rollyson

BURNING A BOOK

Author: William Stafford (1914-1993)
Type of poem: Lyric
First published: 1987, in *An Oregon Message*

The Poem

"Burning a Book" is in free verse, its nineteen lines divided into three verse para-graphs, units of thought of eight, nine, and two lines, respectively. Book burning is of-ten seen as a symbol of censorship and ignorance, but this poem looks at book burning from a unique viewpoint. It is unwise to assume automatically that the poet and the speaker of a poem are speaking with the same voice, but very often such is the case. "Burning a Book" so closely identifies with William Stafford's own views on writing that one can conclude there is no distinction between the two.

The poem begins with a detailed, even graphic description of the burning of a book; it recognizes the destructive nature of book burning and apparently supports the con-ventional symbolism associated with it. Yet there is a hint of the direction the poem will take when the reader is told that lies are burning as well as truth. Apparently, book burning may not be all bad. The last sentence of the first paragraph sets a conversa-tional tone and includes the reader in the process: "You can usually find a few charred words in the ashes." Within the first few words of the second verse paragraph, the poet's viewpoint is stated directly: "some books ought to burn." Stafford's poems of-ten state opposing attitudes. It is almost as if he wants to speak both for and against.

The latter part of the second verse paragraph speaks metaphorically of the per-ceived danger: Worse than the act of burning books (or, by symbolic association, re-jecting written ideas) deemed failures is the fact that some books that should have been written were never written at all; some subjects—good or bad, weighty or insig-nificant—were never explored. There are "whole libraries" of undiscovered subjects, worthy and unworthy, in towns, cities, and countrysides. The ironic crux of the poem's message is in the last sentence of the paragraph: "ignorance can dance in the absence of fire." The implied viewpoint is that fire is needed for knowledge, even the fire of burning books; for even a burned book has had something to say, whether truth-ful, controversial, proved wrong or dangerous, or simply poorly stated. How could its worth be determined if it had never been written?

The final paragraph, which opens with a challenging, defiant tone, unites the reader and the speaker. The poet has burned books and perhaps, as has the reader, has found "a few charred words in the ashes." More important to him are the books he has not written, that "nobody has," whole libraries of potential fuel for knowledge, testing, even controversy.

Forms and Devices

An openness to the possibilities in language characterizes Stafford's poetic method.

He is eager to explore unique modes of perception in language in order to express meanings in objects and ideas. Figures of speech allow the poet to say things in new ways. Stafford uses figures of speech—personification and metaphor—to great effect in "Burning a Book."

Nearly every object and idea in the poem seems alive. The pages protect each other, truth and lies both burn, the flame's attitude is one of indifference, some books are "trying for character but just faking it," and ignorance dances. Personifying these things, attributing human characteristics to the nonhuman, causes the poem to bristle with energy. The effect supports the concept in the poem that what the words say in a book is not as important as the creative energy, the impulse, that takes the writer through the process. If the process leads to a failure, so be it, implies the poet, but one never knows unless the process is brought to life and new ideas and methods are explored. Only ignorance has energy in the absence of creative exploration, and it dances gleefully.

Pages that contain both truth and lies try to protect themselves from the fire. They appear victimized, and the reader is pulled, by the personification, into empathy for the writings being destroyed. One can easily visualize a repressive society burning books that threaten conventional and acceptable standards.

Some of these personified books, however, are fakes whose ideas have no validity. Put simply, books are, like people, all different. Like people, all deserve at least the chance to have their say. As well as infusing energy into the poem, then, the personification also highlights the poem's pragmatic outlook, which explores the abstract, conventional symbolism of book burning in terms with which the reader can identify—and even participate in—by realistically examining it from all sides.

The extended library metaphor in the second paragraph of the poem indicates the vastness of the material that could be written about. Books represent ideas, and libraries are the places where those ideas are found—in towns and cities and countrysides, anywhere there is life. If writers do not explore these places, even the evils—"wild dogs" who terrorize the countryside and who "own anything that moves"—will not be identified. The comparatively small fire a few books make (shown by the description of the burning of one book) cannot compare to the enormous waste and potential danger of not writing at all.

Themes and Meanings

"Burning a Book" is a poem about taking risks—specifically, taking risks in writing. Stafford has always admired, and practiced in his own writing, the quixotic approach of plunging into the unknown. He maintains that no subject, as long as it involves the heart and intuition of the writer, is too small to write about. As Stafford himself says, "[L]ike Don Quixote you must expect some disasters. You must write your bad poems." (Perhaps one must write some poems worthy of nothing better than "burning.") Not to write intuitively, on impulse, is "to guarantee that you will not find the unknown, the risky."

Following a creative impulse may lead to something worthwhile or it may lead to windmills in the sky, but one thing is certain in the poem: Neither truth nor lies will be found without the attempt. Stafford's sense of irony admits that "Truth, brittle and faint, burns easily,/ its fire as hot as the fire lies make," and his wisdom says that if neither is accessible, there is no way to distinguish between truth and lies.

Although book burning is conventionally associated with ignorance, in his usual attitude of openness to both sides of an issue, Stafford observes that, ironically, ignorance dances equally well in the absence of fire. He takes a wry look at the whole concept. Where there are books being burned, there is something with which to disagree; there is knowledge, however faulty. To be judged unworthy, a book must be read and must be written in the first place. How could book burning itself be deemed repressive without the words that can expose its dangers?

The reader is invited to risk being fallible. The imaginative space of the poem includes writer and reader alike. "You" and "I" are almost equated, for the participation of the reader is required if one is to find the words in the ashes. When the poet admits figuratively to burning books that no doubt meet the criterion "trying for character/ but just faking it," he is quite possibly talking about some of his own writing. The tone is finally optimistic as he casually shrugs at his own failures (and perhaps at his critics) and looks forward to the endless possibilities of discovery.

Stafford is one of the most prolific of American poets. In his view, even the most ordinary ideas are worth examining and exploring. "Burning a Book" exemplifies his deep-rooted beliefs about writing; his words are designed to rekindle vigor and excitement in exploring the boundaries of thought.

Marilyn Schultz

THE BURNING BABE

Author: Robert Southwell (1561-1595)
Type of poem: Lyric/narrative
First published: 1595, in *Moeoniae: Or, Certaine Excellent Poems and Spirituall Hymnes*

The Poem

"The Burning Babe," by Robert Southwell, is one of the most famous and powerful Christmas poems in the English language. Written in carefully crafted rhyming couplets of iambic heptameter, the poem is sixteen lines long, and each of its long lines is skillfully broken by a caesura (pause), which occurs after the first four feet and before the last three. Yet, despite its structural complication, "The Burning Babe" relates its astonishing, mystical occurrences in a smoothly flowing narrative.

In the first four lines of the poem, a cold and isolated narrator stands "shivering" in the snow at night when he suddenly senses a comforting "heat" which lifts his spirits and causes his "heart to glow." Nevertheless, he casts a "fearful" glance at the source of the heat and, astonishingly, he sees, suspended in the air, "A pretty babe all burning bright." This "burning babe" is the infant Jesus Christ.

In lines 5 through 8 of the poem, the Christ child's peculiar condition is carefully described: the babe is "scorchèd with excessive heat" and shedding "floods of tears." Finally, this amazing and sorrowful image speaks, not with the joy usually associated with Christmas, but with the complaint that "none approach to warm their hearts." Clearly, the babe is reminding the stunned narrator that the extraordinary miracle of the Incarnation (Christ's human birth) is too often taken for granted and that men too often refuse to undertake a true and necessary commitment to Christ's warming love.

Then, in lines 9 through 12, the love of God is portrayed not only as warming, but also as purifying: "My faultless breast the furnace is" and the "metal in this furnace wrought are men's defilèd souls." Through this extraordinary metaphor (Jesus as a purifying furnace), the Christ child reminds the narrator that the great news of the Incarnation is not only that God is among us, which is extraordinary enough, but also that this Incarnation also initiates a redemption through which all men can purify themselves before God.

In the poem's final four lines, the Christ child reinforces the furnace imagery with a related metaphor of purification and cleansing: the promise to all men to "melt into a bath to wash them in my blood." With these words, the burning babe suddenly vanishes from sights and the amazed narrator immediately recalls "that it was Christmas day." Thus the poem, through the Christ child, reminds the narrator (and the reader) that Christmas and the Redemption cannot be separated and that the best awakening that one could possibly have each Christmas is to remember that the purpose of the Incarnation is one's personal salvation.

Forms and Devices

The great Elizabethan poet Ben Jonson once said that if he could have written "The Burning Babe," he would have been glad to destroy many of his own best poems. There are many reasons this poem is so affecting, but the strangeness of the narrative and the unusual central metaphor are two of the poem's most memorable aspects.

The very incident itself—the encounter with an enflamed Christ child suspended in the air—is both a stunning and miraculous apparition. The babe's strong admonition and unusual language increase the peculiar and marvelous aspects of the narrative. Finally, when the narrator's conscience has been awakened, the babe simply vanishes. Thus Southwell, by combining the traditional "strangeness" of early folk ballads with the miraculous events recorded in hagiographies (lives of the saints), creates a scene that is both mystical and unforgettable.

Even more amazing, however, than the action of the poem is its central metaphor of the infant Jesus as a furnace, explained when the burning babe first appears: " 'Alas!' quoth he, 'but newly born in fiery heats I fry.' " As critic Linda Ching Sledge points out, in her book *Shivering Babe, Victorious Lord: The Nativity in Poetry and Art* (1981), this powerful image of the newly born Christ child literally enflamed in a nonconsuming fire clearly recalls the primary two symbolisms of fire imagery in the Bible: the presence of God (as in the burning bush of Exodus 3:2, the pillar of fire in Exodus 13:21, and the tongues of fire in Acts 2:3-4) and the nature of sacrifice (as in the story of Abraham and Isaac in Genesis and in the many Old Testament burnt offerings to God).

In the poem, the child explains that he burns with a purifying love that burns away men's sins: "My faultless breast the furnace is, the fuel wounding thorns." Thus, through the Passion of Jesus (which included the crowning with thorns), this furnace will consume man's sins. Although divine justice demands retribution for human sin, God's mercy "blows the coals," and the resultant fire is Christ's love. As a result of this extraordinary love, "men's defilèd souls" can now be transformed "to their good."

The poem "The Burning Babe" is a marvelous blend of many striking poetic elements: haunting rhythm and rhyme, powerful language, sharp images, intellectual complexity, and fervid spirituality. It is its very strange narrative and its memorable central metaphor, however, that make the poem more powerfully effective than the many other interesting, but less memorable, nativity poems which have been written by a wide range of English poets, including John Donne, Ben Jonson, John Milton, and William Blake.

Themes and Meanings

"The Burning Babe" is a poem about Christian redemption. It was written by Robert Southwell, a young Jesuit priest, who violated an English decree that no Catholic Masses could be celebrated in England. As a result, Southwell was hunted, captured, and viciously tortured by Richard Topcliffe, one of Queen Elizabeth's most brutal "pursuivants" (priest-hunters). At the time he wrote the poem, Southwell was awaiting trial and certain execution in the Tower of London. In his poem, Southwell clearly reflects on his own coming death and his hopes of personal redemption.

Unlike most Christmas poems that focus on the nativity scene and emphasize the joy of the Incarnation, Southwell's poem is a strange, deep, and often somber meditation which clearly reflects his own situation as a tortured prisoner awaiting death in solitary confinement. At the beginning of the poem, the narrator, as indicated by his isolation and deep "shivering" cold, appears as a lost or misguided soul clearly in need of spiritual direction. Thus the very purpose of the entire poem is to indicate the sudden and astonishing impact which the strange apparition of the burning Christ child has upon the narrator. The lost soul's shock upon first seeing the suspended child is similar to that of the Bethlehem shepherds on Christmas night when the angel suddenly appears to them: "And lo, the angel of the Lord came upon them, and the glory of the Lord shone about them; and they were sore afraid" (Luke 2:9).

Then, when the burning babe has admonished all men (including the narrator) for not apprehending the love and sacrifice of God, he further explains his ability to burn away (and wash away) all human sin. This great and divine power had been foretold by the angel Gabriel when he spoke to Mary of her coming child: "For He shall save His people from their sins" (Matthew 1:21). Finally, at the end of the poem, when the babe vanishes, the awestruck narrator "callèd unto mind that it was Christmas day." Thus, the lost and lonely soul has clearly been awakened by his miraculous experience as he recalls the great significance of the day. Like Dante in *The Divine Comedy* (c. 1320), the narrator has now been directed back to the right and true path.

Robert Southwell sincerely believed that poetry could be used for higher, more spiritual ends, and he was determined to show "how well verse and virtue suit together" (*The Life of Robert Southwell, Poet and Martyr*, Christopher Devlin, 1956). While awaiting his execution (he was hanged at Tyburn on February 21, 1595), Southwell proved his convictions by writing his small masterpiece, "The Burning Babe." In this most unusual and powerful of all Christmas poems, Robert Southwell, who was canonized in 1970, explains that the miracle of Christmas should inspire all men to recall the ultimate miracle of redemption and salvation.

William Baer

BURNING THE TOMATO WORMS

Author: Carolyn Forché (1950-   )
Type of poem: Meditation
First published: 1975; collected in *Gathering the Tribes*, 1976

The Poem

"Burning the Tomato Worms" is a long poem of thirteen stanzas in free verse, the key poem among seven others in the section of Carolyn Forché's *Gathering the Tribes* that bears the same name. At first, the poem seems not to be about the event named in its title. Stanza 5 finally mentions burning the tomato worms, an act that is transformed in stanza 10, when the tomatoes and their worms are brought in for shelter from an early frost. The symbolic significance of the round, red tomatoes and the cylindrical worms that destroy them becomes clear by the end of the poem.

The epigraph for the poem offers a suggestion for interpreting it. The epigraph speaks of the cycles of creation and destruction, a cycle that is readily apparent in tending crops and, in the poem, is applied to human life. Moreover, the epigraph gives the injunction that poetry must be an attempt to "know" and name and order these important patterns of life, that it must strive to capture the roots of birth and death and to tell people what to do in the interim between them.

In the first stanza, the narrator is stimulated by the sights and feelings of autumn into remembering her grandmother. Although the stanza is brief, only seven lines, it introduces the reader to several important aspects of the poem. The dark spines of the pine trees seem to be phallic, an image of masculinity. In contrast, the clouds (perhaps billowy and rounded), the fertility of the plowed ground, and the bulging beaks of the pelicans as they bring food to their young suggest femininity. The narrator is careful to place this scene in the United States. The memory comes during a transitional time, an interim, "Between apples and the first snow." All of this suggests that the poem will reenact a rite of passage for the narrator: from naïve and innocent childhood to the age-old knowledge of womanhood and a kinship with her female ancestor. She will attain the knowledge of creation but also of pain, suffering, and loss.

As the memory of her grandmother becomes more focused, the narrator projects into the circumstances of her own conception and birth by imagining a time prior to her own existence. She divides the society before her birth into communities of men and communities of women, each with their own work to do and images that represent them. Most notable are the climatic contrasts: the frozen blood that thaws at her conception, for example.

She pictures her grandmother in her native Uzbek and imagines her daily occupations. Most of the images surrounding her grandmother evoke sustenance and nurturance; yet, the implication is that the tasks of farm life and motherhood took her away from a life of creativity. At the end of stanza 3, the grandmother beckons to the narrator to join her in a cyclic ritual, and the narrator feels connected, linked to both womanhood and her personal history, despite the differences in the two women's ages and experience.

It is unclear as to where her grandmother leads her; blood reappears here in the footprints pointing away from the house—away from domestic chores and responsibilities. That blood could be creative or destructive; the grandmother seems ready for an escape, a quick getaway. Perhaps she is the victim of a pogrom, or perhaps she is merely running away from the drudgery of being a farm wife.

Stanzas 5 through 10 offer a different cycle, beginning and ending with the tomato worms. Now, more realistically, the narrator paints pictures in the life of her grandmother: her appearance, her knowledge, her lifestyle. Interspersed are comments spoken by the grandmother herself, phrases etched in a young girl's memory but now recalled only in fragments. In all these memories is a sense of loss, of an opportunity that passes all too quickly, leaving one's life already determined and perhaps wasted. All the images used to describe the grandmother are closely allied with the natural world and with religion. The child can re-create the image of the grandmother and walk in her footsteps but with a difference of removal through space and time.

In stanza 5, the narrator burns tomato worms and strings useless gourds. Symbolically, she destroys the male principle and finds her own fertility, or productivity, equally destitute. In stanza 10, the tomatoes, complete with their worms, are brought into the home and retained and accepted rather than destroyed—salvaged at the last minute from the destruction of the frost. Even though the narrator can imaginatively experience the pain of achieving sexual maturity through the life of her grandmother and its expansion to archetypal dimensions, she cannot avoid the experience herself, and her time has arrived. The scene is set, but there is a confusion as to its nature: It can be both destructive and creative. Nature seems to encourage her boldness, offering her examples at every turn. She enacts her rite of sexual passage in stanza 12.

Stanza 13 gives a glimpse of the narrator after becoming a woman. Ironically, the passage has not brought her clarity of vision but rather reveals that the answers are simply in the living. Her grandmother had her own truth and keeps it to herself; the narrator must also find her own answers and cope with the pain of existence on her own.

Forms and Devices

The thirteen sections of the poem intermix memorial reconstruction of the grandmother's life, the actual voice of the grandmother, and the narrator's personal history revolving around the hardships and rhythms of a life linked to the land.

The poem attains unity through alliteration and assonance. Although it does not rhyme, the repetition of consonant and vowel sounds lends the poem an air of mystery and remoteness, as if it were an incantation.

This remoteness takes the poem away from the specific details of the narrator's life and memory of her grandmother and renders it archetypal, that is, an enduring and endlessly recurring pattern of human behavior. All the images and symbols of the poem align themselves along poles of masculinity and femininity. For the male principle, there are the tomato worms, logs, bonfires, cucumbers, gladioli, daggers, and knives; for the female, there are the gourds, tomatoes, apples, beads, candles and the worship of the Virgin Mary, hearts, and the moon.

The recurring image of blood points to the ambivalence that the poem retains from beginning to end. In ancient cultures, the wedding sheets were hung on the clothesline the day after the marriage to show the entire community by means of the bloodstains that the bride was a virgin and that the union had been consummated. Nature teaches the necessity of fertility and renewal, yet blood also appears at destruction, as when animals dying in traps bleed on the snow. Humankind seems to be the agent of destruction indicated by the blood, yet humans are also necessary partners in the renewal of life.

The central section of the poem employs the trope called metonymy, which is the use of a crucial part of something to represent the whole. The hands of the grandmother—both their potential and the actual work that they do—tell her entire story. Other female images reinforce the feeling of magic and transformation traditionally associated with women: worship of the moon, tending to growth and sustenance, the mysteries of birth. Yet, if procreation is a natural and necessary process, it is hard to account for pain in the world. Interestingly, the female initiate feels like an animal of prey, as suggested by the analogy to the rabbit in stanza 11.

Themes and Meanings

"Burning the Tomato Worms" is more of an experience than a statement of specific and definitive meaning. It dramatizes a rite of passage into womanhood, the sexual awakening of a girl who, through that passage, finds the dark bond that links her to all other women. It depicts the necessity of succumbing to the processes of being human, which entails both joy and pain. The poem affirms the importance of relations, especially familial relations, in establishing a personal identity. It enjoins the reader to live according to her own inner promptings and personal history at the same time as it reveals the inexorable and universal processes that unite all women, all humanity.

Returning to the epigraph with which the poem began, the reader may consider the poem an attempt to tell a truth, to capture both the personal and universal inherent in a single experience. "Burning the Tomato Worms" explores the ways in which an individual acquires knowledge and constructs truths, a process that logic and reason cannot necessarily capture. The end of the poem implies, too, that truth is neither simple nor clear. Like many poems, "Burning the Tomato Worms" requires the reader to accept the ambiguous and the paradoxical in life.

Sandra K. Fischer

BUSHED

Author: Earle Birney (1904-1995)
Type of poem: Narrative
First published: 1951; collected in *The Poems of Earle Birney*, 1969

The Poem

"Bushed" is a free-verse poem in lines of irregular length that convey the experience of a man who succumbs to nature's intimidating force. The title's denotations and connotations are all pertinent to the poem's meaning. In the first place, the title indicates location: the "bush," which in Canada refers to those vast areas of wilderness remote from human settlement. Second, to be "bushed" is to be exhausted, to be bereft of strength and therefore incapable of countering force with force or even cunning. In this case, it means also in effect to be swallowed up by the "bush," by the wilderness that, in the man's mind, seems to lie in wait for its prey and at the moment of greatest vulnerability makes its ambush without mercy. The poem is written from the point of view of an observer who tells the story with both emotional intensity and philosophical detachment.

"Bushed" begins with an observation that foreshadows disaster. "He," or humankind, "invented a rainbow" and saw in it divine assurance that nature would not ultimately destroy human life. Then nature's power, through lightning, turned that dream into cold comfort by smashing the rainbow into a mountain lake. At the edge of that lake, far from civilization, a solitary trapper builds himself a shack. He has "learned to roast porcupine belly" and wears the "quills on his hatband." Soon, however, he senses that he has invaded enemy territory whose inhabitants he cannot slay with impunity. That feeling grows in him and gradually unhinges him; he now perceives nature all around him transmogrifying itself into an enemy force. Whether the day dawns in sunshine or fog, the mountain is alive with messages to remind him that he is a puny, unwelcome intruder in the midst of nature. Instead of conqueror, he is its prisoner.

Mountain goats and ospreys guard him in the daytime; in the evening, the night smoke rises "from the boil of the sunset." At night the moon, the owls, and the cedars threaten and mock him with mysterious totems and incantations. The terrible realization penetrates him: While the mountain is asleep, the winds are forging its peak into an arrowhead that will be poised, with him as its single target. Defeated and resigned, the trapper bars himself inside the cabin, his stronghold of civilization, which he now knows is a delusion. All he can do is wait "for the great flint to come singing into his heart."

Forms and Devices

Earle Birney spent his youth in the Banff area, and thus he became intimately familiar with the awesome presence of the Rockies. Much of his poetry reflects a careful observation of the natural world. That observation is often far from dispassionate. As Northrop Frye observed (in "Canada and Its Poetry," *Canadian Forum* 23, 1943,), Birney achieves an "evocation of stark terror" when all the intelligence and cunning of solitary man is pitted against "nature's apparently meaningless power to waste and destroy on a superhuman scale." "Bushed" is such a poem.

Terror is evoked primarily through the imagery. Much of the imagery Birney selects is used in Psalm 104 in praise of a beneficent God who is "clothed with splendor and majesty," who "makes winds his messengers, flames of fire his servants," whose "high mountains belong to the goats," who "touches the mountains and they smoke," who plants "the cedars of Lebanon," who "brings darkness, and all the beasts of the forest prowl." In "Bushed," however, from the first line to the last, it is not the glory and goodness of God's nature but its hostile power that impresses the trapper and inexorably reduces him to a cowed victim.

First, there is the imagery of the heavens. According to the biblical story, God vowed after the flood that floods would never again destroy so much life, and then He chose the rainbow as the eternal reminder and warrant of that promise. Hence the rainbow came to symbolize divine reassurance of human safety and security. Here the fierce lightning of a mountain storm shatters the rainbow and serves notice to the trapper that he has ventured beyond the pale of human and divine protection. Later, the "boil of the sunset" suggests not beauty and peace but a seething cauldron of witches' brew that foreshadows evil to come. In addition, the moon is linked to the sinister work of carving totems, intensifying the trapper's terror. Even when "the mountain slept" at last, the winds of the heavens gathered for the final fatal attack, shaping the mountain's peak to "an arrowhead poised" to attack the victim's heart.

The land imagery is also central. The immensity of the mountain that towers above the man increasingly assumes the personality of an implacable foe with absolute control. It is "so big his mind slowed when he looked at it." Its lap constitutes a lake that swallows the light and the promise of the rainbow. Its messages sweep down "every hot morning," and its proclamations boom out every noon. All nature does its bidding, and the trapper is convinced that all its bidding conspires against him.

Third, there is the imagery of the animal world. The trapper has slain the porcupine and decorated himself with its quills, but not with impunity. A "white guard of goat" now protects the mountain's domain, and the ospreys "fall like valkyries," an ominous allusion to Odin, the all-seeing god of war and magic whose battle maidens (valkyries) chose the heroes to be slain. Here they choose as their victim "the cut-throat," a large trout that, significantly, resembles the rainbow trout. Twice now the rainbow has fallen victim. Besides, the meaning of "cut-throat" as a murderer obviously points to the trapper as the chosen target of the mountain-god's warriors.

Finally, there is the imagery of the spirit world. The moon uses its magical powers to carve "unknown totems out of the lakeshore." These powerful emblems of another, mysterious world terrify the trapper. When, as the element of animism becomes more pervasive, the owl, traditionally linked to the spirit world, derides him, and cedars shape themselves into moose, circle "his swamps," and toss "their antlers up to the stars," the trapper knows he is trapped: The poised "arrowhead" of the mountain-god will be the final mockery of the porcupine "quills on his hatband."

Themes and Meanings

Earle Birney did not follow in the tradition of earlier nature poets such as Bliss Carman (1861-1929) or Archibald Lampman (1861-1899), whose romantic landscape poems celebrated the beauty, peace, and goodness of nature—but then, the rugged Canadian West of Birney's experience hardly resembled the more tranquil scenery of the East that inspired the imagination of his predecessors. The awe-inspiring and fear-inspiring mountain wilderness shaped such poems as "David" (one of his best-known poems, about the fall and death of a young mountain climber) and "Bushed." These poems are as much about the flaws and fears of human nature as they are about the fierce beauty and power of physical nature. As Birney stresses in such poems as "Maritime Faces" and "Climbers," if humans are to survive in a harsh environment that is indifferent to their pretensions and vulnerability, they must come with respect, humility, knowledge, vigilance, and readiness to solve the problems they encounter, both around them and within them.

"Bushed" exposes the folly of a man who fails to take seriously either nature's threat or his own limitations. His journey into the wilderness is a journey into madness and death. At first he presumes that the place he chooses to build his shack is safe and will accommodate his needs and desires. The "quills on his hatband" flaunt his arrogance. It is not so much nature around him that defeats him but his own nature, which is unprepared to take the proper measure of either his external or internal world. The mighty mountain looms high above him, and the confrontation with its shattering force soon seeps into his psyche and begins the unhinging of his mind. Increasingly, his mind mirrors the irrationality of a terror-stricken soul projected onto the vast indifference and impersonal force of his environment. The mountain comes alive, not with glorious splendor but as an ogre-god who wills the intruder's death and marshals all its resources to accomplish its purpose. Thus the lake becomes the god's lap of destruction, the ospreys become valkyries, the goats turn into guards, the lakeshore into totems, the owls into mockers, the cedars into threatening animals. The woods become "beardusky," and the winds become the aerial blacksmiths that forge the fateful arrowhead. The man who came to conquer the bush rather than to seek kinship discovers that he came in ignorance. He retreats to his puny shelter, bars himself in, and waits for the death that his mind has imagined.

Henry J. Baron

BUT SO AS BY FIRE

Author: George Oppen (1908-1984)
Type of poem: Lyric
First published: 1972; collected in *Seascape: Needle's Eye*, 1972

The Poem

George Oppen's "But so as by Fire" is a poem in free verse, its twenty-six short lines divided into thirteen verse paragraphs resembling brief phrases. The paragraphs, or phrases, vary in length from one to four lines. The title suggests an alternative to the effects of fire—effects achieved by something else as though "by fire." Fire often triggers new growth, as seen, for example, in the forest after a fire. Another fitting example within the poem's context is the rebirth of the mythological phoenix from the ashes of its own fiery death. The word "fire" is not in the poem; the regenerative connotation is unspoken.

There is immediacy of place in the first sixteen lines of the poem as the reader observes "this" life that is guarded by the trees' dark shade. Describing and extolling the virtues of nature are frequent themes of lyric poetry. In this poem, the "magic" of the natural world is protected by darkness, a significant departure from most poems about nature, wherein darkness is associated with fear or even death. The darkness here is not forbidding but nurturing.

The first two paragraphs present the larger picture, from a viewpoint of some distance—a general image of thick-foliaged woods covering the rocky ground. Then, suddenly, the author focuses in on his subject, and the images become more specific. The next four paragraphs—lines 7 through 14—detail the world under the trees. Broken boughs on the ground foster the decomposition cycle, as new life sprouts from the rotting matter on the ground. Small animals thrive in protective shadows, and pools, not stagnant but clean with the "trickle of freshwater," nourish the healthy life cycle.

The shift in perspective from the small, detailed world of the woods to the world of humanity begins in paragraph 7. The only punctuation in the poem occurs in line 15 as all that has gone before is identified, emphasized, and set apart by the comma and the white space after the phrase "New life." Oppen's poetry often involves clean-cut silences framing words; the usage here is consistent with the "beauty of silence" of the shadowed world.

The rich compost generates its own gentle heat on the forest floor and engenders new life. Unrealized potential is intimated in the "hidden starry life" that is "not yet/ A mirror like our lives." In paragraphs 8 through 10, the speaker intensifies his focus on struggling humanity and speaks with inclusive spokesmanship, likening "our lives" to a mirror: hiding nothing in light and reflecting mere copy images. Nothing new is produced in a mirror, in sharp contrast to the new life created by decay in the shaded forest.

In the generalizing manner of the sage, the poet muses in the last four lines (three concise phrases) that, paradoxically, light is to be feared more than shadows. He implies that in the silent dark places, literally and figuratively, are found possibilities, creativity, and strength to "Summon one's powers."

Forms and Devices

Precision of language is characteristic of Oppen's poetry. It is evident in the compressed language and spare method used in the poem as well as in Oppen's use of imagery. Oppen's poetry is most approachable through its imagery. As John Taggart states in an essay entitled "Deep Jewels: George Oppen's *Seascape*," in the journal *Ironwood* (1985), "Oppen has chosen to stand fast to the conception of image as center, foundation, and base for composition."

Oppen's imagery renders the abstract in concrete terms throughout the poem. For example, the new life generated by "the dark green moss/ In the sweet smell of rot" conveys the poem's concept of darkness as nurturer. Plain and original dispensing of ordinary words mark the precise and concrete imagery.

As with the objectivist method of poetry that he helped to originate in the 1930's, Oppen strove for a new refinement of imagery toward a poetry of simplicity and most important, thought. Imagery involves only the eye, but objectivism engages both the eyes and the mind equally. Oppen once said that in his poetry he was trying to describe how "the test of images can be a test of whether one's thought is valid." Consistent with that statement, in this poem the imagery is arresting, but its thrust is toward thought.

This thrust toward thought is accomplished in three ways. The first is characteristic of Oppen's bare, terse style. The language may be spare, but with a single word it can establish an attitude or a mood. The "thin ground/ That covers the rock ledge" is rendered beautiful because it is "magic." The darkness is not fearsome for it "guards" life. The rot is "sweet" smelling. Clearly, the organic structures are generated to lead toward thought.

Key patterns of sound accompany the word pictures in the second method of supporting the poem's meaning. The alliteration is subtle, but in this poetry of such reticence that it almost moves toward silence, compression and precision of language give each letter greater significance. Gentle, explosive *b* sounds link and grant "beauty" to "broken boughs." One can sense the forest's subtle regenerative heat in the quiet hiss of the phrase "moss/ In the sweet smell of rot." In contrast, the assonance in "lives reflect light/ like mirrors" is loudly bright and penetrating.

Finally, it is the combination of imagery and didacticism that leads the reader to meditative conclusions. The shadow imagery suggests protection and creativity. When, however, attention is turned to the situation in which humanity finds itself—exposed in light and "gone/ As far as possible"—the tone becomes didactic. The positive connotations of darkness—the images of safety in shadows—are replaced by the shock of rhetoric that defines the stated paradox that the danger to humanity exists in the light, not in the darkness. For example, the poet asks who knew "To be afraid/ Not of shadow but of light." Thus is traditional thought undermined by the restrained but powerful amalgam of statement with imagery. The "test of images" successfully guides the reader to final, thoughtful conclusions.

Themes and Meanings

"But so as by Fire" is a poem about regeneration. A frequent theme in poetry, with roots in ancient mythology, regeneration is typically perceived as a fount of possibility, creativity, and strength. That perception applies literally to organic life, as seen in the womblike environment of the forest in the poem, and figuratively to the mind and to the works of humanity.

In reality, fire often triggers rebirth in the forest, but the poem offers the organic life in the shaded forest as its representation of the beauty of the regenerative cycle. It then explores the subject further and declares that not only has humanity turned away from nurturing its own dark pockets of vision and apparently lost figurative regenerative capabilities but also there appears to be a tragic inevitability about the process.

The poem represents the loss by likening "our lives" (although the pronoun is ambiguous, the poet's inclusivity indicates the modern society all humans share) to mirrors. What is reflected in a mirror is not substantive and is not creatively new—it is a copy. Compared to the activity of rebirth in the darkened, symbiotic forest, humankind can be said to have lost all forward momentum. The poem implies that humans are stalled, creativity blocked, and that they stand exposed and vulnerable in the light that they themselves sought, having rejected the internal quiet, shadowed places out of fear of the dark. The poem does not explain further as to what light it means or in what way humans have "Gone/ As far as is possible." The effort is simply to lay out the human facts more clearly, to describe what it means to investigate the human condition.

The suggested inevitability of the move from the occurrence of regeneration to the figurative loss of it in humanity renders the poem nearly tragic. The perception of the tragic in the poem can be defined as the ceaseless conflict (the terms of which are never quite clear) that cannot be won.

The evidence that the process is inevitable is most clear in two places in the poem. The first is in the finality of the past tense used in the phrase "We have gone/ As far as is possible." The second is in the prophetic outlook that the new life, the "Hidden starry life," is not "yet" attained. The inference is clear: It is merely a matter of time.

"Hidden starry life" is a marvelous transitional image to demonstrate what it means to lose the strength of unrealized potential. A star is "hidden" while it gathers energy in the cool hydrogen gases of dark space, but after it ignites into fiery visibility, it begins consuming its own gases until its eventual death.

The poem ponders whether humanity will regenerate somehow, "as by fire," as life in the forest does, and find new possibilities. There are no answers given in the poem, although the tone remains upbeat. The exhortation is, after all, to "Summon one's powers," even if for no other reason than for courage to face the inevitable.

Marilyn Schultz

BUTCHER SHOP

Author: Charles Simic (1938-   )
Type of poem: Lyric
First published: 1971, in *Dismantling the Silence*

The Poem

Charles Simic's "Butcher Shop" is a poem of four four-line stanzas that shows how the poet and subsequently all humans are caught in a solitary existence. However, through a poet's perspective, people can reach across the distance of solitude toward communication.

The poet (someone who may or may not be the autobiographical Simic) stops before a closed butcher shop where a single light shines in the dark. Accoutrements of the butcher shop—a bloody apron, glistening knives, and a wooden butcher's block—can all be seen inside the store. The light and the other objects serve as images that metaphorically summon further images. The light is "like the light in which the convict digs his tunnel." The apron's bloody smears appear to make a map of continents, rivers, and oceans of blood. The polished knives shine like the altars "in a dark church," where supplicants bring victims of physical and mental infirmities to be healed. The wooden block, "where bones are broken," has been cleaned, but fruitlessly, because it still shows the remnants of the "river" of blood "dried to its bed." In this final image, the poet recognizes that this source nourishes him. That feeding is not physical, however; the poet claims that it is from this dried river that "deep in the night [he] hear[s] a voice."

As in much of Simic's work, the poem operates on a minimalist level. Not much seems to happen within the scene itself. Instead, the action takes place in the poet's act of making poetry—in turning the simple though gruesome effects of the butcher's shop into something surreal. This transformation allows the poet and the reader to speculate on the worldly phenomena that allow humans to reach across the distance of space, time, and language to speak to each other.

Forms and Devices

Simic's vocabulary in this poem—a typical example of his early work—is absolutely approachable. For instance, of the sixty-seven different words used in the poem, "continents" and "imbecile" are the only words longer than two syllables. Similarly, Simic uses a four-line stanza made up of free-verse lines with approximately four beats per line. Such a verse pattern may seem arbitrarily chosen, especially when it is realized that Simic violates this standard several times. For instance, two lines are four syllables or less ("Where I am fed" and "To be healed"). If intentionally chosen, this line may be employed by Simic simply because he finds it comfortable. Yet its facility also aids the reader in simply approaching the poem. The lines are neither overly long nor too short to draw attention to themselves. Overall, Simic seems to be striving for a kind of transparency in his language, where the things named will become what they signify when read.

Other aspects of the poem are manipulated to stress the objects at hand. Each stanza is its own sentence, except the first, which is divided into two sentences. Likewise, each object described—the light, apron, knives, and wooden block—receives a full sentence. When repetition surfaces as perhaps the only overt poetical device, it appears halfway through the poem and again at the end, serving to emphasize the bloody patterns on the apron ("great continents of blood,/ The great rivers and oceans of blood" and "Where I am fed,/ Where deep in the night I hear a voice").

The point of view in the poem is generalized and anonymous. Both the particulars of time and place are removed by the use of the opening word "sometimes" and the setting of the unnamed city or village street. The "I" in the poem could be anyone, and its anonymity draws the reader into a participation in the poet's own meditation. The three sentences that begin with "there is" or "there are" emphasize the factuality and permanence of common experience. Once each of the things named here is shown to actually exist, the poet moves into the less tangible connections brought about by the images' metaphoric comparisons.

Thus, much of Simic's style is characterized by omission rather than commission. Simic has pared down his words and meter, grounding the poem in day-to-day experience. By emphasizing the things at hand, he shows that the metaphysical considerations within this poem are indeed close to all readers and can even be accessed through everyday physical objects.

Themes and Meanings

Central to understanding much of Simic's work is realizing his belief that poetry can be a way to think. By starting with the certainty of the physical, the poet moves into areas that are more uncertain, intangible, and transitory. Simic wants to emphasize that all one knows of the imaginative, intellectual, emotional, and even spiritual worlds is gained from observation of surrounding things. As this poem begins with the certain objects of a butcher's shop and progresses into less tangible considerations, it may symbolize the poet's wish for readers to proceed in the same manner, from the material things of this world into a place that provides less certainty but more insight into the things around them. Thus, on one level, this poem does not supply a meaning as much as invite the reader to create one out of the objects found within it. However, this approach does not mean that a poem by Simic can mean anything that anyone wants. The poet has sent the reader in a specific direction, and that direction has been influenced by the person who is already experiencing the butcher shop.

In a setting typical of much of Simic's work, the speaker finds himself alone in a place that is dark and poorly lit. The scene retains an Old World atmosphere, one that is not often found in modern America. Part of the scene's imagery may be attributed to Simic's own childhood in Belgrade and Paris and his young adult life in the ethnic neighborhoods of New York City and Chicago. It also serves to summon a time before people selected their meat from rows of shrink-wrapped products in well-lit grocery aisles. In both time and condition, the scene calls to mind humans' physical connection to the earth.

The poet's mentioning that "I am fed" refers to metaphysical nourishment. In this way, the objects take on a metaphorical meaning. The single source of light provides the only light in the poet's solitude. Because it is "Like the light in which the convict digs his tunnel," Simic suggests that this small but sufficient light provides a hopeful exit from an otherwise dark perspective. As the poem's first image, the light suggests that observation—the illumination of the scene and the interplay of that illumination upon other objects—provides a way out of darkness. Likewise, the map created upon the apron and the dark church's altar suggested by the shining knives both create a sense of hope that comes from escape. That escape is neither guaranteed nor easy, but it offers hope.

These images may promise escape and comfort, but their connection to the violence that has created them makes them disturbing. The apron's map is drawn with smeared blood, and the church is imagined from the glint of knives that drew that blood. Blood is an ambiguous image here, as it is both a necessary part of life and yet often a sign of violence. One is not usually aware of the source of life—blood—unless the body is wounded or unless one considers a scene such as the butcher shop. Metaphorically, it is through a similarly difficult act of thinking that those things surrounding one all the time are wrested from their "unmeaning" state and made to mean.

The poet seems to be escaping from solitude, from the inability to connect with others. The people referred to individually are distant and alone: the convict in his tunnel, and "the cripple and the imbecile" brought to the altar. Only the "they" who bring these afflicted people to the dark altar are mentioned in the plural. The word "they" often refers to everyone and no one at the same time. This nameless and faceless group serves as the assumed voice of authority; it is the group most often referred to in casual conversation (such as "well, you know what they say. . . ."). In desiring healing for the cripple and the imbecile, "they" seem to want these differences wiped away, to bring same homogenous identity to the entire population. Therefore, the presence of the "they" contrasts with the individual's identity that allows one to truly communicate with another.

In the final stanza, the poet is freed from this subsuming force through a momentary hope of a single "voice" (the last word in the poem). This voice comes from the "river dried to its bed," which has been imaginatively created out of the "wooden block where bones are broken"; again, the violent imagery suggests that this wresting of meaningful communication will be difficult and even painful. Yet just as the block has been "scraped clean," the poet can scrape away the inauthentic identities of the faceless and blinding mob. In doing so, he can reach that single voice that calls to him from the solitude. The poet's wish is for the reader to hear this voice as well. The voice that the reader hears might be the poet's call from this poem; likewise, it may be the reader's voice that the poet himself heeds.

Brian C. Ferguson-Avery

BUTTERFLY

Author: Nelly Sachs (1891-1970)
Type of poem: Lyric
First published: 1949, as "Schmetterling," in *Sternverdunkelung*; English translation
  collected in *O the Chimneys*, 1967

The Poem

"Butterfly," written in free verse, consists of sixteen lines arranged in three groups
of six, six, and four lines. At the core of the poem is a typical nature reverie, except
that here the processes of observation and abstraction are reversed. In conventional
nature poetry, observation of a concrete object inspires the poet to achieve a deeper in-
sight, but in this poem the actual butterfly is embedded in interpretive associations. As
the poet contemplates the butterfly, two different images are summoned. The first im-
age, a visionary flight from the center of the earth, can be regarded as an association
inspired by the second image, a butterfly lighting on a rose.

The poem begins with the poet directly addressing the butterfly and admiring its
beautiful colors. Paradoxically, its colorfulness is tied to the image of dust and the
concept of "aftermath." The presence of dust is easily explained in terms of a natural
phenomenon—when one lightly brushes a butterfly's wings, a powdery residue re-
mains. Yet dust connotes death as well: "For dust you are and to dust you shall return"
(Genesis 3:19). In view of this second interpretation of dust, the connection to "after-
math" and the implied destruction is clearer.

The poet's subsequent observation is equally contradictory on the surface. The
reader is told that the butterfly has made the journey from the earth's flaming core,
passing through the stony outer layer. These cataclysmic images of fire and stone con-
flict with the butterfly's fragility. If one remains on the level of visual association, one
can picture how the butterfly has caught some of the fire's luminosity in the vibrant
coloring of its wings. One might also appreciate the lapidary quality of its markings,
like brilliant enamels fired in a kiln. The final line of this section, however, "Webs of
farewell in the transient measure," invites one to consider the butterfly's journey in
metaphoric terms. One is confronted with the concepts of death and transition.

Next the poet hails the butterfly as a creature of night, not in a demoniac sense, but a
blessed one. This is a highly unusual label for the butterfly, which depends on sunlight
for its survival. It has been suggested by Matthias Krieg that the butterfly's positive
connection to the night lies in its being an image of dreams. If one considers the dream
state as one of transition between consciousness and unconsciousness, then the pro-
jection of life's and death's burden onto the butterfly's delicate wings follows logi-
cally. Finally one arrives at the concrete image of the butterfly coming to rest on a
rose. For a moment the butterfly is only a butterfly, not an abstract fusion of life and
death, stasis and transition.

These ideas, however, permeate the poem's atmosphere and are transposed onto the wilting rose and fading sun in the last line of the second section.

Lines 13 and 14 repeat the opening pair of lines. Here the butterfly's colorful designs become abstract as they are transposed into the realm of metaphor and are transformed into a system of signs. The grammatical ambiguity of the final lines deliberately leaves the reader alternating between viewing the butterfly as a royal sign or as bearing a royal sign. The question is unresolved, but the reverential implication of "royal" bespeaks an optimistic faith in the order of the world. The butterfly becomes the ultimate symbol of signs and their meanings, carrying on its wings a mysterious, yet kingly, system of ciphers.

Forms and Devices

"Butterfly" contains no traditional metrical patterns, but the poem achieves a lyrical quality through its evocative associations and descriptions. It opens with a direct address to the butterfly and continues as an extended apostrophe. The poet's one-sided discourse consists of admiring epithets and descriptions.

The principal poetic device used by Nelly Sachs is the metaphor. This poem provides an excellent example of how she expands and adapts a metaphor, creating an all-inclusive symbol. The multiple possibilities of her metaphor's meaning exist somewhere between conventional references and a highly personal system of associations inspired by biographical experiences and a study of mysticism—both Jewish and Christian.

The butterfly traditionally evokes spring, renewal, and hope. Deeply bound to the sun for survival, it is connected to the symbolism of light, representing optimism and enlightenment. Its vibrant coloring is another aspect of this connection to the positive symbolism of light; hence, the butterfly is ascribed yet another abstract dimension. In many Western cultures it also serves as an icon for the soul, capturing visually the moment of the soul's separation from the body in death. So, too, does Sachs's butterfly carry a message that speaks to the human condition.

For the most powerful implications of this metaphoric butterfly, one must turn to the biological fact that the butterfly is a creature of metamorphosis. Its beautiful, evocative form is but a phase; indeed, it already has one "death" behind it—the death of the pupa. The butterfly carries a dual association: It symbolizes at once death (or the transient quality of life) and a hopeful cycle of renewal. The English version of this poem inclines one to favor the more pessimistic interpretation of the butterfly, for it translates the word *Jenseits* as "aftermath," which has decidedly negative connotations. *Jenseits* literally means "beyond" and indicates the afterlife or immortality. In one other instance the English translation opts for a darker view: The rose "withers," when in the original language it "wilts" in the fading sun. A wilting rose is part of a cycle of regeneration, as is the setting sun, while withering implies a more permanent state of decay. In the German text, then, the concepts of death and renewal do not form a duality of opposition; rather, they coexist as aspects of natural life and allow for a transcendence beyond its limitations.

Themes and Meanings

In Nelly Sachs's mature poetry, one finds echoes of her childhood passion for the fossils and insects that she studied as keys to nature's secrets. Later, as she tried to understand a distorted world which had engendered the Holocaust, she returned to this realm and found a rich source of symbols and metaphors. Her poem focuses on natural phenomena that emphasize constant flux and the potential for transformation, making it an especially poignant statement in the light of the historical background against which she wrote.

Sachs, who received the Nobel Prize for Literature in 1966, was known as the "poet of the Holocaust." This particular poem appeared in a volume of poetry dedicated to commemorating its victims and understanding their suffering. The butterfly is a recurring image in this collection, where it serves most often as an icon for the souls of the innocent. In this poem, however, the individual's metamorphosis through death is placed in the context of the earth's life cycles: The butterfly symbolically embraces a phase of transformation lasting eons (the planet's core is constantly creating) and one lasting a single day. Each end leads to a new beginning. The pain of leavetaking, of death, is not erased, but is mitigated by the promise of renewal. Thus did Sachs attempt to come to terms with the senseless deaths of her people during the Holocaust.

The metaphor is the poem's formative poetic device as well as its thematic content. In writing poetry, Sachs faced an unusual dilemma: The language she used, German, was also the language of the oppressor. Moreover, the experiences of her time seemed overwhelming and inexpressible. Her solution was her system of metaphors. At a time when many poets were experimenting with meaninglessness and with the arbitrariness of language, her metaphoric approach allowed her, in a sense, to reinvent her language. The metaphoric butterfly expresses the paradoxical relationship between death and transformation. It is the "royal sign" which encodes the patterns of this mystery and serves as an example of Sachs's transformed language in which words seem to include concepts and their opposites. When confronted with such paradoxes, one is indeed challenged to reconsider assumptions about how narrowly one perceives the world and one's position in it.

Elisabeth Strenger

BYPASSING RUE DESCARTES

Author: Czesław Miłosz (1911-   )
Type of poem: Lyric
First published: 1982, as "Rue Descartes," in *Hymn o perle*; English translation collected in *The Separate Notebooks*, 1984

The Poem

"Bypassing Rue Descartes" is a poem thirty-five lines long and arranged in ten irregular stanzas. The poem is written in the first person, as is traditional in lyric poetry. The poet remembers a walk taken in Paris, which occasions a meditation on history, exile, and guilt. The poem has the qualities of nostalgia and intimacy that insist the poem is autobiographical rather than a portrayal of a persona.

"Bypassing Rue Descartes" (which was tellingly retitled in translation from simply "Rue Descartes") describes a walk the poet, "A young barbarian just come to the capital of the world," took that initiated his life as an exile from Lithuania and Poland. The title establishes a place and a locus for meditation. The poet, however, bypasses this street and figuratively bypasses what this street signifies: Cartesian certainty, with its insistence on analysis and division. Bypassing Rue Descartes, the poet descends toward the Seine, hence proposing a traditional departure from abstraction and a movement toward nature.

The poem's first stanza establishes the poet's place and identity. In the second stanza, the poet considers himself one among many exiled nationalities, including Poles, North Africans, and Vietnamese. Implicit in his catalog is the history of empires and colonialism. The poem continues, describing the difference between the immigrant's customs, "About which nobody here should ever be told," and the cosmopolitan world. While the poet is speaking from his own experience, he also is describing the condition of the exile. The poet contrasts his homeland's "cloudy provinces" with the "universal" city he enters "dazzled and desiring."

In the fourth and fifth stanzas, both of which are unrhymed couplets, the poet shifts to a conditional future that describes certain specific political conditions. In these lines, the tone is clipped, aphoristic, and ironic. Readers should recall that when Czesław Miłosz permanently left Poland for France in late 1951, France was the colonial power in Algeria and Vietnam. Nationalists of both these countries were active in Paris, hence many of these exiles "Would be killed because they wanted to abolish the customs of their homes." Many of their peers were "seizing power/ In order to kill in the name of the universal, beautiful ideas."

The poem returns to the specifics of the walk in the sixth stanza with the sensuous catalog of a street market: rustling laughter in the dark, baked breads, lemons and garlic, and wine poured from clay pitchers. These sights and sounds return the poet to the immediate and commonplace world, yet his meditations on empire and power are not mitigated, for the poet finds he is surrounded by monuments attesting periods of glory. What these monuments represent, however, is forgotten.

The final four stanzas consist of a movement toward a vision of time where empires always rise and fall. This traditional vision of fortune is then displaced by a more earthly, almost pagan, vision that "the time of human generations is not like the time of the earth." The large vision narrows to focus on the poet, and the poem concludes with the poet's confession of his own guilt.

Forms and Devices

Although "Bypassing Rue Descartes" is essentially a lyric, Miłosz is a poet who never rests easily in a single recognizable form. Like many of his other poems, this one is allegorical and ironic. It also shares with Miłosz's prose writing a philosophical interest in the nature of power. Because the poem continually verges on the allegorical and philosophical, and departs from the personal or lyrical, it contains elements of generalization.

The city of Paris is named through its epithet, "the capital of the world." The city then becomes "the universal," suggesting not only its cosmopolitan atmosphere but also its metaphysical absoluteness. It is a manifestation of *idea*. The poet quickly undercuts this portrayal with the personification of the city behaving in accordance with its nature ("Rustling" with laughter, "baking" breads, "pouring wine," "buying" garlic and fish), all the while shamelessly indifferent. Though this lists the commonplace, Miłosz uses its vitality and the sense of being engrossed with the transactions of life to contrast with the attraction of the exiled to the "universal."

The poem employs the classical allegorical structure of the journey to convey meaning. Like the pilgrim Dante, the young exile Miłosz makes a descending journey toward revelation. The journey from postwar Poland into exile also is implied as part of this allegorical journey. When the poet reaches the Seine and leans on the "rough granite of the embankment," he senses he has "returned from travels through the underworlds." Like Dante, he has witnessed the cataclysms of history. At the river's edge, symbolically another threshold, he "suddenly saw in the light the reeling wheel of the seasons/ Where empires have fallen and those once living are now dead." Not simply a traditional view of the vicissitudes of Fortuna, the poet assumes the role of prophet. Much in the tradition of Ecclesiastes, the poet sees the emptiness of human existence and the need for dispensations other than those offered by politics and philosophy.

If the first part of the poem can be considered ironic (the poet self-deprecatingly calls himself a "young barbarian," which echoes Constantine Cavafy's poem "Waiting for the Barbarians"; the decidedly ironic repetition of "Soon enough" marks the fate of exiles involved in politics) and the second part an allegorical vision; then the third part, the last two stanzas, returns to the personal but without the opening stanzas' ironic detachment. The poem turns to an earlier memory of a walk through a forest, where the poet encountered a water snake coiled in the grass and killed it. The poem concludes with a deeply personal memory and a profoundly symbolic image. While one may wish to assign a biblical meaning to the snake, one must note that it is a water snake and that in Lithuanian folklore these creatures are sacred; hence, it is taboo to harm them, as Miłosz states in a footnote to the poem. The poem describes the poet's exile from nature in that he has committed a transgression against life.

Themes and Meanings

"Bypassing Rue Descartes" is a deceptively complex poem. Among its considerations are exile, the mutability of power through time, and guilt. The poem's journey is in many ways a searching back to reach a personal moment of guilt, an original but personal sin that has resulted in what amounts to a life of punishment and purgation through the condition of exile. That everyone has committed transgressions against life, that everyone is guilty of destruction, is the human condition and not one borne of a strictly religious sensibility. Insofar as everyone is guilty of transgression, everyone lives in a condition of exile.

"Bypassing Rue Descartes" implicitly asks: For what do we live? It does not ask the question of dogma—how do we live?—but the question of choices, responses, and responsibilities. The poem offers many dichotomies: civilized-barbarian, abstraction-sensuousness, metaphysical-tangible, empire-local, universal-specific, and death-life. It traces the poet's movement from desiring the universal to understanding it as part of the complex of empire, dogmatic politics, abstraction, and finally the force of death—the same force that has driven him into exile.

The poem insists on life: the sensuous particularity of life as illustrated by the catalogs of the provincial customs and the details of the street market as well as the symbolic value of the water snake as a sign of generative forces. The emphasis on the fully lived moment is found throughout Miłosz's poetry, as exemplified by "Rivers," "It Was Winter," "A Poetic State," "Reading the Japanese Poet Issa (1762-1826)," or the movement of the entire collection of poems *Nieobjęta ziemia* (1984), translated as *Unattainable Earth* (1986).

Miłosz's poetry exemplifies what has become known as the poetry of witness. His work has revolved consistently around the question of history and the individual's position within history. Poetry, for Miłosz, is the witnessing of history. Poetry thus serves as memory; however, poetry is also moral, in that daily it stands before what is real and it must name that reality. "Bypassing Rue Descartes" is not a rejection of history, but an understanding of mutability. To be a witness, one must also be willing to bear responsibility of one's guilt, which comes at the very moment of the exercise of power. No one can escape the judgment of history, for "just punishment/ . . . reaches, sooner or later, the breaker of a taboo."

James McCorkle

BYZANTIUM

Author: William Butler Yeats (1865-1939)
Type of poem: Lyric
First published: 1932, in *Words for Music Perhaps and Other Poems*

The Poem

"Byzantium" is written in five eight-line stanzas that are, in their metrical precision and complex rhyme scheme, reminiscent of the unique stanzaic patterns of the early nineteenth century odes composed by such English Romantic poets as William Wordsworth, Percy Bysshe Shelley, and John Keats. The twentieth century Anglo-Irish poet William Butler Yeats certainly shares many traits with those, and other, nineteenth century precursors. Nevertheless, despite all the intensity of its emotion and the rich intricacies of its imagery, "Byzantium" is hardly the sort of effusive out-burst one has come to associate with the ode; the speaker seems to be more engulfed in his vision than in any attempt to share its emotional quadrants with the reader.

"Byzantium" takes its name from an ancient city upon whose site the Roman Em-peror Constantine constructed his eastern, Christian capital about C.E. 330. Called Nova Roma, that city eventually became known as Constantinopolis and is the modern-day Turkish city Istanbul. For more than a thousand years the capital of the Byzantine Empire, it was regarded as the premier city of the Western world. While Yeats prefers the city's older name, there is no doubt that his Byzantium is medieval Constantinople.

As the poem begins, night is falling. The day's sights and even the night's sounds draw back, leaving the reader's undistracted senses free to explore other realms of re-ality and ranges of experience. Soon it is after midnight. The soldiers' nightly revel-ries have ended, although a "night walker," who may simply be someone out very late or a streetwalker plying her trade, is singing, and in the "great cathedral," the Hagia Sophia, the gong that calls the faithful to prayer has already rung.

In this dreamy atmosphere, pregnant with mystery and anticipation, "A starlit or a moonlit dome disdains" all that human beings are—human complexities and the "fury and the mire" of human veins. That dome may be the night sky or it may be the dome of the Hagia Sophia. Earthbound in this most worldly of cities, an imperial capi-tal, the speaker reminds the reader of that extreme emblem of power and glory, the boundless heavens that dwarf the scope of the human imagination, let alone human accomplishments, let alone one mere mortal.

As if he, too, has been called to prayer and is inspired by this setting to free his spirit of its sensory limitations, the speaker now has a vision. He cannot be certain if the im-age he sees is a man or a shade—that is, a ghost—although it is an image apparently so awesome in its reality that it overwhelms him to such an extent that he does not know if he is alive or dead—or what life or death is. Yielding to the strength of his vi-sion, he "hail[s] the superhuman;/ I call it death-in-life and life-in-death."

The vision increases in its intensity as the darkened physical world all about him is transfigured. He is "seeing" with the mind's eye—although it would be more proper, given the quasi-religious tone of much of the imagery thus far, to imagine the so-called third eye of the mystic. The reader now sees a golden bird that may be a miracle, a real bird, or a man-made, mechanical bird. The speaker decides that it is a miraculous bird; it is "Planted on the starlit golden bough" and "by the moon embittered." The imagery recalls the disdainful dome of the opening stanza, for the bird also "scorn[s] aloud" the day's commonplaces and "all complexities of mire or blood."

In the fourth stanza, the visionary frenzy increases as the reader is swept up with the speaker "into a dance,/ An agony of trance." Flames are flitting on the pavement. These are not the result of the fires of our physical world, however, but are manifestations of the fire of the spirit. Although they are begotten of blood, those spirits who have finally transcended their physical being—that "fury and mire"—are escaping the purgatorial fires that have cleansed them of their worldliness.

In the last stanza, the vision is fulfilled, and the reader is allowed to see the liberated souls of the dead. "Astraddle on the dolphin's mire and blood," these souls have breached all those earthly and sensory barriers that in life normally confine one to the prosaic plane of this world. As if on a floodtide that bursts like a fountain up from the midnight streets of ancient Byzantium, the spirits make their journey to the Isle of the Blessed across "That dolphin-torn, that gong-tormented sea" that divides the living both from their peace and from the ultimate source of the speaker's vision.

Forms and Devices

Yeats never abandoned the Symbolist tradition that shaped him as a poet in his youth. Though "Byzantium" is a product of his later years, written well after he had transformed himself into a modernist poet, surely the chief device that gives the poem its other-worldly ambiance is the symbol.

Indeed, in Yeats's view, only the symbolic can express the highest truths, for symbols are "hints too subtle for the intellect"—that is, they can speak to the deeper and more enduring faculties that are generally categorized as the soul. Furthermore, the symbol can do so with an incredible economy, whereby a series of symbols in the right combination can encompass the sorts of truths that would require reams of philosophical discourse to approximate.

By the same token, Yeats was himself too serious a student and seeker of human enlightenment to trust to the unregenerate dream imagery that often beguiles the visionary poet. Thus all his life he steeped himself in traditional symbologies—ancient Celtic lore; occult symbolism and ritual, including astrology; and, finally, the rich Christian iconography of Byzantine Europe.

Yeats's studies had taught him that the ancient Romans used dolphins to depict the spirit's voyage from this world to the next; that the starry dome was symbolic of the soul's astral destiny in the ancient mystery cults associated with Mithra and Orpheus; that a crowing cock carved on a tombstone was intended to ward off evil spirits and influences; that the Byzantine emperors had mechanical birds that sang to the delight of visitors; that the golden bough signifies that point at which the temporal and eternal mingle their mysteries. Precisely how these and other symbols that Yeats half appropriated and half created combine to form new or larger meanings in his poetry is left, as it should be, to the creative energies of each reader.

Themes and Meanings

While the symbol may leave the analytical mind that eschews speculative reasoning high and dry, Yeats's poetry is not incapable of yielding precise meanings, even if they remain debatable. If one can balance the symbolic coordinates, "Byzantium" yields a rich harvest.

It is generally accepted, for example, that Byzantium is for Yeats a city of art to which the soul might escape whenever the pressures or sheer corruption of the world in particular and the physical universe in general become too much to bear. Much of this sort of reading of "Byzantium" is based on pairing that poem with comments Yeats made in a long prose work entitled *A Vision* (1925, 1937), as well as with another, earlier Yeats poem, "Sailing to Byzantium," which does seem to express a desire to escape from the decay and tedium of cyclical nature and which also mentions a golden bird.

On a wholly spiritual level, "Byzantium" clearly does contrast the mere mundane level of daylight vision with the infinitely richer possibilities that contemplations of the eternal and the miraculous offer. If the poem seems to trivialize day-to-day despairs and travails, it does so by asserting that enduring glories that are as yet unimagined, albeit hinted at in the symbols and icons of artistic and religious traditions, will eventually reward the patient soul.

The less one categorizes the nature of these glories—whether they are religious or aesthetic—of the eternal and spiritual or of the temporal and perceptual, the more one can appreciate Yeats's main point that they are in fact transcendent and beyond corruption, and are therefore unchanging.

Thus the "superhuman" that the speaker hails can be Yeats's way of suggesting that humanity has yet to achieve its full potential in the capacity to imagine a transcendent reality. The poem also comments on that element of the divine that seems to commingle irresistibly with humanity's mortal nature, creating the complexities and confusions and conflicts on which the poem comments. This divine element could be the Christ, who, in the Byzantine image called the Pantokrator, represented in Yeats's view the apogee of all Western thought and development to that moment in history and so seemed, as an image, to embody the perfection the race is perpetually seeking in its visionary quests.

Russell Elliott Murphy

THE CADENCE OF SILK

Author: Garrett Kaoru Hongo (1951-   )
Type of poem: Narrative
First published: 1988, in *The River of Heaven*

The Poem

Garrett Kaoru Hongo's "The Cadence of Silk" consists of one long stanza of forty-two lines that describes the poet's relationship to the game of basketball in general, and to the play of two teams in particular. The poem begins with the poet recounting how he originally became interested in basketball in Seattle, then continues with a description of his current favorite team, in Los Angeles. The poem directs the reader to the intricate details of the basketball game in such a way that even if the reader is not interested in sports, the cadence of the game will appear interesting.

The poem's single stanza may be deceptive in its simplicity, but the poet is actually very carefully leading the reader from the speaker's initial fascination with one sports team to his interpretations of the intricate details of the sport once he settles upon a home-team favorite. The poet's purpose is merely to reveal his own fascination with the game, rather than to convince the reader that basketball is a worthwhile sport. While basketball is unlikely subject matter for poetry, the poet wins the reader over by mimicking the sounds of the sport through language choice and images.

While basketball is a game of hundreds of quickly executed plays, the poet takes the time in the second half of the poem to describe just one play performed by one of his favorite players. Through his detail of this single event the poet draws out the action of the poem to a conclusion that is as satisfying to the reader as the completion of an attempted basket is to the basketball fan. Thus, the poem imitates the pleasure derived from the sport by delivering the same spontaneity and success within the poem. The poet demonstrates his skills with language just as the sportsman demonstrates his skill with the ball.

Forms and Devices

The combination of lyrical description and narrative is typical of Hongo's technique. His narrative skill lies in his use of specific language, on his ability to tell an interesting story, and on his genuine interest in and enthusiasm for his subject. A successful narrative poem must achieve two goals: tell a story and present the story in a musical or metaphorical manner so that the reader is transformed by the story as one is by any poem. Hongo uses the language of basketball in detailed and effective lines that convey the meaning of the action of the game, while not overburdening the meter of the poem with unnecessary language or meaning. The actual game of basketball is one that requires an economy of movement in order to achieve the goal; likewise, Hongo's poem must make minimal use of language in order to accomplish its simple description without losing the readers who may not be familiar with the game.

"The Cadence of Silk" relies upon ordinary language, a few sports terms which are defined, and the juxtaposition of mundane images to convey the action and nuances of the basketball game the poet is describing. The simple language welcomes the reader like an afternoon spent on a couch watching sports, yet the occasional technical term or rich and aptly placed adjective awakens in the reader the knowledge that some other sort of perfection is being sought by the poet as well. Sports terminology is a language of duosyllabic terms: "rebound," "outbound," "downcourt," "scoopshot," "point guard," and "backspin," for example, all serve to place the poem in an active sort of rhythm. However, the poet can surprise the reader with other descriptions of the play as "undulant ballet" or "action, smooth/ and strenuous as Gorgiasian rhetoric." Here the language asks more of the reader than simply a fan's adoration of the game. Clearly the poet owes more than casual allegiance to the sport as well.

There is no attempt at rhyme in this poem, although a certain rhythm is set up by the aforementioned doubled words, which continue throughout the poem. The point that the poet makes in the narrative of the poem is that the action of play of basketball is smooth and has a certain music and cadence to it caused by the movements of the players. In the last half of the poem, his description of a single basketball shot by his favorite player serves to illustrate this physical music. The poet uses language that moves from one line to the next without hesitation and requires long breaths to speak, just as the successful execution of a basketball shot may require numerous movements all fluidly consecutive to get the ball through the hoop.

In addition to the use of language the poet uses a vivid image in the last section of the poem describing the basket. The play is described in a fluid terms itself: The player is "sleek as [an] arctic seal," then the ball is "slick as spit," and then, finally, the player is a waiter balancing glasses of champagne, the ultimate celebratory fluid. These images flow together easily until they reach the climax of the poem's last lines, where the basketball "slashes through/ the basket's silk net with a small,/ sonorous splash of completion." The poet is generous in his use of images of the player, first characterizing him as a waiter, then characterizing his jump as "popcorn-like," and then describing his arching play as "slung dextrously."

The poet uses conversational language. Phrases such as "in my opinion," "frankly," and "in the parlance of the game," all serve to create a homely image for the poem. However, the poet surprises the reader by comparing the game to "Gorgiasian rhetoric," a term that suggests the complicated nature of the game. Gorgias was a Greek philosopher from c. 483-c. 376 B.C.E. whose highly regarded powers of oratory and persuasion included rhythmic and musical effects, symmetrical clauses and poetic diction. Through this reference, the poet suggests the intricate and carefully orchestrated aspects of the game of basketball.

Themes and Meanings

"The Cadence of Silk" occurs in the middle of the second section of *The River of Heaven*, nestled among other poems about growing up in Los Angeles in a mixed Anglo-American, Asian, and Latino culture. Although this poem does not bring the issues of culture to the forefront, other poems in this book highlight the trials and joys of growing up on the outside of American culture, while finding a place inside. Hongo has described his own work as "a search for origins of various kinds, a quest for ethnic and familial roots, cultural identity, and poetic inspiration."

Hongo's work is easily accessible to young people because he writes with authentic language and humor about the experiences of youth, while crediting these experiences with the importance and significance that they deserve. Hongo has provided some sort of voice for what he called "newly arrived peoples with their boat trails of memories from across the oceans." These comments alone attest to the usefulness of a poem such as "The Cadence of Silk" in talking with young people about poetry, sports, and the perfection of language and action. The poem itself has so much action that it would be an ideal starting point for involving students who are usually unresponsive to poetry.

In "The Cadence of Silk" Hongo directs the reader's attention to the artistic and physical feats of the game and compares basketball to ballet. The language of the poem is designed to make the reader feel comfortable and unthreatened by the action of the poem. Even if the reader does not like the Los Angeles Lakers, the poem can be satisfying, as the point of the poem is not to prove that the Lakers are the best team, or even that basketball is the best sport. Rather, the poet attempts to reveal what is appealing about the game by leading the reader through a perfectly executed play, which is characterized by sounds that cannot be heard by spectators, but only seen—the cadence of silk, when it swishes and undulates and everyone sees that the basket has been successful.

Marlene Broemer

CAGED BIRD

Author: Maya Angelou (Marguerite Johnson, 1928-   )
Type of poem: Lyric
First published: 1983, in *Shaker, Why Don't You Sing?*

The Poem

Maya Angelou's highly romantic "Caged Bird" first appeared in the collection *Shaker, Why Don't You Sing?* in 1983. Inspired by Paul Laurence Dunbar's poem "Sympathy," Angelou contrasts the struggles of a bird attempting to rise above the limitations of adverse surroundings with the flight of a bird that is free. She seeks to create in the reader sentiment toward the plight of the misused, captured creature—a symbol of downtrodden African Americans and their experiences.

The first two stanzas contrast two birds. Lines 1 through 7 describe the actions of a bird that is free; it interacts with nature and "dares to claim the sky." The second stanza (lines 8 through 14) tells of a captured bird that must endure clipped wings, tied feet, and bars of rage; yet he still opens his throat and sings.

The third and fifth stanzas are identical. Lines 2, 4, and 6 and lines 5 and 7 of these identical stanzas rhyme. This repeated verse elaborates on the song of freedom trilled by the caged bird; though his heart is fearful and his longings unmet, the bird continues to sing of liberty. The fourth stanza continues the comparison of two birds, the caged and the free. The free bird enjoys the breeze, the trees, the winds, the lawn, the sky, and the fat worms; the caged bird with his wings still clipped and his feet still tied continues, nevertheless, to open his throat and sing. Like the refrain of a hymn, the fifth and final stanza is a reiteration.

Angelou's characterization of a bird that is free (first and fourth stanzas) provides an effective contrast with the bird that is caged (second, third, fourth, and fifth stanzas). The sentiment that Angelou evokes in the reader is suggestive of Dunbar's inspirational poem.

Forms and Devices

Angelou does not allow meter, rhyme, and stanza to control her poetry. She determines her own structure—or lack of it—and uses form and device for her own means; she searches for the sound, the tempo, the rhythm, and the rhyme appropriate for each line.

"Caged Bird" is an example of unstructured verse. The number of beats per line varies; for example, line 1 has four beats, line 2 has six, line 3 has four, and line 4 has five. The number of lines in each stanza fluctuates as well; stanzas 1 and 2 have seven lines each, but stanzas 3 and 4 have eight. In addition to her use of the intermittent stanza, Angelou repeats stanza 3 as stanza 5; this repetition is reminiscent of the chorus in a song. The only other structuring device that Angelou employs in the thirty-eight lines is sporadic rhyme. For instance, only lines 9 and 11 in the entire first two stanzas use rhyming words ("cage" and "rage"); in the fourth stanza only lines 30 and 31 rhyme ("breeze" and "trees"). The only other rhyming words that Angelou uses—and at her own discretion—are in the third stanza, which she repeats as stanza 5. She rhymes "trill" and "still" with "hill"; she also rhymes "heard" and "bird."

The repetition of the third stanza gives some predictability to the poem and allows the reader to participate actively in the unpleasant plight of the caged bird. By contrast, other parts of the poem are unpredictable and at times even pleasurable; the joy of the free bird makes it possible for the reader to bear the tragic story of the oppressed one.

To convey her message clearly, Angelou applies many stylistic devices in her poem. She employs personification when she writes "his shadow shouts," when the free bird "names the sky," and when the sailing bird rides "on the back of the wind." She uses imagery to advantage in "Caged Bird." Her adjectives enable the reader to see clearly the "orange sun rays" and the "dawn-bright lawn." Her precise verbs make clear the action in the verse. For instance, the free bird "leaps," "dips his wing," and "dares to claim the sky"; conversely, the caged bird "stalks" and "can seldom see through/ his bars." Angelou presents both the dance of the free bird and the impeded hobble of the caged one. The pathetic visions of clipped wings, bound limbs, and prison cell are in direct contrast to the dipping wings of a free bird riding the wind. Angelou does not compromise the cruelty; she unhesitatingly conveys the heartrending message and the sorrowful images to the reader. Likewise, she presents the joy of freedom and flight.

Metaphor is one of Angelou's most obvious stylistic devices. The reader recognizes that the caged bird is Angelou herself—as well as any African American in an oppressive society. The "grave of dreams" is the perch in the confining cage.

Angelou's use of foreshadowing is evident. The fate of the caged bird will be unrelenting misery and death if the imprisonment and oppression continue. The poet hints at this despair and inevitable outcome when she pens the words "grave," "nightmare," "stalks," and "scream." Sounds are an essential part of the poem. The poet refers to songs, to tunes, to "a fearful trill," to singing, and to sighing trees.

Among the most effective of Angelou's stylistic devices are her comparisons and contrasts. She presents similarities between the free and the caged birds: their wings, their physical form. Her use of contrasts, however, is particularly effective; for example, the "nightmare scream" of the caged bird's shadow is in direct opposition to the bird's fearfully trilling his song of freedom. Angelou juxtaposes cultures—the open air and a cage with bars—and the ways that the two birds use their wings: the free bird flies freely in the rays of the sun, but the caged bird endures clipped wings.

Themes and Meanings

Any analysis of "Caged Bird" must begin with the title. The reader knows immediately from the words "Caged Bird" that the story will necessarily involve the restrictions imposed by a cage on the bird within its bars. Dunbar's "Sympathy" gave Angelou both the inspiration and the title not only for this poem and but also for her first autobiographical book, *I Know Why the Caged Bird Sings* (1970); these two works by Angelou celebrate her survival and that of all African Americans in oppression.

Evident in "Caged Bird" are two traditional literary themes: reversal of fortune and survival of the unfittest. By presenting the free bird before depicting the caged bird, Angelou helps the reader visualize what the caged bird must have been like before its capture; the description of the two contrasting environments helps the reader feel the sense of loss of the captured bird because of its reversed fate. Even with its clipped wings, tied feet, narrow quarters, and bars of rage, however, the fragile, caged bird is still able to survive and to soar again through its song; this imprisoned bird truly epitomizes the survival of the unfittest, the major theme in the verse.

These contrasting environments—the freedom of the open world and the restrictive surroundings of the caged bird—create the setting for the poem. The reader can feel the breeze, see the sun, imagine the rich feast of fat worms, and hear the sighing trees of the world of the free creature; in contrast, the reader feels the fear and restricted movement, sees the bars, imagines the wants, and hears the song of the imprisoned bird.

Characterization is important to "Caged Bird." An important way of revealing the character of the caged animal is to pit the exploits of the bird that is free against the stalking of the penned animal; the reader is able to experience the deprivation of the confined creature and the ecstasy of the free one. A description of the shackled feet, small quarters, and clipped wings acquaints the reader with the physical pain that the prisoner has had to endure; the word "fear" conveys its emotional plight. The most significant characteristic of the manacled creature, however, is its singing despite its fear; this song divulges its hope and its inner strength. The reader's own throat is closed with emotion as the bird opens its throat in song, its reaction to the indignities and its way to transcend the harsh environment.

The bird's life reflects more than submission and mere survival. The harsh and painful aspects of the caged bird's existence do not take away its dignity, and the physical and psychological pain do not destroy its style; the bird continues to know the source of its strength and to use its means of expression—song—to pray and to rebuild its life. The melody signifies the ability of the bird to tap its internal, creative resources for its healing. The beliefs of the imprisoned creature anchor its identity and allow the bird to adapt to its situation creatively. One of the lasting images the reader has of "Caged Bird" is the bird's raising its head in song, its answer to fear, oppression, and the pressures of life. The political poem encourages strength in adversity.

Angelou did not intend "Caged Bird" for African Americans alone; she intended the poem for any listening ear. Like the caged bird, she uses her own creativity, prepares her own song, and shows resilience and strength in the face of hardships; the poem is her autobiography. Although the bird is still caged at the end, the reader is left with hope. The delicate bird is a survivor and remembers his song. The reader trusts that the bird can endure the oppression that hopefully will soon lift. The denouement is, however, open; readers—and the bird—can complete the ending as they will.

Anita Price Davis

CALIFORNIA SWIMMING POOL

Author: Sharon Olds (1942-   )
Type of poem: Lyric
First published: 1987, in *The Gold Cell*

The Poem

"California Swimming Pool" is a short poem in free verse. It is made up of five long, descriptive sentences, which form one stanza. In it, the poet evokes the mood—the sounds, the sights, the atmosphere, and the intrigue—of summer afternoons at a public swimming pool.

The scene is described from a young girl's perspective, most likely a girl approaching puberty. She speaks informally in the first person, remembering the scene, using the conversational "you" to describe the place and what she did and saw there. Sharon Olds often describes personal experiences in her poems; in fact, many of her poems are clearly autobiographical. Thus, the speaker, who is actually an adult looking back on herself as a girl, is probably indistinguishable from the poet herself.

The first two sentences set the scene. Around the pool, the poet recalls, the dead leaves "lay like dried-out turtle shells," and the air was filled with summer insects: "sated" mosquitoes and yellow jackets. The bright sun and intense heat of a California summer are easily evoked. The leaves were "scorched and crisp," and mosquitoes hung in the air. As the poet describes it, not only does the weather seem oppressive but also the mood, which borders on the sinister: The dead leaves have "points sharp as wasps' stingers," and the mosquitoes are compared to sharks. Even the yellow jackets, usually harmless if annoying, "moved when you moved," in a threatening manner implying the futility of escape.

In fact, for the poet, there was no escape. A ritual, common and irresistible, unfolded daily, and the boys and girls of summer were participants in the ceremony. The site for the ritual, the "great pool" around which "everything circled," is described as if it were in an ancient temple, its water "blue and/ glittering as the sacred waters at Crocodilopolis." Furthermore, there was even the ritual of mock sacrifice when "the boys came from underwater . . ./ to pull you down." The swimming pool in which the children played becomes in the poet's memory a sacred place where the youngsters performed their own rites of passage, marking their entrances into adulthood.

That transformation naturally included the girl's first knowledge of sex—an awareness of her own sexual feelings and a curiosity about the sexuality of others. That is why "the true center was the/ dressing rooms," because behind the splintered pine wall "were boys, actually/ naked there in air clouded as the/ shadows at the bottom of the pool. . . ." As part of her initiation into adulthood, the girl seeks sexual knowledge. The reader is reminded, however, that she suspected the quest was dangerous: The bottom of the pool was "where the crocodiles/ glistened in their slick skins." Boys—and the power of sexuality—are like crocodiles, fascinating yet threatening, even deadly.

Nevertheless, the urge to sacrifice herself for sexual knowledge was hard to resist—temptation (in the form of a knothole in the pine wall), says the poet, "hissed at me" all summer. Thus, the poem ends with an allusion to Eve's temptation by the serpent and the girl (not yet a woman) considering the invitation to partake of the forbidden fruit: *"come see, come see, come eat and be eaten."*

Forms and Devices

In "California Swimming Pool," the poet's vantage point in time and maturity lends an irony to this description of the summertime experience of a girl on the threshold of sexual awakening. The poet speaks in the past tense; she has had time to reflect on her experiences. In other words, the speaker (and perhaps the reader) fondly recalls as well as painfully relives what will happen—what did happen—in the weeks or months after the summer scene this poem describes. The girl in the poem, however, is still an innocent, no matter how attuned she has become to the forbidden pleasures and hidden dangers of sex and boys.

"California Swimming Pool" is packed so full of concrete language that it has the richness and density of a copiously arranged still life. Olds does not rely on rhyme or strict meter to give her poem unity and form; she uses related images to "hinge" the four sentences together. The dead leaves "like dried-out turtle shells," with "points sharp as wasps' stingers" and the "sated" mosquitoes "like sharks" are similes that suggest not only the summer climate but also the peril later clearly associated with the boys. These images create an aura of danger and prepare the reader for the later comparisons, which are bolder.

The central metaphor describes the boys as crocodiles, coming from underwater "to pull you down" and lying in shadows at the bottom of the pool "in their slick skins." The references to predators—mosquitoes, wasps, sharks, and finally crocodiles—unify the poem and reinforce the sense of unknown danger the poet then felt about her attraction to the opposite sex.

The combined effect of these images is to transform the swimming pool into a magical, almost mythical place of sacred waters and fabulous beasts. The place at the center of the fable, however, is described in literal terms: The dressing rooms are familiar, with their "smell of chlorine" and their "cold concrete." It is almost as if the fantasy of the pool fades to stark reality in the dressing rooms, where "boys, actually naked" were for the girl a temptation all too real.

Themes and Meanings

Danger is probably not all that the girl sensed that summer, but her inexperience hindered a mature appreciation of her sexuality. Sex, a frequent theme in Olds's poetry, is often explored, always celebrated. She reveres and respects its power in human lives and rejoices in its power to express absolute love. For Olds, sex is a fundamental and needed language. So for the girl, the message of the hissing knot-hole was undeniable. The mysterious attraction of sex, for Olds, is similarly not to be denied.

The "clouded" air of the dressing rooms and the "shadows" in the pool are also accurate metaphors. The clouds and shadows hid and distorted the objects of the girl's curiosity; they represent the obstacles that the girl, in her quest for sexual knowledge, would have to confront and overcome. They also could represent her own naïve beliefs, possibly misconceptions, which might have impeded her quest.

The reference to "sacred waters" reinforces the idea of the girls and boys as initiates in an ancient ceremony. "Crocodilopolis" is an allusion to the Acropolis of Athens, Greece, site of some of the best-known ancient Greek temples and a sacred place of worship. This allusion suggests again that what encircled the "great pool" was worship of the sacred power of sexuality and the raw vitality of youth. The summer-long ceremony was a dance for the coming-of-age the youths were experiencing. At this temple of the crocodiles, the youths paid homage to themselves and to the waters of life.

In the popular imagination, crocodiles—direct descendants of prehistoric reptiles—are particularly fierce and terrifying. Their actions are propelled by millions of years of honed instinct. When a crocodile attacks, it is efficient and, to humans, remorseless. Yet these cold-blooded creatures fascinate human beings. They are savage yet awe-inspiring; they are beautiful.

In "California Swimming Pool," the crocodile becomes a symbol for sex, for its impenetrable mystery and powerful jaws, for its primitive attraction, and for its unspeakable beauty. This symbol vitalizes Olds's description of a young girl's first reckonings with her own sexual energy and power. The poem conveys the poet's awe for the beauty and mysterious power of sex and her deep reverence for the life force in everyone.

JoAnn Balingit

THE CAMBRIDGE LADIES WHO LIVE
IN FURNISHED SOULS

Author: E. E. Cummings (1894-1962)
Type of poem: Sonnet
First published: 1923, in *Tulips and Chimneys*

The Poem

E. E. Cummings's sonnet now known as "the Cambridge ladies who live in furnished souls" was originally published without a title in a section of Cummings's first collection of poetry, *Tulips and Chimneys* (1923). That section, labeled "Chimneys," is divided into three subsections: "Realities," "Unrealities," and "Actualities." This particular poem, included in the first subsection, is an example of how Cummings uses a traditional verse form—the fourteen-line lyric known as a sonnet—and remakes it to suit his purpose of startling the reader into a new understanding and into seeing reality in a new way. In this sonnet, Cummings portrays a group of people, "Cambridge ladies," as representations of people who have money and a certain distinguished class in society but who lack the spontaneity and feeling that Cummings believes are the hallmarks of truly human beings. Cummings shows how these people from Cambridge, Massachusetts, the home of such prestigious institutions as Harvard University, are not what they appear to be.

In the first four lines, Cummings describes the ladies whom he is criticizing. They live in "furnished souls"—that is, their souls, as is the case with their lives, are assembled, readymade, and artificially arranged—and their minds are "unbeautiful" and "comfortable." Furthermore, they live with the approval of the society around them, described as "the church's protestant blessings," which is an indication that they are both representative of their culture and held up as model citizens of this culture.

As he proceeds to describe the artificiality of the Cambridge ladies, Cummings notes that they believe in Christ and Longfellow, thus implying that they hold traditional beliefs in Christianity and art: in this instance, the art produced by Henry Wadsworth Longfellow, an American poet who lived from 1807 to 1882 and who was a professor of Romance languages at Harvard. Longfellow's poetry, traditional in form and very American in its subject matter, suggests that these women are careful to read what is noncontroversial and nationalistic, two qualities Cummings abhors. Just as they believe in acceptable religion and art, these women are also involved in acceptable causes, described by Cummings as "knitting for the is it Poles?/ perhaps."

Appearance is not reality, however, as Cummings goes on to demonstrate in the following lines. These Cambridge ladies are described as actually being gossipers who "coyly bandy/ scandal of Mrs. N and Professor D" and, worse, as people who, being caught up in their hypocritical posturing, neglect the beauty of nature around them. In the concluding lines, Cummings describes the moon above them as being "in its box of/ sky lavender and cornerless," rattling "like a fragment of angry candy." The knitting, gossiping ladies, being preoccupied with themselves, do not care to look up to see this natural phenomenon and, as a result, choose for themselves a lifeless, spiritless existence.

Forms and Devices

Innovation is E. E. Cummings's hallmark, and this lyric embodies virtually all of his experimental efforts. Using a traditional verse form, the sonnet, as his structure, Cummings transforms the fourteen-line poem so that it is neither a Shakespearean nor a Petrarchan sonnet (the two types traditionally associated with this verse form). In the former, sometimes called English, three quatrains, each with a rhyme-scheme of its own, are followed by a rhyming couplet. In the latter, sometimes called Italian, the poem is divided into two sections, an octave and a sestet, each with its own particular rhyming pattern. Cummings uses only the basic structure of the traditional sonnet form—its fourteen lines—and discards virtually everything else, most obviously its disciplined rhyme schemes.

Another innovation Cummings introduces into his poetry is a wrenched syntax; that is, a sentence structure that does not follow the expected order of, for example, a subject followed by a verb or an adjective preceding a noun. Thus, the last four lines jumble the expected arrangement of words, forcing the reader to pause and reconstruct the lines to make meaning out of Cummings's experimental arrangement:

> . . . the Cambridge ladies do not care, above
> Cambridge if sometimes in its box of
> sky lavender and cornerless, the
> moon rattles like a fragment of angry candy

By forcing this labor upon the reader, Cummings accomplishes one of his poetic purposes, which is to help the reader stop, look, and listen: stop a process of sometimes too-rapid reading, look at and listen to the words on the page, and reassemble those words so they reveal a new reality.

The reassembling process is a challenging one, especially since Cummings's use (or lack) of punctuation does not reflect a traditional, grammatically correct approach to commas and other marks that might help a reader know when to stop and when to move forward in a poem. A series of adjectives is presented with no commas—"daughters, unscented shapeless spirited"—and a sentence might appear to end with a question mark but actually concludes with a period: "at the present writing one still finds/ delighted fingers knitting for is it the Poles?/ perhaps." If the disregard for punctuation is one challenge, the disrespect for capitalization of letters is still another. Sometimes a sentence does not begin with a capital letter, such as the opening line of the poem, and sometimes it does, such as the last sentence of the poem (which does not conclude with a period). This sonnet, like Cummings's other poems, does not allow for reading in the usual way or at the usual pace.

Just as he creates a new syntax and a new method of punctuation, so Cummings experiments with language, creating his own words and including unusual images. The Cambridge ladies are described as "unbeautiful," one of many examples in Cummings's poems of his use of the "un-" prefix to contrast a world he sees as ugly and artificial with its alternative world of beauty and spontaneity. His images, likewise, reveal these two worlds. The ladies in the poem, described as "unscented shapeless spirited," occupy "furnished souls," while the sky above them—which they never see—is "lavender and cornerless" and home to the moon, which is described with the simile, "like a fragment of angry candy." Not only is this an unusual way to describe the moon, but it is also a startling way to end a sonnet. This is no neat conclusion to a sonnet, as a reader would expect in a traditional Shakespearean or Petrarchan sonnet. On the contrary, it is a typical Cummings conclusion, an assertion that endings are not artificially neat, like the lives of the Cambridge ladies, but are, instead, naturally unpredictable, like the moon rattling above the neglectful women.

Themes and Meanings

Cummings's poem is both satirical and lyrical. It satirizes the hypocrisy and artificiality of people, represented by the Cambridge ladies, who are more concerned with their own images than with the images of nature around them. While appearing to go about their humanitarian tasks with duty and dedication, these ladies actually spread gossip, and they fail to appreciate and become a part of the natural beauty surrounding them (one of the greatest sins of all in Cummings's inventory of sins). In setting his poem in Cambridge and focusing on the ladies who live there, Cummings uses a city he knows well: He was born there, and he was a student at Harvard. His father, a Congregational minister, taught English and, later, social ethics at Harvard. The poet, therefore, is not satirizing an abstract place and set of behaviors but, rather, a specific location that represents his roots and is frequently associated with high culture and the source of what many consider to be true American culture and civilization.

The poem is also lyrical, demonstrating those qualities that typically characterize a lyric poem: imagination, melody, and emotion. Cummings's description of both worlds in this poem—the artificial world of Cambridge and the natural world around the city—do not offer literal, pictorial views. Rather, they provide imaginative perspectives that emphasize the poet's strong emotions: his deep feelings for the beauty of the natural world and his equally deep feelings against the ugliness of the lives embodied by the world created by human beings.

This artificial world, fashioned by the women of Cambridge, is only an appearance. Reality, an important concept to Cummings (this sonnet first appeared in *Tulips and Chimneys* in a section titled "Realities"), is the essence of life. It transcends what a person sees when looking with ordinary eyes at ordinary life. It transforms the ordinary into the extraordinary. It is the "sky lavender and cornerless" that the Cambridge ladies do not know exists above them.

Marjorie Smelstor

THE CANONIZATION

Author: John Donne (1572-1631)
Type of poem: Lyric
First published: 1633, in *Poems, by J. D.: With Elegies on the Authors Death*

The Poem

The forty-five lines of John Donne's "The Canonization" are divided into five nine-line stanzas, a form that suggests a five-act play. The title reflects the speaker's conviction that in opposing the claims of the world (business, courtly ambitions), he and his beloved have become love's martyrs, and therefore saints.

The first-person speaker appears to be addressing an outsider who is unsympathetic to his romantic involvement and who has said as much prior to the first line. The poem, then, is a type of dramatic monologue, in which the speaker defends and later celebrates his love against the outsider's objection. In the first stanza, he commands the outsider to hold his tongue and tells him to scold him about being too old for love if he wishes, but not about being in love. He suggests that the outsider pursue his own ambitions or do whatever he likes, so long as he leaves him alone to love.

In the second stanza, the speaker adopts a defensive tone, arguing that no one is "injured" by his love, as the outsider may have charged. Donne employs several conventional Petrarchan metaphors (poetic clichés by that time), insisting that his lover's sighs have not sunk any merchant ships, nor has his heated passion caused an early spring to be delayed. He concludes that argumentative soldiers and lawyers can still bicker even though he finds contentment in love.

In the third stanza, the speaker reacts to apparent name-calling on the part of the outsider, insisting that he and his beloved are "flies" (in the diction of his age, moths or butterflies) or "tapers" (candles), which gain fullness of life even as they consume themselves. (Renaissance English poets commonly employed the word "die" as a sexual pun, based on the folk belief that each orgasm shortened one's life by a day.) Likening the physically and spiritually united lovers to the phoenix, a mythical bird that was thought to erupt into flame and then be resurrected from its own ashes, the speaker claims that they are proven "mysterious" (in the spiritual sense) by this ideal love. This constitutes the climax or turning point of this small drama.

In the fourth stanza the speaker explains that if they do literally die from their love, it will be a martyrdom, and their saints' legend will be an appropriate subject for poetry (as this poem itself proves), so they will also live because of their love. He expands his point metaphorically by suggesting that if their love is not suitable for chronicles, it will do for sonnets, and that a carefully made funeral urn is as suitable for famous personages as "half-acre tombs" like the pyramids.

The last stanza amounts to an imagined prayer of intercession. In short, the busy world will request a "pattern" or model of ideal love from these martyrs, who have found in each other a peaceful "hermitage."

Forms and Devices

This poem is a triumph in the "complex stanza" form, which derives from the classical ode and which requires that the poet contrive a fresh rhyme scheme (*abbaccca* in the present case) and use a variable line length as well. Donne employs a free iambic foot and a meter that varies from pentameter (ten syllables per line) in the first, third, fourth, and seventh lines to trimeter (six syllables) in the last line of each stanza. The remaining lines are in tetrameter (eight syllables). Donne frames each stanza by closing off the first and ninth lines with the word "love," which accordingly echoes throughout the poem.

Within the formal structure, Donne uses frequent balance and antithesis (as in line 2, in which "my palsy" is balanced with "my gout"). Occasionally this binary pattern, which operates throughout the poem, leads to paradox, for the speaker argues that the apparent dangers of passionate love actually sustain life in the best sense. The paradoxical pairing of the lover's "colds" (chills) and "heats" (fevers) in the second stanza are conventional and even somewhat playful, but the pairing of dying and rising later in the poem is more profound. Antitheses abound in the poem: chronicles/sonnets, well-wrought urn/half-acre tombs, peace/rage. These tend to counter the more obviously balanced pairs in the first stanza: "With wealth your state"/ "your mind with arts," a course/a place (in court, presumably), His Honor/ His Grace, "the King's real"/ "or his stamped face" (on a coin).

The metaphorical play in this poem can be confusing to those who are unaware of the traditions and conventions of Renaissance poetry. The typical Petrarchan lover, for example, who is teased in the second stanza, was pictured as an unfortunate man who was spurned by his mistress and who consequently sighed up a storm, wept floods, and alternately suffered chills and fevers. Donne's lover is beloved in turn, so he does not suffer such maladies.

Donne draws on the emblem tradition for conventional metaphors in the second stanza. Emblem books in that era provided woodcuts or engravings that had moralizing mottoes and poems. The moth drawn to a deadly candle was one such emblem, as was the image of the eagle (representing physical power, often that of the male) and the dove (representing peace or spirituality). The phoenix was also a popular emblem.

Donne concludes his poem with a metaphor in which the lovers, staring into each other's eyes, reflect themselves and indeed the whole world, as represented by "Countries, towns, courts." They become, then, the epitome or summation of the universe.

Themes and Meanings

"The Canonization" argues for the superiority of love's unifying and reconciling potential over the divisive and antagonistic impulses of the ordinary world. In pursuing personal ambitions in business or at court, people like the imagined outsider and courtiers, soldiers, and lawyers trade serenity for strife. The speaker argues that an ideal love, which is both physical and spiritual, can provide a paradigm for the confused world, and he asserts that this poem proves his point.

The reference to the king in the first stanza causes some scholars to associate the poem with the accession of James I in 1604. Only three years earlier, Donne had put a disastrous halt to his own courtly ambitions when he eloped with Ann More, the ward of his employer, Sir Thomas Egerton, Lord Keeper of the Seal. Ann More's father had Donne blackballed, in effect, and the couple experienced severe financial strain for several years. This poem might be seen, then, as an explanation or even a justification of his apparently impulsive behavior.

If his intended audience for the poem was King James himself, Donne's appeal must have fallen on deaf ears, since another ten years were to pass before his fortunes improved. The marriage was apparently a happy one, however, and Ann Donne was to bear nine children before her death in 1617. John Donne did not remarry.

Ron McFarland

CANTO 1

Author: Ezra Pound (1885-1972)
Type of poem: Poetic sequence
First published: 1925, in *A Draft of XVI Cantos*

The Poem

Canto 1 is the first poem in a long sequence of 120 cantos making up what the poet, Ezra Pound, conceived of as a twentieth century epic. Pound worked on the *Cantos* for nearly fifty years, weaving scores of subjects and themes into the longest important poetic work of the modern era. When he set out on his poetic odyssey, Pound conceived of his poem as a modern version of Dante's *The Divine Comedy* (c.1320); his intention was to mirror Dante's epic organization into "inferno," "purgatory," and "heaven." Pound, following Dante, called the individual units of the epic cantos.

When Pound finished Canto 1, in 1921, he had no idea what the final shape of his modern epic would be, but he was aware that this first canto would have to act as an overture to whatever followed. So in many ways, Canto 1 is a capsule form of many of the themes and poetic devices that would come in the succeeding cantos. At the same time, this poem reflects many of Pound's interests in subject and form that appear in his earlier works.

Canto 1 can be divided into two sections: The first, longer section (ending with "Lie quiet Divus") is drawn from the *Odyssey* (c.800 B.C.E.), Book XI, and certain other Homeric works; the second half is a pastiche, which, although it still refers directly to Odysseus, also echoes other classic poems, chiefly a Homeric hymn to Aphrodite.

Although the speaker in the earlier part of Canto 1 is clearly Odysseus, the personae in the poem's later parts are more difficult to identify. Odysseus speaks first, and is followed by a quotation from the blind sage Tiresias, whom Odysseus meets in his journey to the underworld. Then, at the line beginning "Lie quiet Divus," Pound himself intervenes as both epic storyteller and classical scholar.

The first half of the poem retells the story of Odysseus's journey to Hades: Odysseus describes setting out to find the entrance to Hades, which had been described to him by the sorceress Circe. His crew loads the ship, and they push off, sailing until they reach the "place aforesaid by Circe." There they perform sacred rites—pouring wine on the ground, saying prayers, sacrificing a sheep—to summon up the dead.

A number of souls appear, including one of Odysseus's crew, Elpenor, who had been killed accidentally when Odysseus and his men had been delayed by Circe. One night, having drunk too much, Elpenor fell off a ladder, breaking his neck ("shattered the nape-nerve"). He asks Odysseus to build a tomb for him, including his epitaph, "A man of no fortune, with a name to come." Then Anticlea, Odysseus's mother, appears, followed by Tiresias, from whom Odysseus wants a prophesy. Tiresias does foretell Odysseus's future, telling the hero that he will eventually return to his homeland but will lose all his shipmates in the process.

At this point in the poem, it is as though Pound the narrator looks up from the old book in which he has been reading Odysseus's story—the Latin translation by Andreas Divus, produced in 1538. Pound also finds in the back of this book some hymns said to be composed by Homer. One of these is a poem in praise of Aphrodite, and Pound ends Canto 1 by quoting the hymn's description of the goddess of love.

Forms and Devices

Although scholars argue about the exact verse structure of the *Cantos*, it is fair to say that generally Canto 1 is written in free verse—poetic lines that have no set rhythm or consistent number of feet and do not rhyme. This is not to say that Canto 1 is without structure: The first section of the poem echoes the rhythms of Anglo-Saxon poetry, while the final lines loosely mimic certain classic verse patterns.

The language that Pound uses in the first part of Canto 1 is that of the Old English "seafarer poet." The result is a story drawn from Greek literature told in the mock-language of early medieval England. Throughout the Cantos, Pound uses this kind of juxtaposition of subject matter drawn from one literary or historical period and poetic language drawn from another. In making such junctions, Pound's intention was to show the reader certain important similarities—in thought and feeling—between eras that might seem at first glance very different.

In this case, Pound believed that Odysseus and the anonymous seafarer from the European Dark Ages were spiritual brothers. Both were animated by the desire to sail unknown seas in small, perilous ships, simply for the sake of discovery. Both find that the discoveries they make have more to do with their own inner landscape than with the geography of new lands.

Devices echoing Anglo-Saxon poetry include reversal ("Circe's this craft," "unpierced ever,"), alliteration ("swart ship," "sun to his slumber"), and archaic language ("swart," "ell-square pitkin," "ingle," "bever," "fosse"). Overall, the rhythm of this section suggests the rolling of the small ship over the sea's breakers.

"Kennings," compound terms that describe metaphorically some common object, are another Anglo-Saxon poetic device used in Canto 1 ("nape-nerve" for "neck").

Pound wants his readers to pay close attention to his poem's sources, its allusions. Generally, allusion takes place in poetry through mention of a name, place, or idea associated with some other work of literature or with some historical event. More rarely, a poet may quote or mimic another writer. In the *Cantos*, however, Pound goes even further: In the section describing Odysseus's journey to the underworld, for example, Pound is freely translating a Latin translation (that of Divus) of Homer's original Greek. In the last lines ("Cypri munimenta sortita est," or "Cyprus is allotted to her"), Pound even reproduces Divus's exact words. Pound's abundant use of foreign languages throughout the Cantos—sometimes with English translations following, sometimes not—forces the reader to pay attention to the literary and cultural sources of his allusions. Untranslated words and phrases in Canto 1 include "in officina Wecheli" (a reference to the place of publication of Divus's translation); "Venerandam," "worthy of veneration"; "Argicida," "killer of Argus" (a reference to the Greek god

Hermes); and "orichalchi," "coppery." In this canto, all foreign-language phrases are in either Greek or Latin.

There are also abundant allusions to classical myth and Homeric epic. Perimedes, Eurylochus, and Elpenor are all members of Odysseus's crew. Erebus and Avernus are different names for the underworld. Finally, Canto 1 displays a formal device that, although it runs throughout the *Cantos*, is generally nontraditional: Many lines are fragmented, having no clear grammatical subject or object. The final phrase—"So that:"—is characteristic of this device. Moreover, Pound shifts abruptly from speaker to speaker in Canto 1, as in the jump from "And then Anticlea came" (spoken by Odysseus) to "Lie quiet Divus" (ostensibly Pound himself). As a result, fragmentation and abrupt shifts in persona create much disorientation in most readers, but Pound's intention here is to spur the reader to greater efforts, to motivate him or her to participate more fully than usual in generating meaning from the poem.

Themes and Meanings

As difficult as Canto 1 may be in form, its theme is a traditional, straightforward one: descent into the underworld. In fact, Homer's account of Odysseus's search for knowledge among the dead spirits of Hades is the earliest version in Western literature of this motif.

In speaking to the dead, Odysseus acquires knowledge that is normally forbidden to mortals: He learns the cause of Elpenor's death, for example, and, more tellingly, discovers his own fate. This kind of supernatural knowledge can be won only through sacrifice, and Odysseus's journey over unknown seas and the deaths of his crewmen prepare him for this knowledge. The holy, sacrificial rites with which he calls up the spirits of the dead are part of this mystery, whereby mortal human intelligence exceeds the usual limits of reality.

Pound uses this theme for two reasons: so he can create variations on it at the end of Canto 1, and to introduce what he projected to be the grand theme of the *Cantos* as a whole.

Just as Odysseus summons the dead to acquire knowledge, so Pound, the narrator and the scholar, calls up the dead Renaissance translator Divus to step from his own historical and literary period into world culture as a whole. By studying Divus's Renaissance Latin version of the *Odyssey*, Pound animates a dead era and two dead languages. In fact, Pound's admonition to "lie quiet Divus" suggests that the experience has been too enlivening, too overwhelming. Moreover, in another historical layer, Pound discovers that Odysseus and the anonymous Anglo-Saxon seafarer are spiritual brothers.

This swirl of characters and eras may account for the confusion at the end of the poem, at which point the various currents of history and literature threaten to dislocate the narrator's consciousness.

John Steven Childs

CANTO 4

Author: Ezra Pound (1885-1972)
Type of poem: Poetic sequence
First published: 1919; collected in *Poems, 1918-1921*, 1921

The Poem

Canto 4 is one of the 117 cantos, or divisions, that make up Ezra Pound's sequence the *Cantos*, one of the major poetic works of the twentieth century. In Canto 4 Ezra Pound introduces the main factors that promote civilizations: urbanization, writing, and religious worship. He describes the ancient city of Troy sacked and destroyed by the victorious Greeks, its palace "in smoky light," the city "a heap of smouldering boundary stones." Then he speaks of Cadmus, the Phoenician trader who founded the city of Thebes. Cadmus gave the Phoenician alphabet to the Greeks; from it they devised the Greek alphabet as it is known today. Pound refers to religious worship by mentioning the "*Chorus nympharum*"—an assembly of bathing nymphs who are worshipers of Pan, the pastoral god who has the legs and feet of a goat.

Once cities, writing, and religion are combined in such a way as to create a civilization, other things can pull civilizations down: The ignoring of tradition by failing, in the words of Matthew Arnold, "to learn and propagate the best that is known and thought in the world." This reverence for tradition also includes the principles of morality, good government, and economics. In addition, self-discipline on the part of rulers and citizens—the ability to curb the meaner passions, greed, selfishness, revenge, desire for power, hatred leading to murder—is necessary if a culture is to survive. It was the coveting of another man's wife by Paris that led to the abduction of Helen and brought about the Trojan War, which destroyed Troy.

The world has darkened for the poet as he contemplates the burning city of Troy, and he seeks relief by recalling moments of light. He recalls the "victory songs" of Pindar and the "nuptial songs" of Catullus, crying out gleefully, "ANAXIFORMINGES!" ("Lords of the Lyre!") and "Aurunculeia!" (the name of a virgin bride honored by Catullus).

After experiencing some light, the poet returns to the dark side of life by recalling the horrible crimes and violence that were perpetrated by the members of the family of Tereus, the king of Thrace. Tereus had lost control of his sexual passion and raped his wife's sister. Then he had cut out her tongue to ensure her silence. Nevertheless, his wife learned of his crimes. In retaliation she murdered their little son, Itys, and fed his cooked flesh as a meal to the king. When she informed him of what he had eaten, he tried to kill both women, but the gods turned all three into birds.

Then Pound moves ahead in time to medieval Provence, a region and former province of the kingdom of Naples and later of France. Provence was the home of the troubadours, poet-musicians who composed in Provençal and practiced courtly love (*amour courtois*). Courtly love was a contradictory form of love: It was illicit (the love of someone else's wife), yet as "pure love" it was considered passionate, disciplined, and able to elevate the lover morally. The danger was that if it was passionate but without discipline, it could lead to trouble and violence. Now Pound metamorphoses Itys into the troubadour Cabestan (Guillen da Cabestanh), who carried on a love affair with a married woman. Her husband grew jealous and murdered Cabestan, and he prepared a meal of Cabestan's flesh and served it to his wife, whom he considered unfaithful. After his wife had consumed the meal, her husband informed her what she had eaten. She rushed to a second-story window and jumped to her death.

Turning away from this darkness, Pound sees the glittering roof of the Romanesque gothic church in Poitiers, France. This image, emblematic of Catholicism, is followed immediately by recognition of the classical world and the worship of Diana, the goddess of the moon. Then the poet's vision sweeps far away to Japan and then China. In Japan he notes "the pine at Takasago," which refers to the legend of the twin pines of Takasago and Sumiyoshi. They are the homes of a very old married couple who have not only lived very long lives but also remained strictly faithful to each other all their lives; they have become immortal. She lives in the pine at Takasago; he lives in the other pine at Sumiyoshi, and for countless years he has paid nightly visits to his wife; the two converse until the break of day. Thus this immortal couple symbolize longevity and conjugal fidelity. Pound now returns from Japanese culture to classical Roman culture. In the voice of Catullus he again celebrates the marriage of Aurunculeia, hailing Hymen, the god of marriage.

Pound next moves to ancient China, where he considers the political question of the power of the ruler in respect to the common people and in respect to nature. At the same time he introduces the reader to the literary question of the relationship of Chinese poetry in style and subject to the poetry of the West. He discusses the main theme of a poem by the distinguished Sung Yü (in the third century B.C.E.), who served as a courtier at the court of King Hsiang Yü, ruler of the state of Ch'u. One day the king was taking his ease on the terrace outside his palace when the wind blew. The king remarked to Sung Yü: "What delightful breeze!" Then he added: "And I and the common people may share it together, may we not?" Sung Yü replied: "The wind does not choose between the high and the low, but it belongs to the place where it seeks out."

Pound concludes Canto 4 by returning to the theme of the city and its violent crime. Pound's city here is Ecbaton (or Ecbatana), the capital of ancient Media during its decline under King Acrisius in the early sixth century B.C.E. According to Herodotus, it was surrounded by seven concentric walls, each of a different color. It was a planned city that contained "plotted streets." It also contained a brazen tower that was the king's treasure house. King Acrisius had been warned by an oracle that he would be slain by a grandson. A coward, he imprisoned his daughter, Danae, in the tower so that no man could love or wed her. Zeus, however, angry that the king should seek to alter a prophecy of the gods, visited Danae in the form of golden rain and made her pregnant. Although Acrisius tried to kill both her and her child, Perseus, he failed. Later Perseus killed Acrisius accidentally.

Then Pound introduces his reader to the city of Sardis (or Sardes), the capital of

Lydia during the reign of King Candaules (c. 700 B.C.E.). The city contained a temple to Artemis, the goddess of the moon. Sardis is believed to have been the first city to issue gold and silver coins. A story of considerable irony is associated with King Candaules. Much in love with his wife, he never tired of recounting to other men the beauty of her face and figure. He tried to impress his young bodyguard, Gyges, on this matter. The youth listened politely to his master's ravings, but he was unmoved. Thinking that his bodyguard did not believe him, the king insisted that Gyges hide in the queen's bedroom until she came in to retire for the night; the bodyguard was much opposed to this plan. He obeyed his master, however, and saw the queen naked. However, from the corner of her eye she saw him dart out the door. The next morning she sent for the bodyguard. She informed him that he had two choices. He must kill her husband, marry her, and become king or he must forfeit his own life. He chose the first alternative.

Forms and Devices

Canto 4 is only one segment of the *Cantos*, a poetic cultural history of the world that is multicultural and multilingual. Pound's poetry is cryptic and sometimes aphoristic. Reflecting his interest in myth and world history, his verse is peppered with foreign languages and with English translations of foreign languages. The style of the *Cantos* in general is fragmented; one small bit of history or myth bumps against another from a different era and part of the world. To Pound, poetry is a "charged language" that has a definite relation to music and, to a lesser degree, to painting and sculpture. He employs free verse, precise imagery, and the rhythms of common, sometimes slangy, speech. One of Pound's major devices is the so-called ideogrammatic method, which he took from his impression of the structure of Chinese characters: A character is formed from two or more pictographs (or indicators) to suggest a larger idea.

Pound pays strict attention to the consonance of words and music. In every case he tries to find the most appropriate word, not only in meaning but also in emotional resonance. He held that a poet's rhythm and meter reveal the poet's sincerity and commitment.

Pound makes considerable use of mythology—for example, he applies classical myths to the lives of the troubadours—and this practice makes the reader aware of certain types of constant relations, as between the Tereus and Cabestan. Pound uses these myths to present moral problems and create psychic experiences. Myth enables him to record dark passions and crimes and to contrast them with the bright light of the world.

The principal device Pound uses is the *forma* or *virtù*. The *forma* or *virtù* is the pattern (or simply the "something") that lies behind concepts or techniques of artistic, literary, and social phenomena and enables a notable tradition to develop—as with the songs of the thirteenth century troubadours or the strange metaphysics of light of Grosseteste. Canto 4 presents no formal organization; like the *Cantos* as a whole, it represents the personal improvisation of a great poetic sensibility.

Themes and Meanings

The foundation stones of a civilization, according to Pound, are in essence urbanization, writing, and religious consciousness. If a civilization is to survive, the moral law must be respected and observed. There must be self-discipline and control of the meaner passions: Lust, revenge, murder, and greed must be disallowed and foolish wars avoided. In Pound's view history follows organic time and consists of "ideas in action." These ideas in action result from the exercise of human will in conjunction with certain ethical frameworks. The actions occur at certain places and at certain times to produce cultural complexes. Such a complex includes language, knowledge, religious consciousness, myth and legend, morals, government, law, customs, and the arts. Through presenting selected past ideas in action, Pound wishes his reader to learn important truths about the present. To Pound, civilization is the inevitable destiny of a culture that is allowed to develop. He held that civilization follows the laws of the organic world and that cultural processes repeat themselves in cyclic stages.

According to R. W. Dasenbrock, "the pattern or repeat in history that fascinated Pound" was the "close interrelation between cultural achievement and violence." This relationship is the dominant theme of Canto 4. Yet the focus on violence stands in contrast to five kinds of love that are also illustrated in the poem: lustful love (Tereus), courtly love (the troubadours), married love (Manlius and Vinia Aurancules), self-love (King Acrisius), and love of life (the Transcendental Light).

Richard P. Benton

CANTO 29

Author: Ezra Pound (1885-1972)
Type of poem: Poetic sequence
First published: 1930, in *A Draft of XXX Cantos*

The Poem

Pound begins Canto 29 with a reference to a cosmology and a tribute to light (*lux*). This description is consonant with the metaphysics of light proposed by the thirteenth century philosopher Grosseteste, whose thinking was familiar to Pound. According to Grosseteste light is from God and is the basis of matter and form. Any dimming of light in the cosmos indicates a decline and a decadence in matter owing to the privation of light. This view constitutes Pound's notion of *forma*; *forma* is that something which produces "ideas," especially "ideas in action," which is Pound's definition of history.

Then Pound presents his views on the natures of women and love. Because of their biology and their beauty of face and figure, women are natural lures of men; hence they can be agents of enhancement to men or agents of destruction. Pound presents the latter type in Pernella, the concubine of Count Aldobrando Orsini of Verona. Having given birth to two male children, she wishes her second to be the heir to her lover's estate despite the fact that Aldobrando has an heir in his grown son, Niccolò Orsini, Count of Petigliano, a gifted mercenary soldier. Believing that Niccolò's courage will get him killed in battle in the near future, Pernella murders her first child in order to advance the second. Seeing into her ambition, Niccolò kills her second child. Foiled in her scheme, Pernella through false communication starts a war. For her treason Niccolò kills her.

Next Pound introduces the troubadours—those aristocratic poet-musicians whose favorite subjects were courtly love, war, and nature. They are represented here by Sordello di Goito (d. 1270), who loves the noblewoman Cunizza, the wife of Rizzardo di Bonifacio. Sordello runs away with her but soon loses her to a knight named Bonio. The other model is Arnaut Daniel (d. 1210), who loved a noblewoman of Gascony, the wife of Sir Guillem de Bouvilla. Ideally, courtly love was what the troubadours called "pure love": It consisted of the union of the hearts and minds of the lovers without physical possession of the woman, the aim being the ennobling of the lover. In practice, "pure love" held a danger because it involved the fanning of illicit desires. If the couple's spirits were weak, the lovers could lapse into adultery.

Pound now leaves early Renaissance Italy for the early twentieth century in the United States. He presents the allegorical figure of "Lusty Juventus," who represents the spirit of youth as a life force. He confronts an old funeral director in front of the latter's house. This man has daughters whose behavior has caused comment among residents of the town. The undertaker does not know how he feels about his daughters. Apparently these young women have revolted against their Protestant heritage and have become "flappers" of the Jazz Age. "The wail of the phonograph" is that of a "djassban" hammering out sexy music suggestive of a "pornograph" to the father's ear. As the representative of the Protestant conscience, he is confused. He has habitually been opposed to drinking alcohol, smoking cigarettes, playing cards, and, above all, dancing and free love. It may seem that Pound's leap from Renaissance Italy to the 1920's Jazz Age in the United States is a big leap in "clock time." However, in the *Cantos* Pound is not concerned with clock time, placing the emphasis on "organic time." Pound held that cultural complexes as processes repeat themselves in accord with Friedrich Nietzsche's principle of the "eternal return."

Juventus speaks in the voice of Grosseteste on the relation of light to matter and *forma*. The American landscape merges into the European scene and becomes multilingual. The main theme of Canto 29 is now spelled out: "the female/ Is an element, the female/ Is a chaos/ An octopus/ A biological process." At this point the Lord of Light appears in the person of Helios.

Forms and Devices

Canto 29 has a principal theme—the exploration of the power of the female sex and the danger inherent in the practice of courtly love—but it has no formal pattern. Rather, it proceeds in a manner similar to the jazz improvisations of such virtuosos as Bix Beiderbecke on the cornet or Art Tatum on the piano, whose styles were very personalized. Pound considered poetry to be "charged language" closely related to music and to common speech. His main technical devices are the use of a persona and its metamorphosis; he employs changelings and their voices, juxtaposition of facts, events, and quotations (often in foreign languages), and dependence on an ideographic method based on the pattern of a certain class of Chinese characters or ideograms.

Canto 29 is but a section of a whole, the *Cantos*, a modern epic poem that is a cultural history of the world in which the poet seeks to reveal the organic unity of civilizations. Hence it is multicultural and multilingual. Pound intended it to be didactic and personal. He comments on the past in order to shed light on the present from his unique point of view. He might have said of the *Cantos* what Walt Whitman said of his *Leaves of Grass* (1855): "Camerado, this is no book;/ Who touches this touches a man."

Themes and Meanings

The central theme of the *Cantos* as a whole is the poet's search for a philosophy capable of validating an ideal system of ethics, economics, and politics—for a social order that will prove a "city of Light," or an ideal civilization. In line with this search Pound presents examples of social behavior on the part of humanity which not only can prove self-destructive but also can prevent a city of light from emerging or destroy one that is existing. Apart from the theme that beautiful women can prove Circes, possessing enough sexual power to turn men into swine, there is always the danger that a human being can feel irrational desire, whether it be in respect to wealth and power or in respect to irrational attachment to sexual pleasure.

Canto 29 presents an example of both overweening ambition and attachment to sexual pleasure in Pernella, the concubine of Count Orsini of Verona; these weaknesses bring about her destruction. Pound also presents two examples from the Middle Ages respecting the destructive power of lust: the Italian troubadour Sordella di Goito, who loves the noble lady Cunizza, and the French troubadour Arnaut Daniel, who loves the noble lady of Gascony. "Pure love" is bypassed in both cases.

Finally, Canto 29 moves through time and space to the United States of the 1920's. The period between 1919 and 1929 has been called the Flapper Age, the Jazz Age, and the Roaring Twenties. In 1917, while World War I was still raging, the Prohibition amendment, outlawing the sale of alcoholic beverages, had been adopted. With the war over in 1918, the women's suffrage amendment was adopted in 1920. All at once it seemed to older Americans that the younger generation was revolting against all the former Victorian moral standards in fashions and behavior. Young women wore short skirts, bobbed their hair, and applied rouge to their faces. They danced the fox trot and the Charleston. They drank bootleg whiskey, smoked cigarettes, and believed in "free love" and divorce. It was the period of gangsters such as Al Capone and Jack "Legs" Diamond. Corruption and violence reigned. It seemed to many that the United States was rapidly heading for disaster—and with the stock market crash of 1929 and the onset of the Great Depression, disaster did indeed strike.

Richard P. Benton

CANTO 49

Author: Ezra Pound (1885-1972)
Type of poem: Poetic sequence
First published: 1937, in *The Fifth Decad of Cantos*

The Poem

Canto 49—often called the "Seven Lakes" canto—is one of a set of ten cantos appearing in the third book of Ezra Pound's twentieth century epic, the *Cantos*. This long poetic sequence, including 120 cantos, weaves scores of subjects and themes into the longest important poetic work of the modern era. By the time the "Fifth Decad" of cantos was published, Pound had already been at work on his epic for nearly twenty years; he would continue to write new cantos for thirty more.

The time is late autumn, and the persona is evidently someone journeying down a canal, noting the passing landscape. In the poem's first line, however, Pound tells us that "these verses" are "by no man"; his intention here is possibly to suggest that the poem itself is a natural object, swelling up from the landscape like the mist or the flocks of birds who live by the banks of the canal.

The persona is evidently standing in the riverboat's small cabin, lit by a single lamp; later, in stanza 4, he describes the "hole of the window" from which he views the landscape he describes. The canto's second line sets the scene: The persona travels late in the year, when the normally busy canal is empty. The weather is turning cold; during the course of the poem, the rain noted in the second line becomes a snow flurry. Meanwhile, under the heavy rain, plants growing on the banks, the reeds and bamboos, bend and creak. The cold rain and the persona's loneliness evoke an aura of sadness, and he feels that the natural world empathizes with him.

Finally, in the second stanza, the weather clears. The sun sets and the moon rises over the surrounding hills. Although Pound gives the reader too little information to be certain about the exact landscape through which the persona passes, the canal on which he travels may link the "seven lakes" of the poem's first line. As the persona sails over one of these lakes, he hears a distant bell from a monastery. The boat voyages on downstream, floating on the silver river lit by the dying sun.

In the short third stanza, the persona now sees the banner of a canalside wine shop and a small settlement adjacent to the shop. Snow begins to fall. There are signs of other people moving about on the lake; a fisherman's boat hung with a small lamp looks from a distance like one of the floating paper lanterns used during Chinese festivals. The village of San Yin, on which the persona comments in the stanza's fourth and fifth lines, may be either the wine-shop settlement the persona is now viewing or another village the persona simply remembers. Throughout the poem, the persona's current perceptions and past memories are often mixed, reflecting time's unimportance to him. Migrating geese alight on a sandbar for a moment and then take off. Other birds, rooks, circle the fishermen's boats, looking for fish. On the distant shore, small boys with lamps turn over rocks, looking for shrimp.

In stanza 5, there is a definite change of tone, probably caused by a shift in persona, from the anonymous Chinese traveler to Pound himself, who comments on the building of the canal. The canal, built by a civic-minded Chinese ruler, represents to Pound the right use of state wealth. Instead of using the state's riches to accumulate debt, the "old king" has used his resources to improve his country. Pound contrasts this with the lending and borrowing of state money for profit. "Geryon," in the stanza's second line, is a mythical beast used in Dante's *Inferno* (c.1320) to signify usury, the immoral accumulation of wealth through lending at interest—in other words, using money to make money, rather than using money to create the physical means to generate wealth, such as a canal that facilitates commerce.

The next stanza is a Japanese transliteration of a Chinese poem. The lines mean "Bright colorful auspicious cloud/ Hang gracefully/ Let sun and moon shine/ Morning after morning."

Stanza 8 describes in shorthand the natural cycle of ordinary human life and work, which is contrasted with the life of the state. The poem ends with a cryptic reference to classical mythology—probably relating to Bacchus's enchantment of wild beasts.

Forms and Devices

The Seven Lakes canto is generally considered one of the most beautiful portions of the *Cantos*. In theme and language, it reflects Pound's lifelong love of Chinese and Japanese poetry. Although it is impossible to render oriental verse forms into English, Pound here tries to capture the flavor of a classic Chinese poem, using short free-verse lines and syntax that often dispenses with the subject-verb-object structure of English sentences. Largely, then, the canto is made up of traditional natural images drawn from Chinese poetry.

Canto 49 is an imitation of the classical Chinese *shih*, or song, first collected in the ancient *Shih Ching* (Classic of Songs). The main structural characteristic of the shih, which Pound adopts here, is the use of short one- or two-syllable words, grouped in four-word lines. Stanza 6 exactly reproduces one such shih. As a result, the rhythm of the poem is terse and far more clipped than most Western poetic styles.

Even though the language of the Seven Lakes canto is direct, the imagery attempts to suggest emotion rather than state it openly. Thus the persona never tells the reader what he himself is feeling; instead, he allows the imagery of the natural world to do that for him. The heavy rain falling in the twilight of the first stanza, the bent reeds, and the "weeping" bamboos all strongly indicate the persona's sadness and loneliness, and the fire and ice of the cloud in the third line suggest a deep unstated conflict within the persona's psyche.

Contrasted to this imagery of cold, rain, and emptiness, however, is another set of images suggesting delicacy, light, and calm. The poem's second stanza introduces both the light of the bright autumn moon and the silvery blaze of sunset on the canal. The persona is also calmed by what he hears: The thin tune carrying through the canalside reeds seems to echo the chill of the air, and the gong of the monk's bell picks up the echo.

The flag waving in the sunset and the chimney smoke from the village reinforce the imagery evoked by this delicate, transitory landscape, which is as constantly changing as the persona's viewpoint as he moves downstream.

The imagery of the poem's fourth stanza is perhaps the jewel of the canto. The flurried snow, the jade-colored landscape, the pinpoint lights of the fishing boats, and the small boys strongly suggest a classical Chinese painting. In such a painting, elements of line and color are subtly implied, giving viewers the impression of a vivid dreamworld.

Themes and Meanings

In many ways, the Seven Lakes canto is simply a masterly imitation of classical Chinese verse. Thus many of its themes may be treated as the traditional ones associated with Oriental poetry. On the other hand, Pound introduces an important subtheme toward the end of the canto, which throws the earlier, more conventional meanings into contrast.

As in much of the *Cantos* (and as in much poetry throughout history), the theme here centers on a journey. In this case, the poem deals with the voyage of a solitary traveler on a nearly deserted waterway late in the year. Because of the mixture of past and present in the voyager's perceptions and because of his loneliness, his journey readily suggests the voyage this person makes through life. One of the great themes of Chinese and Japanese poetry—perhaps in part because of the strong Buddhist influence in those cultures—is the transience of life, its evanescent and even illusory quality.

Much of what the persona sees as he travels downstream seems insubstantial: The changing weather of autumn, the changing of day into night, the moon, the migrating birds, the chimney smoke—all these images combine to create a picture of a universe that Buddhism views as only partly real. Although the reader is never told exactly what troubles the persona, the speaker's emotions are clearly the most solid element in his world.

A key line in stanza 2—"Sail passed here in April; may return in October"—may reflect the poem's central meaning, the coming and going of human relationships. Here Pound relies upon a conventional theme in Chinese poetry: the departure of a beloved person on a long journey. In poems that employ this theme, the persona, the person being left behind, is often uncertain that the traveler will return.

Thus the smaller incident of saying goodbye to one person—perhaps forever—mirrors the larger course of any individual's life, from which friends, lovers, and family are eventually taken by death or distance.

This theme in the poem might be termed the "personal" one, but the canto concludes with another theme, the "social" one. Here Pound turns his emphasis from the emotions of one lonely person to passions having to do with statecraft. The image that links the private and the public is the canal: For the lonely traveler, the canal symbolizes life's solitary journey through an achingly beautiful natural landscape; but for the social observer, the canal symbolizes the just use of a state's wealth—to promote commerce, to enhance the lives of all the people who live by the thoroughfare. These are the people who live simple, direct lives, untroubled by the more sophisticated worries of the traveler. When the sun comes up, they work; when it sets, they rest. Their efforts are concentrated on not merely observing nature, but making it productive—they dig wells and work the fields.

Pound possibly suggests at the end of the poem that there is another dimension that transcends both the public and the private. In this, he is simply following the Chinese sage Confucius (who was much admired by Pound). Confucius argued that there was no separation between the good of the individual and the good of the people as a whole—that, like the flow of the canal through the lakes, individual health moved naturally into the public realm.

John Steven Childs

CANTO 74

Author: Ezra Pound (1885-1972)
Type of poem: Poetic sequence
First published: 1948, in *The Pisan Cantos*

The Poem

Canto 74 is the first poem in an eleven-poem set called *The Pisan Cantos*, which occurs about midway in the long poetic sequence the *Cantos*. Most Ezra Pound scholars agree that *The Pisan Cantos* contains some of the most powerful and beautiful passages in the entire sequence of 120 cantos. Like the remainder of the poem, *The Pisan Cantos* interweaves scores of themes and motifs into a tapestry containing elements drawn from world history, the literature of many countries and periods, and from Pound's own life. In fact, Pound often described the *Cantos* as "a poem containing history," including his own life history, and Canto 74 is a particularly good example of the ways in which Pound used personal and universal history as the foundation of the *Cantos*'s poetic structure.

The sequence was written during Pound's internment in the Detention Training Camp, a U.S. Army prison outside Pisa, Italy, during 1945 and 1946. During World War II, Pound had sided with Benito Mussolini's Fascists and had spent much of the war making pro-Fascist propaganda broadcasts for Rome Radio. When the Allies captured northern Italy, Pound was arrested as a traitor and held in Italy to await trial in the United States. Pound's incarceration in the camp forms the autobiographical basis for these cantos, and much of their subject matter has to do with Pound's day-to-day life in the open-air prison.

There are two difficulties with presenting a straightforward summary of Canto 74's content. The first is that by the time the reader reaches *The Pisan Cantos* (at page 425 of the American edition of the *Cantos*), he or she is expected to have assimilated dozens of references and allusions developed more fully in earlier cantos. The second is that this is one of the lengthiest of the cantos, running to nearly fifty pages in the standard edition.

In the opening seventy-four lines, for example (ending with "thereby making clutter"), nearly each line contains a different allusion, either to an earlier section of the *Cantos* themselves or to literature or history. The first eight lines allude to the death of Mussolini ("Ben"), who, having been captured by Italian Resistance fighters was killed along with his mistress ("Clara") and hung by his feet in a public square in Milan. Yet this reference immediately flows into one having to do with the "resurrected-god" motif of Mediterranean folklore and religion (in Greek, *Digonos* means "twice born"), and that in turn spurs the persona, Pound himself, to recall his friend T. S. Eliot's famous line about humankind ending with a "whimper" not a "bang"—Pound reverses this idea and thus introduces a note of defiance and even hope in the middle of his own defeat.

Next, a series of references to the writings of Confucius and to classic Chinese poetry intervene ("rain is also of the process"). These lines are followed by allusions to the journeys of Odysseus and of the Argonauts. One line in this sequence, "when Lucifer fell in N. Carolina," remains a mystery to Pound scholars, who are baffled by its meaning. In fact, the "Lucifer" line is typical of many others in this canto, making a coherent summary difficult.

The poem opens with Pound's lament for the death of Mussolini, who, Pound felt, was to lead Italy into a new Renaissance. Pound then contrasts political upheaval with the steady processes of nature praised in the Chinese classics. The reference to Confucius leads to remarks on the financial probity of the Chinese emperors and the contrasting usury practiced against Indian peasants during the last years of the British raj. Pound believed that the economic structure of the modern world was the source of its evils, including war and the loss of freedom, to which he refers in "the Constitution in jeopardy."

Returning to Odysseus, Pound compares one meaning of the Greek hero's name, "no man," with that accorded to an Australian god, Wanjina, who, like the God of the Old Testament, brought the created world into being through naming. The poem now shifts (at "from the death cells") to Pound's own impressions of the landscape in and around the detention camp. That landscape includes gallows for hanging criminals, and the gallows remind him of various executed criminals, including the medieval French poet François Villon and Barabbas. In the lines following, Pound introduces some of his fellow prisoners, "Thos. Wilson" and "Mr. K."; at "there was a smell of mint under the tent flaps," Pound inserts a lyrical passage having to do with the beauties of nature, visible even in the camp.

The Chinese character that then appears ("shien") means "to manifest, shining," and this ideogram is meant to stand for the light of the natural world, which illuminates everything, even the prison, with the clarity of truth. From light, Pound then returns to the darkness of economic falsehood (at "Never inside the country . . . ") and to the hidden machinations of usurers (those who lend money at exorbitant interest— Pound's chief villains).

At "Pisa, in the 23rd year . . . ," Pound describes the execution of a fellow prisoner, Till, and the natural wisdom of another prisoner, called "Snag." The Chinese character here means "mo," or evening; Pound expands the character's meaning to "a man on whom the sun has gone down," such as the executed Till. That is followed by a series of lines contrasting the illumination of mystical light with the darkness of history. The verse paragraphs beginning "Lordly men are to earth o'ergiven" relate Pound's memories of his fellow writers, some of whom are now dead: Ford Madox Ford, William Carlos Williams, James Joyce, and others. These memories are followed by others having to do with various twentieth century events, which had been related to Pound through anecdotes told by witnesses of them.

These main subjects—Pound's life in the camp, his memories, the evils of a corrupt economic system, the beauty and light of the natural world, the fleeting events of history—recur throughout the remainder of Canto 74 and on into the rest of *The Pisan*

Cantos. As the poem picks up its pace, however, the subjects are interwoven at smaller and smaller intervals. For example, in the passage beginning "autumnal heavens under sha-o," Pound moves in rapid succession through Chinese poetry (three lines), Old Testament dictates on money (three lines), the fees charged on an ancient toll road (three lines), Confucius (four lines), a description of a fellow prisoner (five lines), usury (two lines), state funding of the Athenian navy (two lines), and the infamy of Sir Winston Churchill (two lines). Often, the change of subject occurs in the middle of a line, complicating matters greatly for the reader intent on detecting a consistent narrative thread.

Forms and Devices

As are the other cantos in general, Canto 74 is written in free verse—poetic lines that have no set rhythm or consistent number of feet and that do not rhyme. The poem is broadly segmented into verse paragraphs; there are stanzas, which, similar to free verse, follow no regular structure and run anywhere from one line to several pages.

One immediately recognizable structural feature of this canto—again as with nearly all the other cantos—is fragmentation: Normal syntactic patterns are often absent, so that individual lines may lack subjects, objects, or verbs. Moreover, such lines may begin abruptly, in midsentence, and may often be written in a foreign language. A good example occurs at the beginning of Canto 74, where "sorella la luna" ("sister the moon") on one separate line is followed by an imperative sentence ("Fear god . . ."), followed by a noun phrase begun by a conjunction ("but a precise definition").

Another unfamiliar structural device, which Pound used increasingly toward the end of the *Cantos*, is the Chinese character, often inserted to the side of the text as a kind of commentary on the Western-language lines. Pound believed that such ideograms were "picture writing," able to be read as visual images without knowledge of Chinese. Thus, ideograms provided direct, unmediated messages embodying the themes of certain portions of the poem.

Largely, however, it is the striking imagery of Canto 74 that most readers admire. Although a simple paraphrase of the many subjects Pound addresses in this canto makes the poem appear incomprehensible, the poet's imagery helps these divergent motifs to cohere.

The main imagery comprises three elements: light, natural processes, and the Celestial City. Much of Pound's imagery in Canto 74 is in direct contrast to the drab realities of prison life. In fact, Pound uses the simple details of his life in the detention camp as symbols of natural forces that flow on, oblivious to human beings and their history. In the passage beginning "and there was a smell of mint under the tent flaps," for example, the many small, piquant details seem to shine like the universal light that is one of the canto's main themes. The odor of rain-drenched wild mint, the brilliant white of oxen on the road outside the prison, the dark sheep standing out against the rainy mountainside take on the quality of eternal emblems of the natural world. Because this world has nothing to do with Pound, it "upholds" him—keeps him going—

precisely as watching the lizards crawling around the camp keeps his mind off his coming trial.

In the lines that follow the "mint" passage, Pound uses the imagery of universal light "to manifest" (as the Chinese character here says) the underlying reality reflected in individual elements of the natural world. Such light also appears in imagery concerning the Celestial City, where the "light of light . . . virtu" illumines human works as well. The "four giants at the four corners," who appear following the above images, were the colossal ancient statues that marked the boundaries of an ideal city-state; however, the statues also symbolize the "giant" that lies dormant in human potential.

Themes and Meanings

The imagery in Canto 74 suggests that human beings will only fulfill their real potential when they bring themselves into harmony with the light of the gods—when, along with the animals and plants, they move in natural sympathy with the universe.

Standing in the way of such potential are a number of obstacles; not the least of these is economic corruption. For Pound, usury symbolized that corruption, because, he believed, usurers make money with money; that is, they contribute nothing to the actual physical well-being of humankind. Earning money through interest on loans occurs only on paper: Lenders are not manufacturers or farmers or artisans, and thus they are out of tune with the natural world.

Canto 74 frames this generalized theme in Pound's own individual perspective. He places the dry world of economics and the abstractions of history in a human context, his own. An aging poet awaiting trial for treason, Pound sees himself as a victim of the modern world's corruption. He also views himself, with all human beings, as a victim of time itself: Throughout the poem, he is flooded with memories of his own past. Yet, as a citizen of the world, as a well-known poet and thinker, Pound's personal life intersected with some of the greatest events of the twentieth century, and so in the lyrical intensity of *The Pisan Cantos*, he welds together these major themes: the disharmony of the modern world and his own personal tragedy.

John Steven Childs

CANTO 81

Author: Ezra Pound (1885-1972)
Type of poem: Poetic sequence
First published: 1948, in *The Pisan Cantos*

The Poem

Canto 81 is a free-verse poem of 173 lines in Ezra Pound's long epic poem entitled the *Cantos*. "Canto" is an Italian word for song, poem, or chant. Pound worked on the *Cantos* for more than fifty years, from about 1915 until his death. Canto 81 is part of *The Pisan Cantos* (cantos 74-84), which Pound wrote in 1945 while a prisoner of war in the United States Army's Disciplinary Training Center (DTC) near Pisa, Italy. With a naïve and misplaced faith in the economic reforms of Italian fascist dictator Benito Mussolini, Pound had delivered broadcasts over Rome Radio criticizing the United States' actions in World War II. Without visits from family or friends and without his books, Pound wrote the eleven Pisan cantos mostly from memory as he struggled for survival during seven months of solitary confinement before being formally accused of treason.

This poem has two sections. The first ninety-two lines offer a meditation on attempts to find worth in life. Through short narratives and direct quotations, often in colloquial diction, the speaker presents ways of worship as well as rituals of everyday life from ancient to contemporary cultures. The first line grounds the poem in Greek antiquity: "Zeus lies in Ceres' bosom." Zeus is a newer male god resting like a baby or lover on the breast of Ceres, the older female god of corn and nature. The section ends with a journalistic account which states that "my ole man went on hoein' corn." Pound believed in the community-strengthening power of the Eleusinian Mysteries, during which the Greeks celebrated the seasonal plant cycles of "the green world," to which Pound often turns for organic principles of order. The speaker ends images of worship, friendship, hospitality, writing, communal dance, and newspaper reporting in this section, along with a three-line lament on his loneliness in prison.

The poem shifts at line 96, where the second section is labeled "libretto," or words for music. Here the poem becomes more consciously musical. The speaker turns to the supernatural with an image that suggests the goddess of love, Aphrodite, Pound's personal deity: "Yet/ Ere the season died a-cold/ Borne upon a zephyr's shoulder/ I rose through the aureate sky." This god seems to preside over the seventeenth century English lyric community. The speaker considers the ability and inability to see and know until, at line 133, the section shifts into a powerful prayer, probably spoken by Aphrodite, that starts, "What thou lovest well remains,/ the rest is dross." It is an encouraging and comforting message to artists and others passionate enough to "Make it new," Pound's words that served as the motto of the modern era.

Readers must sort through often confusing and apparently esoteric fragments. This process requires interpretation of the poem in order to find its value. The end of the poem can function as Pound's rationale for radio broadcasts intended to improve rather than betray his country, as the goddess may be addressing Pound: "How mean thy hates// Rathe [quick] to destroy, niggard in charity// But to have done instead of not doing/ this is not vanity." In another interpretation, the goddess may be admonishing Pound's critics, so quick to destroy him and so deficient in compassion. It is up to the reader to ponder whether Canto 81 presents a repentant or defiant Pound—or whether it is more important to contemplate love and love contemplation.

Forms and Devices

This poem, like many by Pound and other modern poets such as T. S. Eliot, accumulates images and documents that leap across time and place without explanatory connective material. Pound used an ordering device that he called the ideogramic method. Taking his cue from some Chinese characters called ideograms, he assembles images that present aspects of an idea. For example, he follows an image of nature comforting Zeus with a Spanish priest who helped Pound with research on the troubadour poet Guido Cavalcanti and a Spanish peasant woman who gave Pound bread. Together, these images convey the idea of kindness.

Pound led a transatlantic poetic movement called Imagism, which opposed nineteenth century Romanticism and sentimentality by favoring sharp, clear images, freedom in choice of subject matter, and common speech. Yet Canto 81 and other cantos have images that are not always clear and often seem to dissolve into other images. In this canto images include Greek and Chinese deities, a Portuguese folk dance, a French economic council, John Adams and Thomas Jefferson, the philosopher George Santayana arriving in Boston, and a reporter getting his story. Pound, along with the painter Wyndham Lewis and sculptor Henri Gaudier-Brzeska, extended Imagism to Vorticism, which declared itself free from the need to imitate nature and celebrated energy changed by the artist into form.

Many fragments in the first section are reportorial or documentary in nature. Languages include Spanish, Chaucer's Middle English, classical Greek, and a shift to some Italian in the second section. All these images and documents give Pound's endeavor authority from different times, places, disciplines, and classes. He starts the canto with classical divinity and ends it with biblical diction and rhythm. Clergy, political leaders, and cultural forces help the speaker to present his theme from different perspectives. This Cubist treatment, which modern writers adapted from painters such as Pablo Picasso, deepened and broadened the treatment of a poetic subject, much as Cubist painter Marcel Duchamp presents on one canvas various views of a nude descending a staircase. Pound used multiple perspectives to write "the tale of the tribe"—the human community—and help it to envision a new "Paideuma . . . the gristly roots of ideas that are in action" in the mid-twentieth century.

In addition, Pound uses music as a formal, stylistic, and semantic device. Refrains such as "Pull down thy vanity" and "What thou lov'st well shall not be reft from thee" dramatize what is important. Cadences from authoritative and aesthetic sources such as the Bible, Ben Jonson, and Geoffrey Chaucer modulate within the poem. As a motif in music alters somewhat yet remains recognizable, Pound works with the main motif of worth and uses the related motifs of love and community to sound its importance. Pound loves the metaphor of a community as a musical group in which each person thoughtfully contributes his or her part to a whole energized by diversity. The music of this canto entrances the reader before he or she can understand its meaning.

Themes and Meanings

Canto 81 is a poem about worth. In the larger work, the *Cantos* as a whole, Pound looks across the history of human civilization and contemplates what endures. Pound thought that civilizations fall because of economic reasons. For example, he dearly loved the intellectual and artistic successes of the Italian Renaissance but believed that it disintegrated because of money lust and private banking. He thought that Italy could serve as the locus of a model or experiment that combined honest Confucian government with the celebration of the Eleusian Mysteries. In Canto 81 he demonstrates the process of finding what is worthwhile.

Overall, this poem uses the scientific method. That is, it starts with observations that the speaker believes are important. From his solitary confinement in Pisa, Pound fondly recalls people who helped other people, both individually and through a community. From this evidence, Pound reaches a thesis: "What thou lovest well remains,/ the rest is dross." The next line, the most famous in the *Cantos*, intensifies this image of purification and relates it more immediately to Pound's desperate condition: "What thou lov'st well shall not be reft from thee." Pound uses the authority of the inductive method to test the value of his conclusion that love and anything done with love have enduring value.

As a guiding principle of love Pound uses Aphrodite, known to Romans as Venus and cited in line 3 as "Cythera," a Greek island where the goddess landed. Directly after Pound's profound cry of loss and loneliness as "a leaf in the current" of life and history with "no Althea" to comfort him, a supernatural figure rises like Botticelli's Venus from the sea. With the cadences and rhetoric of God speaking from the whirlwind in the Book of Job and the preacher in Ecclesiastes, she inspires harmonious community by asking of individual artists and craftspeople, "Has he tempered the viol's wood// Has he curved us the bowl of the lute?" Later she states that "it is not man/ Made courage, or made order, or made grace,/ Pull down thy vanity, I say pull down." She asks them to contemplate the source of their creative energies.

Pound sees worth in community. Canto 81 offers a heterogeneous community that includes peasants, political leaders, and gods. Contrary to the elitism that some people see in Pound's poetry, this canto is inclusive. Unlike the more homogeneous world of the Cavalier poetic tradition, Pound's world is global. Love and caring can create a viable new transnational community. As Pound sifts through the pieces of his life, the people of a Europe wrecked by World War II must choose the fragments worthy of creating a new world.

Joanna Yin

CANTO 116

Author: Ezra Pound (1885-1972)
Type of poem: Poetic sequence
First published: 1962; collected in *Drafts and Fragments of Cantos CX-CXVII*, 1968

The Poem

"Canto 116" (or "Canto CXVI," as it was first known) was composed in Italy in 1959. It is a relatively short poem in free verse. Its seventy-four lines vary in length from three to eleven syllables. The figure the poem makes on paper is jagged because of frequent indentation; many of its lines begin in the middle or toward the end of the page.

Upon scrutiny, "Canto 116" reveals a threefold structure: Part 1, so called, extends from Neptunus (Neptune) of line 1 to Justinian, including the next line (line 22), "a tangle of works unfinished." Muss (Mussolini), the "old crank" dead in Virginia, and the vision of the Madonna are stages in this section. Part 2, comprising the next thirty-four lines, begins with the definite emergence of the first-person narrator ("I have brought the great ball of crystal") and ends with a concession in line 56: "even if my notes do not cohere." This median group of lines may be further subdivided into two unequal parts, from line 23 to line 31 and from line 32 to line 56. Finally, part 3 goes from line 57 ("Many errors") to the end of the poem (line 74), "to lead back to splendour." The quest for paradise is brought to a rest here, but it promises a new dawn and a renewed beginning.

The first character to burst upon the scene is Neptune, the god of the seas in Greek mythology, whose mind frolics like leaping dolphins. Then there is talk about cosmos-making in a world of the possible: the political realm of Benito Mussolini, the dictator of Italy from 1922 to 1943, and the poetic sphere of fashioning an epic poem, Ezra Pound's *Cantos* themselves. The "record" (line 8) and the "palimpsest" (line 9) seem to refer back to both. With line 13 Pound himself gets his picture into the text. He will gradually emerge as the protagonist of "Canto 116." Then a picture of the Madonna, the mother of Jesus, is introduced. The next several lines seem to deal with Justinian, the Byzantine emperor from 527 to 565 C.E., famous for his code of laws.

With line 23 the first-person voice proclaims its presence and firmly takes over. Things become clearer, especially for those readers who are familiar with Pound's troubles in old age: his incarceration and trial for treason at the end of World War II, his subsequent thirteen-year-long confinement at St. Elizabeth's (an asylum for the insane in Washington, D.C.), the scandal caused by the first Bollingen Prize being awarded to his *Pisan Cantos* in 1949, and his final release and return to Italy in 1958. In the middle of "Canto 116" the speaking persona of the poet is intent on building an argument regarding his mismanagement of the entire large-scale project of the *Cantos* as an epic poem. In doing so, however, Pound is also keen in pointing out various extenuating circumstances, and even the relative strengths of his whole endeavor.

While hammering out his pseudo-defense, the speaker evokes the strength and encouragement he drew from a range of benefic agencies, including two beautiful and sympathetic creatures "under the elms," "squirrels and bluejays" popping up from Walt Disney's world of animated films, "Ariadne," the famous heroine of Greek mythology who gave Theseus the thread with which he found his way out of the Minotaur's labyrinth, André Spire, the Jewish French poet and humanist, the French symbolist poet Jules Laforgue, Linnaeus, the great Swedish botanist, and "Venere"—the goddess of love and beauty, also known as Venus or Aphrodite. The point is reached that paradise ("paradiso" in the text, most probably in honor of Dante Alighieri) seems still within reach, here on earth: "a nice quiet paradise/ over the shambles" (lines 49-50). The spirit is upbeat. The failure acknowledged in lines 28-29 is mitigated, even reversed, in lines 55-56.

In the concluding section, the speaker's voice ruminates on the balancing act involved: "many errors,/ a little rightness" (lines 57-58) and "To confess wrong without losing rightness" (line 70). To make most of what endures is the lesson in humility that the poet has learned the hard way. At long last, a glimmer of light flickers, showing the way back to splendor. The whole epic cycle comes to rest on this hopeful note.

Forms and Devices

"Canto 116" is part of a large-scale, 800-page epic poem that was forty years in the making, roughly from 1920 to 1960. the *Cantos* (the later poetry of Ezra Pound) bears comparison in scope, complexity, and difficulty with *Ulysses* (1922), the well-known novel by James Joyce, and with the other masterwork that appeared in that same year, T. S. Eliot's poem *The Waste Land.* All three works are representative of English Modernism, the literary trend that dominated the first half of twentieth century Western culture.

As part of a larger whole, "Canto 116" is only a relatively independent piece of writing. However, being practically the last completed unit of the sequence, it represents a vantage point from which the compositional strategies of the *Cantos* can be surveyed and grasped as a whole. In contradistinction to most of the previous cantos—and, for that matter, to any other epic poem—"Canto 116" is written in the first person. Hence it possesses a higher consistency of viewpoint, even though subjective, and greater clarity and accessibility than much of Pound's work.

The engine that drives this canto's unfolding is Pound's usual resort to parataxis: the placing side by side of bits of information, names of important people and places, mythical allusions, and phrases in foreign tongues (sometimes translated, sometimes not)—all in rapid succession, with no grammatical connectives whatsoever between them. Thus words are grouped in rhythmical, self-sufficient units or paragraphs, a fact which renders their meanings more readily available. The lines of varying length yielded by this process are further highlighted by their typographical arrangement down the page in doublets or triplets. The emotional highs and lows that alternate during the unfolding of the canto can be thus followed and plotted. The reader is also urged to spot the instances of hypotaxis, when such syntactical connectors such as "but," "though," or "even if" (see the beginnings of lines 8, 26, 27, 45, 56, and 66) restrict or qualify the significance of the statements. Likewise, inversion of a Miltonic type (a device generally avoided by Pound) powerfully launches the opening line: "Came Neptunus."

Pound's text production, with its reliance on disconnected fragments, arresting images, and recondite allusions, requires considerable critical research. All modernist works demand initiation prior to comfortable enjoyment. Since there is no such thing as an omniscient reader, an industry of modernist exegesis has flourished. The reader who has developed a taste for Pound, Eliot, or Joyce will eventually have to read the findings of Eva Hesse, Walter Baumann, James J. Wilhelm, George Kearns, Christine Froula, and Peter Stoicheff, to name some of the more insightful commentators on "Canto 116." Likewise, periodically interesting and rewarding articles are published in *Paideuma*, the main journal focusing on Pound's work.

Themes and Meanings

"Canto 116" begins with Neptune's divine mind asserting its presence and prompting some summing-up or self-criticism inspired by impending death. Pound's original ambition of structuring the Cantos on a cosmic scale is found wanting. His many errors, such as his involvement with fascism and the scapegoating of the Jews, prevented him from "making things cohere." Acknowledgment of this is the dominant theme of the canto, so a sense of dark despair underlies it. Along these lines, Pound's constant model and source of inspiration, Dante's *Divine Comedy*, provided him with a vision of Paradise that he could not sustain. What he could attain, though, was a kind of private paradise of personal fulfillment and love, a humble experience of purgatorial ascent.

Although Pound resorts to such limiting terms as "palimpsest," "record," and "notes," he seems eager to uphold and defend his work. There is perfection in it ("the crystal ball") or great promise ("an acron of light") or a reassuring permanence (Ariadne's "golden thread"). The whole setting seems to take part in this positive outlook: the luminous gold of Italian geography and art (the golden mosaic at the church on the island of Torcello, the "lane of gold" in the wake of the setting sun across the Bay of Tiguillo), the equally luminous feminine presences, the muses of memory (Sheri Martinelli and Marcella Booth, née Spann) in the arboretum at St. Elizabeth's, the simplicity and elemental alertness of bluejays and squirrels in Disney's films (contrasted with the "metaphysicals"—modern scientists who disregard the radiance and splendor of the created universe). Pound's confidence is shattered only when it comes to the question of the decoding of his message by some future generation.

Beyond that concern, "charity"—the chief Dantescan value—remains one of his genuine experiences, though somewhat frustrated by his own sense of guilt, which does not allow a full rejoicing in it. Finally, "the dim rush of light," symbolizing his love for his infant daughter, lends to his longing for the "splendour" of bygone days with both poignancy and wistful hope.

Stefan Stoenescu

CAPTIVITY

Author: Louise Erdrich (1954-   )
Type of poem: Narrative
First published: 1984, in *Jacklight*

The Poem

"Captivity" is a medium-length narrative poem in free verse, its fifty-eight lines divided into six stanzas which are, respectively, nine, ten, eleven, eight, ten, and ten lines long. The title refers to the subject of the narrative: It is a woman's story of her capture by a band of American Indians in the seventeenth century. No names are given for the narrator or any of the other characters—the man she identifies as her captor, a woman associated with him, and the narrator's child and husband. An epigraph, a short quote from Mary Rowlandson's 1676 narrative about her own capture and travels with a band of Wampanoag, follows the title of the poem. The quote reads: "He (my captor) gave me a bisquit, which I put in my pocket, and not daring to eat it, buried it under a log, fearing he had put something in it to make me love him."

Although the poem is written in the first-person point of view, the Rowlandson reference makes it clear that Erdrich is creating a narrator whose culture, experiences, and beliefs are different from the poet's own. The speaker of the poem is based on a historical figure. Erdrich is a twentieth century poet of German and Chippewa descent; the narrator of "Captivity" is a woman like Mary Rowlandson.

The poem begins with a description of the group's flight through the woods. The narrator states that she had trouble crossing a stream but that someone, referred to only as "he," saved her. The captive has learned to recognize him as an individual, and she is afraid that she understands "his language, which [is] not human." In her fear, she prays.

The next two stanzas describe events that occurred during her time with her captors. They are chased and have to march. The narrator's child cries because of hunger, but she cannot suckle, so a woman feeds the baby "milk of acorns." The narrator promises herself to starve rather than take food from her captors, but she does not keep the promise. One night "he" kills a pregnant deer and gives her "to eat of the fawn./ It was so tender,/ the bones like the stems of flowers,/ that I followed where he took me." The events that close the stanza are not clearly described. "He" cuts the ropes that bind her, and it is night. The next stanza describes natural events that the narrator interprets as God's wrath. These events include a lightning storm. She sees that her captor neither notices or fears God's wrath.

The last two stanzas describe her life after she has been rescued and returned to her husband. Although she is back with her family, she is neither happy nor content. She says that she sees "no truth in things," and despite having food for her child, she does not feel at home. She says "I lay myself to sleep" and "I lay to sleep," two lines that echo the prayer taught to children. Instead of untroubled sleep or a completed prayer, she has a vision of herself back with her captors. She is "outside their circle," but as her captor leads them in what the narrator first thinks of as noise, she finds herself part of the chant. She strips a branch and joins them, strikes the earth "begging it to open/ to admit me/ as he was/ and feed me honey from the rock."

Forms and Devices

The narrative and language of the poem are based on another group of texts: historical "captivity narratives." Erdrich explicitly directs the readers to consider the existence and meanings of the captivity narratives by quoting Mary Rowlandson's narrative and providing basic information about her situation. Rowlandson was taken prisoner by the Wampanoag "when Lancaster, Massachusetts, was destroyed, in the year 1676." In order to understand the poem's themes fully, some knowledge of the historical circumstances is necessary. Rowlandson's narrative has become one of the most well known of numerous published captivity stories, but it is by no means the only one. Frances Roe Kestler, in *The Indian Captivity Narrative: A Woman's View* (1990), identifies approximately five hundred narratives, published in twelve hundred editions, during the seventeenth, eighteenth, and nineteenth centuries. The narratives were written by men and women who were held captive by various tribes during the centuries of conflict between the European immigrants and the American Indians who lived in the areas where the Europeans settled.

According to Kestler, Rowlandson's was the first narrative known to be composed by a woman. The experiences of and perceptions about women who were held captive differed from those of men because of the different cultural expectations regarding women, especially regarding sexuality. Rowlandson had immigrated to Salem with her father and later married Joseph Rowlandson, a minister. They had four children. The three children who survived infancy were taken captive, along with their mother, in February of 1676. The youngest child died during captivity; the older two escaped or were ransomed. Rowlandson was ransomed in May after three months of captivity.

The unnamed narrator of Erdrich's poem cannot be Mary Rowlandson, who was taken captive with three children, the youngest age six, but Erdrich clearly intends readers to view the poem as a captivity narrative by a woman who had similar experiences and fears, especially regarding the possibility of being forced to "love" her captor through some charm or spell placed on food. The narrator, like Rowlandson, fears her captors as being completely different and "other" than human.

Another important aspect of the poem is the imagery, especially the image clusters relating to religion and food. The religious images and allusions would be natural usage to a Puritan woman, and they primarily are references to natural disasters as representing God's punishment. The narrator is dragged from "the flood," a reference to the biblical flood, which was God's punishment of humanity. She prays after realizing that she is understanding some of "his" language, recalling the Tower of Babel, which led to God causing humans to speak in different languages. After she goes apart with him, she believes that she is being punished by God: Trees fling "down/ their sharpened lashes." God's wrath is made clear in natural manifestations ("blasting fire from half-buried stumps.")

Her belief that God punishes humanity through the earth changes in the last stanza when the narrator imagines herself joining in the chant, "begging" the earth "to open// and feed me honey from the rock." The change from earth as a place of sinning and punishment to earth as a nurturing mother implies a change from the Puritan worldview to a belief common to American Indians.

The final stanza links religious and food imagery, but the food imagery begins in the epigraph which speaks of Rowlandson's determination not to eat any food from the hand of her captor because it might make her love him. When the narrator's child is hungry, a woman provides food. The narrator herself plans to starve but ultimately accepts food "from his hands," the second time that he saves her life. The food is the flesh of an unborn fawn, and it causes her to follow him ("I followed where he took me"). At the end of the poem, the speaker begs the earth, through her chant, to feed her "honey from the rock," a new and different kind of food, linked to her captor. The food imagery being associated with children (her child and the unborn fawn) shows the link between food and sexuality or birth.

Themes and Meanings

"Captivity" is a poem about identity and culture. The history of the relationships between "Americans" (as the indigenous peoples were called by the early immigrants) and "Europeans" is a long and complicated one, and Erdrich is re-viewing that history. Erdrich, a twentieth century German-Chippewa woman, creates as her speaker a seventeenth century Puritan woman who travels and lives with a group that she would normally see as her family's and culture's enemies. If the narrator shares Mary Rowlandson's views, shaped by the preaching of Puritan ministers, she would also see her captor and the others as allies of Satan, placed in the "New World" to tempt the Puritans from their religion and culture. Any understanding of or intimacy with a man from this group who are "not human" would be seen as endangering her soul. At the beginning of the narrative, the speaker fears learning to understand her captor, fears accepting food from him, because any intimacy with him will bring down God's wrath on her.

By the end of the poem, the narrator has moved beyond her culture's attitudes about the "Other," and the experience changes her irretrievably. Rescued, she has lost any sense of her own culture's "truth" and longs to join what she formerly rejected. The poem does not explicitly state that physical intimacy occurred, but a woman writing in the seventeenth century would probably not be able to say so explicitly, at least not in any published work. The intimacy has to be understood through images, through what is not said, and through changes in her. Even if no sexual act occurred, her vision at the end of the poem shows that she wishes to join in the circle, to join with them, in a chant which is probably of a religious nature. Even if she remained physically faithful to her husband, she has been spiritually changed. The poem's theme subverts the expectations and attitudes of an earlier time and asks contemporary readers to think about those attitudes and about what has changed, or not changed, in the centuries following the events of this poem.

Robin Anne Reid

CARGOES

Author: John Masefield (1878-1967)
Type of poem: Lyric
First published: 1903, in *Ballads*

The Poem

"Cargoes" is a short lyric poem consisting of three five-line stanzas. In each, Masefield describes a different kind of ship. The first two lines of each stanza describe the ship moving through water; the last three list the different cargoes the ships are carrying.

The ship in stanza 1 is a quinquireme, a large vessel rowed by groups of five oarsmen. Masefield's ship is being rowed from "distant Ophir," a region in either Arabia or Africa at the southern end of the Red Sea, to the northern end of that sea. (Masefield must have intended the term "Palestine" to apply to the land at the farthest reach of the present Gulf of Aqaba.) The ship's goal is a happy one, for Palestine is a safe "haven" with sunny skies. This boat carries a cargo of animals, birds, exotic woods, and wine.

Masefield found many of his details in the Old Testament. Nineveh, an important Assyrian city, is often mentioned there. Many of the details of this stanza—ivory, apes, peacocks, and cedars—come from 1 Kings 10. That chapter also mentions drinking vessels, though not the wine in them, and "almug trees," which may be the same as sandalwood trees.

In stanza 3, the poem moves ahead about two thousand years to the sixteenth or seventeenth century and changes its focus to the West Indies. A galleon was a large sailing ship often used in trade between Spain and Latin America, a part of the world Masefield himself knew well from his days as a sailor. This "stately" (splendid, dignified, majestic) ship began its journey at the Isthmus of Panama, and it progresses with a vessel's normal up-and-down motion ("dipping") through the verdant and beautiful islands of the Caribbean. Its cargo contains precious stones (emeralds and diamonds), semiprecious stones, spices, and gold coins. (A "moidore" is a Portuguese coin; the word means literally "coin of gold.")

In stanza 3 the British ship is neither so pretty as the previous two (it is "dirty") nor so big. A coaster is a small ship designed chiefly to carry goods along a coastline rather than on the high seas. This coaster is propelled by a steam engine (it has a smokestack), and it moves through the English Channel with a force and motion that resemble an animal butting with its head. Part of its cargo are things to burn: wood for fireplaces and coal mined near Newcastle-upon-Tyne on the eastern coast of Britain. The rest is metal that has been processed or manufactured, perhaps in the British Midlands not far from Newcastle: metal rails with which to build railroad tracks, lead ingots or "pigs," items of hardware made of iron, and "cheap tin trays."

Forms and Devices

Masefield's poem is formally precise. Each stanza describes a ship in its historical era. Each ship is pictured in motion, and its cargo is then noted. In each stanza the first two and last lines are long, whereas the third and fourth are short; the second and fifth lines rhyme.

The rhythm of each stanza is very similar. Masefield seems to have abandoned usual English syllabic verse for accentual verse, which was being experimented with in his day. This poem is best read with strong accents, giving two beats to each short line and four beats to each long line. An extra half-accent may be given in the second and fifth lines of each stanza to words such as "white," "green," and "tin."

Because "Cargoes" has no clauses, independent or dependent, it makes no statement, provisional or otherwise. Therefore it must depend for its effect on the associations and connotations of the words Masefield has chosen. These effects differ significantly from stanza to stanza. Readers may not know that the details of stanza 1 describe Solomon's lavish court at the time of the visit of the queen of Sheba. Even so, they will sense the exotic and sensual nature of this cargo. Ivory is lovely to touch; it and sandalwood come from far-off regions, even farther away than distant Ophir. Both sandalwood and cedarwood are pleasingly aromatic; white wine is sweet to taste; apes and peacocks may decorate opulent palaces in sun-drenched Palestine.

Even though a quinquireme had sails, Masefield describes only how it is rowed by human power. Other omissions are significant as well. The Bible says that Solomon possessed great quantities of gold and spices, but Masefield does not mention them. In this stanza Masefield distorts geography and history in order to heighten the poetic effect of his lines. Nineveh was a great distance from the Red Sea and flourished long before the era of quinquiremes. It would have been almost impossible for such a large ship to have navigated down the Tigris River from Nineveh. Moreover, quinquiremes were Roman warships, not cargo-carrying vessels. Masefield probably chose the word "Nineveh" mainly for its sound and rhythm and for its aura of importance.

Stanza 2 is almost as exotic as stanza 1 and even more opulent. Masefield may have omitted gold from stanza 1 because he wanted to save it for stanza 2. The emphasis here is on the riches of gold and gems, not on sensual pleasures. Yet these gems, the galleon, and the palm-green shores have a wonderful beauty that may exceed that of the ancient world.

Stanza 3 offers a stark contrast to the first two. The British coaster is in no way beautiful or exotic or wealthy. Instead of the lovely weather of Palestine and the Caribbean, Masefield now provides unpleasant "mad March" days. The seas that cake the smokestack with salt must be butted through with the help of a steam engine. The coaster's cargo is similarly unexotic,—practical fuels and manufactured goods, some of them ugly.

Masefield varies his sound to suit his subject matter. The first two stanzas are euphonious and slow-moving. Stanza 3 is cacophonous and fairly quick to read; its accents are heavier and less subtle, and its consonants are harsh: "salt-caked smokestacks." One reason "Cargoes" has been anthologized so often is that Masefield's control of his language produces so much pleasure.

Themes and Meanings

Throughout his life Masefield delighted in describing ships and the sea, and the most obvious focus of "Cargoes" simply has to do with ships. Though a dirty coaster is not the sort of vessel to which he usually responded, this poem clearly shows the poet's love of various kinds of ships. Masefield imagines these ships at their most attractive: in action, dipping and butting in both smooth and choppy seas. When Masefield contrasts three very different ships from three very different historical eras, he implies that the wonders of ships and the sea, despite some changes, remain constant. Because the poem contains no clauses and hence no statements, it is tempting to say that Masefield has produced a pretty anthology-piece with very little meaning. Yet the contrast of the poem's stanzas yields a simple but effective view of history as well as a perspective on Masefield's own age.

The ancient world is shown as sensual, given to exotic pleasures. Its boats are propelled by human power over modest distances. In contrast, the world of the sixteenth century is magnificent and heroic. Its wind-driven ships traverse vast oceans and bring cargoes that are beautiful and opulent: gems and gold that are worth a great deal. In both stanzas, the ships are bringing their wonderful things back home for the enjoyment of those who live there.

Regardless of whether Masefield literally believed in these readings of history, they serve as a backdrop for his view of contemporary life in stanza 3. Modern life is one of change. The dirty coaster is propelled by a steam engine, a comparatively recent machine that was supplanting time-honored sail power even as Masefield was serving as a sailor. This world is not a pleasant one. The coaster is not a pretty ship, and it is having a difficult time steaming in the choppy seas. Moreover, it is not bringing wonderful things back home to be enjoyed; it is *taking* a cargo of goods, many of them manufactured goods, away for delivery or sale at some unspecified port, perhaps elsewhere in Britain or across the English Channel in France. These goods are not sensual or beautiful but practical, commercial, utilitarian, and sometimes cheap: rails for railroads, hardware, tin trays.

Even so, this modern ship has an energy that Masefield finds admirable. The coaster suggests the side of British life that Masefield wishes to praise: not the elegant refinements of the Victorian aristocracy but the vigor of the common working people.

George Soule

A CARRIAGE FROM SWEDEN

Author: Marianne Moore (1887-1972)
Type of poem: Lyric
First published: 1944, in *Nevertheless*

The Poem

"A Carriage from Sweden" by Marianne Moore is a sixty-line poem of twelve five-line stanzas celebrating the beauty of a Swedish country cart as well as the virtues of the nation in which it was made. The poet's words raise a utilitarian folk artifact into a museum masterpiece. Thus the poem is an example of ekphrasis (Greek for "to speak out"), the verbal representation of a visual work of art, as a painting or sculpture. Its technique of alternating description and interpretation can be compared with the pure ekphrasis of John Keats's "Ode on a Grecian Urn," in which the art object exists solely and wholly in words, and with W. H. Auden's "Musée des Beaux Arts," which uses several paintings but centers finally upon Pieter Bruegel, the Elder's "Landscape with Fall of Icarus." Had not the Swedish carriage been sold from the Brooklyn museum where Moore first saw it, and subsequently lost, a photograph of it could accompany the poem for comparison.

Ekphrastic poetry involves the remaking of a made thing. Imagery is largely visual as the reader is invited to see the art object from different perspectives. The object is not only described but also interpreted for the reader, who should be alert for the movement from one sort of rhetoric to the other. Even acts of description become interpretation, however, for the poet's selectivity sets thematic priorities. The poet may emphasize, exaggerate, distort, or even omit details of the art object. In the case of the carriage from Sweden, the vehicle made in words by a Brooklyn poet is every bit as impressive as the wooden vehicle made in Scandinavia. Indeed, Moore's theme is the integrity of well-made things, whether carts or arts. Behind every line of the poem (Greek for *poema*, "created thing") lies the notion of the poet (Greek for *poietes*, "maker") as creator, maker of a made thing, as well as the forces that make it poetic (Greek for *poietikos*, "inventive, ingenious").

Forms and Devices

Although Moore's poem is unmetered, that is, without any particular rhythm, it is structured with syllabics and intricate rhyme. As the maker of the Swedish cart may have drawn a plan of what he or she was about to make, so Moore worked according to an elaborate blueprint of syllable count and rhymes. First, she decided to make twelve five-line stanzas. Lines 1, 2, 3, and 5 have eight syllables each. Line 4 in all stanzas but the last has nine syllables, and even in the final stanza it may have nine if one assumes two silent syllables, like the dramatic pause at the end of a symphony before its conclusion.

In every stanza, the second and third lines end with full or exact rhymes or, occasionally, slant rhymes, as in stanzas 2 and 3. Rhyme in these lines is more noticeable than rhyme in other lines. The longer, nine-syllable lines remain unrhymed. The first rhyme of each stanza contains internal rhyme of the third syllable with the last, as in "there/air" (line 1), "resined/wind" (line 11), and "vertical/all" (line 31). These might also be full or exact rhymes and slant rhymes. The last line of each stanza rhymes its first syllable with its last. These might be sight rhyme, as "*some*thing/home" in line 5; slant rhyme, as "*in*tegrity/ve*in*" in line 10; or full, exact rhyme, as "Adolphus/de*cay*" in line 15. These demanding constraints and intricate patterns mimic the elaborate designs of the cart which serve to raise it from being merely utilitarian to being an art object worthy of the muses themselves.

Themes and Meanings

A museum is literally the abode of the muses, goddesses of poetic, dramatic, and astronomical inspiration. The Swedish cart is a "put-away/museum piece." When Moore went to check on it a decade after she first saw it, it was gone. Thus, in a sense, her poem operates like Keats's as pure ekphrasis, for now the cart exists only as words. She remembers it was made in Sweden, "there . . . a sweeter air . . . than we have here;/ a Hamlet's castle atmosphere." Hamlet may have known something was rotten in Denmark, but, on the whole, Scandinavia has a "sweeter air" than the poet's Brooklyn. Yet the poet is very comfortable in her own place: "At all events there is in Brooklyn/ something that makes me feel at home." Like the cart, the poet has been made by her atmosphere. Whatever is true of the cart is likely to be true of her as well.

Not a perfect place, hers is a "city of freckled/ integrity" against which the Swedish cart stands with "resined straightness" as if to take the city's measure. Aware of the shortcomings of her native place, Moore prays, "Washington and Gustavus/ Adolphus, forgive our decay." The rectitude of these two men is proverbial. The fabled George Washington, who could not tell a lie, and the worthy King Gustavus Adolphus, who ruled the land of the cart, are imposing standards of behavior.

A paradox of the carriage from Sweden is that now "no one may see this put-away/ museum piece." Things in museums are meant to be seen. Yet even when they are on display, some inner quality of the art object, "that inner happiness made art," is quite invisible. It is for the words of the poet to make this quality visible to the reader. As a standard of beauty and inner happiness, the carriage has a Platonic otherworldliness, a universality which can be grasped only in bits and pieces. Moore tries, by invoking bits and pieces of Swedish history and culture, to grasp the fullness of the cart's meaning.

The fourth stanza praises the cart's design from "a flowered step [and] swan-/ dart brake" to the "swirling crustacean-/ tailed equine amphibious creatures/ that garnish the axletree." As she beholds the riotous decorations which raise the useful cart to art object, the poet can only exclaim, "What// a fine thing!" Enjambment from stanza to stanza as well as from line to line keeps the poem rolling along like a cart racing down a country road. Moore can even imagine the beautiful woman waiting for its arrival, she "with the natural stoop of the/ snowy egret/ . . . or whom it should come to the door." She herself is that woman.

Stanza 6 is a veritable personification of Sweden: "the split/ pine fair hair . . . gannet-clear/ eyes . . . pine needled-path deer-/ swift step." The cart embodies all these qualities of its homeland; it has a life, too. It is straight like the spruce tree "vertical though a seedling." As the tree is bent, so it grows, but in Sweden, trees and people grow straight. There, people dance "in thick-soled/ shoes!" When the Nazis threatened Europe, "Denmark's sanctuaried Jews" found refuge in compassionate Sweden. The texture of folk arts and material culture, from jugs and rugs to stools to buttons and ornamental braid ("frogs"), captures the essence of Sweden, as does the cart itself.

Moore was a sports fan, so to her the spirit of Sweden was nowhere more visible than in "a runner called the Deer, who// when he's won a race, likes to run/ more." The last Olympic Games before the poem was written in 1944 had been the so-called Nazi Olympics of 1936. World War II forced the cancellation of the 1940 and 1944 Games. In 1948, three Swedish "deer" swept the 3,000-meter steeplechase for gold, silver, and bronze medals. This same exuberant, athletic spirit has produced the cart and is at work in the poem. It is akin to that "spontaneous overflow of powerful emotion" that William Wordsworth claimed to be the very source of poetry itself.

In an apostrophe (direct address), the poet asks, "Sweden,/ what makes the people dress that way/ and those who see you wish to stay?" What made the runner "not too tired to run more"? What made the cart so "dolphin-graceful"? What, she asks, accounts for the genius of a Nils Gustaf Dalen, who invented a "lighthouse, self-lit?— responsive and responsible"? She answers her own question in line 8: "that inner happiness made art."

As the poem concludes, it circles back upon itself dolphinlike, as graceful as the amphibians on the cart. It began with "a Hamlet's castle atmosphere," so it ends with "moated white castles," with the letter *S* picked out in "white flowers densely grown," with *S* for "Sweden," for "stalwartness," for "skill." To be "made in Sweden" is Moore's final metaphor for something that is well made, for the making of her well-wrought poem itself. "Carts are my trade," she says, both seriously and mischievously. The cart and her poem are now one.

R. Parks Lanier, Jr.

CARRION COMFORT

Author: Gerard Manley Hopkins (1844-1889)
Type of poem: Sonnet
First published: 1918, in *Poems of Gerard Manley Hopkins, Now First Published, with Notes by Robert Bridges*

The Poem

Gerard Manley Hopkins's sonnet "Carrion Comfort" displays brilliantly the complex prosody he developed for himself from many poetic sources, including Old English, Welsh, Italian, and various religious traditions. Despite its initial impression of difficulty, with a careful reading both the meaning and the form become clear. This poem must be read aloud, however, if the reader wishes to understand Hopkins's profoundly moving struggle with despair and with God.

"Carrion Comfort" is a variation on the Petrarchan or Italian sonnet form; this poem was one of a series of six sonnets Hopkins wrote in 1885 that have been called the "terrible sonnets" and part of a larger cycle known as the "sonnets of desolation" because of the tremendous power and pain in them. In this poem, though, Hopkins is defying the despair that threatens and even appears to overwhelm him in other sonnets of this cycle. He entitles this despair "carrion," after the dead and putrefying flesh that buzzards and other scavengers devour; he refuses to feed upon it, to find comfort in that despair.

In the first quatrain he resists both the temptation of despair and suicide and proclaims his ability to hope, or, if that is too extreme, at least to wish for day and "not choose not to be." He will not "untwist . . . the last strands of man/ in [him]"; that is, he will not give up his humanity to despair. In the second quatrain the poet speaks to an adversary who is as yet unknown to the reader, calling him only "thou terrible," and questions why the speaker is so cruelly, as well as rudely, treated by him. He uses diction that is biblical in its implications, such as "lay a lion-limb against me" and the imagery of winnowing grain.

In the final sestet, the speaker answers his own questions; he is roughly treated so that he might be clarified and chastened, brought to "[kiss] the rod" of God, and by that submission actually be saved. Thus the winner of the match may be either the "hero whose heaven-handling flung" him, or the speaker himself who, by wrestling with but finally submitting to God, has become a winner in the wrestling match he has endured. Thus salvation comes through surrender, a profound paradox that is part of the Christian tradition.

"Carrion Comfort" is a poem of faith, tested and triumphant, in which the poet rejects the option of suicide, affirms some hope in his life, wrestles with God, and finds himself saved by submission. It displays examples of some of Hopkins's innovative devices, including the preponderance of repetition, alliteration, strong stresses, and a wrenching of syntax that results in a powerful evocation of the emotional and spiritual struggle that is its topic.

Forms and Devices

Hopkins occasionally uses archaic language and portmanteau words in his poetry to express his often convoluted ideas. In "Carrion Comfort" the most noticeable language choices are the use of the word "rude" as a verb; the creation of the compound words "wring-world," "lion-limb," and "heaven-handling"; the coining of the portmanteau word "darksome"; the archaism of the word "coil" to mean confusion or conflict; and the ambiguity and double usage of terms such as "rock" in "Thy wring-world right foot rock?" One of the most striking examples of evocative language is the use of the word "not" four times in the first two lines of the poem, each of them stressed, in conjunction with the phrase "untwist . . . these last strands of man/ in me," thus calling up the idea of unknotting as well the negation implied in the word "not."

The rhyme scheme of the poem begins as a traditional Petrarchan sonnet with an octet of *abba abba*, followed by a variation on the final sestet, which is *cdc dcd* rather than *cde cde*. The meter is not regular iambic pentameter, as found in most sonnets in English. Instead, Hopkins uses the older form of counting the number of stresses in the poem, which he called sprung rhythm. He begins with spondees, in which there are a series of stresses, one after another, as in "Not, I'll not, carrion comfort, Despair, not feast on thee"; this creates the powerful sense that the poet is forcefully rejecting a sentient being.

The point of view in the poem is the first-person voice of a man wrestling in the dark night of the soul first with despair, and then, to his great surprise, with one who turns out to be God. The heavy use of alliteration adds to the sense of struggle, as in "rude on me/ Thy wring-world right foot rock."

Symbolism and allusion are very powerful and prevalent in this poem. Right from the title, which establishes the subject as "carrion comfort"—the comfort to be taken from eating carrion, the term Hopkins uses to describe despair—there is profound metaphoric language used to describe the pain and suffering the speaker feels. After the refusal to feed upon the "carrion" of despair, the speaker also refuses to "untwist these last strands of man," or to become completely unknotted—he will not, he repeats six times in the opening quatrain, become unknotted, nor will he choose not to be. He affirms that he can do something, even if it is only to wish for day or refuse to not be. He continues the description metaphors of physical struggle and biblical allusions, such as the imagery of laying "lion-limb" against him, of winnowing grain, and of kissing the rod.

Themes and Meanings

"Carrion Comfort" describes a struggle of faith that takes the form of wrestling with despair—or, more specifically, of the poet wrestling with God during a period of weakness. It is a Christian allegory of the dark night of the soul, including biblical allusions in images of struggle and winnowing. Despite its inclusion in the six "terrible sonnets," it is actually a profoundly moving affirmation of God's love of humanity and a promise of hope no matter how despairing a person might feel; it also introduces the powerful psychological truth that it is often through surrender, through giving up the struggle, that the greatest peace and victory is found.

It is very difficult, when discussing a Hopkins poem, to separate the meaning from the form, as Hopkins developed his own personal idiosyncratic means to best express the emotional struggles and theological truths he wished to convey. The problem Hopkins poses in the octave of the poem is that of the struggle with despair, even the contemplation of suicide, the greatest sin in the Catholic faith, as it implies a lack of faith, true despair, the rejection of the belief that God can and will solve all problems and forgive all sins. One is led to wonder why God would send such agony, such despair, and such pain upon those he claims to love.

The speaker then goes on to describe his suffering as a physical struggle, a sort of wrestling match, not with despair but with someone else not revealed until the final line. All the reader knows at first is that the opponent is "terrible" and "rude," all-powerful with a right foot that can wring the world, that he lays a biblical lion-limb against the speaker and scans his "bruised bones" with an almost erotic desire—"with darksome devouring eyes." He also fans with tempests the heaped and frantic speaker, making it clear that the opponent is persistent and supernatural. The speaker is forced to ask the purpose of all this suffering.

The response that is presented in the final sestet is that this struggle will bring about two glorious resolutions. One is the winnowing of the sinner, which will leave him "sheer and clear." Second is the complete surrender and submission of the sinner, who in kissing the rod—thereby surrendering to God—becomes in that action triumphant, for it is not the punishing rod which is kissed, but rather the hand of God. In that act of kissing the hand of his opponent, the speaker wins salvation: By losing, he wins far more gloriously. In this night—"That night, that year/ Of now done darkness"—he "lapped strength, stole joy, would laugh, cheer" for the glorious outcome. Finally it becomes clear that this supernatural opponent with whom he has been wrestling is actually God, revealed cleverly with the parenthetical exclamation "(my God!) my God!" emphasizing the terrible and wonderful glory of that struggle.

Mary LeDonne Cassidy

CASUALTY

Author: Seamus Heaney (1939-   )
Type of poem: Elegy
First published: 1979, in *Field Work*

The Poem

"Casualty" is a lament for the unknown citizen, an anonymous victim not merely of the social violence of the poet's native province but also of those tribal attachments that make the violence so aggravated, interminable, and difficult to understand—those elements that are referred to toward the second section of the poem as "our tribe's complicity." Since the poet himself was born and reared in Northern Ireland, he speaks with particular, if understated, eloquence and with an intimacy that is typical of his work as a whole on the complex of human inevitability and historical happenstance of which his subject has fallen foul.

The poem is one of a number of elegies in *Field Work*, a collection that also includes, among other poems of this type, one on a murdered cousin as well as an elegy on the American poet, Robert Lowell. In addition, *Field Work*—the author's first book after leaving his native province and coming to live in the Republic of Ireland—contains numerous poems on the possibility of renewal. The collection's overall concern with death and rebirth and the impact of that historical, social, and natural cycle on an individual consciousness is conveniently, if not necessarily definitively, condensed in the three parts of "Casualty," making it one of the emblematic statements in a pivotal work in the poet's development.

Although the poet has, in a biographical sense, left his native place, in other senses, he is, as "Casualty" shows, very much attached to it. The acts of public respect and private mourning bridge the gap between the poem's sections and provide evidence of that attachment. The event in question is the killing of thirteen unarmed civil rights protesters—not all of them from the Bogside area of Derry, which has become a facile synonym for die-hard Provisional Irish Republican Army (IRA) sympathizers ("the Provisionals" mentioned in the poem)—by British Forces on January 30, 1972, commonly remembered as Bloody Sunday. (Derry is the capital city of the county in which Seamus Heaney was reared.) As the poet is assimilated to, and detached from, that notorious event, so is his subject, and the poem effectively addresses itself to the awkward existence of both distance and intimacy between the poet and his material.

The very anonymity of the casualty becomes a challenge to the poet, like a question he feels he must answer or a ghost ("Dawn-sniffing revenant") he has no desire to exorcise. The three-part division of the poem facilitates a slow, tentative, oblique approach ("my tentative art") to the violent absence that the poet feels obliged to confront. Opening with a fondly detailed evocation of the subject—his habits, gestures, and bearing, which recount the natural facts of his actual presence—the poem moves to the different kind of attentiveness in its treatment of the funeral of the Bloody

Sunday Thirteen. On that occasion, communal feeling held sway. The mourners formed the facsimile of a community ("braced and bound/ Like brothers in a ring"). This communal mode of observance has been denied by the casualty, who met his death indifferently breaking the law, expressing a loyalty to his own nature rather than to reflexes conditioned by larger forces. The poet who "missed his funeral" problematically preserves him in a poem, ensuring that this unassimilated citizen is assimilated in an other-than-communal order of witnessing.

Forms and Devices

Heaney's poetry is widely admired—even by readers without direct access to the poems' contexts or allusions—for its fidelity to the actual and its ability to render the world of things with a direct, sensory appeal. The opening stanza of "Casualty" is a good example of the poet's economical conjuring up of his subject's physical presence. The oxymoronic "observant back" vividly connotes the man's ready presence and complements the sense of his being "a natural for work." This economy of means is underlined by the poem's almost laconic three-foot line—a line that seems to replicate the casualty's "deadpan sidling tact." Immediacy of language and simplicity of metrical structure also make acceptable the disarming candor and the poet's attitude: "I loved his whole manner."

The poem's patent disavowal of rhetoric, the means whereby it is able to "manage by some trick/ To switch the talk" from the loftiness often considered endemic to elegies, makes its larger project of reclamation and commemoration seem feasible. Nothing in the poem seems beyond the bounds of nature, except the various violences that it addresses. The same plain and rather plaintive tone is maintained even in the act of imagining the victim's moment of death ("I see him as he turned"). Sustaining a steady tone to guide the supple range of his associative mode of writing has always been one of Heaney's principal characteristics. The effects of doing so can be readily experienced in "Casualty," where such issues as historical contingency and social solidarity are installed as tributaries to the main theme of individual fate and choice so that the theme is seen more revealingly as a result.

The continuity of the poet's witnessing voice throughout the poem, weaving its chronologically random way through various levels of a recent personal past, also adds greatly to the poem's overall effect. The events recounted in "Casualty" happened with an abruptness that is unanswerable. This fact is preserved in the poem's discontinuous narrative, in which what is the irenic equal and opposite to the subject's death ("that morning/ When he took me in his boat") is kept till last. The poem's relaxed, yet steadfast, tone ensures that a means of both admitting and accommodating those discontinuities can be found, shocking "puzzle" though they may be. The discontinuities are reflected in the poem's form, both in its three-part organization and in the variable lengths of its stanzas. Within those forms, however, the same meter remains constant, and subtle rhymes and half-rhymes supply an understated but persistent sense of order. In other words, the very aspects that are the poet's fundamental attributes articulate a degree of coherence and containment that are lamentably and destructively unavailable to the world outside the poem. With the casualty presented in this manner, the reader as well as the recollecting author should be in a position to admit the tragic awareness that "I tasted freedom with him."

Themes and Meanings

Students of Irish poetry will find many intriguing echoes between "Casualty" and William Butler Yeats's "The Fisherman." Published in a pivotal collection in Yeats's development—*The Wild Swans at Coole* (1919)—this poem conjures up a remote, anonymous, isolated figure and holds him up as an ideal whereby the aspirations of the day might be revealed in all their tawdry (though not necessarily violent) opportunism. In particular, Yeats makes a strong case for the fisherman as the embodiment of cultural integrity based on personal distinctiveness.

Heaney's "Casualty" is less politically ambitious than Yeats's "The Fisherman," and it is much more quiescent in tone, as befits the personal tenor of this elegy. With its emphasis on questioning and on thought as an experience of difficulty rather than of release ("you're supposed to be/ An educated man"), "Casualty" is also less didactic than its Yeatsian predecessor. Nevertheless, Heaney's poem may be instructively read as a critical companion piece to Yeats's, particularly in its Yeatsian tendency to seek redemption in nature for what society manifestly disdains to supply. Since Heaney's fisherman is "A dole-kept breadwinner" (that is, a recipient of unemployment benefits), it is tempting to see him in the poem's concluding section as a poacher, a fisher of waters not his own. Such a view would be consistent with the sense of his going his own way that the poet both admires and is disturbed by, since it is the occasion of his untimely death.

It seems, however, that the poem needs a sense of the sea ("fathoms," "haul/ Steadily off the bottom," "well out, beyond") in order to give a sense of scope to the freedom being "tasted." Such scope is necessary in order for the full measure of risk and self-sufficiency to emerge. The sense of self-sufficiency is present in the reader's introduction to the character, while the understanding of risk emerges in the victim's paying with his life for a forbidden drink. The fact that "he would not be held/ At home by his own crowd" (those to whom by reason of culture, social standing, and background he might be presumed to owe allegiance) is both the unnerving cause of his death and the reason he is the poem's subject.

In the obscure fate of an anonymous citizen, Heaney trawls the emptiness for an image of adequacy. What he comes up with is a potent recognition of independence as something that is not only provided for by militant activity and tribal prescriptions: It may also be something innate. By means of a typical verbal maneuver, Heaney uses the colloquial Irish expression, "he drank like a fish," to invoke a sense of the casualty's larger-than-social existence. It is by virtue of his nonaligned, nonconforming aspects, and the poet's insistence on their relevance, that "Casualty" becomes an elegy for the "cornered outfaced stare" of humanity in Heaney's homeland.

George O'Brien

CATS

Author: Charles Baudelaire (1821-1867)
Type of poem: Sonnet
First published: 1847, as "Les Chats," in *Les Fleurs du mal,* 1857; English translation collected in *The Flowers of Evil,* 1955

The Poem

"Cats" is a sonnet, a poem of fourteen lines, in which the octave is divided into two quatrains and the sestet is made up of two tercets. The poem was first published in the journal *Le Corsaire* in 1847 and was ultimately included in Charles Baudelaire's collection of 1857 known in English as *The Flowers of Evil.* The poem is both elegant and magical in its descriptions of cats. The first line (in the translation by Anthony Hecht) introduces "Feverish lovers, scholars in their lofts," and the second line states that both lovers and scholars will eventually "love the cat." In the first two lines, the poet has given the reader a glimpse of the hold cats have even on people from diverse walks of life. The third line of the first quatrain describes the cat as being both "gentle" and "powerful" and states that this creature is "king of the parlor mat." In the last line of the quatrain, Baudelaire notes that the cat is "Lazy," like the lovers and scholars, and "sensitive to draughts." One can assume that cats, by their nature, exert a hold over those who let them into their homes.

The second quatrain—the second half of the sonnet's octave—presents unsettling attributes of the "Gentle but powerful" creature. The first line speaks of the cat as being "linked to learning and to love." The cat "Exhibits a taste for silences and gloom"; it is more complex than first imagined. It has a dark side, which has been heightened through long silences. The conclusion put forth in the closing lines of the second quatrain speaks of the cat becoming a "splendid messenger of doom/ If his fierce pride would condescend to serve." There is an ominous cloud hanging over the poem now, which could lead to frightening prospects if the cat were so inclined. It is perhaps a small consolation that the cat will not be the "messenger of doom" because of its "fierce pride."

The sestet of "Cats" moves away from the "gloom" of the octave and introduces mystery and magic. The cat is "Lost in his day-dream" as the first tercet begins and resembles "sphinxes in the desert." It has become timeless and almost godlike. The first tercet ends with the image of this royal creature being "Fixed in a reverie that has no end." The cat has transcended the conscious world and has become something that is more myth than reality. The poem closes with a tercet that revels even more in the magical qualities of the cat. The first line points to the cat's loins being "lit with the fires of alchemy"; it has become more than the sum of its parts. From whatever angle the cat is observed, there is some new quality to be discovered. The poem closes with "And bits of gold, small as the finest sand,/ Fleck, here and there, the mystery of his eyes." The cat ultimately remains a mystery, and the deepest mystery is in its eyes.

Forms and Devices

Baudelaire's collection *The Flowers of Evil* was not assembled in a random fashion. The collection is divided into sections, and the poems included in each section help to build a thematic pattern for that section. The American author Edgar Allan Poe had a major influence on Baudelaire. Structure, rhythm, and rhyme, according to both Poe and Baudelaire, should be employed by the poet to give each poem its own independent identity; each poem should create a unique atmosphere. Baudelaire constructed every poem as a unit, and the unit then fit into the larger thematic patterns to create the whole of *The Flowers of Evil*. The most successful poems in the collection have a strong rhetorical structure. Baudelaire's greatest poems are relatively short. The shortness was by design, since Baudelaire (and Poe) believed that the power of one poem to stimulate its reader could not be sustained over an extended length.

"Cats" can be found in the first section of *The Flowers of Evil*. This section, "Spleen et Idéal" ("Bile and the Ideal"), is the largest of the collection; there are eighty-eight poems included, and "Cats" is the sixty-ninth. A number of sonnets are included in "Bile and the Ideal," and "Cats" is certainly one of the best. The sonnet form was ideally suited to Baudelaire's expressed need to create emotional impact in a brief number of lines. A sonnet is only fourteen lines long and traditionally has been employed to express emotional power through a lyrical mood. Each line of "Cats" is an Alexandrine, which means that the line has twelve syllables consisting of six iambics. There must also be a caesura (or interruption) after the third iambic.

In the original French, "Cats" draws much of its power from metrical stresses. Baudelaire also makes use of the compound doublet, which consists of the repetition of two, or possibly more, sounds in the same sequence. Baudelaire's skillful handling of rhythm, marvelous manipulation of rhyme, and strong sense of metaphor all enhance the power of "Cats." The evolution of the cat from a creature of the house to be loved in the first quatrain to a magnificent creature of mystery in the last tercet is beautifully unified. The sonnet form is a precise style of expression, and "Cats" is a concise poem. A subtly magical work is built upon a realistic base; the balance of the poem exemplifies Baudelaire's belief that the emotional content of a poem could be mastered through its formal structure.

Themes and Meanings

The publication of *The Flowers of Evil* in 1857 caused a great scandal. It was ruled by a French court to be an obscene collection, and some of the poems had to be excised in subsequent editions. The preface of *The Flowers of Evil* stated Baudelaire's belief that sin overwhelmed the world, and in each section of the collection, the poet confronted different ways of personal escape. "Cats" was included in the opening section, in which Baudelaire escaped into a quest for beauty in art and love. Within this section there is charm, music, and sensuality; Romanticism is strong in these poems. It is clearly evident in a poem such as "Cats." The spell that is created within this sonnet has close ties to English Romanticism and especially to the work of Samuel Taylor Coleridge.

Baudelaire can also be considered a bridge to modern poetic art. He used the bold repudiation of bourgeois normality found in Romanticism and added his own sharp images, framed within a rigid poetic structure, to legitimize a wide range of topics otherwise thought to be indelicate. "Cats" does not approach some of the more scandalous subjects; it does speak powerfully about a creature that is exotic, however, and the exotic also runs counter to bourgeois normality. The cat of the first quatrain receives love by being different but not existing outside normal boundaries. Baudelaire refuses to leave it at that. In the second quatrain, the cat takes on qualities that are dark, or at least potentially dark (the cat's pride will not allow it to "condescend to serve").

The sestet introduces a magical world. The common house cat is no longer—if it ever really was—common. It assumes a pose comparable to the "sphinxes in the desert"; it is beyond complete human comprehension. When the last tercet begins with an image of the cat's loins being "lit with the fires of alchemy," it is evident that cats are magical creatures with special powers. The last line mentions "the mystery of his eyes," which is a fitting summation of what cats symbolize. The cat represents (as do tigresses or women in other of Baudelaire's poems) a fantastic creature that will consume any human who tries to understand or love it. *The Flowers of Evil* attempted to pierce bourgeois society from every possible angle. In "Cats," Baudelaire created a sonnet that struck at society's respectability through the exotic and mysterious world of cats.

Michael Jeffrys

CAVALRY CROSSING A FORD

Author: Walt Whitman (1819-1892)
Type of poem: Lyric
First published: 1865, in *Drum-Taps*

The Poem

Walt Whitman's seven-line, one-sentence poem, "Cavalry Crossing a Ford," re-
cords an ordinary scene in the American Civil War: the crossing of some unnamed
river by a nondescript unit of cavalry. While the poem is ostensibly a simple sketch of
these soldiers, by showing the soldiers from a variety of vantage points, the poet chal-
lenges the reader's notion of the term "cavalry," replacing the militaristic term with
the image of a group of individual men.

As if the poet were drifting downstream in a canoe, the poem begins by viewing the
soldiers from afar, as a "line in long array." He moves close enough to see that "each
person [is] a picture," then moves away again. All the while, the flags are visible, flut-
tering "gaily in the wind" above the soldiers.

The poem's title presents a clear, concrete image. However, the language of the first
line is oddly abstract. Instead of a group of soldiers, the poet shows "a line" winding
between "green islands." The soldiers are fused as one (the line), and the only con-
crete noun in the first line is the "islands." The emphasis here is on the aesthetic imag-
ery, not the marshal nature of the scene. From the poet's perspective, this military unit
is more of an adornment or adjunct of the natural world than a fighting force.

In the second line the soldiers start to become distinct. The poet notes the flash of
the soldiers's arms and describes the "musical clank" of their equipment. Moving
closer still, the loitering horses become clear in line 3. Finally, in line 4, the reader
sees the soldiers themselves, "brown-faced men, each group, each person a picture."
These men are veterans, their faces tanned by long months in the field. They lean neg-
ligently in their saddles. The word "negligent" here suggests confidence and self-pos-
session rather than disregard.

In the next line, the poet begins to pan back; perhaps he is drifting downstream from
the soldiers. The reader now sees the soldiers as a group again, still a line stretched
across the river. The line is still winding; some soldiers leave the river as others enter
it—a river of soldiers crossing the river of water.

Up to this point in the poem, the syntax of the sentence has bound everything to-
gether. Commas, dashes, and imperative commands, such as "behold," direct the
reader to one thing, then another. Each of these images is somehow independent, self-
reliant. However, the final two lines are connected to the rest of the poem by a con-
junction: "while." The conjunction emphasizes that the red, white, and blue flags that
fly in the last two lines do so as everything else in the poem happens.

In these last two lines, the image of the flags contrasts markedly with the rest of the
poem. Whereas the first five lines of the poem describe men and nature intertwined,

the flags are set apart. While the men are veterans, the flags are bright and clean— "scarlet" and "snowy white," they have not been dimmed and dirtied by months of campaigning. Further, their gay fluttering is at odds with the negligence of the soldiers. Thus the reader is left to wonder whether the flags act as a unifying image, or as something distinct from the river, the horses, and the men.

Forms and Devices

One of the difficulties of "Cavalry Crossing a Ford" is that it appears so effortless, so artless. It seems as if the poet simply wrote about what he saw, without adornment. In fact, however, the poem is highly artful. First, the poet's language controls the pace and flow of the poem, alternately slowing and speeding the reader along. Second, the apparent artlessness of the poem masks the speaker's presence and control of the poem.

The poem is written in free verse. The first five lines contain from fourteen to twenty-three syllables per line and are broken into a series of three-stress units or phrases, such as "Behold the silvery river, in it the splashing horses loitering stop to drink." The three-stress phrases—"Behold the silvery river," "in it the splashing horses," and "loitering stop to drink"—slow the pace of the poem. Each of these units ends with an accented syllable, causing the reader to pause momentarily. The effect is to create lines that contain a series of semiautonomous images. These semiautonomous phrases mirror the cavalrymen themselves. Just as the group of cavalry is made up of individuals, "each person a picture," so too the poem is made up of phrases, each one a picture, each one contributing its part to the whole.

However, the last two lines differ markedly from the first five. These lines contain only eight and eleven syllables, with four and five stresses, respectively. The lines are shorter, and there are no internal stops in the lines. As a result, these two lines read much more quickly than the previous five. The effect of this is to make the flags stand out boldly and distinctly from the rest of the scene. The flags not only fly above the soldiers and the river but also exist in a separate metrical realm, just as the politics they represent exist in a separate realm from the men and the river.

Another important element in the poem is the point of view. In a typical Whitman poem, the speaker is a grand presence, lording over the poem, directing the reader here and there. Whitman opens "Song of Myself" by telling the reader "What I assume you shall assume." In comparison to "Song of Myself" or "Crossing Brooklyn Ferry," the speaker of "Cavalry Crossing a Ford" is almost timid. There is no first-person speaker. At first glance, then, the poem appears to be closer to the Imagist poems of the early 1900's than to the great egocentric poems of *Leaves of Grass* (1855-1892). Although it seems as if the poet is merely describing what he sees, the speaker is in complete control of the scene. The poem becomes a kind of photo survey of the topic. Each three-stress phrase is a different photo, and the poet directs attention to the images only when he is ready. The speaker commands the reader: "Hark," "Behold," and "Behold" again, shifting the reader's attention from image to image.

Themes and Meanings

The Civil War was a time of great upheaval for Whitman personally, as well as for the nation. One of the major themes of his pre-Civil War poetry is the unity of the nation. When the United States fell into civil war in 1861, Whitman was momentarily stunned into silence. He wrote a few jingoistic recruitment poems, such as "Beat! Beat! Drums!," but in late 1862 Whitman discovered that his brother, George Whitman, had been wounded in the Battle of Fredericksburg. Walt quickly went to the front to find his brother, who was only slightly wounded, and stayed with the army for several months. From his experiences at the front, Walt Whitman began to compose a series of short, sketchlike poems, of which "Cavalry Crossing a Ford" is the most well known. In these poems, Whitman attempts to persuade not through argument and personality, as he does in his earlier poetry, but through the arrangement of imagery.

In this Imagistic poem, the speaker is much quieter than that of his earlier work. This speaker, unlike that of "Crossing Brooklyn Ferry," avoids transcendent claims. The soldiers who "emerge on the opposite bank" are no different from those "just entering." Instead, Whitman portrays one of the key themes of his poetry: the relationship between "simple separate person" and "the word Democratic, the word En-Masse," as he wrote in "One's-Self I Sing," the opening poem of *Leaves of Grass*. In the poem, the soldiers are represented as both individuals ("each person a picture") and the "en masse" ("A line in long array"). They represent the democratic army of the Union, a collection of rough, confident individuals joined in common purpose. As in all of *Drum-Taps*, there are no officers shown, just men. These loitering, negligent soldiers, so calm and self-assured, represent wartime versions of the portraits of men found in "Song of Myself," men like the boatmen and clam diggers who stop for him in section 10 of "Song of Myself," or the blacksmiths of section 12.

However, the relationship between the men and the political institutions, represented by the flags, is uncertain. The flags are set off, imagistically, grammatically (with the conjunction "while"), and metrically. From one perspective, the flags fly over the whole action of the poem, from the "line in long array" to the "brown-faced men." In this sense, the flags may represent the unity of the men engaged in the struggle for the nation. However, the flags are also set off from the action, as if the politics are somehow separate. The men, the horses, the green islands, and the silvery river are all fundamentally a part of creation. The flags, however, are abstractions. In this way, the poem reflects Whitman's idea that the nation exists in the bodies of the men and women who constitute it, rather than in political structures and institutions.

Andrew C. Higgins

CELLO ENTRY

Author: Paul Celan (Paul Antschel, 1920-1970)
Type of poem: Lyric
First published: 1967, as "Cello-Einsatz," in *Atemwende*; English translation collected in *Poems of Paul Celan*, 1988

The Poem

"Cello Entry" is one of Paul Celan's later poems. It appears in the fourth of six cycles of short poems published under the title *Atemwende* (turn of breath). These eighty poems are best read together because the images of Celan's refined, referential poems are less cryptic in the context of the collection. The poems describe mind space. Both of Celan's parents were killed in concentration camps. Paul was their only child and subsequently suffered increasingly from survivor guilt, a mental state of grief and self-recrimination. At the beginning of the poem, it seems as if the sound of the cello, with its deep, resonant tones, may distract him from his pain. The second stanza, with its references to "arrival runway and drive," indicates that the poet is moved by the music but is still unsure of where it will transport him.

Any elevation in mood the music may have afforded him is marred in the third stanza by the surreal shift in metaphor. It is evening, and he finds that branches he has climbed are not tree branches but lung branches. This mention of lungs, followed in the fourth stanza by "smoke-clouds of breath," refers almost certainly to the gas chambers and crematoria of Adolf Hitler's concentration camps in which millions of people were murdered simply because they, like Celan, were Jewish. His thoughts are now back on the horrors of the Holocaust. A book gets opened: not just any book, but the book, the story of his people, opened by the noise in his own head, which seems to have drowned out the cello music.

Celan begins the fourth stanza with the word "two" set off in a line by itself, a typographic arrangement indicating that this word is charged with significance. What is this significance? Are the two smoke-clouds of breath from his own two nostrils? Are they from his parents? The poetic effect of naming and placing emphasis on an exact number is to lend specificity while permitting several interpretations. For the poet himself, the dreamlike images are fraught with meaning. His interpretive response to them is one of recognition and validation: "something grows true." This main clause, which stands alone as a single verse and stanza just over halfway through the poem, is like the peak of a musical phrase and may reflect a high point of the cello performance. Its lack of concrete detail places the emphasis fully on the emotional valence of the experience.

Stanza 6 describes twelve flashes of insight. Again, the specific number lends almost magical significance to the events but may also be determined by referents external to the poem such as twelve-tone music or the twelve tribes of Israel. The poet focuses finally on a woman and man engaged in a sexual act that cannot produce offspring. Their intimacy is paradoxical because they are dead, "black-blooded." This powerful image conveys feelings of futility, depression, and horror, all perfectly understandable in a bereaved survivor of extreme persecution. In the last stanza, the poet has stopped the frightening flow of images and comments rationally on them as if awakening from a bad dream: "all things are less than/ they are." That is not the last word, however. Celan cannot dismiss the promptings of his subconscious. He ends the poem with a characteristic reversal that augments the intensity of his experience: "all are more."

Forms and Devices

The twenty-two lines of "Cello Entry" contain a total of only sixty words in the original German. Celan had studied the development of the German language from medieval times to the present and had seen it debased by Nazi propaganda between 1933 and 1945. It had gone, he explains, "through the thousand darknesses of death bringing speech." Celan is therefore extremely careful in his choice of words and avoids the arbitrary frameworks of end rhyme and metric pattern. The length of his poems is dictated by inner necessity. His attention is focused on the sounds and meanings of individual words, syllables, and even letters.

Four of Celan's distinguishing techniques that occur in "Cello Entry" are his tendency to split words to emphasize their component parts, his construction of neologisms, his repetition of words and phrases with or without variation, and his inclination to let the sound of a word lead him to a similar one. In "Cello Entry," for example, "the black-/ blooded woman" is split at the hyphen over two lines, whereas "the black-blooded man" is written together on one line. The effect of the initial split is to place more weight on the word "black" and its negative connotations and to emphasize the highly unusual first part of the compound word. "Black-blooded" is also one of Celan's neologisms, a shocking departure from the familiar "blue-blooded," "hot-blooded," and "cold-blooded." Other such thought-provoking new combinations in the poem are "counter-heavens," "lung-scrub," and "temple-din." Celan's most famous poem, "Death Fugue," written in 1952, is replete with repetitions and recombinations. This technique comes close to replicating human thought processes. People dwell on anything that bothers them. In "Cello Entry," "black-blooded" can also serve as an example of effective repetition. By applying the unusual adjective to both the woman and the man, Celan stresses that they are both dead, that they represent two separate deaths. The fourth technique, that of letting one word determine the next, is often lost in translation but is apparent in the German even if one does not know the language. For example, the second stanza of "Cello Entry" ends with the line "Einflugschneise und Einfahrt," in which Celan seems to have selected the second capitalized word for its felicitous resemblance to the first on the accented first syllable and following *f*.

The positioning of Celan's periods is a reliable guide to the understanding of his poems. "Cello Entry" has just one period. The entire poem is a single sentence. Celan gently leads the reader in and out, but the bulk of the poem consists of a highly figurative account of a personal moment of truth. Twelve poems later in the cycle, a shorter poem encapsulates the meaning, method, even the music of "Cello Entry": "A RUM-BLING: truth/ itself has appeared/ among humankind/ in the very thick of their/ flurrying metaphors."

Themes and Meanings

It is Celan's great accomplishment to be able to transport the reader into a crystalline mind space. Celan refused to interpret any one of his poems, saying that repeated reading should suffice. His most extended commentary on the nature, function, and experience of art is contained in "The Meridian," his 1960 Georg Büchner Prize acceptance speech. Art, he says, is ubiquitous and capable of transformation. This explains the constantly changing imaginative inner landscape of "Cello Entry" as exemplified by the metamorphosis of evening into something that can be climbed like a tree and then into animal matter with lungs. There are no constraints. Celan's remarks about the function of art are particularly apposite. A poem, he says, can signify a turn of breath, a unique short moment. One writes to release something else, and there is no telling how long its effect will last. Turn of breath, or *Atemwende*, is the title of the collection containing "Cello Entry." The turn of breath in this poem is the solitary line that does not further the phantasmagorical visions but rather registers their effect: "something grows true." The space between images, the time between breathing out and breathing in, these are the moments of stasis that allow the mind to move into another dimension.

Celan's poems are designed to communicate with receptive readers, to facilitate a meeting of minds. They are conceived as conversations, albeit often conversations of despair. At the end of his acceptance speech, Celan describes his experience of the creative process: "I find something—like language—immaterial, but earthly, terrestrial, something circular, meeting up with itself again over both the poles and—happily—going through the tropics en route—: I find . . . a *meridian*." Celan finds the meridian when he succeeds in bringing disparate images into line, giving that line the tension of a circle and making it visible to the reader. It is a helpful construct that does not permit any element of the poem to be dropped from the interpretation. "Cello Entry" is an indivisible entity. It is not primarily about a cello or about any of the fantastic images that follow or their derivation. It describes a mind space in which stream-of-consciousness images synthesize with sudden meaning, providing a moment of truth. That truth encompasses the poet's own reality, human history, and alternate universes. It is accessible to all who have pondered their own existence.

Jean M. Snook

THE CEMETERY BY THE SEA

Author: Paul Valéry (1871-1945)
Type of poem: Meditation
First published: 1922, as "Le Cimetière marin," in *Charmes, ou poèmes*; collected in
*An Anthology of French Poetry from Nerval to Valéry in English Translation with
French Originals*, 1958

The Poem
"The Cemetery by the Sea," written in 1920, is Paul Valéry's best-known poem. It
consists of twenty-four stanzas of six lines each. The poet returns in imagination to
the cemetery of Sète, a city on a cliff above the Mediterranean, where he was born and
where he dreamed as a youth among the tombs of his ancestors. He imagines himself
sitting on a tombstone at noon and contemplating the white sails on the calm sea,
which he describes as doves pecking on a roof, while he wrestles with the problems of
life and death, of being and nonbeing, and thinks about the future course of his life.

In his monologue, Valéry thinks of the sea as the roof of the temple of time spar-
kling with diamonds, and he enjoys the idea of mingling with the sky and the sea. As
his shadow passes over the tombs, he realizes that he himself is subject to change; he
recalls his nineteen years of what he calls indolence. (Actually, since 1894 he had
been working first in the Ministry of War and later in the news agency Havas. He was
a married man and the father of two children, devoting his free time to research on the
nature of thought.) He accuses himself of idleness because he has not made full use of
his poetic talent.

In stanza 11, the poet imagines himself a shepherd among the quiet white sheep, the
tombs. He refuses the Christian consolation symbolized by the marble doves and an-
gels and contemplates eternal nothingness, reflecting in stanza 13 that the dead buried
in the cemetery are quite comfortable.

In the next two stanzas the noonday sun, symbol of unchanging perfection, is con-
trasted with ephemeral man—with the poet himself, who is filled with fear, repen-
tance, and doubt. Man, he decides, is the flaw, the changing element in the perfection
of the universe. The dead lose their individuality and return to the great Whole; their
bodies feed the flowers.

In the seventeenth stanza, Valéry chides himself for dreaming of a more perfect
world and asks himself if he expects to write poetry when he is dead. Immortality is
only an illusion; those who compare death to a maternal breast are guilty of a beautiful
lie and a pious trick. The empty head of a skeleton laughs forever. Stanza 19 states that
the true worm is not that which has destroyed the bodies, but is thought that feeds on
life and never leaves man. Even in his sleep, the worm of thought pursues him. Valéry
is referring to the dictum of René Descartes, *Cogito ergo sum*: "I think, therefore
I am."

In stanza 21, Valéry asks Zeno, a Greek philosopher who denied the reality of movement by asserting that a flying arrow is immobile at each instant, if he has pierced him with the arrow that is killing him. He rejects the idea that time does not pass; movement exists, therefore life and time exist and action is possible.

In the last three stanzas, the poet reacts: The weather has changed, and a breeze has sprung up. Its salty freshness returns his soul to him. Like a man who has plunged into the refreshing sea, he emerges from his reverie filled with a taste for life. He will plunge into action.

Forms and Devices

All six lines in each stanza end with a rhyme in the pattern *aabccb*. This rigidity called for great expertise on the part of Valéry and his translators. If a translator is truly faithful to the thought of a poem, it is the music that suffers most in passing from one language to another. If he must limit each line to ten syllables and adhere to a difficult rhyme scheme, he can hardly hope to imitate the music of the original.

This difficult poem requires the reader to penetrate a host of metaphors. The reader must equate the calm sea with a roof and the sails with doves pecking on the shining roof of the temple of time under a blazing noontime sky while the poet meditates on great philosophical problems and on his own existence. Stanza 5 contains a simile: The poet inhales his future as a hungry mouth obscures the contour of a piece of fruit. This is perhaps the only reasonably simple comparison in a forest of unexpected (and unexplained) images used as symbols.

The theme of the poem rests on these original, complicated, and obscure symbols. One eminent critic insists that the whole poem is a metaphor, to which each image refers. Another famous scholar declares that the noonday sun is the symbol of eternity and the sea is the symbol of human consciousness. Less difficult to conceive is the idea that the sea seen through the trees is a prisoner of the leaves. It devours the cemetery grills because the sea, sparkling in the sun, causes them to seem to disappear.

Comprehensible also is the metaphor of the poet as a shepherd among his sheep, the white marble tombs, and the sea as watchdog. The angels and doves (unfortunately translated sometimes as "pigeons") obviously represent the consolation of the Christian religion. He urges the watchdog to frighten them as a sign that he rejects this idea of life after death.

In the second-to-last stanza, Valéry describes in startling images the sea as it reacts to the rising wind: It is delirious; it resembles a panther's skin and a torn Greek cloak; it is a hydra, the serpent with nine heads which, according to Greek mythology, replaced each lost head with two others; it is a serpent biting its tail.

Valéry employed figures of speech and symbols to express philosophic ideas. The metaphor which unifies the structure of the poem, according to one critic, establishes a parallelism among the three separate elements: the sea, the cemetery, and the poet. Each of these elements has two aspects, one on the surface, the other interior. Other poetic devices, such as alliteration, embellish the original but cannot be preserved in translation. For example, stanza 4 of the French has nine pronounced *t* sounds and eight pronounced *s* sounds; the effect is striking.

Themes and Meanings

Scores of books have been written about Paul Valéry and "Le Cimetière marin," as well as hundreds of articles by critics, teachers, poets. In 1928, Gustave Cohen, a professor at the Sorbonne, gave a series of lectures entitled *Essai d'interprétation du "Cimetière marin"* (attempt to interpret "The Cemetery by the Sea") to a large audience that included Paul Valéry himself. The poet expressed his pleasure at having the intentions and the wording of the poem, reputedly obscure, so well understood. Valéry explained in a preface to the publication of the lectures that he had decided to write a monologue that would be at the same time personal and universal, one that would contain the simplest and most constant themes of his emotional and intellectual life. His poem is a meditation on life and death, on mobility and immobility, on being and nonbeing. Since, in the fashion of his friends the Symbolists, he does not explain his metaphors, the reader must puzzle out the meanings. This is harder to do from a translation than from the original, because the translator has had to incorporate English rhymes and meter as well as preserve the meanings.

The personal problem at issue in the poem is how the poet should spend the rest of his life. For the past nineteen years, his chief intellectual efforts have been directed to mathematics, art, music, and linguistics at the expense of his great poetic talent. He is trying to discover his true self. He meditates on life and eternity. The surface of the sea is calm, but underneath there is turbulence; the poet thinks of the activities of life with philosophic disdain, but behind the disdain there is a living organism. The cemetery offers the immobility of the tombs, but underneath them are the remains of the poet's ancestors. As he looks at the sea he is filled with the idea of changelessness, but his own shadow rejects the light. He needs some assurance of the fact of change to prove his own existence. He cannot accept the idea of immortality. The true irrefutable worm is not in the grave but in life.

The story of Zeno's stationary arrow and the tale of Achilles and the tortoise were meant to illustrate the fact that change is illusion. He must reject this idea, however; he cannot escape from change and action. At the end of the poem, the calm sea becomes turbulent, and with a triumphant cry the poet accepts the prospect of an active life.

Dorothy B. Aspinwall

THE CHAMBERED NAUTILUS

Author: Oliver Wendell Holmes (1809-1894)
Type of poem: Lyric
First published: 1858, in *The Autocrat of the Breakfast-Table*

The Poem

In the five stanzas of "The Chambered Nautilus," the poet contemplates the broken shell of a nautilus, a small sea animal which the *American Heritage Dictionary* describes as "a mollusk whose spiral shell contains a series of air-filled chambers." In his contemplation, he moves from a metaphorical description of its beauty and lifestyle to the ultimate lesson that it teaches.

The first three stanzas trace the life cycle of the little animal, emphasizing the various stages of its growth and development and its eventual death and destruction. In the beginning, the poet likens the nautilus to a ship which sets out to sea—beautiful in its majesty as its sails unfurl to the "sweet summer wind." He imagines the many wonderful adventures the nautilus has encountered as it challenged the mighty sea, sailing "the unshadowed main." During its lifetime it ventured into enchanted gulfs and heard the siren songs and has seen mermaids sunning "their streaming hair."

In the second stanza the poet laments the death of the nautilus, whose shell now lies broken and abandoned on the seashore like the wreck of a once beautiful ship—a ship that will no more "sail the unbounded main." Like a ship that once teemed with life and now is silent, the nautilus lies lifeless, useless. Just as when a ship is wrecked, the top may be ripped and torn and its interior laid bare for all to see, so the little sea animal is destroyed—its shell broken, its insides exposed, and every "chambered cell revealed." In the third stanza the poet considers the evolution of the nautilus through the various stages of its life. As it grows, its shell continues to expand in order to accommodate that growth, as evidenced by the ever-widening spirals that mark the shell. The nautilus moves into its new home quite tenuously at first, and for a time it misses the familiarity of its old home. In time, however, the new quarters become familiar and more comfortable.

The fourth stanza is addressed directly to the nautilus, thanking it for the lesson that it has brought him. It is a lesson of great importance, and one which strikes the poet with startling clarity—a message as clear, he says, "as ever Triton blew on his wreathèd horn." This message is stated in the final stanza of the poem, beginning, "Build thee more stately mansions." The lesson is that the growth of the human being should parallel that of the nautilus; the individual should continue to grow spiritually throughout his lifetime.

Forms and Devices

The poet employs three major figures of speech, metaphor, personification, and apostrophe, to create the imagery in the poem—images which are at first quite impersonal but which become increasingly more personal as the poem progresses toward its conclusion. This helps prepare the reader for the intensely personal message of the final stanza.

The poet begins with sea imagery, using a sailing vessel as a metaphor for the nautilus. He refers to it as a "ship of pearl," suggesting not only its beauty and grandeur but also its value as both a living organism and a teacher. The poet's use of the term "venturous bark," in reference to the nautilus, evokes images of the majestic sailing ships of bygone days, eager to explore different worlds. His allusions to the songs of the "sirens," the "enchanted gulfs," and the coral reefs where "sea-maids rise to sun their streaming hair," all help to reinforce the images of grand and glorious adventures reminiscent of the mythological voyages of the great classical heroes of the ancient world. In the second stanza, the poet continues with the ship metaphor, likening the "webs of living gauze," by which the nautilus moves, to the sails which move the ship. The beauty and grandeur of this little ship, however, has now been destroyed and will no longer "unfurl" its lovely sails to the wind.

In the third stanza the imagery becomes personal. Here the nautilus is compared to a human being who, when he outgrows one home, abandons it and moves into new quarters that will better accommodate him. This personal imagery is enhanced by the poet's use of terms usually associated with human behavior to describe the activities of the nautilus. He speaks, for example, of the "silent toil" by which the animal built his new "dwelling," and the "soft step" with which he entered his new home. Finally, the nautilus "stretched in his new-found home," expressing its contentment in the same manner as a human being would. The imagery becomes even more personal in the fourth stanza as the poet abandons the use of metaphor altogether and utilizes the apostrophe to address the nautilus directly, thanking it for the lesson it has brought him, even in death. He refers to it as a "child" cast from the "lap" of the sea—thus using personification to establish a mother-child relationship between the animal and the sea, further enhancing the personal tone and preparing the reader for the final message of the poem.

Themes and Meanings

Much of the poetry of Oliver Wendell Holmes is occasional verse, and as such it is light, witty, and often humorous (as in poems such as "The Deacon's Masterpiece," "My Aunt," and "The Boys"). It is said that such poetry can make delightful reading but that its poetic quality is seldom high. Holmes himself once remarked that his poetry was "as the beating of a drum or the tinkling of a triangle to the harmony of a band." "The Chambered Nautilus," often considered one of his best poems, is not in the vein of his occasional verse and has a more pensive tone than that which generally characterizes his poetry. This poem is not preachy (as is a poem such as "Old Ironsides"), and while its theme is not profound, it is certainly provocative. By observing the nautilus and by essentially "dissecting" its physical body, the poet discovers a profound spiritual truth. To him the "silent toil" of the nautilus as it struggles to achieve physical growth is symbolic of the human endeavor necessary to the growth of the soul.

That individuals should continually be engaged in building broader and more comprehensive lives, growing with age and experience, and that they should be continually concerned with the nourishment of the soul throughout their lifetimes, is the message the poet derives from his experience with the nautilus. Such a conclusion is not only a consequence of a different kind of seeing but also a result of the religious background of the poet, who was born the son of a Calvinist minister. Also, his meticulous "dissecting" of the animal in the earlier stanzas of the poem may well be attributable to Holmes's formal training in anatomy and the many years that he spent as professor of anatomy at Dartmouth and at Harvard Universities.

In developing his theme in the final stanza of the poem, then, it is understandable that the poet makes generous use of biblical allusions. His insistence, for example, that the soul build "stately" or magnificent "mansions" seems to be an allusion to the "mansions" of matchless beauty which, according to the Bible, have been prepared in heaven for the souls of the righteous. He further insists that these "temples" of the soul be "new" and noble, or, as Scripture contends, that the soul should be clean and "undefiled." Finally, the poet alludes to the body as a shell which is discarded after death; in the same manner as the shell of the nautilus, it is cast from the "lap" of the "unresting sea." Implicit in this statement is the notion that only the soul is eternal. Thus, individuals must strive throughout their lifetimes to nourish and develop that which lasts—the soul. Just as the nautilus continues to grow during its lifetime, ever expanding and creating new and "lustrous coils," so should human beings continue growing spiritually throughout their lives, ever moving toward a higher plane of existence, leaving behind all small thoughts, acts, and desires, ever striving to build "new temples"—each one perfect, each one "nobler than the last."

Gladys J. Washington

CHANNEL FIRING

Author: Thomas Hardy (1840-1928)
Type of poem: Narrative
First published: 1914, in *Satires of Circumstance*

The Poem

The title refers to the firing of naval guns on the English Channel, guns apparently engaging in a military exercise. The poem registers a complex response to this event, using nine stanzas, each a quatrain set in an *abab* rhyme scheme, one of the most common forms of English poetry.

In "Channel Firing," Thomas Hardy uses the first-person plural, though the "We" might be thought of as a single individual speaking for his companions as well as for himself. The "We" are all dead and buried in a graveyard situated beside a church. This location is indicated not only by the reference to an "altar-crumb" but also by the word "chancel," which means the space around the altar of a church for the clergy and the choir, as well as by the term "glebe cow," which means a cow pastured on church grounds for the pastor's use.

The first two stanzas describe the arousal of the dead by the sound of the guns, a sound that is interpreted by them as signaling the arrival of Judgment Day. That occasion, according to Christian belief, will see the destruction of the world as humans know it, the resurrection of the dead, and their assignment by God, along with those still living, to eternal bliss or eternal torment.

God does in fact enter but not to proceed to judgment. Rather, He assures the dead that the sounds they have heard are simply those of guns at sea practicing to make war even bloodier ("redder") than it has been in ages past. God accuses the nations preparing for war of being insane. The living, he says, are doing no more for promulgating Christian principles than are the dead, who are helpless to affect the course of human events. God further states that it is a good thing He has not arrived to deliver judgment, because if He had, some of the living would be consigned to hell for engaging in military threats. God's statement, which dominates the middle section of the poem, concludes by His saying that "It will be warmer" if He ever does blow the trumpet signaling Judgment Day. By that, he apparently means the flames of hell will engulf the world.

Assured that Judgment Day has not arrived, the dead, who had sat up in response to the sounds they heard, resume their horizontal position. One of them wonders aloud whether humanity will ever prove to be saner than it was when he and his companions were sent to their death by God. Another, who had been a clergyman, wishes that he had spent his life enjoying himself (smoking and drinking) rather than preaching.

As the poem concludes, the sounds of the guns are heard once again, creating an impression of their readiness to carry out acts of revenge. The guns' reverberations extend inland to Stourton Tower, a structure built to commemorate the victory of Alfred the Great over Danish invaders. The sounds also reach Camelot, the site of the legendary King Arthur's court, and, finally, Stonehenge, a ring of monoliths that may have been used by a sun-worshiping cult or for astronomical observation.

Forms and Devices

Hardy has made a daring choice of speakers for the telling of this curious anecdote, employing not only the dead, whose actions and speech are reported to the reader directly, but also God Himself, who speaks condemningly of humankind. The presence of these beings, along with the graveyard setting, would seem to make for an unrelievedly solemn and moralistic piece, but in fact "Channel Firing" works to subvert such an effect through the use of irony.

Irony comes in various forms, but it always involves a gap or discrepancy of some sort. One such gap occurs between the thrust of the first six lines and that of the next three. The initial somberness and spookiness created by guns shaking coffins, the disturbing of the dead, and the awakening of dogs who then proceed to howl in a "drearisome" manner is undercut by the distinctly unthreatening details of the mouse, the withdrawing worms, and, most of all, the drooling cow. Hardy heightens the incongruous presence of the cow by having it enter the poem in the same line that sees the entrance of God. The setup of that line—"The glebe cow drooled. Till God called, 'No' "—creates the momentary impression that God is enjoining the cow not to drool, a patently ridiculous effect.

Even when the reader continues and realizes that the "No" refers to the fact that God is informing the dead that it is not Judgment Day, irony persists. It now involves the discrepancy between the way one would commonly expect God to talk and the way Hardy's creation speaks. While God's statement is given a touch of the elevated and archaic by His employment of the medieval "Christés" (instead of "Christ's"), His speech is notable for its use of the all-too-human taunting remark, "Ha, ha," as well as for the cliché "Mad as hatters" (which alludes to the occupational hazard once faced by people who made hats because of a chemical used in their production). Even "for Christés sake" carries with it the echo of the common human and secularized expression "for Christ's sake."

Related to God's use of "Ha ha" is the irony involving His attitude. Functioning neither as the figure of mercy nor the solemn deliverer of justice that common belief would expect, God taunts and teases the dead on the matter of Judgment Day. Instead of having the coming of that momentous occasion continue to be regarded as a certainty, He leaves the matter open. He says, when referring to His blowing of the trumpet signifying judgment, "if indeed/ I ever do," bringing into question a fundamental Christian belief under the cover of His solicitousness for the dead ("for you are men,/ And rest eternal sorely need"). It is no wonder that in response to the appearance of this sort of divinity, one of the dead should regret having given his life to being a Christian preacher.

Themes and Meanings

Unless the comic undercutting of the original atmosphere of the poem is recognized, along with the irony attached to the figure of God, "Channel Firing" might be read as a fairly straightforward and unrelentingly serious condemnation of humankind for continuing to make war, a judgment coming from within a Christian perspective. The moralizing figure of the poem, God, cannot be taken seriously, however, or at least not entirely so. Ultimately, He is an unattractive figure.

The poem is registering the fact of war and its cost in human life. Indeed, the piece might be regarded as prescient, for Hardy wrote it in April of 1914, only months before the outbreak of World War I. Yet Hardy is pointing to the costly use of force less to shake a judgmental finger at humankind than to register such use as apparently inescapable. The poem might be said to replace judgments with facts, and Christian theology, which it finds absurd, with history.

It is interesting to note Hardy's handling of place names in the last stanza. They are arranged so as to have the sounds of the guns carry not merely inland through space but also backward through time. The reader moves from Hardy's century to the eighteenth century, the period when Stourton Tower was constructed. The reference to that edifice moves the reader back even further, for it commemorates an event of the ninth century. The mention of Camelot carries the reader still further back, to the sixth century, and the reference to Stonehenge goes back furthest of all, for that prodigious structure is prehistoric.

It is as if Hardy is saying that the use of force, the making of war, has been with humankind for as long as there have been human beings. That, along with the gunnery practice that opens the poem, would suggest that violence will continue to be a fact of human life. A solemnity returns to "Channel Firing" as Hardy offers the reader this bleak but in a way grand perspective on human existence, setting that existence in the framework of the cosmos with the notable phrase that closes the poem, a phrase marked by alliteration and four strong beats—"starlit Stonehenge." Bloody as it has been, the human enterprise acquires a certain substance and dignity here. Unlike the poem's handling of God and fundamental presuppositions of Christianity, it does not undercut that dignity by subjecting it to irony.

Alan Holder

CHAPLINESQUE

Author: Hart Crane (1899-1932)
Type of poem: Lyric
First published: 1921; collected in *White Buildings*, 1926

The Poem

Hart Crane's "Chaplinesque" is a poem in five stanzas, the first two containing four lines each, the last three with five lines each. The title introduces the central metaphor of the poem, the film actor and comedian Charlie Chaplin. The poem is a striking dramatization of the tenuous position in modern society of those who are, for whatever reason, excluded from the establishment. The persona, the "we" of the poem, represents all outsiders, not only poets and other artists—although they are central to Crane's vision—but also all sensitive and feeling people who do not fit into the structured society. Although Crane sees the human condition as rather bleak and tragic, he finds brief but welcome consolation in elements of everyday life as well as in kindness, imagination, and humor.

The first stanza states in simple terms what compromises ("meek adjustments") human beings must make in order to survive in a hostile environment. The world Crane portrays is naturalistic, materialistic, judgmental, and insensitive to the feeling, caring person. No matter what one's expectations, he or she must learn to be satisfied with whatever occasional benefits are supplied, unexpectedly and without rational pattern, by nature or fate.

Both stanza 1 and stanza 2 refer to Charlie Chaplin in his most famous role, that of the "Little Tramp" in his baggy and tattered costume. In the first stanza, Crane describes the large pockets of the tramp's trousers and the oversize elbows of his sleeves. In both stanzas, the "random consolations" derive from the simple, even homely pleasures that come to one unexpectedly, for example, the starving kitten on the doorstep as in need of love as is the poet or, indeed, any other person.

The third stanza describes the tactics necessary for the outsider who wishes to survive against society's hostility. Crane's distrust of business and of businessmen is represented by the traditional gesture of a rather frightening figure counting money between thumb and index finger. The stanza also refers obliquely to the inevitability of death and the amazement with which a person may face it, all the while endeavoring to preserve life.

In stanza 4, Crane employs Chaplin's trick of leaning on or twirling his bendable cane to symbolize human vulnerability. The "obsequies," or funeral rites, which might seem to some false, are, at least to a degree, true, since the heart will endure even beyond death. In other words, feeling endures, even when the physical being fails.

The final stanza offers the best hope for the sensitive human being in a hostile environment, the existence of some sort of ideal beyond the harsh reality of life. Smirk if you will, the persona says to the enemy (authority, the establishment, the law, Puritanism) but one can still hope: There may be no Holy Grail, but imagination can create "a grail of laughter" from a trash can, and there is the kitten, crying, waiting to be saved. The rescue of the kitten embodies humanistic feeling, the existence of which, for Crane, provides the best hope. These "adjustments" make life worth the effort for the persona.

Forms and Devices

The lines in "Chaplinesque" are uneven in length, and there is no predominant meter, although some are in iambic pentameter. There is only one full rhyme ("lies"/"enterprise"), but Crane uses three examples of assonance ("deposits"/"pockets"; "know"/ "coverts"; "quest"/"wilderness"). The tone is conversational and understated, the feelings carefully controlled, even though the subject matter is intensely emotional, concerning pains and disappointments and the difficulty of surviving in an unfriendly world. The way in which Crane employs some words is startling and unique, for example, "coverts," "obsequies," and "grail."

The point of view is that of a first-person plural narrator who seems to speak not only for poets but also for all those excluded from conventional society. In the first four lines he introduces the major metaphor, a comparison of the human dilemma to an easily recognized cultural icon, the "Little Tramp" portrayed by Charlie Chaplin. Several lines refer to specific scenes in the Chaplin film entitled *The Kid*, released the year Crane wrote the poem.

Chaplin's actions in the role are stylized, like pantomime, with jerky exaggerated movements similar to those of a puppet. Chaplin was always identified with his distinctive costume and props, including the cane that contributed, through its flexibility, to the well-choreographed pratfalls or near-falls ("these fine collapses") that were a standard device of his performance. The look on the actor's face, which rarely changes, is a puzzled one, like that of a child or some other innocent creature surprised by the experiences he confronts. Crane endeavored to represent in words the distinctive movements of the actor, the alternate jerky motion and frozen stances. (After reading the poem, Chaplin wrote Crane a letter of appreciation, and later the two of them met.)

In identifying with the "Little Tramp," the poet underscores the Everyman message of the poem—that all sensitive "little" people suffer, that they find hope wherever they can, and that they must ultimately face the same fate, although there is hope in the endurance of the human heart. Further, although Chaplin as the tramp indulged unabashedly in sentimentality, he converted it, the poet felt, into a particularly modern tragedy in his depiction of a poor man shut out of the banquet of American life.

Other figures in the poem include the starving kitten, which represents the sympathetic feelings Crane believed to be an essential part of human nature; the concept of life as a game, frustrating but inevitable; the businessman in the classic pose of the money counter; the moon as imaginaton; and the ash can, which, through the alchemy of laughter is converted into a modern representation of the Holy Grail.

Themes and Meanings

"Chaplinesque" is in many ways Crane's most personal poem, in which he presents a cogent statement of the plight of the poet in modern society. As such, it is one of his major works, for here he combines his fascination with the craft of poetry with distinctive American aspects, with popular culture, and with his own life. Crane's use of intensely personal elements places him in the tradition established by Walt Whitman, whose best-known poem was entitled "Song of Myself." Indeed, Crane was the "most American" poet since Whitman, and he wrote in much the same vein, using American images—the Brooklyn Bridge, the elevated train, motion pictures—although in a quite original way.

Crane admired the contemporary American poet who influenced him most, T. S. Eliot, but he rejected Eliot's belief that poetry should be a vehicle not for displaying personal emotions but for freeing oneself from them. The ash can that is transformed into a "grail of laughter" in the final stanza of "Chaplinesque" is an allusion to Eliot's most famous work, "The Waste Land" (1922), in which the search for the Holy Grail figures as a major symbol. However, Eliot's philosophy of impersonality ran contrary to Crane's belief that the American poet should employ his own personal vision of the American experience to create a new kind of art, and that emotion was of the essence.

There are decidedly individual references in "Chaplinesque"—the kitten Crane himself had adopted and the pun on his own name in the line "the heart lives on"—but more important, the personal elements of the poem center around the fact that Crane always felt in his maturity separated from the mainstream of American life. First of all, as a poet, he did not fit into the corporate system represented by his father, the owner of a candy factory. Not long before the composition of "Chaplinesque," Crane had become permanently estranged from his father, a condition that provided the poet with yet another sense of being among outsiders. Second, in an era in which his homosexuality was not only considered immoral but was also a crime punishable by imprisonment, Crane felt even further alienated from the majority. By extension, however, it should be noted that although Crane is directly concerned with poets and other outcasts, in a sense he sees all human beings as hapless victims of a naturalistic universe, a political and social world, and a fate over which most of them finally have no control. The motif of exclusion and the suffering of the poet and others would ultimately blossom again in the works of the playwright Tennessee Williams, Hart Crane's most devoted disciple.

W. Kenneth Holditch

THE CHARGE OF THE LIGHT BRIGADE

Author: Alfred, Lord Tennyson (1809-1892)
Type of poem: Ode
First published: 1854; collected in *Maud and Other Poems*, 1855

The Poem

Alfred, Lord Tennyson wrote "The Charge of the Light Brigade" shortly after reading a newspaper article about the futile charge of troops at the 1854 Battle of Balaklava during the Crimean War (1853-1856). British and French troops had been sent to the Crimean Peninsula to punish the Russian government for various aggressive and belligerent policies. A newsman for the London *Times* was on the scene and hinted in his report that the debacle resulted from blunders made by British commanders in the Crimea. In Tennyson's mind, the questionable behavior of the British generals did not diminish the bravery of the troops who had acted valiantly in carrying out orders. Moved by these acts of valor and perhaps angered by the mismanagement of senior officers, the poet laureate immediately wrote an ode to commemorate the occasion.

In six irregular stanzas, Tennyson describes the movement of the troops down the long valley at Balaklava. Sitting on the ridge at the end of this depression are batteries of Russian artillery, whose fusillade decimated the cavalrymen as they approached. In stanza 1, the commander's directive to "Charge for the guns" vividly captures the reckless abandon that would lead to disastrous consequences. The reaction of the troops is captured in the second stanza. The poet asks, "Was there a man dismayed?" and immediately responds, "Not though the soldier knew/ Someone had blundered." Instead, the men of the light brigade ride boldly down the valley, carrying out their orders; "Theirs not to reason why," the poet says, "Theirs but to do and die." Like good soldiers, they are willing to follow their leaders' orders, even though they can see for themselves that the mission is sure to be suicidal.

Stanzas 3, 4, and 5 describe the charge and its aftermath. As the cannons along the hills ringing the valley rain down missiles of destruction, the soldiers advance with sabers unsheathed "Into the jaws of Death,/ Into the mouth of Hell." Eventually, despite heavy losses, they break through the Russians' line of defense and slaughter the gunners. The effect of the charge takes its toll on the brigade, however; "Back from the mouth of Hell" a much smaller number of soldiers return to the British lines at the end of the battle.

In the final stanza, Tennyson acknowledges that, though in some ways futile, the charge was a heroic act, and it is the duty of his contemporaries and of ages to come to "Honor the charge they made,/ Honor the Light Brigade." These men had the courage to carry out orders knowing that to do so would almost certainly result in death. Of such heroism are odes and tragedies made.

Forms and Devices

As in many odes, the stanza pattern of "The Charge of the Light Brigade" is irregular. An eight-line opening stanza gives way to two stanzas of nine lines, in which the poet sets the stage for the charge and describes the entry into the valley. The central action of the battle and its aftermath is described in two longer stanzas, of twelve and eleven lines, respectively. The final stanza, only six lines, serves as an epitaph honoring the brave men who sacrificed themselves in serving their country.

The rhyme scheme, too, is irregular. In some stanzas, only two or three lines are rhymed. In others, Tennyson inserts a number of couplets and triplets. The poem may appear to be more regular on first reading, however, because Tennyson skillfully uses repetition and variation to link his six stanzas. The closing phrase "six hundred" is present in every stanza, and in each stanza at least one internal line rhymes with this phrase. These rhyming words, all strong action verbs, capture the key actions of the poem. Someone in leadership "blundered." Cannons on the rim of the valley "thundered." When the men of the light brigade break through enemy lines, the Russian and Cossack gunners are "shattered" and "sundered." Meanwhile, those outside the valley, and indeed "the whole world," Tennyson says, "wondered" about the outcome of the charge. Since each of the rhyming lines ends with a full stop, the attention of readers is focused on these actions.

As he does in many other poems, Tennyson uses repetition and variation of phrases and even whole lines as a key poetic device. The poem opens with a thrice-repeated phrase so that the effect of the rhythm in the first two lines is to mimic the sound of the charge: "Half a league, half a league,/ Half a league onward" suggests the galloping of the horses charging down the valley. Similarly, in stanzas 3 and 5 the poet creates a sense of the pounding of artillery upon the brigade by varying the lines describing the cannons' volley: "Cannon to right of them,/ Cannon to left of them,/ Cannon in front of them" all "volleyed and thundered" as the men approach the guns. As the soldiers leave the field, the third line of this triplet is changed to "Cannon behind them," suggesting that the retreat is as devastating as the charge itself.

Finally, the meter Tennyson uses is particularly appropriate for this poem. Tennyson reported to his son that the newspaper editorial about the Battle of Balaklava, during which this charge took place, had stated that "someone had blundered." From this he instantly saw that the appropriate meter for the poem was dactylic: a stress syllable followed by two unstressed ones. The powerful suggestion led him to use what has traditionally been a meter associated with epic. Tennyson produces lines that are predominantly dactylic, with key stops written as spondees, two-syllable feet. The effect is similar to the dactylic hexameters used by both Homer and Virgil. Readers familiar with classical epic will find echoes of Homer's *Iliad* and *Odyssey* (both c. 800 B.C.E.; Eng. trans., 1616) and Vergil's *Aeneid* (c. 29-19 B.C.E.; Eng. trans., 1553) in Tennyson's tribute to the brave men who charged down the valley at Balaklava.

Themes and Meanings

"The Charge of the Light Brigade" issues a clear call to celebrate the heroism of soldiers who surrender themselves to a greater cause. Throughout the poem Tennyson calls attention to their valor, technical skill, and willingness to trust in their leaders. The theme might be best understood by seeing it expressed in another of Tennyson's poems, *Idylls of the King* (1859-1885). In a lyric sung at the marriage of King Arthur, the knights who have pledged fidelity to him chant that "The King will follow Christ, and we the King/ In whom high God hath breathed a sacred thing." This paean to the benevolent and specially endowed leader is characteristic of both monarchist government and military discipline. The soldiers of the light brigade, knowing that their lives are in danger, nevertheless follow orders and charge the enemy gun emplacements at the end of the valley. Assuming that the mission is important and necessary for the success of the British campaign, these men brave the artillery fire from all sides to carry out orders. Tennyson states clearly that such behavior is to be honored, and that the fame of these soldiers deserves perpetual veneration.

Glancing at the works of other writers, one can see the universality of this theme. In *Voyna i mir* (1865-1869; *War and Peace*, 1886), Leo Tolstoy offers similar praise for the Russian soldiers who fought for Russia against Napoleon's invading troops. Soviet dissident Aleksandr Solzhenitsyn also speaks with great admiration of the courage of Russian soldiers at the tragic Battle of the Tannenburg Forest in his novel *Avgust chetyrnadtsatogo* (1971, rev. 1983; *August 1914*, 1972). The works of American writer Ernest Hemingway frequently celebrate the courage soldiers and civilians sometimes exhibit when they carry out their duty, knowing all the while that they will pay with their lives for their heroism.

Because the charge of the light brigade was ill-conceived and futile, there may be some who would argue that the soldiers' behavior was simply stupid; following orders that were known to be poorly developed, and which would lead to certain death, is hardly the mark of heroes. Tennyson argues that such thinking is wrongheaded. The mark of good soldiers is that they follow legitimate orders even if it means risking their lives. "The Charge of the Light Brigade" is as hard on the British generals as the London *Times* editorial had been; the mistakes of those in authority are not excused. What Tennyson wants to make clear is that these errors should not obscure the gallantry of those asked to carry out military missions in service to the nation. Debates about the wisdom of following orders stretch back into ancient times and continue throughout history. An example from American history, the reaction of the public to the Vietnam War, is a reminder that Tennyson's concerns for the individual soldier asked to obey questionable government policy have relevance far beyond the valleys on the Crimean Peninsula.

Laurence W. Mazzeno

CHERRYLOG ROAD

Author: James Dickey (1923-1997)
Type of poem: Narrative
First published: 1964; collected in *Poems, 1957-1967*, 1967

The Poem

"Cherrylog Road" is a narrative poem, a memory recounted in the first person. The title identifies the setting of the event that the speaker recalls: Cherrylog Road is the location of a junkyard in which the speaker meets his teenage lover for secret assignations. As the title suggests, the poem pays a lot of attention to setting, even identifying Cherrylog Road, in the first and last stanzas, as a roadway branching off of Highway 106. In spite of this specificity, the poet identifies the location only as an unnamed "southern-state." Details reveal that the setting is the rural South—bootlegging country—and that the time of year is summer.

The speaker arrives at the junkyard first for a prearranged meeting with his lover, Doris Holbrook. Little information is offered about Doris except that she lives nearby and must meet the speaker on the sly for fear of retribution from her father. While waiting for Doris, the speaker explores the junkyard, moving from wrecked car to wrecked car and fantasizing about their owners or picturing himself as a race car driver. As his anticipation mounts, his imagination turns to Doris, and he speculates about the unpleasant consequences of being caught by her father. By the middle of the poem, the speaker hears the sound of Doris approaching, tapping the wrecked cars with her wrench (she must return with used car parts to explain her absence from home). However, it is not until the fifteenth of eighteen stanzas that the two lovers are united. Three stanzas describe their lovemaking in passionate and metaphorical terms, and then the final stanza chronicles the speaker's elated departure—from Cherrylog Road to Highway 106—on his motorcycle.

The core of the poem is description, and the junkyard setting occupies most of the poet's attention. The description enumerates automobiles and their parts, detailing the fragmented condition of the cars. The rural setting emerges through the natural denizens of the junkyard: snakes, toads, mice, and roaches. However, the poem also seeks to describe youthful passion, and much of its interest lies in how the poet uses the junkyard to evoke the speaker's anticipation and recklessness. The poem mixes realistic description with fantasies played out in the speaker's mind. Thus, "Cherrylog Road" evokes a vividly remembered scene and explores the emotions of the speaker, who recalls the scene in detail. The poet blends those two levels of presentation—description and psychological analysis—seamlessly.

Forms and Devices

"Cherrylog Road" is an easy poem to read, and its accessibility results from James Dickey's use of straightforward diction, conventional syntax, and grammatical sentences. Yet the poem's 108 lines make up only nine sentences, which are spread over eighteen six-line stanzas. Though the stanza structure is regular, the verse is unrhymed and the line length varies from four to ten syllables. Six- and seven-syllable lines with three stresses are the most common, but the metrical variation approaches free verse.

The most notable poetic devices appear in the use of figurative language, which reinforces the poem's emphasis on connecting descriptive detail to the speaker's state of mind. Some of the figurative language seems natural to the junkyard setting, as when the poet uses a simile to compare the speaker's posture in a wrecked car to a driver "in a wild stock-car race" or when a metaphor presents the junked vehicles as "stalled, dreaming traffic." The automobile imagery becomes more blatantly symbolic, however, when the junkyard is called "the parking lot of the dead" or when the sun is personified as "eating the paint in blisters/ From a hundred car tops and hoods." Other examples of figurative language hint at how the speaker's erotic anticipation colors his description. The sun-warmed interiors of the cars are described as possessing "body heat," the center of the junkyard is its "weedy heart," and the torn upholstery of a luxury car is "tender." When the speaker spins a fantasy about being a wealthy old woman directing her chauffeur to an orphanage where she will dispense toys, the car's brand name ("Pierce-Arrow") combines with the metaphor for the reflected sun ("platters of blindness") to suggest the avatars of love, a blind god served by an arrow-wielding cherub.

The weedy and littered garden of the junkyard has a teeming animal life, and Dickey identifies snakes three times: a "kingsnake" in stanza 6 and a "blacksnake" in stanzas 14 and 15. Given the gardenlike setting and the sexually charged occasion, the associations of the snake with Original Sin and with phallic imagery seem deliberate. Indeed, the developing symbolism of the description helps the reader understand how Dickey describes the passionate encounter. Doris's appearance is heralded by a simile comparing her noise to the scraping of a mouse. Along with the phallic connotations of the snake, this association explains the natural description inserted into the midst of the lovers' embrace in stanzas 15 and 16: "So the blacksnake, stiff/ With inaction, curved back/ Into life, and hunted the mouse/ With deadly overexcitement." The curious phrase "deadly overexcitement" brings together the traditional hunt or chase imagery of courtship with the story of Original Sin, in which a snake and a sexual fall bring death into the world.

At the heart of the poem, the lovers come together in language that suggests union and imprisonment: "clung," "glued," "hooks," "springs," and "catch." Given the dangerous nature of their tryst, they part quickly, and the poet describes them leaving "by separate doors," passing through "the changed, other bodies/ Of cars," just as the union of their bodies has changed them. The narrator's youthful exuberance is visited upon the inanimate body of his motorcycle, which is compared by simile to "the soul of the junkyard/ Restored" and through metaphor to "a bicycle fleshed/ With power." The reader knows that it is the speaker, not his motorcycle, who feels restored and powerful, but the transference of animate qualities to the mechanical vehicles of the junkyard is consistent with the imagery and methods of the poem.

Themes and Meanings

That the speaker's recollection of his junkyard meetings with Doris is positive emerges clearly from his memories and exuberant tone, but one must ask why Dickey chooses a junkyard for this encounter. What significance does he place on wrecked automobiles as a ground for the blossoming of love and sexuality? The landscape of wrecks becomes a sort of code to be deciphered, just as the speaker hears the banging of Doris's wrench as "tapping like code." The speaker himself reads the lives of past generations into their wrecked vehicles. This exercise of imagination works two ways: It suggests how the mind erects its palaces or playgrounds anywhere it must, turning a junkyard into a paradise; but it also suggests how youthful passion, like all things, becomes subject to age and deterioration. The junkyard is a litter of broken parts: A glass panel is "broken out"; upholstery is "spilling," "ripped," and "burst[ing]"; wheels are missing; and every surface shows rust. The "parking lot of the dead" serves as a memento mori, a reminder that death and decay are ubiquitous.

Yet Doris collects working parts from this graveyard, "Carrying off headlights,/ Sparkplugs, bumpers." More important, out of the wreckage young love finds expression. If the snake-filled setting represents a version of the corrupted Garden of Eden after the Fall, Dickey's poem offers an alternative vision of the genesis of sexuality. In Dickey's version, the sexual moment engenders life out of death rather than mortality out of ever-youthful paradise. In the decayed junkyard, death lingers: "Through dust where the blacksnake dies/ Of boredom, and the beetle knows/ The compost has no more life." These lines are filled with images of a wasted world. The explicit association of the snake with death and the reference to dust (symbolic of mortality) and the beetle (also traditionally associated with death) reveal that the compost, which should generate new life out of waste, "has no more life." It is this morbid landscape that the lovers' sexual passion spurs back into vitality, as the snake "curved back/ Into life" and "The beetles reclaimed their field."

The imagery of the final stanza conjures up the youthful pride of a boy experimenting with sex and, typically, projecting his enthusiasm onto his motorcycle, the powerful machine between his legs. Alliteration connects the key words of the closing lines: "Wringing the handlebar for speed,/ Wild to be wreckage forever." However, this closing paean to wildness has grim overtones. Does the boy's desire to be wreckage become a death wish on the highway? Perhaps that connection back to all the wrecks of the junkyard he is leaving behind is meant to remind the reader that the speaker's experience is an initiation into the fallen adult world, where the ultimate result of passion is wreckage. The speaker conveys the message, but his desire does not allow him to hear it. The reader captures the poem's bittersweet "forever," poised against the fleeting brevity of the remembered encounter.

Christopher Ames

CHICAGO

Author: Carl Sandburg (1878-1967)
Type of poem: Lyric
First published: 1916, in *Chicago Poems*

The Poem

"Chicago" is a poem in free verse, one without a set meter or rhyme scheme, running twenty-three lines. The title gives the name of the city that the poet is praising, which does not appear elsewhere in the poem. Without the title, this poem could refer to any industrial city, suggesting a universal love of place.

The poem, written in the first person so that the poet addresses the reader directly, celebrates both the virtues and vices of the city. It begins with a staccato list of occupations found in Chicago (hog butcher, tool maker, stacker of wheat), followed by three adjectives that attach an emotion to those occupations. Carl Sandburg calls them "Stormy, husky, brawling," creating an aura of vitality. This first section of the poem is abrupt and rapid, like the city being portrayed.

The second section departs from the brief phrasing and turns to long, flowing, melodic sentences. Each of the first three sentences acknowledges a vice of the city in the first half of the sentence. It is wicked, corrupt, and brutal. The poet agrees to each accusation, supplying a specific detail that supports the charge in the second half of the sentence. There are "painted women," "gunmen," and "wanton hunger." The city does, in fact, have its failings.

The poet more than accepts the failings of his city, however; he answers in the remaining lines with a list of positive attributes. His city is singing and loud, "proud to be alive and coarse and strong and cunning." Sandburg celebrates this strength, and it is clear that the vices are a small enough price to pay for the overwhelming vitality and life the city contains.

In the last four lines, an important shift of perspective occurs. The poet personifies the city, saying it laughs as a young man does, laughs "as an ignorant fighter who has never lost a battle." This suggests a sense of innocence despite the previously mentioned corruption. Only youth laughs and feels confident regardless of circumstances. Only youth swaggers with the assurance of victory. Hence, a sense of immaturity mingles with the confidence and vitality.

The last line repeats the major attributes the poet grants the city. It is laughing, stormy, and proud. This line concludes with the repetition of the poem's beginning, but as fragments of a single line rather than separate lines. This gives the poem a circular effect, ending right where it began, and creates a sense of closure.

Forms and Devices

Sandburg wrote in free verse, but this does not mean that the poem lacks any structure. The structure supports the subject matter. A poem about a loud, brawling city would hardly be appropriately conveyed in a tightly constructed sonnet. Sandburg sought to capture the mood of the city in the arrangement of the poem's language. The short phrases in the first section are simply a list of occupations. This suggests that the city is primarily a place of industry, all efficiency and business. When the second section begins, the lines are long compound sentences that capture the depth of emotion the poet feels. The poet is in awe of the city even as he admits its weaknesses.

Sandburg was greatly influenced by the poetry of Walt Whitman. Both poets wrote of the common man, democratic society, and celebrations of the ordinary rather than the sublime. Sandburg utilizes the free-verse form that Whitman had made so popular in the nineteenth century, but Sandburg owes other debts as well—particularly to the Bible. The repetition of "and" in the first several lines, for example, is distinctly biblical. By using "and" rather than writing sentences with dependent clauses, Sandburg creates the effect that each independent clause is equally important. The poet's emotions are equally significant regarding the city's vices and its virtues.

This parallelism is one of the chief poetic devices employed. In addition to the repeated "and," the use of the "-ing" form of the verbs after line 13 implies that the action is occurring presently. These are the things the city is doing; it is not resting on its laurels and traditions like other "little soft cities," but moving rapidly.

The poem is written in the present tense, which lends it immediacy. The poet is currently experiencing the city and its emotion, which is a radical departure from what the nineteenth century English poet William Wordsworth said poetry ideally was: emotion recalled in tranquility. There is nothing tranquil about "Chicago," and the use of the present tense helps convey this.

Sandburg's use of metaphor further supports his themes. He compares the city to a dog to show its fierceness. He compares it to a young man, endowing the city with youth and enthusiasm and energy. These comparisons are commonplace; there is no elaborate use of mythology or classical allusions, so the reader has immediate access to the meanings. Sandburg does not employ traditional poetic devices such as alliteration or assonance, preferring the rhythms of natural speech. This is a conscious appeal to the common man, as Sandburg believed that poetry should address the common man.

Perhaps one of the most outstanding devices the poet uses is the personification of the city. Personification, giving human characteristics to inanimate objects, is clear in the attribution of physical traits to Chicago, such as saying the city has a mouth and head. The city behaves in a human fashion, laughing and brawling and singing. In this way, Sandburg furthers the concept of the city's vitality and life.

Additionally, Sandburg addresses the city directly—the poetic voice is speaking to the city. "They tell me you are wicked," he says, as if the city will answer him. This conveys the idea that the city will continue, in the same fashion, regardless of the occupants. Indeed, if people move away, the city's character will not change, and Sandburg acknowledges this self-perpetuating ability in the direct address.

Themes and Meanings

"Chicago" is a celebration of America's vitality. It is about boundless energy, about love of life, about the zest and laughter that Sandburg found. Granted, the city has its dark side, but Sandburg's city laughs in the face of terrible destiny. This attitude is a prominent theme in American literature, especially in the latter half of the twentieth century.

The destiny to which the poet refers is death. Many of Sandburg's poems address this theme directly, but in "Chicago" it is implied rather than directly stated. The terrible destiny is inevitable; no matter how much life is packed into the sprawling city, its inhabitants will perish. The spirit of the city will eventually soften and become like other cities. This impression of death is reaffirmed in the metaphor of the ignorant fighter. Fighters do lose eventually, even if it has not happened yet. Despite the certainty of destiny, however, the important thing is to live. The affirmation of life lies in the attempts to live life fully, to work, and most of all, to laugh.

Unlike many of his contemporaries, notably T. S. Eliot, Sandburg was a poet of the people. He was widely read in his own time, and his poetry reflects his preoccupation with the common person. The people of his city may be underfed, criminal, or immoral, but they are real people. He writes of workers and farmers. He writes of those people who strain and sweat and swear and laugh and cry in order to celebrate the very existence of humanity. His concern for common people is more than intellectual; throughout his life, he kept in close contact with the laboring classes and was motivated by his experiences with the Populist movement. It is no coincidence that in addition to his many volumes of poetry Sandburg wrote a massive biography of Abraham Lincoln. He viewed Lincoln much the same way that he viewed his city, Chicago—as a folkloric figure of the people, standing for the average worker.

Sandburg contributed an important dimension to the poetry of his time. His use of blunt language helped liberate poetry from the nineteenth century's formal prettiness. His subject matter appealed to working people rather than to strict intellectuals. The form was loose and free, like the dreams of the people. This poem, perhaps his greatest, provides a glimpse of the talent and power of one of America's early twentieth century poets.

Christine F. Sally

THE CHICAGO *DEFENDER* SENDS
A MAN TO LITTLE ROCK

Author: Gwendolyn Brooks (1917-2000)
Type of poem: Narrative
First published: 1960, in *The Bean Eaters*

The Poem

A number of Gwendolyn Brooks's poems, particularly those written in the years of the Civil Rights movement, highlight major events in the African American struggle for legal equality. The title of this poem clearly conveys its historical context: A reporter from Chicago's black newspaper, the *Defender*, travels in the fall of 1957 to Little Rock, Arkansas, during that city's battles over school desegregation. In the actual historical events, the first nine black students ever to be admitted to Central High School were forbidden to enter the school by the governor of Arkansas, who used the state's National Guard to block them from entering. Hostile mobs from the community cursed and spat at the children, and they attacked both black and white journalists covering the incident. Eventually President Dwight Eisenhower sent federal troops with orders to safeguard the children and allow them to attend the school. The landmark incident marked the first serious test of the Supreme Court's 1954 *Brown v. Board of Education* decision forbidding segregation in public schools.

Creatively linking these real events with a poetic (re)creation, Brooks's poem reflects a reporter's first-person account of life in this racially charged southern city. Instead of beginning with descriptions of violence and hatred, the narrator records the everyday lives of ordinary people who look for jobs, have babies, repair their homes, and water their plants. On Sunday in church they sing hymns; afterward they have tea and cookies. Like Americans from coast to coast, they celebrate Christmas and enjoy baseball and music. In the tenth stanza, however, the mood shifts as the reporter, scratching his head, makes a crucial observation: "there is a puzzle in this town." The citizens appear to be "like people everywhere." There is no observable sign of the hatred and evil contained in the human heart. After hurling insults and launching vicious attacks, community members return to their ordinary lives.

The narrator imagines how disappointed his Chicago editor would be to hear such a banal account of Little Rock citizens, when in fact he has witnessed them harassing, spitting, and hurling rocks. Yet he cannot forget the shocking reality of their dualistic nature. Brooks closes the poem with the reporter's thought of another mob of ordinary people—those at the crucifixion of Christ—thereby forcing readers to reconsider how they recognize evil and to look within for evidence of hatred or bigotry that might not be immediately apparent.

Forms and Devices

References to music and love permeate Brooks's poem. Readers who know her work will not be surprised, for such images appear often in her poetry about the black community. However, their use here in describing the white community is quite different. Ironically, even in a time of racial conflict, when people are behaving in inhuman ways, they "sing/ Sunday hymns like anything" and attend musical events where the beauty of Beethoven, Bach, and Offenbach fill their ears, if not their hearts. These musical images at first seem paradoxical in a protest poem, but they have a definite function. As critic and poet Haki R. Madhubuti writes in his introduction to *Say That the River Turns: The Impact of Gwendolyn Brooks* (1987), "it is her vision—her ability to see truths rather than trends, to seek meaning and not fads, to question ideas rather than gossip—that endears her to us." In this poem the truth for Brooks is that music is not an antidote to hate. Avid listeners are not necessarily transformed by its beauty; they may still embody evil.

The seventh stanza examines another paradox: how the capacities for love and hate coexist in the same place and even in the same people. The narrator notes that there is love as well as music in Little Rock. Images of "soft women" giving and receiving pleasure point to the people's desire to dull the pain or, as Brooks writes, "To wash away old semi-discomfitures." Such physical expressions of love appear to clarify uncertainties, but they actually cover up, rather than confront, the most serious problems of society. Many images are suggestive, their meanings not completely spelled out, and Brooks links ideas ordinarily kept apart: love and music appear in frightening juxtaposition with bigotry and violence.

The inextricability of form and content is another important aspect of "The Chicago *Defender* Sends a Man to Little Rock," one of the most compelling poems in her collection *The Bean Eaters*. The apparent normalcy of Little Rock lives is emphasized by the conventional line lengths and prosaic language. Yet after four stanzas, when the narrator finally interrupts the smooth litany of their days and nights, the lines are short, clipped. The reporter speaks: "I forecast/ And I believe." One expects his revelation to expose the evil in the community. Instead he makes a prediction about the festive holiday season. Then the poem quickly resumes its original form. Mirroring reality, no change occurs, the usual flow of events continues, and for the next three stanzas Brooks re-creates the laughter and tinsel of Christmas, the baseball games, and the twilight concerts. Readers experience through the poem's structure the frustrating inability to recognize and destroy the enemy easily, for the enemy is well hidden in this city of ordinary people. What is perhaps most striking about a poem on such a harsh subject is its overall lack of shocking detail. Only near the end does Brooks show the violence that lurks beneath the calm exterior: "And true, they are hurling spittle, rock,/ Garbage and fruit in Little Rock./ And I saw coiling storm a-writhe/ On bright madonnas. And a scythe/ Of men harassing brownish girls."

The unusually wide spaces between the last three lines allow readers time to read between the lines, to imagine what lies beneath the surface of this apparently placid poem and community, and then to compare what they find with their own understanding of the history of persecution and oppression.

Themes and Meanings

"The Chicago *Defender* Sends a Man to Little Rock" contains themes found in much of Gwendolyn Brooks's poetry. Undeniably it is a thoughtful criticism of contemporary society. In an interview from her autobiography *Report From Part One* (1972), Brooks says that much of a writer's use of themes depends upon the climate of America at the time: "I think it is the task or job or responsibility or pleasure or pride of any writer to respond to his climate. You write about what is in the world." Examining the United States in the late 1950's and early 1960's, she could not escape the existing racism and violence. The point of the poem is that people often do fail to see its existence in their communities, their neighbors, and even themselves.

For the most part, the poems in *The Bean Eaters* are about commonplace people, and this poem is no exception. Brooks demonstrates the extraordinary effects that "ordinary" lives can have on the course of history. She also shows that violence is often perpetrated by people who present a benign exterior. The poem attempts to see behind the mask. Brooks strips away illusions about evil and immerses readers in its very real, very conventional nature.

The eighth stanza shows how Little Rock citizens feign politeness, answer the phone, and respond to questions about the problems in their community. Even as they converse with reporters they remain firmly in denial about their own complicity in the social and psychological oppression. The voice of the poet then becomes the conscience for the larger community of readers who must sort through this series of paradoxical events to separate truth from lies.

There are two particularly notable ways in which "The Chicago *Defender* Sends a Man to Little Rock" differs from other poems on the theme of racial injustice. First is its basis in an actual confrontation that shocked the world and underscored the anguish of a people searching for equality in a country that continued to deny it. The poem invites the reader to identify with a narrator who is appalled that these oppressors "are like people everywhere." The second important distinction is the skillful way Brooks compresses a history of oppression into the final two lines of the poem as if to imply that little has been resolved in the years since Jesus' death.

With a gift for seeing truth no matter where or how it is hidden, Gwendolyn Brooks throughout her career has questioned suppositions about equality and justice. As she writes in her autobiography, a writer "needs to live richly with eyes open, and heart, too."

Carol F. Bender

"CHILDE ROLAND TO THE DARK TOWER CAME"

Author: Robert Browning (1812-1889)
Type of poem: Narrative
First published: 1855, in *Men and Women*

The Poem

The title is a direct quotation from a song of Edgar in William Shakespeare's *King Lear* (c. 1605-1606). It has traditionally been assumed that the persona is Roland, although such an assumption is unwarranted. This poem is an interior monologue, a hybrid of the soliloquy and the dramatic monologue, and the "narrator" is simply thinking aloud. The thinker-narrator is a quester of many years, something that the mythical Roland was not. Moreover, the persona does not appear to be a very young man preparing for knighthood, as the word "childe" would suggest.

"Childe Roland to the Dark Tower Came" begins *in medias res*. Since no background or explanation is given for what is happening, the reader is initially confounded. Gradually, it becomes clear that the persona is searching for the "Dark Tower" and has just asked an aged cripple for directions. Suspicious that the cripple has maliciously misdirected him even to his death, he nevertheless proceeds on the appointed path. He is exhausted by his search, "drawn out through years," and would be glad to reach an end of any kind, even if the end should mean failure or death.

At line 43, the persona turns away from the ominous cripple-guide to continue his search. Immediately on entering the gray plain, the safe road vanishes. The protagonist finds himself amid gathering darkness, entrapped in a grotesque, alien environment. Much of the remainder of the poem describes changing scenes from this landscape of nightmare, which in many ways parallels the diseased garden of *The Sensitive Plant* (1820) by Percy Bysshe Shelley, one of Robert Browning's favorite poets. From the tenth stanza intermittently to the thirty-first, the poem is, in large measure, a series of vivid verbal pictures that put one in mind of the surreal paintings of Hieronymus Bosch, Pieter Bruegel, and Salvador Dalí.

As he continues his search for the Dark Tower, the persona confronts not only the physical horrors of a stunted, deformed nature but also the memory of earlier comrades who, in their quest for the Dark Tower, came to miserable ends. His memory of "Cuthbert's reddening face" and Giles, "the soul of honor," is more harrowing to him than the "starved ignoble nature" by which he is surrounded. At last, the plain gives way to mountains, and in a final ray of sunset between two hills the Tower is revealed to the persona. His mind filled with the names of "all the lost adventurers" who had gone before him and feeling like a helpless prey for the gigantic hills, which are "Crouched like two bulls locked horn in horn in fight," the persona is dauntless and sounds his horn in defiance and triumph: *"Childe Roland to the Dark Tower Came."* On this note the poem ends—as abruptly as it began.

Forms and Devices

The poem consists of 204 lines divided into thirty-four stanzas. As is the case with many of Browning's dramatic poems, the meter keeps to a conversational (in this case thoughtful) rhythm while remaining predominantly iambic pentameter. "In the dock's harsh swarth leaves, bruised as to balk" is a telling exception. The rhyme scheme of the six-line stanzas is fixed at *abbaab*. A powerful effect of emphasis and finality is often achieved by means of the rhyme of the final line of the stanza echoing that of the third line. Stanzas 2, 9, and 16 are good examples of this sound effect.

In the hands of a lesser poet, the use of a fixed stanza form could inhibit the free flow of thought and reduce credibility by making the reader question the appropriateness of the form for the substance. Such is not the case, however, with this poem. Through the frequent use of enjambment and internal stops, Browning is able to approximate the fluidity of consciousness. In this freeing of the restraints of form, this poem is a tour de force in the manner of Browning's "My Last Duchess," in which naturalness of speech is achieved within the confines of rhymed couplets.

In *"Childe Roland to the Dark Tower Came,"* Browning makes extensive use of cacophony, simile, and metaphor. The harsh ugliness of the landscape is conveyed by means of such shrill words and phrases as "cockle," "spurge," "blotches," "chopped," "bespate," "ugh," "ragged thistle stalk," "dank/ Soil to a plash," and "ugly heights and heaps." Browning was especially comfortable using unpleasant sounds to create desired effects, as one may see in "Soliloquy of the Spanish Cloister" and "How They Brought the Good News from Ghent to Aix."

Similes in this poem are what might be called "organic." They are vital embodiments of the persona's perceptions. The persona's comparison of the "sudden little river" to a serpent indicates his sense of danger; the phrase "quiet as despair" in stanza 8 suggests his exhaustion. That he has "supp'd full with horrors" is seen in his perception of the cleft in the oak tree as "a distorted mouth that splits its rim/ Gaping at death" in stanza 26.

The various states of the persona's consciousness are similarly delineated by metaphors. As he leaves the public path in stanza 8, he sees himself as a lost farm animal: The sun "shot one grim/ Red leer to see the plan catch its estray." The doomed ship in stanza 31 and the exposed, vulnerable prey of gigantic hunters in stanza 32 are additional indications of the persona's acute fear and sense of danger.

Themes and Meanings

According to Browning, *"Childe Roland to the Dark Tower Came"* descended upon him as a sort of dream and was written in a single day, January 2, 1852. Browning denied any allegorical intentions in writing it and was characteristically reluctant to offer any help in interpreting it. Many years later, Browning said that the poem had demanded to be written and that he was aware of no particular meaning when he composed it. When a friend asked if the poem's meaning could be described as "He that endureth to the end shall be saved," Browning replied affirmatively.

"Childe Roland to the Dark Tower Came" has been the subject of numerous stud-

ies. William Clyde DeVane has found in Gerard de Lairesse's *The Art of Painting* (translated into English in 1778), a book that had a profound and permanent influence on Browning, the origin of many of the poem's images, including the cripple, the pathless field, the diseased vegetation, the river, the water rat, the claustrophobic mountains, and the malevolent sunset. The image of the tower was suggested by one he had seen several times in Italy, and he told Mrs. Orr, his early biographer, that the horse came to him from a figure in a tapestry he owned.

Because of its suggestion of allegory, this poem has been a favorite subject of interpretation of Browning societies. Some see in the poem a dark pessimism reflecting unresolved conflicts in the poet's psyche. Others see it as a study of courage. Clearly, the poem draws heavily on the conventions of quest literature, and it has many affinities with *Sir Gawain and the Green Knight* (fourteenth century). Both Browning's persona and Gawain traverse dangerous and frightening terrains in their search; they are beset with self-doubt and fear; they are forced to look deep within themselves and summon up their last vestiges of courage and will. Finally, the objects of their quests are disappointing. The Green Chapel is merely an earthen mound, and the Dark Tower is no more than a "round squat turret" made of brown stone. The tower has no intrinsic beauty or value. What is important is the quest itself. Considered in this way, *"Childe Roland to the Dark Tower Came"* is a clear statement of "success in failure," a theme Browning explored often. Making the effort to overcome obstacles to Browning is far more spiritually fulfilling than anything the world regards as success. Browning's heroes embrace life and death fully and fiercely. The "ungirt loin and the unlit lamp" are sins that loom large in Browning's writing. Timidity and a turning away from challenges have no place in Browning's strong optimism.

The persona of *"Childe Roland to the Dark Tower Came"* is a hero. His life is fulfilled in a splendid expenditure of energy; he has far more in common with Alfred, Lord Tennyson's Ulysses than with T. S. Eliot's J. Alfred Prufrock. Taken in the broad context of Browning's poetry, *"Childe Roland to the Dark Tower Came,"* despite its general ambience of gloom, affirms the ultimate value of human effort. It is a poem of unbridled optimism.

Robert G. Blake

CHILDE-HOOD

Author: Henry Vaughan (1622-1695)
Type of poem: Lyric
First published: 1655, in *Silex Scintillans*, second edition

The Poem

This religious poem by metaphysical poet Henry Vaughan idealizes childhood as a time of purity and superior insight, contrasted to the sin and misleading predilections of adulthood. The narrator wishes to recapture this innocence and piety, but he is able to see it only "as through a glass darkly," tainted by years in the corrupting adult world. Thus the poem is both hopeful and sadly nostalgic, since it describes a state of holiness that exists in this world but is unreachable to the speaker. The only hope, offered at the end through a biblical quotation, is to emulate the state when he finds it—as in the play of children or in the scriptures of the church.

The first stanza, beginning "I cannot reach it," both describes the ideal state of childhood and expresses the impossibility of an adult even fully understanding it. If the speaker could recapture that view, he states, he would surely go to heaven, as easily as children play games—in fact, through playing, instead of through suffering. "With their content too in my power" is a play on words: the content (substance) of the childlike thoughts would make him content (satisfied) on his path to heaven.

However, the next stanza makes clear how debased, even dangerous, the adult state is. The questions beginning the stanza do not ask whether adult men are corrupt, but why. Humankind's perverse nature (as expressed in Romans 7:19 and John 3:19) leads him to prefer the wolf to the lamb and dove, "hell-fire and brimstone streams" to "bright stars, and God's own beams." The more the speaker examines worldly existence, the more he values untainted childhood: "Since all that age doth teach, is ill/ Why should I not love childe-hood still?" Unlike the earlier questions, this one has an implied answer. The lessons of age are wrong, and so are the reasons they suggest for giving up childhood's spiritual state: "Those observations are but foul/ Which makes me wise to lose my soul."

However, the final stanzas not only celebrate childhood but also pine over its unreachability. It is "a short, swift span" that passes quickly; in one image, virtue is depicted as driven away, weeping like a rejected lover. The only answer, allowing one to understand this "age of mysteries," is to "live twice": to be born again in Christ, to become as a little child to enter the kingdom of heaven (John 3:3, Matthew 18:3, Luke 18:17). When the speaker states that he studies "Thee, more than ere I studied man," "thee" can mean "God's face," childhood's virtue, and perhaps the scriptures, all at once. This life is "the *narrow way*," difficult and disapproved of by the world, but one's only chance for salvation (Matthew 7:13-14, Luke 13:24).

Forms and Devices

"Childe-hood" is composed in rhymed couplets, grouped in stanzas of varying lengths. The first stanza establishes the desired goal: recapturing the innocent piety and spiritual insight of childhood. Next, a longer stanza depicts the many barriers to this goal that are created by adult nature as well as the lessons taught by the fallen world. Finally, four shorter stanzas in more traditional lengths—three quatrains and a sestet—try to balance these two and find some solution.

Metaphysical poetry such as Vaughan's is known for its intellectual complexity conveyed through striking (sometimes incongruous) imagery; in "Childe-hood," this is seen in the references to, and often the reversal of, biblical imagery. In the second stanza, men embrace thorns, not in altruistic suffering as Christ did, but because of the "ill" lessons that this world has taught them. That stanza concludes by comparing the lure of these lessons with the temptation of Christ, when Satan told Jesus to jump off a cliff so the angels could hold him up. Unlike Christ, people too often give in, their dedication to "the world" leading them to "gravely cast themselves away."

Vaughan uses imagery of light for childhood and darkness for the adult state. In the first stanza childhood is described as a bright light, "white designs" that "dazzle" the adult eye, no longer accustomed to such spiritual brilliance. In the final stanza the speaker studies "through a long night" wishing for the reward of being able to see God as clearly as the bright light of "mid-day."

More subtly, the poet reinforces the unreachable nature of childhood's spiritual state by describing it in negative terms: It is "harmless," "love without lust" and "without self-ends" (that is, unselfish). Even the light is so bright as to make description impossible. Moreover, in the final stanza, all that the speaker can see and study is "Thy edges, and thy bordering light," while yearning to see "thy Center." The buried imagery is one of a book, of which the speaker can only perceive the white margins, unable to read the text in the center of the page. The speaker, despite his disdain of the world, is already too far gone to be able to understand or describe what he glimpses, unless he is reborn through Christ.

The poem also demonstrates metaphysical wordplay, such as that on "content" in the first stanza. Similarly, "gravely cast themselves away," in the third stanza, refers both to the perils of the (misguided) seriousness of adulthood and the literal grave to which the eternal life with Christ is the only alternative. In that same stanza, "Business and weighty action all/ Checking the poor child for his play" refers to serious adults criticizing children (who are actually their spiritual betters); it also implies a metaphor of literal weight, a burden to children that inhibits their play and a contrast to the guardian flight of angels in the next stanza.

Themes and Meanings

The religious significance of the poem should be clear. After a less distinguished career in secular poetry influenced by the school of Ben Jonson (1572-1637), Vaughan experienced a religious conversion in the late 1640's and began writing poetry drawing on many sources, including the Bible and the works of religious poet

George Herbert (1593-1633). Many critics see Vaughan's works as traditional theology expressed in unconventional images. Yet Vaughan was also influenced by neo-Platonic and occult ideas, perhaps learned from his twin brother Thomas, an alchemist and mystical philosopher. The idea that children maintain some memories of eternity, lost as they settle into the material world, can be found in the Hermetic texts and the works of Jakob Boehme (1575-1624), Cornelius Agrippa (1486-1535), Plotinus (205-270 C.E.), and even Plato (c. 428-c. 348 B.C.E.).

The biblical influences are central, however, as is the influence of Herbert's poem "The Collar," about the pursuit of the soul by God. Its last two lines are: "Methought I heard one calling, *Child!*/ And I reply'd, *My Lord."* The state desired by the speaker of Vaughan's poem is both that of actual childhood and the pre-Fall innocence of Adam in Paradise. As Vaughan's contemporary, Jeremy Taylor, wrote, "In Baptism we are born again," free of Adam's sin.

Much of Vaughan's religious poetry is concerned with the relationship of the individual soul to God and, as in "Childe-hood," sadly notes the difficulty of knowing God's presence in the fallen world humans inhabit. Because of this, some critics have called Vaughan a poet of frustration or even failure, especially when his work is compared with the greater assurance—and reassurance—of religious verse such as Herbert's.

Some critics find a political dimension to Vaughan's nostalgia and rejection of the world he saw around him. In his prose, such as *The Mount of Olives* (1652), Vaughan bemoans the harsh measures of the Puritans and their effect on the church. Certainly, the effects of the Civil War in England were far-reaching, and Vaughan's unhappiness with it may have provided further motive for a wish to retreat to childhood. Still, despite the condemnation of T. S. Eliot in a 1927 review of a study of Vaughan's poetry, one cannot dismiss it as mere immature failure to face the present.

Vaughan's view of childhood, which he shared with fellow metaphysical poet Thomas Traherne, would not be explored by a major artist until it became a primary concern of the poet William Blake, especially seen in his *Songs of Innocence* (1789). Many critics believe that Vaughan influenced the Romantic view of childhood, especially in the poems of William Wordsworth.

Bernadette Lynn Bosky

CHILDHOOD

Author: Rainer Maria Rilke (1875-1926)
Type of poem: Lyric
First published: 1906, as "Kindheit," in *Das Buch der Bilder* (expanded edition); English translation collected in *Translations from the Poetry of Rainer Maria Rilke*, 1938

The Poem

"Childhood" is a poem of thirty-three lines divided into four stanzas. The title would generally lead the reader to expect a poem describing a time of innocence and joy, and while "Childhood" does this to some extent, it also describes a contrasting sad side to childhood. The poem is written in the third person, which often serves to distance the poet from the speakers or perspectives in the poem. However, in "Childhood" the unnamed, pale child and his feelings of loneliness, isolation, and sadness resemble Rilke's remembrance of his own childhood quite closely.

"Childhood" begins with a short description of school; it is shown in an entirely negative light. The atmosphere is stuffy, the hours spent there are long and boring, and the feelings the child experiences are of anxiety and loneliness. The relief and joy of dismissal contrasts sharply with the "heavy lumpish time" in school. The streets ring out with children's voices, the town squares are full of bubbling fountains, and the outdoor world has endless space and possibilities. At the end of the first stanza a small child is introduced as different from all the others. Though he shares in the exultant feeling of release from school, he walks a different path, alone and lonely.

The second stanza shows the wider world from the child's perspective, one both distanced and perceptive. He watches men and women, children in brightly colored clothes, houses, here and there a dog. This description of the physical world suddenly changes to intense emotions underlying the seemingly simple neighborhood scene; feelings of silent terror alternate with trust. The stanza ends, as they all do, with a few words or phrases expressing the child's and poet's emotional perspective of the scene or event described. After observing the peaceful setting and sensing the conflicting emotions of fear and trust, there is a feeling of senseless sadness, dreams, and horror.

The third and fourth stanzas narrow their focus to the child's more immediate environment and playtime. As daylight begins to fade, the small, pale child plays with balls, hoops, and bats, rushes around blindly playing tag, and bumps into some grown-ups in the process. Evening quietly arrives; playtime is over as the child is led home firmly by the hand. Sometimes the child plays for hours at the pond with his sailboat, trying to forget the others whose boats are prettier. The poem ends with the boy contemplating his reflection in the water, "looking up as it sank down," wondering where childhood is taking him, where it all will lead.

Forms and Devices

"Childhood" was published in *Das Buch der Bilder* (the book of pictures), a collection of poetry that reveals a transition between Rilke's earlier phase emphasizing emotion and his more mature phase aiming for more precision in imagery and style. "Childhood" demonstrates both these phases of firm structure and impressionistic emotion. Though it appears to have an irregular form, divided into uneven stanzas (ten, seven, eight, and eight lines), there is a regular meter (iambic pentameter) and rhyme scheme. With the exception of the last verse, which introduces a third rhyme in the last line of the poem, there are two rhymes in each stanza, though the pattern varies. No rhymes are carried over to the next stanza.

"Childhood" makes its strongest impact on the reader through the use of juxtapositions of sounds and images. Rilke employs both alliteration and assonance to bring his descriptions to the reader's attention. The repeating of sounds, whether consonant or vowel, makes the phrase stand out and emphasizes the image. Rilke employs alliteration more frequently, and "Childhood" is full of consonantal pairs, for example: "dumpfen Dingen" (musty things), "Welt so weit" (world so wide), "großen grauen" (great gray), "Haschens Hast." Repetitious use of vowel sounds is also used effectively, but to truly notice these, the reader must read the poem aloud: "o Traum, o Grauen" (o dream, o horror), "kleinen steifen" (small stiff), "o entgleichende Vergleiche" (elusive comparisons).

Even more than sound, the juxtaposition of contrasting images and emotions alerts the reader to the child's perception of differences in the world he sees and the sense of otherness in himself. The anxiety, depression, and ennui of the school experience is sharply contrasted with the streets, squares, and gardens coming alive with children and movement. The wonderful time of release is diminished, however, by the continued loneliness of the child. The peaceful image of men, women, and children, and their houses and dogs is diminished by the silent terror alternating with trust, and again with a sadness and horror. A joyful game of tag closes with feelings of anxiety and worry. The final stanza begins with the idyllic image of children floating their sailboats on the pond but ends with a sad call to childhood, asking what the meaning of it all is.

Themes and Meanings

"Childhood" is a picture or evocation of childhood from Rilke's collection *Das Buch der Bilder*, which he intended to resemble a picture gallery full of paintings. The interest in pictures came early to Rilke, beginning in his childhood with a love of the visual arts. He later studied art history (among other subjects) at the university, and as a young man he lived in the artists' colony at Worpswede. There he became involved with several artists, befriending the painter Paula Modersohn-Becker and marrying the sculptor Clara Westhoff. Later in Paris he also worked for the sculptor Auguste Rodin. Rilke wrote monographs on Worpswede and Rodin, and his interest in and exposure to the visual arts played a significant role in his vision of poetry. He cultivated an artist's eye, and his obsession with *Schauen* (observing), a word that appears in this and another childhood poem ("From Childhood") in this collection, dominated his vision of what a poem should convey to its reader.

The child in "Childhood" is an observer of the outer world of school and play and the inner world of his reactions and emotions. The poem contains abundant visual images. Streets of children sparkle with "lights and colors," the children's sailboats are colorful "at a grayish pond," the day's "light fades away" slowly into evening, and a child's panoramic view can "see into it all from far away." Indeed, the poem's last image is a child staring at his own reflection as he ponders the meaning of childhood. As painters employ chiaroscuro, an arrangement of light and dark elements, so does Rilke juxtapose light and dark images and emotions to produce a dramatic effect. The bubbling fountains, colorful children, and lively streets contrast sharply with the heaviness and stuffiness of school. The ecstasy of freedom is followed by loneliness, silent terror "all at once replaced by total trust," the game of tag with anxiety. Rilke's picture of childhood is not one-dimensional; it presents multiple shades of experience and feeling.

A recurring image of "Childhood" and other poems is that of *Einsamkeit*, which can be translated as both aloneness and loneliness. In other poems in this collection, Rilke writes of a "child still and alone" ("From Childhood") and of being "so entirely alone" ("Vorgefühl" [foreboding]). He titled two of the poems "Einsamkeit" and "Der Einsame" (the solitary one or lonely one). In "Childhood" the feeling of otherness, aloneness, or loneliness is repeated throughout. Although literature is not necessarily biography or autobiography, in Rilke's case much of his work reflects his personal experience. Some background to Rilke's childhood can provide insight into the emphasis on the child's feeling of isolation. Rilke was the only child of a mother who had wanted a daughter. He was dressed as a girl and treated as a daughter during the early years of his life. His father tried to counterbalance the influence of his mother by sending the boy to military school. The harsh discipline and other boys' hostility toward him made a lasting impression. The atmosphere of the school was alien to his character, and he felt his lack of inclusion keenly. It was this and the loneliness he faced because of the boys' shunning that turned him to writing. Rilke mentioned several times his feeling that he had been deprived of a happy childhood, and in his poetry he tried to redeem some image of a happier childhood for himself. "Childhood" does indeed contain some idyllic scenes of a carefree childhood, but the lurking shadows of sadness, anxiety, and otherness continually peer through the lighter images of play.

Shoshanah Dietz

CHILDREN IN EXILE

Author: James Fenton (1949-   )
Type of poem: Narrative
First published: 1982, in *The Memory of War: Poems, 1968-1982*

The Poem

"Children in Exile" is written in forty-nine stanzas of four lines each, an extra line space being inserted in the last stanza. The poem begins with a direct quote from a child in exile, who states one of the keynotes of the poem, that what one is is less important than what one does. Readers then are made aware of the general subject of the poem—that it involves children from Cambodia in exile in a strange country (readers later learn that this is Italy) in roughly the late 1970's. Though still children, the exiles "have learnt much." Far from being innocents, they have experienced ordeals that most of the adults who take care of them cannot even begin to imagine. They have escaped from the mass killings perpetrated by the Cambodian regime of Pol Pot, in power from 1975 to 1979, which was preceded by a civil war (in which the United States intervened) in which many were also killed and wounded. The children have physically escaped from their ordeal, but psychologically they are still wounded, and their dreams are troubled.

The "I" of the poem, a friendly Western adult observer, sees that the children are still in pain from their experiences. He muses on the tragic situation; these children were punished not for their own actions but because they happened to be children of people who were political opponents of the regime or who were otherwise persecuted. The children also, in a way, symbolize the entire Cambodian nation, which was so rent by civil conflict and government-sponsored killings that its own survival seemed in doubt. The children in exile are now free, but they do not realize their own freedom. The fear from their old experiences still troubles them, even in safe, touristy locales such as the Leaning Tower of Pisa, where a child becomes afraid even though there are only friends around who want him to have fun. Yet amid the Italian spring the children's suffering begins to heal, and they evince curiosity about the landscape and people that surround them. Duschko the dog and the doves in the hayloft are part of the harmony of the landscape, which welcomes and accommodates the children.

Surrounded by love instead of fear, the children hurry to catch up on the education they have missed in their native land and to assimilate the culture of the West. One of the children has a twin sister who had escaped to America and has given birth to a baby. The children see America as the promised land; the narrator, on the other hand, deems the United States to be partially guilty of Cambodia's ruin. Regardless of whether they find the happiness they associate with America in America itself or in Europe, the children will flourish in the future. The narrator wishes them well and wishes them the freedom to dream of whatever future they want. Though the children are in exile from their homeland, they have found freedom and safety at last.

Forms and Devices

The most striking aspect of "Children in Exile" is that it is at once a serious political poem and an old-style, melodic ballad. Its stanzas are quatrains (four lines each), of which the second and fourth line rhyme. This form allows tremendous clarity, but it also allows breeziness and wit. Most of all, it connotes the poet's desire to tell a story. Given the subject of the poem, this is by no means an inevitable choice: The poem could be an elegy for the dead in Cambodia, for example, or a lament for the psychological trauma sustained by the children. However, the ballad form structures the poem as the story of the children's recovery in exile. It provides a kind of reassurance to readers, shielding them from the horrors of war much as the lush Italian landscape begins to shelter the children in the poem.

Fenton often plays havoc with the reader's expectations, as with the long digression about Duschko the dog and the doves in the hayloft, which not only provides a lighthearted, almost nonsense element that alleviates the poem's seriousness but also lulls the reader into accepting the children's safety and happiness, rather than their suffering, as a given. There is an exuberance about the poem that gives it an air of celebration despite its stern witness to the horrors of the Cambodian killings that have forced the children so far from home.

There is also a mock-epic aspect to the poem, as when Duschko the dog goes "mad" and eats "all those chickens," mimicking in a far more minor key the killings in Cambodia. The chickens are animals, not people, and in this mini-play a kind of restitution unfolds that is not admitted in the outer world. The dog, first suspicious of the children, comes to share his home with them and to love them. Within the fictive world of the poem, the brutal laws of external reality are softened and inverted.

Fenton's style is urbane and sophisticated, yet the poem is understandable to an educated reader after reading it once or twice. The poem's occasional nonsensical tinge may distract those who are looking for a traditional sort of political poem that seeks to rally people to a cause. For instance, the last line, with the children dreaming "Of Jesus, America, maths, Lego, music and dance," seems curiously anticlimactic; it is not a peroration that will whip a crowd into a frenzy. Its very modesty, the way it looks into the hearts of the children and sees what is there rather than imposing a grandiose adult agenda, is at the heart of the poem's winning combination of modesty and eloquence.

Themes and Meanings

When *The Memory of War* (1982), the volume including "Children in Exile," first appeared in Britain, many readers were immediately reminded of the 1930's political poetry of W. H. Auden. (Fenton makes this debt clear in "Children in Exile" by citing Auden's 1962 prose book *The Dyer's Hand* in the latter portion of the poem.) Fenton, like Auden in the 1930's, was a young poet writing about conflicts in distant countries and making them immediate for the British reader, but there are certainly differences between them. Auden often implied that he was essentially an apolitical poet whom the onslaught of fascism in the Spanish Civil War and after had forced into a partisan position. Fenton, on the other hand, had gone to Vietnam and Cambodia as a working journalist, freelancing for several newspapers and magazines. Among other things, he was a witness to the fall of Saigon to the Communist North Vietnamese in 1975. This event came only days after the Communist takeover in Cambodia that occasioned the suffering from which the Cambodian children in the poem are fleeing.

Although Fenton displays political sympathies of a center-left sort in the poem (as evinced by his giving the United States partial blame for the problems of Cambodia after 1975, a position with which some on the right would disagree), the poem is not a politically committed poem in the manner of Auden's "Spain" (1937). The poem's most explicit sympathies are noncontroversial; they are for civilization and common human decency. These values are made newly cogent by the suffering from which the children have escaped.

The poem should be read at least twice, once to comprehend its surface meaning and again to appreciate the considerable feeling that Fenton puts into the poem, as well as the way he uses whimsy and slight-of-hand to make the children's experience both special to them and also somehow representative. The setting of the Italian landscape, for instance, might be bypassed on the first reading in order to focus on the agony and redemption of the children, yet Fenton's laid-back evocation of this landscape is a crucial prerequisite of the poem's sense of earned affirmation.

The poet, insofar as he projects himself in the poem, is successful at empathizing with the children yet distancing himself from them. One recognizes that he sees the children's dreams of Jesus and America as naïve, yet he does not mock these ideals or the childlike innocence, marred by untold suffering yet still resilient, that inspires them.

Despite his clear aspirations to emulate Auden, Fenton's techniques are also reminiscent of those used by his contemporaries, particularly Craig Raine, who in *A Martian Sends a Postcard Home* (1979) applied a metaphorical perspective to ordinary phenomena, and Andrew Motion, who in *Secret Narratives* (1983) related skewed verse-tales similar to Fenton's. Fenton's imaginativeness helps ballast his poem's political wisdom. The directly committed Auden was compelled to repudiate "Spain" within five years once his views had changed, but the humanity and compassion of Fenton's poem persist decades after the events they describe.

Nicholas Birns

THE CHILDREN OF THE NIGHT

Author: Edwin Arlington Robinson (1869-1935)
Type of poem: Book of poems
First published: 1897

The Poems

At its publication in 1897, Edwin Arlington Robinson's *The Children of the Night* consisted of eighty-seven poems, forty-four of which had appeared in *The Torrent and the Night Before*, a pamphlet printed at the author's own expense the previous year. In addition, the new volume contained another forty-three poems. When the author incorporated *The Children of the Night* into later collections of his poetry he made some alterations, a situation that can be very confusing for readers. For example, some poems were eliminated altogether, and because of deletions the "Octaves" in the collections do not bear the same numbers that they did in the 1897 book. Nevertheless, while scholars find both the originals and revisions of interest, most students will find the later versions of *The Children of the Night* as useful for study as the original.

Robinson believed that he would be remembered primarily for his thirteen long narrative poems, beginning with *Merlin* (1917) and including *Tristram* (1927), which not only won for him a Pulitzer Prize but also was his only commercial success. Ironically, however, it is his short poems, many of them contained in *The Children of the Night*, on which Robinson's literary reputation now depends.

The poems in this collection fall into several different categories. Some of them are addressed to people who actually lived. For example, "Zola" pays tribute to the French novelist Émile Zola for his dedication to truth, while "Verlaine" is a defense of the French poet Paul Verlaine, who is believed to have influenced some of Robinson's works, notably "Luke Havergal." Other poems are about fictional characters from "Tilbury Town," which represents Gardiner, Maine, where Robinson spent most of his early years. Although all of them are relatively short, crisp in style, and ironic in tone, the Tilbury Town poems vary in subject matter and in pattern.

"John Evereldown," for instance, is written as a dialogue. In the first stanza an unnamed person asks John Evereldown where he is going so late at night. In the second Evereldown replies that he is on his way to Tilbury Town but is taking an indirect route through the woods so that no one can see him. Now even more puzzled, the interrogator urges Evereldown to come in and warm himself by the fire rather than continuing on his journey. In the fourth and final stanza Evereldown admits that he is drawn into the cold, dark night because in Tilbury Town he may find a woman to satisfy his obsessive lust.

"Luke Havergal" is one of the most obscure poems in the collection. The single speaker is not identified, except as a voice from the grave or perhaps from Havergal's own subconscious. This spirit speaks of the "hell" through which Havergal is passing as somehow related to a lost "paradise." It is evident that death has taken the woman

Havergal loved, but since she is referred to in the third person, obviously it is not she who is addressing him. When the spirit urges him to "Go to the western gate," it is not clear whether Havergal is to transcend his grief and move on, trusting that he will meet his lost love in the next world, or whether he is being urged to pass through the gate of death immediately—to commit suicide.

While some Tilbury Town poems, such as these, are essentially static descriptions of emotional states, others are like short stories, moving toward a dramatic conclusion. The first twelve lines of "Richard Cory" could well be just another character sketch. Speaking in a single voice, the ordinary people of Tilbury Town describe the wealthy and elegant Cory, whom they admit they envied, noting his unfailing courtesy to those below him. The fourth stanza begins with the townspeople summing up their dull and desperate lives, but in the last two lines Richard Cory once again becomes the focal point of the poem. Robinson now sets the stage ("one calm summer night") and bluntly describes Cory's suicide. It is now clear why the townspeople were speaking of Cory in the past tense. It is also evident that, in the light of this ending, what they said must be reinterpreted. Moreover, the earlier part of the poem, which seemed static, was in fact preparing for the final dramatic action.

The Children of the Night also contains a number of poems in which, instead of voicing his opinions obliquely, the writer addresses his readers directly. In "Ballade by the Fire," Robinson is sitting by the fire, smoking, while his imagination creates ghostly figures from the past. In the second stanza, he wonders what the future may be. In the third stanza, however, the mood changes. Suddenly recognizing that death could well be close at hand, he urges himself into action. The envoy reflects this new resolution. Since everyone knows that life "is the game that must be played," people should "live and laugh" rather than be depressed by the "phantoms" with which everyone lives.

Forms and Devices

In *Children of the Night* Robinson demonstrates his knowledge of his craft and his poetic skill by utilizing a number of traditional forms. "Three Quatrains," "Two Quatrains," and "Richard Cory," for example, consist of Sicilian quatrains; the tetrameter poem "Two Men" is written in long measure, or long hymnal measure; and for "Boston" Robinson uses two Italian quatrains, shaped into an envelope stanza. The collection also includes an ode, "The Chorus of Old Men in Aegeus," and though "John Evereldown" does not have the most common ballad format, its question-answer pattern and its incremental repetition recall such well-known ballads as "Lord Randal" and "The Three Ravens."

Robinson is also adept in the most exacting French forms. "Ballade by the Fire" and "Ballade of Broken Flutes" meet the strict requirements of the *ballade*, including the refrain at the end of each stanza, the envoy, the limitation on the number of rhymes, and the rhyme pattern itself. Another difficult French form that Robinson handles superbly is the *villanelle*, as seen in "Villanelle of Change" and "The House on the Hill."

The poetic patterns that appear most frequently in *The Children of the Night*, however, are the Petrarchan sonnet and the blank verse octave. The poet uses the sonnet for a wide variety of poems. It is highly effective in the philosophical "Credo," in which the statement of despair in the octave is answered in the sestet by the proclamation that, despite the darkness all around him, the speaker can "feel the coming glory of the Light." Just as impressive are the Petrarchan sonnets that describe the people of Tilbury Town, often (as in "Cliff Klingenhagen") narrating a story to do so. In the octave of that poem, the speaker sets up a mystery. After their dinner together one evening, Cliff, the host, downs a glass of wormwood, while offering his guest the usual wine. In the sestet, Cliff smilingly refuses to explain, and all the speaker can say is that Cliff seems to be amazingly happy. It is left to the reader to guess the significance of Cliff's action and of the speaker's comment. Still another poem that illustrates Robinson's skill with the Petrarchan sonnet is "Fleming Helphenstine." Here, though it begins with a suggestion of distrust, the octave proceeds to establish Fleming as an open sort of man, who talks as easily as if he has known the narrator for a long time and, in fact, is an intimate of his. In the sestet, there is a dramatic reversal. The two men look closely at each other, and something happens that makes both of them "cringe and wince." Then the stranger apologizes and exits, both from the scene and from the narrator's life. Again in this poem, Robinson has used the Petrarchan sonnet with its two-part structure for high dramatic effect.

The octaves in the collection are not Robinson's most memorable poems, though they do provide some insight into his thinking at the time they were written. In the octave that starts "We thrill too strangely at the master's touch," for instance, the poet accuses human beings of backing off from the unhappy events which are part of life, forgetting that God has his own plans for human beings. The octave beginning "Tumultuously void of a clean scheme" is not quite as abstract as the previous one and, indeed, is built on an interesting image—humanity as a great "crazy" legion, controlled only by instinct and "Ignorance" and led "by drunk trumpeters." However, again, it is not quite effective. For some reason, Robinson's octaves lack the force of his other poems, even of those which, like the sonnets "Dear Friends" and "Credo," have the same sort of abstract subject matter. It may be that when he used traditional forms such as the sonnet, in which the octave establishing the topic or the situation is followed by a sestet with some kind of reversal or at least a resolution, Robinson was prevented from rambling toward an inconclusive conclusion, as he so often does in these octaves. At any rate, the poet evidently sensed that the blank verse octave was not effective. After *The Children of the Night*, Robinson wrote no more poems in that form.

It is unfortunate that so fine a craftsman as Robinson began publishing his work just when the fashions in poetry were changing. Through no fault of his own, Robinson was largely eclipsed by writers who were considered more modern, such as the Imagists. However, Robinson never abandoned traditional forms. While everyone else seemed to be writing free verse, he worked on perfecting blank verse in his long narrative poems. Ironically, those later works, which Robinson believed were his highest achievement, are now read far less often than his short poems, especially those that tell of Tilbury Town and its residents. At least, in one way, the changing styles have worked to his benefit, for now that the free verse flurry is over and some writers have turned once again to traditional forms, Robinson's skill can be fully appreciated.

Themes and Meanings

It is particularly ironic that so many critics and scholars classified Robinson as an old-fashioned writer because he clung to traditional forms, when in subject matter he was as unconventional as any of his contemporaries. There is not a trace of nineteenth century sentimentalism in Robinson's poetry. He does not believe that in this world God makes everything right. However, though they are pitiable, human beings are so blind, so intent on rejecting divine direction, that one can hardly blame God for permitting them to suffer. Nevertheless, Robinson believes that beyond the darkness there is light, and once they pass beyond their suffering, human beings can perceive God's plan.

Many of the poems in *The Children of the Night* deal with misery, failure, and death. Admittedly, some of Robinson's characters, such as the materialists in the octave beginning "To me the groaning of world-worshippers," do not realize that their lives are empty. The miser Aaron Stark, who represents the very worst in human nature, is actually pleased with his reputation for heartlessness; the pity of a tenderhearted soul, who recognizes his friendlessness, merely provides Stark with an excuse for laughter. However, not all of the prosperous are so blind as to be contented with their condition in life. Some, like the glittering Richard Cory, find that wealth and social status are not enough to bring happiness.

A nineteenth century sentimentalist might have had his characters find fulfillment in romantic love. However, Robinson is a twentieth century realist. Often, he knows, what others call love is merely a sexual obsession, like that which drives John Evereldown. In fact, love is so often both obsessive and possessive that it seems to make disaster inevitable. The husband in "The Story of the Ashes and the Flame," even though his wife has first been unfaithful and then deserted him, loves her so much that he retreats from life in order to dream of her return. Similarly, when the beloved one dies, as in "Luke Havergal," "Amaryllis," and "Reuben Bright," the person left behind is so grief stricken that his own life virtually ends. One might take refuge in friendship, but Robinson shows it, too, as imperfect. In "An Old Story," the speaker recognizes in himself the human depravity which blights all relationships. Perversely, the more his friend demonstrated his loyalty, thereby earning the praise of others, the more violently the speaker disliked him. Now that the friend is dead, however, he realizes how much he has lost. The sad fact is that none of Robinson's characters really know one another. Thus in the poem "On the Night of a Friend's Wedding," the poet is surrounded by "Good friends" but is well aware that what they praise in him is a "mirage" that may "crumble out of sight" at any moment.

Nevertheless, Robinson's view of life is not unrelievedly pessimistic. Though the house described in "The House on the Hill" reeks of "ruin and decay" and Tilbury Town is filled with repressed people and broken dreams (like those of "The Clerks") one does not have to stay there. In "Boston," Robinson speaks of a town that has both "something new and fierce" and a "charmed antiquity." Such places are filled with the true aristocrats, who are dedicated to the search for truth and may, like Zola, in discovering it find also "the divine heart of man." In "Dear Friends," Robinson makes it clear that he holds his pursuit of art far more glorious than others' pursuit of wealth.

Robinson does not pin all his hopes for humanity either on reason or on creativity. His sympathy for even the most desperate souls in Tilbury Town, such as John Evereldown, lost in lust, and Reuben Bright, sunk in grief and despair, is intensified by his faith in God. The poet seems to believe that a dark night of the soul may be essential to a human being's development. In the octave "We thrill too strangely at the master's touch," he suggests that by enduring misery, by accepting "the splendid shame of uncreated failure," one may rise to a new level of life and bask in the light of eternity. This is the point of "The Torrent." In this poem Robinson describes a natural paradise, which will be destroyed by "hard men" with "screaming saws." However, the poem does not end there. Moments of "gladness" culminate in true joy; finally the speaker welcomes the destructive saws, because he knows that loss can clear the way for something better, failures can be "steps to the great place where trees and torrents go." In such passages Robinson makes it clear that, while a realist and a modernist, he is no pessimist but a man strongly influenced by the Transcendentalism of Ralph Waldo Emerson. It is significant that in "L'Envoi," the final poem in *The Children of the Light*, Robinson speaks of "transcendent music," which comes from no human source but directly from the hand of God. Thus the collection ends on a hopeful note, which is the more persuasive because the poet has not ignored either the pervasiveness of human unhappiness or the inevitability of death.

Rosemary M. Canfield Reisman

THE CHIMES OF NEVERWHERE

Author: Les A. Murray (1938-   )
Type of poem: Meditation
First published: 1987, in *The Daylight Moon*

The Poem

While Les Murray is much admired for his realistic descriptions of life in his native Australia, his poetry also reflects the broader literary heritage common to all English-speaking peoples. It may not be far-fetched to wonder whether "The Chimes of Neverwhere" was inspired by the famous poem by the English writer Thomas Gray, "Elegy Written in a Country Church-yard" (1751), in which Gray wonders how history would have been different if those buried around him had lived somewhere other than in their obscure, isolated village. "The Chimes of Neverwhere," too, deals with what did not happen, but in a very different manner.

Murray's poem is composed of eight four-line stanzas. In the first, italicized stanza, Murray asks, *"How many times did the Church prevent war?"* He then answers himself by pointing out that one cannot count events which did not occur. These nonhistorical wars, he then suggests, live in a place called "Neverwhere," where they are *"Treasures of the Devil."* In the second stanza, the poet explains that Neverwhere contains everything that did not happen or has been lost.

In the five stanzas that follow, Murray lists examples. In Neverwhere are the lost buildings, those destroyed after the German leader Adolf Hitler started World War II. There are also events that never happened. There was never a second chance for the Manchu dynasty in China or a written language for the Picts. Cigars were not imported into England early enough for either James I or James II to smoke one of them. The history of Armenia has long been a sad story of oppression, starvation, and misery. As for Peter and Heloise Abelard, they had only one child, for her parents had Peter castrated, and the lovers spent the rest of their days apart.

Murray continues with his odd assortment. There is an anonymous girl with whom the reader might have had an affair but did not, along with poems never written, inventions never finished. The Australians never gave anybody a title, nor did they have to fight in a Third World War.

In the sixth and seventh stanzas, Murray moves to the subject of religion. Neverwhere, he says, contains "half the works of sainthood," for divine grace has saved many of those threatened with martyrdom. Because of Christ's sacrifice, the poet adds, much evil that would otherwise have found its way to the earth will remain in Neverwhere.

The final stanza is again italicized, and it starts with a variation of the poem's opening question. This time, however, instead of answering the question, Murray indicates that a reply is unnecessary. It is enough to know that the Church, the earthly manifestation of God's grace, is always attempting to act for the benefit of humanity on this earth. Sometimes it does not succeed, and therefore in Neverwhere there is peace that never came to be, but then, Murray muses, such goodness is needed where there are also so many unborn children, a place which, by and large, is the home of the Devil.

Forms and Devices

"The Chimes of Neverwhere" is unlike many of Murray's poems in that it is more theoretical than realistic. However, while it lacks the detailed descriptions of the Australian landscape and the stories of rural life for which Murray is so much admired, it is consistent with Murray's poetic theory and with his other works in that it is clearly directed not toward an elite audience but to the average reader. Murray's poetical populism is evident even in his choice of words. Words of one and two syllables dominate the poem; in fact, several lines have no multisyllable words at all—for example, "is hard to place as near or far" and "in which I and boys my age were killed." Even the longer words are familiar: "happiness," "waterbed," "pointlessly," "enslavements," "sacrifice."

In his effort to be reader-friendly, Murray devotes his second stanza to explaining just what he means by Neverwhere. Moreover, even his allusions are either common knowledge or easy to trace. The girl with the come-hither look, for example, needs no annotation, nor do poems, inventions, soldiers, saints, or Christian concepts such as divine grace. Admittedly, outsiders might not know that the "Third AIF" was meant to remind one of the Second Australian Imperial Force that fought in World War II or that, unlike the mother country, Australia has no hereditary hierarchy. However, other than those rather localized references, there are only six allusions, all in the third stanza, that might require a glance into an encyclopedia.

Despite the fact that "The Chimes of Neverwhere" often alludes either to the possibility or to the reality of human suffering, the tone is generally good-natured, even lighthearted, in part because of the whimsical nature of the underlying idea, in part because of the poet's skillful use of meter and rhyme. In lines such as "and the mornings you might have woke to her" and "in which I and boys my age were killed," anapests speed up the tempo; if in the second instance a rollicking rhythm seems inappropriate, one must remember that the poet is celebrating the prevention of war.

The poem also jingles with a profusion of rhymes. Sometimes they are exact, placed at the end of a line, as "Neverwhere"/"there"/"despair"; "far"/"cigar"/"are"; and "took"/"look"/"book." They can also occur at the ends of alternate lines. More often, though, either conventional rhymes or near rhymes are sprinkled into the poem just often enough to keep the sound alive. Thus, as in a musical composition, one can hear not only "her" and "were" but also slight variations, such as "war"/"occur"/ "Neverwhere"/"near"/"far"/"there." These sounds are found just in the first two stanzas of the poem. As a result of this intricate patterning of meter and sound effects, "The Chimes of Neverwhere" has a lilting quality that is perfectly in tune with the poet's thematic intentions.

Themes and Meanings

Although Murray writes in a simple and direct fashion, hoping thus to express his ideas to a wider audience, he never descends to sentimentality or suggests that there are simple solutions to life's problems. In "The Chimes of Neverwhere," the poet does not ignore either the fact of suffering or the existence of evil. Individuals suffer from the cruelty of others, as Abelard did; nations are oppressed, as Armenia was; and one tyrant like Hitler can bring about a terrible, destructive war. There is always the possibility of evil; not once, but twice, the poet places the Devil in the country of what could have happened, but did not.

If one is to rejoice that such evils did not come to pass, one must lament the good that remains in Neverwhere, unrealized. Like Gray, who wondered if a poet who could have been as great as John Milton lay in that quiet churchyard, his epic of sin and salvation never written for the illumination of humankind, Murray believes that unfulfilled potentialities are to be lamented. They may even be considered a passive evil. No one's life was made easier by poems that were not "quite" finished or by inventions that were blocked from reaching the market. Similarly, though one cannot know that the love affair suggested in the fourth stanza would have turned out well or that the birth of children would make someone's life better, the fact that these possibilities are marooned means that good never had a chance. More specifically, divine grace did not have a chance to operate.

That the grace of God is the real subject of "The Chimes of Neverwhere" becomes clear in the last three stanzas of the poem. Because of Christ's sacrifice for the sins of the whole world, saints have been saved from martyrdom, and "billions" of human beings from agonizing death. The poet concludes by suggesting a new dimension to the question he posed at the beginning of the poem. At that point, one might assume that by "Church" Murray meant Roman Catholicism and that he was about to examine the peacemaking efforts of that body. At the end of "The Chimes of Neverwhere," however, it is evident that the word has a very different meaning. The Church, or Christianity, has brought peace not by its temporal efforts but by merely existing, thus enabling individuals to avail themselves of the grace bought by Christ's sacrifice. Finally, Murray returns to his whimsical construct. If there are failures of the Church in Neverwhere, at least those attempts at good can perhaps shield the children, unborn because of human evil, who are doomed to spend eternity in the presence of the Devil.

Rosemary M. Canfield Reisman

THE CHIMNEY SWEEPER

Author: William Blake (1757-1827)
Type of poem: Lyric
First published: 1789, in *Songs of Innocence*

The Poem

"The Chimney Sweeper," a poem of six quatrains, accompanied by William Blake's illustration, appeared in *Songs of Innocence* in 1789, the year of the outbreak of the French Revolution, and expresses Blake's revolutionary fervor. It exposes the appalling conditions of the boys known as climbing boys, whose lot had been brought to public attention but had been only marginally improved by the 1788 Chimney Sweepers' Act. Blake published a companion poem in *Songs of Innocence and of Experience* in 1794.

The speaker is a young chimney sweeper, presumably six or seven years old, and the style is appropriately simple. Much of the imaginative power of the poem comes from the tension between the child's naïveté and the subtlety of Blake's own vision.

In the first stanza, the sweeper recounts how he came to this way of life. His mother—always in Blake's work the warm, nurturing parent—having died, he was sold as an apprentice by his father, the stern figure of authority. His present life revolves around working, calling through the streets for more work, and at the end of the day sleeping in soot, a realistic detail since the boys did indeed make their beds on bags of the soot they had swept from chimneys.

The second stanza introduces Tom Dacre, who comes to join the workers and is initiated into his new life by a haircut. As Tom cries when his head is shaved, the speaker comforts him with the thought that if his hair is cut it cannot be spoiled by the soot. The consolation is, from any adult point of view, totally inadequate, but for Tom it is effective. He falls asleep and dreams happily.

The next three stanzas give the substance of the dream. Tom dreams that thousands of sweepers locked in coffins are released by an angel. Suddenly, they find themselves in a pastoral landscape, where, freed from their burdens, they bathe in a river and then rise up to the clouds. There, the angel tells Tom, "if he'd be a good boy,/ He'd have God for his father & never want joy." The dream is an obvious instance of wish fulfillment, and its pathos rests on the fact that while it reveals the child's longing to escape, the opening and closing of the poem make it clear that his only ways of escape are dreams and death.

The last quatrain opens with a brutal contrast. Having dreamed of playing in the sun, Tom awakes, and the sweepers begin their day's work, a day to be spent in the total darkness of the cramped chimneys. Yet, restored by his dream, Tom is happy, and the poem ends with the pious moral, akin to the angel's speech, "So if all do their duty, they need not fear harm."

Forms and Devices

The poem is built around a series of powerful, closely related contrasts. The first, introduced in the second line, is that of bondage and freedom, for the child is literally sold into a state of both servitude and imprisonment within the chimneys. This contrast is reinforced by the parallel contrast between black and white. Covered in soot, the sweepers are habitually black; Tom's white hair is cut off, and the whiteness of his skin is only regained in the dream, when he, along with the other boys, is able to wash in the river. The color contrast suggests the condition of the African slave, whose plight Blake, an ardent supporter of abolition, describes in "The Little Black Boy." Like that little boy, the blackened chimney sweeper suffers the injustice of a white society that puts commercial values before moral ones and treats him as an outcast from the human condition.

A second group of contrasts juxtaposes work and play, sorrow and joy, tears and laughter. In the streets, the sweeper can only call, "weep weep," and Tom cries when his head is shaved, but in the dream, the scene that is the subject of Blake's illustration, the boys leap, laugh, and play.

The final antithesis is that between death and life, coldness and warmth, darkness and light. The sweepers endure a death-in-life, the literal cold and dark of their days matched by their deprivation and the cold indifference of society. In Tom's dream, however, the washing in the river assumes the significance of a baptism into a better life and counters the ritual head shaving of the entry into prison. The child glimpses a new heaven and a new Earth before he returns to the fallen world.

From these contrasts, certain images acquire symbolic significance. The bags, abandoned in the dream and picked up again with the brushes the next morning, suggest the terrible burden of the child's life; the soot indicates the corruption of a society that uses and abuses him; and the coffins represent both the chimneys in which he works and the actual death to which he will soon come. In contrast, the sun, river, and plain express the joys that should be natural to childhood. Yet, even symbols associated with happiness intensify the harsh facts of existence. The bright key recalls imprisonment; the harmony of the leaping boys emphasizes their isolation in the chimneys; and the lamb, whose curling fleece Tom's hair resembles, is often, as is the sweeper, a helpless victim.

These emotionally charged contrasts and images underscore the ironic understatement. The speaker describes his life plainly, indulging in neither denunciation nor sentimentality. The facts speak for themselves, however, forcefully opposing the three pieces of comfort in the poem, the first provided by the speaker for Tom, the second provided by the angel, and the third offered by the speaker as a final moral. When God the Father, like the father on earth, seems to have turned His face from the child, injunctions for Tom to be good and to do his duty betoken a bitter irony.

Themes and Meanings

While presenting the nonjudgmental viewpoint of the child, Blake makes a passionate indictment of a society that exploits the weak and at the same time hypocritically uses moral platitudes about duty and goodness to further its selfish interests. Moreover, the reader is made aware of his own complicity in social evil when the sweeper addresses him directly with the words "your chimneys I sweep."

Yet, the poem is more than social criticism. In *Songs of Innocence and of Experience*, Blake contrasts the two states of being. Usually the condition of childhood, innocence is that state in which evil is not known; it is characterized by joy and love, is normally associated with the peaceful harmony of a pastoral background, and is often guarded by the presence of the good mother. Experience, on the other hand, brings awareness of evil; it is accompanied by feelings of outrage and hatred; and it finds its appropriate setting in the city. In Blake's philosophy, passage through experience is necessary before entrance into a final state of vision, a higher innocence in which joy is regained but transformed by deeper spiritual awareness.

Although most poems in *Songs of Innocence* directly reflect the happiness of innocence, a few—notably, "The Chimney Sweeper," "Holy Thursday," and "The Little Black Boy"—place innocent children in a world of experience. Surrounded by evil, these children still retain their innocence, an innocence marked not so much by their own freedom from guilt as by their unawareness of the guilt of others.

The chimney sweeper is robbed of everything that should be the accompaniment of innocence. Yet, he bears no ill will, accepting without question both his lot and the moral clichés of a corrupt adult world. He transcends circumstances and in a sense re-creates his world. Deprived of his own mother, he becomes Tom's protector as he soothes the sobbing child. Thus comforted, Tom enjoys, in a dream, the light, laughter, and freedom denied him in real life. Significantly, the joy does not dissipate with the start of the day's work, and Tom, secure in his innocence, remains "happy & warm."

The last line, "So if all do their duty, they need not fear harm," is then a paradox. On the level of social protest, the moral is deliberately inadequate and ironic. Yet, it also asserts a fundamental truth, since duty implies not the obligation to climb the chimneys or to acquiesce in the social pattern but the need to retain as long as possible an innocence that allows its possessor to triumph over the restrictions of the material world.

"The Chimney Sweeper" juxtaposes two points of view: that of the poet, who attacks society by indirections, and that of the sweeper, who presents directly the mode of perception characteristic of innocence. The interplay of the two gives the poem its unique depth and complexity.

Muriel Mellown

CHRISTABEL

Author: Samuel Taylor Coleridge (1772-1834)
Type of poem: Narrative
First published: 1816

The Poem

   Christabel is a long narrative poem, most of which is written in tetrameter couplets. As Samuel Taylor Coleridge himself pointed out in the original preface to the work, although the meter is standard, the number of syllables is somewhat irregular, varying from seven to twelve. The simple title emphasizes the fact that the story told by the poet is indeed Christabel's story, the story of her struggle against possession by a demonic force.

   From the scenic description in part 2 of *Christabel*, critics have deduced that the geographical setting Coleridge chose for his poem was the Lake District of England, where he had lived for some time near his friend and fellow poet William Wordsworth. The historical setting is the Middle Ages and, appropriately, the physical milieu is the castle of a baron, Sir Leoline.

   Christabel begins in the forest outside the castle. Although it is a chilly night in early spring, the protagonist, Christabel, has sought the solitude of the woods to pray for her absent lover. Suddenly a mysterious lady emerges from the darkness. After introducing herself as "Geraldine," she says that she was abducted from her own home by five knights, who deposited her in the woods but will return for her. Taking pity upon Geraldine, Christabel helps her into the castle, ignoring such warnings of evil as the lady's seeming inability to walk across the threshold, which had been blessed against evil spirits, and the growls of the usually good-natured old mastiff as the guest passes.

   When they reach her room, Christabel speaks of her dead mother, who she believes still guards her from evil. The statement calls forth a strange, defiant exclamation from Geraldine, but Christabel attributes it to her guest's frightening experience, and the two settle down to sleep. While she holds the sleeping Christabel in her arms, Geraldine puts a spell on her, so that although she will be able to recognize evil, Christabel will not be able to speak about it.

   When Christabel awakens the next morning, she has a confused sense of having sinned, perhaps in a dream. It is difficult for her to believe that Geraldine is evil, however, especially after Sir Leoline discovers that their guest is the daughter of his former friend, Lord Roland de Vaux of Tryermaine, from whom he has long been estranged. Resolving to heal the breach between them, Lord Roland commands the bard Bracy to take word to Lord Roland that his daughter is safe.

   Bracy asks for a day's grace, so that he can expel from the woods the evil which he senses is lurking there. He tells the Baron of a troubling dream, in which he saw a snake devour a dove. Unfortunately, Sir Leoline assumes that the dove is not Christabel but Geraldine. When Christabel begs him to expel the guest, he accuses her of jealousy and, in a fury, sends Bracy on his mission. The poem ends with a few lines about the relationship between a father and a child.

Although Coleridge published the poem unfinished, he left an account of his intentions for two or three more parts, which would bring it to a conclusion. Geraldine would vanish, to reappear in the guise of Christabel's lover, and Sir Leoline would insist on proceeding with a wedding. The real lover would appear just in time and prove his identity. The evil spirit would disappear forever and all would end happily.

Forms and Devices

In the late eighteenth century, the Middle Ages had once again become fashionable. Readers were fascinated with the Gothic: knights in armor, ladies in distress, exotic religious trappings—such as rosaries, matins, bells, guardian spirits, and prayers to the Virgin—and, above all, supernatural suspense. It was this side of Romanticism that Coleridge had claimed when he and Wordsworth divided up the subject matter to be included in *Lyrical Ballads* (1798), and even though it appeared in a later collection, *Christabel* also clearly illustrates this kind of work.

The images in *Christabel* are those conventionally associated with mystery and the supernatural; for example, the sounds mentioned in the first lines: the chiming of the midnight hour, the hoots of owls, and the howling of the mastiff. The poet stresses the fact that the cock is crowing at the wrong time; clearly, this is a hint of disorder in the natural environment. The full moon is significant, too; although it brightens the dark woods, it is partially covered by a gray cloud, symbolizing the struggle between light and dark.

As the poem proceeds, this conflict becomes more explicit, and the images suggest the theme. Conventionally, light represents good, and dark, evil. It is also light that reveals the truth. Thus, when Geraldine enters the castle, the cold brands flare up so that Christabel can see Geraldine's snakelike eyes. Later, it is Christabel who lights the lamp, Geraldine who seems to shrink from the light. The fact that Geraldine is garbed in white, denoting goodness and purity, indicates that she is involved in a carefully planned deception.

The snake or serpent is the major symbol of evil in part 2 of the poem. Sir Leoline applies this symbol to Geraldine's supposed attackers, who he says must have "reptile souls." Later, he misinterprets Bracy's warning about the dove and the snake by assuming that the innocent-looking Geraldine is the dove. It is Christabel who now begins to see her as a snake or a serpent. It is clear that the images in the poem do more than create a mood; they are integrally related to the central conflict of the poem.

Themes and Meanings

Christabel is a poem about the conflict between good and evil. Christabel is good; Geraldine is evil. Geraldine has appeared at the castle with the obvious intention of drawing Christabel into evil, perhaps, it is implied, through a sexual seduction.

Early in the poem, the forces on both sides of the conflict are clearly lined up.

Christabel has her faith, as expressed in her prayers to God and to the Virgin Mary. Moreover, she has a spiritual guardian in her dead mother as well as an earthly guardian in her beloved father.

Although Geraldine does not actually call upon satanic powers, it is clear that she has their skills. Like the biblical serpent, she is a deceiver. She can invent plausible lies; she can feign goodness; and, as Coleridge's projected continuation suggests, she can appear in any guise, even that of another living person.

The reason that Geraldine is so successful in deceiving Christabel and Sir Leoline is that she appeals to the very vulnerability of virtue. Because she has been taught to be compassionate toward others, Christabel pities Geraldine. The fact that Geraldine seems to be another girl of high rank, almost a second self, makes Christabel's action even more predictable.

Sir Leoline, too, is made vulnerable by the seeming helplessness of a daughter so much like his own; however, his greatest weakness is his devotion to the code of chivalry. A knight is bound by hospitality; he cannot honorably cast out a guest and certainly not if she is a helpless damsel who has put herself under his protection.

Even in the fragment of *Christabel* which was published there are hints that while recognizing the power of evil, Coleridge did not intend for it to win. Despite the spell placed upon her, Christabel feels an increasing revulsion toward Geraldine; Bracy believes his dream, warning of evil; and certainly Sir Leoline will eventually once more be governed by his love for Christabel. In the conclusion, just as in Coleridge's *The Rime of the Ancient Mariner* (1798), nature will be justified; the woods, as well as the castle, will be rescued from evil by the power of good.

Rosemary M. Canfield Reisman

CHURCH GOING

Author: Philip Larkin (1922-1985)
Type of poem: Meditation
First published: 1955, in *The Less Deceived*

The Poem

"Church Going," a poem of seven nine-line stanzas, is a first-person description of a visit to an empty English country church. The narrator is apparently on a cycling tour (he stops to remove his bicycle clips), a popular activity for British workers on their summer holiday. He has come upon a church and stopped to look inside. Not wishing to participate in a worship service, the visitor checks first to make "sure there's nothing going on." He will eventually reveal that he is an agnostic and that his interest in churches is not derived from religious faith.

This church is empty, so he walks in, observing all of the usual accoutrements: "matting, seats, and stone,/ And little books." His irreverence is captured in his tone as he observes "some brass and stuff/ Up at the holy end." Yet he is not totally irreverent. He knows that he should take off his hat, but he is not wearing one. Instead, he removes his bicycle clips.

As he moves around the building, he touches the baptismal font, observes the roof, and climbs into the lectern to look at the large-print lectionary. He even plays church for a moment, speaking the words ("Here endeth the lesson") that are usually announced at the end of each scripture reading. Clearly, he has some familiarity with religious practices. He also knows enough to leave an offering in the alms box at the door of the church. All he leaves, however, is an Irish sixpence, a coin worth less than its English equivalent.

After the narrative/descriptive beginning, the poem changes direction. The narrator wonders why he stopped at the church, why he often stops at churches. What is he looking for? Before answering that question, however, he asks another. What will happen to church buildings when we stop using them as churches? This is not an entirely irrelevant question for a man who has lost his faith and who assumes that others will do likewise.

He imagines that some churches will become museums, while others will fall to ruin. They might be avoided as places of bad luck, or approached as places for magical cures. Certainly, there will be superstition associated with these places for a time, the narrator observes, but even superstition will eventually fade.

Who will be the last to remember what church buildings were used for, he wonders: an archaeologist perhaps, who would know the name for the rood-loft, the high beam between the choir and the nave that held a cross or crucifix, or someone looking for an antique or a decorative artifact. It might be a "Christmas-addict," assuming with comic irony that the celebration of Christmas will go on long after Christianity has been forgotten. Or it might be someone like the narrator, someone who comes to "this cross of ground" (traditional English churches are laid out like crosses) looking for *something*. This last thought returns the narrator to his original question: What is it that he is looking for? And now he is ready to venture a tentative answer. This place has held "what since is found/ Only in separation—marriage, and birth,/ And death, and thoughts of these." The importance of these moments was recognized here. Furthermore, church buildings have been places for serious thoughts, and even when they are no longer used for worship, they will still be sought by people who need to be serious. It is a place that is "proper to grow wise in,/ If only that so many dead lie round."

Forms and Devices

"Church Going" looks and sounds almost casual in its structure, but that appearance is deceptive. The poem is, in fact, an expertly constructed work. The rhyme scheme of each stanza is complexly intertwined: *ababcadcd*. The middle lines (lines 5 and 6) reverse the expected alternating rhymes.

Furthermore, the rhyme is so subtle as to be almost unnoticed in the reading. Only a few of the rhyming words are exact rhymes, and these are often very ordinary words (for example, "door" and "for" in stanza 2, and "do" and "too" in stanza 3) that do not call attention to themselves. Other rhyming words are half-rhymes (also known as imperfect rhymes, near rhymes, or slant rhymes). These words have similar vowel sounds, or similar consonant sounds, but not both. Some of the many half-rhymes in "Church Going" are "on," "stone," and "organ," and "silence" and "reverence."

The other dominant structural device in the poem is rhetorical. "Church Going" carefully follows the structure of the meditation, beginning with a detailed description of a place, leading to an internal debate, and finally reaching a tentative conclusion. Larkin's place, a church, is evoked in sufficient detail to let readers re-create it in their minds and imagine themselves there with the narrator. The internal debate begins in stanza 3 and continues through the beginning of stanza 6. Here the narrator raises many questions, answering none of them. The questions explore the possible significance and uses of church buildings once people no longer use them for religious worship. What will happen when their purpose has been forgotten? The questions lead inevitably to considering why the narrator himself is drawn to these places.

His conclusion, which begins halfway through stanza 6, remains tentative. The narrator discovers some important purposes for church buildings, at least for himself, and he offers them for his readers to consider. True to the meditation format, the poem does not seek to prove a point logically or solve a problem absolutely. Instead, it allows the mind to take direction from the external environment and consider various aspects of an issue, letting the discussion lead to a new discovery. That discovery may be a momentary resolution, not the final answer.

Themes and Meanings

"Church Going" records the spiritual longings of a man who has lost religious faith. It may be seen as representing the spiritual longings of a generation of British citizens for whom the church has ceased to be important.

That religion has lost its central position is assumed. After all, the narrator would have observed the serious decline in church attendance in England since the nineteenth century. He would also, perhaps, think of Stonehenge, a religious site whose purpose has been forgotten. The narrator does not wonder *if* churches will fall out of use. Instead, he wonders what will happen *when* they do. Understanding the rest of the poem requires the recognition of that assumption.

The discussion about what will become of the unused church buildings is, in fact, an exploration of what has caused religion to be so important to so many for so long. Uncovering those reasons also reveals the needs that must still be met in the secular world.

The church, the narrator discovers, "held unspilt/ So long and equably what since is found/ Only in separation—marriage, and birth,/ And death, and thoughts of these." People have always turned to the church for these major life events. Weddings, baptisms, and funerals are conducted in churches (or at least by ministers), and even in an age that lacks religious faith, people need to affirm the special significance of these events. They want God to take notice of them, even if, paradoxically, they don't believe in God. Love, birth, and death all transcend the ordinary and must be "recognised/ And robed as destinies."

Finally, the church is a place that is "proper to grow wise in." The secular world, the world of work, bicycling holidays, suburbs, and sheep, can do very well without the influence of the church, but "someone will forever be surprising/ A hunger in himself to be more serious." That hunger, a spiritual longing, can be met only by going to a place where it is valued, where it has been valued for centuries.

Bruce H. Leland

CHURCHILL'S FUNERAL

Author: Geoffrey Hill (1932-   )
Type of poem: Elegy
First published: 1994, in *New and Collected Poems, 1952-1992*

The Poem

"Churchill's Funeral" is a poem in five sections. The poem begins by flashing back to London during World War II. The stained-glass windows of the great churches of London have been damaged by German bombing. The people inside the churches, or those who are seeking to rescue the victims, have been wounded, maimed, or killed. There is a curious nobility about their deaths, however, a grandeur equal to the devastated beauty of the churches. This nobility is brought to mind, years later, by the state funeral of former British prime minister Winston Churchill at St. Paul's Cathedral in January, 1965.

The second section begins to explore the poem's theme in depth. The innocent soul—that exempt from politics or worldly damage—has a guilty twin, involved in both giving the laws and violating them. In the third stanza of the second section, "res publica" means "public thing" in Latin (it provides the origin for the English word "republic"). "Res publica" is usually spoken of as something positive, but the poem sees it as responsible for both war and those who seek to restore peace. Toward the end of the section, the benevolent aspects of the res publica are emphasized, "fierce tea-making/ in time of war" signifying a kind of healthy respect for custom and triviality in the midst of crisis, then, even more directly, praise of the "courage and kindness" that, for no other reason than a simple dedication to what is right, kept the faith in the midst of the Nazi attacks. These virtues are seen as those of ordinary people, beyond the grasp of the "maestros of the world" who dominate political affairs.

The third section begins with an epigraph from eighteenth century poet William Blake. "Lambeth," a London ecclesiastical building that is home to the archbishop of Canterbury, the head of the Church of England, is "the house of the lamb" if one considers both Hebrew and English etymologies (not its literal etymology, but one coined by the poet). Yet lambs symbolize peace, and if Lambeth is bombed in wartime, then it can be no more the house of the lamb. A catafalque is a hearse for use in carrying the dead at a funeral; the droning Heinkels (German bombers) render the scene a kind of ghastly performance in which Fame, personified as a woman, renders the meek victims of the past morally victorious even as they die; their reputation will long survive their deaths, as, inferentially, will that of the more visibly famous Churchill.

The fourth section commemorates three specific London churches damaged in the wartime bombings. All the churches are dedicated to St. Mary the Virgin, and symbolism of Mary (as the "Pietà" or mourning mother) is juxtaposed with the survival of ragwort and other lowly weeds after the blast to show that both grand and simple things help sustain the human spirit in a time of crisis.

The final section shows the city after wartime, recovering from the destruction. The hour of the valorous poor who were victims of the blast is over; in peacetime, ordinary hierarchies return. "The last salvo of poppies" at the end of the poem refers to the red flowers placed on wartime graves. The image is a tribute to the spirit of sacrifice that saved democracy during the two world wars. Yet it is also a questioning of the cost, the innocent human life that was sacrificed. Even after Churchill's funeral and all that it signifies, will the victims of the war ever be fully recompensed in spirit?

Forms and Devices

The poem is written in stanzas of four lines each; the poem's five individual sections have as few as four of these stanzas or as many as seven. There is little direct rhyme in the poem, though Hill, a master prosodist, often uses assonance or verbal echo to give his words a certain ring or to create undertones. In the last stanza, the presence of "bones" and "poppies" at the end of the second and fourth lines respectively produces a kinship of sound, in the repetition of the "-es," that juxtaposes the bones and poppies in a way that makes the final image meaningful to the reader. The beauty of the poppies attempts to cover the horror and symbolic poverty of the bare bones, but in a sense the poppies are no more than the bones' external manifestation. Were it not for the dead bones, there would be no need for poppies as a symbol of mourning. Hill's verbal juxtapositions make the reader think about the underlying issues of the poem.

The poet never makes an explicit declaration of his theme, allowing the reader to piece together the poem's overall thrust from hints and images. This being so, each image, even each word, gains more importance and seems chosen by the poet with exquisite, almost excruciating, care. Hill sometimes uses very common words, but he also includes very obscure words in his diction—words such as "lourd," which is not in most standard English dictionaries, being the French word for "heavy." More characteristic are words such as "catafalque," a rather formal and obscure English word. Hill's verse is dense with meaning, each small stanza packed with resonance and reverberation.

Another device that calls attention to each individual word is Hill's use of space on the page. Despite the erudition and density of Hill's verse, it is actually very spare, not taking up much of a page. There is therefore a great deal of "negative space," of whiteness on the paper, which serves to concentrate the reader's attention on the bare words themselves.

The poem is not a direct narrative; indeed, in the tradition of elegy, it is far more meditation than narration. Each section of the poem is like a scene in a play or, more apposite to the poem, one of a series of stained-glass windows on a linked theme. At times, as in the second section, the focus is broad and public. At others, as in the fourth section, the one devoted to Mary, the poet contracts his focus and looks at a particular section of the entire tableau. It is notable that Churchill himself never makes a direct appearance in the poem, even though it is ostensibly concerned with his funeral. This is typical of Hill's oblique and indirect approach to his material.

Themes and Meanings

The reader of "Churchill's Funeral" must first determine the poem's stance toward Churchill and his funeral. Churchill almost single-handedly rallied the British people to resist the aggression of Nazi Germany. His funeral is therefore the end of an era as well as a recapitulatory celebration of the victory over fascism. Hill's sketching of the damaged churches, however, implies that healing from the war will not be as total as it might seem to those who conveniently forget history in their pursuit of the pleasures of the present. Churchill's funeral also calls to mind the end of the British Empire, which had crumbled rapidly as many of Britain's colonies were given independence after the war. In earlier poems such as "An Apology for the Revival of Christian Architecture in England" (1978), which has a subsection entitled "A Short History of the British in India," Hill has very subtly and ambiguously considered the theme of British imperialism, so the end of empire could certainly be an aspect of Hill's interest in Churchill. In this light, the "last salvo of poppies" could refer not only to mourning but also to the last manifestation of traditional British valor as seen in Churchill's attitude toward empire and war.

Hill's interest here, though, lies less with Churchill himself than in how Churchill's funeral provides a point of closure for the many deaths suffered in the bombing of London. Churchill's funeral takes place in a great old London church, which recalls the many churches devastated in the war Churchill fought. In the epigraphs surrounding the poem's sections, Hill quotes such earlier British poets as William Blake and John Milton, both associated with a Protestant democratic optimism. Hill implies that this vision is what saw Britain through the war but also that the carnage of war to some degree mocks and satirizes the utopian aspects of the earlier poets' thought. For the ordinary Londoner killed in the bombing, no amount of utopian rhetoric can provide compensation, despite the nobility of the ideals associated with Britain during the war and throughout Britain's history.

Ultimately Hill's stance toward Churchill is unclear. It seems generally admiring, but he is at pains to focus on the ordinary victims of the bombings who did not have Churchill's fame or position of privilege. This focus may be partly attributable to the fact that Hill was a young boy during World War II. To a certain extent he is pleading that the immediate impact of wartime death not be swept under the rug in a search for reconciliation or transcendence.

Nicholas Birns

CINDERELLA

Author: Anne Sexton (1928-1974)
Type of poem: Narrative
First published: 1971, in *Transformations*

The Poem

"Cinderella" by Anne Sexton retells the traditional version of this fairy tale but gives it a sardonic twist. The poem appears in *Transformations*, a collection of poems in which the speaker, introduced in the first poem, "The Gold Key," is a "middle-aged witch" and author of "tales/ which transform the Brothers Grimm."

As befits oral storytelling, the speaker opens the poem with a direct address to the reader and undercuts Cinderella's rags-to-riches story in four short stanzas that give examples of contemporary success stories: the plumber "who wins the Irish Sweepstakes," the nursemaid who marries her employer's son, the milkman who makes his fortune in real estate, and the charwoman who collects insurance from an accident. Three of these examples are followed by the sarcastic refrain "That story," which mocks the happy ending of this fairy tale and perhaps its hopeful readers as well.

The following six stanzas retell the Grimm's tale keeping faithful to its details for the most part but with occasional observations by the narrator telling readers to pay attention to an important part of the story or commenting on characters or plot. In the fifth and sixth stanzas of the poem, Cinderella becomes maid to her stepmother and stepsisters and plants a twig, given to her by her father, on her mother's grave. On the tree that grows from the twig perches a dove who grants all her wishes. The sixth and seventh stanzas continue the familiar story. When Cinderella must pick a bowl of lentils out of the cinders before she can go to the ball, the white dove comes to her rescue, not only picking up the lentils but also providing her with a golden gown and slippers to match. The prince dances only with her.

The poem continues in the next three stanzas to describe the prince's escorting Cinderella home, where she disappears into the pigeon house, until the fateful third day when, by covering the palace steps with wax, the prince captures Cinderella's slipper. The eldest sister cuts off her toe and the youngest her heel in order to fit into the slipper and thus win the prince, but in each case the dove alerts the prince to the trail of blood that gives away the sisters' ruse. At last the prince fits the shoe on Cinderella. The stepsisters attend the wedding, where the vengeful dove pecks out their eyes.

In the concluding stanza, which echoes the tone and structure of the opening stanzas, the narrator reveals that "Cinderella and the prince/ lived, they say, happily ever after," ending the poem with the sardonic refrain "That story."

Forms and Devices

Sexton transforms this tale not by changing its details but by using tone and imagery that mocks the happily-ever-after motif of fairy tales. She employs these devices to keep reminding readers that "Cinderella," or any idealization of romantic bliss, is a fairy tale, indeed.

The first four stanzas, which act as a sort of preamble to the actual story, establish the speaker's tone and deprecating attitude toward the tale. The plumber's luck is summarized and reduced in the phrase "From toilets to riches." The nursemaid is described as a commodity, "some luscious sweet," who moves "From diapers to Dior." Sexton creates variety in the structure of this prelude in the third stanza by changing the number of lines and dropping the refrain "That story," but the tone is no less biting. The fourth stanza parallels the structure of the first two, and the opening section concludes with the dismissive "That story." Thus, before the middle-aged witch has even moved to the particulars of Cinderella's tale she has established that all such stories are somewhat comic and completely unrealistic.

The speaker reinforces this mocking attitude by interrupting her narration to address the reader and comment on the tale. For example, in addition to calling attention to the importance of the dove, the narrator points out the meanness of the stepmother—"That's the way with stepmothers"—and the impossibility of a dove's delivering a gown and slippers—"Rather a large package for a simple bird." When the stepsisters' trickery is revealed by their bleeding feet, the narrator says with dark humor, "That is the way with amputations./ They don't just heal up like a wish." These asides inject reality into the fairy tale and work against the suspension of disbelief.

The speaker's attitude toward her material, crucial in conveying theme, is inseparable from the imagery and diction of the poem. Informal language, almost slang, serves to further debunk the romanticism of the fairy tale. Cinderella is described as "gussying up" for the ball. The birds pick lentils out of the cinders "in a jiffy." In addition, the imagery, primarily drawn from domestic life or popular culture, emphasizes the speaker's cynicism. The stepsisters have "hearts like blackjacks." Sooty Cinderella looks "like Al Jolson"—a comparison that points up the inauthenticity of the tale's outcome—and she calls to her mother for help "like a gospel singer," hardly a delicate image.

Sexton comments on the economics of the tale and of heterosexual relationships in general when she describes the ball as "a marriage market." She further develops this sense of relationship as commercial transaction by comparing the prince to a "shoe salesman" as he hunts for Cinderella. Both these images hearken back to the images of the first four stanzas, which present success in terms of money rather than love, with the marriageable nursemaid, in particular, as a kind of delectable product to be consumed.

When the prince finally finds Cinderella, the domestication and confinement of romance in marriage is hinted at by the way Cinderella fits "into the shoe/ like a love letter into its envelope." Furthermore, when the dove pecks out the stepsisters' eyes, rather than presenting an image of gore and disfigurement, the speaker tells readers "Two hollow spots were left/ like soup spoons." Even the most violent acts are tamped down by domesticity, and literal loss of vision becomes equated with the metaphorical loss of vision entailed in domestic life.

The most damning imagery, however, comes in the final stanza. The structure of this concluding stanza is similar to that of the opening four stanzas. However, whereas the beginning stanzas are filled with images of change, albeit sardonic, the final stanzas are filled with images of stasis, suggesting a lack of vitality in married life. In addition to questioning the happily-ever-after ending by inserting the phrase "they say," the speaker compares Cinderella and the prince to "two dolls in a museum case" with "their darling smiles pasted on for eternity." If "they say" posits the happy ending as hearsay, the picture of the unchanging dolls with their artificial smiles undermines it entirely.

Furthermore, the list of mundane annoyances to which Cinderella and the prince are not subject only emphasizes the fairy tale's unreality. The very specificity of the list—diapers, dust, the timing of an egg, repeating stories, getting a "middle-aged spread"—serves to remind readers of the tedium actual married life involves. The speaker concludes by comparing Cinderella and the prince to children—"Regular Bobbsey Twins"—implying this tale of romance and marriage infantilizes its main characters as perhaps does actual, real-life marriage. The poem comes full circle in its last line by repeating the refrain from its opening stanzas, "That story," thus juxtaposing the strangely static happiness of Cinderella with the equally unlikely good fortune of the plumber, nursemaid, milkman, and charwoman.

Themes and Meanings

Although the poems in *Transformations* are a departure from the confessional mode for which Sexton is so well known, many of the poems in this collection, including "Cinderella," are, like the confessional poems, concerned with issues of family and relationships between the sexes. The dark humor and structure of "Cinderella," as well as its contrast between the magical details of fairy tales and the mundane realities of daily life, are characteristic of the poems in *Transformations*, which show the influence of psychoanalyst Sigmund Freud as well as feminism.

"Cinderella," in particular, pokes fun at the willingness to believe in the lucky break that will transform ordinary life as well as the willingness to idealize love and marriage. The fairy tale's happy ending is depicted as trivial and stultifying, a kind of emotional and psychological death. However, by implication, actual married life fares no better. It is characterized by petty annoyances and quarrels as the once-young married couple becomes overweight and middle-aged.

The poem explores the tension between the ever popular Cinderella tale and reality. In the persona of the experienced and cynical middle-aged witch, Sexton enters the debate on marriage and the relationship between men and women, encouraging readers to view the marriage plot with a mixture of skepticism and humor.

Kathleen Aguero

CIRCULATIONS OF THE SONG

Author: Robert Duncan (1919-1988)
Type of poem: Ode
First published: 1977; collected in *Ground Work: Before the War,* 1984

The Poem

"Circulations of the Song" is a long poem divided into twenty-two stanzas of various lengths. There are 306 lines in this highly developed irregular ode. The title suggests circular as well as cyclic patterns among the stanzas, while the subtitle ("After Jalal al-Din Rumi") indicates the model that Robert Duncan is using, that of thirteenth century Persian poet Jalal al-Din Rumi. Rumi, as he has been known for centuries, was one of the founders of a sect of the Sufi religion called the Dancing Mevlevi Dervishes; he was also one of the supreme poets of Persia. He had been a sober and strict theologian and preacher of the Sufi religion until he fell in love with a young man named Shams al-Din, who became Rumi's "beloved." After that transforming experience, Rumi began composing ecstatic odes, which were accompanied by dancing and music from the reed pipe and drum.

The subject of Duncan's poem is his longtime companion, artist Jess Collins. Duncan used the term "beloved" in many of his poems, but it is in this poem in which he most clearly identifies Jess as the beloved, though he does not use his name. The mood of the poem is ecstatic declamation, as Duncan seeks to find images and metaphors that can adequately express his devotion to Jess. Each major section is built around metaphors and image clusters that Duncan used throughout his poetic career, such as the tree and leaves, the stars, water wells, speech itself, sexual orgasm, the mythic fall, and the power of Hermes in his role as alchemist and gnostic guide. The poem concludes with the metaphor of the house, not only as a Jungian symbol of the psyche but also as the domestic household that he and Jess created in a world hostile to homosexual unions.

Many motifs surface as the poem moves along, some coming from Duncan's other major collections of poems, such as the fields and meadows of his early collection *The Opening of the Field* (1960) as well as trees, roots, leaves, and branches from his second collection, *Roots and Branches* (1964). Stanza 19 (none of the stanzas are numbered in the poem) features the bow of Eros, a principal motif in Duncan's third major collection, *Bending the Bow* (1968). All these motifs come together and flower in his final collection, *Ground Work: Before the War* (1984), in which "Circulations of the Song" was first collected. In this volume the earth is a collective metaphor for all of Duncan's work.

Forms and Devices

The formal requirements of the ode determine the structure of this long, complex poem, but the ecstatic, declamatory tone is taken from Rumi's odes in honor of his young lover, Shams al-Din. Duncan could not find a poetic tradition in Western literature that could serve as an adequate model for the ecstatic, visionary utterances of love that combine both human and divine aspects, a condition he saw as an expression of the "sublime." The search for the "divine beloved" does appear in highly sensual images in the Song of Songs, but that work stands out from the other, more somber books of the Old Testament. Duncan's poem opens with the assertion that the beloved can never be found and attained in reason or intellectual pursuits. Duncan, like his great model, William Blake, believed that reason, without imagination, was essentially destructive: "If I do not know where He is/ He is in the very place of my not knowing." Only when the seeker abandons all rational pursuits does he have a chance of attaining union with the object of his love. Yet what leads him to love is passion guided by the imagination.

Each stanza entertains possible avenues to the beloved and displays Duncan's ingenious use of parables—sometimes quite similar to Rumi's—to articulate what is basically impossible to express: the depth of his devotion to Jess, who embodies the divine beloved. "The Mind is that fathomless darkness" which leads to nothing but the enemy of love: the self. Duncan gives direct credit to the odes of Rumi in stanza 7 when he states: "The rest is an Artesian well, an underground fountain// . . . Rising thru me/ the circuit Jalāl al-Dīn Rūmī/ in which at last! I come to read you, you/ come to be read by me."

Stanzas 14 through 17 trace the process of Duncan "falling" in love with Jess, a happy fall that saves him from his dangerous lean toward solipsism: "I am falling into an emptiness of Me," an emptiness that ensures that he will never "return into my Self." One of the requirements that Rumi records throughout his ecstatic love poetry is the necessity of abandoning the self and using the alchemy of divine love to attain union with the beloved. Yet only by becoming a servant of both human and divine love can he find true satisfaction. The fire of that love comes from the heart of the lover, and Duncan expresses its effect in unmistakably alchemical terms: "Molten informations of gold/ flood into my heart, arteries and veins,/ my blood, racing thruout with this news,/ pulses in a thousand chemical/ new centers of this learning." He directly quotes Rumi on the beloved—"He has climbed over the horizon like the sun"—and refers to Rumi's text as the agent of this love: "a wave of my own seeing you/ in the rapture of this reading."

In the final stanzas, Duncan identifies Jess as Eros, who wounds him with his arrow of love, an allusion to *Bending the Bow*'s use of the myth of Eros and Psyche as an example of the mystery of love. Duncan invokes Hermes and his "gnostic revelations" as the hidden source of both divine and sensuous love. Duncan's attainment of the beloved is demonstrated in serpentine images from the Garden of Eden, images that proclaim the mythic Fall as a victory, rather than a defeat, for the initiates of Dionysus, who celebrate in "the honeyd glow of the woodwind dance/ singing." The dance, a favorite metaphor of Duncan's, proclaims the full integration of the divine and the human in natural process and change. The final stanza commemorates the establishment of the House; that is, the household—one of Duncan's favorite words—of the love between Jess Collins and himself. Their household becomes "the Grand Assemblage of Lives,/ the Great Assembly-House/ this Identity, this Ever-Presence, arranged// . . . now in the constant exchange/ renderd true." Jess as the divine beloved has enabled Duncan to establish an actual place in the world of process and change, anchored always in the "sweet constancy" of their shared lives.

Themes and Meanings

"Circulations of the Song" is a poem about love and about the frustrations of expressing the depth of that love fully. However, Duncan also wants to explore the connections between human and divine love. Throughout his writing life, he used the word "beloved" to embody the range and intensity of the love he held for Jess Collins. Duncan finally found an adequate model in the ecstatic utterances of Jalal al-Din Rumi, the founder of the Whirling Dervishes. Rumi was forced to create these modes of ecstatic expression so that he could articulate the sensuous and spiritual intensity of his devotion to his lover. The use of the ode and the dithyrambic verse form allowed Duncan to imitate and, at the same time, pay homage to one of his great poetic idols, Rumi, a fellow homosexual and practitioner of ecstatic passion. Duncan also revered the Greek god of the dance and sensuality, Dionysus, who combined human and divine rapture.

A devoted and proud romantic all his life, Duncan found Rumi's poetic models a perfect vehicle for expressing his own antirationalistic position and for celebrating feeling as the key to unlocking the power of the imagination to transform the fallen world into a bower of bliss. Only by "falling in love," or surrendering the self to the fires of passional love, can human beings attain higher knowledge and experience the profundity of love. Duncan's poem participates in the identical process that Rumi delineated in his odes. He called his poem "Circulations of the Song" because the quest for the beloved circulates throughout the history of poetry and has circulated from ancient Greece down to the present day. The heart was one of Duncan's principal poetic figures, and he used it both metaphorically and literally; the circulation system exchanges oxygen and carbon dioxide to sustain life itself. Duncan frequently used objects which serve on both literal and metaphoric levels.

Patrick Meanor

THE CIRCUMSTANCE

Author: Hart Crane (1899-1932)
Type of poem: Lyric
First published: 1933, in *The Collected Poems of Hart Crane*

The Poem

"The Circumstance" exists in draft versions that Hart Crane composed before his death in 1932. It was not published in Crane's lifetime and might best be regarded as a complete draft rather than as a poem the poet considered finished. Dedicated to Xochipilli, the Aztec flower god referred to in the poem, its twenty-four lines are divided into three stanzas of uneven length.

The poem is the speaker's effort to find, in pre-Columbian America, a better way of responding to time than he has found in his own culture. The first stanza describes the ruined site of a ritual sacrifice. The remains of a throne and a stone basin where sacrifices were performed remind the speaker of the bloody history of the Aztecs, including their fatal conflicts with the exploring Spaniards. The stanza may be interpreted as a description of the clash of the Aztecs with the Spaniards, each of whom saw the other as "a bloody foreign clown." On one hand, the Aztecs, who had not seen horses before, "dismounted" the Spaniards from their horses in battle. On the other hand, the Spaniards "dismounted" the Aztec rulers. It might be the blood and bones of either group floating in the stone basins. The history of conquest is bloody, no matter who wins, but Crane's sympathy seems to lie with the Aztecs.

The second stanza proposes ways to absorb, or at least take intellectual possession of, history, "more and more of Time," as the Aztec god has. Buying stones and displaying bones, as in a museum, represent a desire to stop time. Xochipilli, often portrayed with flowers and butterflies, might be said to "drink the sun" as flowers do—another way of dealing with time, by living in the moment. The Aztec flower god, by celebrating the cycle of nature and by existing as a stone statue, may have it both ways.

The phrase "stumbling bones" refers directly to the remains of those sacrificed by the Aztecs (or—less likely—those killed by the Spaniards). "You" may be taken as a way of addressing the reader, but it may also be taken to mean that the speaker is addressing himself as "you" as he tries to enter imaginatively into the past. The stanza struggles somehow to see love as triumphant over time, but the diction is halting, the link to Xochipilli is tenuous, and the victory is, at best, tentative. The glittering crown at the beginning is paralleled by the winds possessed "in halo full" at the end. Xochipilli's crown of gold or golden flowers parallels a Christian halo. Yet these parallels are not fully explored as variant answers to the questions that human mortality raises about time.

The third stanza gives the poem its central concluding statement, "You could stop time." Xochipilli participated in the history of his time, but he also stood beyond it as a god. Xochipilli's answer to the vastness of time is to be memorialized with monuments and statues that have endured "as they did—and have done." But Xochipilli stands more prominently for the cycle of nature, the living and dying by which life continues on earth.

Forms and Devices

Repetition and rhyme create parallelism and contribute to the hammering rhythm and insistent tone of the poem. These devices also take the place of consistent meter, though iambic pentameter is still the basis for the poem. The opening line is metrically regular, as are other lines in the poem, including line 18, which begins the last stanza. Iambic trimeter lines, such as lines 6 and 7, as well as more unusual lines, such as the single trochee "Shins, sus-," contribute to the poem's tonal variety while not violating the regular underlying rhythm.

The poem is rich in rhyme. The rhyme "crown/clown" in lines 1 and 3 in the first stanza leads to an off-rhyme with "bone" at the end of the fourth line. "Bone" also concludes the first stanza's sequence of internal rhyme, "stone/throne." The rhyme and repetition resume in the second stanza with "stones/bones." The phrases "stumbling bones" and "unsuspecting shins" evoke an image of a person being led to a sacrifice, where one-third of the syllables in "sustaining" will be lopped off like a head. Difficult though the poem is, its rhythms are insistent. In the second stanza, the series of present participles, "urging," "unsuspecting," and "sustaining," creates a rhythm and a parallelism enhanced by the rhymes and consonant rhymes on "nothing," "shins," and "in." As the speaker struggles to find meaning in the figure of the flower god, the word "answer" is repeated three times in the concluding stanza.

The second stanza is a long sequence of phrases comprising two dependent clauses: "If you could buy the stones" and "If you/ Could drink the sun." Crane does not resolve these conditional clauses with an independent clause until the final stanza, where he concludes the "if" sequence on the independent clause, "You could stop time." In fact, syntactical resolution is played with, suspended, or delayed until that single independent clause around which the whole poem turns. The lines "as did and does/ Xochipilli,—as they who've/ Gone have done, as they/ Who've done" in stanza 2 prepare the reader for "As they did—and have done" at the very end. This repetition may be taken to represent the cycle of nature, words and phrases returning in slightly different contexts, as flowers return each spring.

Some passages resist paraphrase but carry clear sensuous and emotive force. "Desperate sweet eyepit-basins" manages to sound gory and tender at the same time. "If you could die, then starve, who live/ Thereafter" may seem confusing at first because it places death before starvation, but it clearly describes the fertility cycle. Seeds die, then "starve" all winter before being nourished by spring rain and warmth. Crane never exactly states who "Mercurially might add," but the phrase refers to time, which defies logic by adding to life as it subtracts from and concentrates life.

Themes and Meanings

While in Mexico in September, 1931, Crane went with an archaeologist on a five-day trip to an Aztec village called Tepoztlan. By accident, Crane and the archaeologist arrived during the yearly festival honoring Tepozteco, the Aztec god of pulque, a native alcoholic beverage. Crane drank with village leaders and was encouraged to participate in the festival, including being invited to beat an ancient drum in a ceremony at dawn. In his letters, Crane expressed pleasure at joining uninhibitedly in the festival and winning the goodwill of the villagers. It was apparently after this experience that he wrote "The Circumstance."

Xochipilli was associated with pleasure—feasting, dancing, games, and frivolity—as well as with love. His mate was Xochiquetzalli, goddess of domestic labor and the harvest. It is easy to see why Crane, who led a short and reckless life, would find this Native American Dionysus appealing among the grim gods of the Aztec pantheon. Compared to the human sacrifices in other Aztec rituals, sacrifices to Xochipilli were relatively humane: The Aztecs used obsidian knives to draw blood from earlobes. The blood was then touched to plants to ensure their continuing fertility. Xochipilli, however, appears not to have been completely benign. Small doves were also sacrificed. He is frequently portrayed carrying a staff on which a human heart is impaled. Both the joyous and the bloody aspects of Xochipilli seem to have suited Crane's mood. Crane refers to "A god of flowers in statued/ Stone," but in a parallel phrase also describes Xochipilli as "death . . . in flowering stone."

"The Circumstance" is a difficult poem made more difficult by the knowledge that it may be incomplete. Critics have seen the poem as an echo, even a repetition, of "The Dance" from *The Bridge* (1930). "The Dance" is also a poem in which the poet tries to imagine himself into a primeval Native American world, violent but in harmony with the life and death that are inevitable in nature. Similarly, the central effort of "The Circumstance" is to respond to the dilemma of the brevity of human life in the vastness of time, but its imagery, though vivid and disturbing, is sometimes obscure. Art and religion, as represented by the ruins of Aztec culture, seem to both participate in and endure beyond (if not triumph over) the bloody events of history. The focus of the poem is more on the poet's subjective desire to overcome time, to live imaginatively in the past while recognizing the brevity of life and the inevitability of death.

By "the circumstance" Crane seems to mean the opposition between cultures, such as the Aztec and the Spanish, and, in a larger sense, between the cycle of nature and time, in which mortality finds itself. "The Circumstance" expresses both empathy for the Aztecs and envy that the poet cannot actually enter the pre-Columbian world. Crane seems to see Xochipilli, intimate with the blood and beauty of life, as a "more enduring answer" than rationalism (and perhaps than Christianity) to the problem of the hugeness of time and the smallness and brevity of life.

Thomas Lisk

THE CIRCUS ANIMALS' DESERTION

Author: William Butler Yeats (1865-1939)
Type of poem: Lyric
First published: 1939, in *Last Poems and Two Plays*

The Poem

"The Circus Animals' Desertion" is a five-stanza poem in three parts. Part 1 introduces the poet's problem: a lack of inspiration. Part 2 explores three earlier writing experiences, and part 3 offers a solution to the problem.

The circus animals of the title are William Butler Yeats's earlier symbols and themes, which until now "were all on show," but now have deserted the elderly poet. In the first stanza, the speaker bemoans that desertion: "I sought a theme and sought for it in vain,/ I sought it daily for six weeks or so." When inspiration does not come, he blames old age.

The list of circus performers that concludes part 1 begins the references to Yeats's earlier works which fill the poem. The "stilted boys" are probably young men suffering from unrequited love. They were like acrobats performing on stilts, and they were "stilted," artificially formal, in their love (such as the "lovers who thought love should be/ So much compounded of high courtesy" in Yeats's 1902 poem "Adam's Curse"). The burnished chariot may belong to Helen of Troy or to Cuchulain, frequent subjects of Yeats's earlier work. The lion and woman is a direct reference to the sphinxlike "rough beast" of "The Second Coming."

Part 2 of the poem discusses three of Yeats's major early works in specific detail. Since his inspiration is blocked, he can do nothing but "enumerate old themes." The first of these is the narrative poem *The Wanderings of Oisin* (1889). In that poem, the hero Oisin tells Saint Patrick of his adventures with his fairy bride visiting three islands (which may be seen as youth, middle age, and old age).

The second early work to be recalled is the play *The Countess Cathleen* (1892), in which the title character offers to sell her soul to the devil in order to save the souls of the peasants on her land. Yeats explains that Maud Gonne ("my dear") had inspired the play. Like Cathleen, Maud risked her own well-being for others in her fanatical opposition to British occupation of Ireland. Once that theme was developed into a story, however, the thought that inspired it diminished. The "dream itself had all my thought and love."

The final work considered is the play *On Baile's Strand* (1904). Just as the Fool in the play is tricked by the Blind Man, Cuchulain is tricked by Conchubar into fighting a young hero who has arrived on the shore. Cuchulain kills the young man, only to learn that the stranger was his son. In remorse, "Cuchulain fought the ungovernable sea," attempting to chop the heads from the waves until he drowned. Here again, the art itself finally took control. "Players and painted stage took all my love/ And not those things that they were emblems of."

All three of Yeats's specific examples reveal the pattern of thought of the artist. Specific people, events, or stories may inspire him, but the act of creation, the details of the particular poem or play, quickly become the center of the artist's attention. Thus removed from life, the creations become complete and perfect in a way that life can never be. Part 3 of "The Circus Animals' Desertion" asks where they began. The answer comes quickly: They began in the messiness of life. In a stunning list of images of corruption and chaos, Yeats exemplifies that origin:

> A mound of refuse or the sweepings of a street,
> Old kettles, old bottles, and a broken can,
> Old iron, old bones, old rags, that raving slut
> Who keeps the till.

This "foul rag and bone shop of the heart" is the only source available to the poet for the creation of new poems.

Forms and Devices

The six stanzas of "The Circus Animals' Desertion" are written in iambic pentameter with a regular rhyme scheme: *abababcc*. Though Yeats wrote occasionally in blank verse (most often in his plays), his poetry usually works with traditional rhyme and meter. Within the tradition, however, Yeats felt free to experiment. He uses half-rhyme from time to time in the poem ("vain" and "man," "enough" and "love"); the occasional use of imperfect rhymes keeps the rhyme scheme from becoming insistent.

There are also variations from the iambic meter. For example, line 8, "Lion and woman and the Lord knows what," ends with three accented syllables following three unaccented syllables. The phrase "the Lord knows what" is thus emphasized, underlining the speaker's frustration. Further, the emphasis of this colloquial phrase helps to create a less formal tone for the poem.

Yeats's division of the poem into three parts provides a clear rhetorical structure. Part 1 presents the problem, part 2 examines it via specific examples, and part 3 reaches a conclusion. The conclusion—that poetic inspiration begins in the sordid chaos of the heart—is predicted from the beginning: In part 1, he suspects that "I must be satisfied with my heart." References to the heart continue through the second part, and the poem concludes with a resounding final image of the "foul rag and bone shop of the heart."

The image of the heart is such a conventional poetic symbol that readers may be tempted to ignore its significance here. In "The Circus Animals' Desertion," Yeats does not use the heart to symbolize romantic love. Rather, "heart" here refers to the wide and confusing range of human emotions. It is clearly distinguished from thought, themes, and art. That distinction between the feelings and the art is central to the theme of the poem.

An unusual device that Yeats uses in the poem is the reference to his own earlier works. While poets regularly use allusions to other famous works of literature, they do not as often allude to their own works. There may even seem to be arrogance in the assumption that readers will have read *The Wanderings of Oisin* or recognize the sphinx image from "The Second Coming." On the other hand, it seems not only appropriate but also right for an introspective poem which reflects on a lifetime of poetic work to include details of that work.

Themes and Meanings

That poets find inspiration in chaotic life is not a new theme for Yeats. In fact, the whole poem can be seen as a new occasion to "enumerate old themes." As early as "Adam's Curse," Yeats was noting the distinction between art (and artifice) and life. In that poem he speaks of lovers who worked hard at love, turning it into a work of art, but "now it seems an idle trade enough." The work of love is too exhausting to sustain; the lovers weary of it.

Much later, in "Sailing to Byzantium," an old man seeks to leave the messy world which celebrates "Whatever is begotten, born, and dies." In contrast to that all-too-human life is the city of Byzantium, symbol of eternal and unchanging art. That symbol is developed further in "Byzantium," where the world of art "disdains/ All that man is,/ All mere complexities,/ The fury and the mire of human veins." In these poems the world of art, because organized, unchanging, and eternal, seems superior to mere humanity and mutable human feeling. Yet there is ambiguity throughout. Lovers become tired with the art of love. The golden bird in "Sailing to Byzantium" sings only of events from the world of nature that was left behind. Images of death pervade "Byzantium."

"The Circus Animals' Desertion" addresses this ambiguity directly and seeks to reconcile it in a balance between messy human feeling and idealized, unchanging art. Yeats explains what happened to him in the process of creating three works. In each instance, he began with real human feelings. For example, when he began *The Countess Cathleen*, he was genuinely concerned that Maud Gonne was destroying herself in her political work on behalf of the Irish peasants. He hoped to warn her of the dangers of such self-sacrifice. From that source in human feeling, however, the play emerged as something quite different.

The works of art are thus removed from life and human feeling. The very process of creation forces this removal: "Players and painted stage took all my love/ And not those things that they were emblems of." The contradiction is resolved in the final stanza, when Yeats recognizes the creation of art requires a continually repeated process of returning to chaotic human feelings. The heart, the symbol for those feelings, must finally be recognized as the source for art. Art is not generated by the intellect; one cannot merely seek a theme. The feelings of the heart, no matter how sordid, chaotic, messy, and unartistic, are the only source for poetry.

Bruce H. Leland

THE CISTERN

Author: George Seferis (Giorgos Stylianou Seferiades, 1900-1971)
Type of poem: Lyric
First published: 1932, as "E sterna," in *E sterna*; English translation collected in *Collected Poems, 1924-1955*, 1967

The Poem

"The Cistern" is a lyric poem of twenty-five stanzas (if one counts the blank twenty-third stanza); each stanza contains five lines. The variable rhyme scheme utilizes off-rhyme in a resourceful and modern way.

"The Cistern" is prefaced with a quotation from the Cretan painter Doménikos Theotokópoulos, called El Greco, who worked in Toledo, Spain. The quotation is from the artist's inscription to his *View and Plan of Toledo* (c. 1609). The significance of the quotation has to do with the artist's poetic license to change reality to fit his aesthetic purposes. El Greco thought it "preferable" to shift the hospital's position and aspect to fit the painting's composition. "As for its actual position in the town," he says, "that appears on the map."

The poem's cistern is no ordinary reservoir to catch rainwater. The reader knows immediately that this cistern exists only in the mind; its symbolism is resonant in the opening line: "Here, in the earth, a cistern has taken root." Though it is an organic part of the landscape, the cistern gathers only "secret water" for one's interior life.

Above it the world goes on, time passes, and human cares and joys resound on its dome like "pitiless night." The cistern is as unconcerned about the world as the heavens are about mortals: "The stars/ don't blend with its heart." In pursuing their "destined suffering," human faces light up for a moment and die out. Caught up in "the pulse of nature," man bends toward earth like roses, thirsty with love, but "turns to marble at time's touch," returning to the earth and "sweetened" in his grave.

Though the world does not touch it, the cistern gathers human suffering, replenished by "pain, drop by drop." It hoards tears, "the groan of each body in the air," hopes that fail "at the edge of the sea." It "casts its nets far into a world" and feeds on the "bitter undulation" of human passion, taking away the embraces it once gave. In sleep one comes close to the cistern's hidden "garden where silver drops," but only in "the cave of death" is one able to talk to "the black roots."

The cistern is closer to "the root of our life/ than our thoughts and our anxiety." The regard of others or one's own pain does not affect this inner resource of one's being, for the cistern is "nearer than the spear still in our side." That one is unable to express this inner resource is a "crime," because if one could, perhaps he or she "might escape" both the painful knowledge and the hunger with which life leaves one.

Suffering is what intimates to men and women that they have this inner resource. The "body's bitterness" nourishes "our souls" so that beauty may "bloom in the blood of our wound." In this rebirth, which is a kind of death, everything may "become as it was at first," like a snake shedding its skin. Then one may find "Great and immaculate love, serenity."

Even though the cistern is known, "the blind earth/ that sweats from the effort of spring" drags human beings from the cool of the cistern back into the "Flames of the world." They know that " 'We are dying! Our gods are dying,' " but are as powerless as the statues who watch "the crowds of death pass by." (Here, a stanza consisting entirely of ellipses represents the silent procession of the dead.) When the dead have passed, the "magic spells" have been broken, but one's vision of the thirst-quenching cistern has already taught him or her the value of "silence," even in the midst of "the flaming city."

Forms and Devices

"The Cistern" is considered the culmination of George Seferis's early period, before the influence of T. S. Eliot's free verse and dramatic method have taken hold, as in *Mythistorema* (1935). The cinquains experiment with off-rhyme and a line resembling English pentameter, showing Seferis to be turning away from the traditional Greek pendecasyllabics and other formal restrictions, toward a rhythm more suitable to the modern Greek idiom.

Nevertheless, the language of "The Cistern" is abstract in a way that Seferis never repeats. The narrator speaks from a spiritual height, aloof from any specific scene or direct human experience. As Zissimos Lorenzatos says, in *The Lost Center and Other Essays in Greek Poetry* (1980): "the language is hardly audible. It has surrendered. In the end, you find you have received the poem's message without anyone having given it to you." There is power in the poem, but it is the power of seduction rather than persuasion; the reader must surrender to the poem as Seferis has surrendered to the language.

"The Cistern" is full of phrases that attribute human feelings to inanimate things. The characters, if they can be called that, are all abstractions. The cistern is an organism with a life of its own; it has "taken root" and has a heart. The day "grows, opens and shuts," like a flower. In such metaphors, the symbol is asserted rather than achieved.

Abstractions are personified. Night is "pitiless," cares "tread," joys "move by," fate has a "quick rattle," the fates "have woken gently," hope "may follow," expectation is "open-eyed," shadows are "mournful," the earth is "blind" and "sweats," warmth is "tame" or "calmly avoided fear" or "knocked on sleep to ask" directions. One also hears of "the wind's breath," "the skin of silence," "the root of our life," "the thirst of love," "the pulse of nature," and "the effort of spring."

What human presences do arrive on the scene are ghostly: "faces light up, shine a moment/ and die out." Otherwise, they appear only as bodies, living or dead: "Man's body bends to earth," "the groan of each body," "the body's bitterness," "a body hidden" in "the cave of death." Bodies may appear only in parts: "fingers eyes and lips," eyes that "roll in a gutter," the victim "full of eyelids," "palm on the temple," "Faces that go!" When the narrator addresses an unspecified "you," who "bent humbly, naked curve,/ white wing over the flock," the erotic possibility of a human presence dissolves in the apostrophe to the abstraction of "Great and immaculate love, serenity."

Themes and Meanings

"The Cistern" is a poem that locates the source of the poet's inspiration in what Philip Sherrard calls "a still centre of contemplative understanding." The poem leads away from the world of action to the poet's inner resources; for the cistern, where all human experience is gathered in secret, "teaches silence/ in the flaming city."

This view of poetic inspiration owes something to ancient Greek and Christian ethics as well as to modern psychology. The heroic ethic of Homer held that suffering leads to wisdom not only personally but also for the race in general. The ancient dead of the statues, for example, "our stern brother/ who looks at us with eyelids closed" communicates, however obliquely, what he has learned. Similarly, Christ in his martyrdom suffered for humanity's sins, and through him is felt "the spear still in our side." Yet the cistern, which gathers all this mythic and historical pain "drop by drop," is "nearer the root of our life" than these, just as it is nearer than the "destined suffering" of personal fate.

In modern psychology, the cistern replenished by individual experience has an analog in C. G. Jung's idea of the "universal unconscious." In sleep and dreams, as well as in meditative states such as artistic creation, one taps this storehouse of archetypal images, which have a power and significance of their own, derived from but no longer dependent on the things of the world. The "secret water" of the cistern is gathered from human experience but is not subject to the world, which "doesn't touch it."

It is toward the cistern that "Man's body bends" when it is "thirsty" for love or art, to nourish the root of his life. Then is when "our souls," like roses, put forth shoots of beauty, "so that we may escape the body's bitterness/ so that roses may bloom in the blood of our wound." There in the cistern of tears the poet finds his inspiration. Like the night that "does not believe in the dawn," or like love that "lives to weave death," the poet is a paradox, aloof from the world, yet distilling his unique vision of the world, observing a contemplative "silence/ in the flaming city." It is in this way that he becomes a "free soul."

Richard Collins

THE CITY IN THE SEA

Author: Edgar Allan Poe (1809-1849)
Type of poem: Lyric
First published: 1831, as "The Doomed City," in *Poems*; collected in *The Raven and Other Poems*, 1845

The Poem

"The City in the Sea" is a poem of four uneven stanzas, the divisions between which Edgar Allan Poe reworked in the several editions of this lyric. The title of the poem and the revisions Poe made in that title suggest connections with the biblical Sodom and Gomorrah, ancient cities condemned for their wickedness and licentiousness. The city that Poe depicts here is certainly a doomed, dreary, and lonely place, one characterized by death rather than life, by stillness rather than human activity.

The poem is primarily descriptive, and by beginning as he does with the exclamation "Lo!"—meaning "Look closely!"—Poe emphasizes that he wants the reader to pay careful attention to the surprising and important picture he is about to paint.

Poe begins by introducing the sole inhabitant of this city in the sea, death, for death has erected his throne here and rules the unusual and alien landscape. The city is located in the "West," the land of the setting sun and endings rather than the land of beginnings and hope, and eventually everyone—both the good and the bad—arrives in this region for "eternal rest." The city seems, however, deserted, and a sense of hopelessness, resignation, and melancholy prevails. Poe infuses the poem with the quality of a nightmare—something familiar but terrifyingly abnormal—by asserting that the city resembles nothing that anyone would recognize while at the same time describing the city with conventional words and concepts ("towers," "shrines," and "palaces"). A vast stillness dominates the scene, and even the wind has forgotten to blow here.

Poe turns his attention to the distance between this city and heaven when he comments on the light. This light is not a holy or natural light (as light from heaven would be) but rather one that gleams from the "lurid" sea onto walls that remind the poet of Babylon, another condemned and sinful city of the ancient world. Despite the fact that the domes, spires, and halls are highly decorated in this city, they remain deserted and forgotten. Poe focuses again on the surreal quality of this landscape when he tells the reader that the turrets and shadows seem to blend and to hang suspended in air. With this assertion, Poe implies that there is no distinction here between what is real (the turrets) and what is unreal (the shadows). Substance and shadow become one, and death rules majestically over all.

The feeling that everything is reduced to immobile similarity is intensified in the third stanza, where Poe shows that both churches (fanes) and graves, symbols of life and death, are "level" with the waves. The scene is so threateningly still that it causes one to think that there may not even be normal, "happier" seas elsewhere in the world. The stillness of both sea and air enhances the unnaturalness of this city, and both make the apparent serenity of the scene hideous rather than comforting. Poe concludes his description, however, with a final appeal to the reader to look carefully, for he again says, "lo," and calls attention to the fact that movement finally occurs: The city seems to sink and settle, and as it does so, hell rises to meet and honor the city.

Forms and Devices

One characteristic of the lyric poem is its focus on pictorial and melodic aspects of experience. "The City in the Sea" is no exception to this rule, for in this work a detailed picture of a city is offered, and the language in which the picture is rendered is intensely melodic and beautiful. The pictorial aspects of "The City in the Sea" are conveyed primarily through imagery, that is, language that appeals to the senses. The sense to which this poem makes its greatest appeal is the visual. Poe wants the reader to see this city; he wants him or her to visualize this beautiful and yet doomed human edifice. His choice of language reveals his preoccupation with sight; words such as "gleam," "shadow," "sculptured," "resemble," "streams," "open," "ripples," "glass," and "diamond" remind the reader that he or she is looking at something, that Poe wants his readers to see what he places before them.

The visual beauty of this city is further emphasized by the melodic beauty of Poe's skillful versification, his use of rhyme and meter. While the poem does not conform to a fixed form (such as a sonnet or a rondel), it does employ various patterns of sound that enhance its appeal. All the lines are arranged in rhymed couplets (two lines), tercets (three lines), or quatrains (four lines), and some lines and words are repeated for emphasis and effect ("Resignedly beneath the sky/ The melancholy waters lie"). Poe makes frequent use of rhymes other than these end rhymes (rhyming words at the end of the line). He uses initial rhyme, or rhyme that comes at the beginning of a line ("Streams up the turrets silently—/ Gleams up the pinnacles far and free"), as well as internal repetition of sounds ("The viol, the violet, and the vine") to intensify his description. In general, each line has four metrical beats, but because the number of syllables in each line varies, the rhythm of the poem is sometimes surprising and emphatic (as in the longest line of the poem—"Where the good and the bad and the worst and the best"—in which the stress falls heavily on the significant words of the passage: "good," "bad," "worst," and "best").

The poem also contains allusions to several real places, although it clearly presents a fantasy of these places rather than a realistic depiction of them. Babylon is mentioned in line 18, a reference to the ancient city devoted to material and sensual pleasures, and the entire poem reminds the reader of the story of Sodom and Gomorrah, which—as is this city—were utterly destroyed for their wickedness. That the city Poe has created is, indeed, evil becomes even more obvious when one considers how unnatural it seems—the wind does not blow, nothing moves, the light is strange—and how far from heaven it is: The light does not come from heaven, the waters are sad rather than joyful, and the gods there are death and "idols."

Themes and Meanings

Essentially, Poe's "The City in the Sea" is not obviously metaphoric; that is, it does not talk about one thing as though it were something else. (It does not, for example, discuss a beloved woman as if she were a rose.) Rather, this poem presents what Poe wants to discuss—a city—in nightmarish and frightening terms. When Poe asks his readers to consider this city, however, he is also asking them to think about all that cities have come to represent for civilized humans—activity, work, pleasure, art, music, and society ("The viol, the violet, and the vine"). This city is filled with the accomplishments of human beings, with "shrines and palaces and towers," but the city is ruled over by death, and the city exists in a land where resignation, melancholy, and stillness prevail. While no one is present in the city save death, everyone comes here eventually, and the poem seems to hint that all human efforts are vain and hopeless and—according to the final lines of the poem—honored only by hell and death.

Poe would probably resist this reading of the poem since he did not believe that poetry existed to teach; he believed rather that poetry existed for its own sake, for the beauty of its lines, mood, atmosphere, and feeling. For Poe, the importance of this poem would lie in how eloquently and elegantly he had represented this doomed city, how poignantly he had sketched the city's fall, how fully he had developed the atmosphere of resignation and sadness. Yet, it is exactly for this reason that many readers find Poe objectionable. No one would argue that Poe has depicted here a healthy and moral environment. The city is clearly corrupt; however, Poe has made something beautiful of this corruption. The reader must decide for himself or herself whether such an effort is laudable, whether a poem should be more uplifting and hopeful.

Given all the stillness in the poem and in the city, a rising or hopeful movement would finish the poem with some triumph, with some sense of morality, but the movement at the end of "The City in the Sea" is instead a sinking that ends with hell "rising from a thousand thrones." Only hell seems ascendant at the end of the poem. In this sense, the poem very much embodies the nightmarish state of mind that so fascinated Poe. He seemed to look at the world of familiar objects the way one looks at the elements of a very bad dream: Things look familiar, but they are really evil and terrifying. It is as if Poe takes a slightly different focus, an altered perspective, on the city, and in so doing he reveals it to be a place of death not life, stillness not activity, melancholy not hope, resignation not determination.

Kathleen Margaret Lant

CITY WITHOUT A NAME

Author: Czesław Miłosz (1911-   )
Type of poem: Lyric
First published: 1969, as "Miasto bez imienia," in *Miasto bez imienia*; English translation collected in *The Collected Poems, 1931-1987*, 1988

The Poem

"City Without a Name" is a long, biographical poem in free verse divided into twelve sections. The speaker, the poet Czesław Miłosz, is physically traveling through Death Valley, California, but the landscape of memory and the people who inhabit his own personal city of remembrance, his "city without a name," are emotionally and spiritually more real to him than the heat, sand, and salt of the desert. The first sections of the poem set up this juxtaposition between past and present in which, paradoxically, it is the present that seems motionless and almost lifeless; the only other person within three hundred miles of the poet is an "Indian . . . walking a bicycle uphill." The past, however, changes constantly in a kaleidoscope of time and images of his native Lithuania.

The greater part of the poem's beginning is made up of long, three-line stanzas, but, in the fifth section, the lines suddenly become short, curt, almost flippant as the poet tries to put the past behind him. "Who cares?" and "Rest in peace" he says, but this almost sarcastic mood soon changes back to the dominant meditative tone of the poem and its correspondingly longer lines when, in the seventh section, the poet considers his own personal situation as a man carried "By fate, or by what happens" far away from his homeland and his physical past. "Time," he cries, "cuts me in two." An emphatic "I" (distinct from "them") governs this section but, as the perspective shifts again and the images or dreams return, the poet places himself within this movement of time as he realizes that he is a being whose own present time may be drawing to a close. He will then become part of the past as the people he remembers have become part of the past of their ancestors and country.

What is his country? Does the poet now belong in the past or the present? He asks himself why all these precise, generally trivial memories keep coming back to him and why they are more real than reality. Why, in the desert, does he think of, smell, and hear "the lands of birch and pine" and "the hounds' barking echoes"? Why is the past "offering" itself to him? This questioning continues throughout the middle sections of the poem until, as if overwhelmed by the accumulation of images, the poetic line lengthens almost into prose and the poet sees himself living in the visions of the past. The last lines dwell on the poet's seeming inability to reconcile this paradox. Even in his poetry, he cannot reconcile his two worlds or find the "desired" word so that the "bygone crying" of the past "can be transformed, at last, into harmony." However, the poem does not end on a note of defeat. A final paradox or perhaps a moment of intuitive understanding is revealed as the poet asserts that perhaps he is "glad not/ to find the desired word."

Forms and Devices

"City Without a Name" is very representative of the poetry Miłosz has written in the United States. He has relaxed the structural formality of his earlier poetry by lengthening and shortening the lines at will (the last section is almost prose), and little effort is made to rhyme. In the English translation (by Miłosz himself), the fifth section does contain short bursts of rhyme: "lashes/Masses," "night/light," and "pity/highly"; the same device is also used in the more pensive but still short lines of section 7: "weepily/stupidity," "snow/know," and "new/two." However, this is not typical of Miłosz's later poetry or of the structure of "City Without a Name." In fact, its presence is meant to highlight thematic mood rather than poetic form.

The absence of metaphor, simile, and symbolism is very typical of Miłosz's later poetry. Nothing is a symbol of anything, and nothing resembles anything else; everything is concrete and is exactly what it is. Miłosz has said that "the accidents of life are definitely more important than the ideal object." He perceives no difference between the language of poetry and the language of the "real" world and wants no poetic finery or linguistic gymnastics that, in his opinion, separate rather than reconcile. In "City Without a Name," the dialectic between past and present is accomplished not through symbols or allusion but through the naming of concrete objects and people. Anna and Dora Druzyno, for instance, are real people rather than memories because they are named.

One poetic device that is dominant is the juxtaposition of a succession of dualities. The starting point for "City Without a Name" is the contrast between the sterility of Death Valley and the fecundity of the landscape of memory in the poet's mind or, more generally, between inner and outer reality. While camping in the desert in spring, the sound of bees unleashes the floodgates of memory as, in an almost cinematographic technique, the waterless silence of Death Valley, marked by the absence even of birds, dissolves into the shores of a river; the sound of flutes and drums is heard, and swallows fly over a pair of lovers. Something in Death Valley, perhaps a reaction to its aridity, has triggered the poet's own valley of the dead. Together with this cameralike fade-in/fade-out of sensory images, the poet lengthens and shortens his lines to represent the contrast between the past and the present and to underline the changing moods of the poem. A long line indicates remembrance and corresponds to more reflective passages, while shorter lines identify the present and the poet's reactions, often ironic and biting, to this involuntary time traveling. For example, the fifth section, with the shortest lines, is almost staccato in its sarcasm—"Doctors and lawyers,/ Well-turned-out majors/ Six feet of earth"—while the likewise short lines of section 7 mirror the poet's sardonic contemplation of his present situation: "So what else is new?/ I am not my own friend."

Themes and Meanings

The dominant theme of "City Without a Name" is self-definition. This questioning of identity, which has been paramount in all of Miłosz's work since his relocation to the West, is strongly linked to the inward musings of a man in the twilight of his years.

However, "City Without a Name" is not an egocentric poem. In fact, if the poet can affirm anything, it is that individuality is, paradoxically, communal. One must be defined by the past and, above all, by the people who share that past. In his book *Radzinna Europa* (1958; *Native Realm: A Search for Self-Definition*, 1968), Miłosz speaks of a "world defined by memory" in which "each experience branches into a series of associations, demands to be given permanency, to be linked up with the whole."

Nevertheless, the admission of such a perspective does not automatically bring acceptance. At times the poet gratefully relives the past or grudgingly perceives its importance, but, in other, blacker moments, he rails against the fact that he may only be the medium through which other experiences are filtered. He is afraid that the past may overwhelm the present, and, when past images begin to dominate, when he loses the present and only gains the past, he strikes out with anger and sarcasm. He cannot reconcile what is with what was. This striving for reconciliation is the corollary to the main theme of self-definition as the poem charts the poet's struggle to find the meaning of his life, to find his own place and time amid the multitude of voices and times that assail him. He has run through his life just as he is now running though the images of memory looking for the "last door," the one that will open on to knowledge and reconciliation, joining everything as one. At times he despairs of ever finding an answer: "And the gift was useless, if, later on, in the flarings of distant nights, there was not less bitterness but more." However, soon after this sad statement, the poem finishes with an entirely different perspective. Many critics have spoken of the epiphanies present in Miłosz's poems, the sudden moments of intuitive clarity in which his "last door" starts to open. "City Without a Name" ends with such a moment as the poet, who has striven to define his life and bring into harmony past and present, suddenly stands mute before images of a peaceful death and the sound of music. He does not want to speak; he does not want to define. Perhaps the experience, the feeling, is the harmony.

Charlene E. Suscavage

CLAREL
A Poem and Pilgrimage in the Holy Land

Author: Herman Melville (1819-1891)
Type of poem: Narrative
First published: 1876

The Poem

Herman Melville wrote *Clarel: A Poem and Pilgrimage in the Holy Land* during the twenty years that followed his journey to Europe and the Middle East in 1856-1857. Although he had earlier achieved fame through his novels of adventure, he was weakened physically and mentally, a condition exacerbated by his now unsuccessful efforts to provide for his family through his writing. Melville accepted the trip as a gift from his father-in-law, Judge Lemuel Shaw. Judge Shaw and Melville's wife, Elizabeth, hoped the extended tour would ease the author's debilitating depression. The trip, which covered fifteen thousand miles and touched on three continents and nine countries, began with a visit to his old friend Nathaniel Hawthorne in Liverpool. From Liverpool, Melville sailed through the Straits of Gibraltar into the Mediterranean Sea, visiting Constantinople and the pyramids before coming to port in Jaffa. From Jaffa he traveled inland to Jerusalem. Like many tourists of the time, Melville arranged to make a three-day trip eastward from Jerusalem to the Dead Sea, passing through Jericho, down the Jordan River to the Dead Sea, and returning to Jerusalem through the ancient monastery of Mar Saba and the village of Bethlehem. This experience provided the basis for the two-volume narrative poem about the spiritual pilgrimage of a young divinity student named Clarel that Melville published in 1876 with a bequest from his uncle Peter Gansevoort.

Melville struggled through the late 1850's and early 1860's. Having abandoned fiction, he tried his hand unsuccessfully at the lecture circuit, wrote poetry about the Civil War that was published as *Battle-Pieces and Aspects of the War* (1866), failed in attempts to procure a consulship, and was troubled by bouts of rheumatism and sciatica. Financially drained, he sold his country home in Pittsfield, Massachusetts, in 1863. In 1866, he was appointed to a four-dollar-a-day job as a customs inspector in New York City. This position placed Melville in the center of one of the most corrupt bureaucracies of postwar America, but it provided him with a steady income and the freedom to write without the pressure of pleasing a public that had long forgotten him. *Clarel*, the narrative of a young theologian's attempt to regain the faith he lost during his years of study, is Melville's personal effort to come to terms with the philosophical uncertainties that troubled him throughout his life.

The poem is divided into four parts, each part culminating in death. Beginning in Jerusalem, the four parts take Clarel and a changing band of companions and guides on a symbolic, circular journey in an ambiguous search for meaning across a debilitated and infertile wasteland.

In part 1, Clarel is repulsed by the barrenness of Jerusalem and overwhelmed by feelings of loneliness. Instead of the traditional vision of a sacred and glorious city, Clarel is confronted by "Dismantled, torn,/ Disastrous houses, ripe for fall," dwellings that look like "plundered tombs." A bleak and confusing maze of walls and enclosures, Jerusalem seems a city forsaken by God and hostile toward humanity. Disillusioned by the decay and disorder of the city, Clarel is overwhelmed by the diversity of people and beliefs he encounters in Jerusalem. He feels surrounded by people "in each degree/ Of craze, whereto some creed is key," people who, in the privacy of their personal visions, "Walk like somnambulists abroad."

In an effort to clarify the confusion he feels in Jerusalem, Clarel seeks spiritual guides. While wandering in the dry, stony lands outside the city's walls, and while visiting the faded monuments and shrines of the ancient city, he meets Nehemiah, a millenarian dispenser of tracts, who has traveled from America to be witness to the Second Coming; Celio, a hunchbacked renegade Catholic, whose sudden, unexplained death seems the terrible price of religious rebellion; Vine, a sensitive, meditative, middle-aged American, who is reminiscent of Nathaniel Hawthorne; and Rolfe, an assertive, argumentative American, who is a partial self-portrait of Melville. During the course of the poem's narrative, Clarel turns to these and other possible guides whom he meets along the way for help, but none of these diverse characters is able to provide him with the guidance he desires.

Clarel's desperate yearning for some hope in existence is answered when he meets a beautiful young Jewish woman named Ruth with whom he immediately falls in love. Impulsively he asks for her hand in marriage, but their courtship is interrupted by the death of Ruth's father, and Clarel decides to pass the required time of mourning by joining his newfound guides in a pilgrimage toward the Dead Sea.

In part 2, Clarel and the other pilgrims are joined by Derwent, a melioristic Anglican priest, and together they journey down from Mount Olivet toward Jericho. Their physical descent is paralleled by a building sense of doom. When they reach Mount Quarantania, the traditional site of Christ's temptation, Mortmain, a cynic whose belief in human progress has been destroyed by the failure of the French Revolution of 1848, leaves the group to spend the night alone under the mountain. As Mortmain leaves, the group is joined by the geologist Margoth, who argues coldly for the primacy of science. Set amid the formidable and barren landscape of the Siddom Plain, part 2 moves through ominous banks of fog toward the encampment on the shores of the Dead Sea. There Mortmain, visibly aged by his nightlong vigil, recklessly drinks the bitter water of the Dead Sea, "Hades water shed . . . the Sodom waters dead," and has a vision of his own coming demise. That night, Nehemiah, hallucinating a vision of the New Jerusalem, walks somnambulistically into the waters. The grim pilgrims find his corpse the next morning floating near the shore.

In part 3, the pilgrims ascend the rugged Judah ridge toward Mar Saba, the ancient Coptic monastery and oasis. At Mar Saba, the starkness of the pilgrims' journey is relieved by the conviviality of the monks, the comfortable quarters, and the plentiful food and drink. The humanism of this center of Christian belief stands in contrast to the closed doors and dust-covered shrines of Jerusalem. A lone, majestic palm, which grows from the side of the mountain, becomes a problematic symbol of the hope for immortality, but the reader is reminded that the intricate passages of Mar Saba lead down as well as up. In this place of reassessment, the pilgrims once again encounter death when they discover the corpse of Mortmain, its open eyes transfixed upon the sacred palm and an eagle feather at its lips. Mortmain's ambiguous demise, which hints at both beatitude and annihilation, leaves the poem's young protagonist feeling "Suspended 'twixt the heaven and hell."

In part 4, the pilgrims stop in Bethlehem on their return journey to Jerusalem. In this portion of their journey they are joined by two others: Agath, an illiterate Greek seaman who has survived the brutality of a hostile world through the tenacity of his will, and Ungar, an embittered Confederate who has fled America and the defeat of his cause to become a soldier of fortune. Clarel, who has had second thoughts and dark premonitions regarding his betrothal to Ruth while on his journey, discovers that she has died while he was traveling. Confused and alone, Clarel is last seen joining another band of pilgrims.

The poem concludes with a brief epilogue that asks "If Luther's day expand to Darwin's year,/ Shall that exclude the hope—foreclose the fear?" Critics have argued over the interpretation of the poem's conclusion. Some see in it a Melville who, near the end of his life, had made peace with the conflict between disbelief and belief. Others, however, see in it a reaffirmation of Melville's lifelong inability to resolve this conflict and his conviction that it could not be resolved.

Forms and Devices

Clarel is a massive work, comprising more than eighteen thousand lines of iambic tetrameter in which lines rhyme at irregular intervals. Melville's decision to use short octosyllabic lines and his decision to create a rhyme at the end of each short line, a particularly difficult task in English, decrease the readability of the poem and help to explain why many critics have dismissed *Clarel* as bad poetry; however, others have argued that the limitations of the form Melville selected are the result of a conscious effort on the author's part to force his reader to experience an uneasiness similar to the spiritual disorientation that confronts the protagonist. In a sense, the reader feels as trapped between the narrow walls of the iambic tetrameter lines as Clarel feels between the conflicting pressures of faith and cynicism.

The poem is divided into four parts of roughly equivalent length. The poem's 150 cantos average about 120 lines each. The cantos are thematically or narratively gathered in groups of two to five and are irregularly divided into sections that indicate a minor change in subject or merely relieve visual monotony. Within each of the four parts, the groups of cantos form a pattern of nine to ten movements. Some slight relief from the confines of the poem's rigid structure is provided by more than forty short lyric pieces—hymns, songs, invocations, and chants—that are interspersed throughout the narrative.

Although limited in its prosody, the poem is rich in symbolic imagery. The topography of the Holy Land provides Melville with his most powerful images. The pilgrims' physical journey down toward the Dead Sea, 1,300 feet below sea level, mirrors their increasing gloom, just as their ascent to Mar Saba's towers offers a brief hope of beatitude. Throughout their journey the sterile images of the desert remind the reader of the sterility that plagues their spirits. The walls and winding alleyways of Jerusalem echo the confusion of the young protagonist; the brackish waters of the Dead Sea serve as a frightening image of annihilation. Most of the poem's landscape is a wilderness, separated from the civilization the pilgrims have voluntarily abandoned. It is at once a place of potential revelation and a place of possible spiritual death. The bleakness of the desert landscape is frequently juxtaposed with the pilgrims' fond memories of lusher landscapes at home, the green fields, orchards, and of families that they have left in their pasts. The poem's setting also offers numerous biblically significant sites that provide Melville with opportunities to elaborate on his theological themes. Most often, however, these holy places are portrayed as ruined or defiled, becoming additional symbols of disillusionment and loss of faith. Finally, it is not surprising that the author of *Moby Dick* (1851) uses sea images throughout his desert poem, for in his earlier work Melville frequently described the vast loneliness of the oceans as a kind of wasteland.

Freed from the pressure to make his writing pay, Melville clearly did not overly concern himself with the commercial potential of *Clarel*; however, his narrative does relate to some important literary and social interests of his time: the popularity of letters from abroad, which related travelers' reactions to famous places; nineteenth century Protestant America's fascination with the Holy Land; and the still popular English genre of the Oriental romance.

Themes and Meanings

Despite its length and intellectual complexity, Melville's *Clarel* has one overriding theme. The poem focuses on the major philosophical crisis of the later nineteenth century, the apparent destruction of the credibility of revealed religion in the wake of Darwin's discoveries. Although the poem is filled with disillusionment and death and permeated with a sense of gloom, it draws no final conclusion regarding the conflict between reason and faith.

The question of faith was always central to Melville's thought. In Liverpool before departing for the Holy Land in 1856, Melville visited Hawthorne, and his friend wrote a remarkable description of their afternoon: "Melville . . . began to reason of Providence and futurity . . . and informed me that he had 'pretty much made up his mind to be annihilated'; but still he does not seem to rest in that anticipation; and, I think will never rest until he gets hold of a definite belief. It is strange how he persists . . . in wandering to and fro over these deserts, as dismal and monotonous as the sand hills amid which we were sitting. He can neither believe, nor be comfortable in his unbelief." The multiple characters with whom Clarel travels represent a broad range of beliefs, from the self-satisfied, comfortable faith of Derwent to the cold, scientific analysis of Margoth, but none of his fellow pilgrims can serve as a model for Clarel, and in the end he leaves to continue his spiritual pilgrimage alone. In the epilogue to *Clarel*, Melville's narrator calls this conflict the "running battle of the star and clod" that will "run forever—If there be no God" to settle the matter by divine intervention. The poem shows Clarel's failure to find belief, concluding with his murmured complaint that " 'They wire the world—far under the sea/ They talk; but never comes to me/ A message from beneath the stone.' " Yet the poem's epilogue advises the protagonist to "keep thy heart," for "Even death may prove unreal at the last,/ And stoics be astounded into heaven."

As a corollary to the examination of faith, *Clarel* confronts the prevalent optimism of American civilization in the late nineteenth century, questioning the inevitable triumph of Protestant democracy. The poem shows that humanity's technological and commercial advances have not dented the age-old questions at the heart of existence. In fact, the poem implies that modern people are turning away from even the consideration of such questions.

Finally, the poem explores the limitations of human relationships, their inability to stem the overwhelming tide of spiritual destruction that washes away humanity's hopes and dreams. The love theme that is brought forth with such promise in part 1 of the poem, quickly fades during the long, dry pilgrimage and the endless theological discussions of the pilgrims. Long before he returns to Jerusalem, Clarel senses that his love for Ruth will not be consummated. When he discovers her funeral upon his return to Jerusalem, the sight merely confirms the tragic intuition he has already felt. During his journey, Clarel turns from one companion to another, seeking companionship as well as revelation. In part 2, as he and Vine rest in a secluded bower, Clarel feels strongly attracted to his countryman: "O, how but for communion true/ And close; let go each alien theme;/ Give me thyself!" But Vine rejects the young man's advances by asking, "Why bring oblations of thy pain/ To one who hath his share?" and asserts that "Lives none can help ye; . . . Go live it out." Vine's gentle rebuke underscores the poem's assertion that companionship cannot assuage the pain of spiritual unrest. Most of the characters in the poem are Ishmaels, renegades who have turned away from the comforts of home in the hope of embracing some higher comfort, but like the ceaseless wanderers of Melville's fiction, they seem destined to find no rest.

Carl Brucker

CLEAR NIGHT

Author: Octavio Paz (1914-1998)
Type of poem: Lyric
First published: 1962, as "Noche en claro," in *Salamandra*; revised in *Poemas*, 1979;
English translation collected in *The Collected Poems of Octavio Paz: 1957-1987*,
1987

The Poem

"Clear Night" is a long poem of 141 lines in free verse. It is divided into seven stanzas of varying length. The poem is dedicated to André Breton and Benjamin Péret, two influential Surrealist poets with whom Octavio Paz became associated in the 1940's while he lived in Paris. From the opening two stanzas, one is led to believe that the three characters in the poem correspond directly to Paz, Breton, and Péret, and the rest of the lyric confirms this belief. The poet uses the first person with no suggestion of artifice; that is, one can safely assume that the speaker of the poem is Paz himself and not a fictional persona. The poem is cast as a recollection of an experience, so much of the time the past tense is used. At moments of special importance the poet shifts to the present tense, as if he were reliving those moments.

Contrary to the suggestion of the title, the poem begins with the three poets sitting in a café at ten o'clock on a misty autumn evening. They are the only ones lingering there. They feel the ominous approach of autumn, which is compared to a "blind giant" (line 5) and "faceless man" (line 8) advancing toward the city. Suspending such dark thoughts, the poet shifts the reader's attention to scenes of the city, and the reader views these scenes as if through the same window as the three friends in the café. It is this experience of carefully attending to the city—not only to its main streams but also to its underground life—that informs the poet's observations throughout the rest of the poem. In particular, he focuses on a teenage couple. The boy is streetwise and tough. The girl is more innocent, small and pale but also resilient and surprisingly durable, like a "pale branch in a patio in winter" (line 54). She is wearing a red jacket on which one sees the boy's hand. The word "love" is spelled on his fingers. One imagines the boy grasping the back of the girl's neck as they pass by the poets' window. Although they seem an unlikely match in some ways, their interaction is characterized by an entwining passion and sexual energy.

The poet's attitude toward the boy's gesture is ambivalent. In the apostrophe to the hand, he seems at first to deplore the predatory relation between the boy and the girl implied in the grasping. The hand as "collar" (line 64) seems to choke the "eager neck of life." In the next lines, however, the poet admires the sign of love painted on the hand. The hand becomes a symbol of redemption rather than a fetter.

In the fourth stanza, there is a shift back to the three friends who now are walking through the city. The language here is highly symbolic—they see at least two distinguishable rivers, the river of centuries and the river of stars. The poet re-creates the excitement of the moment by adopting the present tense and by recalling the urgent voices that direct and manipulate his gaze. It is at this point that the night "opens" (line 79). This marks the first epiphany, or revelation, of the poem.

The fifth stanza returns to a more narrative mode. It begins by describing the friends' separation and a brief observation about the wind and the river which remind the reader of the literal setting of the poem. This literalness is, however, short-lived, for the poet quickly moves to pondering the violence of time. He seems to conclude that humanity inevitably loses the battle with time. Poetry is the only means of defeating time. Paz is not invoking the classical idea that poetry is a means to immortality through fame; rather, he is defining poetry as a particular way of experiencing reality that does not view time as linear and death as an end.

The last long division of the poem describes a second epiphany, one which the poet experiences apart from his friends. It is here that Paz explores in erotic imagery the relation between poetry and the point of silence from which poetry begins and toward which it leads. This silence is not negative; rather, it is the necessary condition for the observer who would penetrate the surface of reality with "the light push of a thought" (line 17).

Forms and Devices

The reader of "Clear Night" is rewarded when she or he perceives the network of images that Paz has woven into the poem, for the interconnectedness of these images offers an interpretative key to the poem. In the central image of the night as it "opens" (line 79) its hand, for instance, one recalls the earlier description of time, not progressing as one normally understands it, but as opening up—the "minute opened into two" (line 20). Shortly after, the poet perceives the city as revealing itself in a similar way: "The city opens like a heart" (line 28). Finally, in the last long section of the poem, the city "unfolds" (line 106) itself to the sensitive poet. Thus, Paz invites the reader to link thematically the images of the hand, time, the city, and the clear night.

Such attention to imagery helps interpret the most enigmatic parts of the poem. In section 3, one is given a sense of a great disaster in a London subway, but the poet speaks in a highly symbolic code and depends on imagery rather than literal description to convey the significance of the event. It is no accident that the poets sit in "Café d'Angleterre" (line 1) as this event is recalled. Although their café is situated in Paris, its name (café of England) reinforces the sense that the poets are connected to the tragedy. The mutilation of the victims is described in a way that evokes the earlier image of autumn. Just as autumn is a "faceless man," so these victims become "faceless" and lose their identities through the mutilation. The poet uses the first person plural to speak for the victims as if all humanity, past and present, share in that disaster. Paz is exploring the relation between human identity and a reality that seems intent on erasing it.

Much of the difficulty and much of the beauty of "Clear Night" derives from Paz's reliance on imagery and the narrative discontinuity that results from this emphasis. Once the poet sets the scene in the first section, he quickly moves to a meditation cast in opaque symbolic language. Although he does mark a break in thought by capitalizing the first letter of a line, the absence of punctuation throughout the whole poem gives the sense of fertility, abundance, and overflow of energy. This energy is precisely what the poet hopes to capture of the city's activity. Lines such as "walking flying ripening bursting" (line 23), "a vagabond grey sparrow streetsmart a bully" (line 51), "embracing splitting joining again" (line 75), "centuries generations epochs" (line 83), "echoes calls signs labyrinths" (line 87), and "towers plazas columns bridges streets (line 109) not only describe the variety of ways one can experience reality at the same time, but more important, such lines also convey the energy with which the poet is manipulating language in order that it correspond to the richness of his experience.

Manipulating language is one way to convey the wealth of experience. Another way is to go outside language. The most noticeable device in the poem is Paz's simple illustration of the hand of the boy, which is set within his verbal description of it. In a very basic way this drawing challenges the reader's preconceived notions about poetry; poetry is more than words organized in a certain way. The simplicity of the drawing is in marked contrast to the network of images in the poem, and although this hand is linked thematically to the more complex corpus of the poem (the hand is not completely devoid of language, for the hand contains the word "love" on its fingers), it remains apart, as if to hint that this image remains the seed of the poem.

Themes and Meanings

"Clear Night" is about the poet's revelation of the interconnectedness or coexistence of things that are usually seen as opposing and separate, such as life and death, past and present, and the heavenly and the mundane. "Everything is a door" (line 16 and line 69), one reads, and "everything a bridge" (line 70). If one waits and observes closely, one will see beneath the superficial divisions in the world and understand that everything is comparable to everything else. The "light push of a thought" (line 17) is all that is needed for such a revelation.

The vision that is celebrated is one that depends on the viewer's arrival at a point that is neither a door nor a bridge, but a point prior to time and space, pure essence. Quite simply, in order to perceive that everything is connected, one must be outside the network of connections. At this point outside time and space, the poet is most aware of, and sensitive to, chance occurrences which would challenge the appearance of reality and reveal something more fundamental than convention or unearth something below consciousness. This is the point of expectation—the expectation that is returned to several times in the poem with the refrain, "Something's about to happen" (lines 18, 32, and 113).

One could also say that this isolated point is the point of pure desire, for desire that is sullied with appetite and acquisitiveness must be suspended in this state. This pure desire could be called poetic desire, the desire to challenge the common view of reality through daring comparisons, through the linking together of things that seem very different. This desire is what allows Paz, in the final long section of the poem, to see woman and city as connected. The effect of this extended comparison is double. Woman becomes objectified and fragmented. This objectification of woman has been a source of criticism of Surrealist art by recent scholarship; Paz's poem certainly bears the marks of Surrealism's influence on him, and this treatment of woman is one of them. More positive, the second effect of the comparison is that the city is transformed from a mere construct to a living organism. Both effects, however different, show the transforming power of poetry.

In stanza 5, Paz makes an explicit claim about the power of poetry. Lamenting the human failure to defeat strife, cruelty, and misfortune, the poet finds hope in the transformative power of poetry. Even though time, which is connoted by the advance of autumn, brings death, the poet takes consolation in the fact that poetry allows one to suspend time—to get outside it. It is poetry that allows Paz to view time in a new way, as opening up. It is poetry that inspires him to link boldly life and death in the present: "the living are alive/ walking flying ripening bursting/ the dead are alive/ oh bones still hot" (lines 22-25).

Poetry is a way of experiencing reality, of reading the signs in the world. It is not a fanciful or delusory indulgence in language. It is the perception of the elusive and mysterious love painted on the hand of the world that redeems and renews the world.

"Clear Night" is a difficult poem that presents the reader with a series of paradoxical images that are finally resolved when one gets outside the poem and views it as a structure of interlinking images rather than a linear process with a beginning, middle, and end. In this way, the experience of the poem demands as much from the reader as the experience of life demands from the poet.

Thomas Mussio

CLEARANCES

Author: Seamus Heaney (1939-   )
Type of poem: Sonnet sequence
First published: 1987, in *The Haw Lantern*

The Poem

An elegiac sequence of eight sonnets on the death of Seamus Heaney's mother, "Clearances" is a reworking and revisiting of many of his early domestic and agrarian poems. At the same time it represents an attempt to confront the importance of his mother in his life and work. As the eldest child, Heaney occupied a somewhat privileged place in the family, and his mother figured in many of his earlier works. The sequence emphasizes the private moments—folding sheets, peeling potatoes together, even the oedipal struggle he calls "our *Sons and Lovers* phase"—the two of them shared.

Even the entry point of the poem involves a private legacy, as he meditates on a cobble thrown at his maternal grandmother by an outraged fellow Protestant when she married a local Catholic man. The cobble is both an emblem of his attachment to his mother's side of the family and a literal keepsake, given to him by her. The intimate nature of that bequest represents the intensely private nature of the entire sequence. Similarly familiar—and familial—the second poem veers between memories of his grandparents' house and a vision of them welcoming their newly deceased daughter to their heavenly home, which, significantly, bears the same address as their earthly home.

Having placed his mother's death, Heaney is prepared to deal with his memories of their relationship. This he achieves in a series of four sonnets in which mother and son are isolated together. In number 3, the two of them sit at home peeling potatoes while the rest of the family attends mass. In number 4 his education separates them, as she typically declines to pronounce words that are "beyond her," deferring to his greater acumen. For his part, he finds himself reverting to a grammar of home rather than of his schooling, although even that stratagem, consciously undertaken, pushes them apart. In the remarkable number 5, the shared act of folding sheets becomes an intricate dance that paradoxically requires them to pull away from each other as it brings them closer together. In number 6 he recalls the shared rituals of church attendance during Holy Week.

The seventh sonnet shows the family attending to his mother's death, with his normally taciturn father showing a surprising aptitude for the right words. Both numbers 7 and 8 play with the notions of presence and absence. When his mother dies, the family members all know that the space they surround, the space she has heretofore occupied, has "been emptied/ into us to keep." Similarly, in the final sonnet, Heaney imagines walking around a space that is "utterly empty," a beautifully realized metaphor for this elegiac sequence, in which Heaney circles around the space in his life which has been emptied by the death of his mother.

Forms and Devices

While the sequence consists of sonnets, no particular type of sonnet predominates. Heaney adheres rigorously to the fourteen-line sonnet form, yet as with his use of all forms, he bends it to his own ends. There are Shakespearean sonnets (as number 6 is), blank forms (number 7), and others that can only be described as Heaneyesque. He bends rhyme schemes to his own uses, varying patterns from poem to poem, thwarting the reader's expectations, so that the standard Petrarchan sonnet form, for instance, fails to materialize, and the rhyme scheme sends the poem in unexpected directions.

At times Heaney employs very regular rhymes, while at others (as in number 7) he rhymes "soul" with "oil," "breathed on" with "incensation," and "pride" with "bread." In the first two lines of the sestet (a sestet consists of the final six lines of a sonnet) in number 5, he rhymes "happened" with itself, thereby upsetting any expectations of formal regularity, yet the rhyme works beautifully, because he causes the stresses of the line to fall in slightly different ways. Heaney is typically mischievous in the matter of rhyme, partly because of his awareness of the irregularities of pronunciation in his native Northern Irish Catholic dialect: He has written elsewhere that in his native speech, "hushed" and "lulled" are exact rhymes for "pushed" and "pulled." That personal linguistic history, together with the early influence of the work of William Butler Yeats and Robert Frost, leads Heaney to maintain a tension between the formal regularity of the sonnet (and of the rhymed poem generally) and the rhythms of everyday speech. The use of slant rhymes, run-on lines, and rhymes on unexpected words allows Heaney to maintain the conversational mode within a highly regulated form.

As with rhyme schemes, the traditional split between a sonnet's octave (its first eight lines) and sestet stands open to reinterpretation. The meaning in several of the sonnets in "Clearances" follows the traditional split, with the opening octave acting as a single unit of meaning and the concluding sestet comprising a second unit. In other poems, however, Heaney introduces the directional break after line 7 (number 5), line 9 (number 8), or line 10 (number 7). What is consistent is that the poems contain two distinct movements, often striking out in quite different directions. The second sonnet, for instance, moves from a memory of childhood visits to his maternal grandparents' house in the octave to his mother's foreseen reunion with her parents in the afterlife. Similarly, in number 3, the octave concerns itself with the memory of the shared privacy of mother and son peeling potatoes on a Sunday morning. That glowing moment takes on different coloring in the sestet, where the speaker recalls it during the priest's deathbed work. At that moment, while others are crying or engrossed in their own thoughts, he recalls that that morning, with their breaths mingling, was the closest they would ever be. Throughout the sequence, the sonnets offer similar shifts and changes; they must be read as single units, to be sure, but as single units made up of two distinct segments.

Themes and Meanings

As one would expect in an elegiac sequence, "Clearances" is about mortality. Rather than understand mortality narrowly as "death," however, one does well to consider mortality as pertaining broadly to life and death. His mother's death occasions in Heaney a meditation on his relationship with her, on the effects of death upon a family, on his own aging, and on both life and the afterlife.

Most immediately, the poems concern themselves with loss: To lose one's mother is inevitably to discover a hole in the world. Heaney's image, in the final poem, of walking around an empty space is a remarkably apt description of that condition of loss. Throughout the poem he has considered his relationship with his mother in its various nuances, from the initial closeness to the inevitable separation and distancing brought on by his education and career. Yet during his whole life the one constant of his relationship with his mother has been her presence. Now he finds that her absence will color both his future and, in a sense, all that has gone before.

The occasion of this particular death also takes on a universal quality. At her deathbed scene in number 7, Heaney declines to name any of the participants. His father is simply "he," the assembled family "we" or "the others." They are both recognizable as themselves and generic: This is any family standing around the deathbed of a parent as well as the very specific family to which he belongs. Such a strategy invites readers to identify with the scene, to see their own losses in his.

Certainly the confrontation with his mother's death leads him to consider his own. In number 8, the empty space in the world is both that which his mother occupied and the space formerly occupied by his birth tree, planted by his aunt and now cut down by subsequent owners of the family farm. That tree, "my coeval," becomes a "bright nowhere," a brilliant image of what it means for a being to go out of the world. The prospect of leaving the world has led to a consideration throughout the sequence of being in it, both in terms of his mother and in terms of his own career. The sonnets contain echoes and traces of his earlier work. The poem about folding sheets is a return to, and in a sense a critique of, his earlier "Churning Day." That poem was about textures— dense, close, even clotted. Sonnet number 5 here is about lines of force, about connecting and pulling away simultaneously, and about, as he himself has said, clarifying and simplifying the excess of words in "Churning Day." Similarly, the great closing image of the empty space is borrowed from the third poem in Heaney's "Station Island" sequence, here turned to a new and more poignant use. Throughout the sequence he works at coming to terms with his agrarian past, which received such strong treatment in his first three books, then was laid aside beginning in *North* (1975).

For Heaney, death is inextricably linked to life, and just as many of his earlier elegies celebrate the life of the deceased—a cousin, a friend, an old fisherman, the poet Robert Lowell—so here the elegy for his mother stands as both a meditation on her death and a celebration of her life and of his life with her.

Thomas C. Foster

THE CLERK'S TALE

Author: Geoffrey Chaucer (c. 1343-1400)
Type of poem: Narrative
First transcribed: 1387-1400, in *The Canterbury Tales*

The Poem

Geoffrey Chaucer's "The Clerk's Tale" is one of twenty-two tales completed—two more exist as fragments—of *The Canterbury Tales*, begun about 1387 but not completed at the time of Chaucer's death in 1400. Scholars later arranged the tales in what they considered to be the most plausible order; "The Clerk's Tale" appears as the ninth tale, sandwiched between "The Summoner's Tale" and "The Merchant's Tale."

"The Clerk's Tale" retells the story of Griselda, already made popular by two literary figures of the fourteenth century, Giovanni Boccaccio and Petrarch. The original source was a folk tale. Coming from this oral tradition, the tale was disseminated in many different forms from those found in the works of Boccaccio, Petrarch, and Chaucer, but the main characters, the major plot elements, and the narrative sequence of events retain basic similarities. The Griselda tale also embodies the Cinderella theme, in which the protagonist rises from a lowly rank to the highest rank by proving her worthiness through a number of tests, in this case, of her patience, obedience, and faithfulness to her husband.

In Chaucer's tale, Walter, a noble king held in high esteem, has refused to marry. When some lords entreat him to do so, and even offer to find a suitable bride, Walter is so favorably impressed with their petition he agrees to marry, but he insists on finding his own bride. The day of the wedding comes, and Walter still has no bride. Shortly before the time of the ceremony, however, Walter asks Janicula, a poor old man, for the hand of his beautiful, virtuous daughter Griselda, whom Walter has seen frequently while traveling about the kingdom. Janicula grants permission to marry Griselda, and she consents. Walter places one condition on the arrangement, however: She must promise to always obey his will cheerfully and without question, even if it causes her great pain.

Fearful and conscious of her lowly state, Griselda agrees to Walter's conditions, and they are married. All the subjects love and admire Griselda for her goodness, her wifely arts, and her wisdom. Soon, a daughter is born, pleasing everyone in the kingdom.

Soon after the birth of the child, however, Walter begins to impose a series of increasingly cruel ordeals to test Griselda. First, maintaining that his subjects wish it and pretending that he is only concerned with keeping peace among them, he commands her to give up the baby daughter. She asks only to kiss the baby farewell before she gives her up. Four years later, when a son is born, he has the child taken away as well. Finally, Walter tells Griselda that his subjects wish him to take another wife. Returning everything she has to him except for a smock to wear back to her humble home, Griselda leaves.

Walter now sends for their daughter, whom he has sent to Bologna, and says that she is to be his new wife. Through all of this Griselda never complains or fails to obey; Walter is finally moved to pity and reveals what he has done, assuring her that he is now convinced of her patience and steadfastness. She returns to him, and all is happy thereafter.

Forms and Devices

In "The Clerk's Tale," Chaucer uses a line containing five stresses or beats, in seven-line stanzas, a form that would later be called rime royal. In fact, Chaucer's greatest contribution to the technique of English verse was the arrangement of this five-stress line in rhyming couplets. In general, his rhymes are carefully matched sounds. In some cases, he availed himself of alternative pronunciations to achieve rhyme. For example, "again" could rhyme either with "main" or with "men." This use of optional variants is one way in which Chaucer is flexible in his use of language.

Chaucer consciously uses language as technique in "The Clerk's Tale" in the way he employs a simple style to parallel Griselda's lowly station in life. Only after Griselda has proven her inner nobility of character even to her husband does she allow herself a sudden release of emotion, weeping and swooning with joy when she is reunited with her children, in contrast to the utter self-control that she has maintained throughout the period of her testing.

The Canterbury Tales is often used as an example of the "frame tale," in that the larger story sets up a situation, or "frame," inside which various characters tell their own stories. The clerk is one of those characters who tells, in this case, his story of Griselda and her patient forbearance. In like manner, Chaucer has the clerk in "The Clerk's Tale" tell his traveling companions that he is telling a story that has been told to him by another learned clerk, a poet laureate (one skilled in Latin grammar and versification) of Italy named Frances Petrarch, further enforcing the idea of the story within a story.

The technical aspect of point of view, the vantage point from which the author presents the actions of the story, is of interest in Chaucer's *Canterbury Tales*. In the larger tale, the frame tale, Chaucer tells the story in the third-person omniscient point of view; however, he has various characters within the story present their stories as they understand them, restricting information to what a given character sees, hears, feels, and thinks. In "The Clerk's Tale," the clerk, who claims to be telling a story told to him, controls who knows what: The reader, for example, knows that Griselda's children are not killed, though she does not. Likewise, Griselda is patient and is obedient to the harshest of tests, losing her children and even being cast aside by her husband, but she does not know, as readers do, that these demands are to test her.

Symbolically, clothing is important in this tale. Walter has a new wardrobe made for Griselda when he takes her from her humble house and her poor, subservient father. When he chooses a woman of low estate and elevates her to the highest social rank, her old clothing must be left behind with her old life. Likewise, when he puts her aside, she must leave behind all of her finery; if it were not for her request to at least cover the womb that has borne his children, she would have returned home naked.

Themes and Meanings

The meaning and interpretation of "The Clerk's Tale" is perhaps best seen in relation to how the tale fits in with the other tales of *The Canterbury Tales* as well as the tale as a separate entity. For one thing, the stories of *The Canterbury Tales* are told primarily for entertainment. Explicit morals are relatively few, and no single, unifying theme is laid down for the whole series. The storytelling is set up as a game and not for the purpose of preaching morals. It is not to be a set of exempla, but a contest.

The placement of the tales within *The Canterbury Tales* is important. The juxtaposition of the tales of the patient wife, "The Clerk's Tale," and of the tale of the unfaithful wife, "The Merchant's Tale," is not happenstance. Likewise, the relationship of the completely subservient wife Griselda in "The Clerk's Tale" to the wife who had complete sovereignty over her husbands in "The Wife of Bath's Tale" is not coincidental. In fact, it is hard to think of any one of these tales in isolation from one another.

In "The Clerk's Tale" itself, Chaucer shows how a drastic imbalance of power in a marriage can lead to suffering for women and sinfulness for men. Like many authors of Chaucer's day, he sees the popular story of the patient Griselda as a cautionary tale. While all Christians were taught to face life's inevitable trials with patience and humility, since they were believed to have been sent by God for His own incomprehensible purposes, no human was justified in inflicting suffering on another just to see how well it was endured. Thus, Walter and Griselda represent extremes of behavior that teach a moral lesson in literature, but that, Chaucer apparently believes, should be avoided in real life. In testing the worth of a woman who is already his moral superior, Walter becomes increasingly evil himself. He can torment Griselda all he pleases because she is a poor man's daughter. Had Griselda been a woman of noble birth, Walter would have risked that family's retaliation if he had mistreated his wife. Griselda is so explicitly an exemplar of virtue that it is easy to accept the shift at the end of the tale from the literal to the parabolic mode. The tale is puzzling, for it is a story at odds with Walter's own meaning. Virtue must serve an apparently wicked cause, and thus, for all the moral of the ending, it is not allegorical, for Griselda is an impossible role model: Her behavior is presented for admiration, not for emulation.

Victoria Price

THE CLOUD

Author: Percy Bysshe Shelley (1792-1822)
Type of poem: Lyric
First published: 1820, in *Prometheus Unbound: A Lyrical Drama in Four Acts*

The Poem

In six stanzas of between twelve and eighteen lines each, the first-person narrator of "The Cloud," who is the cloud itself, describes its various forms and functions throughout its life cycle. The first stanza captures the range of the cloud's moods. Gentle, it brings rain to nourish the earth's flowers and shade for the leaves of trees. The cloud can also be ferocious, however, bringing hail that whitens the ground, followed by thunderstorms.

Peaceful again in stanza 2, the cloud describes how it shrouds the snow on mountain peaks and sleeps during the storm. Then the cloud explains how it is controlled by atmospheric electricity (a belief that was common in Shelley's time but has since been disproved). The poet pictures the cloud as possessing a positive electrical charge that interacts with earth's negative charge to produce rain, either a fierce thunderstorm or more gentle showers. The attraction between the two kinds of electricity is depicted as love.

Stanza 3 describes a sunrise and a sunset from the cloud's perspective. At daybreak, just as Venus (the "morning star") becomes invisible, the sun's rays leap onto the mass of clouds driven by the wind; at sunset the cloud rests, with "wings folded," like a "brooding dove." In stanza 4 the moon, "that orbed maiden," rises at dusk and "Glides glimmering" over the cloud's "fleece-like floor." The type of cloud suggested here is altocumulus, a "thin roof" that sometimes breaks to reveal the stars. To the cloud the stars are like a "swarm of golden bees." When the breeze blows stronger the cloud breaks up, and through it the sky appears, "Like strips . . . fallen through me on high," until the reflection of the moon and stars can be seen in rivers, lakes, and seas.

In stanza 5 the cloud has become cirrostratus, a high cloud that produces a halo, "a burning zone," around the sun and a "garland of pearl" around the moon when they shine behind it. Then the cloud changes yet again and becomes stratocumulus, a low gray cloud that hangs "like a roof" and is "Sunbeam-proof." The second half of the stanza describes a cumulonimbus rain cloud that marches through the "triumphal arch" of the rainbow as it delivers its contents onto the "moist Earth."

The final stanza is a summation. The cloud explains its relationship to the elements in intimate terms: It is the "daughter of Earth and Water" and is nursed by the sky. In the life cycle of the cloud its endlessly circulating particles pass through the "pores of the ocean and shores" (the latter are the rivers). The cloud constantly changes its form, and yet it does not die. After rain has come and the sky is once more clear, the cloud laughs at its own "cenotaph," which is a monument erected in honor of someone who is buried elsewhere, and like a child emerging from the womb it arises and once more "unbuilds" the "blue dome of air."

Forms and Devices

Each stanza is composed of several quatrains that rhyme like a ballad stanza, *abcb*. There is also an internal rhyme in each stanza ("I bring fresh showers for the thirsting flowers," for example) in line 1 and in each subsequent uneven line number (line 3, line 5, and so on). The effect of this consistent rhyme scheme is to give the poem a sense of order and cohesion, since the meter, although it consists basically of iambic and anapestic feet, is constantly varied.

The imagery Shelley employs has the effect of humanizing nature. For example, flowers "thirst," and leaves, lazy in the noon sun, "dream." Buds "waken" after they have been at rest in the earth, like a child, "on their mother's breast." The earth does not merely rotate around the sun, it "dances"; the trees "groan" in the wind; thunder "struggles"; the sunrise has "meteor eyes"; it "leaps on the back" of the clouds; sunset "breathes"; the movement of the moon is the "beat of unseen feet"; stars "peep" and "peer"; heaven has a "blue smile," and the earth is depicted as "laughing" after a storm. The effect created is of a universe alive with feeling and divine influences, reminiscent of some of William Blake's *Songs of Innocence*.

Crowning all these images is the metaphor of the cloud itself as a laughing, winged child-god. The word "laugh" occurs three times in this context. In stanza 1 the cloud laughs in the midst of the thunderstorm; in stanza 4 it laughs again at the sight of the stars as they "whirl and flee," and in the final stanza the cloud silently laughs at the presence of the clear blue sky, which appears to be a memorial to the cloud's own demise. The cloud laughs because it knows this is an illusion. This image occurs elsewhere in Shelley's work. In *Prometheus Unbound* (1820), for example, published in the same volume as "The Cloud," the spirit of the earth is a winged child and, like the cloud in stanza 2, sleeping in the storm, is shown asleep, its lips moving, "amid the changing light of their own smiles," a close parallel to the laughing cloud.

The other notable quality of the images is that they make poetry from scientific processes. Shelley took a close interest in scientific matters, and his descriptions of the various forms and changes in this protean cloud are scientifically accurate. This accuracy applies also to other observations in the poem, such as the image of "sunbeams with their convex gleams." This phrase refers to the phenomenon of atmospheric refraction, in which the earth's atmosphere bends sunlight around the earth in a convex arc, as seen from the cloud's point of view (the same phenomenon would be concave if viewed from the earth).

Themes and Meanings

In an earlier poem entitled "Mutability," Shelley used clouds as a symbol of impermanence and likened them to human life, which is never the same from one day to the next. In *Prometheus Unbound* the cloud takes on a different meaning as a symbol of the material human form, which is illuminated by the transcendent light that shines from within it. "The Cloud" builds on both these meanings and adds a third. Certainly the cloud is transient, but impermanence is not the last word; everything in the poem goes through a cycle of dissolution and rebirth; nothing is forever lost. This is why the cloud is depicted as laughing: It knows this truth, and its laughter suggests that the essential reality of life, underlying all temporal phenomena, even its apparently dark or distressing elements, is bliss and joy. This bliss is propelled through the material world through the power of love—another belief that Shelley expressed frequently, especially in *Prometheus Unbound*.

The image of the cloud at sunset, resting with wings folded, "as still as a brooding dove," is also significant. It is a clear allusion to Book I of *Paradise Lost*, by John Milton, in which the Holy Spirit is described at the creation as sitting "Dove-like . . . brooding on the vast Abyss." The image suggests that the cloud is also a metaphor for the creative energy, which elsewhere in his writings Shelley saw embodied in an absolute One that effortlessly manifests its power through the material world. This power is usually hidden, as, for example, in "Hymn to Intellectual Beauty," but it is indestructible—the eternal dimension of existence which persists unchanged through all the cycles the material world undergoes. In this sense the cloud resembles the skylark in "To a Skylark," a poem Shelley wrote at about the same time that he wrote "The Cloud." The skylark sings in joy; its song comes not from itself but from an unmanifest creative source that merely uses the bird as its instrument. So it is with the cloud. All these meanings combine to suggest a world in which truth is effortlessly manifested and joyously perceived, an unpolluted paradise free of the ugliness that ignorant humans, who mistake illusion for reality, appear (but only appear) to impose upon it.

Bryan Aubrey

THE COLLAR

Author: George Herbert (1593-1633)
Type of poem: Dramatic monologue
First published: 1633, in *The Temple*

The Poem

"The Collar" is George Herbert's most extensive and detailed poem of rebellion. Thirty-two of its thirty-six lines describe what the poem itself calls the ravings of a person growing "more fierce and wild" as he strains to release himself from the restrictive pressures that surround him. Much like John Donne's energetic complaints to God in several of his Holy Sonnets, "The Collar" gives full expression to the speaker's resentment of the pain and rigor of leading a life that is moral and holy. Only after these complaints are freely, almost hysterically voiced is the speaker taught how quickly they can be banished by a patient God who ultimately gives more than he asks.

The poem begins with a dramatic statement of refusal—"I struck the board, and cried, No more"—and the following lines give examples of the kind of life that the speaker wants to leave behind. He is a person of ambition and desire, yet everything in life seems to conspire to frustrate or torment him. His life is one of "sighs" and "tears," a situation he finds particularly distressing because he can readily imagine the joys and glories, the wine, fruit, and flowers, that are withheld from him.

The process of describing his past failure to seize the available pleasures of life makes him more determined to change his ways immediately and exchange his tears for the pursuit of "double pleasures." Like a libertine, he suggests that inhibitions and moral laws are only a "rope of sands" once a person decides not to be bound by them. Instead of being blind to the forbidden pleasures of life, he will now serve only his needs and desires. Enraptured by his own enthusiasm, even the death's-head, the traditional reminder of mortality and the nearness of judgment, is no longer intimidating and will certainly not be part of his luggage as he prepares to go abroad. He is confident that all of his fears can be neatly bundled up and left behind, and he attempts to wind up his argument with what sounds like a proverb celebrating his new creed of practical selfishness: "He that forbears/ To suit and serve his need,/ Deserves his load."

This is not, however, the true finale of his argument, which is provided by the intervention of a holy voice, a device used in several other key poems by Herbert. All the ravings of the speaker are answered by one gentle word, "*Child*," an almost miraculous reminder that not only is the speaker always overheard by God, but, more important, he is always protected, instructed, and accepted. This is the way the world of rebellion ends, not with a bang but with a whisper, and when the speaker replies "*My Lord*," he acknowledges not only that his rebelliousness is at an end but that devotion to such a Lord is not painful servitude but joyful freedom. In a curious way, the story of this poem is thus foretold by the multiple meanings hinted at by the title: "The Collar" suggests a restrictive collar that the speaker wants to slip and the angry "choler" to which he gives voice throughout most of the lines; yet even in the depths of his anger and rebelliousness, the speaker is a "caller," and God is always ready to answer.

Forms and Devices

One of the most interesting aspects of "The Collar" is the way the form of the poem helps to convey not only the dramatic rebelliousness of the speaker but also the concluding resolution. The speaker's anger and nervousness are underscored in several ways. His speech pattern is halting and constantly interrupted. Many of the statements are short, and the frequent punctuation in the lines gives them a clipped, staccato sound, adding to the impression of uneasiness. Any sense that this is the speech of a confident and determined man is also undermined by the fact that much of it takes the form of questions. These are meant to be rhetorical questions, but still they suggest that the speaker is plagued with doubts.

At first glance, the overall structure of "The Collar" seems to mirror the state of mind of the speaker. The line lengths alternate in an apparently irregular pattern, and the rhyme scheme is difficult to assess. As a result, the structure of the poem may be taken as an embodiment of the rebelliousness of the man who is in the process of swearing off all laws and restrictions. "My lines and life are free," he says, and the irregular lines of the poem signify his first step toward a life of pleasurable transgression. From another perspective, the form of the poem seems not so much free as chaotic, thus subtly indicating that a person who repudiates the legal and moral restrictions of life abandons the basic principles of order and thereby begins a descent into incoherence, the necessary by-product of rebelliousness.

The structure of "The Collar," however, is neither completely free nor chaotic, but extremely subtle, discernible only after careful and patient analysis. Beneath the superficial disorder, or developing progressively through it, is an orderly pattern that climaxes in the last four lines of the poem. This is best seen in the rhyme scheme. As Joseph H. Summers points out in *George Herbert: His Religion and Art* (1954), every line in "The Collar" finds a rhyme somewhere, but through most of the poem there are many off-rhymes, and because rhymes do not occur at predictable, regular intervals, they sometimes undermine rather than create a sense of closure. Near the end, the rhyming lines begin to occur closer and closer, but the speaker's last assertion that he is tying up his fears is still belied by the irregular off-rhymes (abroad/load, fears/forbears). Only in the last four lines do the rhymes become regular (alternating *abab*) and purposeful: The designation of the speaker as "wild" is replaced by the new name given to him, "Child," and his every "word" of rebelliousness gives way to "Lord," the divine word capable of redeeming human anger, weakness, and folly.

Themes and Meanings

The recurrent topic of Herbert's poems is not perfection but correction. Perfection is unreachable, but constant correction is one of the rules of religious life (and religious poetry) for Herbert. The speaker of "The Collar" is by no means wicked or reprehensible. He is, in fact, all too human, and his protest against the inevitable disappointments, restrictions, and pains of life is one with which most of the readers of this poem can sympathize and identify. Much to his credit, Herbert never denies the validity of the experiences described in "The Collar" or suggests that such feelings, however confused or disordered or angry, are unworthy of expression. Herbert knew that the Bible, especially the book of Psalms, one of his great spiritual and poetic models, dwells repeatedly on laments and complaints as radical as those in "The Collar."

Alongside the Bible, perhaps there is also something of a different kind of social and religious ritualism here—the carnivalesque spirit. Carnival is a festival time of at least temporary release from the obligations and restraints of daily life, and one is not only freed but even encouraged to abuse, parody, or otherwise flout the figures of authority and "cold dispute[s]/ Of what is fit, and not" and grab for the physical pleasures at hand. Carnival functions not only as an individual and societal relief valve, letting off pressure that might otherwise build to intolerable levels, but also an important acknowledgment of the claims of the body and a person's legitimate right to cry out against the strains of religion, law, and morality.

In works by William Shakespeare, according to C. L. Barber in *Shakespeare's Festive Comedy* (1959), carnivalesque release leads to clarification, and this is precisely the pattern of "The Collar," where Herbert allows the speaker full expression of his freedom as part of a rhythm of spiritual life that returns him to a deepened understanding of his obligations and his relationship to God. One of the ironies of the speaker's protests throughout "The Collar" is that everything valuable that he seeks by rebellion is available through religious obedience. God surfaces dramatically at the end of the poem, and this is a surprising, wondrous moment. Yet there are signs of God subtly in evidence long before the last two lines: in the "board" of line 1 that the speaker strikes, which calls to mind the Communion table, and in the thorn, tears, blood, wine, and corn (by which Herbert meant grain or wheat) which the speaker mistakenly thinks are absent from the holy, moral life or are signs only of his pain and disappointment. Properly understood, the true desires of the speaker reinforce not his momentary rebellion from but his ineradicably close connection to God. As in so many of Herbert's other poems, in "The Collar" one comes to God in a surprising way, in this case after exhausting oneself in an impatient struggle against a God who is overwhelmingly patient, kind, and understanding.

Sidney Gottlieb

THE COLOSSUS

Author: Sylvia Plath (1932-1963)
Type of poem: Lyric
First published: 1960, in *The Colossus*

The Poem

"The Colossus" is a fairly short poem in free verse, with six stanzas of five lines each. The title of the poem, which also serves at the title of Sylvia Plath's first collection of poetry, suggests both the classical world in which huge statues or monuments were constructed (for example, the Colossus of Rhodes, an ancient wonder of the world) and the enormity of the subject for the writer.

The poem is written in the first person, but the speaker of the poem does not place herself in a recognizably contemporary world; instead, she chooses a strange environment that seems to be partially a reconstruction of classical Greece and Rome and partially a bizarre world of exaggerated, nightmarish metaphors. As with many first-person lyrics, this poem is addressed to a specific "you"; however, the identity of the person addressed is withheld from the reader through the first three stanzas.

Plath begins with an image that suggests Humpty-Dumpty rather than the classical world. She can never get her colossus "pieced, glued, and properly jointed" together, no matter how hard she tries. Despite her attempts to "dredge the silt" from the throat of this thing (is it monster, statue, human, or animal?), all she hears are the untranslatable brays, grunts, and cackles proceeding from its lips. Because the oracles of Greece and Rome communicated by nearly incomprehensible messages, Plath thinks that perhaps these sounds are coming from a "mouthpiece of the dead, or of some god or other." Although she has worked for thirty years on her dredging project, she is "none the wiser"; no god's message has been heard.

The third and fourth stanzas remain focused on the image of the incomprehensible head, but they move from the lips to the brow, the eyes, and the hair. In addition, the fourth stanza finally removes some ambiguity by stating specifically that the "you" she is trying to recompose and listen to is, in fact, the speaker's father. The images become increasingly bizarre and macabre as the speaker crawls all over the "skull plates" of her father, trying still to clean and mend him. She then proceeds to eat her lunch in this huge burial ground. The father's enormity is clear not only because of the physical size of his ruined corpse/statue, but also because of the exaggerated comparisons he elicits from the speaker: Her father, all by himself, is "pithy and historical as the Roman Forum." The reader is convinced that the father is immensely important to the speaker by the sheer size and outrageousness of the comparisons.

The final stanzas end one workday for the tireless speaker and begin another. During the night, she protects herself from the elements by squatting "in the cornucopia/ Of [his] left ear," but she still hears nothing from him. The morning sun rises "from under the pillar of [his] tongue," but it rises silently: No message comes from the land

of the dead. The speaker is "married to shadow," not substance, because she is still en-
amored of her deceased father. The poem ends with a striking image, taken once again
from the classical world, of a boat's keel scraping the shore as it lands; she no longer
listens for this sound of rescue or deliverance—either because she does not expect a
husband-type figure to win her or because she has resolved herself to the fact that her
father will never return.

Forms and Devices

The chief literary technique employed by Plath is the conceit, or extended (and of-
ten exaggerated) metaphor. A reader can easily accept a quick metaphor which com-
pares a person with a statue, but Plath allows this metaphor to surprise the reader
when she insists on focusing her attention on the comparison for the entire poem.

Because of its subject matter, the poem could have easily become a macabre or sen-
timental piece, but because of the exaggerated and therefore humorous nature of the
conceit, the poem is saved from the problems inherent in a poem about mourning a
parent. The poem's seriousness is undercut by the oddity of her comparisons.

The scattered remains of a dead parent are horrific, but Plath's conceit allows her to
challenge the horror by placing the absurd alongside it. The speaker imagines herself
"crawl[ing] like an ant in mourning/ Over the weedy acres of [his] brow," but she com-
plicates the picture by having the metaphorical ant scale "little ladders with gluepots
and pails of Lysol." The poem becomes cartoonlike in its images: The ant carries glue
to fix the "immense skull plates" and Lysol to clear his eyes. When the poem regains
its seriousness with an allusion to Aeschylus's *Oresteia* (458 B.C.E.), the Greek trag-
edy, Plath again disrupts the sober scene by explaining, "I open my lunch on a hill of
black cypress." She eats surrounded by her father's bones and hair "littered . . . to the
horizon line." She has followed the metaphor for so long that the normal biological
demands, the ingredients usually of comedy, interrupt the poem, and she picnics amid
the littered scene. Finally, at night, when she protects herself from the elements near
the poem's close, she squats in "the cornucopia" of her father's severed left ear. This
hyperbolic, or exaggerated, comparison between a cornucopia and an ear, as with the
other metaphors in the poem, becomes oddly humorous because the conceit, or the
analogy between the father and the ruined statue, has become strained: He is her fa-
ther, a Greek or Roman ruin, litter, and a cornucopia.

Plath's successes come from her ability to risk the excesses of her metaphors, and
her work is important at least partly because of the extremes—in both subject matter
and style—she was able to reach in her writing.

Themes and Meanings

Many American poets writing after World War II concentrated on their own per-
sonal histories or family trees for poetic subject matter. Sylvia Plath is often linked
with Anne Sexton, Robert Lowell, and John Berryman, all poets writing in postwar
America, because of the self-analysis and self-reflection present in the poems. Often
these writers are called "confessional poets" because they reveal their own personal

obsessions, psychological quirks, or tawdry misdeeds in the poems. Plath's "The Colossus" fits into this school of poetry because of its self-absorption and the ambivalent feelings the speaker has toward her father.

Sylvia Plath's relationship with her father, who died when she was eight, is the subject of much of her poetry. In later poems, especially "Daddy," she reveals astonishingly strong and disturbing feelings toward her father. She imagines herself as a Jew and her father as a Nazi and confesses that she, in some way, relishes the role: "Every woman adores a Fascist,/ The boot in the face, the brute/ Brute heart of a brute like you." The poet seems to enjoy the need for punishment, perhaps to erase feelings of guilt about her father's death.

"The Colossus," an early poem, does not go quite so far in examining the psychologically disturbing relationship of father and daughter as "Daddy" does, but it does examine archetypal patterns of behavior. It is no accident that the poem's one direct allusion to a classical text comes with the "blue sky out of the Oresteia." That trilogy by the Greek tragic playwright Aeschylus deals in part with Electra's attempt to come to terms with the death of her father, Agamemnon. Sigmund Freud, working with this Greek myth, thought the Electra complex paralleled in many ways the male Oedipus complex, and he suggested that daughters often want to displace their mothers in order to capture totally their father's affections.

Plath's obsessive quest to reestablish contact with her father in "The Colossus" participates in some ways in this Freudian theory. The mother is invisible in the poem (and in most Plath poems); she is removed from the scene by the author's inattention to the relationship. The speaker confesses that her "hours are married to shadow" because of her devotion to her father's memory. In the poem, she labors to piece together her father in order to establish some type of relationship with him again; she wants to hear him speak, to listen to his words of advice.

The fact that the father lies scattered across the poem, littering the horizon, perhaps suggests the ambivalence the poet feels for her father. On one hand she wants to become reunited with him, but on the other the image she creates of a dismembered ruin perhaps suggests her anger at her father for leaving her when she was a young girl.

When a poem deals with a psychologically complex relationship, its meaning is often difficult to pin down. The seriousness of the poem's subject combines with the comic exaggerations of the conceit, and the desire of the speaker for reunion with her father is linked with Plath's own capacity to "create such a ruin" in the first place. To say that the poem's meaning is difficult to express is to say that Plath's relationship with her father was extremely ambivalent. Like most good poems, "The Colossus" creates its power from the tensions and ambiguities it contains.

Kevin Boyle

THE COMPANY

Author: Robert Creeley (1926-   )
Type of poem: Lyric
First published: 1988, in *The Company*

The Poem

In the poetry Robert Creeley wrote during the 1980's, he began to turn back to the early stages of his life, placing his present thoughts in a larger perspective through reflection on decisive moments of the past. The recollective sense of "The Company" is immediately established by the first word, "Backward," which is instantly qualified by the phrase "as if retentive," suggesting how experience accumulates. Creeley's placement of the well-known line from William Wordsworth's "My Heart Leaps Up," "The child is father of [Creeley says "to"] the man," then gives the poem specific direction; a dual track from childhood is drawn in terms of "use" (or personal choice) and "circumstance" (the outside world). The first quatrain, written in open verse in a flowing line dense with information, is followed by three similarly shaped stanzas that examine the implications of this formulation. The poet draws conclusions from his experience, summarized in terse, almost aphoristic form. The randomness of existence and the difficulty in determining the presence of any form or meaning in most human actions are posed as a central theme, as the "great expectations" of the "next town" repeatedly turn into an "empty plate" in actuality.

The fifth stanza epitomizes this situation. The poet looks back at the young men such as himself who were reaching maturity in the historical moment of World War II. The war pulled them out of a comparatively privileged cultural position and set them between "all the garbage/ of either so-called side." The poet remembers clinging to "an existential/ *raison d'être* like a pea/ some faded princess tried to sleep on," but this turns out to be merely a trendy philosophical scheme with no real value for the poet.

In the last three stanzas, the poet shifts to the present and reaches beyond it toward the future. Proposing a philosophical position that would permit an understanding of his generation's (or company's) life and times, the poet envisions a "recorder" (another version of the writer) who must attend not only to the official version of events of historians ("in books") or archaeologists ("under rocks") but, more crucially, to what is central to human survival—"some common places of feeling."

Although there is clearly a positive aspect to "the good times" that people must "take heart in remembering," there is also a constant consciousness of an almost nameless dread, referred to as "whatever it was,/ comes here again," a chilling indicator of the tenuousness of existence. The terrifying abruptness with which life can end engenders a feeling of unease, yet an adult's awareness of this threat might enliven each moment in an oblique fashion through the energy generated by the fear of extinction. The repeated use of the word "last" in the final stanza suggests both closure and a continuance into the unknown.

Forms and Devices

Creeley has said that he is "very at home" with colloquial language, and "The Company" is written with "a sense of source in common speech" characteristic of Creeley's voice. The vernacular is qualified by interposition of quotations from familiar poetry and brief catch-phrases with origins in foreign languages, which have become a part of American culture. These provide a contrasting context, establishing a tension between an official version of history and what Creeley feels are the genuinely significant elements of most people's lives. The Wordsworth quote recalls not only "My Heart Leaps Up" but also the much more famous "Ode: Intimations of Immortality." The Wordsworth reference seems to set a direction for the poem, but the data from one's early years are called into question by a barrage of words such as "banality," "vacant," "disjunct," and "ambivalent," which question the data's validity. Similarly, the line "Out of all this emptiness/ something must come . . . " is countered by the diminution of "great expectations" into "empty plates." In both cases, the somewhat portentous, lofty prospects promised by official culture have been turned into hollow shells. Even the adventure and excitement of foreign travel combined with the epoch-making danger of a global war, turn into a groping for meaning through reliance on historical slogans.

Creeley describes himself as "one who has been long in city pent," quoting from a sonnet by John Keats that also echoes John Milton's *Paradise Lost* (1667, 1674) and Samuel Taylor Coleridge's "Frost at Midnight" and "This Lime-Tree Bower My Prison." The references again set up a mood of expectation, but while "trying to make sense of it," Creeley's generation was "blasted" out of what he calls "humanistic" obligations. The use of the word "humanistic" is a reduction of the much more positive "human" of the last three stanzas, while the "*oblige*" of "*noblesse oblige*" carries again the pressure of externally imposed responsibility. The culmination of all these attempts to control "the company" Creeley speaks for is the failure of the more hip academic mind to offer some kind of explanation, its "existential *raison d'être*"— replete with sophisticated European connotations—collapsing into the simile of a "faded princess" (an exhausted Old-World image) who "was expectably soon gone."

The clash between the dominant political and cultural ideas and a growing awareness of their inadequacy is ingeniously developed through the close control of words and their location, an important element of Creeley's style in all of his work. There is a sense of qualification, even resistance, when the scientifically precise "scale" of the second stanza becomes the poetically suggestive "implication"; in the third stanza, the removal of the article before "small, still" compresses and intensifies the image of emptiness. The implication, without actual statement, of "we were" before "moving along" in the fourth stanza contributes to a growing sense of urgency expressed in rhythmic momentum. The first four stanzas are written in short word bursts, hesitant and incomplete, which mark the poet's confusion and distrust. An expository section that follows (stanzas 5 through 7) is composed of longer lines, a flowing narrative that encapsulates the deceptive and unsatisfactory "solutions" presented in polished rhetoric by the spokesman for a settled society. The last three stanzas occur as a single long, deliberative line. In a final rejection of what is expected, the repetition of the word "last" produces a pattern of continuance, so that even the feared end of life is qualified by the resonant reverberation of the words themselves.

Themes and Meanings

Robert Creeley has spoken of his friends and fellow artists as "a *company*, a kind of leaderless Robin Hood's band, which I dearly love. . . . There is no company dearer, more phenomenal, closer to my heart." He further describes this loose community as writers for whom poetry is "not a purpose, not discretion, not even craft—but *revelation*, initial and eternal." "The Company" is an attempt to express the sensibility that informs this conviction and to describe some of the conditions that contributed to its occurrence.

Creeley begins with negative assumptions because so much of his education and cultural conditioning seemed to interfere with the goal of his writing, "an actual possibility of revelation." While he respects the literary achievements of various canonical writers, the weight of their reputations and the force of their mastery of form tended to narrow his own possibilities. Even while accepting many of the traditional aspects of a New England upbringing, his inclusion of the phrase "ages hence," from Robert Frost's "The Road Not Taken," suggests that for him, neither road was appropriate, that he and his "company" had to blaze their own trail.

The tentativeness, the hesitancy, that characterizes much of Creeley's poetry is not evident here in the commanding, declarative tone the poet uses to dismiss the false assumptions that he and his contemporaries had to overcome. The last section attempts, as Creeley did in much of his work during the middle and late 1980's, to mingle (as Charles Molesworth says) "quiet acceptance" with "ineradicable doubt" in search of some enduring human qualities. The "common places of feeling" recall the Ezra Pound dictum "Only emotion endures," which Creeley often uses as a guiding precept. The tension between the "good times" one wants to remember and "whatever it was" (the nameless dread) one "can't forget" is part of the ultimate burden of human existence. This final juxtaposition of hope and fear defines the poet's existence, while the poem is itself an instrument in the maintenance of an optimistic attitude. It is typical of Creeley that by using language to confront and frame his fear in the repetition of an occasion ("the last, the last") that haunts his thoughts, he is doing all he can to overcome it.

Leon Lewis

COMPOSED UPON WESTMINSTER BRIDGE, SEPTEMBER 3, 1802

Author: William Wordsworth (1770-1850)
Type of poem: Sonnet
First published: 1807, in *Poems in Two Volumes*

The Poem

This poem's title, "Composed upon Westminster Bridge, September 3, 1802," tells the reader its setting: William Wordsworth is in London on the bridge that crosses the Thames River by the houses of Parliament, close to where Big Ben's Tower stands today. When he tells the poem's place and date of composition, however, the poet may not be strictly accurate. He probably began composing the poem on July 31 as he crossed the bridge at the beginning of a journey to France; he may have then finished it by his return on September 3. His sister, Dorothy Wordsworth, records that on July 31 as they drove over Westminster Bridge they saw St. Paul's Cathedral in the distance and noticed that the Thames was filled with many small boats. "The houses were not overhung," she reports, "by their cloud of smoke, and they were spread out endlessly, yet the sun shone so brightly, with such a pure light" that it seemed like "one of nature's own grand spectacles." Dorothy Wordsworth's description can help one to read the poem.

The reader may first think that the poet is musing to himself, but his somewhat public tone suggests a general audience. One may first be puzzled; if it were not for its title, the general subject of the poem would not be immediately apparent. Lines 1 through 3 make a forceful assertion, but it is a negative one: Whatever the "sight" turns out to be, nothing on earth is more beautiful, and only a very insensitive person could ignore it. All one knows of this "sight" so far is that it is impressive ("majestic") and moving ("touching").

In line 4, the reader discovers that the subject of the poem is the beauty of the city. One should probably take "City" to mean all the parts of greater London that could have been seen from Westminster Bridge in 1802, and perhaps in particular the sections called the City of Westminster (located by the bridge) and the City of London, with its towers and spires visible downriver on the north bank of the Thames. The poet, echoing his sister's description, describes the panorama of this vast city in the silence and clear air of an early morning in summer. He sees the tops of many different structures; he sees ships on the river, but most of all such urban landmarks as theaters and churches. The dome must be that of St. Paul's itself. His eyes move easily from these buildings to the sky and to the open hills and fields that in those days lay close to central London to the southwest and were visible on hills to the north.

At line 9, the poet stops his description of London and begins to compare it to those wonderful sights he has seen in nature. He has never seen anything in nature more beautiful than this view of the city. He has never seen a sight any more calm than this, nor presumably has any sight ever caused him to feel more calm himself. In the poem's final three lines, the poet returns to give vivid, even extravagant pictures of the beautiful city and the river. He exclaims to God that London's "mighty heart" is alive and motionless in houses that themselves "seem asleep."

Forms and Devices

This poem is a sonnet—a fourteen-line lyric poem with a moderately rigid rhyme scheme. In his sonnets, Wordsworth rhymes in the manner of the Italian Petrarch and the Englishman John Milton, not in that of William Shakespeare (the most famous sonneteer in English). Here Wordsworth rhymes *abba, abba, cdcdcd*. Two groups of four lines (or quatrains) form the octave (or opening eight-line grouping). This sonnet does not break down into units as markedly as do more traditional examples of the form. Although like most sonnets it changes direction after the octave, the change is less sharp than usual. The sestet's meaning shifts between lines 10 and 11, but the shift is not abrupt.

In spite of its rather strict form, the poem seems unconstrained. In most ways, its sentences proceed in a normal conversational English way, with a list here or a parenthetical remark there. One exception to this generalization is that the poet often inverts normal word order to achieve emphasis: "Dull would he be," "Never did sun," "Ne'er saw I." As a result, the poem reads somewhat like dramatic prose, even though the reader does feel a regular musical pulse. Wordsworth said elsewhere that he tried to write poetry in a language close to real speech, and here he appears to succeed. As in ordinary conversation, this poem's language has few extravagant figures of speech. A simile compares the city's morning beauty to "a garment" that it wears; valleys "steep" in sunlight. In the last three lines, the poet employs obvious personifications: The river has its own will, houses sleep, and London has a dormant mighty heart.

The force of the poem's language lies in its vigorous emphasis and its descriptions (and perhaps one allusion). As noted above, inversions of words often create strong emphases. Many lines, particularly in the octet, are enjambed; that is, many lines run into the next, propelling the poem's rhythm forward. The last six lines provide successive short, forceful, and somewhat unconnected exclamations and statements. Most readers can respond to the sights of the city that this poem provides. The image of the London skyline is vivid even to those who have never seen a picture of London, as are the separate pictures (the river, the houses) evoked by the personifications in the last three lines of the poem. (Note that Wordsworth has simplified what he must have seen; the boats that Dorothy mentioned do not appear in William's account.)

The poem reads easily. It presents its ideas forcefully by means of comparatively simple devices and vivid images. Nevertheless, many readers come away with a sense that there is more to the poem than an uncomplicated, vigorous description of what Wordsworth saw from Westminster Bridge.

Themes and Meanings

Between July 31 and September 3, 1802, William and Dorothy Wordsworth traveled to France to visit William's former lover, Annette Vallon, and William and Annette's illegitimate daughter, Caroline. Even though at this time Wordsworth was preparing to marry someone else, one should not assume that the visit was at all traumatic. The reader gets quite the opposite impression from the poet's account of a walk with his daughter that he describes in another sonnet, "It Is a Beauteous Evening." War had separated Wordsworth and Annette for ten years, and any idea that they might marry had been put aside. Undoubtedly, Wordsworth was living intensely at this time, but the reader should resist trying to find any specific autobiographical meaning in this poem.

To a reader of Wordsworth's other poetry, the most unusual thing about "Composed upon Westminster Bridge, September 3, 1802," is its subject matter. In most of his poetry, Wordsworth describes natural scenes: streams, hills, mountains, woods, and meadows—natural sights located in Switzerland, Wales, and most of all in the Lake District in northwestern England. He not only describes those scenes but also explains how experiencing them refreshes and ennobles the human spirit. In contrast, he usually pictures cities in general, and London in particular, as the opposite of the country, as places where those ennobling experiences do not happen, places where human nature is degraded. He celebrates his own escape from a city in the opening lines of *The Prelude* (1850), and later in that poem he describes the depravity of London at great length. He often sympathizes with his friend Samuel Taylor Coleridge because he was unlucky enough to have spent much of his boyhood in London.

So it is unusual that in this poem Wordsworth finds the city fully as beautiful as natural scenery. He celebrates London's beauty in many of the ways he talks about natural sights. As in "Lines Composed a Few Miles Above Tintern Abbey," what one sees on the earth's surface in London blends into the sky and harmonizes with it. The London scene is suffused in glorious light. As in other poems, this scene and its observer are "calm"—a word that to Wordsworth never means simply "without motion," but rather describes a profound and life-giving peace.

Wordsworth knows that he is not seeing the city in all of its aspects. He sees London at its best, early in the morning of a beautiful summer day. He knows that, later, the city will awake and that the streets will fill up with their normal noise and bustle. In colder seasons, smoke from fireplaces will darken the sky. Wordsworth's simile in lines 4 and 5 makes this point clearly: The beauty of the morning is like a garment which makes its wearer beautiful, but which can be taken off—presumably to reveal a different, less lovely city underneath. If line 6 contains an allusion to the insubstantial, soon-to-disappear "cloud-capp'd towers" of William Shakespeare's *The Tempest* (1611; act 4 scene 1), one sees even more vividly how ephemeral is Wordsworth's vision.

Nevertheless, the vision is real. Its effect is powerful, and it lasts in the memory. It is a vision of calm beauty—and something more. In other passages in his poetry, most notably in Book 1 of *The Prelude*, one senses a force outside the poet, pressing upon him. This force can be terrifying (as when great hills stride after him) or simply exciting or invigorating. In this poem, many readers sense that the poet has seen and evoked such a force in the autonomous river gliding "at his own sweet will," in the soon-to-awaken houses, and in the energy and potential activity of the sleeping collective heart of the inhabitants of London.

George Soule

CONCERNING EXAGGERATION, OR HOW, PROPERLY, TO HEAP UP

Author: Charles Olson (1910-1970)
Type of poem: Lyric
First published: 1953, in *In Cold Hell, in Thicket*

The Poem

"Concerning Exaggeration, or How, Properly, to Heap Up" is a long poem of one hundred lines describing the ideal poet and the fully realized human being, both of whom reject conventional limitations for identification with the totality of reality through exaggeration (literally, from the Latin root, "to heap up"), requiring a movement of the self into a reimagined world of fulfilling possibilities.

Written in 1951, the poem first appeared in *In Cold Hell, in Thicket*, edited by a poetic disciple, Robert Creeley, in 1953. The volume was the only book of short poems to be completed when Charles Olson was rector of Black Mountain College, an experimental alternative to conventional colleges, located in North Carolina. Both Black Mountain College and this collection of poems were intended as antidotes to the status quo in modern Western literature and culture, and the poems established Olson as a new force in American poetry.

In part 1, the speaker advises circumspection (meaning both "caution" and "a fully rounded perspective") regarding conventional notions of "blood" (restricted social perceptions of one's inherited identity). The advice is that people must all take a revolutionary look at all their "economies" and conventional systems and assumptions. The speaker then makes a major affirmation; namely, that he is more than the restricted, detached, or conventional self conditioned by society; he is everything, feels and affects everything, and expresses (or poetically sings) everything, be it wild or indifferent (lines 1 through 9).

Part 2 focuses on "How, Properly, to Heap Up"—in other words, how the speaker and the reader can best create such oneness with the totality of reality through conjuring up epic exaggeration in Greco-Roman, Hebraic, and other cultural myths of birth and engendering, as in the cases of Venus ("She/ came out of a wave"), Agamemnon ("who came back from the war to find his double," Aegisthus), and other legendary personages. The mythological figures in this section all suggest a reaching out (their "heaping up") beyond the individual self into a plethora of complex, even if grotesque, familial relationships. As such, they are mythic role models for human identification with a whole universe of becoming, yet they are no more fantastic ("No wonders") than the setting sun that in its descent touches everything, from tree branch to earth root (lines 10 through 37).

Part 3 changes the focus from blood and birth to the head and celebrates a mythic hero of the mind, a leader rendered all the more powerful from his union (his "heaping up") with a hawk whose wings encircle "the sides of his head." This role model had appeared in a dream that had generated exaggerations or fancies in the mind of the speaker, who thereby moved out of the self (his "heaping up") into a universe of possibility, becoming a "horse on both sides of a river" fondled by others, "each on each side." There is more self-aggrandizement in a charade converting a single individual into "two of us" in the united form of a "centaur." Such is the process of reorienting the self and reimagining the world ("And I twist,/ in the early morning, asking/ where/ does it stop") in order to enter the totality of reality (lines 38-57).

Part 4 begins with a statement of Olson's literary and philosophical creed. The totality of reality and its infinity of possibilities transcend the bounds of conventional realism that pigeonholes one's identity and perception of things. To apprehend infinity within the moment requires a receptivity within one that is as all-inclusive as reality is. One must exaggerate and "heap up" beyond the self. People must become living metaphors, creating vital bridges between their selves and the otherness of existence. Such living metaphors are the liberating movement of selves into a universe of multiple possibilities ("than as fabulous as to move") and express human achievement of an integration with total reality worthy of the Hindu goddess Shiva, who unites the opposites of destruction and creation ("he who is presented with her answer is/ that answer"). The poem closes as it began, with a call for circumspection (an all-encompassing perspective on things) and with a warning against restricted notions of "blood" that delimit one's identity, whose very symbol of imprisonment appears in the typography of the last three lines:

> (was what he said,
> at that point of
> his time).

Forms and Devices

"Concerning Exaggeration, or How, Properly, to Heap Up" is an experimental lyric poem divided into four parts and written in free verse. Its form was directly influenced by the poetic techniques of Ezra Pound. Pound helped to spearhead a modernist revolution in early twentieth century poetry of the Western world, and Olson was perhaps the most prominent, if not uncritical, follower of the methods practiced in Pound's *Cantos* (1917-1970). Both men shared an abhorrence of vague abstractions, with Olson going so far as to consider the generalizing tendency of the modern mind to be the major obstacle preventing the achievement of fulfilling totality of being.

Both poets strove for the exact word (*le mot juste*) and the precise image and discarded discursive poetic statement. Both favored intense compression and ellipsis—the deletion of all unnecessary words ("All, is of the matter")—to achieve a complex suggestiveness of meaning and a mythic resonance with an absolute economy of language.

They both indulged in maximum allusiveness by references to both Eastern and Western literary and historical figures and events to lend mythic richness and universality of significance to their poems. Olson, for example, piled on cryptic references to legendary figures serving as role models for a human totality of being in this poem, especially in parts 2 (lines 10 to 17 and 22 to 37), 3 (lines 38 to 45), and 4 (lines 72 to 87).

Finally, Olson imitated Pound's penchant for exploiting the literal and pictorial character of words that reached its zenith with the use of ideograms (word signs capturing a physical actuality in place of detested abstractions). Olson's poem literalizes words such as "exaggeration" and "circumspection" for a dramatic communication of his philosophy of experiencing the totality of reality. The poem does not merely represent but at times also presents meaning, as in the series of metaphors and similes (lines 72 through 87) expressing self-realization in the living act of metaphor (lines 68 through 71). Similarly, the concluding three lines constitute an ideogram picturing the circumscribed identity trapped in delimiting notions of conventional thought.

Themes and Meanings

"Concerning Exaggeration, or How, Properly, to Heap Up" is about the full flowering of the ideal poet and human being through movement beyond delimiting social conditioning (literally, the exaggeration of the self in the form of a "heaping up") into a whole universe of being and becoming.

Olson's influential essay "Projective Verse" (1950) rejected the partitioning of reality separating the human from the natural world as well as the subjective from the objective realm of being. Poetry is to assist readers in breaking down conventional boundaries and in experiencing the totality of things by avoiding abstraction and logical deduction and by striving for a cumulative inductive barrage of disordered feelings and thoughts to humble the intellect into a reoriented perception of a whole universe of being and becoming. Poetry is, therefore, inherently an exaggeration because it reimagines the world, enabling readers to transcend socially conditioned boundaries and grasp at new possibilities of seeing and self-realization.

As Sherman Paul wrote in *Olson's Push: "Origin," Black Mountain, and Recent American Poetry* (1978), such self-actualization through projective verse is the ultimate end of the poet's art and thought: "Felicity comes of obeying what [Ralph Waldo] Emerson called the soul's emphasis." In another of Olson's experimental essays, published in *Origin*, there is an attack on Socrates for fathering the delimiting Western system of education: "his methodology still the RULE: 'I'll stick my logic up, and classify, boy, classify you right out of existence.' "

Olson's "Concerning Exaggeration, or How, Properly, to Heap Up" is one of many experimental poems designed to dispel the conventional rule-mongering of his contemporaries and to extend the reach of the human psyche into the totality of reality. To achieve this end, the poem must not simply represent reality; it must also present and project a total reality to its readership through elaborate exaggeration.

Thomas M. Curley

CONCERNING NECESSITY

Author: Hayden Carruth (1921-   )
Type of poem: Narrative
First published: 1973, in *From Snow and Rock, from Chaos: Poems 1965-1972*

The Poem

"Concerning Necessity" is a narrative poem of forty-two lines, which are divided into seven six-line stanzas. Each stanza has inexact, or slant, rhymes in an *ababcc* scheme. The poem is written in the first person. Although authors often create a persona that is distinct from themselves, the persona of this poem is commonly seen in Hayden Carruth's poetry: The speaker is a man (a husband and father) who is living in a difficult environment filled with physical labor. To anyone who is aware that Carruth spent more than twenty years of his life as a laborer and handyman in a rural area of Vermont, it is clear that this poem arises from Carruth's personal experiences.

The poem begins in the first-person plural ("we"), indicating that there are many people who live in the rural hardship described. Stanzas 1, 2, and 3 depict a work-filled, arduous existence, in which he and others live in a "kind of rural twilight." These stanzas contain precise details of this existence, beginning with stanza 1 and its references to "hard dirt" and "difficult woods." The emphasis on work is continued in stanza 2, with a catalog of the types of work performed. The use of cataloging, which often occurs in poetry as a list of supportive examples or statements in parallel order, works well here because it intensifies the sense of the relentless labor of these people. The work involved is very physical—for example, driving a wedge, and making a chain saw "snarl once more." Stanza 3 shows dramatically that everything is "falling to pieces" and creates a near-despairing tone. The mood of the first three stanzas is dark and foreboding.

In stanza 4, however, the poem turns from physical description to meditation. The speaker now ruminates upon his situation, realizing that he had been deluded in thinking, like "that idiot Thoreau," as he says, that "necessity could be saved" by the natural facts of his rural existence. He now sees his delusion in believing that the "necessity" of his life, including hard work, suffering, and, eventually, death, could be compensated for solely by the objects of nature.

The poet again uses a catalog of natural objects in stanza 5 with references to trees, bird, mountain, and stars. Carruth, a noted observer and lover of nature, often turns in his poems to such natural phenomena for solace. Yet the stanza ends with the realization that "these things do serve/ a little though not enough," and the reader is left wondering what would be "enough." Carruth gives the answer in stanzas 6 and 7, in which the speaker states directly what "saves the undoubted collapse/ of the driven day and the year": He sees a woman "asleep in the field" or "telling a song to a child." These observations of tenderness and love in stanza 7 enable the speaker to "fall in love/ all over with human beauty."

Forms and Devices

"Concerning Necessity" has a formal structure of seven six-line stanzas which employ an *ababcc* slant-rhyme scheme and a line that varies between six and ten syllables. Within this structure, the poet uses strong images and direct, colloquial statement to convey his concerns. Although this combination may seem contradictory, it is often seen in Carruth's poetry, with the formal structure helping to "contain" the message of the content.

The slant rhymes are not exact, but each set of rhymes contains an echoing vowel or consonant. For example, the last word of line 1 "live," echoes the last word of line 3, "giving." This use of inexact rhyme gives the poem a structure which, at the same time, does not force it into a rigid pattern (as a full rhyme might). In the same way, the six-to-ten-syllable lines give the poem a sense of regularity without a strict syllable count. Most of the lines are six or seven syllables, and this repetition of length creates a strong rhythmic expectation, as may be seen clearly in the last four lines of stanza 2: "dig the potato patch/ dig ashes dig gravel/ tickle the dyspeptic chain saw/ make him snarl once more."

Appropriately for a poem about the difficult lives of people living in rural areas, Carruth often uses simple declarative statements that contain colloquial words and direct, easily understood images. Since this is a poem about people working in a natural environment, the actions are fundamental ones: cleaning a hen house, cutting corn, and watching a woman "telling a song" to a child.

Images are also basic: "dirt," "weeds," "potato patch," "white birch." The strength of these images dramatically re-creates the scenes and also anchors the speaker's meditations in the physical world. For example, the major meditation, "that necessity could be saved/ by the facts we actually have," is followed by a catalog of natural images such as the "white birch," "hemlock," "baybreasted nut-hatch." This pattern does not allow the speaker to drift off into abstraction; rather, it brings his thoughts back into the world.

Also appropriately for the simple, rural context of the poem, Carruth does not use figures of speech or thought, such as similes or metaphors. Since the poem is about the bare, unadorned lives of rural people, the poet creates a poetic language that is also bare and unadorned. Digging a potato patch, or watching a woman who is "done in or footsore," is not like anything else, Carruth implies; the reality portrayed must be taken for what it is, and this imbues that reality with importance and solidity. He does, however, present this reality in catalogs. For example, stanza 3 contains a catalog of the deteriorating situations in which the speaker finds himself: "the house is falling to pieces/ the car coming apart/ the boy sitting and complaining." These catalogs intensify the individual images and, through accumulation, give them a power they would not have separately.

Themes and Meanings

The essential question of the poem is hinted at in the title, "Concerning Necessity." What, the poet asks, can sustain the speaker in the face of his difficult, rural existence?

How can "necessity," or the determinants of one's life, be compensated for? This question is often raised in Carruth poems, which usually have a speaker who is alone in nature and is meditating on the meaning of his usually difficult life. In his poem, as in other Carruth poems, the speaker does not turn to metaphysics, to intuitive responses, or to nature for his answers: He looks for and finds them in his loved one— or, as the speaker says at the end of the poem, "right here where I live."

After depicting the hard work and deteriorating situations of his existence, the speaker says, "this was the world foreknown," meaning that he had sensed his life would come to this end. He admits to his "delusion" that nature could provide him with the answers he seeks. Like "that idiot Thoreau," he had held romantic notions that nature can provide the meaning for man's existence, if he would only search for such meaning. This notion, that man can find the answers to the basic questions of his existence in nature, was one of the dominant ideas of the great Romantic period of American literature, during the nineteenth century. Authors such as Ralph Waldo Emerson, Henry David Thoreau, and Walt Whitman were the more optimistic representatives of this period, and it is their belief in nature's ability to give complete meaning to man's existence that the speaker of the poem no longer accepts. Nature, he says, does "serve/ a little though not enough."

Instead, the speaker realizes, it is "human beauty" that "saves" him and, by implication, also saves "necessity" by compensating for all the hard work and suffering the man and his loved ones undergo. This human beauty is seen in the woman portrayed in stanzas 6 and 7, the one who is "down asleep in the field/ or telling a song to a child," the one who moves "in some particular way" and makes the speaker "fall in love all over with human beauty" again. Thus, the poem, which begins on a somber, laborious note and turns, in stanza 4, to a meditation on the speaker's condition, ends with a confirmation: It is the beauty of human beings in his everyday world that provides the speaker with meaning.

This poem, as are so many of Carruth's poems, is similar in an essential way to the poems of Robert Frost. Using nature as a backdrop, the poets place their personae in extremely difficult, almost overwhelming situations. These personae do not find easy answers in God and nature; rather, they must rely upon their own dogged perseverance and constant searching in order to find meaning in their lives. Carruth, though, goes one step beyond Frost, for he has his speaker find meaning in another human being, in love.

Len Roberts

CONCORD HYMN

Author: Ralph Waldo Emerson (1803-1882)
Type of poem: Lyric
First published: 1837, as "Original Hymn"; collected as "Hymn, Sung at the Completion of the Concord Monument," in *Poems*, 1847

The Poem
 This poem was first distributed as a leaflet on the occasion of the dedication of a monument (July 4, 1837) commemorating the battle of Lexington and Concord. However, since the cornerstone of the monument was laid late in 1836 and the monument carries the date 1836, some printed versions of the poem give that date. The poem was not printed again until it was included in Ralph Waldo Emerson's *Poems* (1847). The poem's original title was replaced in subsequent years by the now commonly accepted title "Concord Hymn." This short poem is composed of four stanzas of quatrains written in iambic tetrameter rhythm. The alternating lines rhyme in a pattern of *abab*.
 In the first stanza Emerson briefly reenacts the early American Revolution battle that took place at Concord bridge on April 19, 1775. The first line describes the location as being by an arched, rustic ("rude") bridge crossing a stream. Patriotic dedication is expressed in the subsequent line, "Their flag to April's breeze unfurled." The release of the flag to the wind symbolizes the fact that there is no going back to the conditions preceding this battle. The third line emphasizes the location by repeating the word "Here." The phrase "the embattled farmers" reminds the reader that the Americans were soldier-farmers fighting a professional British army. The most famous line of the poem, "And fired the shot heard round the world," expresses another anomaly: These farmers changed not only their own lives but also the lives of people living in far distant countries. The United States' successful fight for independence from England inspired the oppressed people of other nations also to protest tyrannical conditions.
 As the first stanza emphasizes the location of the battle, the second stanza emphasizes time—the period that has elapsed between the battle and the monument being erected to commemorate the battle. In the first line the identification of the enemy as "The foe" is softened by the concept that "the foe" has now been asleep (or perhaps dead) for many years. The second line semantically balances the "foe" (the English soldier) of the first line with his opponent, "the conqueror" (the American farmer), and then unites them in the same action of sleeping in silence. The third line explicitly identifies "Time," the great equalizer that has "swept" the "ruined bridge" away from that spot and into the stream that moves slowly ("creeps") toward the sea. Through time, nature removes political differences: "Foe" and "conqueror" are united in time's dissolution.
 The third stanza describes the immediate location ("On this green bank, by this soft

stream"), the immediate action of dedicating a monument ("We set to-day a votive stone"), and the purpose of the monument ("That memory may their deed redeem"). The last line projects the poem into the future, at the same time alluding to the action of the past. Like "the sires" of the group gathered at the dedication, their "sons" will certainly recall the deed of the "embattled farmers."

The fourth and last stanza expresses an address to a "Spirit." This apostrophe or prayer unites the heroes who "dare/ To die" with their children who are "free" and requests that the Spirit "Bid Time and Nature" spare "The shaft" (the monument raised to the dead "embattled farmers"). The poet is praying that the monument will not meet the fate of the ruined bridge.

Forms and Devices

Emerson believed that all of life consists of organic wholeness, and he wanted the form of his poetry—its rhyme, rhythm, symbolism, diction—to embody this view. His philosophic purpose did not always produce felicitous verse; indeed, critics of his first volume (*Poems*, 1847), which contained "Concord Hymn," highly criticized his use of poetic elements, finding philosophy and poetry at odds. However, they applauded "Concord Hymn" as an exception to this criticism.

Because of his belief in poetic liberty, Emerson himself wrote that he wanted "not tinkling rhyme, but grand Pindaric strokes" and "such rhymes as shall not suggest a restraint, but contrariwise the wildest freedom." Certainly, the drumbeat rhythm of "Concord Hymn" mimics its martial content; the line "the shot heard round the world" almost seems an echo of the actual fact. On the other hand, the rhythmic beat points to the original occasion of its publication; this poem was intended to provide lyrics for a hymn, both a song of patriotism and a prayer to the Spirit. In addition, the frequent masculine rhyme, both simple and effective, underscores the effectiveness of the historical action being commemorated by dedicating a memorial stone, that is also a "votive stone"; the poet intends the audience to remember the action of the past, the dedication of the present, and the people living in the future, all bound by the "Spirit" invoked in the final stanza.

The simple diction—most words are monosyllabic—also indicates strength, the strength of the farmers who fought and the simple stone that honors them. Action words in the first stanza ("arched," "unfurled," "embattled," "fired," "shot") relate to the farmers. Action words in the fourth stanza ("dared to die," "leave," "spare," "raise") relate to the Spirit. The use of these action words connects the farmers' actions with the Spirit's action, thus expressing Emerson's and the other American Transcendentalists' organic view of life.

Probably Emerson's most important contribution to American poetry was his use of the symbol. For him, Nature was itself a symbol of the Spirit. In "Concord Hymn," Nature, Time, and Spirit are capitalized; these abstract words provide a backdrop for the other actions. The poem uses natural actions ("slept" and "swept," "sleeps" and "creeps") to suggest that natural life pervades historic actions and political determination.

Diction used in the poem is filled with natural images ("the dark stream," "this green bank," "this soft stream"). Through the use of natural visual images of location, the poet indicates that nature and humankind share experiences when the individuals ("the embattled farmers") are true to the Spirit that Nature has placed within them.

Emerson's central symbol is the use of the bridge to represent a man-made object which has disappeared since the battle that took place on it. Likewise the monument (the North Bridge Battle Monument) represents a man-made object that will, like "the rude bridge," disappear and become part of the sea unless the Spirit bids "Time and Nature [to] gently spare/ The shaft." Although the "votive stone" represents a stronger man-made symbol, it will avoid the destruction of Nature only if humankind and the Spirit work together.

Themes and Meanings

Emerson's first collection, *Poems*, indicates an introspective thinker whose idiom was highly intellectualized. Yet a few poems toward the end of the volume, such as "Concord Hymn," deal more concretely with Emerson's life in Concord. In fact, Emerson's personal life and the lives of his family were tied very closely with the erection of the monument. The famous fight with the British redcoats had taken place near the Manse, the Emerson family home. Emerson's grandfather, Samuel Ripley, gave the town of Concord a piece of land on the condition that a monument commemorating the battle of April 19, 1775, would be erected there. On the occasion of the dedication of the monument, Ripley recited the original hymn, written by a "citizen of Concord" (Emerson), which was then sung by a choir to the tune of "Old Hundred." Thirty-eight years later, Emerson was part of the committee that hired Daniel Chester French to sculpt a statue of the "Minute Man"; the first stanza of "Concord Hymn" was engraved on its base. These circumstances connect the poet closely with the historical event, the Concord location, and his audience.

In addition to his personal connection with the circumstances celebrated in "Concord Hymn," Ralph Waldo Emerson saw himself as a prophet to the American people. In turn, many of the American people saw Emerson as a person who embodied the rugged individualism of the American pioneers and the minutemen who opposed the British Empire. In "Concord Hymn" Emerson expressed the "Self-Reliance" he described (in his famous essay of the same name) as essential to the individual's personal development. Against all odds, the "embattled farmers" faced death in order to acquire the liberty to express their own beliefs.

Emerson believed the power of this self-reliance arose because each individual is a microcosm of the Oversoul, the "Spirit" the narrator addresses in the fourth stanza. Since Nature and Time reflect the power of this Oversoul, the narrator appeals to the Spirit to "bid" them spare the shaft (the monument).

The conflict between Nature (exemplified in the destructiveness of Time) and the Spirit (expressed in the heroic patriotism of the minutemen) is a central theme of "Concord Hymn." This conflict somewhat qualifies the nationalistic spirit of the poem by pointing to the transience of human works (the bridge and possibly the monument). In the past, Time swept the ruined bridge "Down the dark stream." The persona prays to avert the changing of a "soft stream" to a "dark stream." However, while his exhortation to the Spirit provides a feeling of aesthetic conclusion, its tentative nature does not inspire any great religious confidence.

Agnes A. Shields

A CONNACHTMAN

Author: Padraic Colum (1881-1972)
Type of poem: Ballad
First published: 1907, in *Wild Earth: A Book of Verse*

The Poem

Padraic Colum's "A Connachtman" consists of nine ballad quatrains in which the lyric persona, an old singer from the west of Ireland, imagines his own wake. In a song full of pity and sadness, as well as humor, he views death, on one hand as a mythic continuum of past, present, and future and, on the other, as an irretrievable closure of life. Death makes him look back to his past and remember the numerous joys of life he has shared with his friends. Also, his wake helps him realize that the account of his travels and exploits, retold by the old and admired by the young, has given his life the aura of a Celtic bard. It is this mythic quality that makes it possible for the lyric persona to reunite with the land and its ancient spirit. Yet, together with emphasizing the importance of tradition as a repository of racial identity, the ballad draws the reader's attention to the idea that death severs humanity's direct connection with nature and the simple pleasures and beauty of life.

In the opening stanza of the ballad the old peasant singer presents to the reader, in a rather humorous way, his greatest "fear": a large and noisy wake at which "hundreds" of people come to show their respect. Considering himself modest and insignificant, he remembers, in the second and third stanzas of the ballad, his past travels in the rural, and, thus, most authentic, Irish provinces of Connacht and Munster. A friend of many "good men," he lets no one surpass him in physical strength, skill, or generosity. He is "foremost" in sports and arts: "In music, in song and in friendship/ In contests by night and by day," traditional masculine qualities that earn him his companions' respect and affection. These joyful memories, however, are interrupted in the fourth stanza by the coarse reality of death. The lyric persona addresses those present at his wake, and one of his friends in particular, with a request—he asks him to "Make smooth the boards of the coffin/ That shortly will cover my face."

This brief loss of confidence, however, is counterbalanced by the next four stanzas, in which the singer envisages Ireland's response to his death. "The old men," the repository of folk history, will remember him and spread gallant stories about him, while the young generation's "sure and clear . . . praise" of him promises further life to his "deeds." No one is silent, not even "the young girls" who, with heads bent in respect, "will pray" for him "near the door."

The ballad reaches its climax in the eighth stanza with the appearance of the "Three Women," a mythic trio closely associated with Mother Ireland, who have come to complete the wake by singing their funeral song of lamentation for the peasant bard. The mythic qualities of this appearance close the circle of life and death by reuniting hero and land. However, despite death's heroic characteristics, in the last stanza the lyric persona redefines the nature of his "grief": the sad realization that he will never "hear,/ When the cuckoo cries in Glenart" and that "the wind that lifts when the sails are loosed/ Will never lift [his] heart."

Forms and Devices

Colum is known for the simple and lyrical quality of his verse. Although he writes his verse in English, he is considered one of the most talented representatives of the Catholic peasant tradition in Ireland during the first decades of the twentieth century. Thus, as a folklorist, storyteller, and poet, he strives to reproduce in his verse the vitality of rhythm and the simplicity of Irish folk songs and traditional ballads. In "A Connachtman" Colum demonstrates this by following the quantitative meter (determined by the relative duration of sound), a characteristic feature of Old and Middle Irish prosody, instead of the accentual-syllabic (qualitative) rhythm used in English versification. For example, Colum employs predominantly the anapestic foot—a three-beat foot with stress on the third syllable—which allows him to achieve the musical and songlike qualities he desires. Also, the end rhymes the poet uses in the *b* positions of the rhyme scheme *abcb* of the ballad are primarily masculine—it is the final accented syllable that contains the repetition of sounds: "place" and "face," "say" and "pray," "day" and "away." This results in a powerful rhyme, easy to remember and quite frequent in folk songs.

In addition to rhyme, Colum emphasizes assonance and alliteration in end rhyme or internal rhyme positions—two factors that also contribute to the musical quality and the simplicity, in a very positive sense, of "A Connachtman." Assonance, for example, is frequently substituted for true end rhyme in the *b* lines: "boys" and "voice." The first stanza presents an instance of alliteration: "my wake won't be quiet,/ Nor my wake-house a silent place." Other examples of vowel and consonantal alliteration include: "going home in the dawning," "down from the Mountain," "I bore the branch," and "the deeds in my days."

In "A Connachtman" Colum's efforts to preserve ancient Celtic elements in contemporary Irish life are also revealed in the notable combination of traditional Irish versification, mythological subject matter, and symbols with commonplace situations of contemporary peasant life in rural Ireland, such as the wake of a dead peasant singer. Thus, the mention of the country fairs with their traditional Gaelic sport and music "contests by night and by day," together with the central role of the divine female trio, the "Three Women" who "come down from the Mountain" in order to sing "the Keen" for the dead poet and escort his body, help re-create an image of ancient Ireland and some of its most respected men—the minstrel-poets.

Themes and Meanings

"A Connachtman" is one of the twenty-five short poems that comprise Colum's first collection of verse, *Wild Earth: A Book of Verse*. Critics agree unanimously that it is this collection that provides the groundwork for his future poetic work and achievements. Known for their focus upon Catholic rural Ireland, its oral tradition, and its ancient past, Colum's ballads sing of the noble spirit of those whose lives and identity are firmly rooted in and depend upon the land. Despite all hardship, these men and women have preserved the vital link with the Irish soil and continue to define themselves through the natural cycles of life and death, sowing and reaping, hope and despair. Because he takes a keen interest in the language, structures of expression, and symbols of the rural west, Colum's diction and methods of versification remain basically untouched by current developments in modern Irish and Continental poetry.

This does not mean, however, that Colum does not participate actively in the social processes of his time. An ardent supporter of the cause for Irish national independence from Great Britain, Colum takes upon himself the task of becoming Ireland's peasant poet. Because of his Catholic and rural origins and upbringing, nationalist activists recognize his work and aspirations as authentic, unlike those of Anglo-Irish poets such as Lady Augusta Gregory, William Butler Yeats, or Æ.

Although his ballads lack the militant edge and didacticism of the verse of most nationalistic poets, Colum's use of mythic symbolism in "A Connachtman" does allow for some, though hardly profound, nationalistic interpretations. Thus, the image of the "Three Women" in stanza 8, in addition to its associations with the Christian Trinity or Mother Ireland, could be also seen to represent the ancient trio of female deities from the Tuatha Dé Danann ("people of the goddess Danu"), the prehistoric Irish race of gods. Significantly, Morrigan, one of these three goddesses, is a goddess of battle, strife, and fertility. There is another trio of Celtic goddesses that has special importance in this context: the Irish sovereignty goddesses Eriu, Banba, and Fotla. Eriu, associated with the land, is a personification of Ireland; Banba represents the spirit of Ireland and is used as a poetic name for the country, and Fotla, having ruled the island before the Gaels arrive, gives Ireland its name.

Again, like the trio from the Tuatha Dé Danann, the sovereignty goddesses are also closely connected with warfare. Such deep and nuanced possibilities of mythic symbolism, which combine natural (rural) and spiritual dimensions, creativity and warfare, national and all-human characteristics of Irish identity, allow Colum's "A Connachtman" to reach a balance between what is essential in the identity of an Irish person and has been preserved since antiquity and what is gained through individual experience. The result is a vital dialogue between Ireland's past and present in the language of the past. "He has brought once more the peasant mind into Anglo-Irish poetry," Ernest Boyd wrote about Colum in *Ireland's Literary Renaissance* (1916), "which is thus renewed at the stream from which our national traditions have sprung, for it is the country people who still preserve the Gaelic element in Irish life, the beliefs, the legends, and the usages which give us a national identity."

Miglena Ivanova

CONNOISSEUR OF CHAOS

Author: Wallace Stevens (1879-1955)
Type of poem: Meditation
First published: 1938; collected in *Parts of a World*, 1942

The Poem

"Connoisseur of Chaos" is a short poem divided into five boldly numbered stanzas of very loose blank verse—unrhymed lines, each with five stresses. While II, III, and IV are full stanzas of ten to twelve lines, the opening and closing units (I and V) do not work as stanzas so much as brief propositions of only two and three lines.

Stanza I, in fact, is an opening gambit consisting of two ruthlessly opposing propositions, as if this connoisseur (an expert in chaos) is beginning a logical proof: *A*, any violent order is finally merely disorder; and *B*, any great disorder is really a kind of order. The mind-tease of *A* and *B* can be illustrated endlessly, and the rest of the poem seems, at first, to be an attempt to illustrate the point.

Stanza II contains more propositions, but now readers have several "if x, then y" proposals cast in material of a rather whimsical nature—if flowers are bright in both Connecticut and in South Africa, which obviously they are, the speaker states, then there is an essential unity in the world. Disorder is really orderly if the big picture is considered.

Yet in stanzas III and IV the speaker damns this sense of order as being perhaps too easy, even sentimental. Things fall apart when readers remember how "squamous" (encrusted) human minds become when confronted with all the squirming facts in a world that can never be ordered. Finding illustration or lovely order in the world is not enough to endure a realization of vastly limited human perception. There are things in this part of the poem which indicate that humans in the twentieth century are at an impasse. The speaker uses a collective voice which states the impossibility of returning to a simpler world order—to the "old order," say, of the church. Because that order seems violent—forced and even destructive—it is strongly implied that the way orthodoxy or institutions attempt to impose order leads to repression and war. The knowledge that old orders end badly almost forces an acceptance that all new orders will have a similar fate. Despair is the result. Each human attempt at making sense of life falls into "the immense disorder of truths," as if dropping into an abyss. By implication, the contemporary world will end there as well.

One last time the speaker makes a proposal: What if the disorder of truths itself should ever become so largely perceived, by minds with unvested interests, that another great order is suddenly perceived? The result is "the pensive man"—a person who can live with ideas and not fall hopelessly into despair when order is again elusive.

The connoisseur abandons his argument in stanza V and gives one last teasing set of lines. He gives up his propositions for a quick image of the one-in-the-many paradox.

Forms and Devices

An important device, almost a trick, in this poem is in the extralogical jump from the cold, unpromising propositions of "*A*" and "*B*" to the lovely matched brevity of the eagle image at the end. Readers have to make a violent connection between those cold, opening propositions and that lovely closing image.

Wallace Stevens helps by putting rather proselike, longer stanzas in the middle of his poem. There are many repetitions of Stevens's "if [x is true] . . . and it is" in these longer stanzas. He perhaps does this in order to provide a strongly implied "therefore." This is the language of logical argument; it is also the impasse out of which the poem must find its way. If readers hear how prosaic and logical Stevens sounds in his sentence structures, they may also hear this "if/then/therefore" language suddenly given up with a kind of shrug—"Well . . . " (IV, line 1).

Up to this point, the connoisseur has not been the kind of speaker who uses conversational shrugs. In adopting more relaxed phrases from this point, he also abandons the collective "we" in favor of the personal "I." He locates himself in an intimate way by declaring, almost out of nowhere, that it is April as he writes and that the wind is blowing after days of constant rain. This relaxing of the language and mood is part of the poem's formal strategy. A mock-pedantic tone has been set up and then discarded so that readers might be given something linguistically fresh, if still puzzling, at the end. Section V is yet another proposition, but it comes from an entirely different realm from that of the propositions given at the beginning.

Themes and Meanings

The thematic thrust of this poem is in its demonstration of using poetry to make a leap from one realm of thinking to another. Stevens had a very long career as a poet, and he never tired of composing poems which get at the nature of what it means to think poetically. Thinking poetically is not whimsical for Stevens; it is separate, but no less real than other ways of thinking. "Connoisseur of Chaos" is a poem about Poetry with a capital *P*—the aesthetics of human experience and what Stevens called the "Supreme Fiction." The persona in this particular poem (the cold-eyed pedant) speaks convincingly of a possible impasse leading to despair in Western twentieth century thinking if people did not have access to poetry's truths. Stevens thought it might be a despair which cuts deeper than anything previously experienced in the history of humankind. During the poet's life, emerging areas of scientific discovery—of non-Euclidean mathematics, to offer only one example—made uncertainty the only certainty in the universe. Science prevented a return to the confidence of Sir Isaac Newton's so-called laws of nature, which once explained much about the physical world while enabling people to imagine a god having set those laws into motion. That order had been deposed. The poem suggests that many experience the bliss and then the horror in the vastly limited powers of everyday perception. The speaker himself is skilled at illustrating how language encourages him to make gorgeous order (nonsense?) of the world. He states, in effect, "I can make all the lovely correspondences in life and nature seem 'as pleasant as port.' " Stevens is making fun of his own task as a poet quite possibly immersed in mere pleasantries. Even ordinary use of language forces those who speak it into analogies they do not wish to make. Some of the despair over reaching impasses in everyday thinking is related to Stevens's sense of his times. Not stated here, but lying behind the dilemma of the poem, is the following address to the collective "we" at the center of this poem: Living in an age of advanced linguistic and psycholinguistic studies, findings have made people aware of what has been called an imprisonment in language.

The connoisseur/speaker strives for a way out of the impasse. One way is for the connoisseur to play with the independent domains of art and science and turn those domains on their heads. Late in the poem he likens his "*A*" and "*B*" propositional thinking, which initially got him started, to that which is rigid, "statuary, posed/ For a vista in the Louvre." Science can lead straight to the prison house if discoverers begin to worship their own discoveries. The discoveries themselves become museum pieces.

To find the domain of truth which is only possible in art, Stevens eschews museums for something more fleeting—for "things chalked on the sidewalk." The chalk, associated with a scientist doing complex mathematical proofs, is placed in the hands of the poet ("the pensive man"), whose blackboard is the exposed, vulnerable sidewalk slate where proofs are temporary.

The pensive man is the other side of the pedantic-sounding speaker, the connoisseur of chaos. Both modes of being—pensive and pedantic—can exist in the same mind. Most people have "*A*" and "*B*" ways of thinking. Such thinking must be integrated; it must become consonant with all other ways of thinking. Only the pensive man, the person perhaps ready to give up every proposition he ever chalks, has the ability to see an eagle float in the sky and to perceive that one bird as part of a huge scheme. Implied is the idea that the eagle's nest is only briefly available as an order, and a vision of God is presented here in Stevens's near-religious wording. The meaning in this Imagist ending is all created by implication: The mind presumably returns to doubt, in the same way the mind goes back and forth between a certainty of huge orders and disorders. From this sense of all that is out there, all poetry springs. Hence the mind is not defeated by chaos, whose vastness the mind cannot begin to fathom. Poets and their readers have in them the courage and the vision to be the connoisseurs of chaos. The vast spheres of chaos will never be tapped, but neither will the sheer human verve to think on chaos and make it one of life's richest experiences.

Beverly Coyle

CONSTANTLY RISKING ABSURDITY

Author: Lawrence Ferlinghetti (1919-   )
Type of poem: Lyric
First published: 1958, in *A Coney Island of the Mind*

The Poem

Lawrence Ferlinghetti's "Constantly Risking Absurdity" is a free-verse poem consisting of thirty-three lines, broken into three progressively shorter sections of eighteen, nine, and six lines. The poem examines the role of the poet in society, the risks a poet must take, the relationship of the poet to the reader, the qualities of perception a poet must possess, and the relationship of poetry to beauty and truth.

This poem is one of twenty-nine poems grouped together under the title "A Coney Island of the Mind," one of three sections in the collection of the same name. In an author's note preceding these poems, Ferlinghetti says he felt "as if they were, taken together . . . a kind of circus of the soul," suggesting their variety and vitality. "Constantly Risking Absurdity," one of two poems in the group that actually uses circus imagery, is untitled in the book, appearing only as poem Number 15 and subsequently taking its name from its first line.

The core of the poem is the assertion in line 6 that the poet is "like an acrobat," with the entire poem taking the form of an extended comparison between poetry and acrobatics, both of which (as the opening lines suggest) are performances risking "absurdity/ and death." The poem develops this comparison by portraying the poet as a tightrope walker performing on a "high wire of his own making," risking his life, dependent not only upon his own skill but also upon the audience, because he is "balancing on eyebeams." Poetry needs an audience, Ferlinghetti suggests, to complete and sustain the creative act of the poet.

At the end of the first section of the poem, Ferlinghetti introduces the idea that as the poet-acrobat performs his tricks, he depends upon clarity of perception, not "mistaking/ any thing/ for what it may not be." This idea is further developed in the second section, with the assertion that a poet is a "super realist" whose success and whose very life are contingent upon perceiving "taut truth." Just as high-wire artists must place their feet carefully upon the wire, poets must keep their eyes on the truth they wish to convey in their poems. Poets not only are concerned with truth but also attempt to capture beauty in their work, and so Ferlinghetti personifies "Beauty" as a female circus performer who is part of the act. At the end of the second section, she "stands and waits," readying herself to leap into the air and be caught by the poet-acrobat. In other words, Ferlinghetti suggests, poets must not only perceive truth but also catch beauty in their work.

Does the poet-acrobat in this poem succeed? Ferlinghetti does not say, but the third and final section vividly portrays the plight of the poet,

                            a little charleychaplin man
                                who may or may not catch
                        her fair eternal form
                                spreadeagled in the empty air
                            of existence

Interestingly, the poet is referred to here in the concluding lines as "a little charley-chaplin man," adding to the portrait of the poet the idea that, like Chaplin's famous "Little Tramp" persona, he is an Everyman constantly trying to beat the odds and whose attempts are touched with humor and pathos.

Forms and Devices

The placement of the lines on the page is typical of many of Ferlinghetti's poems, but it seems particularly appropriate for this poem: The lack of a fixed left-hand margin and the irregularly staggered lines, ranging in length from two to eight words, suggest the poet-acrobat's teetering motions as he tries to maintain his balance. Nearly half the lines begin near the middle of the page, approximating a center of balance, with other lines to the left and right suggesting the precariousness of equilibrium. Thus there is a strong visual component to the experience of reading the poem. Ferlinghetti's free-verse technique also avoids punctuation, which adds to the free-floating quality. Although each of the three sections begins with a capital letter, the poem can be read as one long sentence, the final clause of which is incomplete, stressing the risks poets take, as well as the inconclusive nature of any judgment of poetic success.

The lines containing the simile upon which the poem is based,

                    the poet like an acrobat
                        climbs on rime
                            to a high wire of his own making

illustrate Ferlinghetti's playful way with language by imperfectly rhyming "climbs" and "rime," the latter an obsolete spelling of the word "rhyme," the root meaning of which includes both the coupling of words with similar sounds and the rhythmic structure of a poem. Thus the importance of poetic devices and techniques to the poem's success is emphasized. Ferlinghetti is also reminding readers that the root meaning of the word "poet" is "maker."

In addition to irregularly appearing rhymes, both internal and external, other devices of sound are found throughout the poem, including assonance (the long *a*'s and *i*'s in the lines quoted above) and alliteration ("who must perforce perceive/ taut truth/ before the taking of each stance or step"). Together with the density of stressed syllables in the phrase "perceive/ taut truth," the alliteration here accentuates the importance of Ferlinghetti's point—that clear vision is necessary for the poet.

Ferlinghetti's playfulness can be seen elsewhere in the poem, for example in his coining of the phrase "slight-of-foot tricks," a play on the phrase "sleight of hand," which again emphasizes the idea of poetry as a performance, poets being like verbal magicians. Ferlinghetti is also fond of puns, as when he says, "Beauty stands and waits/ with gravity/ to start her death-defying leap," which suggests the critical nature of the situation, its serious demeanor, and the force of gravity that will cause its fall.

Informal yet precise in tone, the language of the poem is a blend of the ordinary and the somewhat obscure ("entrechats"), with occasional neologisms, like "slight-of-foot tricks" and "charleychaplin man." The poem also skillfully combines abstract and concrete language. Continuing the abstract language that concludes the first section, the second section begins abstractly and then starts to turn concrete with the word "taut," before moving on to a more concrete description of the poet-acrobat's movements. With regard to figurative language, in addition to the controlling simile of the poem, several key metaphors advance its argument. For example, the assertion that the poet-acrobat "paces his way/ to the other side of day" suggests that poetry pierces through the world's appearances to discover significance hidden from ordinary perception. "The other side of day" may also suggest night, a realm of mystery in which the poet feels comfortable.

Themes and Meanings

The notion of risk taking is central to Ferlinghetti's portrayal of the poet's role in the world. To say that the poet is "Constantly risking absurdity/ and death" is to remind the reader of how poetry is marginalized by a society that often finds the language and assertions of the art absurd and meaningless. This is partly because poetry refuses to yield to the forces of conformity and standardization, but poetry can also pose a threat to the state. In Plato's *Politeia* (*Republic*, 1701), Socrates advocated the banishment of poets from the ideal society because of their tendency to depart from reasoned discourse.

Many poets have literally risked death by having the courage to confront the injustices of their society. Osip Mandelstam and Federico García Lorca both lost their lives for standing up to totalitarianism and fascism. The poet can risk other types of death as well, such as a death of the spirit when creativity fails or the reader loses interest. Stage performers often speak of dying on stage when the audience fails to respond. In fact, Ferlinghetti's poem strongly asserts that a poet needs the support of his readers. He may perform "above the heads/ of his audience" because he takes chances that most people do not take, but he is "balancing on [their] eyebeams."

For Ferlinghetti, therefore, the poet's role is highly public and entails performance, which is in keeping with the role of poetry proposed by the Beat poets, with whom Ferlinghetti has been associated. The Beats, after all, were largely responsible for creating the popularity of poetry readings in the twentieth century, and Beat poets such as Gregory Corso, Jack Kerouac, and Allen Ginsberg, all of whom were published by Ferlinghetti's publishing company, City Lights Books, were well aware of the risks of challenging society's established values.

In order for the risks taken by poets to be meaningful, their visions of reality must be clear. To say that poets perform "without mistaking/ any thing/ for what it may not be" is to say that they see things for what they are. A poet is not merely a realist but a "super realist," able to pierce through mere appearance, perhaps even able to perceive a mystical reality unobscured by the illusions society creates.

   With an echo of John Keats's "Ode on a Grecian Urn," Ferlinghetti emphasizes the importance of the concepts of truth and beauty to the poet. By maintaining contact with the truth, however tenuous, the poet approaches Beauty and in fact must catch "her fair eternal form" for the poem/performance to succeed. Whether the poet in Ferlinghetti's poem succeeds is not known, for the verse concludes with the image of Beauty "spreadeagled in the empty air/ of existence," a wonderful image that also suggests the existential vulnerability of the human condition. For the poet, Ferlinghetti implies, the rewards of the perilous and exhilarating attempt to capture beauty are worth all the risks.

David L. Elliott

CONTEMPLATIONS

Author: Anne Bradstreet (1612?-1672)
Type of poem: Meditation
First published: 1678, in *The Tenth Muse Lately Sprung Up in America: Or, Several Poems Compiled with Great Variety of Wit and Learning, Full of Delight*

The Poem

"Contemplations" is a poem of thirty-three seven-line stanzas that consider various aspects of nature and biblical history and reflect upon their spiritual significance. The title suggests that the poem is a collection of isolated reflections, but within the poem are several sequences that each develop an idea over a number of stanzas.

The poem begins with Anne Bradstreet noticing the beauty of fall colors in New England as the sun sets. Many readers have shared the experience of delight in the beauty of nature. Bradstreet does not stop with her description of nature and the effect nature's beauty has on her. She goes on in the next stanza to relate this common experience to her spiritual beliefs: If God is known by his works on Earth, and since nature as experienced is so beautiful, then how wonderful must God be, who created all of this. Selecting a single oak tree from all the beauty around her, the poet marvels on the longevity of the oak and is inspired to think about the spiritual parallel—eternity.

In the next four stanzas Bradstreet contemplates the sun, acknowledging its glory, which caused it to be considered a god by some societies. In language reminiscent of the biblical Song of Songs, Bradstreet compares the sun to a bridegroom rushing from the chamber to make his daily and seasonal journeys. At the end of the sequence, Bradstreet again uses the physical phenomenon as an emblem reflecting the glory of the Creator.

In the next section she describes herself wandering alone. She looks toward heaven in the hope of being able to glorify God in some way, but she is stymied by a sense of her own inadequacy. This leads her to consider the lowly grasshopper and cricket, both of which seem able to praise God in their own way. She wonders again at her own incapacity as she contemplates the ease with which these humble creatures worship.

The poem takes a major turn after Bradstreet remarks that even the lowliest of creatures can praise God adequately while she remains "mute." She turns to a major preoccupation—time and eternity. Memory makes the past alive, as does history, and thinking about the past makes a person older in imagination than Methuselah. Thus Bradstreet shifts from looking at nature to looking at the Bible.

Stanzas 11 to 16 review the history of Adam and his progeny, Cain and Abel. Just as nature has a deeper meaning for Bradstreet, biblical history also has a lesson: Even though current lives are much shorter than the lifespans of humanity's biblical forefathers, they are shortened even more by foolish sensuous practices. Bradstreet compares human mortality to nature's cyclical process of dying in winter only to be rejuvenated in the following spring: When a person dies, there is no rejuvenation the next spring. Human mortality seems a curse. When Bradstreet wonders if she should then praise the trees, she reminds herself that only people, not nature, can aspire to immortality.

In the next section, she moves from contemplating the woods to the rivers and streams. She acknowledges the constancy of the stream that moves swiftly forward, despite obstacles, until it reaches its desired goal, the ocean. Thus, the stream's faith and determination are a model for humanity to follow. The fish in the stream simply follow their own nature to be happy. The poet's attention is next drawn to a bird, which she calls a Philomel. The bird does not worry about the past or fear the future; it simply enjoys its present. People, on the other hand, in stanzas 29 and 30, lead wretched lives, filled with worry, sickness, and pain, yet still do not yearn for eternal life. People are like mariners who think everything is fair sailing until a sudden storm arises to remind them of their precariousness.

The last stanza reminds the reader that only above can humanity find security. Indeed, only eternal salvation will survive earthly time. Time and the ravages of earthly life will be conquered only by those who have faith and by those who are chosen for everlasting life.

Forms and Devices

The poem is a series of seven-line stanzas, with each stanza using the rhyme scheme *ababccc*. The closing triplet of each stanza provides a sense of an end, and the finality of each stanza is further confirmed by the strategy of an extra foot in each final line. The first six lines of each stanza are regularly iambic pentameter (five feet consisting of an unstressed syllable followed by a stressed syllable). The last line of each stanza has six feet (hexameter). This is an adaptation of the Spenserian stanza.

More important than rhyme and meter is Bradstreet's adaptation of emblem form in this poem. Emblem books were popular in the sixteenth and seventeenth centuries, and Bradstreet probably had access to many while she lived in England at the estate of the Earl of Lincoln at Sempringham. Emblem books featured a pictorial image or woodcut and an accompanying poem that explained the moral lesson of the image. In "Contemplations" Bradstreet looks at a natural image—the trees, the sun, the river, the fish, and so on—and then explains for the reader the spiritual significance and the lesson to be learned. Rather than using an actual woodcut or some kind of pictorial image, Bradstreet creates her image with words. The poem is thus more descriptive than many Puritan poems, and the description leaves the impression that Bradstreet really looked at and enjoyed the scenery around her. After the vivid descriptions come the lessons. This poem can be looked at as a series of emblems related to a central theme, that of the meaning of time and eternity.

The emblem idea accords well with the poem's title. To contemplate something suggests looking at it carefully and thinking about it. An emblem poem does just that: It takes a visual image and looks at it carefully, thinks about it, and derives a lesson from it.

It is somewhat surprising, however, that in this poem in which enjoyment of nature is both manifest and genuine, Bradstreet nevertheless resorts occasionally to a more artificial, poetic, or bookish description. One example is her reference to the nightingale or Philomel. Because nightingales were not found in the New England colonies, it is clear that Bradstreet is relying on her learning rather than her personal experience. The poem thus reveals Bradstreet as a daughter of the Renaissance, educated in proper English diction and the literature of Greece and Rome. Allusions to Greek gods, such as Neptune and Thetis, fit right in with allusions to figures of the Old Testament.

The transition from nature to the Bible is effected through a stanza on the function of memory and its power to make people who are dead seem to be alive. This would seem to negate the effects of death and mortality, but in this poem as elsewhere the possibility of eternal life is the only answer to the problem of human mortality.

The stanza on history's backward reflection makes a smooth transition to the biblical account of Adam's fall. The absurdity of wasting one's short time on Earth in "vain delight" becomes clear in the perspective of eternity. Thus, the Bible has its lesson for humanity just as did nature earlier in the poem.

Eternity is the focal point of the last major development of the poem, as it shifts to an appreciation of human hope for immortality. Natural phenomena—the trees, the earth, the streams, the fish, and so on—may have the better of time on Earth, but immortality finally gives people the upper hand. Bradstreet's last symbol, the white stone from Revelations, unifies the two subject areas of the poem, nature and the Bible, and yields the spiritual significance of her "Contemplations."

Themes and Meanings

"Contemplations" is a poem about time and eternity. It looks at the natural world and studies it for its implications for the spiritual world. The poem looks at various aspects of time in the natural world. Trees, for example, can survive many hundreds of years, while human lifetimes are very limited in comparison; rocks and stones endure much longer. Bradstreet wonders if this means that these long-enduring natural phenomena should be praised. In considering the natural world, clearly other natural phenomena may appear to have greater claim to glory than humanity.

From another perspective, that of eternity, humanity is superior, for only people, and only a select few among them, have the hope of eternal salvation. If one's name "is graved in the white stone," then he or she will outlive and outlast all earthly phenomena.

Even the Bible is considered for what it has to say about time and eternity: Human lifespans are growing shorter, so time should be spent wisely and well. In a stereotypical Calvinistic view, Bradstreet notes that human time on Earth is wretched; the human condition sustains sickness, misery, and loss, yet surprisingly no one longs for death. What one must do with whatever time is granted is to work in the hope of a glorious eternity with God. Earthly achievement and status, memorials and records, are meaningless in the perspective of eternity. Only salvation can triumph over time.

The poem shows that Puritan poets characteristically looked to two sources for spiritual lessons: nature and the Bible. The lessons from these two different sources were surprisingly alike. Both nature and the Bible teach people to use their limited time on earth wisely and in the hope of eternal life in heaven. Earthly life is insignificant from the perspective of eternity.

What is unusual for Bradstreet's time is the poet's enthusiastic appreciation of nature. She anticipates the American Romantics when she says in the opening stanza, "Rapt were my senses at this delectable view," in reference to brilliant fall foliage. Also noteworthy is her expressed understanding for sun worshipers of earlier civilizations—"Had I not better known, alas, the same had I." In both cases, she remains characteristically Puritan by pulling herself back to the spiritual significance of such natural beauties. Nevertheless, the hearty appreciation of nature remains in the poetry for all to enjoy.

"Contemplations" is an interesting poem to read from the Bradstreet canon because it marks a middle ground between the conventional and derivative poetry of her early years—the poems published in *The Tenth Muse Lately Sprung Up in America* (1650)—and the more personal and lyrical poems referred to as the Andover Manuscripts, not published until after her death. "Contemplations" bears hints of the personal Bradstreet while at the same time couching her thoughts and experiences in the conventional religious wisdom of the time.

Paula Kopacz

CONTINUOUS

Author: Tony Harrison (1937-   )
Type of poem: Sonnet
First published: 1981, in *Continuous: Fifty Sonnets from "The School of Eloquence"*

The Poem

Tony Harrison calls this poem and the others in this collection "sonnets" although they are not, strictly speaking, since they consist of sixteen rather than fourteen lines of rhyming iambic pentameter. They are sometimes metrically uneven, quite deliberately, to enhance their informality and the themes of the individual poems. The title refers to a major subject of the book: the relationship of a son to his parents before and after their deaths. The poem, written in the first person, takes as its beginning a memory of the father and son enjoying a visit to an English motion-picture theater in 1949, when the narrator was a child.

He remembers that they both enjoyed James Cagney, the American actor famous for his portrayal of gangsters. The experience is a common one, only slightly complicated by the English setting. The narrator remembers, for example, that his father bought him a "choc ice," the British equivalent of an ice-cream bar or Eskimo Pie. At that time, some larger theaters in England and America used to employ an organist who would play between showings of films, and who was often positioned on an elevated platform at the front of the screen. As the curtains parted for the beginning of the film, the platform would descend and the organist would disappear into the pit. The narrator remembers two further things: the ring that his father wore, which had belonged to his father before him, and the fact that in 1949 his father would have been the same age as he is at the time the poem is written.

In the third stanza, he remembers his father's cremation, and the connection is made between that sad affair and their times at the films. The organ music is there, as at the films, but on this occasion, his father's coffin is on the platform and is lowered into the furnace of blinding flames, an image which is something of a counterpart to the blinding light of the film as it begins out of the dark. The ring is on his father's finger and is the only thing that will come through the flames unscathed.

In the last stanza, the speaker is wearing the ring, retrieved from the cremation ashes. He now goes to the films alone wearing his grandfather's ring, and he thinks of his father's hands, cold from holding the choc ice, so much colder now in death—as if they held the ice-cream bar through an entire film. *White Heat* (1949), a famous Cagney film, is appropriately titled for the juxtaposition of the chill of death and the heat of cremation.

Forms and Devices

Harrison is something of a late twentieth century Metaphysical poet in that he likes to manipulate images in clever (and sometimes slightly tasteless) ways but often so tenderly that the reader is willing to accept them even if slightly uneasy about their propriety. He has, in this poem, at least five points of comparison which he uses to deal with this memory of the dead father: the film, the temperature of the "choc" and the fact of its melting, the organ, the disappearing platform, and the ring.

In the first, second, and third stanzas these objects are subtly (and sometimes not so subtly) manipulated to explore the relationship between the loving, if inarticulate, father and the worldly-wise son, now looking back on their simple, somewhat banal moments of togetherness. It is deliberately antiromantic, and fittingly so in the context of the wider meanings that are revealed in a reading of all the poems in the collection. Harrison, born into the English working class, often writes of the simple lives of his parents, attempting to express the narrowness of their lives and their lack of sophistication without patronizing them. In this poem, the mundane objects of a childhood memory are established in the first two stanzas. Then, in a manner reminiscent of the practice of Metaphysical poetry, they appear again, shifted ever so slightly, but sufficiently to create aesthetic pleasure in the modification. The motion picture becomes the tape upon which the music is played in the crematorium; the organ is now mute, reduced to holding the body of the dead father; the music which was "live" in the theater is now, in a sense, dead, simply a recording. Given the serious nature of the occasion, it is religious as opposed to popular, as it would have been in the theater. The "choc ice" is now the cold, dead hand of the father; the light on the screen becomes the light of the furnace. The platform remains, and descends as it did in the theater, but this time at the end of a life rather than the end of an organ concert. All is changed save for the ring, which goes through the flames and, in the final stanza, is worn on the finger of the son who, when he goes to see a Cagney film, remembers his time with his father and buys himself a "choc ice." These correspondences, or parallel images, are somewhat far-fetched, as is often the case in Metaphysical poetry; it could also be argued that Harrison is "metaphysical" in the word's other sense: in writing about the mystery of humankind and its relation to life and death.

It is a deceptively interesting poem, complicated in its use of image and time. It starts back in 1949, then moves to the cremation of the father sometime later, then to sometime around 1980 when the poem was written, and back into time in the choice of the old Cagney film and the ice-cream bar. The "circling" image pervades the poem, and is most obviously represented by the ring.

Themes and Meanings

Harrison is often a strongly autobiographical poet and, as such, is not shy about the difficulties he had with his parents as a result of being educated out of his class. He comes from the working-class world of northern England; his parents never left the area around Leeds, Yorkshire, where Harrison was born. His father was a baker; Harrison became a classical scholar, a part-time academic, a poet, and eventually established connections in the theater and the opera through his translations of classical and European texts. He had continuing difficulty in relating to his parents as his world expanded, and they, in turn, had considerable suspicion of the life he led, despite his determination to keep his connections with northern England open. Harrison writes about working-class life and keeps a home in the north when he is not working in London or New York. The battle with his parents shows up regularly, somewhat ruefully, in his poetry.

In this poem, it takes an elegiac turn since he is contemplating the death of his father. That death is put in the context of a further theme: the inability of his father ever to express love for his son openly, a common idea which the poet often explores and sees as an example of the stunted emotional lives of the working classes as he knows them. The idea that his father was so incapable of expressing his feelings that he could never show his love openly is a common theme in Harrison's poems, and the act of dropping a cold bar of ice cream into his son's hands as a measure of his love is an appropriate symbol for his incapacity to love his son with any show of warmth.

The poem also hints at the problem of the way in which the son's life has separated him from his parents. Significantly, father and son shared two enthusiasms, for ice-cream bars and Cagney movies. The movies, something of a minor art form, give Harrison an opportunity to comment upon the fact that those films were the only "art" the two ever shared. Harrison seems to expect the reader to know that he is an artist with wide-ranging interests in literature, theater, and the opera house. It could be argued that the idea of the problem between Harrison and his father might still have force as an example of the general problem that grown children often have with parents whom, through no one's fault, they have outgrown intellectually. Its deep poignancy is best felt in knowing that Harrison often writes about how hurt he often felt because of his parents' inability to understand his work, and how his parents, in turn, had sometimes been confused and ashamed of the frankness and ribaldry of some of his poetry.

The poem can then be read as a personal statement or as a general statement on the matter of mutual failures of children and parents. Its tone, however, is basically tender and forgiving, and its wittiness is tempered by the sense that for all their differences there is something that connects father and son which goes beyond the ring, and that it lies in this grieving memory that the poet, a middle-aged man, sitting in a theater watching Jimmy Cagney and nursing his ice-cream bar, has of his childhood moment of union with his father. Like his father, he seems able to express his feeling only in a roundabout way.

Charles Pullen

CONVALESCENCE

Author: J. V. Cunningham (1911-1985)
Type of poem: Lyric
First published: 1947, in *The Judge Is Fury*

The Poem

The title "Convalescence" focuses on the recovery from illness and despair. The poem dramatizes the moment of crisis in a man's perception of himself in which "consciousness" puts into question his earlier life. This awareness seems to threaten the stasis that the speaker has apparently created in his life. It is described as a betrayal of long-established patterns of behavior.

The speaker seems to be the voice of the poet himself. He is attempting to preserve his integrity against the threats of a "consciousness" that attempts to bring unwelcome change. J. V. Cunningham does not make himself into a heroic figure in his poems but treats himself as rigorously and harshly as he does the negative types he satirizes.

"Convalescence" speaks of a betrayal of a way of life that had earlier been established. "Consciousness," knowledge of oneself, is not a guide; rather, it betrays the silence and resignation that had earlier been achieved. "Consciousness" betrays the protective "silence" and is described as manifesting itself in the "fever" that has attacked the speaker. Illness brings on awareness that is seen as a threat rather than an insight.

Prior to this betrayal, the speaker had nearly achieved "simplicity," described as a renunciation that is not an escape from loss but an acknowledgment of it. The language of this simplicity is curiously "to recite as if it were not said" and "to renounce as if one lost instead." It is the reverse of what the reader might expect "simplicity" to be; simplicity usually suggests a purification of one's life, but this approach is quite different. It is declamatory in style and acknowledges loss rather than true renunciation.

In the fourth stanza, there is something of a counterattack on the intruding "consciousness" and change. His "unabandoned soul withdrew abhorred." He retreats from awareness to the sustaining and defensive knowledge that "oblivion was its own reward." It seems to be a description of a state of despair in which nothing is of value. All that is sought is oblivion and its dubious rewards. There is only silence and oblivion to overcome unwelcome consciousness.

The last couplet beautifully balances the contending forces of the poem. "But pride is life, and I had longed for death/ only in consciousness of indrawn breath." There is no escape from pride; it is "life," it is what keeps people motivated. The longing for death is contrasted with the life-giving act of breathing. Life and death are joined as the speaker longed for death at the moment of preserving it in breathing.

Forms and Devices

The poem is written in rhyming couplets in which the first line of the couplet runs on and the second is end-stopped. Each couplet, then, becomes an independent stanza, an unusual stanzaic structure. The couplets work out a struggle between two opposing forces that is finally reconciled and balanced in the final couplet. Cunningham is a master of the couplet form, especially the balance and antithesis that couplets seem naturally to use as a structural principle.

There are a few intriguing rhymes in the poem. Cunningham rhymes "infirmity" with "simplicity," showing the clash of opposites that make up the poem. The last couplet sets "death" against "breath." Death is longed for at the very moment when life is asserting itself in the act of breathing. The pairing of the two central elements of the poem and the victory of "breath" over "death" is an effective way to resolve the conflicts.

The meter is a generally regular iambic pentameter. The last line, which is the crucial break in the struggle of the poem, does vary the meter in some significant ways. The first foot of the line is trochaic, and the last foot is a spondee, demonstrating how Cunningham varies the meter at the crucial moment in the poem. Clearly, the meter, despite its regularity, is not monotonous but is varied when the meaning changes. There is also an important caesura in the penultimate line that mirrors the movement of the poem. The first part of the line is "but pride is life," and the second part is a contrasting "and I had longed for death." The sharp division of the line into two separate parts is a mark of couplet form. It is one of the many ways in which balance and antithesis are maintained.

An important metaphor can be found in the final couplet of the poem. In this couplet, the metaphor "pride is life" makes the crucial reversal that takes the reader from "oblivion" to "life." Pride is usually seen as a negative quality, but here it is a saving one. It returns the speaker to life and its complexities and difficulties.

The images of the poem are, perhaps, the most significant device. They also are opposing images. A shadowy image of "death" is set against the natural and human image of "breath." "Silence" and "simplicity" come under attack from the sudden burst of "consciousness." Yet, when the word "consciousness" is used a second time in the poem, it takes on a different meaning. Now, it is "consciousness of indrawn breath" rather than the earlier and more common meaning of awareness. There are also images of "fever" and "infirmity," which are a part of the illness that brings on the crisis in the poem.

Themes and Meanings

After examining the workings of the poem, one can see more fully the significance of the title. The word is not used within the poem, but it frames the whole poem by defining the occasion and suggesting the recovery the speaker makes. Convalescence brings on an unwelcome consciousness that breaks down the barriers of silence and loss. The consciousness of "indrawn breath" overcomes the destructive armor the speaker has built around him. The life force manifests itself as an antidote to the oblivion that was sought.

The poem at first glance seems very simple. There are no difficult words or elaborate figures of speech, and it is only ten lines long. It is, however, a complex poem. The reader must come to terms with all the overtones of "consciousness" and then work out the special way in which "simplicity" is used. Furthermore, there is nothing less than a struggle between the concepts that Cunningham sets against one another. Cunningham is a precise and a rigorous poet. Each word must be carefully considered and weighed before the full meaning of the poem is revealed.

Consciousness is an important theme in the poem. Consciousness is seen as a sudden awareness that comes on the speaker when he is in a feverish condition. People usually associate "consciousness" with a Romantic concentration on the self. This association was resisted both in this poem and in other pieces by Cunningham. He often used mockery in his poems and criticism to challenge the inflated claims of Romanticism, especially the morbid concentration on the self. "The Man of Feeling," a poem that was written at about the same time as "Convalescence," is one of many examples that can be found in *The Collected Poems and Epigrams of J. Cunningham* (1971).

The poem is not a satire, but it does seem to have a mocking tone toward both the forced "simplicity" of the speaker and the workings of "consciousness." For example, "simplicity" is described in terms of a declamatory reciting and in an acknowledgment of loss; the attempt to achieve "simplicity" at the price of life is seen as pretentious as well as unattainable. "Consciousness" is a much stronger force than "simplicity," and it is resisted with everything the speaker can marshal against it, but it finally gives way to the simpler and more natural "consciousness of indrawn breath."

The portrayal of "pride" in the poem curiously has a positive effect on the speaker of the poem. "Pride" is equated with "life"; it is not a destructive but a preserving force that asserts the rightful place of the self against the claims of "oblivion" and "death." Cunningham does not merely echo traditional concepts; he is also continually testing and challenging them.

James Sullivan

THE CONVERGENCE OF THE TWAIN

Author: Thomas Hardy (1840-1928)
Type of poem: Lyric
First published: 1912; collected in *Satires of Circumstance*, 1914

The Poem

After the "unsinkable" steamship *Titanic* hit an iceberg and sank on its maiden voyage from London to New York in 1912, Thomas Hardy wrote "The Convergence of the Twain" to be printed in the program of a charity performance given at the Royal Opera House to aid the victims. Exactly how comforting the bereaved found this ironic eleven-section work has not been recorded. For Hardy, the disaster was an occasion for reflecting on the relationships among humans, nature, and an impersonal supernatural force controlling or at least foreseeing events.

The poem is written in eleven three-line stanzas; the three lines of each stanza rhyme. The first two lines of each stanza have six to eight syllables, and the last line of each has twelve or thirteen syllables. The stanzas fall into two groups: The first five stanzas describe the sunken ship, and the last six trace the events leading up to the sinking.

The omniscient speaker of the poem first sees the sunken ship and the changes in its situation. The first stanza emphasizes how the shipwreck is now wholly separated from the "human vanity" and "Pride of Life" that led to its building. Thus, from the very beginning, the speaker disparages the possibility of creating an unsinkable craft. The speaker then turns his attention to the ironic changes in some of the more striking parts of the ship. The enormous fire-boxes, intended to burn coal to create power for the engines, almost magical with their "salamandrine fires," are now cold. The costly mirrors and jewelry, meant for the wealthy passengers and "in joy designed," are now lying in the dark with only sea worms and fish to see them. These creatures ask, at the end of stanza 5, what the "vaingloriousness" of the ship is doing in their submarine world.

In the second part of the poem, the speaker answers the question, ironically tracing the circumstances leading to the disaster. He points out that just as the ship took time to build, so the iceberg that hit it was growing. Although "no mortal eye" foresaw what would happen to bring ship and iceberg together, some supernatural force, the "Immanent Will" or "Spinner of the Years," could see that they would be "twin halves of one august event." Finally, in stanza 11, each object—ship and iceberg—hears the supernatural "Now!" and what had seemed unconnected suddenly comes together with enough force to "jar two hemispheres," referring to the impact of the disaster in both England and the United States.

Forms and Devices

Hardy uses an omniscient speaker and elevated, abstract diction to place the events of the poem in a cosmic context. Instead of identifying with any of the participants in the action, the speaker views them all from a detached, lofty viewpoint that reinforces the sense that no one close to the events genuinely understands them. The structure of the poem, beginning with the result and moving back in time to describe everyone's ignorance of the impending doom, further reinforces this sense of lofty detachment.

The omniscient speaker in "The Convergence of the Twain," as in many of Hardy's poems, uses irony as the dominant approach to understanding life. On the verbal level, this irony appears in the contrasts between the *Titanic* before the sinking and after the sinking in stanzas 1-5: "Solitude of the sea" is as different from "human vanity" in stanza 1 as the "fires" from the "cold currents" in stanza 2 or the "grotesque" worm from the "opulent" mirror-gazers in stanza 3. In stanzas 6 through 11, verbal irony contrasts the "smart ship," with its "cleaving wing," planned and built by humans, with the iceberg, a "sinister mate" growing without human knowledge in "shadowy silent distance." All these ironic contrasts heighten the sense that what actually happened to the ship was the opposite of what was expected to happen.

On the narrative level, the irony appears most strongly in the second part of the poem, as Hardy tells two stories at once. The story of the ship seems triumphant, a human technological success; yet at the same time, Hardy tells of another object growing—the iceberg—which is the opposite of technology and human planning. Whereas the ship is "smart," the iceberg is only a "Shape," taking form in "shadowy silent distance" from the observable "stature, grace, and hue" of the ocean liner. Yet, despite human plans and powers, the dumb iceberg will conquer the "smart" ship.

On the structural and situational levels, the irony emphasizes the narrowness of human knowledge. The people building the ship are unaware of the parallel growth of the iceberg; only the "Immanent Will" or "Spinner of the Years" knows in advance the fate of the ship. Thus, the humans are shown as plunging ahead with their project, taking insufficient account of nonhuman forces in the world.

Themes and Meanings

"The Convergence of the Twain" directly questions the significance of this maritime disaster. Hardy chooses not even to mention the drowned victims, the monetary losses, or the grief of the survivors; for him, the important element is the tragedy in the Greek sense, the inevitable bringing down of humans with too much pride in their own powers. Just as all Greek tragedy is ironic, with heroes unaware of their folly until too late, so this poem explores the ironies of people doomed because of their overweening self-confidence. "Human vanity" and "Pride of Life" ultimately lead to a downfall both literal and figurative.

Hardy saw the supernatural forces in the universe as at best indifferent to human suffering, and at worst—as in this poem—arranging events to demonstrate to humans how powerless they are. Ultimately, even the best-planned and most technologically advanced human efforts to conquer nature are at the mercy of these forces.

Furthermore, the "Immanent Will" prepares a "mate" for the ship, the "welding" of ship and iceberg is "intimate," and their collision is a "consummation"; the shipwreck seems like a marriage in the supernatural scheme of things. This line of development raises further questions about how the supernatural forces regard humans: One usually expects marriage to be a happy conclusion, not a tragic one. The marriage here, however, as inevitable as any romantic cliché could make it, is a destruction of life instead of a celebration of continuing life.

In this poem, then, the significance of catastrophe is its demonstration of human powerlessness in the face of nature and supernatural forces. Like many of his contemporaries, Hardy could see little evidence of divine benevolence in the universe, and the wreck of the *Titanic* served as one more incident confirming this view.

Julia Whitsitt

CONVERSATION OVERHEARD

Author: Quincy Troupe (1943-   )
Type of poem: Satire
First published: 1975; collected in *Snake-back Solos: Selected Poems, 1969-1977,*
1978

The Poem

Quincy Troupe's "Conversation Overheard" is an extended free-verse diatribe using indention rather than spacing to mark the breaks between sections of the single, continuous stanza. The speaker observes the repetition and stagnation of routinized American life, characterized as a "treadmill" that does not allow forward progress. Images from popular culture, especially television ("idiot tube") images and advertisements, are used as symbols of meaningless, unprogressive experience. The speaker of the poem is asked by his "love" to consider the absurdity of commercialization and misinformation on television, exemplified by the political situation of the day: the corrupt activities of U.S. president Richard Nixon's administration, particularly of Vice President Spiro Agnew, who is mocked and accused of being a liar and who manipulates public opinion through television. Agnew's disingenuousness is compared to the false television commercials that glorify the success of sports figures.

The speaker continues with an extended critique of football star O. J. Simpson and his portrayal by advertisers. The mockery of Simpson is achieved through brief descriptions of commercials he made for Chevrolet automobiles. The image of Simpson running with a football and attempting to outpace a Chevrolet Corvette is juxtaposed with Simpson's early intention to be a social worker. Simpson's name is manipulated—"overjoyedsimpson"—and the football is described as "tucked under [his] brain" rather than under his arm. The poem is prophetic in that it foresees Simpson's future as a film star but also warns that race may be a factor in the kinds of roles he will receive—preference will be given to Joe Namath, "broadway joe," another highly talented football player who, as a white star, is more likely to be cast in romantic roles.

The repeated metaphor of the treadmill moves the poem toward a comparison of the wealthy and the "starving" masses. The images of wealth focus on excess of material possessions and vapid intellectual pursuits—"spacious/ bookshelves with no books on those shelves." Other Hollywood figures are ridiculed and questions of judicial correctness are raised. The plight of well-known white figures is contrasted to the dilemmas of black political prisoners, especially the Black Panthers and Angela Davis. The media is also indicted by the poet, who sees an obvious injustice in the treatment of black groups such as the Black Panthers as compared to the treatment of white racist organizations such as the Ku Klux Klan, the Minutemen, and the John Birch Society. These injustices are symbolized by police actions during the 1967 Detroit riots and the infamous 1960 incident in Sharpsville, South Africa, in which black protesters were killed by white police officers. The poem concludes with an unanswered question concerning the continuation of the treadmill as well as the inefficacy of the "truth seeking poet," implying that the author, whose recourse is the "street corner" and lovemaking with his "woman," escapes from his ability to act and therefore contribute to changing the inequities addressed in the poem.

Forms and Devices

The poem is written in a free-verse form that is conversational in tone and structure. The poet is situated in relation to his "love" who, like the poet, questions the truths presented on television, which some assume to be a "bible," a metaphor that refers to the alleged veracity of television statements. Certain metaphors and devices of language give structure to the poem, which uses satire to ridicule various personalities from popular culture and politics. The treadmill metaphor suggests the meaningless routine of American life, and expressions found in commercials are modified to achieve a mockery of the jargon of absurd television messages (for example, "no money down all we want is your life!").

In the conversation between the poet and his "love," the questions challenge the way the general public reacts to the hypocrisy of Nixon ("tricky dick nixon"), a symbol of deceit. The poet manipulates language to create patterns fashioned from the joining of words and the alteration of spelling: "ohjaysimpson," "orangejuicesimpson," and "overjoyedsimpson," each based on the use of the letters *o* and *j*. In addition to the satirical symbolism of Simpson, the poem uses Joe Namath to discuss racism in typecasting.

The treadmill metaphor is also used to refer to those wealthier members of American society who, like the common folk, are also caught up in a relentless pursuit. The images of excess expressed through hyperbole—"five cadillacs," "25 diamond rings," "1000 silk suits," and "2000 pairs of alligator shoes"—imply that striving for material success, especially in the context of Hollywood, is an exaggeration of reality. Figures from Hollywood are used as symbols of emptiness and superficiality. Hopalong Cassidy, the cowboy character from popular Western films of the 1930's and television of the 1950's, is joined to descriptions of overabundance and fakery. The pretense of Hollywood creations is equated with the political falsehood represented by developments in the "test tube in washington," a metonymy that echoes the earlier references to Nixon and Agnew. Additional Hollywood personalities such as Zsa Zsa Gabor and Elizabeth Taylor are satirized, but Troupe also introduces Linda Kasabian, the coconspirator of Charles Manson, who induced a number of men and women to commit murder; Kasabian became a film personality in a production about the Manson murders.

The treadmill metaphor is used to conclude the poem, as is the questioning device. The poet's frustration is represented in the use of both exclamation marks and question marks to emphasize the principal trope: "why are these people dancing and singing on this/ treadmill!!??" The suggestion of social stagnation and the lack of progressive political or cultural development is linked to images of celebration, implying that those who are "dancing and singing" are oblivious to the underlying reality of "the chess game," a metaphor indicating control of world economies and political activities by a select few.

Themes and Meanings

The overall theme of the poem concerns the complacency of Americans, corruption within national politics, the inanity of television, and blatant injustices of the criminal justice system, especially relating to racial issues and African American activists. The poet also questions his inability to be an agent of social transformation. Although the principal satire is directed toward certain figures of popular culture and politics, the poet concludes with an ironic note concerning his own reaction to the unresolved dilemmas of popular culture and social justice. The mockery is based on the satirical treatment of personalities from the political arena, television, and the commercial world of Hollywood. Satire is achieved through exaggeration and ridicule.

The indictment of American culture of the late 1960's includes the mockery of Nixon and Agnew; the White House is a symbol of deception and trickery. However, political corruption is not the only form of deception: Corruption in the form of false advertising can be found in the marketing devices of television commercials, as in the image "selling suntan lotion with foul breath." The central absurdities of television are found in the methods of selling products. The satire of popular culture mocks not only white images but also the pretensions of black personalities such as O. J. Simpson. The critique of Simpson directs the poem toward racial themes such as the upward mobility of black athletes and their manipulation by the Hollywood system. Simpson is portrayed as a black sellout who is unaware of the racial implications of Hollywood typecasting and who lacks intellectual depth. Beyond Simpson's role in deceptive advertising lies the larger dilemma: the huge profits garnered by certain people involved in the television and film industry while "millions of people are starving." The social conscience of the poet is implicitly anticapitalist, and he condemns profligacy and the accumulation of status symbols (as opposed to intellectual development). Acquisition of numerous material possessions affects the "soggy brains" of the wealthy. Images of beauty symbolized by Hollywood women of public renown are presented as grotesque and constructed.

"Conversation Overheard" also protests inequities in the criminal justice system, particularly the differing treatment of black and white groups and individuals. The falsification of truth through television coverage is linked to images drawn from controversial and politically oriented coverage of Charles Manson, Angela Davis, and the Black Panthers. The focus on racial bias in the criminal justice system is part of the overall criticism of American culture. The poem also attempts to explain the social upheavals of the 1960's as complicated by a racist social order. Especially important are the white organizations known for their hatred of African Americans—"the minutemen/ the white citizen's committee, the birch society"—groups that have not been subject to police action. The interrelated themes of corruption, deception, economic inequities, and injustice point to the imbalance of a world order sustained by a minority of the powerful. The poet ultimately blames the international power structure and suggests a worldwide conspiracy of manipulation.

Joseph McLaren

A CONVERSATION WITH LEONARDO

Author: John Ciardi (1916-1986)
Type of poem: Lyric
First published: 1974, in *The Little That Is All*

The Poem

"A Conversation with Leonardo" is a brief poem in free verse, its forty-five lines divided into fifteen three-line stanzas. Speaking in the first person, the poet recalls one "stew of a night" he dreamed of conversing with Leonardo da Vinci, the great Renaissance artist, perhaps because his own "spread-eagled" body recalled the artist's famous drawing that illustrated this position.

Once the narrator falls asleep, Leonardo, attempting to re-create his drawing with the narrator as the living model, pounces and draws a circle around him. The endeavor to fit real body into "turned ratio" provokes the modern poet to mildly rebuke the old master for his antiquated desire to coerce humanity into an ideal proportion: " 'I could have told you,/ . . . you're sketching the wrong times.' " Stung by this implied challenge, Leonardo responds with an offensive truism of his own: Although the narrator is a "deformity/ among examples," the "collector" can still use him if a hidden "memory of man to illustrate" remains.

The poet-narrator is quick to point out that the artist is not really referring to him at all: It is the idea of man that interests Leonardo. Representing a misguided search for illusory truths, this "memory" really has nothing to do with man at all. Man, suggests the poet is "measured not by absolutes," but rather by the blemished and imperfect reality of "genre." "Other examples/ of the same school"—specific flesh-and-blood individuals molded by the trifles of daily life and the monotony of unremarkable existence—are the real human yardstick. With perhaps more pride than apology, the narrator declares, "I am, alas, *that* man."

Leonardo sees the poet's measuring of humanity by his own poor standard as "an absolute irrelevance" and a "poor excuse" for such a degraded view of man. Claiming to revere "what was never there," the narrator declares that "God measures perfection and crock measures pot." When the narrator thus implicitly alters the Renaissance credo from "Man is the measure of all things" to "Man is the measure of the tangible, the everyday, the insignificant," Leonardo disdainfully comments that he is grateful he died when he did.

With the tenth stanza, the narrator shifts his focus from the unprovable, supposed relationship between man and God to the identifiable, actual relationships between man and man. The question he poses—" 'Master . . . do you imagine God/ is thinking you in this sequence?' "—points to their own situation, and to the probability that he thinks more admiringly and reverently of the artist than God would, " 'were He inclined.' " Clearly disturbed by this new thought and by the perspective it opens on the modern existential theme of man alone in the universe, Leonardo approaches the revelation in the best way he knows how: He will try " 'a drawing of it. If it lives on paper—/ if I can make it live—I may understand.' "

The poet wistfully wishes to share this promised redrawing of the human condition but must wait for another time, another dream: " 'I will live for that,' " he pledges, and immediately wakes "to the dark" of his uncomfortable room.

Forms and Devices

"A Conversation with Leonardo" is a loose adaptation of the "tenzone," a poetic debate, usually between abstract qualities such as Body and Soul, often employing invective and formal verse. John Ciardi parodies this traditional form to create a slyly secular dream vision in which the argument occurs between two individuals—one living and one dead—with very distinct personalities. Instead of adopting the clearly designated formal divisions of the tenzone, Ciardi modernizes it with the rapid exchange offered by normal conversation.

The familiarity of the conversational structure and the language of daily speech establishes a realistic tone for the poem. Common vocabulary, regular syntax, and subtle repetition of key words all emphasize the prosaic qualities of the poetry, a goal Ciardi consciously pursued because he believed that poems should be read aloud so people could "speak the piece as the poet heard it."

Another important device the poet uses to heighten and communicate the mundane reality behind his own poetic vision is concrete imagery. For example, the specific, unpleasant sensations of a sweltering night are completely, yet concisely, conveyed when the poet says the narrator "flailed off the one sheet" before he "wilted to sleep."

This keen observation of significant details also helps to structure the poem. By focusing on the narrator's physical discomfort at the beginning and end, the poet creates a realistic frame around the dialogue itself. The unrelentingly "really real" world expressed in this framework provides an important contrast to the philosophical matters debated, while also providing a concrete example of the narrator's own unswerving vision of the world as it is.

In addition to structuring and contributing to the poem's realistic vision, another function of Ciardi's imagery is evocation. For example, when Leonardo appears in the dream, he is not merely an empty symbol; rather, he is the embodiment of vital, complex human values and of dynamic, affirmative qualities in the human spirit. As a man of the Renaissance, he simultaneously represents both its heritage and commitment to concepts such as harmony, proportion, order, balance, and clarity. As artist, he affirms the faith that art, like man, is inherently worthwhile and significant, for it expresses visions capable of transcending even death and time. Finally, as an individual person, he demonstrates a firm and self-possessed, distinctive personality.

Leonardo's drawing, sometimes titled "Vitruvian Man," also evokes its own network of associations. In stanzas 5 and 6, its image conjures revered names such as Protagoras, Praxiteles, and Plato, while it also summons thoughts from the Bible, scholastic logic, and Plato's theory of ideas. All are linked by their creation of an abstract, idealized vision of man, which results from their attempts to connect the hu-

man with the divine, the transient with the eternal, the tangible with the intangible.
It is precisely this kind of endeavor that causes the narrator to exclaim, "Ah, the greatness of lost causes!" By doing so, he is making an important, personal judgment about the amalgam of values, beliefs, and methods Leonardo and his idealistic humanism represent. Unprovable absolutes such as Good, Truth, Beauty, and God, all of paramount importance to the Renaissance, are to him merely "the idea/ of the abstraction of nothing." The narrator's clear allegiance to a cynical, rational, empirical vision of man and the world is evidenced in his association with emphatically concrete particulars ("I am, alas, *that* man"), and in his smug, worldly-wise attitude toward Leonardo.

Themes and Meanings

"A Conversation with Leonardo" presents a complex debate between past and present, idealism and realism, faith and skepticism, art and nature. The dialogue, however, ultimately revolves around one central theme: the observation Protagoras made more than two thousand years ago that "Man is the measure of all things." Leonardo is the heir and representative of a venerable tradition, which first defines man in absolute, nonhuman terms, and then measures man against that model. Either as the container of its feeble spark, the pinnacle of its creation, or at the very least, its imperfect image, for the traditional humanist, humankind's significance depends upon some alleged connection with divinity.

Against this religious version of humanism, Ciardi places another, more modern form, which developed out of René Descartes's assertion, "I think, therefore I am." When the narrator tells Leonardo, "I'm/ thinking you," he is clearly echoing the revolutionary words that place humanity at the center of humanity's understanding and significance. No longer the shadow, idea, or handiwork of something intangible and incomprehensible ("the abstraction of nothing"), this vision secularizes man, making of him the first and only measure of himself, of what he actually is.

As Miller Williams writes in *The Achievement of John Ciardi* (1969), this kind of secular humanism is only attained when one gives "his whole attention to the moment he is living. . . . [This is] the affirmation of the eternal present." Such an affirmation, however, often requires a high price, as the title of another Ciardi poem, "Nothing is Really Hard But to Be Real," suggests. The stubborn attachment to the here and now, to scientific proof and sober reason, prevent the towering visions that stir and lift the heart: Renaissance men such as Leonardo have little place in a humanism of human proportions, except perhaps in its dreams and memories. Closing with an air of melancholy, the poem hints that both sides inevitably suffer loss and disillusionment, notwithstanding their respect for and commitment to the same central belief in humanism. The narrator's awakening in the final stanza is not only literal, but metaphorical as well, for only by disillusioning Leonardo does he see clearly the extent of his own disillusionment. For him, it is now "pointless to try for sleep again in nature"; he has woken and faces his own solitude in a diminished world unilluminated by faith in God, man, or ideals.

Terri Frongia

THE COOL WEB

Author: Robert Graves (1895-1985)
Type of poem: Lyric
First published: 1927, in *Poems: 1914-1926*

The Poem

This poem of four stanzas makes an unusual observation about the relationship between the emotions and the language used to express them. The cool web of the title is a metaphor for language itself, which, rather than intensifying and clarifying what one feels, may actually dull or cool the passions.

The first quatrain presents the plight of those who presumably have limited ability to put feeling into words: "Children are dumb to say how hot the day is." The other three lines name other experiences that induce emotion in children: the scent of roses, the darkening of the evening sky, and the sound of drums and marching soldiers.

The second stanza states that "we," presumably meaning adults, though it might have more specialized application to poets, have speech, with which to cool the heat of the day, dull the scent of the rose, and "spell away" our fears of approaching night and marching soldiers.

The third stanza characterizes this effect of language as a "Retreat from too much joy or too much fear," as though these contradictory possibilities were equally ominous to the fragile psyche. Yet such protection produces its own disaster: "We grow sea-green at last and coldly die/ In brininess and volubility."

The last stanza, having six lines, suggests an alternative to this miserable drowning. "But if we let our tongues lose self-possession,/ Throwing off language and its watery clasp" before we actually die, instead of when we die, then we would again face the "wide glare of the children's day" as well as the rose, the dark sky, and the soldier's drum. This would probably drive one mad, and one would die that way.

The poet's cool and orderly analysis of this function of language suggests that he is demonstrating how words display this cloaking, muffling property. Immediately under the surface is a raw sensibility that finds experience almost more than he can bear. The poem provides some hints, but it conceals the actual nature of the reality that lies beneath. Real fear and joy are so muffled in metaphor and symbol that the reader cannot know what actually inspired such emotion. Yet one believes that under the well-crafted phrases and the smoothly controlled lines lies a primal scream.

Perhaps the most successful of the poet's verbal cloaking devices is the clear implication that the undisciplined fears are characteristic only of children. This is a person remembering childish nightmares, perhaps. Knowing of Robert Graves's actual experience of protracted war neurasthenia during and after World War I, however, one must suspect that it was not in childhood that he experienced that extraordinary terror. The dumb—that is, speechless—child that cannot say what it feels is a child within, whom the poet strives both to reveal and to conceal in language.

Forms and Devices

The poem achieves a remarkable tension between meaning and form, and form seems to "win," successfully submerging the desperation of the message. No matter what the words mean, the technical control is precise. The argument proceeds with the cool logic of a deductive syllogism, with each stanza expressing one aspect of the case. The final line wraps up the analysis, stated in impersonal tones almost like the written report of a doctor who does not personally know the patient and perhaps does not really care to know him. If a certain thing occurs, then the patient will go mad and "die that way." This objective approach to the matter seems to imply that, since everyone dies anyway, there is no real cause for alarm. Yet both methods of dying sound horrible.

Under the calming influence of language, the dying is described in images of suffocation and drowning. The web of language "winds us in"; we are trapped, turn green, and "coldly die" in "brininess" (somehow worse than fresh water) and "volubility," suggesting some degeneration into meaningless babble. In fact, of the two ways of dying, that sounds almost worse than going mad—except that the mad death apparently involves reliving the most dreadful of one's memories. The poem does not say that explicitly but repeats the relatively innocuous experiences listed in the first stanza: "Facing the wide glare of the children's day/ Facing the rose, the dark sky and the drum."

By this point in the poem, some of the more suggestive words that revealed unaccountable terror behind the images have been cleared away: The rose is mentioned, but not its "hot scent"; "dark sky" is easier to take than "black wastes"; drums are mentioned but not soldiers; and the two "dreadfuls" of the first stanza are gone ("How dreadful the black wastes of evening sky,/ How dreadful the tall soldiers drumming by"). Not only has the poet apparently chosen language over raw emotion, he has also curbed his tendency to use loaded words.

Since the images used for painful experience are so clear in literal terms yet so veiled as to their underlying significance, one can do little more than guess from possible connotations what they mean to the poet. "Hot" has traditional associations with both anger and sexual passions. The rose is certainly traditionally paired with love. If attributing this dread to children is to deflect attention from the grown man, then uneasiness about sexual passions makes sense. In fact, Graves wrote other poems devoted to this attitude. Moreover, though little boys are hardly ever worried about drums and toy soldiers, big boys such as Graves, who was nineteen when he knew the hell of trench warfare in World War I, suffered both physical and psychological wounds. Many of his generation shared what was then popularly called shell shock. There can be little doubt that the soldiers mentioned in the poem are known from a brutally realistic, adult perspective, not from a child's view. Graves was so badly wounded at one time that he was listed as dead. Moreover, the war neurasthenia lingered for many years after the war ended.

Themes and Meanings

There is another ambiguity of word meanings: "Dying" probably does not mean physical death so much as it does mental or emotional or spiritual death. Whether one smothers in pointless words or becomes violently psychotic, one's identity is lost.

Graves had a curious attitude toward his war neurosis as it related to his poetic powers. Although he was acquainted with and much influenced by a prominent Cambridge neurologist and psychologist, W. H. R. Rivers, Graves avoided actual treatment for his war neurasthenia. Rivers was a Freudian psychoanalyst and a specialist in that kind of neurosis as well as in the relationship between the troubled subconscious and poetic creativity.

While Graves did not go into psychoanalysis, sometimes called the "talking cure," he believed, at least for some years, that writing poetry was a way of working out one's psychological problems. He believed that a poem must originate as an internal conflict of opposing forces, which one seeks to resolve in the act of expressing them. Thus, poetry might serve as a therapeutic exercise and might also help the reader who shared the same internal conflicts.

Of possible relevance to this particular poem, Graves worried at times that if he actually did cure his psychological difficulties, he might no longer be inspired to write poetry. Thus, writing poetry as a "talking cure," if actually successful, might deliver him into the stagnant, dead sea imagined in this poem, where the web of language has destroyed him as a poet.

In later years, Graves discarded his psychological explanation of poetic creativity, but not before he had produced considerable poetry haunted by subjective feelings of guilt, fear, despair, and a sense of entrapment. He seldom wrote poems actually about war experience, preferring the traditional subject matter of the Gothic mode: haunted houses, nightmarish castles, lust as destructive to romantic love, and the sinking into insanity ("The Pier Glass," "The Castle," "The Succubus," "Down"). "The Cool Web" demonstrates a significant step away from the emotionalism of the Gothic mode, or perhaps a kind of graduation into another kind of problem: how to be more cool and objective while retaining the sensitivity and feeling appropriate and necessary to a poet.

Graves eventually found the orientation that fulfilled his twin needs of an anchor for his runaway emotions and a suitably romantic and inspiring muse in the mythology of the White Goddess. Not only was she (in Freudian terms) the anima of his subconscious, she was also a pervasive presence in ancient myth and religion, which became a fascinating subject for scholarly research. Moreover, the ancient goddess rules over both life and death, retaining a certain cruelty and sacrifice as the price for the gift of love and inspiration. As the oracle for the White Goddess, Robert Graves evaded both of the fates he imagined in "The Cool Web." He neither succumbed to madness, nor drowned as a poet in the cool web of language.

Katherine Snipes

COOLE PARK, 1929

Author: William Butler Yeats (1865-1939)
Type of poem: Lyric
First published: 1931, in Lady Augusta Gregory's *Coole*; collected in *The Winding Stair and Other Poems*, 1933

The Poem

"Coole Park, 1929" is a thirty-two-line poem composed of four stanzas. William Butler Yeats wrote the poem to honor Lady Augusta Gregory (1852-1932). Lady Gregory was an important playwright and cofounder of Dublin's Abbey Theatre; she also received many Irish writers as extended guests at her elegant estate, Coole Park, in western Ireland. There they were surrounded by great natural beauty and were free to spend uninterrupted days writing their poems and plays. Coole Park represented an oasis of calm and beauty that contrasted sharply with the poverty that existed in Ireland during the first three decades of the twentieth century.

The poem is written in the first person. Yeats meditates upon the many visits he and other writers had made to Coole Park, where the aged Lady Gregory is now dying from cancer. At first reading, "Coole Park, 1929" can be interpreted simply as an extended compliment to Lady Gregory, but at a more profound level it is also a lyrical meditation on death and dying. The inclusion of the poem in Lady Gregory's 1931 memoir *Coole* was especially appropriate because in this work, which dealt largely with the architecture and gardens of Coole Park, she wrote eloquently about the intense grief she had experienced after the deaths of so many family members and friends who used to visit the estate.

In the first stanza Yeats speaks of the flight of a swallow. A swallow is a migratory bird that does not stay for lengthy periods of time in a single region. This image of a swallow reminds one of the transitory nature of human life. Yeats then speaks of Lady Gregory as "an aged woman" whose stay in this life would not be very long. He recalls not the exquisite beauty of the formal gardens at Coole Park but rather his recollections of a beautiful sycamore and the beautiful blue sky of western Ireland. He contrasts these impressions of the constant changes in life and in nature itself with the permanent nature of the literary works created at Coole Park.

In the second stanza Yeats refers to five people who had experienced the beauty of Coole Park, three of them deceased and two still living. Those deceased were Lady Gregory's beloved nephews John Shawe-Taylor, a well-known Dublin painter, and Hugh Lane, a collector of French paintings who was killed when German torpedoes sank the *Lusitania* off the coast of Ireland, and the Irish dramatist John Millington Synge, whose *Playboy of the Western World* (1907) had sparked a lively controversy because it portrayed Irish people in a realistic but not always favorable light. Those still living were Yeats himself and the Irish folklorist Douglas Hyde, who would later serve as president of the Republic of Ireland.

In the third stanza, Yeats compares those people whom Lady Gregory had befriended to swallows, but he adds that her "powerful character" persuaded her guests to use properly the precious time they spent at Coole Park and on this earth. In the final stanza, Yeats suggests to his reader that even though the gardens and mansion at Coole might not be preserved for future generations, readers should never forget the importance of Lady Gregory's contributions to the cultural life of Ireland. In Greek mythology, laurel wreaths were placed on the foreheads of heroes and heroines. In the final verse of "Coole Park, 1929," Yeats compares Lady Gregory to a Greek heroine worthy of admiration when he asks his readers to pay homage to the "laurelled head" of Lady Gregory.

Forms and Devices

For modern readers it is almost impossible to separate this poem about Coole Park from Yeats's very famous 1917 poem "The Wild Swans at Coole," in which he describes both the exquisite beauty of fall at Coole and the grief he felt because so many people whom he had met at Coole were now dead. The second poem in the book entitled *The Wild Swans at Coole* (1919) was an elegy for Lady Gregory's only child Robert, who was killed in action in World War I. Lady Gregory never really recovered from her grief. In "Coole Park, 1929," Yeats refers to five swallows who came to and then left Coole, but in the third stanza he writes that there were "half a dozen in formation there." The sixth and unnamed swallow is clearly her beloved Robert.

"Coole Park, 1929" effectively contrasts the continuing presence of an aged woman with the repeated departures and returns of swallows. Yeats's very choice of swallows may seem paradoxical because few people associate swallows with beauty. Swallows, however, mysteriously return to the same places for brief periods of time each year. The writers and artists who came to Coole found the inspiration and moral support which enabled them to reach their full creative potential. Yeats had the pleasure of returning to Coole several times between his first visit in 1896 and Lady Gregory's death thirty-six years later. He realized that she had helped him to develop from a writer with a "timid heart" into a richly complex poet. The artists who created works of lasting beauty at Coole had differing personalities. Yeats refers to Synge as a "meditative man" who found inspiration in the solitude of the Aran Islands. Lady Gregory's nephews Hugh Lane and John Shawe-Taylor were "impetuous" men convinced of their own importance, but their aunt persuaded them to use their wealth and interest in painting to improve the cultural life of Ireland by developing the talents of younger and poorer Irish painters.

Each time Yeats refers to swallows in this poem, the meaning is different. In the first stanza Yeats refers to a real flight of swallows, and readers can interpret this as the evocation of a pleasant memory of a visit to Coole. In the third stanza, however, the flights of swallows remind one that several of these "swallows" have completed their final flights and are now dead. Real swallows can fly, but the swallows whom Lady Gregory guided at Coole were free to dream and to create works that continue to bring pleasure to others long after their deaths.

Themes and Meanings

"Coole Park, 1929" evokes the complex nature of artistic creation. For writers such as Yeats and Synge, who lived through traumatic periods in Irish history, the tranquillity at Coole and the firm but gentle guidance that they received from Lady Gregory enabled them to produce poems and plays that continue to fascinate readers long after their deaths (Synge in 1909 and Yeats in 1939). Certain "swallows," such as Yeats, were privileged to return to Coole many times because these lives were long. Others, such as Synge and Hugh Lane, died at relatively young ages. Their artistic and literary creations, however, survived them.

In the final stanza of the poem, Yeats calls his reader "traveller, scholar, poet." All three are richly evocative terms that lead one to appreciate the complex nature of the creative and aesthetic experiences. People travel from one place to another, but they also undertake voyages of personal discovery. (Yeats does not need to add that everyone also travels toward death.) All thoughtful people are scholars in the sense that they reflect on the meaning of the past in their lives and strive to communicate their insights to others. The word "poet" derives from the Greek word "to create," and all people are thus poets because they attempt to create meaning in their lives.

Coole Park itself was demolished in 1941, nine years after Lady Gregory's death. Even the formal gardens no longer exist; the new owners decided to sell the land so that many modest houses could be built there. The beautiful architecture and natural beauty of Coole Park can, however, still be appreciated by readers of Yeats's poetry and Lady Gregory's memoir *Coole*. "Coole Park, 1929" continues to touch readers because it explores the importance of memory and friendship. When he wrote this poem in 1928, Yeats was sixty-three years old and had already survived many of his closest friends. Lady Gregory had been diagnosed with breast cancer in 1923, and her two operations had not been successful. It was obvious to her close friends that she was dying. The poem remains an eloquent meditation on the meanings of creativity, memory, and friendships.

Edmund J. Campion

CORINNA'S GOING A-MAYING

Author: Robert Herrick (1591-1674)
Type of poem: Dramatic monologue/pastoral
First published: 1648, in *Hesperides: Or, The Works Both Humane and Divine of Robert Herrick, Esq.*

The Poem

The title of this poem is particularly interesting in that it asserts unequivocably that Corinna will take part in the activities of May morning, although there is no certainty in the text that she will do so. The poem is a dramatic monologue, with the lover-speaker seeking to persuade his sweetheart to get out of bed and join the other youths "to fetch in May." Her reactions to his entreaties are unrecorded. She remains no more than a name, as the interest of the poem resides in the speaker's rhetorical strategies to work his will upon her.

The opening words, "Get up! get up for shame!" are jarring, as if he is trying to startle her into wakefulness, but the tone softens with "Get up, sweet slug-a-bed." The burden of his argument in the first stanza is that it is "sin" and "profanation" to stay indoors when "a thousand virgins on this day/ Spring, sooner than the lark, to fetch in May."

In the second stanza, the lover's tone changes perceptibly. Harsh urgency gives way to soft flattery, as indicated by the sibilance of the lines. Do not bother with jewels, the lover argues, since nature will make you as sweet as the goddess of flowers herself. Even Titan is standing still as he awaits her entrance into the natural world. The last line of this stanza ("Few beads are best when once we go a-Maying") shows the lover's wit and ambiguity. The line is certainly a cavalier allusion to Puritanism as a religion of restraint. It also prepares for the pagan worship of nature in the following stanza.

Like the first two stanzas, the third opens with an imperative, of which there are more than twenty in the poem's seventy lines. Here the lover tries to pique his sweetheart's curiosity to see the wonderful transformation of the village into a celebration of the May. This transformation has religious overtones. The ornamenting of the trees with whitethorne is an act of devotion. Each house is as sacred as the Hebrew Ark of the Covenant. The speaker repeats his earlier admonition that to stay indoors on this day would be sinful.

In the next-to-the-last stanza, the speaker refrains entirely from enjoining his sweetheart to do anything. Instead, he simply states that "not a budding boy or girl this day/ But is got up and gone to bring in May," enumerates in some detail their joyous activities, and concludes, "yet we're not a-Maying."

Since cajolery and flattery have apparently not worked, the speaker-lover resorts to fear as a motivator in the final stanza. The tone darkens dramatically as the speaker, echoing the words of Job, warns that "our days run/ As fast away as does the sun."

Life's brevity is emphasized in powerful images of loss and oblivion. Once lost, time can never be regained. The conclusion is inescapable: "Come, my Corinna, come, let's go a-Maying."

Forms and Devices

"Corinna's Going A-Maying" consists of five stanzas of fourteen lines. It is written in rhymed couplets, and although there is some enjambment, there is none of the conversational authenticity that is sometimes found in the dramatic monologues of John Donne and Robert Browning. This poem has more the nature of a set speech than of an urgent appeal. Its artificial quality is the result of both the subject matter and the form. May Day celebrations and pagan nature worship are far removed from the reader's everyday concerns, and the complex metrical scheme that is repeated in each stanza draws attention to itself. In every stanza, lines 1, 2, 7, 8, 13, and 14 contain ten stresses, while all other lines are shortened to eight. The effect is one of variety, enhanced by the combinations of iambic and spondaic feet, but it is also one of patterned artificiality.

Anticipating English Romanticism by a century and a half, the speaker perceives the natural world as organic. Consequently, the most prevalent figure of speech is personification. In the first stanza alone, four inanimate objects are endowed with human characteristics: "the blooming morn," "The dew," "Each flower," and "the birds." In the first line, the morn, imaged as Aurora, is said to be presenting Apollo, the god of dawn whose hair is never cut: "the god unshorn." Aurora, seen as throwing "her fair/ Fresh-quilted colors through the air," is a complicated figure suggesting both the human and the sublime, a woman impatient to be out of bed throwing off her bedclothes and a goddess showering the world with light. If Aurora is not content to stay in bed, the implication is that Corinna certainly should not be. Metaphor is used subtly to advocate the speaker's argument. The other personifications have been similarly aroused to greet the day. The birds saying "matins" and singing "their thankful hymns" prepare for the religious dimensions of the May Day celebration in the third stanza. In the second stanza, the light of dawn hanging "on the dew-locks of the night" is replaced by the "endless night" of the final stanza. Therefore, to take advantage of the light while it yet shines becomes a matter of supreme importance.

In addition to personification, the poem is richly endowed with other rhetorical devices, such as metaphor, simile, and allusion. "Spring" (line 14) is used as a verb to indicate youthful energy while also suggesting the season of youth and rebirth. Corinna is admonished to put on her "foliage," to join every "budding boy or girl" in the celebration, to affirm youth and life while she is "but decaying." "Rise" (line 15), like "Spring," is richly connotative. It suggests vitality and energy as opposed to the oblivion of old age and death in the final stanza. Up to the last stanza, all metaphors and similes relate to spring and rebirth. In the last lines, however, the images of nature are abruptly transformed to signify the brevity of life and the finality of death. Life lost is as irretrievable "as a vapor or a drop of rain."

Themes and Meanings

"Corinna's Going A-Maying" draws extensively from elements of pastoral and *carpe diem* poetry. Both types of poetry tend to be dramatic, spoken by a lover to his beloved. Pastoral literature envisages an ideal world of nature far removed from the transitory one of human experience, a world of youthful lovers. In the evergreen pastoral world, golden lads and girls do not "As chimney-sweepers come to dust," as a song in William Shakespeare's *Cymbeline* (c. 1609-1610) says. Christopher Marlowe's "The Passionate Shepherd to His Love" describes such a happy world, one which Sir Walter Raleigh later debunks in "The Nymph's Reply to the Shepherd."

Carpe diem poetry was developed by Horace in pre-Christian Rome. *Carpe diem* is Latin for "seize the day," and poetry that advanced this theme became extremely popular in the strife-torn England of the seventeenth century. *Carpe diem* poetry always expresses the philosophy of "Eat, drink, and be merry, for tomorrow we die." Time is fleeting, life is short, and beyond this life lies only the darkness of eternity. Since there is no afterlife in this philosophy of hedonism, the pleasures of earthly existence become all important. It is doubtful that Robert Herrick, an Anglican priest, literally subscribed to the tenets of hedonism. It makes more sense to regard this poem and his "To the Virgins, to Make Much of Time" as literary exercises or, at most, as political statements against the restraints of Puritanism. "To the Virgins, to Make Much of Time" is perhaps the best-known example in English of the *carpe diem* theme. The poem is brief, and the language is simple, unlike the elaborate "Corinna's Going A-Maying." "Corinna's Going A-Maying" is similar to Andrew Marvell's "To His Coy Mistress" in its strong dramatic element, especially its rhetorical strategies that shift from flattery to fear.

Collectively, pastoral poems, such as Marlowe's "The Passionate Shepherd to His Love," and *carpe diem* poetry represent "the poetry of seduction." This poetry is always dramatic, spoken by the male lover, who is seeking to persuade his sweetheart to submit to him. Its main interest is the character of the speaker and the ingenuity of his argument. The lady's response is never made known, except in Raleigh's exceptional "Nymph's Reply to the Shepherd." "Corinna's Going A-Maying" and Marvell's "To His Coy Mistress" are among the finest examples in English of the poetry of seduction.

Robert G. Blake

CORONA

Author: Paul Celan (Paul Antschel, 1920-1970)
Type of poem: Lyric
First published: 1952, in *Mohn und Gedächtnis*; English translation collected in *Selected Poems*, 1972

The Poem

"Corona" is a short lyric poem about the difficulty of loving, honestly and truly, for two people who have experienced the catastrophes of World War II and the Holocaust. The memory of disaster and the busy pressure of the time period immediately after the war affect the private life of the two lovers and shape the tone of this love poem.

A corona is a halo or a ring of bright light around the object that obscures or blocks a source of light in an event such as an eclipse. In this poem, love is in eclipse, but the corona of light remaining for the lovers is a source of hope in an eerie darkness. An eclipse provides a chance to learn about the sun and the body that obscures it, and "Corona" provides an opportunity to reconsider the nature of love and to learn much about the couple and their dark world. A corona is also a crown, and the poet offers this poem, with its bright ring of light, as a crown to his beloved in praise of their love.

The poem's eighteen lines fall into three groups of six lines. The opening, arranged in two three-line stanzas, establishes that it is autumn, a season in which one is reminded of mortality, and a Sunday, when the lovers are able to sleep longer and to spend time together. The next six lines form the center of the poem. The couple speak "dark words" while together during an intimate time that they have freed for love.

The final six lines step back from the intimacy of the central section and attempt to reconcile this tender intimacy with the harsher, public world. People on the street notice the two lovers embracing by a window, and the poet reacts to the fact that they have been seen, taking a kind of public position on the matter.

The poem frames the tender and intimate central section with an opening and a closing that place that moment in the context of a hostile era. The hidden question of the poem is whether or not love has a place and can survive between people in a time such as the postwar years when forgetting the recent tragedies is not possible or desirable. Perhaps if the couple could forget, they could love—or if they could love, they might forget for a time. In either case, love would be reduced to an evasion, a flight from the truth, a mere temporary escape. Add to this the difficulty of finding time for love in a busy world, and love becomes difficult indeed.

The poem tries to move beyond this impasse by suggesting that a new time might be beginning in which one could love without fleeing reality. In the last lines, Paul Celan writes: "It is time the stone made an effort to flower,/ Time unrest had a beating heart./ It is time it were time." The stone and the unrest, emblematic of postwar disillusionment, do not cease to exist but rather begin to flower, to love with the heart, to move to a new phase and a new beginning.

Forms and Devices

Probably the most difficult feature of Celan's style is his use of concise, surrealistic images. Presented in very few words, these dreamlike images are seductive and disturbing, and seem to halt our reading and call for more attention. In "Corona," things that are suggested by such images, but never directly stated, have a way of turning out to be central. Critics are fond of saying that Celan's poems lie in the silences after such compressed images are presented, or in the spaces between the lines where interconnections between images might be traced.

In the first six lines, for example, the temporal setting is presented in dreamlike images in which the usual course of events is transformed, animated and often reversed. Autumn becomes an animal tamely eating its leaf from the poet's hand, and its return is a familiar domestic ritual. The kernel shelled from nuts in the fall is, oddly, "time," and it must be nurtured like a child and taught how to walk. In a strange reversal, time decides it is not yet prepared for the world and returns to its protective shell. These concise, surreal images set up an important tension. Autumn returns for its food and life shortens, but the time we need, which lovers might attentively nurture for the sake of love, fatefully and constantly retreats to its hardened shell. Time is running out, but the times remain at odds with love.

The Sunday of late sleep and dream, a time freed for love, is first seen in a mirror whose depths reverse the logic of waking reality. Usually one says that one dreams in sleep, but here sleep occurs within the dream; in that sleep, rather than in waking, the mouth speaks the truth. For Celan, the inner mirror-world and the weekday world it supposedly reflects and reverses are like halves of one reality. The truth of both sides must be captured in speech that includes dream, as in the condensed, surreal images of the opening six lines.

In the central section of the poem, surreal images are used in several very compressed, striking similes to describe the relationship between the two lovers. They are said, for example, to love one another "like poppy and memory." Memory, an important theme in Celan's work, is often a responsibility and a burden. Celan lost both parents and suffered himself for many years in concentration camps in Adolf Hitler's Germany. Memory needs poppy, a flower and the source of opiates, to soften the horrible burdens of memory and to make the responsibility of remembering more bearable. Poppy relies on memory, invoking and even reveling in memory. Like poppy and memory, the lovers depend on each other, each meeting the other's anxieties, providing the other's release, and shaping the other's dreams.

They also sleep like "the sea in the blood ray of the moon," an image that invokes restlessness. The moon, which pulls the ocean in its ceaseless tides, bathes it also in red light, compared here to blood. As passionate and beautiful as this image is, it is not an escapist image for their sleep together. The problem of the memory of the Holocaust and the difficult restlessness of the postwar years penetrate deeply into their private mirror-world, coloring the qualities of their dreams and of their love for one another. The blood-red moon coloring a restless sea, though a dream image, epitomizes the true reality in which the couple live. For them, true love is not an escapist illusion.

The image reflects their restless struggle to remember, to dream, to love, and to live in a hard time.

Celan felt the true reality he wished to capture or present; but this reality is not easily conveyed in the words of a language meant to serve as a puppet to other purposes. For Celan, the German language in particular was suspect because it had so often been abused for the sake of propaganda and commercialism. Language had to be strained—broken apart and reassembled in compressed images—in order to free itself of false values and do its work in Celan's poetry.

Themes and Meanings

The poem concerns the difficulty of loving for people who do not want love to be an illusion or an escape from everything else they know must be acknowledged as fact. It is also for those who deeply distrust a world that cheapens life by separating its contents in separate, sealed categories, so that Sundays are separate from other days, and love, dream, and memory are separated from the rest of reality, which must suffer from the separation. The memory of the Holocaust and the ironic temperament of the postwar years, seen by the need for vigilance and engagement to prevent the return of disaster, would make such an escapist form of love seem both an emotional cheat and an intellectual dishonesty as well as a moral failure.

Thus memory, irony, and business, invoked in small, suggestive, and surreal images, nearly eclipse the possibility of love. Yet what shines around and through the images of the poem, surfacing clearly in the emphatic rhythmic and rhetorical structures of the last lines, is the need to find and to give love in a true and honest way. Around the difficulty, the prematurity of love in the autumn of Europe, shines this corona of hope and of possibility.

The title "Corona" may be taken as the first and last of Celan's compressed symbols. The corona that is made visible around the outline of these lovers embracing in a window affirms the possibility of love. This ring of light crowns their relationship and is seen as a source of sincere hope of moving beyond the difficult but honest impasse the poem describes. Celan's poem also transcends his particular time and place. Love is confronted with the same dangers, in various manifestations and degrees, in any time. "Corona" reflects every lover's hope that love can be more than peripheral, delusory, and invisible; it is in such a world that we may then truly begin to live.

Von E. Underwood

CORRESPONDENCE

Author: Henri Coulette (1927-1988)
Type of poem: Lyric
First published: 1990, in *The Collected Poems of Henri Coulette*

The Poem

"Correspondence" is a short, three-stanza poem without rhyme or meter, but with a loose 4-4-5-4 beat pattern in each stanza. "Correspondences" is a traditional title or subject of a poem. The French Symbolist poet Charles Baudelaire, for example, published a poem in *Les Fleurs du mal* (1857; *Flowers of Evil*, 1909) entitled "Correspondences," and the modern American poet Robert Duncan also used the title "Correspondences." It is a word with two meanings. Poems are often addressed to someone and are therefore a kind of letter, a form of correspondence with that person. At the same time, poems often bring out previously unseen associations, or correspondences, by techniques such as imagery, simile, and metaphor. Since Henri Coulette evokes both traditions by giving his poem this title, the poem must be examined for evidence of both.

The poem's relation to correspondence by exchange of letters is announced in the first line. There is no first-person pronoun, only an unidentified speaker describing a "letter" that "lies" on top of something. It has been where it is "all day," and sunlight has passed across it as hours have gone by. In this first stanza, while the description of the letter is physical, the speaker describing it is clearly concerned with its contents. The letter is examined by both the speaker and the bright sunlight, which was even "changing the hues of the ink," but it is not read by either. Its "truths" are also examined, but only the tangible ones of its presence as a fixed, "stationary" object and as something written on leaves of paper (on "stationery"). Whatever is written, however, is left unread.

In the second stanza, the letter itself is no longer the focus of attention. Instead, images of distance and nearness, strangeness and familiarity, are raised. The day that has illuminated the letter is gone. The darkness of night comes from and is associated with the letter's distant origin and its writer by the phrase "from your zone to mine." The moon is not strong and certain and piercing, as the sunlight was, but is "tentative," unlike her usual self. In this unworldly and uncertain nighttime, the owl and its mate "bell" to each other; they are familiar to each other and are able to communicate in a "dialogue of sorts." So, while the letter is no longer visible and is still unread, a form of correspondence is occurring.

In the third stanza, the distance and strangeness of the writer of the letter become the focus. The second-person "you" is asleep, and "East" of the sleeper the next day "is already chronicled." That "Tomorrow," with its illumination, will come to the sleeping writer of the letter first, but will come to the speaker eventually, bringing the unanswered letter to his attention once again.

The final line tells the reader that despite the fact that the speaker has not yet read the letter, he has already guessed its contents and even knows, with a kind of submission, what his response to it will be.

Forms and Devices

In addition to the dual meaning of the title, "Correspondence" uses several puns, beginning with the play on the double meaning of "lies" in the first line and on "stationary" in the fourth. The word "chronicled" in the eleventh line is a play on recorded chronicles of history and on "chronical," an archaic adjective that means regulated by time. These puns are not mere jokes. Each of them represents two alternatives: action and inaction. A letter that "lies" on a table does nothing; it is inactive, immobile, fixed. For a person to write "lies" in a letter is an action. "Stationary," in one sense, means "still," "unmoving," but, in another, means the pages (stationery) upon which one writes letters. The chronicle of time passes without any action by any person: Day turns to night and night to day no matter what anyone does. The chronicle of history, however, is written only by human effort. These puns play on images of activity and inactivity, and the specific activity they are concerned with is writing. This exactly mirrors the concern of the writer of the poem: what has already been and what will be written.

To return to the title pun, while the speaker is concerned with what is written and what he will write, the poem also shows other kinds of correspondences: The "tentative" light of the moon is a counterpart to the light of the sun; the planets and zodiacal stars influence each other and the earth. The owls have an unwritten form of communication that enables them to correspond in their "dialogue of sorts," in which questions can be answers and vice versa.

The poem uses personification to emphasize this second form of correspondence. The light of the sun is spoken of as a person, a being that "travelled the crowded pages" of the letter as if it were a busy train station (perhaps a distant pun with "stationary"). The moon is spoken of as a person too, one who is "not wholly herself." Further, the sunlight "shifts shadows" and "changes the hue of the ink," seeming to have an effect on the contents of the letter. The personified sun and moon, and the signs of the zodiac also function as allusions to the classical mythological deities and heroes who intervene in human affairs. These devices indicate that the celestial bodies all participate in a kind of correspondence that in the poem is represented by the letter, but has nothing to do with reading it.

Themes and Meanings

This poem tells of wanting to answer a letter but does not provide the answer to the letter. In that way, it is about wanting to write but knowing that to begin is to cut off the possibility of telling the truth. There are neither "lies" nor "truths" in the letter so long as it remains unanswered, and the speaker knows that once he begins his answer, it will only be what someone else wants to hear. In this way, the poem is about poetry itself. The theme of truth and lies, tentativeness, and the failed attempt to be wholly oneself is very much the poet's, because the poet is concerned with trying to tell the truth, speaking wholly with his or her own voice. As long as one has never begun to write a poem—or a letter, history, or "true" story—one has never written a false thing. If one never begins, however, then one never communicates at all.

The repeated images of the cosmos—the sun, the moon, and the zodiac—give an impression of great distance and great silence, yet they move with one another in a great dance. By using them as a symbol for regulated movement, Coulette invokes the image of "the music of the spheres." This natural harmony is like the "natural language" of the owls who "bell" to each other (with another kind of "music"): They have a communication that is perhaps not so fraught with difficulty as human speech, in which even the distinctions of question and answer are blurred.

By using these two themes together—the inaccuracy and potential falsehood of human communication, and a more instinctive communing represented by nature, the planets and the owls—the poem implies that even when the correspondence of letters is suspended, another kind of correspondence can go on. The speaker is not reading the letter before him, and he has not, by the end of the poem, begun his answer. Yet, in the course of the poem, a form of communication between the writer of the letter and the speaker has taken place.

Because the belling is between the owl and his "mate," the poem also carries a theme of love. But the "dialogue" of the owls is a happier one than that between the speaker and the writer of the letter: The final exclamation tells us that this is a relationship of submission, that love has led this poet to place pleasing the beloved above everything else, including concerns about telling the truth.

Laurie Glover

CORRESPONDENCES

Author: Charles Baudelaire (1821-1867)
Type of poem: Lyric
First published: 1857, as "Correspondences," in *Les Fleurs du mal*; English translation collected in *Flowers of Evil*, 1936

The Poem

"Correspondences" is a sonnet, its fourteen lines divided into two quatrains and two tercets, in the rhyme pattern *abba, cddc, efe, fgg.* One of the most influential poems in modern literature, it has been translated into English in many forms: unrhymed free verse, sonnet rhyme patterns, and prose. The American poet George Dillon, for example, kept the original French twelve-syllable line but changed the rhyme pattern to *abba, cddc, efg, efg.*

The title names the topic of the poem—the discovery that one makes during certain states of mind that one's sense perceptions blend. Sound becomes a symbol of color; perfumes evoke sights; color reveals emotion. The senses not only correspond with each other but also bear a moral influence in the direction of either purity or corruption.

The importance of this poem comes from its suggestion that the physical world—nature—is imbued with symbols of moral meaning. Later poets such as Stéphane Mallarmé and Arthur Rimbaud, called Symbolists, used the correspondence theory to evoke emotional states by describing objects: A dry mineral field might symbolize boredom or emotional sterility. Since nature's "messages" are presented in words by the poet, the subject of language, specifically poetry, pervades such a poem. This rich poem speaks of communication and reception of truth. Stanza 1 makes the bold generality that all of nature is a single, holy meeting place ("a temple") where one hears confusing messages and feels that one is known and watched. It is a "forest of symbols," full of meanings one cannot quite grasp.

Stanza 2 compares these messages to echoes coming from far away that blend into one sound, as vast as the light of day and the dark of night; the senses of smell, sound, and sight correspond to one another in their meanings. The third stanza illustrates the working of the principle of correspondence with the sense of smell. Some soft, sweet perfumes remind one of musical sounds, children's skin, or green fields. Other perfumes are the opposite: They evoke messages of corruption or oppression.

The final stanza continues the description of odors that speak of dark forces. These are expansive, even infinite, such as frankincense and myrrh. They sing in praise of mental and physical ecstasy. The next-to-last line, naming four exotic spices, recalls the precious ointments brought to the Christ child by the Three Kings. The very words "frankincense and myrrh" have associations with richness and bitterness; they carry a biblical authority and hint of religious celebrations in music and ritual.

Forms and Devices

Analysis of tone and sentence structure in "Correspondences" demonstrates Charles Baudelaire's mastery of formal devices. Although the subject of symbolic meanings in nature may be difficult for the reader to grasp, the poet's tone projects a confidence that adds to the poem's power. The opening metaphor directly equating nature with a temple commands one's attention with its boldness. The use of simile, a weaker device, would have less power. Later in the poem, the blending of sensory perception is compared to echoes one hears in the background: a train passing, a machine humming, the wind blowing, a tap dripping. Here the simile works well, underscoring a point. Throughout the poem, in three clear and grammatical sentences, the poet firmly controls the unfolding of his idea.

The four lines of stanza 1 complete one sentence—a compound sentence with a break exactly in the middle, at the end of the second line. It begins with its subject and verb declaring a proposition; the proposition's effects in human life unroll in the third and fourth lines. The second stanza also begins and ends as one sentence, but the opposite placement of subject and verb makes this stanza grammatically a mirror of the first. Here, three lines of an introductory phrase, an extended simile, lead into the main clause in line 4. Here one comes to the heart of the poem, in which the plainly spoken "correspondence" of sense perception is stated. These two sentences are called "right-branching" (starting with subject and verb) and "left-branching" (ending with subject and verb), respectively. They balance each other and provide a rhythm in the movement of the poem that the reader may feel subconsciously. The balance of sentence style sets up an echo or dialogue effect that mirrors the first stanza's report of humanity feeling "watched" by nature and the second stanza's simile about echoes.

The remaining six lines, divided into two three-line stanzas, make the third and final sentence. The correspondences of perfumes (a favorite sensory reference in Baudelaire's poetry) result in various effects. Odors can evoke, for example, sweetness and freshness, or they can stimulate one toward dark, infinite, and dangerous powers that enchant the mind and senses.

Critics such as Roman Jakobson have found layers of grammatical parallels embedded in Baudelaire's poetry. Balanced vowel and consonant patterns, general and concrete noun patterns, and verb tense patterns show a delicately crafted subsurface structure that affects the reader. This extraordinary perfection of form resembles the "hidden" patterns of sound and word in the sonnets of William Shakespeare.

"Correspondences" would seem to present an unlikely marriage of form and meaning. The tightly controlled sonnet form would not seem to be conducive to the subject of confused half-awareness with which one understands nature's symbols. The final line praises ecstasy of mind and body—hardly an orderly concept in the usual sense. Yet one can find a profound rightness in this apparent contrast. The human imagination, Baudelaire believed, was as accurate and truthful as any scientific instrument. Beyond the confusions of sensual perceptions lies an encompassing, ordained, and beautiful balance, a justice that human imagination can picture.

Thus, in a confident and assured tone, Baudelaire can speak of disorder and dimly perceived correspondences, with the expression remaining classically coherent. Like the expression of many moods in Ludwig van Beethoven's music, Baudelaire's poetry encases emotion within the controlling power of mind.

Themes and Meanings

"Correspondences" is a poem about the unity of nature, human perceptions of interdependence in sense perceptions, and the multiple worlds those analogies reveal. One becomes aware of this unity only at rare moments. When one loses one's ordinary state of mind, when one no longer separates oneself from one's surroundings and objects from one another, one may be able to perceive the equivalence of one sense impression to another—perfume to sight, sound to color.

The word "ecstasy" means a state of "standing outside" oneself—a trancelike state. Such an altered state of consciousness may be induced by hallucinogenic drugs. Baudelaire admired Thomas De Quincey, the English writer of *Confessions of an English Opium-Eater* (1821), and Edgar Allan Poe, whose dreamlike poems and stories were extremely influential in France—thanks largely to Baudelaire's writings about Poe's aesthetics. Baudelaire himself took opium and hashish. Another inducement to a unitary state of mind, a traditional and universal way, is the practice of meditation in many forms: quieting the analytical mind by dancing, chanting, repeating a mantra, or putting the service of others before one's own ego demands. Most religious sects enable devotees to attain "oneness" with God by such practices. For centuries, "out of body" experiences have been recorded by mystics. Baudelaire's Roman Catholic upbringing, in conjunction with the Romantic idealism of his time, may be seen in many poems. "Correspondences" suggests a mystic holiness surrounding one's presence in nature's temple. One's own body becomes nature's temple—the meeting place of mind and sensation.

Art provides a third avenue for the loss of one's ordinary conscious awareness of time and space. "Correspondences" suggests that the artist is attuned to the animated world of objects and can perceive analogies in the natural world. One should not assume by this that Baudelaire was a "nature lover" in the modern sense. He had no love for vegetation or biology as such. An urbane Parisian art critic, he much preferred the artificial presentation of beauty in art to an unadorned, "natural" spectacle. The law and order of abstract nature was indeed his ideal, however, and the senses could introduce one to that world.

The point to which the poem advances, with the illustration of perfumes, is the revelation that the universe of nature is not unitary, but plural. One universe is pure and sweet; its mirror opposite is attractive but evil—heavy, sensual, exotic, and domineering. Many of the poems of Baudelaire's mature creative period come from this second universe; flowers plucked from all the doubt, disgust, and disease that he felt inside himself and in the bourgeois culture of nineteenth century France.

Doris Earnshaw

CORSONS INLET

Author: A. R. Ammons (1926-2001)
Type of poem: Meditation
First published: 1965; collected in *Corsons Inlet,* 1965

The Poem

"Corsons Inlet" is a poem of 128 lines recounting the poet's reaction to what he sees, thinks, and feels during a morning walk along a seashore. It becomes an almost ecstatic celebration of change, of form as temporary but beautiful because it cannot endure. The poem is written in what seems to be free verse, but while it avoids rhyme there are frequent echoings of sound. While the line lengths vary from one syllable to as many as fifteen, there is something approaching a pattern in the arrangement of the lines; while there are no stanzas or strophes, the patterns formed by groups of lines bear a shifting resemblance to one another.

This avoidance of clear patterns while suggesting that patterns do exist is a reflection of the central idea of "Corsons Inlet." As the poet walks, he finds himself liberated from the "straight lines, blocks, boxes, binds/ of thought" into a world of sensation and motion. His mind can move freely, and he characterizes his work as "swerves of action" like the changing shape of sand dunes. He can cope with details, no matter how small, but the question of whether there is a single meaning in the process, some all-encompassing pattern, is not his to answer: "overall is beyond me."

Having rejected wide-ranging philosophies, the poet proclaims his openness, his willingness to accept what he sees and to allow the forms to define themselves. He describes the transitions in the natural world, which have no clear boundaries, no sharp edges. He paints a vivid picture of the violence of nature: a gull eating to the point of vomiting, a different gull cracking and eating a crab. In the natural world "risk is full: every living thing in/ siege: the demand is life, to keep life."

His attention then turns to a small system. Autumn is bringing "thousands of tree swallows" to eat bayberries and to gather themselves for flight, and he sees that what appears to be chaotic may be part of an order: "the possibility of rule as the sum of rulelessness." He recognizes that there is order also in the small details. Still, he insists that there are, "in the large view, no/ lines or changeless shapes."

As the poem moves toward its close, he arrives at a point of serenity; he will accept, but not try to force anything. There are orders, but around them "the looser, wider forces work." In his poetry he will try to "fasten into order enlarging grasps of disorder" but will revel in the freedom of the knowledge that he will never find definitive answers, that change will continue, "that tomorrow a new walk is a new walk."

Forms and Devices

The appearance of total disorder when in fact there are large kinds of order is both the theme of "Corsons Inlet" and its form: change is "not chaos." The poem is divided into groups of lines too irregularly to allow the divisions to be called stanzas, but these divisions are not random. Many consist of two or more long lines followed by very short lines, sometimes consisting of a single syllable or a single word, which are followed in turn by more long lines. The divisions are of different lengths, but generally range between three and nine lines, with most containing six or seven.

The movement of the poem is also less random than it seems at first. If there is no regular meter, there is rhythm, conversational for the most part, with stresses used chiefly to emphasize significant passages. The narration follows the course of a walk along the dunes, returning "along the inlet shore." The imagery of sight, sound, smell, and touch is all drawn from the natural surroundings, as are the metaphors; early in the poem, the poet says, "I allow myself eddies of meaning," drawing the metaphor from the movement of water and sand. In his poetry, he says, there is "a direction of significance/ running/ like a stream through the geography of my work."

The imagery is precise, for the most part, but it is sometimes complex, as when he plays with different meanings of the concept of order: "pulsations of order/ in the bellies of minnows: orders swallowed,/ broken down, transferred through membranes/ to strengthen larger orders." Throughout the poem, imagery alternates with his thoughts about what he is seeing; conclusions are drawn constantly, not saved for the end, and these conclusions also change. At one point, he sees what appears to be chaos in small things but suspects that there are larger orders which he cannot see; at a later point, the order he sees is in the minuscule.

The observer notices shapes in small things—flowers and the shells of small animals. The actual appearance of the poem on the page suggests order in movement and change:

> I have reached no conclusions, have erected no boundaries,
> shutting out and shutting in, separating inside
>   from outside: I have
>   drawn no lines:
>   as
>
> manifold events of sand
> change the dune's shape that will not be the same shape
> tomorrow.

Throughout the poem, the idea of formlessness becoming form, at least temporarily, is presented in A. R. Ammons's descriptions of his ideas and conclusions, interwoven among his observations of the natural world. Even the punctuation used in the poem maintains Ammons's theme: He uses only commas and colons to mark pauses and rests. Until the end, where a single period closes the poem, there are no periods or even semicolons used, as if to suggest that such marks would be too positive and final. Except for the personal pronoun "I," he capitalizes only two words, both for ironic effect: "Overall" and "Scope" are capitalized to suggest godlike qualities too huge for his comprehension.

Themes and Meanings

Throughout his early work, Ammons employed his observations of nature as a means of conveying his sense of the fragility as well as the fascination of life. The mood of other poems may be depressed, playful, or self-mocking, but in "Corsons Inlet" he expresses a kind of ecstasy at the recognition that life is risky, various, and full. Most important, it is in constant flux. What he sees keeps moving him toward and away from the idea that all this natural activity is planned. He finds paradox in nature ("an order held/ in constant change"); there is terror, but it is not planned. It "pervades but is not arranged."

For Ammons, even an ordinary walk by the ocean on an overcast day is an experience which informs his view of life and confirms his conviction about what his poetry should be. Moving through the scene he describes, he is not a detached observer but part of the events: Birds fly away when he comes over the crest of a dune, an event which may lead to the birds' stripping the berries from a different bayberry bush somewhere else. The other creatures cling to life as tenaciously as he does, and they are as certain to find death. This is an unavoidable part of the process and can also be celebrated; "entropy" is a physical law decreeing the eventual death of all systems, but in Ammons's ecstatic view he can see "a congregation/ rich with entropy."

The poet can reach conclusions, but they are paradoxical: He will determine only that he will make no final determinations. "I see narrow orders, limited tightness, but will/ not run to that easy victory:/ still around the looser, wider forces work." "Corsons Inlet" is noteworthy not only because it is a clear and forceful expression of Ammons's attitude toward life and toward his work, but also because it is a poem in which the different elements all work in the same direction. The images, metaphors, and forms, even the punctuation and the way in which the poem appears on the page, all contribute to the effect. All the elements are employed to a single end, in a coherence which contains the very paradox that is the subject of the poem.

John M. Muste

COUNTING SMALL-BONED BODIES

Author: Robert Bly (1926-   )
Type of poem: Satire
First published: 1967, in *The Light Around the Body*

The Poem

Robert Bly's "Counting Small-Boned Bodies" is a short poem of ten lines, written in free verse and carefully divided into four stanzas. The poem initially invites the reader to participate with the speaker (or persona) in the singular action of recounting bodies. The process Bly refers to is one of counting the bodies of enemy dead following a battle, a military practice used to determine the extent of damage inflicted on the opposing force. The satire of the poem protests the Vietnam War, and more specifically the Pentagon practice of releasing body-count statistics to the press on a daily basis. The last three stanzas show the bodies shrinking and becoming ostensibly less important. Bly uses a succession of unusual metaphoric images to demonstrate the horror of trivializing death in this manner.

The title of the poem gives immediate notification that something out of the ordinary is taking place, as Bly stipulates that the bodies are small-boned, bringing images to mind of the skeleton rather than flesh and blood. The title thus suggests something other than the gory images usually associated with day-after descriptions of battle scenes. The title even reduces the size of the bodies, preparing the reader for the starker reductions that follow. The conversational tone of the first stanza involves the reader in the "we" of the remainder of the poem, setting up a tacit agreement that to read on is to participate in the experimental testing of the practice of counting bodies. The first word, "Let's," is encouraging in tone and hints at an equal participation between speaker and reader.

Each of the next three stanzas begins with the same line, a wistful thought that if it were only possible to make the bodies smaller, then—the speaker surmises—they would become ever more manageable. In each of the three dreamlike visions that follow, the reader and body-counter move closer to the bodies, which occupy first a moonlit plain and then a desk, until finally a single body is shrunken to a size that would fit into a "finger-ring." However, the bodies resist any reduction of their importance, thanks to the shocking and surreal images Bly uses: a field of skulls, a year's worth of kill on a single desktop, and finally a body inserted into a ring. The speaker seems unaware that each reduction in size also reduces the distance between the counter and the counted.

The ending of the poem presents a singular finality in which the bodies are all but lost while at the same time one could be contained within a ring, a trophy to be prized as a token of achievement. In this particular poem, Bly relies on what critics call "deep images" to convey the anger and energy of his dissent. Bly prefers to describe this as looking inward to connect with the spiritual self, a process that is important even though the results may seem mysterious and disturbing. The effort produces images that are strange and surreal, yet often healing. These images in Bly's war poetry are similar to those found in the political protest poems of Pablo Neruda. Bly's overall work as a poet, translator, critic and publisher has enlarged American poetry by popularizing images drawn from the collective unconscious, transformative images previously found primarily in non-English-language writers.

Forms and Devices

Much of the effectiveness of "Counting Small-Boned Bodies" in attacking body counts as a method of measuring "progress" in the Vietnam War lies in the structure Bly develops. The poem spirals downward through ever smaller yet ever more potent images. The single line of the first stanza simply portrays the speaker's conspiratorial approach, providing a narrative hook—inviting the reader to play along.

The second line of the poem continues in the reasonable tone already established, but it proposes a connection between a real event and imaginative world where a human body could be made smaller and smaller for the sake of convenience. How the body size is reduced is never explained; however, the impact of the reduction comes in the brief third line, in which the bodies have become skull-sized. This is followed by a compelling vision of a moonlit plain filled with skulls, each representing a body. The vast numbers of skulls filling the whitened landscape is suggestive of a Romantic painting. Bly accentuates the satiric miracle of the moonlit scene by ending the stanza with an exclamation mark.

The last line of the stanza is the longest of the poem. It also achieves the final element of the pattern Bly follows in the rest of the poem; in this case stanzas 2, 3, and 4 enclose a small line between longer first and last lines. Each stanza is a tercet, fashioned from a sentence broken into three separate lines. The structure of the poem is an outgrowth of the content and meaning, one of the basic attributes of free verse.

The poem continues to tighten while growing even more emphatically satirical. Stanza 3 proposes that a "whole year's kill" might be shrunk so small as to fit on a single desk. Using the symbol of a desk, an image of bureaucracy, focuses the anger in the poem toward the Pentagon's use of body counts and kill-ratio statistics. The military establishment is indicted for creating a view of death as a statistic and dead enemy soldiers as objects of proof. Again, Bly ends with the satiric exclamation mark.

In the final stanza the satire overwhelms by turning from the vastness of the compiled statistics to a single body made small enough to fit inside a ring. This is the most personal and potent image of all, an ultimate reminder to everyone of the horror being masked by the sanitized language of body counts. The final phrase of a "keepsake forever" implies the falseness of the entire body count procedure by alluding to an advertising slogan popular at the time.

In "Counting Small-Boned Bodies" the first line of each stanza repeats a suggestion of the inexplicable process whereby bodies are made smaller, while the last line embodies a surrealistic vision that drives home the horror of death. In this way Bly trumps the manner of speech that he criticizes, creating a wrenching vision of the horror of war by using a bloodless set of images.

Themes and Meanings

Bly calls on his personal imagination to create the stages the bodies pass through as they are made smaller. By contrasting the concrete images of plain, desk, and ring with the surreal idea of shrinking the bodies, he heightens the satire. Readers can see that the Pentagon method of scoring progress in the war really does make the bodies smaller, the deaths less important, and the enemy something other than human. Indeed, Bly makes his view clear that the body-count method of tracking the progress of the war is evil.

While death has always been a result of war, previous methods of calculating progress in conflict involved measuring geographic territory taken and held. This proved to be impossible in Vietnam for several reasons, the main one being that in a guerilla war in a jungle setting, the enemy can return and may at any time be only a few feet away. In addition, the United States forces found it difficult to distinguish between civilians and soldiers, Vietnamese allies and Viet Cong enemies.

Because honors were meted out to American units based on their reporting of body counts, such statistics were often inflated—in fact, a "partial body count" process was created to help make U.S. forces appear superior. Disparaging comparisons were made between body counts and baseball scores. Bly read "Counting Small-Boned Bodies" and other antiwar poems during rallies and readings, often while wearing a frightening patriarchal mask. He became a prominent member of the antiwar movement, which held that the United States should withdraw and leave the conflict to be settled by the Vietnamese themselves.

"Counting Small-Boned Bodies" may be read as a powerful statement against all war and especially against the war it was written to denounce. It demonstrates that all war remains visceral and abhorrent. As published in Bly's second collection of poems, *The Light Around the Body*, the poem appears in a chapter simply entitled "Viet Nam." When Bly won the National Book Award for the collection, he contributed the prize money to a group he had helped found in 1966, Writers Against the War.

"Counting Small-Boned Bodies" is especially effective in its final image. In war, soldiers often take souvenirs consisting of a piece of the equipment, personal effects, body or hair of the defeated enemy. Bly's final image of the shrunken body as a keepsake suggests both the horror of plunder and the casual aplomb with which the results of victory may be flaunted. The reader is left with the warning that the practice of counting bodies and, by implication, other such misrepresentations of the truth will result in lasting psychological damage to the warring culture.

Margaret A. Dodson

COUNTING THE CHILDREN

Author: Dana Gioia (1950-   )
Type of poem: Narrative
First published: 1990; collected in *The Gods of Winter*, 1991

The Poem

Dana Gioia's "Counting the Children" is a long narrative poem, comprising fifty-six stanzas (fifty-five of them unrhymed tercets) across four sections. The poem's first section details the investigation of a Mr. Choi, a court-appointed auditor (and the persona of this poem), who is led into the house of a deceased woman by a neighbor. "When someone wealthy dies without a will," Mr. Choi is "sent out by the State/ To take an inventory." The neighbor recounts to the auditor the dead woman's eccentricities: "She used to wander around town at night/ And rifle through the trash. We all knew that." The neighbors, however, apparently never took time to notice what it was the woman was digging for in the trash. Certainly, it could not have been for anything valuable: She was a wealthy woman.

What both the investigator and neighbor discover, in the aftermath of the woman's death, is that she had been collecting cast-off dolls. The neighbor, shaken by the discovery of this grotesque collection, tells Mr. Choi, "Come in, . . . I want to show you hell. . . . Stretching from floor to ceiling, wall to wall," "A crowd of faces looked up silently./ Shoulder to shoulder, standing all in rows,/ Hundreds of dolls were lining every wall." Significantly, this is "Not a collection anyone would want—/ Just ordinary dolls salvaged from the trash, . . . Some battered, others missing arms and legs." In this macabre scene, the dolls "looked like sisters huddling in the dark,/ Forgotten brides abandoned at the altar, . . . Rows of discarded little girls and babies—/ Some naked, others dressed for play—they wore/ Whatever lives their owners left them in."

Mr. Choi recognizes this scene as tragic: "Where were the children who promised them love?" He realizes, "Now they have become each other—/ Anonymous except for injury." While the dolls' tragedy is clear, implied is the dead woman's own tragic situational irony. Wealthy as she was, she had no wealth in friendship. Like the dolls, she was "anonymous except for injury." Her attempt to rescue the unloved dolls was also her attempt to rescue her own unloved heart. So full of love herself, so needful, she gives her affection to the dolls who, like herself, had been cast away. As Mr. Choi notes, "all affection is outgrown," and "Dust has a million lives, the heart has one." Ironically, despite this momentary epiphany, Mr. Choi does exactly as all had done to the old woman and to the dolls: He "turn[s] away" to make his report.

In the second section of Gioia's poem, Mr. Choi recounts the dream he subsequently has that same night. In his dream he is "working on a ledger,/ A book so large, it stretched across my desk,/ Thousands of numbers running down each page." He has an account to settle, but, as he calculates, the numbers begin "slipping down the page." He realizes that nothing he ever did would fit together, that all his calculations would turn up "back to nil." He remarks, "In my hands even 2 + 2 + 2/ No longer equaled anything at all." At the culmination of the dream, Mr. Choi sees his whole family standing beside and behind him, including "cousins I'd never seen,/ My grandparents from China and their parents." This vision shifts from the family to the realization that "now I wasn't at my desk/ But working on the coffin of my daughter/ And she would die unless I found the sum." However, the numbers caught fire, and the dolls were there, "screaming in the flames."

The third and shortest section leaves the surreal dream to Mr. Choi's waking aftermath. He sits up in his bed, certain he has screamed; however, when he looks over at his sleeping wife, he realizes he has not. This transitional section places Mr. Choi amid the incongruities of the dead woman's world, his surreal nightmare, and a reality where his night terror brings him to his infant daughter's room in vigil. The poet writes, "I felt so helpless standing by her crib" because "In the bare nursery we had improvised/ I learned the loneliness that we call love."

The last section provides a summary of the effects all these stimuli have upon Mr. Choi. He feels as if he has had a vision, something one might believe accountants are incapable of having. Yet, in that vision, he sees that "We die . . . and we are one/ With all our ancestors . . . The ancient face returning in the child,/ The distant arms embracing us." The vision illustrates how people are the products of all past loves and all past promises as much as they are the products of the injuries they suffer when those loves and promises fail. Mr. Choi determines he will not let go of his daughter, that she will not endure the death of lovelessness as prophesied by his dream. Yet, in the darkness of his daughter's bedroom, he sees that she has lined up three dolls on her shelves, in the manner the old woman had placed her salvaged loves. He remarks, "I felt like holding them tight in my arms,/ Promising I would never let them go,/ But they would trust no promises of mine."

Forms and Devices

Gioia is highly regarded as a neoformalist or expansionist poet, as he and others of this contemporary generation call themselves. As a new postmodern, or twenty-first century school, the intent of the expansionist poet is to revive the old traditional forms of poetry and to expand them in new, innovative ways. Gioia's "Counting the Children" is written in unrhymed tercets, with the exception of a final, single line that closes the dramatic narrative. Sectioning the poem, as he does, Gioia moves readers through the poem's plot and subplot, from the macabre scenery of the old woman's doll room, to the surreal nightmare that coalesces Mr. Choi's occupation to the dolls, to his daughter and ancestors, and then to the real fear of losing his promise of love. As the poem moves in three-line stanzas, the readers are taken to three types of realities, each nightmarish in their own fashion. Consequently, the form of Gioia's poem mirrors the thought.

When the neighbor woman tells Mr. Choi, "I want to show you hell," Gioia sets up a well-executed allusion to Dante's Inferno, from *La divina commedia* (c. 1320; *The Divine Comedy*, 1802). The neighbor woman acts as Vergil, who will lead Mr. Choi, the Dante-visionary, into the chasm of the old woman's doll room. In the Inferno, Dante must pass through the various chasms of hell before he can come to enlightenment and redemption; he must become accountable and know the abomination of sin. Appropriately, the accountant Mr. Choi must take inventory of all those "lost" dolls and, in his dream ledger, the lost ancestors, those forgotten, broken, anonymous masses. Just as Dante takes the trip into hell and returns, Mr. Choi's vision takes him on a similar journey. Whereas Dante's hell is the afterlife, Mr. Choi's hell is very much the present world where promises do not last. The sin of Choi's hell is "the loneliness that we call love."

Gioia also alludes to William Butler Yeats's "The Dolls." Just as Yeats's dolls disdain the dollmaker and his wife for bringing a baby into their home, the dolls of Gioia's poem disdain and would scream at a man they cannot trust. In both poems, the undying artifact—perfect because it does not die—has reason to scorn the impermanence of human love. The live baby in Yeats's poem is a thing of filth; in Gioia's poem, the filth is the human betrayal of love, no matter to whom or what it was originally given.

Themes and Meanings

Since Gioia's "Counting the Children" alludes so poignantly to Dante's Inferno, one of the poem's themes must be about loss of Paradise and the pain humans endure in hell. What is clear, here, is that the hell humans endure comes from the injuries they suffer when promises of love are broken and they are cast away. Unless someone equally loveless rescues and salvages them, they are condemned to perpetual torment. Ancestors stand beside and behind every person; ghosts haunt with the reminder that one will become them—anonymous and forgotten—and that one's children will also become them. The sum of all accounts, existentially speaking, is constant zero. Mr. Choi's determination to persist in the love of his daughter, to attend fearfully to her nightly as she sleeps, is futility. Passing through the gateway of hell, one abandons all hope of permanent love and despairs. Those whom one loves should, like the dolls, scream out angrily; already, it is understood that one will fail, despite good intentions. What becomes of the dolls the old woman rescued when she has died? Despite her love and care for the dolls, they will become refuse again. Tragically, even those whom love rescues face much the same fate.

Mark Sanders

THE COUNTRY OF MARRIAGE

Author: Wendell Berry (1934-   )
Type of poem: Lyric
First published: 1971; collected in *The Country of Marriage*, 1973

The Poem

"The Country of Marriage" is a pastoral lyric in free verse with seventy-eight lines and seven irregular stanzas. The title suggests the poem's dual celebration of country life and marriage. Both farming and marriage are valued as complementary expressions of love, fidelity, trust, and commitment. The poem is written in the first person, using the Berry persona of the "Mad Farmer," who reflects Berry's agrarian perspective. It is implicitly addressed to Berry's wife, Tanya, as a love poem, though she is not named directly but addressed throughout the poem in the second person.

As a poem about courtship, marriage, and the married life, "The Country of Marriage" echoes the form and sentiments of Edmund Spenser's "Epithalamion" (epithalamion means "wedding song or poem"). Berry, however, forsakes Spenser's classical allusions in favor of pastoral images drawn directly from the Berrys' marriage and life together on their Kentucky farm.

Stanza 1 opens with a dream: The speaker envisions his wife "walking at night along the streams/ of the country of my birth," merged with the forces of nature, "holding in your body the dark seed of my/ sleep." This discreetly eroticized dream of love and procreation sets their conjugal love within the context of the wider reproductive powers of nature.

Stanza 2 contrasts the security of their union with the prior loneliness and isolation of the speaker, who depicts himself as "a man lost in the woods in the dark," a wanderer who has lost his way and seeks "the solace of his native land." Berry's persona finds reassurance in his wife's words in a dream that he did not know he had dreamed, "like the earth's empowering brew rising/ in root and branch." Their life together reminds the speaker of a clearing in the forest, revealing a well-tended farm, with orchard, garden, and bright flowers. The pastoral images in stanza 3 reinforce the connection between country and marriage. Images of light and dark also dominate in this stanza, the light in the clearing accentuated by the darkness of the surrounding forest.

Stanza 4 reveals a pattern of the speaker launching out and returning to the emotional comfort of their relationship, filled with joy, surrendering and trusting to their love like a man venturing into "the forest unarmed." Images of descent, arrival, and rest suggest the pleasures of their love. In stanza 5 the poet affirms that the bond of their love surpasses a mere economic exchange: It is rich and limitless in its possibilities for their mutual growth and development. Again, his wife serves as a guide and source of support. The speaker stresses his unworthiness and affirms the blessedness of their union as an unearned gift, to be accepted as the plants accept "the bounty of the/ light."

What their love has taught him, the poet affirms in stanza 6, is the freedom of surrender to its bounty, as conveyed by the simile of their drinking the waters of a deep stream whose richness surpasses their thirst. Berry's water images imply the freedom, surrender, and trust essential to love. The last stanza unifies the images of light and darkness, water and rain, and flowers, orchards, and abundance in the promise of the marriage that they have "planted in this ground." The poet closes by praising his wife as a type of "all beautiful and honest women that you gather to/ yourself."

Forms and Devices

"The Country of Marriage" is the title poem of Berry's fourth poetry volume, which was dedicated to his wife Tanya. Each of the seven stanzas is organized around a series of metaphoric assertions of the poet's love for his wife. Berry, like Denise Levertov, is committed to the use of organic form, in which the content of a poem shapes its form. Berry's use of the confessional form also allows him to celebrate their conjugal love in a personal but discreet manner.

Each stanza opens with a poetic assertion or question which is then expanded through the use of a dominant metaphor, linking their love with nature. The delicacy and intimacy of the lines create a sense of rhetorical privacy, as in a love letter or courtship poem. The basic movement of each stanza is from separation and isolation to union, from dream and desire to surrender and union. The organic metaphors express a series of oppositions that convey the richness of their love: limited/limitless, known/unknown, possessed/unpossessed, worthy/unworthy, light/darkness, life/ death.

Another dominant trope for their love is expressed through the words trust, approach, surrender, descent, union, rest, and peace, which echo the Elizabethan conceit of "dying" into each other's love, often found in courtly love poetry. The energy of the poem seems to alternate between separation and union, losing and finding each other, suggesting the task of finding and defining oneself through love. There is a sense of indirect erotic tension and energy diffused throughout the poem, conveyed through the organic metaphors, which parallels the fecundity of nature.

The speaker celebrates the joy, happiness, and fulfillment of their marriage, always from the speaker's own point of view. His wife is addressed but never replies. The poem also conveys a tacit religious sensibility, reminiscent of St. Paul's celebration of love in I Corinthians 13, in that the qualities of conjugal love—its paradoxical, mysterious, generous, unpredictable, unbounded, and transcendent nature—suggest a parallel with divine love. A husband's and wife's love for each other mirrors God's love for humanity. These religious overtones are implied through Berry's consistent use of light and dark imagery throughout the poem.

Themes and Meanings

"The Country of Marriage" is a subtle, delicate celebration of married love. Through the intimacy of the confessional form, the poet reaffirms the ardency of his courtship and his fidelity to his marriage vows. Each stanza offers a subtle variation on the theme of the bonds of love and fidelity, mutual trust and affection, giving and receiving. The pastoral setting and organic form provide an appropriate context for the celebration of marital love.

Stanza 2 echoes the opening stanzas of Dante Alighieri's *The Divine Comedy*. Like Dante the pilgrim, Berry's speaker envisions himself lost in a dark wood in which the vision of the beloved appears to him as a spiritual guide as Beatrice did for Dante. Berry, like Dante, imagines himself a wanderer in his native land, spiritually lost, seeking the level ground to avoid the abyss. The metaphoric implications of Berry's persona as a pilgrim who has lost his way and seeks a guide suggests the belief in the transforming power of love shared by both poets. A crucial difference is that while Beatrice served as both muse and idealization of love, Berry's persona celebrates the fully realized marital relationship. He finds his way to a kind of "salvation" in the present life through the pleasures of marriage.

A central theme in the poem is the rejection of mere economic or utilitarian calculations of love. The poet asserts that "our bond is no little economy based on the exchange/ of my love and work for yours." Instead, their love is unbounded, immeasurable, a mystery, a blessing to be accepted "as a plant accepts from all the bounty of the/ light/ enough to live, and then accepts the dark." Their mutual love and surrender is an exercise in freedom and a way of accepting their mortality and the mysterious gift of life. Their relationship provides a continuous education and self-liberation in which "what I am learning to give you is my death/ to set you free of me, and me from myself/ into the dark and the new light." As husband and wife, they constantly renew themselves and each other through their marriage.

Their love is a mystery, an unbounded, constantly renewable gift, a mutual surprise and delight, as figured in the pastoral images of the last stanza: "a night of rain," "a clump of orange-blooming weeds beside the road," "the young orchard waiting in the snow." The last stanza ends with the poet's rededication of his love for his wife.

Berry's use of the pastoral form and the images of farming and husbandry to celebrate conjugal love places his poem within a long tradition of pastoral poetry that stretches through English poetry to the Greek and Roman classics of Theocritus, Vergil, and Horace. Most of all, perhaps, he resembles the Elizabethan and Metaphysical poets—Edmund Spenser, Andrew Marvell, and John Donne—who reinvigorated the English pastoral form. The subtle mastery of "The Country of Marriage" demonstrates why Berry is widely considered the foremost contemporary American pastoral poet.

Andrew J. Angyal

COUNTRY STARS

Author: William Meredith (1919-   )
Type of poem: Meditation
First published: 1976; collected in *The Cheer*, 1980

The Poem

"Country Stars" is a short poem consisting of two five-line stanzas with a rhyme scheme of *abbab, cdcdd.* The title not only evokes a scene of supreme beauty—the dark night sky studded with stars—but the term "country" also draws the reader into experiencing the sights, sounds, and scents associated with the country.

Contrary to expectations, the poem does not open with a celebration of the sublime beauty of nature, but with a domestic scene where a myopic child "comes downstairs to be kissed goodnight." The poet follows her actions as she blows on a "black windowpane until it's white" and digresses to describe a constellation of stars, "a great bear," passing over the apple trees. This scene of beauty escapes the child, who sees only darkness—a darkness that she distrusts. By taking off the glasses through which she sees, by clouding the windowpane, she is responsible for the barrier between her and the beauty of the night sky, for her own personal state of limited vision and obscurity.

In the second stanza, the poet relates the scene within the country home and the actions of the child to actions taking place within "two cities." The poet animates cities, chemical plants, and "clotted cars" and visualizes them to be breathing pollutants into the air. The most likely pollutants suggested by the images are chemical fumes and carbon monoxide. The poet holds humanity responsible for the growing man-made darkness that acts as a barrier between humans and the starry sky, like the clouded windowpane that prevents the child from appreciating the beauty of the nocturnal scene outside her window. The child's fear dissolves into a collective fear as the poet ends his poem with lines that shake the reader's faith in "the bright watchers" looking down on them. The afterthought, "or only proper fear," in the lines "But have no fear, or only proper fear:/ the bright watchers are still there" instills that element of doubt in the stars that are initially viewed as guardians watching over humanity. Perhaps the thought occurs that a time may come when the curtain of pollution may be so thick that the darkness may be impregnable, thus severing the bond between people and the sublime beauty symbolized by the stars forever.

Forms and Devices

From the very beginning, William Meredith makes effective use of contrasts. The bright stars are seen against the backdrop of the black night sky. When the "nearsighted child" takes off her glasses, she moves from the state of seeing to that of unseeing. As she blows on the windowpane, she transforms it from "black" to "white." Such key terms as "country stars," "apple trees," "cities," "chemical plant," and "clotted cars" establish the contrast between the serene, fresh, natural beauty of the country and city smog, chemical fumes, and dust. The warmth, trust, and love inherent in the word "kissed" is contrasted with such emotions as distrust and fear. Finally, the protected state of the child within the room is contrasted with the fear of abandonment as the poet questions the presence of the "bright watchers" in the sky.

Throughout the poem, Meredith uses words associated directly or indirectly with vision. "Country stars," the constellation passing over the apple trees, and "the bright watchers" all call upon the reader to appreciate a scene of beauty from a distance. The nearsightedness of the child expresses a state of blurred vision. Haziness again is suggested by the image of the clouded windowpane used to describe the thick layer of pollution hanging over the city. Beyond the blurred vision is the fear of total loss of vision. This is expressed through the predominance of the color black in the poem.

The act of seeing takes another dimension when the reader examines Meredith's use of frames. The child's lenses are contained within frames. The window through which she views the darkness presents two differing framed pictures: one constructed by her, the other by the poet. She sees a black-framed scene, whereas the poet distinguishes the pattern of the stars above the apple trees. Both the poet and the child are viewing the same scene, but the child does not possess the clarity of vision that the poet does. Again, the extension of the image of the clouded windowpane to the second stanza gives another framed picture: the picture of dimly perceived stars viewed through a cloudy film.

Meredith's power of animating inanimate objects is evident in the way he personifies cities, chemical plants, and cars as living, breathing things. The stars also seem to be alive as they watch over humanity from afar.

Above all, there is a unifying principle linking the first and second stanzas, as individual actions, images, and emotions in the first stanza are related to collective actions and sentiments in the second stanza. The blurred vision of the child is related to the blurred vision of the masses; the clouded windowpane of one room is related to a huge windowpane obstructing the vision of the multitude of city dwellers; and the fear of the child is related to the collective fear of humanity in general. This reconciliation of the individual with the collective gives the poem an air of universality.

In "The Language of the Tribe: William Meredith's Poetry," in *Southwest Review* (1982), Neva Herrington writes of "the marvelous mystery of the associative power of words." Indeed, the poetic cosmos of Meredith's "Country Stars" is a world in which words, images, actions, and sentiments interact with one another in such a way that through the power of association, the poem grows in significance with each new reading.

Themes and Meanings

"Country Stars" is a poem about vision and the bond between humankind and nature. The poem presents many perspectives on vision. There is the blurred vision of the child, the clouded vision of the city dwellers viewing the sky through polluted air, and the total loss of vision expressed through the blackness of the night. Scenes are viewed from a distance as well as from close proximity. They are even viewed through such different mediums as glass and polluted air. There is, though, one who sees with a penetrating vision and clarity all that escapes the multitudes. This is the omniscient poet, who rejoices in the beauty of the country stars passing over the apple trees and the "bright watchers" in the sky over the city and wishes to share this joy. The poet as seer, however, also realizes that the joy he experiences in this relationship between himself and the beautiful night sky is doomed to be a solitary experience if humanity is not more conscious of the environment. Through "Country Stars," Meredith attempts to instill this consciousness in his readers.

The poet sees humanity through its own means destroying a very special relationship with beauty and nature. The theme of a relationship begins with the poet's depiction of the trusting relationship between parent and child in the scene in which the child comes without her glasses to be kissed goodnight. This relationship is extended to that between nature and humankind when the poet perceives the stars to be watching over the earth's population, as a parent watches over a child. Words such as "distrust" and "fear" implant the idea that relationships can change for the worse, which is what the poet sees happening on earth. Consciously or unconsciously, by polluting the earth's atmosphere, humans are harming the relationship they have with nature. The poem expresses the fear that a time may come when the bond between humans and nature may be totally severed. The spiritual beauty of the night sky will be there, but it will be unperceived by the people on Earth.

By making readers of "Country Stars" aware of the loss that will be experienced through specific words, images, and scene painting, Meredith illuminates for his readers the danger of pollution. A key sentiment in the poem is that humans have the capacity to transform things. This is illustrated in the way the child transforms a black windowpane into white. The glittering stars brightening the dark night therefore become symbols of hope as the poet puts the fate of the relationship between humanity and the sublime beauty of nature in the hands of the people of the earth. Meredith seems to be urging readers to work unitedly for a pollution-free atmosphere so that they can continue to rejoice in the sublime beauty of the "country stars."

Aparajita Mazumder

A COUNTRY WALK

Author: Thomas Kinsella (1928-   )
Type of poem: Dramatic monologue
First published: 1962, in *Downstream*

The Poem

"A Country Walk" is representative of Thomas Kinsella's middle period in a number of important respects. Together with the title poem of the collection in which it occurs, its tensions, themes, and restless movement anticipate numerous tendencies in his later verse. At the same time, it marks a transition from the predominant, though not exclusive, use of lyric, which characterized the collection that is *Downstream*'s important predecessor, *Another September* (1958).

This sense of transition is not merely indicative of the development of Kinsella's poetic career, it is also vividly present as a pretext and motif in the poem itself. The abrupt antilyrical opening of "A Country Walk" is an overture to a world beyond domesticity, the world at large, in effect, with its minute particulars and large abstractions ("Mated, like a fall of rock, with time"). The seeds of these abstractions are minutiae: The actual physical evidence of the locality is so keenly apprehended in its physical presence that only a metaphysical artifact can consolidate the moment of seeing, as the quotation suggests. Walking is not only a means of traversing a given landscape but also a means of going over the various levels for which that landscape stands.

The world beyond "the piercing company of women" is both a natural world and a historical world. Nature offers a nonhuman dimension—flora and fauna—which, ironically, offer human comfort. Almost as soon as the walker sets foot in the natural environment, each step becomes "a drop of peace returning," and the simplicity of a drink of water is restorative to a degree that he "inch by inch rejoiced." The poet is careful not to sentimentalize nature, however. The candor of "rejoiced" is at once modified, "Or so it seemed," and brambles are considered "melancholy."

Nevertheless, the world of nature, if not exactly fertile ("The littered fields where summer broke and fled"), is at least provisionally equable, even if the atmosphere is thickened by "a silence full of storms." Nature is apprehended in a transitional, unsettled moment, which allies it to the poem's larger thematic interests. The antilyrical tenor of "A Country Walk" inhibits a view of nature as a bountiful opposite to the works of humankind, just as the actual view of the natural terrain is made incomplete by the evidence of the town that keeps getting in the way. Images of humanity, which the landscape provides and suggests are, on the other hand, fraught with the tempests of history.

The recollection of the old Irish sagas ("the tales") gains significance from Kinsella's enduring interest in literature in the Irish language, ancient and modern. He is his generation's most important translator of Irish texts, and one of his major artistic accomplishments is his rendering of one the most celebrated works of pre-Christian Irish literature, *Tain-Bo-Cuailgne*. The poem modulates from a sense of being present in nature to a vision of Irish history. Many of the most important events of Irish history in the Christian era (the reference to "the day that Christ hung dying" is intended to condense the complex heritage of Irishness) are imaginatively glossed in terms of their recurring blood sacrifice. Beginning with the Norman Conquest of the twelfth century, and proceeding by way of the Cromwellian invasion of the mid-seventeenth century, the poem comes to contemplate not only the events of the Irish War of Independence (the victim commemorated by "A concrete cross") but its aftermath in civil war: "brother met brother in a modern light."

This review of what the landscape has seen culminates in a bitterly ironic depiction of "the gombeen jungle," which is considered contemporary Irish society's translation of its legacy of historical suffering. "Gombeen" is a belittling term applied to a land-grabber or other economic exploiter who is of the same social origins as those he exploits. The phrase is a richly satirical insight on social Darwinism as practiced in independent Ireland. The names of the merchants are a deliberate echo of William Butler Yeats's "Easter 1916," which commemorates in laudatory terms the names of some of the principal participants in the Irish rebellion against British rule that took place on the eponymous date.

Yet despite the ill-concealed animosity to the landscape of contemporary Irish society ("A lamp switched on above the urinal"—there can hardly be many lines of poetry less celebratory than this), the poet persists with his walk. The culminating view of the river, with the "troubled union" of its impermanent, fretful, and recurring surface, may be considered a metaphor for the tide of human affairs. It is also a pretext for poetry, as the closing statements of "A Country Walk" suggest: "Heart and tongue were loosed."

Forms and Devices

The principal gesture in "A Country Walk" is one of comprehensiveness. Stage by stage the poem builds up a complete vision of a world, from the narrowness of stifling domesticity to a perspective on the inspirational evening star, "*Hesperus* . . . bringing sweet trade"—not that of the commerce abjured in the "open square" sequence but that of poetry, which proposes an adequate rate of exchange between world and consciousness. This act of cultural and existential cartography is carried out with "intensity," as the poem admits, but is devoid of the schematic or the mechanical.

Such limitations are resisted by a number of means. In the first place, the poem's intense language must be noted. This language derives its voltage from two sources. One is its unadorned and unqualified honesty: A poem that introduces itself to the reader with the word "sick" is clearly not interested in pulling punches. In addition, the strength of the verbs throughout, together with a willingness to convey a sense of the world's mundane ugliness, may also be taken as a further example of the completeness of the poet's hard-hitting commitment to his material. Another source is the language's visionary appeal, as in the fusion of brutality and courtliness in the Norman warlords, or in the condensed finality of "generations that let welcome fail." The poem's language arrests and disturbs the reader in ways that make it an enactment of the landscape's effect on the poet's consciousness.

A sense of the programmatic accumulation of detail and effect is also resisted by virtue of the comparatively brief span of attention that the poem's authorizing consciousness devotes to each of the poem's details. The details are not arranged in a particular order. When order may be thought to supervene, as in the town, "jungle" is the term used to describe it. Even the historical chronology should not be regarded as in any way exhaustive. Its elements pertain specifically to the poem's actual locale. The poem itself functions as the elements in the extended river simile: "a shape/ That forms and fructifies and dies."

This shape is borne out by the use of ellipses, compound sentences, blank verse, and an unstable verse form. The poem's basic five-line stanza provides the momentum of the walk, but that stanzaic structure is an option of ordering that is honored as much in the breach as in the observance. In formal terms, too, the poem articulates the shapeless but exact nature of the landscape it addresses.

Themes and Meanings

Many Kinsella poems are conceived as either quests or ordeals, debating either how best to proceed or how best to abide by the present's intransigent grip. Part of the exemplary character of "A Country Walk" is that it mediates between those two polar options. The walk functions as a release and as an intensification; as an enactment of witness and of rejection; as a depiction of ruin, despoliation, and unfulfillment; and as an impetus to poetry. The apparent entailment of negative and positive, which is evidently thought to be as inevitable as the placing of one "slow footfall" after another, allows the poem to reach a nadir, "the valley floor," perhaps, and an apex, "the green and golden light" of Venus, an inspirational star by which to steer.

Despite the sense of resolution, however, which the close of "A Country Walk" suggests, the poem's main burden is premised on a notion of the incompleteness of each of the worlds it surveys. The idea of resolution is conveyed in the closing line, where, by the simple means of quotation marks, poetry is resorted to as an option owing something in permanence and beauty to the evening star. Yet what that line—presented as though it might be the opening line of another poem—speaks of is flux and turbulence. It is not difficult to imagine that the material of this poem will also find a focus in "an omphalos of scraps," particularly when that phrase comes from a poetic treatment (a simile) of the one element of natural continuity in "A Country Walk," the river.

Yet, as the river's presence suggests, there is not merely change in the sense of an aimless succession of fluctuations; there is also persistence, or what the poem invokes by the use of the past participle "endured." Not only does the river possess a dual, ostensibly contradictory nature, but so does the phenomenon of human time, which has for its signature "the sucking chaos" of history and the "potent calm" of the asylum that is art.

George O'Brien

THE COURTESY

Author: Alan Shapiro (1952-   )
Type of poem: Narrative
First published: 1983, in *The Courtesy*

The Poem

"The Courtesy," the title poem in Alan Shapiro's second book, is composed of thirty-eight lines of loose iambic pentameter and divided into three irregular-length stanzas. In the poem, dedicated to a deceased friend of the narrator, Shapiro creates a complex narrative about meeting this friend and sharing some dreamlike moments with him.

The first line of the poem makes the reader expect a traditional narrative: "I walked from my house down Coolidge Street last night" could lead to a variety of poetic stances, from simple narrative about what happened that night to a meditation on love, the heavens, or family life. However, the comfortable opening soon shifts when something ominous seems to happen: The air shakes "down a hushing from the branches." The reader is prepared by this preamble for some action or thought that could be out of the ordinary. When the homes on Coolidge Street become "solid shadow, blocks of silence," the eerie feeling is continued, and readers are prepared to meet the narrator's old friend, Saul; from the dedication, the reader knows that Saul Chessler has died years before.

The second stanza begins, just as the first did, with a matter-of-fact statement: "I wanted to ask you what it was like to die." This realistic tone, this down-to-earth conversational voice makes it appear as if nothing remarkable is happening, and a reader might not catch on immediately to the fact that this poem, while being a narrative with a story line, is also a very dreamlike, visionary experience. The narrator has met a dead man and wants to have a conversation with him, but the character of Saul speaks first and says the only words that the two exchange during this surreal moment: " 'The doctors made me better. We can run again.'" The poem that began with one man walking now becomes a poem with two men running, one dead and one living, both breathing that air that created the hushing sound at the start of the poem. Suddenly the poem, which began on Coolidge Street with no hint of snow, now shifts to a field with the runners' "footsteps patter(ing) the smooth crust."

Just as the reader has begun to feel comfortable with the idea of a dead man running on snow with his old friend from childhood, the third stanza opens with a strange but flat, matter-of-fact statement: "And we returned by train." The dreamlike effect of the poem is heightened in the next few lines, when the narrator sees his friend Saul outside the train lying "like a dark slash in the snow," but Saul is also, at the same moment, sitting beside the narrator in the train. The narrator still wants to ask the question he felt like asking the moment he saw his friend—"What is it like to die?"—but again the question is deferred. The answer is never given because Saul seems so intent on convincing the narrator that he is alive, not for some selfish reason, but simply because Saul feels the reality of his own death might embarrass the speaker.

Forms and Devices

One of Shapiro's main accomplishments in this poem is to blend the surreal with the real in a way that seems both plausible and dreamlike. In a poem that moves from walking to running to riding a train without any clear transitions, the "strange familiarity" that Shapiro mentions at the close of the poem is the guiding principle or technique Shapiro uses to construct his piece. If the poem were simply wildly surreal, with bizarre images joined with eerie metaphors, the emotion of the poem would not be as strong. Shapiro makes the poem both familiar and strange and allows the reader to believe that such a meeting could take place.

One way this notion of "strange familiarity" functions is evident in the first stanza. After the peculiar images of homes as "blocks of silence" and the violet light that is "dim without dimming," Shapiro writes a clear, direct sentence: "I saw you, Saul, my old friend, waiting/ For me at the corner where our two streets met." On one hand this image is entirely familiar: Two friends meet on the corner where their two streets meet. Yet on a metaphorical level, the image is strange: These two streets that join at a corner are, in one sense, the avenue of life and the avenue of death; it is a liminal world, a world of boundaries between not only life and death but also sleep and waking. The poem inhabits both worlds.

Other images in the poem work in the same way to convey this idea of occupying two worlds at the same time. The most obvious is the train image, in which Saul is both in the train, sitting next to the narrator, and lying in the snow, "arms flung up" and "legs crossed." This kind of doubling is also present in other less obvious images. A normal, scientific image of breath becoming a brief cloud takes on a resonance in this poem: Their breath "scrawled" in the chilling air and then vanished, just as Saul, and eventually the narrator, have their moments on earth and then vanish into the realms of the dead.

In addition, the moment of running on snow allows Shapiro to have an image that replicates what is taking place in the poem: As they run on the field of snow, Shapiro feels as if they might break through; again, it is an image of boundaries being crossed, of a surface being penetrated. Just as life turns into death, and the dead come back to life, therefore erasing the boundaries between the two worlds, so too these images echo this idea of being in one place only temporarily.

Themes and Meanings

No poem exists in a vacuum; all poems are part of a long tradition of writing. By placing a poem in the context of literary history, its themes and meanings can become more apparent. Shapiro is writing in a literary tradition that dates back to the era of classical myth. Both Odysseus in Homer's *Odyssey* (800 B.C.E.; Eng. trans., 1616) and Aeneas in Vergil's *Aeneid* (c. 29-19 B.C.E.; Eng. trans., 1553) make trips to the underworld, penetrating the boundary between the living and the dead. There, through blood sacrifices, the dead are able to speak, and the Greek and Roman heroes are able to see the sufferings of those, such as Sisyphus and Tantalus, who offended the gods.

La divina commedia (c. 1320; *The Divine Comedy*, 1802), by Dante, is another example of this type of writing. In this fourteenth century epic poem Dante is led by Vergil through hell, purgatory, and heaven. Here he is able to hear directly from the dead which sins they committed that caused them to suffer, or which acts of generosity brought them to heaven. In a more modern version of this story, Seamus Heaney, a poet Shapiro reveres, writes of a deceased cousin who was killed in sectarian violence in Northern Ireland. In "The Strand at Lough Beg" (1979), Heaney does not speak with the dead man, but he meets his dead cousin, washes mud from his body, and lays him out as if to bury him.

In this context Shapiro's poem stands out in sharp relief. There is no moral to this poem, as there is in Homer's, Vergil's, and Dante's. The reader is not spoken to in a didactic way by Shapiro, or warned of the evils the dead have done or the punishments they have received. There is no blood sacrifice to conjure up the dead; there is also no healing moment as there is in Heaney's poem. Shapiro's poem is an American, secular version of the meeting between the dead and the living. It is also a very gentle poem, one that the rules of politeness control rather than the rules of religion. Shapiro's narrator is unable to ask the central question that all mortals want to know—"What is it like to die?"—because he does not want Saul to know that he recognizes him as a dead man. Saul tries so hard not to seem dead because he senses that this might embarrass the narrator; this leads to the narrator being unable to broach the question. Saul, the dead man, is courteous enough not to trouble the narrator with his death, so the narrator returns the courtesy and acts as if the man is in fact as alive as he seems.

Kevin Boyle

CRAFTSMANSHIP AND EMPTINESS

Author: Jalāl al-Dīn Rūmī (1207-1273)
Type of poem: Meditation
First published: Early thirteenth century, as part of *Maśnavī-ye Maʿnavī*; English translation collected in *One-Handed Basket Weaving*, 1991

The Poem

"Craftsmanship and Emptiness" consists of a relatively few lines (lines 1369-1420 of book 5) from Jalāl al-Dīn Rūmī's enormous work *Mathnawi*. The Persian title *Mathnawi* refers to the verse form used (rhyming couplets) and came to mean an extensive didactic work that could include a variety of tales and other material. Rūmī's *Mathnawi*, left unfinished at his death, includes stories from the Qur'an (Koran) and Islamic tradition, folk stories, and anecdotes. Even though its intent is serious, his *Mathnawi* is funny and even bawdy at times. Written mostly in Persian, the book also includes passages in Arabic, Turkish, and even Greek. Traditionally, it is referred to as the "Qur'an in Persian," an indication of its high status. The title "Craftsmanship and Emptiness" is not Rūmī's, but was added by the translators. This translation makes no effort to reproduce the rhyming couplet form of the original but instead is rendered in free verse.

Rūmī is speaking to the reader in this poem; the relation is one of a spiritual teacher instructing a disciple. The poem moves associatively from one topic to another closely related topic. Its several sections illustrate the value of emptiness. Rūmī begins by reminding his audience of a topic he has spoken of before—emptiness as an opportunity for the craftsman to practice his craft. He lists examples that would be part of the original audience's everyday experience. In the third stanza, Rūmī addresses the reader directly, admonishing the reader that it is foolish to fear death and emptiness, which are a "beautiful expanse," while being deceived by the destructive things of the world ("a scorpion pit").

Having admonished the reader, Rūmī turns to a story from an earlier Persian poet, Attar, to expand and clarify what he has said. The story tells of a Hindu boy, captured by a Muslim ruler and shown favor. The boy's parents have taught him to fear King Mahmud; raised to a high standing (the king's vice-regent), the boy weeps in delight and wishes that his parents could be there to see that their fears were all wrong.

Rūmī interprets the story's details by applying them to his audience. The parents, whose fears previously governed the boy's feelings, are seen as human attachments. These attachments keep one blind to the "beautiful expanse" of one's real situation and keep one imprisoned in the "scorpion pit" of fears and selfish desires. Rūmī promises readers that one day they will experience the boy's tears of joy.

The theme of attachment suggests the body, to which Rūmī next turns. Rather than advocating an extreme ascetic attitude toward the body, Rūmī suggests that the body is useful as well as frustrating and that one's best attitude toward it is patience. The next few lines take up the theme of patience, using both natural images (the rose and the camel) and human images (the prophets and the embroidered shirt) to show the reader how patience is part of life. Rūmī concludes with three stanzas advising the reader to "live in" God—the Eternal—or be burned out like an abandoned campfire.

Forms and Devices

The comments in this section refer to Coleman Barks's translation (as collected in *Rūmī: One-Handed Basket Weaving, Poems on the Theme of Work*, 1991, and *The Essential Rūmī*, 1995). Other translators of Rūmī have used very different styles. For example, Reynold A. Nicholson, who edited, translated, and commented on the entire *Mathnawi* (1925-1940), translated each couplet into a prose line, as in these lines: "Even such is the seeker at the court of God: when God comes, the seeker is naughted/ Although union with God is life on life, yet at first that life consists in dying to self" (*Tales of Mystic Meaning*, 1931, reprint 1995).

Barks used free verse divided into twenty-five verse paragraphs of varying length. Free verse allows Barks to focus on the meaning of Rūmī's verses and to use line breaks to provide emphasis and rhythm. Barks has translated many of Rūmī's poems in this style, including material from Rūmī's quatrains and ghazals (a Persian poetic form) as well as the *Mathnawi*. Overall, Barks's translations have the effect of direct and colloquial speech. This effect, combined with Rūmī's pungent stories and metaphors, accounts for the popularity of Barks's renderings.

The style Barks uses does not call attention to itself—there is no rhyme, no noticeable alliteration, and no strong rhythms. The sentences are worded directly and vigorously, with no unusual word choices. Sentence structures are varied, thus avoiding such devices as parallelism. The line endings are the major indication of rhythm. As a result, the language is lively, concise, direct, and transparent.

The lack of poetic ornament makes these thirteenth century poems seem very contemporary. Lack of ornamentation may also be particularly appropriate, since Rūmī discounted the value of poetry and wrote the *Mathnawi* only at the urging of a close associate. In *Fīhi mā fīhi* (*Signs of the Unseen*, 1994), Rūmī says that he is "vexed by poetry" and only composes it as a way to communicate with people who respond to poetry. Consistent with this attitude, the poems in the *Mathnawi* are intended to teach by entertaining the reader with entrancing stories.

Rūmī uses metaphor, simile, allegory, and symbolic images to express his meaning in a vivid and appealing way. In the first few lines, he uses simple descriptive images—the builder, the water carrier, and the carpenter. He endows these images with symbolic meaning by pointing out the value of emptiness to each of these craftsmen. "Emptiness" then refers to the mode in which Rūmī encourages the reader to experience God, but the word does not remain an abstraction. Instead, it is an "ocean" in which the reader is presumed to fish and a "beautiful expanse" in contrast to the "scorpion pit" where the reader has chosen to live.

After retelling Attar's story of King Mahmud and the young man, Rūmī gives an allegorical interpretation, using details of the story to encourage the reader to abandon attachment to the fleeting things of the world and to not be afraid of the "emptiness" of God. Then, in comparing the body to a shirt of chain mail, Rūmī uses a simile that would be more familiar to his original audience than to a modern one, but nonetheless is clear and forceful. Finally, in describing the individual mixing with God as being like honey mixing with milk, Rūmī uses another simile that not only makes Rūmī's point but also uses traditional Muslim imagery associated with paradise to reinforce the appeal of his advice.

Themes and Meanings

"Craftsmanship and Emptiness" is about surrender to the Divine. Rūmī was a spiritual leader and teacher in Sufism, the mystical tradition in Islam. He founded the Mevlevi order, the group popularly known as Whirling Dervishes. As spiritual teacher, Rūmī focused on the transforming experience of God that a human might have. "Craftsmanship and Emptiness" shows "misapprehension"—fearful clinging to the passing and unsatisfactory things of this world—as the thing that hinders one's experience of the divine emptiness.

Rūmī's teaching about emptiness involves a paradox related to existence. The world that people ordinarily experience, which Rūmī often calls "this world," seems to exist but really does not. The spiritual world, which Rūmī often calls "that world," seems not to exist but is really the emptiness that is necessary for existence, and so is more real than this apparently real world. Thus, what seems most real to the ordinary human is not real at all, and what seems unreal and empty is the only reality.

In a favorite image, Rūmī refers to "this world" as the foam on the ocean of reality ("that world"). The paradox of emptiness goes a step further. Humans as such are as void of reality as is this world. In "Emptiness," another selection from the *Mathnawi* translated by Barks, Rūmī writes, "We are/ emptiness." For Rūmī, emptiness is not discouraging; rather, human emptiness is necessary for humans to come to know God. Paradoxically, what seems negative is actually positive.

The story of King Mahmud and the Hindu boy presents this paradox in vivid narrative terms. Rūmī tells readers that Mahmud represents the spirit's emptiness—that is, the state which is spiritually desirable. Yet the boy's parents have taught him to fear Mahmud (emptiness) and cling to "beliefs," "bloodties," "desires," and "comforting habits," those seemingly real aspects of life which are void of reality. Unlike some other spiritual teachers, however, Rūmī does not say that this world has no value at all. He knows that the body can be bothersome, but he also acknowledges that it can be helpful in teaching one patience.

The craftsmen at the poem's beginning are aware of the paradoxically greater reality of emptiness since they must find emptiness in order to practice their crafts. In this, they are like God, who brought forth the world out of emptiness. Rather than discouraging readers, Rūmī's insistence on the value of emptiness is intended to leave them aware of the creative potential of the "invisible ocean" and to encourage them to enter it.

Gene Doty

CRAZY JANE TALKS WITH THE BISHOP

Author: William Butler Yeats (1865-1939)
Type of poem: Lyric
First published: 1932, in *Words for Music Perhaps and Other Poems*

The Poem

"Crazy Jane Talks with the Bishop" is a short poem in three six-line stanzas. The poem is the sixth in a series of seven in which Crazy Jane is the persona. The title refers to a fictional character whom William Butler Yeats based upon an old woman who lived in a little cottage in Gort, a small village near Galway in western Ireland. He admired her for her audacious speech, her lust for life, and her satirical eye. She had clearly become an important symbol for him by the time he came to write this poem; for some time, he had been thinking about what it was that such a cantankerous old woman might represent.

The poem begins as a confrontation between Jane and a bishop, who happen to meet on a road. The bishop speaks in the first stanza, and Jane is the sole speaker in the second and third stanzas. That is the extent of the poem's actions, and they can be understood easily enough at face value. The reader, however, cannot fail to be struck by the emotionally charged content of the conversation, which is highly personal in tone. The bishop condemns the woman, apparently for her unkempt appearance. The implication seems to be that she is leading an unchaste life. Jane responds somewhat defensively, but even more defiantly. In fact, she seems didactic, as if she is attempting to teach the bishop a lesson of some sort.

Since the first stanza notes that the two said "much" to each other, the implication is that the conversation recorded here is only part of what transpired, or, more likely, that the persona believes that she has distilled the incident into something of greater significance than its brevity might at first suggest.

Forms and Devices

This poem can be appreciated and understood on its own. Insofar as Jane introduces the reader to a bishop as "the" bishop, however, and thereby suggests some familiarity between them, there is an implication that one is coming upon this scene *in medias res*—that there is a prehistory, which may be culled from a reading of the other poems in the Crazy Jane series. In this regard, therefore, it shares somewhat in the balladic tradition, where poems frequently begin without much explanation of all that led up to the current situation being narrated.

The rhythm in each stanza is basically iambic, alternating each line between tetrameter and trimeter. The last two lines of each stanza are less regular, ending with a more emphatic spondaic pulse. The rhyme scheme is *abcbdb, efgfhf, ijkjlj* (every other line rhymes).

For such a short poem, with a rather humble woman as its central focus, there is a surprising gravity of tone. Yeats achieves this effect through his masterful use of several devices. The regular rhythm and rhyme, first of all, call the reader's attention to an artificiality in the discussion, a careful crafting of the supposedly spontaneous interchange between the bishop and the woman. This artificiality is accented by the surprising juxtaposition of a childlike nursery-rhyme rhythm and a blunt reference to the woman's bodily parts by the bishop. The singsong effect and the crudity of the bishop's gaze raise further questions in the reader's mind when one looks more closely at the scriptural overtones of the bishop's language (the parallelism of the consonance in "flat and fallen," the biblical allusion to one's "heavenly mansion," and the possible allusion to the parable of the prodigal son in "some foul sty").

The woman's language is also heavily referential, and it might be said that allusion is the "shaping" device in this poem. By avoiding any biblical references of her own and replacing them with religious allusions that are less clear, she makes her message even more earthy than the bishop's. Lines 7 and 8, for example, call to mind the opening scene of William Shakespeare's *Macbeth* (1606), in which three witches frame what is to follow: By setting a countervailing anti-Christian tone, their words and presence suggest that there may be a fate controlling Macbeth and all other humans that cannot be easily contained within any theological explanation. Lines 17 and 18 seem an allusion to the sexual violence of Yeats's own poem "Leda and the Swan" and bring with the allusion all that earlier poem's respectful references to a pre-Christian philosophy of life.

Such simple yet highly referential language maintains a lyrical and even lilting sound to the lines while forcing them to carry more freight than immediately meets the eye. In effect, Yeats asks the reader to look beyond the niceties of poetic diction to the brutal dichotomies (nursery rhyme/lyric ballad of loss; man/woman; religion/sex) that are central to the controlled discussion between these two characters. These dichotomies are most obvious in the use of puns in the last stanza, specifically the play on the words "sole" and soul, hole and "whole." "Rent" may pun on the double meaning of tearing something in two and leasing rather than owning outright.

Themes and Meanings

The Crazy Jane series, like much of Yeats's poetry, remains enigmatic. Why, after all, choose such an unlikely persona for this series? Why, in this particular poem, is there the harshness of this encounter with a bishop? Every poet develops a personally significant vocabulary and set of place names and images, but this is especially true of Yeats. Part of the reason for the particularity of his imagining in this poem can be explained by its theme, but, as with much of Yeats's vision, part of the reason remains (probably intentionally) mysterious.

The claim made for him by many to be the greatest lyric poet of the twentieth century rests upon his unique expression of three worlds: that of the rustic Celtic imagination he found in Sligo in western Ireland, that of the politics of Dublin, and that of the literary sophistication of London. Crazy Jane arises from the world of Sligo. To these influences Yeats added a truly extraordinary interest in finding something meaningful

beyond the material world, while at the same time celebrating the material world spe-
cifically as a manifestation of the ethereal. This quest for a non-Christian, quotidian
"incarnation" is the key to this poem and to many of his best poems.

What becomes clear from the other Crazy Jane poems is that one is to listen more
respectfully to her insights into life than one is to those of someone like the bishop. He
has far more importance in the eyes of the world, and he represents an orthodox inter-
pretation of life's meaning, but his pharisaical judging of Jane suggests that it is he
who is essentially dead inside. The reader also learns from the earlier poems that the
bishop may, himself, have loved her at one time.

The dichotomies of this poem are, in fact, the key to its theme, which has to do with
the resolution of "antinomies" (as Yeats called sets of opposites) that obsessed him
throughout his poetic career. It is true that Jane's breasts are flat and fallen, but her re-
tort is an exuberant celebration of the fact that this very body remains for her the phys-
ical location of love. That is a painful and difficult "resolution," but Yeats seems to
suggest that it is the only one possible for a human being to make. Rather than reject
love (and lust) as worthless because impermanent or somehow filthy, Jane takes what
may seem to be a *carpe diem* position: make hay while the sun shines. The implication
of her lesson to the bishop goes further, however, since the sun is no longer shining for
her and she is nevertheless affirming the value even of transient love.

Yeats was almost seventy when he wrote this poem, and, like many of the poems
from this period, it expresses his own renewed passion for life and for love. Among
the closest in theme to this one is "The Circus Animals' Desertion" (1939), especially
in its closing stanza. "Crazy Jane Talks with the Bishop" might also be read in con-
junction with "Among School Children" (1927), a poem concerned with Maud Gonne
and aging love. Very much aware of his own failing body, the poet seems nevertheless
to embrace it, in spite of—or because of—all of its "holes." Fixated on the body/soul
dichotomy that has dominated Western philosophy, Yeats celebrates the body as the
seat not only of excrement, but also of all that is transcendent.

John C. Hawley

CREDENCES OF SUMMER

Author: Wallace Stevens (1879-1955)
Type of poem: Meditation
First published: 1947, in *Transport to Summer*

The Poem

"Credences of Summer" is a blank-verse poem divided into ten sections, or cantos, of three five-line stanzas each. The title suggests a set of "truths" or declarations about this season; to Stevens summer was the epitome of the year's natural fullness, and it is often associated in his poetry with the creative process. This process, as described in canto VII of the poem, is a three-stage or "thrice concentred" activity. "Credences of Summer" is arranged accordingly, with cantos I through III devoted to the moment of experience that the individual artist or writer wishes to express in art or poetry. His cantos IV through VI describe the ordering of that moment in the artist's consciousness; cantos VII through IX are devoted to the finished articulation or rendering in art of that experience. Canto X, like the final sections in many of Stevens's longer meditative poems, serves as a coda that reiterates the imaginative process which the poem as a whole defines and exemplifies.

Canto I sets the poem's tone of contemplation with the pun on the word "broods" and with the declaration that at midsummer "the mind lays by its trouble," repeated with the addition of "and considers" in the next line. This moment of contemplation begins the poetic act—what Stevens called elsewhere the "act of the mind." Full of sensation, this moment will be accorded the mind's full attention, without "evasion" (canto II). The poet must look at a subject directly, not relying on the words or prescriptions of others, nor even on the poet's own previous perceptions: "Look at it in its essential barrenness/ And say this, this is the centre that I seek." Once the experience itself has been identified, it assumes an essential importance, becoming a "tower more precious than the view beyond" (canto III). For the duration of the moment, the creative intelligence satisfies itself with the directness and immediacy of sensory experience.

Canto IV illustrates the difficulty of ordering or understanding such experience, here represented by the harvested hay fields of Oley (Pennsylvania). The poet admits that reality tends to resist attempts to order it—for example, language's attempts to render in rational discourse one's most visceral experiences. Therefore he calls for a language that will be more than mere "secondary sounds" describing experience. In canto V he aims at a poetry that "contains" reality "without souvenir." That is, he would dispense with the devices and systems of the past in his own apprehension of the moment, hoping to compose a poetry that enriches rather than merely embellishes or decorates: "stripped of remembrance, it displays its strength."

The third and final phase of the poetic act, in cantos VII through IX, involves the satisfactory articulation of experience. Each canto in this phase presents a kind of "poet figure" who will "proclaim/ The meaning of the capture, this hard prize" called understanding. Then and only then, the poet argues, will one have arrived at a fully experienced reality. In canto VII the singers fill this role. In canto VIII the "trumpet of morning" sounds its "resounding cry," and in canto IX the "Soft, civil bird" of morning heralds "the spirit of the arranged"—the power of the poet's art to express experience in a way meaningful to others.

The final canto of "Credences of Summer" recapitulates the three-part process that has been in evidence throughout the poem, but here it is the "inhuman author" of summer itself that meditates like the "mind" of canto I, and that finds an "appropriate habit" or ordering principle as in canto V, and that then "completes" reality rather than succeeding merely in decorating it.

Forms and Devices

Stevens employs a highly formal structure and an elevated diction throughout "Credences of Summer," lending the poem's language a pronouncement-like gravity. His use of literary allusion and symbolism strengthens the tone of seemingly incontrovertible rhetoric in the poem.

First, the division of the poem into numbered cantos suggests an orderly argument as opposed to an impassioned lyrical poem such as an ode or sonnet. The blank verse (unrhymed iambic pentameter) allows Stevens a rhythmic flexibility that approaches prose discourse at times, furthering the reader's sense of being in the presence of an eminently reasonable, thoughtful persona speculating on the mind's ability to comprehend the phenomena of human experience. The diction heightens this effect; highly wrought terms abound: "infuriations," "inhalations," "apogee," "ancientness," and "clairvoyance." Elsewhere Stevens resorts to foreignisms: *douceurs, tristesses.* The long compound and complex sentences reinforce the formality. (No fewer than half a dozen sentences here extend to a five-line stanza or more, with the poem's final sentence stretching across three stanzas in all.)

In a poem that urges the mind to dispense with received metaphors and accepted systems of perceiving the world, it is ironic that Stevens should make such use of literary allusion. With his opening line—"Now in midsummer come and all fools slaughtered"—Stevens invokes the famous opening lines of Richard of Gloucester in William Shakespeare's *Richard III*: "Now is the winter of our discontent/ Made glorious summer by this son of York." A few lines later it is Hamlet's "there is nothing either good or bad but thinking makes it so" as well as the gloomy Dane's divided self that one can hear echoed: "There is nothing more inscribed nor thought nor felt/ And this must comfort the heart's core against/ Its false disasters." Indeed, in the poem's insistence on seizing the moment of experience many critics have pointed out that "Credences of Summer" bears out Edgar's advice in *King Lear* that "ripeness is all."

Another influence is Walt Whitman, whose poems of ecstatic merging with natural phenomena are recalled repeatedly in "Credences of Summer." In this "folk-land [of] mostly marriage-hymns," Stevens places a hearty Whitmanesque character "[w]ho reads no book" and whose "ruddy ancientness/ Absorbs the ruddy summer" (canto III).

Symbol is another of Stevens's main devices. The Whitmansque old man, the "bristling soldier," the hermit, the king and his princes, the characters garbed in summer's motley—these are, to varying degrees, representative of human perspectives or ways of ordering reality. Against these traditional figures, Stevens seems to prefer poet-figures of a more rudimentary sort: the unidentified singers in the wood, the trumpet of morning, the brown-breasted robin. Opposite these, Stevens symbolizes physical reality as whatever is ultimately irreducible: "The rock [that] cannot be broken. It is the truth" (canto VI).

Themes and Meanings

Like much of the poetry of Wallace Stevens, "Credences of Summer" is deeply philosophical, concerned with the processes by which the human mind perceives and comes to understand the external "reality" it is at once separable from and itself a part of. Critics have cited several themes extending from this concern.

First, the poem can be read as a kind of prologue to Stevens's more famous "Notes Toward a Supreme Fiction," in which the poet proposes that the creation of literary art should have a force equal to nature's creative powers. "Credences of Summer" thus concerns the effects of a poet's creation upon the individual consciousness. Because people tend to perceive the world through the images, metaphors, and symbols ("fictions," as Stevens conceives them) with which artists, philosophers, and theologians have supplied them, the poet's task is to examine how such fictions or constructs of the mind are employed, eventually providing new fictions with which people can apprehend the world around them.

Other critics have pointed to the sense of crisis in the poem, suggesting that "Credences of Summer" expresses the poet's own doubts about his creative powers as he entered the latter stages of his literary career. Images of slaughter and of catastrophe begin the poem, which proceeds to invoke other terms of finality that may be read as spiritual or intellectual fatigue: the final mountain, last choirs, last sounds, and so on.

Steering between the extremes of a "supreme fiction" and a barren imagination, one might see the poem as a successful treatment of the problem that confronts any writer, that of expressing in a fulfilling way the experience of "being." Stevens once claimed that the chief difference between philosophers and poets was that philosophers sought to *prove* they existed while poets *enjoyed* their own existence. If so, then the sensory richness and rhetorical force with which "Credences of Summer" captures such a moment of accord between mind and matter, language and experience, can be cited as sufficient evidence of Stevens's credo. As Thomas Hines puts it in *The Later Poetry of Wallace Stevens*, "Few poems in modern literature so thoroughly meditate the meaning of fulfillment, ripeness, and completed desire. . . . [It] shows the full value of the continuity of the creative process and how the projected fulfillment comes true in the completed vision of summer."

James Scruton

THE CRICKET

Author: Frederick Goddard Tuckerman (1821-1873)
Type of poem: Ode
First published: 1950, in *Frederick Goddard Tuckerman: The Cricket*

The Poem

Frederick Goddard Tuckerman's posthumously published "The Cricket" is an irregular ode of 131 lines divided into five sections of unequal length. The titular insect, at first glance almost comically inconsequential, provokes in the poet a meditation on death that leads him ultimately to affirm the value of life.

The introductory section presents a lyrical consideration of sound-producing insects. Both the "humming bee" and the "dogday locust" have their bards, but the cricket, whose voice is "bright" among "the insect crowd," has not been sung of before. After identifying the cricket as the subject of the ode, the poet also invokes the insect as his muse: "Shall I not take to help me in my song/ A little cooing cricket?"

Although the rest of the poem is written in the first person, the second section utilizes a second-person voice. The speaker addresses his audience directly, inviting the reader to imagine a setting in which "our minstrel's carol," the song of the cricket, can be heard and appreciated. First a shady spot beside a brook is pictured, then "a garden bower" with overhanging leaves and vines. In both places, the sleepy afternoon produces a half-waking, half-dreaming state. As consciousness thus becomes receptive to the natural world, the landscape suddenly seems filled with crickets and their singing.

In the third section, the mood of the poem changes as the poet begins to contemplate the meaning of the ubiquitous cricket's song. During the day, it is joyful; at night, it brings "rest and silence." Along with these cheering notes, however, the speaker hears first the sound of the sea and then "dim accents from the grave." In many of Tuckerman's other poems, the sea appears as a symbol of impermanence and mutability; and the grave represents death and the end of human loves, desires, and attachments. The third section concludes with the poet reminded of loved ones who have died, "faces where but now a gap must be."

The fourth section offers a meditation on the history of the cricket's song. As the poet now hears notes of death, so too ancient people listening to this insect must have heard the same melancholy murmur. Impermanence and death, then, are recognized as central, lasting concerns in human history.

The fifth section is the longest of the poem. The speaker imagines an "Enchanter old" who knows a plant that will make the "cry of beast, or bird, or insect's hum" understandable. The poet wishes that, like the enchanter, he could comprehend the language of the cricket and be its "true interpreter." Since the cricket's song has become associated with "dim accents from the grave," however, the interpretation of that song—his poetry—would necessarily be associated with death as well. He realizes that his desire to understand the cricket is unwise because a knowledge of death would blunt his creative response to the living beauty around him. He therefore accepts the ultimate incomprehensibility of the natural world and chooses life, impermanent as it is, over death as a theme for his poetry. The conclusion of "The Cricket" firmly announces this choice: "Rejoice! rejoice! whilst yet the hours exist."

Forms and Devices

As an irregular ode, "The Cricket" belongs to a time-honored poetic genre. Odes are poems on elevated subjects such as death. Regular odes maintain a predictable stanzaic pattern, while irregular odes uses stanzas (often called "strophes") and lines of uneven length. Originally a classical form, the ode achieved a new popularity during the Romantic period at the hands of William Wordsworth and John Keats.

In "The Cricket," Tuckerman uses the formal freedom of the irregular ode to create an almost musical composition. The five sections of the poem alternate in mood and intensity. The first section is light and airy as the cricket is introduced; the second is slower, more somnolent, as a contemplative mood develops. The third section turns suddenly dark and somber as the poet considers death, while the fourth offers limited relief by urging that death has always been a human concern. The fifth section builds slowly from the speaker's desire to understand the cricket's song to his triumphant realization that in the face of death, life can still be enjoyed.

While these changing moods originate in the literal meaning of the poem, they are strongly reinforced by its form. Although the meter is predominantly iambic, the irregular style allows Tuckerman to utilize lines of as few as four syllables and as many as twelve. These short and long lines intermix to create a flexible, varying rhythm throughout the poem. This rhythm is interrupted only in the third section, where the formal consideration of death begins; there, stately lines of iambic pentameter fit the serious mood.

Tuckerman adds a further rhythmic dimension to the poem by repeating syntactical patterns. The following lines from the second section provide a basic example of this practice: "The falling water and fluttering wind/ Mingle and meet,/ Murmur and mix." The most obvious poetic device in these lines is the alliterative repetition of *f*, *w*, and *m* sounds, but the quotation also shows how the poet creates a cadenced passage by substituting one word for another in a repeated grammatical construction. For example, in the first line, "falling water" is mirrored by "fluttering wind," both nouns preceded by adjectives; the grammatical structure in the second line, two verbs separated by a conjunction, is reproduced exactly in the third line where "mingle and meet" is replaced by "murmur and mix."

Tuckerman often joins this syntactical patterning to other rhythmic devices, as the following lines from the fifth section demonstrate: "Content to bring thy wisdom to the world;/ Content to gain at last some low applause,/ Now low, now lost." Again, in the first two lines the syntactical structure is partially repeated; in the last line, the words are divided into two grammatically equivalent halves. The alliteration in the lines reinforces the syntactical patterning by repeating *t*, *th*, and *l* sounds. In the second and third lines, the repetition of "low" and the consonantal rhyme of "last" and "lost" amounts almost to a chiasmus, a poetic device in which repeated words or phrases are reversed (last/low, low/lost) in successive syntactical units. These examples suggest how rhythmic cadences can be created without reliance on strict metrical regularity. Arguably, "The Cricket" is a poem about which one learns more by simply listening carefully as it is read aloud than by formally analyzing its metrical characteristics.

Themes and Meanings

"The Cricket" intentionally establishes its relation to other famous Romantic odes in order to differentiate itself from their thematic resolutions. For a full understanding of "The Cricket," familiarity with another ode, such as Keats's "Ode to a Nightingale," is very helpful.

The first clue that places "The Cricket" in a specific tradition is the invocation to the muse in the opening section. Calls for inspiration are standard in certain kind of poems, such as epics and elegies, although they do not always appear in odes. The poet, however, has included this invocation to link "The Cricket" with other Romantic odes in a gently ironic way: The animal chosen as muse seems deliberately odd since crickets are usually not symbolically connected with elevated poetry. Unlike Keats's nightingale, the cricket does not soar and sing, but rather crawls through the undergrowth and murmurs.

Curiously, following the ironic invocation, the poem settles down to the materials and practices so prevalent in other Romantic odes. It is almost as if, after encouraging his readers to believe that "The Cricket" would not be typical, Tuckerman changes his plans and his audience's expectations by writing a poem very much like others of its kind. The description of the setting, the introduction of the theme, and the placement of that theme in its historical context are all common.

In the fifth section, however, Tuckerman reawakens the reader's initial expectations by veering away from standard practice. As many scholars have pointed out, "The Cricket" provides an alternative to the traditional Romantic notion of a consummation with nature through death. Romantic poets tended to look to death as a way of merging with nature, of becoming part of the totality from which the status of human beings excludes one. The "Ode to a Nightingale" provides a famous example of this tendency when its speaker claims to be "half in love with easeful Death."

Unlike Keats and others in the Romantic tradition, Tuckerman chooses a limited but ultimately affirmative way of interacting with the natural world. Death would make the poet the "true interpreter" of the cricket since the insect's song reminds him that all life must end. Nevertheless, to surrender to this reality would mean that the beauties of life, which remain beautiful even though they will fade and die, would have to be devalued. By accepting death as an unavoidable human experience, and yet refusing to give in to grief and sorrow, Tuckerman suggests an almost existential understanding of life that anticipates twentieth century outlooks.

Jeffrey D. Groves

CROSS TIES

Author: X. J. Kennedy (Joseph Charles Kennedy, 1929-   )
Type of poem: Lyric
First published: 1969, in *Growing into Love*

The Poem

This lyric poem is composed of sixteen lines (counting lines 14 and 15 as a single unit) that follow the poet through two journeys: a solitary walk along a railroad track and a spiritual quest. The first two lines of the poem set the scene—the poet is walking "left over" ties of an unused train line, where "nothing" travels now but "rust and grass." The next two lines reveal a surprising observation: Reminded of the use of railroad ties and track, the wanderer realizes he "could" find it worth his while to step in front of a train bearing down from behind. Strangely, the thought does not stir his emotions. He remains as detached as the imagined train itself, "Far off, indifferent" (line 6). The nature of trains accounts for machine indifference. Nothing yet accounts for the wanderer's detachment, but the thought of the train's indifference is associated with the "curfew's wail" (line 6) on the gusting wind. The moon catches his eye and reminds him again of the train (lines 8-9), hinting of death, offering annihilation.

Threat is in the air; tension pervades the first eleven lines, and the night walker feels it. The hawk that swoops down is seen to "strafe" (line 9) the grass, which is "bristled" (line 10), and the hawk's cry is "Like steel wrenched taut till severed" (line 11). If the threats of violence are projections of his own fears, the tension reflects his own as well. Although his mind has circled back to the menacing presence of an imagined train, he continues to regard his situation from a distance: He is "Out of reach" of the deadly forces around him, which may be Devil-sent (he sees the imagined train as "Hellbent"), and beyond the reach of his own impulses (beneath his own "desiring"). For the moment, he goes "safe," though "tensed for a leap" (line 13), not yet resolved to the apparently contradictory nature of death, which appears to be "a dark void" yet "all kindness."

Having presented his state of mind, his situation, and his choices, the wanderer pauses (line 14) and considers any resolution that might come to him. His dilemma is caused, at least in part, by conflicting loyalties. Referring to the practice of throwing spilled salt over the shoulder to ward off the Devil (or bad luck), he admits to irrational superstition, yet he pays tribute to formal religious faith by allowing his child to be baptized. Instead of finding double safety in two beliefs, he appears to be shut out of both, left in a limbo of unresolved faith.

Forms and Devices

If it were not for line 8 and the break in line 14, this poem would comprise four regular quatrains; instead, the rhyme scheme in the second quatrain breaks the pattern found in the first four lines and in the final eight: *abba, cdd[e], fggf, hiih.* A pause also marks the end of the three regular quatrains, as if to set them further apart from the second quatrain, whose fourth line lacks a pause. The break in line 14 focuses attention on ties—broken structurally, but reinforced by the concluding ideas.

The lines contain five stresses each; most of the metric feet are iambs, but the rhythms are modulated to underscore meaning, as in line 4 ("Béariňg dówn Hěllbént") and line 13 ("Wǎlk ón ténsed fǒr ǎ leáp . . . "). Mostly, however, metric regularity keeps time with meaning and forms a backdrop that highlights the irregularities.

Grammatical ties are used to give some words more than one possible reference point. In line 1, "left over" refers to "ties" but could modify the "I" in line 3. In line 12, "desiring" could refer to the "I" immediately following, to the "Devil" in the penultimate line, or to the forces that menace the wanderer. Again in line 14, the phrase "all kindness" is in apposition to "void," but the lack of a comma hints at another meaning: "void [is] all kindness." Complicating the grammatical "ties" in these ways reinforces the poem's theme of cross ties, just as the disrupted rhyme scheme of the second quatrain reinforces the poem's focus on disharmony and incongruity.

The poem's argument develops in a world of concrete objects, vivid imagery, and sounds reinforced by alliteration, rhyme, and other devices. In line 4, alliteration and sense combine to suggest the ominous nature of the train: "Bearing down Hellbent from behind my back." The imagery generally connotes danger—the wind flings, the hawk strafes and falls, and the grass is "bristled"—and is often reinforced by discordant sounds. A simile in line 7 ties the violence of the wind to the image of the threatening train: "flings like a sack of mail." Though a flight of birds is suggested in "flock of cloud," the sounds are "hard" (because of the *k* sounds in "flock" and "cloud"), and the violence suggested by "flings" (line 7) is echoed in "flock." In lines 11 and 12, the sense is heightened by a combination of alliteration, assonance, and "hard" sounds: "screech . . . steel wrenched taut till severed."

Wordplay is most evident in the use of "ties," which appears in both the title and the first line. Its various meanings not only inform the argument of the poem but also provide the principal image, that of bonding or entangling. Its negative implications suggest collision, danger—while walking the cross ties, the speaker "could" collide with a train. In a spiritual sense, the speaker ponders his "ties" to the Devil and his child. Spiritual and emotional ties may be as complicated (or uncertain) as some of the grammatical ties. The wanderer feels tied to the tracks, the wind, the hawk, in ways that reflect his mood and could determine his fate. The threatening nature of these intertwining forces is suggested in one of the meanings of "Cross"—angry. As the poem's sounds unfold, the ties between the world of the senses and that of meaning are revealed. Bonding develops even out of conflict and discordance.

Themes and Meanings

The poem is about a solitary wanderer suspended between two worlds: a "dark void" and a world that represents "all kindness." Though the poet seems detached throughout his journey, he is nevertheless deeply involved in conflicting emotions and meanings. The poem's title—"Cross Ties"—suggests conflict from the very beginning, and by repeating the word "ties," the first line emphasizes the central theme of bonding. Past beliefs ("ties left over") do not bind the poet tightly, but they remain. Wandering in the night along a rusted railroad track, the poet discovers a way to "sever" those ties that keep him uncommitted—he can "sidestep or go down before."

Between the thought of self-destruction and the final acquiescence ("I let them sprinkle . . . "), the poet finds himself amid a swirl of violent motions—the imagined train, the wind that "flings," the hawk that strafes. In a world of random disorder, he ties together its parts. Belief synthesizes as he makes invisible connections. He is at the center but has no center. Instead of sure belief, he finds indifference, discord, and the threat of violence. The way out of this swirling dilemma is to commit himself to an "indifferent" mechanical yet demonic force or to one that seems to be "all kindness." Both demand obeisance. For the Devil, he throws spilled salt. For the other, he lets "them sprinkle water" on his child.

While the poet walks the tracks of his dilemma, the poem's construction subtly suggests a resolution. What the spirit cannot find, art will provide. The regularity of meter and rhyme yokes the poet into a path that, for the moment at least, he is not prepared to commit to, at least not wholly. The colon at the end of line 4, immediately after "back," brings meaning and structure together to underscore the poet's predicament: He is backed up against his own dilemma. At this point in his journey, he comes to a temporary stop in his poetic line. Bound by "ties left over," he faces what lies beyond the colon, a journey dependent on his poetic vision and his ability to proceed. The colon both stops him and signals an imperative to continue. The image in line 11 foreshadows the break in line 14: "Like steel wrenched taut till severed." Seeing the poetic process as railroad tracks that keep him in line and on line, he "severs" one of the lines (line 14) and in that way perhaps discovers a resolution of his conflict. Though the poet pays tribute to the Devil and to the spirit that requires water baptism, the poetic process can reconcile everything, for it gives order and ties belief into a meaningful whole despite the temporary halts, the breaks, and threatening cross ties. The poem is not the world, but it can help the poet discover order in a world of doubt. It can resolve a dilemma by bringing him to an understanding of the one tie that promises continuance: his "child."

Bernard E. Morris

CROSSING BROOKLYN FERRY

Author: Walt Whitman (1819-1892)
Type of poem: Dramatic monologue
First published: 1856, as "Sun-Down Poem," in *Leaves of Grass*

The Poem

"Crossing Brooklyn Ferry" first appeared in 1856 under the title "Sun-Down Poem." It was one of the twenty new poems added to the twelve originally untitled poems of the first edition of *Leaves of Grass* (1855), the collection that Walt Whitman thought of as a single poem that he continued to expand and revise over the course of nine distinct editions. "Sun-Down Poem" became "Crossing Brooklyn Ferry" in the third, and again expanded, edition of *Leaves of Grass* published in 1860. The poem, in its final form of 132 lines, develops a single major idea throughout nine sections, the last of which serves as both reprise and climax.

The original and revised titles introduce the temporal and spatial figures that play such important parts in the poem and in the context of Whitman's other writings. With the sun still "half an hour high" and the flood tide running, the narrator—not Whitman the man or Whitman the poet but the Whitmanic persona—is seen making the crossing between Brooklyn and Manhattan aboard the Fulton Street Ferry. Just as the literal ferry carries him from shore to shore, the figurative ferry and the equally figurative flood tide carry him "far away" to that purely poetic place from which his highly metaphorical meditation on time and space, doubt and faith, issues.

The extensive panorama of city and river as seen from the ever-moving (yet in a sense seemingly stationary) ferry gradually comes to coexist with the narrator's imagined sight of those who, in a hundred years or even hundreds of years, will occupy the place he occupies now, who will see what he sees and feel what he feels. The curiosity of the Whitmanic I/eye thus extends from the physical to the imagined, from the perceptual to the conceptual, as he draws his "impalpable sustenance" from each and all. Poem and narrative poet alike cross from shore to shore, from tangible to intangible, sight to feeling, object to subject, and, more important, from present to future as Whitman attempts to go beyond the doubts, questions, and fragmentation of (then) modern experience caused by various psychological, political, and spiritual uncertainties. He crosses to the future less as a pilgrim in search of his faith than as teacher, prophet, and comrade (three of Whitman's favorite poses). He offers the consoling vision of a "well-joined scheme" in which all things (natural and man-made) are "dumb, beautiful ministers" and in which everything and everyone, now and ages hence, has its, his, or her part to play, whether "great or small," in the making of a soul that seems to resemble more closely the Hindu atman than the individualized Christian spirit.

Forms and Devices

The title, "Crossing Brooklyn Ferry," announces the poem's basic structure and line of development: the movement from separation through similarity and identification to the eventual fusing of I (or eye) and other, of part and whole (or the Emersonian "each and all"), present and future. The specific stylistic means by which Whitman accomplishes this integration are individually noteworthy.

One is Whitman's idiosyncratic Transcendental style—less philosophical than Ralph Waldo Emerson's and less learned and literary than Henry David Thoreau's but no less effective than either and, in terms of its political implications, far more radically democratic. Whitman's style is at once minutely inclusive and broadly expansive. It involves the merging, or juxtaposing, of the particular and the general, of private confession and public announcement, of the self-reliant individual and—democracy's flip side—mass humanity. Whitman's preoccupation with the crafting of a completely new and entirely democratic poetic becomes especially pronounced in his catalogs, including the one that takes up all but the first five lines of the poem's relatively long third section.

The second stylistic element derives from Whitman's decision to forgo conventional poetry's reliance on narrowly defined rhythmical patterns and his willingness to explore the possibilities of a more fluid and organic rhythm based upon repetition of various kinds—of words, for example, and similar syntactical structures (rhetorical questions, exclamatory statements, noun, verb, and prepositional phrases, and, as in the "crossing" of the poem's title, participles). All of these, and the latter in particular, create a paradoxical sense of simultaneous motion and stasis to which Whitman dedicated himself in his self-proclaimed role as "uniter of here and hereafter."

The third element, and the one that distinguishes "Crossing Brooklyn Ferry" from nearly all Whitman's other poems, is his deft manipulation of verb tense. The poem opens in the present tense. It is the speaker's present and is carefully distinguished from the reader's future identified at the beginning of section 2. Soon, however, speaker and reader merge, by means of a trick of tense. What was future now becomes present, and in section 3 what was present (section 1) now becomes past. Such a summary does not do justice to the subtlety with which Whitman accomplishes his grammatical coup, not merely moving unobtrusively to another age but transcending time altogether. (Although the temporal shift will remain in effect through section 6, some additional blurring of the temporal edges occurs in section 3: the change of seasons—but not time of day—in lines 28 and 31, and the sudden passage from sundown to night in lines 47-48.) A still more daring shift occurs in the poem's three concluding sections, as past, present, and future become indistinguishable. Free of verb tenses and of psychic tensions, the poem/speaker posits the reality of the eternal moment of time itself, or rather of timelessness.

Themes and Meanings

The question that Whitman poses midway through "Crossing Brooklyn Ferry"—"What is it then between us?"—sums up his and his poem's twin preoccupations and perspectives. The one is personal, though not narrowly autobiographical, the other more or less philosophical. The question serves as the pivot on which the entire poem turns and from which, like a pendulum, it depends, moving back and forth (like the tide's ebb and flow). The word "between" plays a similarly double and thematically crucial role in that it implies both separation (temporal, spatial, ideological, and psychological) and connection (the bonds that transcend all differences).

By means of the usual Transcendentalist intuitive leaps and metaphorical correspondences (the poem's "similitudes"), "Crossing Brooklyn Ferry" moves well beyond the seeming narcissism, even solipsism, of the opening line ("Flood-tide below me! I see you face to face!"). Whitman's transcendent as well as Transcendentalist narrator penetrates the "appearances" and "usual costumes" of the world of phenomena in order to discover the noumenal truth that binds each and all together in one "simple, compact, well-join'd scheme." That scheme is nothing less than the cosmic design, the former house builder's poetically prosaic version of Emerson's more abstract Over-Soul.

In one of the poem's most affecting and psychologically penetrating lines, "I too had been struck from the float forever held in solution," Whitman creates the central image in his drama of the conflict between the individual ego and the self's desire to identify or merge with a reality larger than itself. Against the exclusion, exile, and helplessness implied by the passive form of the verb "to strike," Whitman holds out the possibility of a shared experience, a return to the wholeness of the protecting, all-satisfying "solution" of the cosmic womb.

The mood here and throughout the poem is one of joyous celebration. Instead of violent transgression of the boundaries delimiting space, time, and person, the poem offers a fluid and fluent crossing over. The speaker's faith is firm, the questions never more than rhetorical. This is not to say that the poem provides any actual answers. Instead, it proves its point by cheerfully and confidently insisting on its affirmative vision of a truth that must remain ineffable—a truth that can be approached but never reached. (The line "Closer yet I approach you" applies as much to this truth as to the poem's imagined reader.) The poem's meaning thus lies beyond the poet's power of articulation but well within his power of imagination. It lies, that is, in the realm of the ecstatic and the prophetic to which Whitman's operatic style always aspires and which, as in the case of "Crossing Brooklyn Ferry," it occasionally attains.

Robert A. Morace

CROSSING THE BAR

Author: Alfred, Lord Tennyson (1809-1892)
Type of poem: Lyric
First published: 1889, in *Demeter and Other Poems*

The Poem

Alfred, Lord Tennyson's "Crossing the Bar" is a sixteen-line poem divided into four four-line stanzas of differing metrical structure. The predominantly iambic lines vary in length, ranging from four-syllable lines (dimeters) to ten-syllable, iambic pentameter lines. The stanzas follow a consistent *abab* rhyme pattern.

The opening line establishes the poem's temporal setting, an unspecified ship that is ready to sail at sunset. As the sun descends, the light of the evening star, a beacon for mariners, rises. Line 9 again draws attention to the approaching evening but calls it "twilight" rather than "sunset." Once the final rays of light disappear, darkness will cover the world. This element neatly divides the poem into two sections, each containing 2 stanzas.

On the literal level, Tennyson's poem begins with the barest elements of setting. A ship is about to set sail on a long voyage at "Sunset and evening star." After a formal announcement, the "one clear call," the vessel will sail out of the harbor, across the sandbar at the harbor's entrance, and into the sea. The anxious passenger, the poem's persona, hopes for a gentle crossing out of the harbor, one without turbulence associated with "moaning of the bar." Instead, he hopes for a tide that is "Too full for sound and foam" because such a gentle tide would be like the one "which drew [him] out the boundless deep" and into port. This realization allows the traveler to think of this voyage out as if it were merely a voyage "again home."

The second section of the poem (stanzas 3 and 4) echoes the poem's first line with a second reference to the approaching night. Instead of the clear call, the sound of the "evening bell" signals the darkness and the scheduled sailing. Hoping for a cheerful departure, one with "no sadness of farewell," the persona senses the importance of this journey, whose course will lead far beyond the limits of "Time and Place." Still, the persona takes confidence in the hope of seeing the "Pilot face to face" after crossing the bar that separates the harbor and sea.

Perhaps one of Tennyson's best-known short poems, "Crossing the Bar" also has a interesting history. Written in October, 1889, the poem was conceived as an expression of thanksgiving. Tennyson, then eighty, had recently recovered from a serious illness. Biographers point out that the poem was written on the back of an envelope in twenty minutes, the length of the ferry crossing from Lymington to Yarmouth on the Isle of Wight. The poem gained immediate popularity and was eventually set to music. It was one of two anthems sung three years later at the poet laureate's funeral in Westminster Abbey on October 12, 1892. At Tennyson's request, the poem is included as the final poem in all editions of his poetry.

Forms and Devices

At first glance, "Crossing the Bar" seems simple and uncomplicated in its rhyme scheme and metrics. The four-line quatrains resemble ballad stanzas, with their alternating rhymes that are consistently masculine and exact. Tennyson, however, carefully manipulated the rhymes, making "bar" a rhyming word in the first and last stanzas of the poem. Another skillful variation occurs with the metrics. Rather than employing the traditional pattern of the ballad, Tennyson extends one line in each of the first three stanzas into a single, graceful iambic pentameter line. In the final stanza, the first and third lines are pentameters. This changes the rhythm and even creates a wavelike motion. The poem's rhythm slows down with the final line, "When I have crossed the bar," and ends powerfully on a final, accented syllable, the word "bar."

The simple language of this poem again recalls the ballad, and like the ballad the poem uses familiar vocabulary. Most of the words are common and monosyllabic, such as "star," "call," and "home." In fact, the poem contains no words of more than two syllables. The word "bourne," however, deserves attention. The one-syllable word, an obsolete term meaning "boundary" or "limit," stands out. Here it refers to a geographical boundary between harbor and ocean. At the same time, it applies equally well a spiritual boundary, one that separates the temporal world and the limitless regions beyond. In addition, "bourne" resembles words found in folk ballads, but the word's simplicity and eloquence suit the poem perfectly.

The eloquence of "Crossing the Bar" lies in its use of metaphor. Like so many works dealing with the sea, its central metaphor compares a sea voyage to the final journey that is part of the human condition, the journey from life to death. Tennyson's numerous correspondences raise the poem beyond the level of mere metaphor to the realm of allegory. Almost every aspect of the poem works on two levels, literal and allegorical. Thus the journey across the bar becomes the crossing from the harbor of life into the dark, unknown sea or the afterlife. The twilight setting lends a sense of foreboding, for the approach of darkness and the sun's setting in the west are traditional references to death. Images such as the "moaning of the bar" and the "sadness of farewell" enhance the somber tone and apply aptly to both dying and the voyage. The sandbar that separates the harbor from the sea becomes the demarcation between life and death.

Even the tidal motion of the sea has significance. Like the traveler, everyone hopes for a peaceful crossing of the bar, one whose "moving seems asleep" because it is "Too full for sound and foam." No one knows what the moment of dying will actually be like, so the journey into death is generally frightening. The traveler finds comfort in the paradoxical nature of the journey, which is both a departure and a homecoming. Furthermore, it will allow Tennyson's traveler to see the Pilot "face to face" after crossing into to death. In capitalizing "Pilot," Tennyson equates the Pilot with God, but God in the guise of a specially qualified mariner who guides the ship through difficult waters in and out of the harbor.

The presence of the Pilot, however, has caused considerable controversy. The poem suggests that the Pilot appears only after the ship has "crossed the bar" rather than quitting the ship after passing the obstacle. Tennyson explained that the Pilot had been aboard all along, identifying him as "that Divine and Unseen Who is always guiding us."

Themes and Meanings

The enduring popularity of this short, meditative lyric lies in its ability to appeal to many people on many levels, despite attempts to limit it to one interpretation. The poem's themes of death and dying have made it a popular selection for memorial services over the years, including Tennyson's own. The poem, however, has significance for all readers. Daily life, a journey in itself, requires individuals to travel regularly from the safety of home, across a threshold, and into the unknown. Like the world of Tennyson's traveler, the world beyond the safe region is dark and mysterious, yet at day's end, people return home.

In this way, "Crossing the Bar" draws parallels between familiar and repeated patterns of ordinary, daily routine with nature's daily cycles, such as night and day and the flow and ebb of the tide. Similarly, Tennyson includes the "evening star" and the Pilot as reminders of sources that guide individuals. These elements eloquently diminish the horror of death by drawing attention to the fact that the journey into death is merely part of a cycle: The going out is also a return home to "the boundless deep," from which this traveler, like all people, came.

The themes of sea and death recur frequently in Tennyson's life and work. As a child, Tennyson first saw the sea on a family vacation at Mablethorpe on the Lincolnshire coast, a place he revisited often for comfort and solitude when an adult. One critic posits that the poet somehow mentally linked the sea at Mablethorpe with the Mediterranean and the Aegean. This seems to be the case in works like "Ulysses"(1842), a poem about the famous epic hero's final voyage at the end of his life. Like the traveler in "Crossing the Bar," Ulysses, now an old man, sails off into the Mediterranean for one final adventure rather than simply yielding to death at home. In "The Passing of Arthur" (1869), Tennyson again connects voyage and death, giving readers the enduring picture of King Arthur's bier floating out on the dark lake into the unknown. In each case, as in this simple lyric, the final voyage is majestic and dignified.

Even with its strong Christian overtones, "Crossing the Bar" appeals to a universal audience of all faiths and even nonbelievers. Everyone can respond to the image of the journey into the unknown. Tennyson carefully avoids using the words "heaven" and "hell," "reward" and "punishment." In Tennyson's view the final crossing includes no judgment. Dying, then, is simply a stage, and the afterlife, a return home to the same unknown place from which individuals emerge. The Pilot, perhaps the clearest reference to God, is, in the poet's own words, "the Divine Presence"—God and yet not necessarily the Christian God, but all the same some greater power that controls and guides human activity.

Stephen V. Myslinski

CRUSOE IN ENGLAND

Author: Elizabeth Bishop (1911-1979)
Type of poem: Dramatic monologue
First published: 1976, in *Geography III*

The Poem

"Crusoe in England" is a poem of 183 lines spoken by Robinson Crusoe (after his return from his island exile) that actually expresses Elizabeth Bishop's own summation of her difficult creative life as a poet.

The poem opens with Robinson Crusoe, back in England, reflecting on his past life of more than fifty years on an island alone but in fact giving utterance to Bishop's apologia for her poetic career. News that a volcano has created a new island somewhere causes Crusoe to recall his own island, to explore it in memory in order to discover the real significance of the island experience that no one else has ever correctly evaluated (lines 1-10).

The raw creative energy for writing poems rests on the cumulative and fully realized ("heads blown off") experiences of fifty-two volcanic years that have generated a poetic inspiration and an overwhelming poetic vision verging on glorious intuitions, despite the difficult and sometimes depressing lot of being a writer. It is the wonderful conjunction of "left-over clouds" in the writer's lived and literary past and the parched "craters" of the writer's artistic genius that releases the energy for poetic creation in the form of multicolored lava shaping the exotic island of fanciful flora and fauna (lines 11-54). This is the poem's "waterspout" conception (lines 46, 52-53) of the writer's creative process: "And I had waterspouts. Oh,/ half a dozen at a time."

Unfortunately, poetic creation could be as lonely as Crusoe's long island exile, and it did provoke some self-pity in response to the heavy responsibility of being a creator. This self-pity is tempered by an acceptance of the artist's role and poetic gifts. The memory of the island is described simply but symbolically. A snail grubbing "over everything" could signify the observing self of the artist creating beauty ("beds of irises") out of the raw material of existence (lines 69-75). As in pastoral poetry, so also in these verses, the speaker tends sheep and sings ecstatically like a dancing Dionysius—the Greek god of wine, song, and frenzy—after ingesting "home-brew" of red berries.

One small area of the poetic self proved a handicap of destructive insecurity, stemming from feelings of ignorance, of an inability to answer the great questions about life, and a failure of vision to drive away the primal fears and doubts lurking in the unconscious. Such insecurity and loneliness provoked escapist thoughts of a sturdy oak tree, fancies transforming the boring landscape of the artistic self, and dreams "of food/ and love," but to no avail. Escapist dreams quickly turned into frightening nightmares of infinite islands of infinite creative possibilities and, therefore, of infinite artistic responsibilities requiring endless self-exploration and repeated literary discovery (lines 90-142). Crusoe's Friday did alleviate the loneliness of the speaker's artistic self-absorption, but the companionship was a limited blessing because of a limited compatibility.

The poem ends with the speaker returned to the everyday world of boring and unproductive old age in England, far from the former island life of dynamic artistic creativity, when the simplest detail exploded with literary meaning and literary possibility ("The knife there on the shelf—it reeked of meaning, like a crucifix"). Instead of the dynamic vitality of poetic creation, there is now a moribund preservation of the aged speaker's past creations in the archives of museums for scholars to study and dissect. The culminating disappointment is that even the inadequate companionship of Friday has been taken away by death. If it was lonely on the island of bygone creativity, then it is a worse deprivation to be a stagnant has-been without any companion at all in the England of tired old age.

Forms and Devices

"Crusoe in England" is a dramatic monologue uttered by the protagonist of Daniel Defoe's classic novel, *Robinson Crusoe* (1719).

A dramatic monologue is a literary form in which a single speaker reveals the totality of the self and the society conditioning that self, often at a moment of crisis for the speaker. Elizabeth Bishop, however, employs the dramatic monologue in an unconventional manner. In "Crusoe in England," the self revealed is not Crusoe but Bishop herself, and there is little attempt at going beyond that poet's self and exploring the outer social world that gave her being and shape. Instead, the focus is autobiographical and intimately psychological. The poem is about her poetry, her difficult poetic life, and her stagnant later life when her fame has replaced her fire.

The poem is written in the confessional mode of simple free verse to capture the ruminating process of summing up a life's significance. The diction is simple ("Do I deserve this?"), casual ("a sort of cloud-dump"), and sometimes shocking ("with their heads blown off"). Blunt informality is the norm.

There is an overriding allusion to Defoe's Crusoe and Friday. Lines 96 and 97 contain a major allusion to William Wordsworth's "I Wandered Lonely as a Cloud" to provide a contrast underscoring the speaker's failure of vision. There is also a veiled allusion to a pastoral Dionysian ecstasy of poetry in lines 76 through 84.

Finally, symbolism lies at the heart of the poem's effectiveness. For example, the goats and turtles, gulls and snails, signify elements or emanations of the speaker's creative process, as they transform into beach-creating lava and back again into creatures of Bishop's poetic imagination. Waterspouts embody in miniature the creative process of poetry. In fact, Crusoe's entire island experience, as remembered in old age, constitutes one grand symbol of the difficulties and complexities of Bishop's inner poetic life and the loss of artistic energy in old age.

Themes and Meanings

In an essay entitled "The Waterspout," published in 1925, Robert Frost wrote of a poet's creative process in a way that provides a fitting commentary on Bishop's unflinching review of her own artistry. Frost used the image of a waterspout to indicate creativity. A poet, Frost wrote, begins as a "cloud" of the other writers the poet has read:

> And first the cloud reaches down toward the water from above and then the water reaches up toward the cloud from below and finally the cloud and water join together to roll as one pillar between heaven and earth. The base of water he picks up from below is of course all the life he ever lived outside of books.

When Bishop wrote about her life, as she did in several poems and stories in the 1950's and last did in her extraordinary final volume entitled *Geography III* (1976), she resisted self-pity and sentimentality and favored understatement and lucid honesty about herself. As M. L. Rosenthal noted about her earliest work in *The Modern Poets: A Critical Introduction* (1960), "Her perfectionism is not such as to keep her from expressing emotions spontaneously."

Exile and travel were at the heart of her poems from the start, and her landscapes often stressed the sweep and violence of encircling and eroding geological powers as observed by a poet with a botanist-geologist-anthropologist's curiosity.

These lifelong poetic traits can be found in her meditation about lonely artistic creation and old age's lost poetic energy in "Crusoe in England." This poem's inspiration is Bishop's own life, as deflected through the distancing literary lens of two English classics, Defoe's *Robinson Crusoe* and Wordsworth's "I Wandered Lonely as a Cloud." Robinson Crusoe's island experience and memories of that exile provide the symbolic landscape for Bishop's autobiographical exploration of the poet's inner creative life—its rigors, ecstasies, loneliness, and insecurities—and the poet's sapped artistic vitality in old age when she became a museum piece for literary analysis.

Midway in the poem (lines 96-97), a quotation from Wordsworth's haunting lyric underscores the discrepancy between a transcendentally optimistic Romantic poet and an insecure modern poet unsure of herself, her power to apprehend great truths, and her ability to stifle the doubts and ugly intimations of her unconscious. Bishop's brutally candid examination of her literary career ("My island seemed to be/ a sort of cloud-dump") sometimes happily echoes but sometimes sadly undercuts Wordsworth's confident lines about the poetic process that generated for him such joy, vitality, and companionship with nature overcoming the artist's loneliness and insecurity.

Thomas M. Curley

CRYSTALS LIKE BLOOD

Author: Hugh MacDiarmid (Christopher Murray Grieve, 1892-1978)
Type of poem: Lyric
First published: 1949; collected in *Collected Poems of Hugh MacDiarmid*, 1962

The Poem

"Crystals Like Blood," a twenty-seven-line free-verse lyric, develops an analogy between mechanical processes and memory to create a synthesis of external and internal experience. Standing at the grave of a person he loved, the speaker remembers finding a fragment of stone containing red crystals. As the poem unfolds, he compares the process of extracting mercury from cinnabar to the process of memory.

In a single two-line sentence, the first of the four verse paragraphs introduces the memory of discovering the stone containing the crystals but does not mention the present setting or the dead friend. In nine lines, the second verse paragraph describes the speaker's picking up "a broken chunk of bed-rock" and examining it carefully, turning "it this way and that." The weight of the stone surprises him. One face of it is brown limestone; the other contains crystals of "greenish-grey quartz-like stone" in which magenta lines appear. The verse paragraph confines itself to carefully chosen description without overtly introducing metaphors.

Repeating "I remember" from the opening of the poem, the third verse paragraph, ten lines, shifts to a time between the "long ago" discovery of the stone and the speaker's present. During this intermediate time, the speaker had observed the mechanical process by which "mercury is extracted from cinnabar." A spiderlike pile-driving machine hammered the stone to fragments of ore, which then moved on a conveyor belt up to an opening in a huge kiln, where the stone was heated to extract the liquid mercury.

The six lines of the fourth verse paragraph return to the present and the process of memory to introduce the unidentified "you" to whom the poem is addressed. The speaker compares the violent mechanical process of mercury production with his "living memory." As the speaker thinks about the "you" who is dead and buried and at whose grave he is standing, memory releases in him "bright torrents of felicity, naturalness, and faith." The living memory is thus contrasted with the dead body as the crystals contrast with the brown limestone.

The poem operates by comparisons and contrasts: between the dull limestone and the bright quartz, between brown stone and the green and red of the crystals, between the mechanical process of extracting mercury and the organic process of memory, between living memory and dead clay, between the speaker and the person or memory to whom the poem is addressed, and between the rigid beauty of naturally occurring crystals and warm, life-giving blood.

Forms and Devices

"Crystals Like Blood" is written in rhythmic free verse, in which the line breaks coincide either with punctuation or with breaks in syntax. The variety in sentence lengths contributes to the conversational tone of the poem's voice and keeps it from becoming monotonous. The unforced, asymmetrical structure of the poem suggests naturalness, in contrast with the "symmetrical" mechanism of the pile driver. The poem moves in a circle from graveside to graveside.

The conveyor in the third stanza is reiterated in the "treadmill" to which the speaker likens his memory. What at first seems to be a mixed metaphor of "torrents" produced by a treadmill is resolved in the implied image of liquid mercury flowing from the kiln. The process of memory releases "felicity, naturalness, and faith" in the speaker, just as the kiln's fires release the quicksilver. The phrase "felicity, naturalness, and faith" uses abstract terms that convey an emotional message intellectually rather than through sensuous specifics. In fact, readers know very little of the "you" in the poem, except that the speaker draws inward sustenance from the memory of the person.

Although the poem is not rhymed in a regular pattern, the third verse paragraph is based on couplets using near rhymes (repetition of vowels or consonants), such as the long *i* and *er* sounds in "piledrivers" and "spider," the *ci* in "precision" and "circle," the long *o* in "force" and "ore," and, less emphatically, the *a* sound in "saw" and "cinnebar," along with the *i* in "high" and "kiln," although the last is a visual rather than an auditory rhyme.

Perhaps not surprisingly, it is the paragraph about the pile-driving machine that uses the most mechanical of poetic effects, rhymed couplets, though the fact that the rhymes are not exact suggests MacDiarmid's resistance to the machine. The machine's "monotonous precision," "endless circle," and "thunderous force" all contrast with the quick "bright torrents" of feeling memory liquefied in the speaker's imagination. The "Crystals like blood" at the beginning of the poem have come to yield the speaker's living memory.

The alliteration of "blood in a broken stone" suggests the living memory in the clay later in the poem. The *k*'s in "chunk" and "rock," as well as the *g*'s in "greenish-grey" and the *d*'s in "dappled" and "darker" subtly suggest Anglo-Saxon alliterative verse. Assonance is also a feature of MacDiarmid's sound effects in the poem. In the opening sentence, the circularity of the poem is hinted at by the repetition of the letter *o*: long *o*'s in "ago," "broken," and "stone," the diphthongs in "how," "found," and "blood," and the short *o* in "long." Assonance also appears in the *o* in "ago" and "stone" and the *a* in "face" and "caked."

The line "Crystals like blood in a broken stone" is strongly cadenced, with four strong stresses ("crystals," "blood," "broke-," and "stone"), in addition to the hammering alliteration. Circularity is also indicated by the "double ring of iron piledrivers." Three of the four verse paragraphs begin with "remember," suggesting rhythmically the repetitive hammering of the pile drivers. All these sounds compose a verbal music that seems quite natural, a subtle interplay of sound and sense without regularized meter or perfect rhyme.

Themes and Meanings

MacDiarmid is a poet of vast though sometimes helter-skelter erudition. Many of his poems are written in "Lallans," a Scottish dialect he synthesized out of several existing dialects, along with words that had fallen out of use but that MacDiarmid found in John Jamieson's *Etymological Dictionary of the Scottish Language* (1808). A Scottish nationalist, MacDiarmid saw himself as doing something akin to what Geoffrey Chaucer did with English and Dante did with Italian, writing in the vernacular rather than in the approved language of the dominant academy (Latin in the case of Chaucer and Dante, English in the case of MacDiarmid). Though he sometimes regarded the English as the enemy and often wrote caustically about English political and poetic domination, in "Crystals Like Blood" MacDiarmid uses English to good effect.

If the whole poem is rather mechanical, working out the intersecting comparisons as persistently as the pile drivers work on the cinnabar, the language is quite simple and precise, and the end result is more nearly sentimental than mechanical. MacDiarmid's aesthetic choice is to confine himself to clear, simple statements of fact in order to concentrate the poem's emotional impact at the end. Until the last verse paragraph the poem is virtually without emotional language. In the first two verse paragraphs there are no words suggesting emotion at all. In the third verse paragraph emotion creeps into the poem in the word "fantastically" as a reaction to the "symmetrical spider" of the pile driver, and in "monotonous" as a judgment of the way the machine works. The word "spider" may also be taken to have vaguely negative emotional associations for some readers, but until the last verse paragraph nothing in the poem gives a hint that its actual subject concerns the relationship between two people.

MacDiarmid's description of the process of mercury production suggests how mercurial the things people remember can be, for at the moment of remembrance memory and the thing remembered are one. Contrasted with the detailed description of the crystal-bearing stone and the mechanical process of mercury extraction, the description of what he remembers of the dead person is conveyed in a single fleeting line. Even the line in the last verse paragraph limits itself to those three abstract words, "felicity, naturalness, and faith," which arguably have less emotional weight than the phrase "dear body rotting."

By concentrating his poem's explicit statement of emotion in three abstract words, MacDiarmid runs the risk of being criticized for vagueness, but the sensuous evocation of a rotting corpse (also in three words) in juxtaposition with "bright torrents" drawn from memory precisely focuses the tension between the living and the dead that is the point of "Crystals Like Blood." To describe what endures, MacDiarmid deliberately avoids using language drawn from sensory experience. The body dies, but the spirit lives on.

Thomas Lisk

CUMBERLAND STATION

Author: Dave Smith (1942-   )
Type of poem: Elegy
First published: 1975; collected in *Cumberland Station*, 1976

The Poem

"Cumberland Station" is a free-verse elegy with nine stanzas that vary in length. The station in the poem's title is in Cumberland, Maryland, a town at the end of the Potomac River that was once considered the "Gateway to the West." While the station at one time served as a gateway, the poem explores how a station can change from a gateway to a "godforsaken/ wayside." Throughout the poem, the station reflects the speaker's moods. Like much of Dave Smith's work, the poem is autobiographical, exploring the effect of place and history on individuals who struggle against changing times and struggle to maintain their sense of self.

In the first stanza, the speaker mentions objects that he sees as he enters the Cumberland train station: "gray brick, ash, hand-bent railings, steps so big/ it takes hours to mount them, polished oak/ pews." These objects are fragments of a grand old station, a place of giants where "Big Daddy" once collected children for thunderous rides on steam engines, where crowds of people had food and purpose, where children rode free. The speaker identifies himself as a child who once ". . . walked uphill/ through flowers of soot to zing/ scared to death into the world." In the first two stanzas the images and bits of narrative create a nostalgic mood—even the soot and ash are beautiful, flowerlike.

Cumberland Station is no longer a place of giants, however; it is now a deserted and damaged hall. It presents a scene that disturbs the speaker: "I come here alone, shaken." In stanza 3, the changes in the speaker and the station are corroborated by the fallen state of Cumberland, a town where jobless, penniless families "cruise" the city with no purpose, a town of "shaken" people. To help the reader understand why Cumberland declined and why the town incites both fear and repulsion in the speaker, he recounts not only Big Daddy's death but also the death of a child who was "diced on a cowcatcher" and the deaths of two male relatives, an uncle who "coughed his youth/ into a gutter" and an alcoholic cousin who "slid on the ice."

After the speaker chronicles Cumberland's fall, in the center of the poem he asks a rhetorical question that stops the narrative: "Grandfather, you ask why I don't visit you/ now you have escaped the ticket-seller's cage." The question and the answer return the reader to themes introduced early in the poem—Cumberland is a fallen place, a place to which no one would wish to return. Yet the grandfather's question forces the speaker to contemplate the guilt and ambivalence that the return causes him. The speaker's intentions are good—he promises often that he will return, that he will free the grandfather, his only surviving relative, that they will escape "like brothers." When in Cumberland, however, the speaker is no longer himself—he is like "a demented cousin" who steals an abandoned newspaper. While he fears Cumberland and the memories that the place evokes, he also longs for the past. He even wishes his grandfather were there to punish him, to tell him what is right and wrong.

Forms and Devices

Since the speaker in "Cumberland Station" tells a story, the poem could be labeled a narrative. Since the poet uses the narrative to express the speaker's psychological state (a state that the speaker only half understands), the poem could also be called a lyric. Finally, since the poem explores the transience of life, is reflective, and laments the loss of a time and place, it is also elegiac. The narrative style, the serious subject matter, and the elegiac form reveal the extent to which Smith draws on a poetic tradition that dates to the Anglo-Saxon period. In anonymous Old English poems, such as "The Seafarer" and "The Wanderer," isolated speakers journey, lamenting the loss of their lords or their families. Like the speakers in those poems, Smith's speaker also journeys, lamenting the loss of heroes and heroic times.

Since the lines vary in length and lack end rhyme, "Cumberland Station" could be called a free-verse poem. The line length is not completely irregular, however. Like "The Wanderer" and "The Seafarer," "Cumberland Station" has long lines, averaging ten syllables. Like Old English poems, there are also at least eight syllables in most lines, and the poet relies on accent and alliteration, rather than on a precise number of syllables or a precise meter, to create rhythm. Long lines usually indicate a serious subject, which is true in Old English poetry and in "Cumberland Station," so the form and the content reinforce each other. In addition, the poem, like Old English elegies, has a two-part structure: The first half of the poem is descriptive, with bits of narrative and concrete imagery; the second half is contemplative, with ruminations on morality, guilt, and responsibility.

While the elegiac form and the long line length draw on a tradition, Smith breaks with tradition by using enjambment throughout the poem, as is evident in the final three lines: "I wish I had the guts/ to tell you this is a place I hope/ I never have to go through again." By breaking these and most lines in mid-thought, by not ending lines with natural pauses where punctuation marks would usually appear, the poet denies a sense of closure, forcing the reader onward from one line to the next. In addition, the enjambment allows one to read a line in several ways. In the above passage, the "I hope" at the end of the second line is first read as modifying the place, but this "hope" is shifted to the speaker in the final line. The avoidance of closure at the ends of lines reinforces the speaker's inability to find closure in his life. Although there are periods at the ends of stanzas, and although the poem comes to a dramatic finish, the closure is only partial. The speaker is left wishing he had the "guts" to escape Cumberland station but not knowing whether he does. By using enjambment, the poet reinforces the speaker's psychological confusion, a confusion that is prototypically modern.

Themes and Meanings

"Cumberland Station" was first collected in a volume entitled *Cumberland Station,* which is divided into three parts. In part 1 the speaker is near the Atlantic coast, near Tidewater, Virginia, but by the end of the first section, he has traveled to Cumberland, Maryland, a journey inland that continues through part 2, a movement to a fallen world that lacks vitality. In part 3 the speaker returns to the water (Tidewater), where there is a sense of renewal. In a poem from part 3, "Sailing the Back River," the speaker is a waterman who fishes for something other than fish; he sits in "the toy wheelhouse of fathers." He fishes the past, but he fishes to save his own life, not to rescue dead relatives, and he throws "out love/ like an anchor." While the speaker of this poem does not escape the past and does not live in a carefree land of plenty, he is optimistic, unlike the speaker in "Cumberland Station."

Images of fish, fishing, and water appear most frequently in part 3 of the collection, but they surface throughout the book, even in "Cumberland Station." In the center of the poem, the grandfather asks the speaker why he does not return to fish. On a literal level, the speaker does not fish because "soot owns even the fish" and the Potomac River is "sored," but on a symbolic level, he does not return because the town is a wasteland that he associates with too many tragedies. Fishing will not return the clean river, the healthy fish, or the dead (his nephew, his uncle, Big Daddy, or the "ash-haired kids"). In Cumberland one will only catch "bad/ news."

The mood of "Cumberland Station" is tragic. The city once offered pioneers a gateway through the mountains to the West and offered industrialists access to rich coal fields. Now, however, it is a fallen place that never fulfilled its promise. Like the Old English poets, Smith laments the loss of heroes and heroic times, the loss of what might have been—he mourns the loss of men such as Big Daddy and others who might have guided him. He also laments the modern industrial age that has fouled the Potomac to the point that one cannot fish. In addition, he laments the modern condition that allows generations to drift without moral guidance, without mentors to teach right from wrong, and without a sense of purpose or past.

Roark Mulligan

CURRICULUM VITAE

Author: Samuel Menashe (1925-   )
Type of poem: Lyric
First published: 1986, in *Collected Poems*

The Poem

"Curriculum Vitae" is a short lyric in two stanzas. It is written in verse that is not rhymed, but which uses the number of syllables in a line to organize the poem. The title means "course of life" in Latin. It refers to the brief biographical account that people (particularly academics) usually include when applying for jobs or other positions. In this poem, the phrase does not refer to an ordinary vocation: It refers to the tasks and experiences that go along with the vocation of being a poet. The title is partially ironic. When one normally hears this phrase, one expects a list of previous occupations or achievements. Instead, the poet presents a stark yet highly vivid picture of the basic texture of his daily life.

As the poem is about the life of a poet, the speaker of the poem is probably Samuel Menashe himself. The poem opens with the image of a "Scribe out of work." It is the poet himself, whom the reader assumes is not employed in a conventional, wage-earning job. This, though, is not the only meaning here. In the second and third lines, it is revealed that the poet is "At a loss for words/ Not his to begin with." The truer meaning of being out of work has to do with the momentary lapse in his poetic inspiration. The poet cannot think of what words he should write.

The first stanza concludes with a scene of the poet standing at his window, waiting for the inspiration to come so that he can write more poetry. By this time, though, the reader is alerted to this poem's nonidealistic view of the artist. The artist does not exist in a realm of perpetual rapture. The fallow moments of standing at the window are not the opposite of poetry; they are the very pauses of contemplation from which poetry may emerge.

The second stanza begins with the poet climbing up a set of stairs, presumably to his home. These are stairs that he has climbed over and over. Yet the image conveys not a sense of weariness and repetition, but one of suspense as it leads to the poem's ending. Once the poet unlocks the door of his apartment, the reader is made aware of everything he has and does not have. He does not have a family or a steady job. His recognition by the outside world is so meager that he has "No name where I live." Yet this namelessness is a paradoxical boon for his poetry. The poet is likened to an animal, alone in his lair. His power, though, is not an aggressive one, but one that turns inward. At the end, the poet sees that he has "one bone to pick/ And no time to spare." The poet confronts his frailty and his limits, yet in doing so, he comes to know what it is to live a poetic life.

Forms and Devices

Considering that it is so short and uses such simple language, "Curriculum Vitae" is a very difficult poem. The language is so compressed that it is left up to the reader to supply the connections the author does not provide. There are no words wasted; each one is crucially important.

Rhyme is not the central organizing feature of the poem. In the second stanza, there are three end words that rhyme. These words are "stairs," "lair," and "spare." This rhyme helps build up the intensity toward the self-knowledge won at the poem's close. Yet the poem's tight organization comes mainly from word choice. Most of the words in the poem are of one syllable, with a small few being of two. The brevity of the words fortifies the minimal, pared-down atmosphere of the poem. The language, like the poet's emotions, is stripped to the essential. The number of syllables in each line of the poem is also important. They are never fewer than four nor more than six. The syllable lengths provide a backbone for the poem, rigorously reining the plight of the poet in a network of form. This taut intensity makes the long, six-syllable lines peaks of energy and aspiration. It also makes lines such as "Alone in my lair" all the more affecting because the sense of loneliness in the poem is expressed by the loneliness of the few short words that make up the line.

The language used in "Curriculum Vitae" at first seems disorienting. Many of the phrases in this poem would be clichés if used in ordinary language. Examples of this are "Time and again," "Biding his time," and "At a loss for words." They do not appear clichéd in the poem, because they alone are virtually all the language that the poem has. Thus, they take on the urgency of the poem's emotional situation. The reader's empathy for the work of the poet is strengthened by the awareness that the building blocks of his art are not ready-made pieces of beauty, but the same jaded truisms with which everyone else operates.

The control maintained in "Curriculum Vitae" also makes the subject matter less exclusively personal. The poet is not indulging himself in self-pity; the poem regards him with, if not total objectivity, at least a sober detachment. This is partially achieved by the way the first stanza describes the situation from a third-person vantage point. Only in the second stanza, after the reader has focused on the poet from an external viewpoint, does he speak in the first person. The poet stages the transition between these two viewpoints by using the word "time" as the last word of the first stanza and the first word of the second stanza. The internal and external may merely be two ways of approaching the same subject, but the poet wants the reader to see both sides. By doing this, he signals that he does not wish approval as much as understanding.

Themes and Meanings

"Curriculum Vitae" addresses the reader's ideas about the work of the poet. One is used to certain stereotypical images of poets. It is familiar to see poets as wild-eyed bards, doomed and persecuted by society. Menashe's view sees the poet as living on the margins of everyday existence. Yet he sees the poet as part of that existence, not liberated or estranged from it by his art. The poet is not a better person than his fellow citizens, nor does he lead a richer and fuller life. This poet does not sit solitary in an ivory tower. As Menashe has said, "My ivory tower is in a tenement on Thompson Street." (Thompson Street is in downtown New York City, where the poet resides).

Menashe does not glorify the life of the poet. Instead, he lets the reader know that it requires extraordinary demands without necessarily producing extraordinary rewards. The poet is solitary. His is an ordinary, almost dreary solitariness, not a special one. There is an artistic breakthrough at the end of the poem, after the poet has withdrawn from the outer world into his own sphere. It is not, however, a revelation of otherworldly beauty. Instead, the poet looks inward to the very skin and bone of his own being. There is little exaltation here, and even less frenzy.

Yet the poem does not leave the reader with a sense of disillusionment. Its belief in poetry is an intense and strong one. By denying both poet and reader easy, gratifying rewards, the poem raises the stakes of the nature and meaning of being a poet. One can understand what the poetic task means more readily because one has seen that the poet is so much like everyone else in many respects. Menashe is no ordinary man. He is widely learned and holds an advanced degree from the Sorbonne, the leading French university. He is at pains to show that it is not his outer but his inner life singling him out.

In this regard, the most crucial image in the poem may be the closing: "With one bone to pick/ And no time to spare." Picking a bone indicates indulging a small, even banal grievance. The poet does this rather than pretend to create great truths. The one bone that the poet has to pick is not something outside himself, but the very marrow of his existence. The urgency and power of the poetic mission are no less normal because they are worked out within a tawdry and ordinary setting. Menashe does not link poetry to any higher cause or belief, whether religious, political, or even artistic. He lets the brute facts of the poetic experience stand on their own. Where others would see pointlessness and meaninglessness, however, Menashe sees the authentic reality of the creative act. Others might surrender or resign to the surrounding bleakness, but this poet vows to continue on with his craft.

Nicholas Birns

A CUT FLOWER

Author: Karl Shapiro (1913-2000)
Type of poem: Lyric
First published: 1942, in *The Place of Love*

The Poem

"A Cut Flower" is a poem of twenty-seven lines divided into three nine-line stanzas with no apparent rhyme scheme. Most of the lines fall into regular iambic pentameter, which means that each line has ten syllables, with five stresses, or accents, and the stress is on the second syllable in each metrical unit of two syllables. This meter is considered to mirror the natural rhythms of English speech most closely, and it contributes to the illusion that the poem is spoken testimony. Several of the lines deviate from this strict meter, which prevents the pattern from becoming monotonous and obtrusive.

From the first word, "I," it is clear that the poem is written in the first person, and by the second line it is apparent that it is not the poet speaking, but the flower itself. At the beginning of the poem the flower is growing in the ground. The first four lines speak of the freshness and beauty of the flower, qualities that attract bees who "sack my throat for kisses and suck love." The remainder of the first stanza hints that all is not well. The wind causes the flower to bend, because it is sick from lack of water and longs for rain.

The second stanza begins with a description of the creature who takes care of the flower, posed in the form of a question. The reader knows that it is a woman, and she seems to inspire love and awe with her tender acts of loosening the soil and touching the flower. The flower speculates on the origins of this creature and wonders if she is "Sent by the sun perhaps to help us grow." The remaining lines of this stanza introduce a darker theme with the opening of the seventh line, "I have seen Death," and the stanza concludes with a description of another flower, which apparently died a natural death. After opening on a positive note, the last stanza builds quickly to its conclusion. By the third line it is clear that something horrible is occurring from the speaker's point of view. The flower does not really understand what is happening, but it describes the experience of having been cut by "The thing sharper than frost" and its own subsequent sufferings in a vase of water. The stanza builds in intensity to the anguished cry of the last line: "Must I die now? Is this a part of life?"

The poem was written in 1942, when Shapiro had been in the U.S. Army for a year and was stationed in Australia. "A Cut Flower" appeared first in a privately printed collection that is not available because one of Shapiro's senior officers bought out almost the entire printing. It appeared subsequently in *Person, Place, and Thing* (1942), his first American collection, and was reprinted in *Selected Poems*, 1968.

Forms and Devices

"A Cut Flower" is a conceit, a type of intricate metaphor in which the spiritual qualities of the described subject are presented in a vehicle that shares no physical features with the subject. The vehicle in this case is the flower that wonders, questions, and tries to make sense of what he sees happening around and to him. In the first stanza, when the flower speaks of its own physical attributes, the reader accepts the idea of a talking flower, an example of the poetic device, personification. Yet by the second stanza, when the flower questions the identity of his caretaker and wonders where she comes from and where she goes, the reader understands that the poem is not about a flower. The subject is really a person who describes what is happening to him through the vehicle of the flower.

This realization that the poem is not about a flower is part of the irony used to heighten the effect of the poem. The title suggests a poem about a flower, yet a surprise occurs when it becomes apparent that the cut flower is not the true subject. Other ironies unfold. The flower wonders what kind of an animal the creature who tends him is, whereas the reader knows immediately that she is a woman tending her flower bed. The "thing sharper than frost" is recognized as scissors or garden shears, and the reader understands what is happening although the flower does not. Another irony is that the flower longs for angry rain that "bites like cold and hurts" in the first stanza, but in the last stanza the flower is "waist deep in rain," and dying. An important irony that provides tension in the poem is the difference between the flower's point of view and the woman's point of view, although the poem never describes what the woman is thinking. The reader understands that tending, cutting, and displaying the flower give the woman pleasure. Poetic compression allows the poet to suggest a great deal in a limited space.

Eight recurrent images have been identified in Shapiro's poetry. The second most common one is glass, often used to symbolize human barriers or painful confinements that must somehow be shattered to achieve release. The glass objects are typically items common in everyday life. This early poem foreshadows the prominence of Shapiro's glass imagery with the vase that will eventually be the flower's passageway to death. "My beauty leaks into the glass like rain," the flower says. The word "rain" occurs four times in the poem, twice in the first stanza and twice in the third. Rain has some of the same qualities as glass; it is transparent and, when it collects, can reflect objects.

Another use of a recurring image in Shapiro's work is the flower's confinement. Images of confinement, containment, encasement, and imprisonment abound in his poems, often in obvious ways. In "A Cut Flower," imprisonment in the vase where the flower finds itself trapped, awaiting death, is a logical outcome of the action. "Conscription Camp," "Troop Train," "Terminal," and "Garden in Chicago" are other examples of Shapiro poems that use images of confinement. In "Garden in Chicago" he finds himself confined by "elegant spears of iron fence." In another poem, "Surrounded," the poet suddenly sees his suburb confined by churches, "hemmed in by love, like Sunday." The churches themselves are surrounded by a ring of missiles with atomic warheads. Both positive and negative images can suggest confinement, and sometimes the image is both—as is the vase-enclosed flower, a lovely image that is nonetheless horrible to the flower itself.

Themes and Meanings

"A Cut Flower" is about life and death in an indifferent universe. It holds a mirror to the human condition: The flower tries to make sense of what is going on in its small world just as generation after generation of human beings have tried to make sense of theirs. At first the flower sees the world as beneficial; even when it bends from lack of rain, the woman tends it and brings it water. The flower believes that the woman is somehow a servant of the sun, sent to help it grow. The flower has mistaken the woman's purpose, however, and is horrified at what happens to it—just as human beings are sometimes shocked when their apparently benign world seems to turn on them with earthquakes, tornadoes, accidents, wars, or other disasters.

One can interpret the poem as a statement about religion without forcing the metaphor. The flower sees the sun as a divine, life-giving force and speculates that the sun may have sent the woman to tend it, yet the woman kills the flower. In the same way, human beings try to make sense of the universe and interpret as benign certain forces that in fact are indifferent; they are merely working out their own processes. Although many people have seen others die, they remain shocked at and even deny the idea of their own death. The flower understands that it is fading and tries to make sense of approaching death. The conclusion to the poem, "Is this a part of life?" is poignant and ironic, for the reader knows the answer.

Karl Shapiro was a loner whose poetry is related to, but does not completely belong to, several movements in modern poetry. Shapiro, Robert Lowell, and Randall Jarrell are the three major poets to have been influenced by the Fugitive school, a movement that flourished in the 1920's and was centered at Vanderbilt University in Nashville. The Fugitives' poetry was inclined toward irony, wit, satire, death, subtle cruelties, and indifference to suffering, many of which can be seen in "A Cut Flower." The Fugitives were a southern, regional movement, and Shapiro wrote a great many poems about the South and his place in it as a Jew. Later Shapiro was associated with the Beat generation of Allen Ginsberg, Gary Snyder, Gregory Corso, and Jack Kerouac, yet he maintained his individuality and distance.

Sheila Golburgh Johnson

DADDY

Author: Sylvia Plath (1932-1963)
Type of poem: Dramatic monologue
First published: 1965, in *Ariel*

The Poem

Written on October 12, 1962—four months before her suicide—Sylvia Plath's "Daddy" is a "confessional" poem of eighty lines divided into sixteen five-line stanzas. The persona, a daughter speaking in the first person, seeks to resolve the manifold conflicts with her father and paternal authority that have dogged her life. Her readiness for the task is unambiguously evident in the first stanza's opening lines: "You do not do, You do not do/ Anymore."

"Daddy," begins the second stanza, "I have had to kill you." The deceased, titanic patriarch, first represented as "Marble-heavy, a bag full of God," has his godliness immediately modified when he is referred to as a "Ghastly statue," with that phrase's related intimations of corpses and ghosts. The death of her father, an awesome figure with "one gray toe/ Big as a Frisco seal" and "A head in the freakish Atlantic," had not daunted the speaker's hopes of reunion; as she puts it in the third stanza, "I used to pray to recover you./ Ach du." Her belief in the power of prayer is, however, a thing of the past, no longer tenable.

The father's European roots—he is imaged as a Nazi in the fourth stanza—prove elusive to the speaker, a relatively unimportant handicap, given the significant affliction she discovers in the fifth stanza: "I never could talk to you./ The tongue stuck in my jaw." A less circumscribed and more dire speechlessness emerges in the sixth stanza.

In the seventh stanza, the Holocaust is introduced, and the speaker recovers her powers of speech in the context—if not as a result—of having pointedly established herself as a Jew. A couple of overworked Nazi emblems are demythologized in stanza 8: "The snows of Tyrol, the clear beer of Vienna/ Are not very pure or true," while she identifies herself with gypsies, another group much hated by the Nazis. In stanza 9, she brazenly mocks Fascist discourse as "gobbledygoo," and does much the same to her father's Nazi image: "And your neat mustache/ And your Aryan eye, bright blue./ Panzer-man, panzer-man, O You—." When, in stanza 10, one reads "Not God but a swastika/ So black no sky could squeak through," one is confronted with a profoundly potent evil capable of overwhelming the heavens.

The penultimate patriarchal image appears in stanza 11: father as teacher-cum-devil. Although, she recalls, "You stand at the blackboard, daddy,/ In the picture I have of you," the innocuous snapshot of a pedagogue does not distract her from perceiving the father's demoniac nature. The hauntingly sadistic image, in the twelfth stanza, of the father who, before dying, "Bit my pretty red heart in two," is juxtaposed with her vain pursuit of him ten years hence, in an attempted suicide. Failing at that, she tries, in stanzas 13 and 14, a more effective, somewhat less self-destructive tactic: "I made a model of you/ A man in black with a Meinkampf look/ And a love of the rack and the screw," and marries the surrogate.

Predatory and erotic, the ruinous, eerie image of the father as vampire in stanza 15 anticipates the speaker's ritualistic solution. "There's a stake in your fat black heart/ And the villagers never liked you," begins the poem's sixteenth and final stanza. The speaker's decisive, triumphant patricide permits her to say, "Daddy, daddy, you bastard, I'm through," and, for the first time, call her life her own.

Forms and Devices

Given the emotionally damaged speaker's mercurial discourse and her father's protean nature, Plath's characterizations of the two and their interrelations—particularly the series of continually modulating images of the father—are among the most psychologically sound, aesthetically impeccable, and effective formal accomplishments in "Daddy."

There is a significant conceptual corollary to the poem's frequent nursery-rhyme rhythms when, in the first stanza, the speaker echoes, with wit and irony, the nursery rhyme about the "old woman who lived in a shoe . . . [who] didn't know what to do." This character, however, is a woman who knows exactly what to do in order to end her thirty-year habitation in her old man's shoe and to exorcize the related intimidation, control, passivity, and entrapment: She must commit a symbolic patricide.

For all the speaker's strident declamations, however, there is nothing to obscure the fact that hers is an ambivalent discourse. Savior and tormentor, the object of nostalgic affection and vituperation—these are the conflicting dualisms that form her troubled attachment to the first man in her life (and to his reincarnation, her husband), dualisms that have set the terms of her persecution and imprisonment. Although she "used to pray to recover [her father]," her present goal, transformed by experience, no longer aimed at *re*covering, is to *un*cover—to lay bare the inventory of her heart's wounds, which shaped and dogged the future, all father-inflicted during childhood. The resulting narrative, awash with untrammeled emotion, produces an intricately wrought compound image of the father.

The permutations that produce the compound image of the father follow a devolving trajectory. In broad terms, the father, first imaged as a god of titanic proportions (stanza 2), is transformed in short order into a sadistic devil (stanza 11) before being finally described as a vampire (stanza 15). Introduced as a worshiped and scorned god-cadaver-statue, the paternal image is modulated and degenerated into the image of a viciously racist, sadistically misogynistic Nazi. When, with bitter irony, the speaker says, "Every woman adores a Fascist," the statement is cast as an affront to feminist sensibilities, so typical is it of male presumptions about what "every woman" wants. The feminist theme continues into the succeeding image of the father as teacher-devil, as traditional gender roles would typically represent, as complementary images, male tutors and untutored females. The semantically dense imagery and characterization that occur here are typical of Plath's poetry.

In the poem's final degenerative permutation, the speaker integrates her father and husband into a single ghastly image of a vampire, a parasitic male who has been drinking her lifeblood. The father's precipitous fall from deity to evil incarnate, conveyed in the serial pattern of paternal imagery, sets up the poem's denouement: a ritual killing of evil, the one necessary prerequisite for the speaker to regain a life worthy of the name.

Themes and Meanings

In the course of discussing Sylvia Plath's poetry, Joyce Carol Oates has contended that the poet did not like other people because she doubted "that they existed in the way that she did, as pulsating, breathing, suffering individuals." The ostensible subject of "Daddy" is the speaker's somewhat belated acknowledgment of her unhealthy attachment to and anger toward her father, and her eagerness to explode the Oedipal prisonhouse in which she has been captive so that she might have a life that is truly her own. Accordingly, it could be said that "Daddy" is about individual freedom and two of its principal prerequisites: self-knowledge and courage.

Like all good poetry, "Daddy" raises many questions, none of which is more compelling than "What is the speaker's understanding of the predicament from which she seeks to escape?" Certainly, the sincerity of her testimony is as apparent as her anguish and rage. She speaks as if she were the victim of an error that her current insights empower her to rectify. Herein lies a major source of the poem's pathos: Plath's speaker fails to detect the resemblance between her situation and that of the Greek hero for whom Sigmund Freud named her presumed psychopathology: Oedipus. She suffers from the intractable consequences of fate.

Her account also implies a subscription to a bizarre mutation of the doctrine of Original Sin, whose central postulate is that all errors are the result of unconscious guilt. This moral drama entails two shaky assumptions: that the world is just and that, despite all contrary evidence, people who suffer have only themselves to blame. Dorothy Van Ghent, however, once pointedly asked about tragic heroes: "Is one guilty for circumstances?" One must deal tactfully if not compassionately with human fictions—while under one's breath lamenting their folly—and Plath's speaker surely deserves such consideration. Unfortunately, redefining herself and reclaiming her life by assuming full responsibility for her dilemma offer the same prospects for complete success as railing at the world for not being just. Perhaps Plath understood the speaker's inadequate sense of her situation sufficiently for suicide to emerge in her life as the more decisive, if unhappy, alternative.

Jordan Leondopoulos

THE DANCE

Author: William Carlos Williams (1883-1963)
Type of poem: Lyric
First published: 1944, in *The Wedge*

The Poem

William Carlos Williams's "The Dance" consists of twelve lines of rhythmic verse written in response to a painting by Pieter Bruegel the Elder (c. 1525-1569). The painting, "The Kermess," or "Peasant Dance," depicts sturdy, well-fed peasants on holiday—dancing, drinking, making music, venting the sexual impulse, and abandoning themselves to the spirit of carnival. Williams's poem captures the hearty vitality that the painting evokes. Through concrete visual and auditory images and through the strong, measured rhythm, Williams renders the hearty jubilance of common, working folk enjoying a day of recreation. The celebrants in the poem dance with vigor: They "go round, they go round and/ around" to the "squeal and the blare and the/ tweedle of bagpipes." In their portliness, they tip "their bellies" (and they might be a little tipsy), which are "round as the thick-/ sided glasses whose wash they impound. . . . Kicking and rolling about/ the Fair Grounds, swinging their butts" to the "rollicking measures," they "prance as they dance." Yet this seemingly formless abandon is shaped through the traditional, communal forms of the folk dance, just as, through the discipline of language and measure, the poem is given form and structure.

Williams was fascinated by Bruegel's scenes of peasant life with all its drudgery, its matter-of-fact violence, its ugliness, and its enduring vitality. In fact, Williams titled a series of poems *Pictures from Brueghel* (1962); "The Dance," however, had been written earlier and was not included in this collection. The word *kermess* (or *kermis*) in Bruegel's title and in Williams's first line refers to an outdoor fair or carnival, but it originally meant the celebration of a local patron saint; thus, the dancers in the painting and in the poem celebrate both a holiday and a holy day. Their vigorous dance and rough festivities extol the value of life vis-à-vis the inevitable dissolution of death. They set traditional religious values in abeyance to give an airing to the desires of the flesh: lust, gluttony, and ribaldry. Their return to their everyday lives of labor and abstemiousness will be rendered more endurable by the earthy sensuality of the holy day.

Forms and Devices

"The Dance" evokes, through the medium of words, the emotions that the picture, through the medium of paint on canvas, rouses in the viewer. The circular shapes of the painting—the full-fleshed bodies of the dancers as well as their fat faces and rounded heads, the round ewer and tankards that hold the "wash," the bladder-shaped bagpipes, the bouffant skirts of the women—as well as the circular movement the painting demands of the viewer—find poetic expression in the circular shape of the poem. The eye device of the parentheses also reproduces the circle—"(round as the thick-/ sided glasses whose wash they impound)"—as does the repetition of the word "round": "the dancers go round, they go round and/ around."

Just as the peasants in the picture dance heedlessly forward, so Williams's poem moves forward at breakneck speed. The enjambed lines provide no stopping point. Williams ends line 2 with the conjunction "and"; he separates the article "the" and the adjectives "those" and "such" from the nouns they modify; he separates the preposition "about" from its object; he even hyphenates a word ("thick-") at the end of a line. There are no capital letters at the beginnings of lines to provide a new beginning. The poem's beginning and ending with the same line not only reproduces the circular movement of the painting but also suggests something endless. When the poem arrives at the last line, it has returned to its beginning; thus, the poem could go on forever, just as the life of the peasant, timeless and eternal, is symbolized by the circle.

Williams also paid careful attention to what he called "measure," which he opposed to "free verse." Eight of the twelve lines contain nine syllables; each of the twelve lines contains either three or four stresses, with variable feet. The first line contains four stresses—"In Breughel's great picture, The Kermess"—with the word "great" getting full stress. Thus the poem begins with a rough, irregular rhythm, just as the dancers in the painting might get off to a halting start; they then begin to move with the measure of the music, as the next two lines exhibit a more regular rhythm, with three stresses each. Williams uses the variable foot in other places as well to evoke the coarse rhythms and the uneven measures of the dance itself—"Kicking and rolling about/ the Fair Grounds, swinging their butts." One can imagine the peasants good-naturedly clashing into each other during their spirited dance. The only full caesura occurs at the period in the middle of line 8, which crashes to a sudden stop, and then the poem rollicks forward again.

The onomatopoetic diction suggests the cacophonous music that fills the hamlet: "the squeal and the blare and the/ tweedle of bagpipes, a bugle and fiddles." Much of the diction is colloquial: The dancers swing "their butts," they tip "their bellies," the dancers have sound "shanks," their "hips and their bellies [are] off balance." Such usage, although twentieth century American, suggests the kind of language that these dancers, unhampered by the demands of polite society, might use. The internal rhyme of "prance as they dance" is the only rhyme of the poem, but the assonance of "dance," "blare," "glasses," and "shanks" suggests the cacophonous "rollicking measures" of the musicians. The word "wash" is an unexpected and appropriate choice of words, connoting a cheap, undistilled liquor such as peasants might drink. The fact that the peasants "impound" it connotes several meanings; one meaning of the word is to gather a liquid (which they have done), but it also carries overtones of something slightly illegal (as in "impounding a document"), and it takes the vague coloring of animals (as in "impounding an animal"). These peasants have impounded the wash, and their unselfconscious animal instincts dominate for the day.

"The Dance," by re-creating a moment, stands as a powerful antidote to those who think a poem should have "meaning." It lets the readers participate vicariously in the celebrations of simple people who live not by the intellect but by the powerful rhythms of the earth.

Themes and Meanings

"The Dance" reveals several of Williams's preoccupations as a poet, preoccupations that mark him as a modernist. First, he said, a poem demands careful attention to the object itself without consideration of the object's meaning. "No ideas but in things," he declares. "The Dance" concentrates on a single moment in time. Yet because it focuses so closely on the details of that moment, the dance acts as a synecdoche for the cultural life that the poem depicts. Beginning as an Imagist, although he later disassociated himself from the movement over its insistence on free verse and called himself an Objectivist, Williams remained true to the Imagist principle of depicting the "thing" or the object itself through vivid images without reference to what the image may symbolize.

Another of Williams's modernist concerns was to find or invent a new language for poetry that would render a new way of seeing. He found part of the answer to this problem in the colloquial speech patterns of the ordinary American. Ironically, the language of "The Dance," by being based on the speech of twentieth century working people, captures the spirit of sixteenth century Dutch peasants.

Third, Williams believed that to be universal, an experience must be lived fully within the local. In "The Dance," peasants celebrate a holiday that is entirely local. The peasants' life is by necessity confined to the local, but they live in it fully and with great verve; they work hard and they play hard—they dance.

Throughout Williams's lifelong career as a doctor in his native New Jersey, he was necessarily tied to the chthonic: He dealt in birth and death, delivered babies, and treated people's sometimes embarrassing ailments. He perceived that the instinctual life, which urban conditions have almost bred and educated out of men and women in the twenty-first century, is a necessity for meaningful existence. That instinctual life is less confined in the conditions of simple people like the ones in Bruegel's painting than in those of twentieth century urban society. Rural people—peasants—see life as a constantly revolving wheel, manifest in the recurring holy days, and this cycle of life is especially expressed in dance.

Williams was fascinated by the dance in all its forms; in fact, he wrote two different poems entitled "The Dance" (although the second one is not so well known as the earlier poem), and he wrote of dancing in several poems. He liked to dance himself, although he acknowledged that his own efforts lacked finesse; in fact, he chuckled at his own satyr-like style. Williams saw the dance as an ancient, life-renewing ritual. Through dance, he believed, men and women reenact enduring myth. Dance celebrates a moment when linear time crosses vertical time—when the temporal crosses the universal. The spirit celebrated in "The Dance" is innate in humankind, and for twenty-first century men and women, its life and vigor and earthiness, chastened by the form and structure of art, provide a much-needed antidote to the disease which ails them.

Jo N. Farrar

DANCE SCRIPT WITH ELECTRIC BALLERINA

Author: Alice Fulton (1952-　　)
Type of poem: Lyric
First published: 1983, in *Dance Script with Electric Ballerina*

The Poem

"Dance Script with Electric Ballerina," at eighty-four lines, is one of Alice Fulton's longer poems; it is an important one because it provides insight into Fulton's artistic objectives. Written in four stanzas of varying length, the free-verse poem presents the persona of a ballerina dancing and discussing her theory of dance. At times the ballerina seems to be addressing the ballet's audience, but at other times she seems to be speaking to a sympathetic co-conspirator, perhaps a fellow ballerina.

The poem begins with the ballerina "limbering up" before going on stage while explaining that she will not be performing the familiar, conventional ballet the audience might be anticipating; she warns, "If you expected sleeping/ beauty sprouting from a rococo/ doughnut of tulle, a figurine/ fit to top a music box, you might want/ your money back." As opposed to these visions of stylized female beauty, Fulton's ballerina wants to be "electric," with a "getup/ functional as light:/ feet bright and precise as eggbeaters,/ fingers quick as switch-/ blades and a miner's lamp for my tiara." In this way, the "electric ballerina" suggests the goals behind her rather unorthodox "dance script"—not grace, beauty, and lightness but power, daring, and illumination.

Fulton's ballerina is aware that her unusual aesthetic choices might not be well received. She notes that although ballet audiences like to discuss "brio" (vigor) and "ballon" (the lightness of a jump that seems to make the ballerina float in the air longer than possible), "spectators prefer/ gestures that don't endanger/ body and soul." In contrast, Fulton's ballerina seems to value what endangers, because the spectators' fear or surprise might shock them from passivity and cause them to reevaluate beauty. An excerpt from Fulton's journal, published in *The Poet's Notebook* (1995), sheds some light on this poem. Fulton discusses the Scottish dancer/choreographer Michael Clark. Clark has his dancers "gasp for breath above the music" in order to make an audience "aware of the effort." Clark sees "the hint of disequilibrium as a gain," and so does Fulton's ballerina, who is not interested in presenting a smooth, seamless ballet. Instead, she wants her "leaps angular and brief" to have the same disjointed and startling quality that Clark's choreography has.

As the poem progresses, the ballerina begins dancing. Predictably, the dance critics who watch the ballet do not understand what she is striving to accomplish. The second stanza ends with an italicized section which presents the criticisms that they will, presumably, publish in their reviews. The critics mistake her deliberate attempt to present the "strain" which is "a reminder/ of the pain that leads to grace" as ineptitude. They fault the ballerina for being "*ragged barbaric hysterical*" and say that she lacks "*authority fluency restraint*," among other things.

As the ballerina nears the end of her dance, she "can sense the movement/ notators' strobe vision/ picking the bones of flux into/ positions." Like a strobe light, the critics have only flashes of illumination, and their dependence on naming recognized positions shows how they are trapped by the conventions of time and space, absolutes which she battles to overcome as she dances. Instead of passively watching and labeling, the ballerina wants them to enjoy the gaps, to "see the gulf/ between gestures as a chance/ to find clairvoyance." Ultimately, however, the critics are too limited by their own conventions to understand her particular brand of iconoclasm. The ballerina wishes for a metaphor or model with which she could make the critics understand her; she seems to feel that such an understanding may one day be possible, but "till then" she is at a "stand-/ still" as she strikes her final position. She notes that "my chest heaves,/ joints shift, eyes dart—" rather defiantly reminding the reader that even then, despite appearances, she is still dancing.

Forms and Devices

In this poem Fulton does not heavily rely on some of the traditional poetic devices available to a poet, such as rhyme and meter, but other devices she uses with great skill. Fulton's choice of line breaks makes an interesting study, for example. On the page, "Dance Script with Electric Ballerina" looks somewhat ragged because the lines are of varying lengths and are not cordoned off into even-length stanzas. Here form reflects theme, because the ballerina is arguing in favor of ragged edges and "disequilibrium." In addition, Fulton uses her line breaks to create a rhythm that can pull the rug out from under the reader's feet. After strongly end-stopped lines, she might break a hyphenated word in half; this sudden enjambment leads to a halting music. Often Fulton, like the poet Marianne Moore before her, uses line breaks to underscore wit or puns. When Fulton cautions that the audience might want a refund if they expected "sleeping/ beauty," her line break reveals what audiences are really after when they choose such sugary, harmless concoctions—a type of reassuring stupor in which no one is changed because no one is challenged.

Another way that the poem seeks to disrupt equilibrium is by presenting sudden and shifting metaphors and rapidly juxtaposed images. The dancer asks, "You've seen kids on Independence Day, waving/ sparklers to sketch their initials on the night?" She continues, "Just so, I'd like to leave a residue/ of slash and glide, a trace-/ form on the riled air." The ballerina's language does "slash and glide" through the poem, shifting from one metaphor to another; moreover, the metaphors are all located in different worlds. Fulton follows her "strobe" metaphor with one from the world of geography, "fissures," followed by a "footage" metaphor from the film industry, in turn followed by mention of an "electrocardiograph," from the world of medicine. In this way the poet reproduces for the readers the unsettling effects of the ballet, hoping that the readers now have enough insight into her methods to rise above the critics' shortsightedness. Instead of requiring familiar "positions," the readers should enjoy the "flux" and leap the gulfs with the ballerina. As Fulton noted in an interview (*TriQuarterly*, 1995), gaps and gulfs are important to her concept of poetry; she questions "continuity and unity. . . . My notion of poetry itself suggests quick cuts—those moves that used to be called poetic leaps. They allow the readers to fill in the gaps and participate by recreating the poem's meaning in their own minds." Fulton, in relying on what is not on the page as well as what is written there, is influenced by Emily Dickinson; Fulton's admiration for Dickinson continued to deepen in her books that came after *Dance Script with Electric Ballerina*, such as *Sensual Math* (1995).

Themes and Meanings

On one level, "Dance Script with Electric Ballerina" is very clearly about a ballerina discussing her moves and delineating her beliefs about the correct aim for dance. Another layer of meaning is present, however: Fulton is presenting her own poetic credo; she hopes to do on the page what her ballerina does in performance.

Many images and metaphors in the poem can be read as pertaining to both dance and poetry. Early in the poem the dancer describes her "script" by saying, "I've dispensed with some conventions// I'm out to disprove the limited orbit of fingers." While one might first interpret this line to mean that the dancer wants to use her material—parts of her body, such as her hands—in new ways, Fulton also tries to use her material to push beyond the "limited orbit of fingers"—the expected output from a writer's hand. Within the italicized section of critics' comments, many statements could have come from literary, not dance, reviewers. For example, the only positive critic in the section states, "*I'm mildly impressed/ by her good line*," a comment which could easily refer to a poet.

In addition to using metaphors that can be read in two ways, Fulton uses metaphors that directly apply to writing. The ballerina wants to be like sparkler-waving children who "sketch their initials on the night." She talks of the "air patterns/ where I distill the scribbling moves" and wishes that her dance moves left a physical trace in the air that could be read like a language. She dreams of a perfect understanding when the critics overcome their lack of imagination but knows that until such communication can take place, she is only "signing space," and her signature so far is unintelligible to the critics.

If Fulton had tried to write a poem that only discussed her poetic credo, the poem might have failed because of self-consciousness. By creating her ballerina, Fulton wisely does two things at once: She presents a character who provides insight into the world of dance, and she articulates her unconventional views of what a poem should do. "Dance Script with Electric Ballerina" might serve as an introduction to the rest of Fulton's work. After seeing the dance critics fail because of their faulty expectations, her readers have enough information to judge her work more fairly. They should not expect a sugar-coated, soothing kind of poetry for a passive reader but a poetry that needs a fellow dancer to complete the electrical current she has begun.

Beth Ann Fennelly

DANNY DEEVER

Author: Rudyard Kipling (1865-1936)
Type of poem: Narrative
First published: 1890, in *Departmental Ditties, Barrack-Room Ballads, and Other Verses*

The Poem

"Danny Deever" is a description of a military execution: the hanging of a British soldier in India for the murder of another soldier in his own regiment. In a combination of responsorial verse reminiscent of a ballad or a hymn, and the observations of a third party, the structure of the four-stanza poem uses the common speech and points of view of representative members of the nineteenth century British army to express one of the most harsh demands of military life.

Danny Deever is the guilty soldier, but the reader learns of this only after an introductory question-and-answer half-stanza. The opening question, "What are the bugles blowin' for?" is asked by Files-on-Parade, a single voice that represents all the soldiers being "turned out" (called to formation); they are the files of "rank and file." Files asks his questions of the Colour-Sergeant, who would have been, in Kipling's time, a noncommissioned officer promoted for distinguished service, a soldier of significantly more experience than his juniors. The elder's face is white, and he is afraid of what he must watch. Why, when he has seen more of war than his subordinates? The observer makes the moment clear: Danny is to be hanged. The regiment is formed ("in 'ollow square"), and the prisoner is ritualistically stripped of the signs of his profession: the buttons on his uniform and the insignia of his rank.

Files then asks for explanations of his observance of behaviors that are not soldierly. In a formal military ceremony, some men are falling out of ranks breathing hard when the rapt stillness of attention is required. The Colour-Sergeant appears to make excuses—the sun, or the cold, has caused these things—but these accountings are as curt as the replies in the first stanza. They are the answers of a man with his own thoughts. The observer notes that Danny is paraded in front of his comrades and walked by his own coffin, and then he clearly indicates that Deever is "a sneakin', shootin' hound–."

Files then exclaims, with perhaps a tone of incredulity, that he has shared, as all soldiers do, the closeness and friendship of barracks life with the doomed man. Danny's cot was close to his, and Danny treated him to a drink many times. The observer sternly states that such things may be true, but those are not the soldiers' concerns now. Danny committed the unspeakable act of killing a comrade in his sleep, so the members of the regiment must face him even as they attend to his execution.

Finally, Files asks about indications that Danny's passing is one of darkness and struggle, and the Colour-Sergeant essentially concurs, although he does not explain why. From the view of the observer, the reader see the regiment march away. The observer gets the last word: The younger soldiers are severely shaken, "an' they'll want their beer to-day."

Forms and Devices

Rudyard Kipling, born in India, raised during the height of the British Empire, the first English writer to win the Nobel Prize, was immensely popular, and he served for some time as a "national voice." He told stories to common countrymen of the travails and hardships of soldiers and sailors far away from home, and he used the accented speech of the lower classes to tell them. "Danny Deever" combines that colloquial context with a question-and-answer conversation that brings with it the tradition of old English ballads. The rhythm, particularly the alliteration of the opening line and the repetition of the response, is militaristic and suggests a march from the outset.

The construction of the first half of each stanza is revealing. In the first, the Colour-Sergeant's repetitious responses to Files's questions are dismissive; Files mocks him with his next question, and the Colour-Sergeant is suddenly serious and revealing. In the second stanza, the Colour-Sergeant is again brusque and so quick to answer Files's pestering questions that only the reader sees the contradictions in his answers. After all, the weather cannot be both hot and cold, so there must be another explanation for the soldiers' behavior.

By the third stanza, Files is disturbed and confused at the circumstances in which he finds himself, and he probably does not understand the Colour-Sergeant's answers. The latter expresses Files's observations as one would describe a soldier in the field, away from post ("sleepin' out an' far") and away from his mates, "drinkin' beer alone." The Colour-Sergeant is saddened at these circumstances, while Files is unnerved. In the last stanza, the rhythm of each of the two speakers is the same, as the experienced and the neophyte soldier watch the same event, Danny's death, at the same time.

The observer is situated in an interesting, and interested, fashion. He can overhear the conversation between Files and the Colour-Sergeant. His comments illuminate the give-and-take of the two speakers and slowly reveal the context in which the two soldiers discuss what is happening. He knows what is about to happen before Files does. He knows that Danny is the worst kind of criminal. He essentially tells Files and the Colour-Sergeant, at the end of the third stanza, that they must both "look 'im in the face" and admit to the horrible fact that they must participate in killing one of their own for killing one of their own.

Finally, in the fourth stanza, the reader sees that the observer is himself a soldier: "The regiment's in column, and they're marching us away." "Us" is the important word. He has overheard the conversation because he is in the ranks. In addition, his position allows him to note with certainty, but without condescension, and even with sympathy, that the forty-four "young recruits are shakin', an' they'll want their beer to-day." He is more experienced than either of the other men, and his position is intellectual. He has seen these things before, more often than has the Colour-Sergeant, and he knows what this ceremony means.

Themes and Meanings

"Danny Deever" captures the irony, comradeship, and demands of military life in a single ceremony. Those who serve in the military are expected to endure hardship, face death, obey orders, and do all these things willingly even though they may not have the experience to understand what is being asked of them.

Danny is the focus of the poem, but the stories Kipling tells are of the three other characters. In civilian society, the state carries out the trials, sentencing, and punishment of those who do wrong. In the military, all those functions are performed by the same organization of which the accused is a member. In Kipling's time, life in a regiment in India was arduous, but for many soldiers the army was the closest thing to a family they had ever known. The unit was hierarchical, to be sure, even castelike, but the business of fighting and protecting the empire was for many an adventure. Men relied upon one another, and on their shared experience, to enjoy the few things they could and to survive in battle.

Imagine then, the shock of finding a murderer in the midst of the regiment—and then realizing the irony that those who have put others to death must now do the same thing to a soldier who was once a friend. Hanging Danny is just as much a requirement, a mission, as fighting in battle, and it must be carried out in the same professional manner. From the inexperience, fear, and insecurity of Files, to the experienced and wiser Colour-Sergeant, to the observer, the chain of thematic effect is built. The conversationalists are the foundation, but the house of the army is built by those who know what the observer knows.

He knows that the ceremony begins with the Dead March, that all who commit crimes of the magnitude of murder will, eventually, see their own coffin. Yet he also knows that the man who made himself "nine 'undred of 'is county an' the Regiment's disgrace" must still somehow be considered a comrade and that the others must appreciate his fight for life and recognize the passing of his soul. Knowing all that, the observer thinks only that the soldiers will want beer to calm them, not sympathy or an explanation of the ways of the world and the army. They must learn those things for themselves. The final irony is certainly that of Files-on-Parade, for he, the youngest, the one who is too young to have seen battle, sees his first death not on the field but in his own camp.

David P. Smith

DARK HARBOR

Author: Mark Strand (1934-   )
Type of poem: Poetic sequence
First published: 1993

The Poem

Dark Harbor is a book-length poem in unrhymed verse, divided into forty-five sections that are identified sequentially by roman numerals. There is also an introduction in verse entitled "Proem." Each section, including "Proem," is written in tercets, but six of the sections end with stanzas of only one or two lines.

The title resonates with echoes of some of Strand's earlier books: *Sleeping with One Eye Open*, his first book of poems; *Reasons for Moving*, probably fueled by his life as the son of a salesman who moved his family too often for them to form long-term relationships with other people; and *Darker*, perhaps the first of Strand's books to convince the critics that his apparent preoccupation with the darker aspects of life was actually a vehicle for explorations of the human ability to find the light hidden in the darkness. Beyond these first three books, all of Strand's books of poetry (and even his children's books) push and pull readers through the dark harbors of the human journey.

Although *Dark Harbor* is not a narrative poem in the classic sense of a work that has a definable beginning, middle, and end, it has a combined sense of form and unity that gives it the sort of through-line of thought that one normally expects from a narrative. The narrator of the poem is a poet on a journey, an odyssey that takes him through a return to his places (both physical and spiritual) of origin and eventually brings him to a place of closure.

Each of the forty-five numbered sections is written from the first-person perspective of the narrator, but "Proem" is written from the perspective of an omniscient narrator. This narrator serves as a sort of Greek chorus who introduces the narrator of all that is to follow, the poet/narrator: " 'This is my Main Street,' he said as he started off/ That morning, leaving the town to the others." These opening lines set the stage for the poet/narrator to take the reader on a journey. Halfway through "Proem" comes the first hard evidence that the narrator who is being introduced is indeed a poet, almost certainly Strand himself or an image of himself that he wants to project for the reader: "he would move his arms/ And begin to mark, almost as a painter would,/ The passages of greater and lesser worth, the silken/ Tropes and calls to this or that, coarsely conceived."

In section I the narrator describes the place of departure for the journey to come. He is in a dark place lighted by streetlamps, but he is wearing a white suit that outshines the moon. "In the night without end," others await his arrival at "the station" before they begin their journey somewhere beyond those still on Earth. In section II he describes the village or hamlet as a place where the reader has never been, a place where there are no trains or places for planes to land. (One might wonder from what sort of station they departed.) It is somewhere in the West that has considerable wind and snow. It is a place where people are not up on fashion and sleep well at night, an indication that those who dwell here have cleaner consciences than people elsewhere.

In section III the place begins to sound more like a small town. Midway through this section the narrator provides a bit of information that appears to contradict what he had said earlier about the reader having never been to this place: "And you pass by unsure if this coming back is a failure/ Or a sign of success, a sign that the time has come/ To embrace your origins as you would yourself." It is possible to interpret this "you" as the travelers that were waiting for him at the beginning of the journey or as someone to whom the reader has not been introduced. Throughout this poem it is often difficult to discern the identity of the narrator's "you." The final tercet of this section might even suggest that the narrator is referring to himself in the second person: "life looked to be simpler back in the town/ You started from look, there in the kitchen are Mom and Dad,/ He's reading the paper, she's killing a fly." It is possible that there is no single "you" consistent throughout the poem. Each usage could be relative to its particular section, leaving the reader to discern identity from the context.

Overall, the narrator paints a picture of returning home to the small town that he left long ago to live in a large city. Most of the sections are vignettes of the narrator's rediscovery or new evaluation of this small town, his place of origin. However, some of the sections are so abstract that they add little, if anything, to the geography of the poem. They appear more as commentaries on life in general. A few others make such sudden turns into sarcasm that they come across as comic, but the comedy, in perfect keeping with the title and the general mood of the poem, is always dark.

The final section, XLV, rounds out the collection by echoing elements of the first two sections: the cottages, unidentified people grouped together, angels singing, images of life after death. It gives both a feeling of completion and a sense of the cyclical nature of everything. This is the dark harbor of souls.

Forms and Devices

The first easily recognized device the poet uses in *Dark Harbor* is the introductory poem, "Proem." This is not a proem in the sense that some critics now use the term, a portmanteau created by combining the words "prose" and "poem." It is a proem in the classical sense—an introductory passage to a longer work that provides clues to the nature and origin of the work that is to follow.

Ironically, *Dark Harbor* reads very much like a prose poem. The rhythms are dictated more by syntax than by lineation. Strand uses a combination of three physical devices to give the poem a structured, poemlike appearance. First, he breaks the poem into lines; there are usually between ten and fifteen syllables to each line, but this is by no means a strict rule. Sometimes the lines end on weak or unstressed words, but the breaks usually wrap logically into the next line. Second, he begins each line with an uppercase letter. This accomplishes two things: It emphasizes the line breaks, and it adds a touch of formality, a punctuating element that helps define each line as a component that exists both within and outside of syntax. Third, he breaks each section into tercets. This gives a consistent appearance to all forty-five sections of the poem as well as "Proem," and it serves as a framing device, using white space to sometimes enhance, sometimes override the ostensible logic of the syntax. It also adds another element of formality that complements the high level of diction and wide variety of sentence structures employed throughout the poem.

Form is essential in all of Strand's poetry. In his essay "Notes on the Craft of Poetry," published in *Claims for Poetry* (Donald Hall, ed., 1982) Strand writes:

> [A]ll poetry is formal in that it exists within limits, limits that are either inherited by tradition or limits that language itself imposes. . . . [F]orm has to do with the structure or outward appearance of something but it also has to do with its essence. . . . [S]tructure and essence seem to come together, as do the disposition of words and their meanings.

For Strand, poetry is a marriage of form and function, and, for better or worse, without both elements there is no marriage, therefore, no poetry.

The most common and interesting images in *Dark Harbor* are those one sees upon looking up: stars, clouds, the sky, moon, sun, falling snow, even angels. These images do not, as might be expected, serve as counterpoints to the dark images of the earth and earthbound things, implying a good-versus-evil dialogue. Rather, they are symbolic of those elusive qualities that define the human spirit as distinctly different from anything else in nature. The dark is not a place of evil; it is simply a point of departure, a place from which people start their quests and inquiries. The light is what one seeks, and Strand is critical of anyone who belittles that. "O you can make fun of the splendors of moonlight,/ But what would the human heart be if it wanted/ Only the dark, wanted nothing on earth/ But the sea's ink or the rock's black shade?"

There are no intentional end rhymes in this poem, but alliterations are not uncommon. Section XXVII makes good use of anaphora, the first six of the seven tercets beginning with the same word, and of alliterations and assonance. Together these tropes add a rich musical quality and an air of nobility to this particular section.

The overall tone of the poem is elegiac, but there are a few sections that provide comic relief, sometimes bordering on zaniness (as in section XIX, the shortest section) and sometimes slipping into a sarcastic mode that adds a different kind of bite to a work that already has a formidable set of teeth. Surrealism is the order of the day. From the very first scene, in which the unnamed group of travelers bands together to begin the journey from darkness, to the final scene, in which there are rumors of dead poets wandering, wishing "to be alive again," everything seems to happen somewhere between dream and reality. Strand's choices of forms and poetic devices give each section of this poem an individual character that allows each to stand on its own. Overall, the same choices give *Dark Harbor* the power of one uniform work that drives all of its component parts in a single direction.

Themes and Meanings

In her 1994 review of *Dark Harbor* for *Antioch Review*, Judith Hall said that the theme of the poem "is the poet's counterlife in art, from his initial departure from the enclosure of family and home, to his journey through a place of darkness and uncertainty, to his final sense of safe harbor within the community of other poets." At least in part, this could have been said about any of Strand's books. Strand has often been criticized for solipsism, an extreme form of concern for self, but these accusations have not deterred him from his search for self nor from his conviction that poetry is his means of discovery.

This is not to say that Strand sees only himself; nothing could be further from the truth. He, like all poets, is constantly examining, evaluating, and speculating about life. By unrelentingly seeking a clearer picture of himself within life and creating poems as windows through which to view his explorations, he makes it possible for those who lack his particular vision to become part of his quest.

More than any of his previous books, *Dark Harbor* exhibits Strand's concern with the community of poets, both living and dead, that has helped shape him as a poet and that continues to influence his poetry. No artist creates in a vacuum, and no poet seems more aware of this than Strand. He has often mentioned a handful of poets that have greatly influenced his work, and a few poets seem to drop in and out of this group. One who is always there, however, whether Strand is talking about himself or whether a critic is talking about him, is Elizabeth Bishop. Although their styles are very different, both wrote often about the relationships of art to life and life to art. The angels that appear and disappear in *Dark Harbor* are poets that have died, and it is not unreasonable to think that the last angel in the book, "one of the good ones, about to sing," is Bishop.

As might well be expected, darkness is one of the major themes of *Dark Harbor*. This darkness is not a Joseph Conrad type of darkness, an impending doom or a void into which one falls and from which one never returns. Strand's darkness creates more an air of nostalgia. It is a world of dreams in which the darkness is usually earthbound with at least some touch of heaven within reach. Sometimes, however, Strand's heaven is within the darkness or, as in section VIII, darkness, death, and heaven are inseparably bound to one another:

> . . . Oh my partner, my beautiful death,
> My black paradise, my fusty intoxicant,
> My symbolist muse, give me your breast
> Or your hand or your tongue that sleeps all day
> Behind its wall of reddish gums.
> Lay yourself down on the restaurant floor
> And recite all that's been kept from my happiness.
> Tell me I have not lived in vain, that the stars
> Will not die, that things will stay as they are,
> That what I have seen will last, that I was not born
> Into change, that what I have said has not been said for me.

This passage expresses one of the greatest fears of poets and other artists, the fear that their ideas and creations are either ephemeral or simply add nothing new. It also expresses a fear held by many people, artists and nonartists, that the world will change so much that nothing currently considered sacred will endure.

In several places in this poem "dark" refers to the future—not in a negative sense, but in the sense that one is not privy to what it holds. In these places Strand leads readers to believe that the dark that is the human inability to see the future is also the playground of imagination. People prefer to stare "Into the dark and imagine a fullness in which/ We are the stars, matching the emptiness/ Of the beginning, giving birth to ourselves/ Again and again." This is an old theme, dating back to Ecclesiastes and probably before. Everything is cyclical: We have been here before, and we will be here again.

Edmund August

THE DARKLING THRUSH

Author: Thomas Hardy (1840-1928)
Type of poem: Lyric
First published: 1901, in *Poems of the Past and Present*

The Poem

"The Darkling Thrush" is a thirty-two-line lyric poem in four stanzas of eight lines each. The first two stanzas provide the setting of the poem. Hardy's poetic persona is standing at the edge of a "coppice," a thicket of bushes or small trees. He surveys a desolate scene at the end of a winter day. He is alone in that "haunted night"; all the rest of humankind "had sought their household fires." The second stanza continues the description and provides two important pieces of information. One concerns the time when the poem was written, December of 1900, which is always included in the printing of the poem. The words "the Century's corpse" and "the ancient pulse of germ and birth" refer to the turn of the century. The other important information is about the poet's state of mind. He is deeply depressed, stating that the dismal scene is "fervorless as I."

These first two stanzas comprise line after line of lyrical description. Details pertaining to death (the bine-stems "like strings from broken lyres," the "crypt," the "death-lament," the "ancient pulse" that is "shrunken hard and dry") add up to a depressing total. The scene of icy, clear death images and the harsh, austere feeling are firmly set in the reader's mind.

Now that the reader's mood has been captured by the frosty, deathly winter scene, surrounded by images of the land's and the century's death, the third stanza opens with a sudden, sharp contrast. A song bursts forth, a "full-hearted evensong/ Of joy illimited." Then another contrast unfolds as the source of the song is revealed: "an aged thrush, frail, gaunt and small." A weak, bedraggled, drab bird somehow has managed to overcome the cold, gloom, and death of winter and sing with its whole heart.

Does the bird sing because it knows some greater joy of which the poet is unaware? In the fourth stanza the poet reveals his agnostic lack of faith. There is "So little cause for carolings," he asserts. The bird's "ecstatic sound" is not founded in reason or faith. For a moment perhaps there is a note of hope, but the poet reveals his feelings in his verb tense. He "could think" there was some hope for the frosty world, but he cannot sustain his belief. In the end, the persona of the poet has no hope; he only observes with a touch of irony that the thrush seems to have hope.

The entire poem sustains an image of desolation. Even the song of "joy illimited" does not relieve the poet's depression. There is no transformation from the mood of death into human optimism, so the contrast of the thrush's song serves to heighten the poet's despair. The corpse of the old century never gives way to the birth of the new.

Forms and Devices

Thomas Hardy is a transitional poet, a bridge between the nineteenth and the twentieth centuries, and between Romantic Victorian and modern thought. "The Darkling Thrush" is particularly apt as a transitional poem, since it was written on and for the turn of the century. There is a strong contrast between form and meaning in the poem, just as there is a contrast between the bleak despair of the scene and the unreasonable joy of the thrush's song.

The form of the poem is traditional, of the nineteenth century, though the meaning is modern, of the twentieth. Hardy was sixty years old in 1900 and was technically competent in the meter and rhyme schemes that were already rooted in the past. The meter never varies from the da-dum da-dum of the basic English iambic tetrameter; the rhyme scheme is a perfect *ababcdcd*. While Hardy is sometimes criticized for lack of originality in this form, the effect of this controlled meter and rhyme scheme is remarkable in a poem about modern despair. The poet cannot control the chaos and decay around him, but he can control the form of the poem. The formal strictness of the verse is a bulwark against disorder.

At times the poet's language seems to be dictated by the unvarying ballad-like form of the poem even more than by his search for meaning. Hardy coins "nonce words," words invented for a single occasion, to fit the meter. "Blast-beruffled" is an example of a nonce word that is effective in description and musicality of language. On the other hand, the nonce word "outleant," coined to rhyme with "death-lament," is difficult to visualize and breaks the flow of the rhythm as the reader puzzles about the meaning.

Again, the meter of the poem demands that the poet write "strings from broken lyres" (line 6) instead of the more apt death-image of "broken strings of lyres." Yet, through his mastery of his form, Hardy manages a broader emotional tone and complexity of imagination and irony than is normally found within a strict folk ballad or hymn meter.

The controlled, traditional form of "The Darkling Thrush" addresses Hardy's response to the lack of control he feels in the historical context of the event he is describing. The entire poem is a metaphor for the turn of the century. The death and desolation of the first two stanzas parallel the dying of the old century. The frost and winter and haunted night of the first stanza are the setting for the crypt in which the "Century's corpse" lies lamented by the wind. Hardy reveals his modern temperament when he breaks with the traditional rhythm of death and rebirth. This old century is not about to give way to new, vigorous life. "The ancient pulse of germ and birth/ Was shrunken hard and dry." The poet's persona is not the only depressed spirit; rather, "every spirit upon earth" is "fervorless as I."

Hardy departs from the traditional again in the effect of the bird's song. In the expected pattern of folklore or mythology, the joyful song of the thrush should herald the hope for the future that the new century must represent. In Hardy's metaphor, however, the thrush is aged, not a symbol of rebirth at all but a caroler without cause. His thrush is not singing a morning song of rejuvenation, but an evensong, a goodnight air. Even in the new century, hope is fleeting. The metaphor seems at first to promise rebirth, but the poet has lost faith. He cannot believe.

Themes and Meanings

The primary theme of "The Darkling Thrush" is the despair of the modern temperament. Hardy describes in lyrical, descriptive detail the dying of the old world, but he cannot positively replace the dying with the new. Something is over, all is changed, civilization has decayed, and he does not know what will replace it. In "The Darkling Thrush," Hardy poses one of the central questions of the modern age and reveals himself as a significant voice of the early twentieth century.

Hardy the modern poet is an isolated man. He has lost his connection with those nineteenth century people who are inside by their household fires. They are connected with one another, and with the natural cycle of death and rebirth, but Hardy, the twentieth century persona, is alone in the cold, surrounded by images of death. He may yearn for that simpler, truer world, and he may seek to recapture something that is lost by using the form of folk themes, but that old century is dead, and the outlook for the new century is bleak indeed.

Hardy saw traditional agricultural society decaying, the earth destroyed by industrialization, and in "The Darkling Thrush" he clearly reveals that he cannot believe in a note of hope. He finds "so little cause for carolings" that he cannot picture the new century or describe it for the reader. Hardy is "unaware" of any hope for the future.

With his tale of the "darkling thrush," a thrush of evening rather than morning, Hardy rejects the Romantic themes of the nineteenth century. While the song of the thrush is the force that crystallizes his fervorless spirit, Hardy's thrush is aged, "frail, gaunt and small," not symbolizing new life but belonging to that dying old century. Even after hearing the thrush's "full-hearted evensong/ Of joy illimited," Hardy's depression is lifted only as far as a state of puzzlement. He comes into the new century unable to believe that even the thrush, that representative of nature, can have a reason to hope.

Susan Butterworth

DARLENE'S HOSPITAL

Author: John Ashbery (1927-   )
Type of poem: Lyric
First published: 1984, in *A Wave*

The Poem

John Ashbery's "Darlene's Hospital" is a seventy-five-line free-verse lyric poem in four verse paragraphs of roughly equal length. The poem explores the process of the poet's mind as it focuses on the phrase "Darlene's Hospital." Like many other Ashbery poems, this one concerns itself with memory and time while both describing and evoking the flow of language and association through the present. Perhaps the simplest thematic statement one could make about "Darlene's Hospital" is that it is a meditation on the way memory and imagination deal with loneliness and the passage of time, an ever-present reminder of mortality. The daydreaming in the poem is more realistic and less romantic than the daydreams in nineteenth century poetry, but an uneasy tension between realism and romance remains.

Although it is tempting to suppose that Ashbery had been reading Alfred, Lord Tennyson's poem "The Lady of Shallot" or looking at one of the Pre-Raphaelite paintings based on that poem, "Darlene's Hospital" is not a straightforward retelling of Tennyson's narrative. The room on the island of Shallot where the lady in Tennyson's poem weaves a "magic web with colors gay" based on her view in a mirror of the landscape around Camelot is mimed in the "colors" and daydreams in Ashbery's poem. In Tennyson's poem, the lady is cursed if she looks on the scene directly and can view Camelot only in her mirror, though "She knows not what the curse may be." Eventually, however, she looks directly at the handsome Lancelot as he rides by. Her mirror cracks, and she secures a boat, leaves the island, and dies, mysteriously cursed, floating on the river.

In "Darlene's Hospital," the Lady of Shallot is mentioned in the second verse paragraph in a light and mocking way: The Lady is "in hot water again," Ashbery's strategically placed cliché making a joke of Tennyson's earnest romanticism. The Lady's presence lingers in the third verse paragraph, where a river flows "Hard by the hospital from whose gilded/ Balconies and turrets fair spirits waved," as if "Darlene" might be the modern equivalent of the Lady of Shallot, but bounded by the realities of hospitals—perhaps even a mental hospital, with "hospital stay" as a euphemism for time spent in an insane asylum. It is noteworthy that the "fair spirits" are "lonely like us," for the poem is about both imagination and loneliness.

Now "a different kind of work/ Of the imagination had grown up around" stories that "weren't true." The line "and so you looked/ And saw nothing, but suddenly felt better/ Without wondering why" seems to play with the story of the Lady of Shallot as if "you," the reader, were to look in the real world of your own imagination for a vision such as the Lady's but see nothing and, instead of dying, suddenly feel better. This is the climax of the poem, the place where the hospital treatment might be said to succeed, so the patient (Darlene, Ashbery in the space of the poem, the reader) feels better. However, "the serial continues:/ Pain, expiation, delight, more pain," as life rarely has the neatness of a Victorian romantic poem.

In the end the "she" of the poem lingers. The phrase "And if she glides/ Backwards through us, a finger hooked/ Out of death" suggests that the Lady's modern incarnation need not die completely.

Forms and Devices

Evocation, the drawing out of sensory and emotional associations, is central to the method of "Darlene's Hospital." A reading of the first verse paragraph foreshadows Ashbery's method throughout the poem. The first line picks up the word "hospital" from the title, but what follows the phrase "The hospital" is disorienting. Instead of being given a description of a building, readers are taken into "her" mind, only to be told that "the colors" were not "her idea." "The colors" seem to be the paint on a picture in progress, and though they are "muddy," they spew "random evocations everywhere." By association, the hospital becomes "A secret lavender place you weren't supposed to look into," the sky, an unlikely place to hide something.

The phrase "Provided that things should pick up next season" seems to refer to the colors' evocations but is perhaps just a random clause that might fit into any sentence. Ashbery's ear is tuned to the clichés, idioms, and commonplace phrases that litter discourse, in contrast to Tennyson's carefully chosen poetic diction. The next sentence seems to relate to the first but also might appear anywhere. The "it" in "It was a way of living" refers vaguely back to "things" picking up next season, but the only "thing" that has occurred is colors sliding "from the brush" and spewing evocations. The whole beginning of the poem evades saying that anything at all has happened, since "it wasn't her idea" in the first place.

The phrase "way of living" suggests a way of making a living, so it should come as no surprise that in line 6 "she took a job," and either the job was not odd or it was not odd that she took the job, though Ashbery never says what her job was. In line 7, "the way many minds have been made up" echoes "her way of thinking" in line 5. Line 8 begins with another unclear reference to "It," but immediately clarifies the reference as being to "the color," which takes one back to the beginning of the poem. To disorient readers further, the color climbs "the apple of the sky," described incongruously as a "secret lavender place."

The tone of the whole verse paragraph is light and whimsical, as "the apple of the sky" (a slight shift from clichéd "apple of her eye") might emphasize, confirmed by the line "And then a sneeze would come along." "Sneeze," suggesting an ailment, is the first word that seems to have anything to do with hospitals. The sneeze blows one from the sky to the shore as, again toying with readers' expectations, lines 10-14 say the sneeze has the beneficial effect of keeping "us" from being "too far out from shore," and goes on to mention "a milky afternoon/ Somewhere in late August" with "traffic flowing like mucus," a natural associative link with a sneeze. The last two lines of the verse paragraph refer to an unspecified "they" and an unclear "its," along with an idiomatic phrase, "it's too bad," which is later echoed by the last phrase of the paragraph, "it's too late."

Themes and Meanings

"Darlene's Hospital" blurs the distinction between lyric and narrative poetry. Although it tells a story, or at least flirts with narrative, it is more about shifting perceptions than about the narrative. Though the poem seems to center on an individual's perception of a situation, it is not easy to identify either the individual or the situation. A simple statement of the poem's thesis, its controlling emotion, or even a paraphrase of the sensuous content is tricky. Instead, the associations of the poem weave in and out, making as much sense as the phrases and images drifting in and out of anyone's consciousness. Although the poem is divided into paragraphs, each ending with a period, the flow of imagination resists compartmentalization into paragraphs or neat stanzas. The constant shifting between past, present, and future suggests the volatility of consciousness.

"Darlene's Hospital" operates by association and disorientation rather than by the more traditional logic of assertions, evidence, and qualifications. Although the poem is ostensibly in Ashbery's voice, it tells almost nothing personal about him. Rather, the poem is concerned with what comes to mind as he follows the image suggested by the poem's title. At first the title may seem silly, deliberately whimsical—"Darlene's Hospital" instead of, for example, "County General Hospital" or "The Darlene Smith Memorial Hospital." The idea of an individual having his or her own hospital is foreign to the usual way of thinking.

Reading beyond the title, however, one finds in the poem evidence that in the mind's shifting landscape, a hospital belongs as much to the individual's perception of it as to some objective reality. In other words, Darlene's experience of the hospital is subjective and internal. Similarly, Ashbery's invention and evocation of Darlene creates a shifting subjectivity in which it is difficult to tell not only who Darlene is but also who the speaker is, let alone who John Ashbery is. Behind all this, like a palimpsest, lies "The Lady of Shallot."

Ashbery challenges the idea of a unified and consistent self by "backing through the way many minds had been made up." Instead of the Lady of Shallot, so easy for Victorian painters to visualize, in "Darlene's Hospital" Ashbery offers a complex force field of consciousness in which evasive pronouns blur the distinction between characters, speaker, and audience, all of whom take the place of a single, clearly delineated heroine. Never mentioned by name in the poem, "Darlene" may be the "she" at the end of the poem who "glides backward through us," effectively disrupting one's settled notions about the poem—even the way readers' "minds had been made up" about her identity.

Thomas Lisk

THE DAY LADY DIED

Author: Frank O'Hara (1926-1966)
Type of poem: Meditation
First published: 1964, in *Lunch Poems*

The Poem

"The Day Lady Died" is written in free verse. It describes Frank O'Hara's activities on the day he found out that Billie (Lady Day) Holiday had died. Although the poem appears to be a straightforward narrative, the title emphasizes the day itself rather than Holiday's death or O'Hara's activities, and thus it hints at something larger, something that perhaps combines both Holiday and O'Hara. It suggests that the poem should also be read as something other than the narrative it may first appear to be.

The poem is written in the first person. Poets often use the first person either to address a particular person or the world, while the reader is a witness rather than the addressee. O'Hara, however, uses the first person differently. One of the striking features of this poem is its conversational tone; combined with the first-person point of view, it creates the impression that the poet is talking directly to his readers, including them in the seemingly innocuous moments of his life.

This effect brings an intimacy to the poem. O'Hara furthers this intimacy by including the names of friends and places that are meaningless to almost anyone who does not know him or his social circle without ever explaining who or what they are or what their significance is to him or his life. He appears to be telling readers about his life as though they already understand all the references; the poem becomes a conversation, O'Hara talking directly to each reader every time it is read. The details, however, still remain meaningless; O'Hara, it may be assumed, knows this and is using it to point again beyond the narrative, toward something else.

The poem lists O'Hara's activities on July 17, 1959 ("three days after Bastille day"). He locates his readers in a very particular time and place, then tells them what he will be doing that evening. Following him as he runs errands and makes purchases in preparation for dinner that night, the reader joins him as the poet sees the front-page headline of the newspaper announcing that Billie Holiday has died. He suddenly remembers a particular night that he heard her sing in a nightclub; he conveys the power of her singing by ending the poem with wordplay involving death: "everyone and I stopped breathing." The image of the audience being so enraptured by her singing that they forget to breathe parallels Holiday's death, when she actually stopped breathing. Her ability as a singer to make people figuratively leave their bodies is analogous to her spirit leaving her body. Thus the poem, at its end, represents a transcendence of the daily activities that it has narrated.

Forms and Devices

Though the poem's narrative structure looks simple, O'Hara employs devices that ultimately break down ordinary concepts of time and perception. For many years he was an art critic, and many of his friends were abstract painters. One of the developing thrusts of visual art at that time was that the painting itself became a record of the process of painting; so, too, O'Hara makes the poem a record of the process of the contents of the poem.

O'Hara accomplishes this through the impressionist quality of the writing, telling of events as he goes about his day. He does not link them together through metaphor, imagery, or any other standard poetic device, but merely sets them down as they occur. Yet this seemingly innocuous jotting down has a peculiar effect; the poem becomes not only a record of the day but also a mirror of the actual process of going through the day. Clearly, when people are standing in line at the bank, they are not linking that action, on some larger scale, to eating a hamburger in a restaurant half an hour earlier; neither does O'Hara. What he does instead is mimic real life. Readers see him as he goes around New York, and the poem becomes a record of that process rather than a poem of any one particular event.

This mirroring of the process of going through a day has a peculiar effect on time. The poem is written entirely in the present tense, and the sense of going through the day while reading heightens the present tense. When O'Hara then flashes back into the past at the end of the poem, he not only continues to write in the present tense but also brings his reader with him as he goes through the process of having the flashback. Yet, when O'Hara wrote the poem, all these events were already in the past. The reader thus experiences past events in the present tense, experiences something further in the past in that same present tense, and then experiences the transcendence at the end of the poem as it happens. All time becomes present. The poem brings the reader into some eternal present where standard concepts of time no longer operate.

O'Hara also appears to include any event or thought, no matter how seemingly trivial. This not only adds another level of intimacy to the poem but anchors the poetry in the mundane, ordinary world rather than in some larger, metaphoric, more traditionally poetic one. It is through the events of one's daily life, he is saying, that art can be found.

Again, however, he makes a shift at the end by juxtaposing this ordinariness with a sudden transcendence. Daily life, which seems so concrete, is suddenly shown to be fragile and easily torn away. This shift has the effect of a veil being lifted; O'Hara celebrates the ordinary for its own sake, but he then pulls the ordinary away to reveal what is extraordinary behind it. By doing this, he again takes the reader out of this world into something more eternal.

Themes and Meanings

"The Day Lady Died" is a visionary poem, one in which the ordinary world is pulled away to reveal something much larger. The poem becomes a poem about how disparate things, people, and events are all interconnected, even when they apparently have no connection whatsoever.

This sense of interconnectedness is foreshadowed by the title. Many have asked, or been asked, where they were or what they were doing when some great world event occurred; O'Hara, in his title, seems to be pointing to that question.

In the poem, however, he does not leave himself and Holiday as separate entities the way one normally would do. Rather, he connects himself to her, not only by focusing on the day itself and by remembering her singing, but also by depicting a moment of epiphany. In this moment, the ordinary concept of time is pulled away to reveal an eternal present, and ordinary, concrete reality is pulled away to reveal something extraordinary, something much larger than one's ordinary senses reveal.

This world behind the world is paralleled to Holiday's ability as a singer to "stop time," or to make people forget their bodies. In that moment, Holiday herself is an instrument of transcendence, able to take people beyond the ordinary. In this sense, the poem is O'Hara's hymn of praise to the singer.

Yet it would be a mistake to leave the poem at that most literal reading. For what O'Hara is ultimately doing is showing the reader the fragility of what is thought of as the ordinary world; it can be torn away by, for example, the beauty of a voice or by a shock of recognition. This does not mean that what is considered to be the world does not exist, but that there is something behind it, something greater than it, some larger form of knowledge or being that brings everyone together.

In its statement that there is a world other than this one, the poem can be read as a religious poem. Yet O'Hara's vision is completely nondenominational; it is more accurate to read the poem as an ecstatic visionary statement of the poet's belief that there is a world beyond ordinary knowing. That world is one of extraordinary beauty and, ultimately, freedom from the constraints of ordinary life and all the rules and regulations (both perceptual and social) that maintain it.

Although O'Hara raises the question of where to find freedom and answers it with his vision, he does not answer the question of how to move beyond the ordinary in order to enter into that eternal present, or how to bring that eternal present into one's life. By reminding the reader of it, though, he is at least pointing in a particular direction. Only in this mundane world are people isolated entities. In that larger one, all are connected, and the knowledge of that eternal present may be a first necessary step.

Robert Kaplan

THE DAY ZIMMER LOST RELIGION

Author: Paul Zimmer (1934-   )
Type of poem: Meditation
First published: 1976, in *The Zimmer Poems*

The Poem

"The Day Zimmer Lost Religion" is composed of three seven-line stanzas of blank verse (unrhymed iambic pentameter). The poem's tone is strongly colloquial as the adult speaker, or persona, recounts the events of a particular day in his childhood when he tested God by missing Mass "on purpose." The phrase "on purpose" focuses the poem on the idea of the test. The child Zimmer assumes that God will punish such behavior immediately, and when no such thing happens, the child concludes that God has evidently recognized that Zimmer is too mature to be frightened by his threats. That day becomes the day named in the title: "The Day Zimmer Lost Religion." Like many poems by Paul Zimmer, the persona of this poem shares the author's name, but it would be a mistake to assume that the two are exactly the same. The Zimmer of this poem, like that of the many other Zimmer poems, is a character created to relate and react to this set of events.

In the first of the stanzas, the persona looks into his past to remember how he expected God to punish him for missing Mass. His fantasies focus on some painful experiences of childhood. He first expects that Christ will show up like a flyweight boxer to pummel him for his failure to attend Mass. The boxing scene is extended as he remembers imagining the devil "roaring" in the stands to cheer his painful humiliation. The second stanza looks back further ("a long cold way") into the speaker's early life to the time when he served as an altar boy, wore a cassock and surplice (a black gown worn under a loose, white, knee-length robe), and assisted the priest during Mass by giving the appropriate Latin responses. In those days he evidently attended a Catholic school; his experience there was permeated by his sense of God's presence so that he imagined the eye of God overlooking all the activities of the school yard, ready to accuse any wrongdoing. The third stanza restates Zimmer's expectations of punishment; this time he imagines Christ as the "playground bully" who might arrive to beat him up for his betrayal of his faith. God's failure to deliver any of Zimmer's imagined punishments seems to confirm for him that God has met his match and is giving up, perhaps because Zimmer is now too old for religion. That, at least, is the young Zimmer's conclusion, although the adult Zimmer who narrates this poem implies something more.

Forms and Devices

The world of this poem is the world of the Catholic schoolboy, and the imagery of the poem grows out of the details of the boy's life in that world. It is a world of grubby little boys who admire boxers and who sometimes do their own share of unofficial fighting in the school yard (particularly if they must defend themselves against the school bully) regardless of what the priests may say to warn them against bad behavior. The boxing and the reference to the "dirty wind that blew/ The soot . . . across the school yard" suggests that it is an urban school.

Boxing establishes the first set of images for the poem as the child Zimmer waits for Christ to "climb down " from the crucifix on which the child usually sees him and to appear as a "wiry flyweight" boxer. Zimmer expects Christ to "club" him in his "blasphemous gut" and his "irreverent teeth" as if they had been sent into the boxing ring together. This imaginary fight even has a spectator: the devil himself. Like a spectator at a boxing match, he sits in reserved seats, roaring with delight at the rebellious Zimmer's punishment. The fighting imagery is extended in the last stanza in which Christ is no longer pictured as a boxer but as the playground bully who will appear in order to "pound" Zimmer until his "irreligious tongue" hangs out.

The language of religion also informs the poem, since the child Zimmer's offense is against God (as well as against his religious instructors who have warned him about the consequences of missing Mass). That is why the poem is furnished with details from the child Zimmer's religious life. The flyweight Jesus will drop him, he says, like a "red hot thurible" (an incense container that is swung from a chain, which an altar boy such as the young Zimmer might carry in a religious procession in church while wearing the cassock and surplice). Another example of the poem's religious diction is the use of "venial" to describe the soot that blows across the school yard. When used to describe sins, venial refers to relatively less important sins, unlike the more serious mortal sins that, the boy's teachers would have told him, could deprive him of God's grace. Like venial sins, the soot smudges everything in this tarnished world. Another component of the poem's diction is its colloquial language. The angry Christ will "wade into [Zimmer's] blasphemous gut," the devil roars until he develops hiccups, and Zimmer uses the slang term "mice" to refer to the bruises on the face of the crucified Christ.

One last image in the poem deserves discussion—the reference to God reigning as a "One-eyed triangle" as he glares down at the playground. That image of God comes from the picture on the great seal of the United States, represented on a one-dollar bill, in which a pyramid is crowned by a huge eye from which light radiates. The child has evidently tied the idea of the pyramid to his teachers' explanation of the concept of the Trinity—God as Father, Son, and Holy Spirit—which is sometimes represented as a triangle. Tellingly, the child sees the image as threatening.

Themes and Meanings

"The Day Zimmer Lost Religion" looks back, half humorously, at a time when the persona decided to test God by missing Mass. His teachers have surely told him that he is obligated to attend Mass, and the fact that he is missing it intentionally may even raise this to the level of a mortal sin, one that is committed with one's full knowledge and volition. The child's teachers may also have warned him against testing God since the desire to control God by forcing Him to take a particular action is also usually considered sinful. Significantly, the child tests God with the expectation that God will immediately punish his wrongdoing, probably in the same very personal way that his teachers might give him corporal punishment. He imagines God first as a boxer and then as a playground bully, the result of his vision of God as the omnipresent threat looming over the playground. In fact, his understanding of God seems confined to a picture of Him as judge. Even his memories of his days as an altar boy seem negative. His role in the service was to "mumble" the Latin responses, and he describes the bell he rang (the bell that marks the holiest point in the Mass, the point when Christ is actually present in the bread and wine) as "obscure."

The poem has an additional level, however, that establishes the irony at its heart. When the threatening God fails to deliver Zimmer's punishment, the child assumes that God feels that he has met his match: "of course He never came, knowing that/ I was grown up and ready for Him now." That final line leads the reader to the poem's point. Instead of the child's assumption that being "ready" for God means that one is ready to win a conflict with him, the reader is invited to see this readiness in another sense: When the child is truly grown up, he will be ready for another understanding of a god who is more interested in love than punishment. An ironic point of view in poetry, as in fiction, often arises from the disparity between what the speaker understands and the deeper understanding that is offered to the reader. That disparity is intrinsic in adults' views of what they understood in childhood. In "The Day Zimmer Lost Religion," it invites the reader to gently laugh with the adult Zimmer, who looks back at his juvenile testing of God and his childish fantasy about the punishments God might inflict on him while hinting at a grown-up understanding of what being ready for God might mean.

Ann D. Garbett

THE DAY'S CHORES: A LIST

Author: Patricia Hampl (1946-   )
Type of poem: Meditation
First published: 1978, in *Woman Before an Aquarium*

The Poem

"The Day's Chores: A List" is in twelve numbered sections. In section 1 (one stanza of eight lines), the speaker sleepily encounters a cup of tea, noting the cup's color and contemplating its ingredients. She opens one eye at a time, perhaps reluctant to come fully awake. Section 2 identifies the first actual chore and issues the first command: Water the plants. The plants are seen as a substitute for a pet; they will at least respond ("purr with pleasure") to being tended. Section 3, the briefest section with only two lines, issues the second command: Observe the sun. This will be remembered in the final stanza, where it will have become a metaphor for living fully awake.

Section 4 expresses the importance of having work to do. Although work is seen as a stand-in for something more dramatic or romantic ("The back of my dreams has been broken"), the speaker announces that since she now understands the importance of her work, it is like a lover to her. Section 5 includes more advice about being awake and attentive, in this case just sitting and listening to the chair creaking and to the person who sat in it before her. This is clearly a spiritual cue to be open to all manner of awareness: Someone who was much older, spoke another language, and was not even present can still offer spiritual company. Section 6 speaks of listening to people now present or to other writers, as long as these writers are truthful about their inner selves.

Section 7, the longest so far with twenty lines, finds the speaker of the poem riding the city bus, "once in daylight/ and again at night." There, she is confided in by an old woman, and again she listens attentively. This section stresses the need for getting out, mingling, and connecting with others. In section 8, she goes to the grocery store and attends to the quality of the food she eats and the nutrients her body needs. She pretends each item is written on one of her fingertips, again stressing the conscious physical involvement in life that she demands of herself. Section 9 involves housework— cleaning, laundering, responding to the mail, all before dark. In this section and in section 8, there are new mentions of the world of sleep and shadow and a sense that the speaker is aware of the dangers of not keeping her eyes wide open to life.

In section 10, the speaker yields to temptation and allows herself a brief nap, justifying it as a way to have a "second morning" or new energy for the balance of the day. Section 11 lets the day begin to die—a late dinner with someone she loves, candlelight, taking inventory in a diary. The speaker celebrates a sense of having met the day's demands and takes pride in the thought that the list of chores is not "tattered" and has no "crossed-off" items; she has attended to the chores single-mindedly and efficiently, leaving virtually nothing undone and having adhered to an original plan.

Section 12, the last and longest section (two stanzas and twenty-nine lines) steps back, reconsiders and reaffirms the speaker's definition of what her chores or tasks have encompassed with a "list within the list," and again celebrates her success in having lived the day as fully awake as possible. She has been careful to observe the sun (section 3) as a hero worthy of honor and now has a sense of "his heart." The reader imagines that her sleep will be both peaceful and deep.

Forms and Devices

The poem has 123 lines and twelve sections that vary in length from 2 to 29 lines. There is no observable meter or rhyme scheme; pattern and stress are inherent in line length and line break. Stress is sometimes pounded out by several successive spondees: "the night not one star sang out." The twelve stanzas are numbered in a manner similar to some of William Blake's work, and they constitute, very ostensibly, a list to be checked off as the day progresses. Yet not all of them are like items taken from a "to-do" memo pad: Some do not involve an imperative at all and clearly have nothing to do with any work or physical action. Often, an object is merely named, and the implication is that this object deserves attention and contemplation: "A pale blue cup/ with tea in it." Only three give a directive (water plants, shop, keep house); the rest are habits to be cultivated and have to do with being, listening, mingling, seeing, and reflecting.

The first stanza sets up the "list" or sets the precedent for its nature: a simple object, a precise image, and a sharp contrast between night and day:

> A pale blue cup
> with tea in it,
> melted-down flowers
> first thing in the morning
> after one brown eye opens,
> and then the other,
> shining
> like the night they came from.

Sharp as the images are, Hampl requires little in the way of simile and metaphor. Eyes shine "like the night they came from"; she has redefined her life's direction, claiming that "The back of my dreams has been broken"; grocery items are "decisions"; there is a "slump in the afternoon"; waking from a nap is "a second morning"; her diary is either "fat" or "slivered," depending on the rigor of the day's demands; and the day's chores, when completed, make up "a set of filed cards." More important is the painting created by the poem and the delicate colors that wash over and through its lines: pale blue, purple, orange, brown, and white, the colors of a cottage still life.

Themes and Meanings

Though written in 1978, this poem could easily be claimed by the proponents of the "voluntary simplicity" movement of the late 1990's as their creed. The speaker of the poem has learned to see through the busy surface of life down to its rock-bottom essentials, and what she identifies as her life-shaping force is work. The numbered stanzas are not the only similarity between Hampl and William Blake: Hampl's poetry is also comparable to Blake's in its use of imperatives, either direct or implied. One of Blake's imperatives is a perfect gloss for Hampl's theme: "The most sublime act is to set another before you." The speaker in Hampl's poem has learned that her "duty" is her work, and she meets it willingly: "Now that I understand/ who it is, I try not/ to keep a lover waiting." She lives with the conviction that "The first task is always before me." Its identity changes as the day progresses, and she must merely acknowledge its claim on her attention: "I call it/ groceries, laundry,/ poem, paint kitchen table." She keeps inventory: "a precise diary," "a set of filed cards." She claims with pride that "The list is not tattered,/ no crossed-off thoughts." Since she knows what her work is, she has rarely had to revise the list, and it seems to be a new list every morning ("the list is not tattered") by having had its chores carried over to another day.

The sun and "a wizened orange" are important to this assurance. She tosses the orange up, exercising complete control, holds it in her hand, and says she thereby has "a sense of the sun,/ his heart" as though she has sucked this day's orange dry, every chore, every piece of wakeful living noted and accomplished.

Her list contains both private and public chores; it allows her to remain a whole, integrated person. Evidently, her chores occasionally feel like mere chores to her. She is slow in waking and longs for the short nap, maybe even "the reentry of shadows," but she remains proudly committed to her covenant with life: "the sun has been observed/ personally by me today." Her index cards have no index; she attends to the day's demands as they present themselves to her, not bound by any proscribed idea of order. Like the orange, the chores have been "perfectly held/ wedge by wedge."

Carla Graham

DEAD GALLOP

Author: Pablo Neruda (Neftalí Ricardo Reyes Basoalto, 1904-1973)
Type of poem: Narrative
First published: 1933, as "Galope muerto," in *Residencia en la tierra*; English translation collected in *Residence on Earth and Other Poems*, 1973

The Poem

"Dead Gallop," also variously translated from the Spanish as "Death Gallop" or "Gallop Toward Death," is the opening poem of Pablo Neruda's Residence cycle. The poem is written in five stanzas, each consisting of an uneven number of lines, the longer opening stanzas ending with considerably shorter lines. In reading the poem through, one gets a feeling of galloping or moving rapidly toward an abrupt ending. Feeling the dramatic impact of the poem is important to understanding the various disjointed images that describe the speaker's movement toward death.

The poem begins with what appear to be sagacious observations about nature; each element seems connected to a crucial function in the universe. Ashes, seas, bells, and plums constitute some of the many sights, sounds, and smells of life. Oddly, however, these objects do not have any obvious connection with one another, although they are linked by the fact that they are "like" or "as" one another in certain ways.

In the second stanza, elemental and essential things are further examined in images such as wheels, the limbs of trees, and lilacs. The third stanza continues the span across the natural world, although the emphasis is on the way things move or remain still, depending on "what my pale heart" expects from the experiences themselves. With the first reference to a personal "my" in the poem, the speaker introduces himself. Now the reader realizes that a human source has made these subjective and wise-sounding observations.

There is a shift in the poem's tone in the fourth stanza. It begins with the locution "Well now," as though to denote a change in the speaker's perception. Momentarily, then, he reflects on the fullness of the world. Even as he pauses, he considers how his thoughts, like the sounds he hears, grow "suddenly, stretching without pause."

The feeling of endless motion carries into the last stanza, where the poem ends tersely. Throughout, the speaker has moved headlong toward something, but at the end, the outcome is anticlimactic; he does not seem to have revealed anything concrete to the reader. The inconclusive closure corresponds to the speaker's sense of nothingness in the face of the world's plenitude. In the earlier stanzas, the outside world has affected him so much that he contemplates images of it. The images had not appeared to him in any coherent way even though he was able to posit a relationship among them. He is able to make sense of the images when he turns them inward toward himself. Figuratively, he gallops toward his inner self and ponders the meaning of the images and impressions. While he does not speak directly of death, he does suggest that the opposite of something is nothing.

If life is characterized by a particular fullness, the opposite might be true: Death, which lies on the other side of life, could be nothingness itself. The speaker does not go completely beyond the end, however, and the poem's last image of things growing suggests that life will still go on.

Forms and Devices

Neruda was in his twenties when he composed the Residence poems. The tone and subject matter of "Dead Gallop" reveal a youthful cynicism about the world, despite the abundance of energy contained in that work. The reader enters into the speaker's subjective vision of the world.

The images appear before the speaker in disjointed fashion, although he presents them as though they somehow connect or correspond with one another. The lines are linked by the poem's dependence on simile, a figure of speech in which unlike things are compared. The repetition of "like," "such as," and "as if" serves to join the various images. As the reader "gallops" along with the speaker, however, it becomes more obvious that the images are in fact disjointed and incomplete. The opening stanza itself is an extensive catalog of dismembered images which do not add up to a tangible whole. This strategy reappears in successive stanzas.

Simile is employed as a poetic device throughout the poem. The speaker compares seemingly incomparable things: shapes to sounds, places to moving things, and silence to flowers. Each comparison ends by moving onto still other comparisons, until the stanza ends with a period. In fact, the images do not necessarily have an external correspondence to the material world. They do not appear to be naturally or logically ordered. The subjective observations are conveyed by the speaker's authoritative manner in presenting them. He thus depends on certain locutions to uphold the correlations he makes.

In the third and fourth stanzas, the speaker begins with "therefore" and "well now," respectively, as if to indicate that he would now offer a summary of what went on in the earlier two stanzas. It is a false start, since he then proceeds to move along again in disjointed fashion. In this accumulation of unconnected images and movement without concrete ends, the speaker reveals a growing discernment beneath the mask of certainty.

The endlessness of the comparisons suggests that the external world is collapsing or, more specifically, that the speaker senses the breakdown and tries to appear confident in this understanding. Paradoxically, the tone of confidence betrays his uncertainty. As he senses his growing despair, the speaker turns inward, "to me who enters singing," and he realizes that it is important, nevertheless, to continue thinking about the world in all its "vast disorder."

"Dead Gallop" is often considered a depressing, or pessimistic, poem in which the speaker seems to shut himself away from the world. More accurately, the poem reflects the anguish of not knowing what death actually is and when it will come. The speaker seems reluctant to bring up the subject of death itself and chooses, instead, to create an atmosphere of uncertainty about the living world. In this way, he prepares for the unknowable by moving through living and growing things.

The poem ends abruptly, without positive reassurance, in an effort to capture what the speaker believes to be the only truth of death: It is a sudden and startling event that intrudes on life, leaving things unfinished.

Themes and Meanings

Many years after their publication, Neruda denounced the Residence poems, calling them harmful and atrocious. Understood in the context of Neruda's work, "Dead Gallop" may be considered an early poem in which the youthful poet experiments with a negative vision that nevertheless accurately reflects a reality of life and death.

The effect of "Dead Gallop" is unsettling, because uncertainty about death naturally makes humans anxious. In a world with so much movement and energy, how could an event suddenly eradicate and silence everything? The speaker does not go gently into this nothingness, and the "gallop" hints at the speaker's strength and determined spirit.

In what seems at first an entirely disordered and meaningless poem, the idea of a "gallop" itself restores meaning and credibility to the speaker's observations. A gallop is literally a manner in which horses move; a dictionary definition states that a gallop is "faster than a canter and slower than a run." It is a very specific and ordered way of moving. Associating the gallop with horses also makes one think of the classical metaphor of death as a horseman who seizes the living when their time on earth has expired. The poem as a whole is, therefore, this movement away from earth and toward the speaker's consciousness as he considers the inevitability of death.

The last two stanzas do not propose a joyous version of this state of affairs. In what "exists between night and time," one can only move along the external world and allow images to impress one with their vitality or their progressive decomposition. The world itself is "oceanic," and one's gallop through earth should be directed at finding meanings even though one cannot be sure exactly what things mean. One may never know.

Even when things die, though, other things continue to live, and new things are born. The speaker stops short of an easy optimism because, truthfully, he does not know any more than this. At the end, even "the great calabash trees" and "pity-laden plants" emphasize the state of unknowing; even in their fullness, they are "dark with heavy drops."

"Dead Gallop" is at times burdened by the philosophical queries it proposes. By the end, it exhausts itself; all that was swift and moving has become "motionless, like the pulley loose within itself." One may take this to mean that futility governs much of what one does in life and that everything is guaranteed only by the fact of death; however, if the poem refuses to give simple answers about the mysteries of death, it also disavows the possibility of such an easy summation. Its strength lies in the ponderous effect it creates as it proposes a collected series of thoughtful images that relate to both life and death.

Cynthia Wong

THE DEAD SEAL

Author: Robert Bly (1926-   )
Type of poem: Narrative
First published: 1972, as "The Dead Seal near McClure's Beach"; revised and republished as a pamphlet, *The Dead Seal near McClure's Beach*, 1973; collected in *Point Reyes Poems*, 1974

The Poem

When Robert Bly wrote "The Dead Seal near McClure's Beach" and other poems in the Point Reyes series, he was, in his own words, attempting to "describe an object or a creature without claiming it, without immersing it like a negative in his developing tank of disappointment and desire." These poems, set in the exquisitely beautiful but often violent part of the Northern California coastline around Point Reyes, focus on an unforgiving natural setting, whose very beauty is the siren's call that can lead ultimately to destruction.

The narrator in this prose poem is walking north toward Point Reyes near McClure's Beach when he spies ahead of him what appears to be a beached brown log. In line 1, even before he introduces the log metaphor, he tells his readers, "I come on a dead seal," lying on its back. Just as he speculates that the seal has been dead for only a few hours, he notices that it quivers, sending out a momentary sign of life, and is dismayed.

He moves into a physical description of the seal, back arched, small eyes closed. Its back is covered with oil, the "oil that heats our houses so efficiently." One flipper is folded over the stomach, "looking like an unfinished arm," while the other "lies half underneath." Bly compares the seal's skin to an old overcoat, noticing that it has scratches possibly made by sharp mussel shells.

When the narrator reaches out to touch the dying seal, it rears up and voices its objection in three cries: "Awaark! Awaark! Awaark!" It lunges toward the narrator, who has now become an antagonist. As the narrator leaps back, the seal "starts flopping toward the sea" but does not have the strength to make it. The seal looks up at the sky, resembling "an old lady who has lost her hair." Settling into the sand, it waits for the narrator to go. Bly writes merely, "I go."

The next day, the narrator returns to say his goodbye to the now-dead seal but does not find it where he left it. Rather, the seal is a quarter of a mile up the beach, "thinner, squatting on his stomach, head out." It is, much to the narrator's dismay, still breathing, still waiting to die. The seal looks at the narrator as a wave comes to shore and touches his muzzle. Bly now compares the crown of the seal's head to "a boy's leather jacket bending over some bicycle bars." The narrator comments matter-of-factly, "He is taking a long time to die." Then he says his goodbye, asking forgiveness "if we have killed you," wishing the dying animal comfort in death "when the sand will be out of your nostrils, and you can swim in long loops through the pure death, ducking under as assassinations break above you."

Forms and Devices

Bly chose the form of the prose poem because of its urgency and directness. He said, "The difference between lulling prose and the good prose poem is that the urgent, alert rhythm of the prose poem prepares us to journey, to cross the border, either to the other world, or to that place where the animal lives."

In "The Dead Seal near McClure's Beach," later titled simply "The Dead Seal," the poet writes in short, clipped sentences, many of the most crucial lines less than half a dozen words long: "My God, he's still alive," "He is dying," "I go," "He's dead now," "But he's not." The simplicity and economy of Bly's words and sentences help to make this prose poem vivid and effective. Bly's masterful control and restraint strip the poem of any mawkish sentimentality that a subject like this might engender.

Prose poems do not have any set rhyme scheme, although at times they may have incidental internal rhyme. Rather than depending on conventional rhyme patterns, they often employ such devices as alliteration, the repetition of consonant sounds, and assonance, the repetition of vowel sounds.

Although this poem involves both alliteration and assonance—"The body is on its back," "looking like an unfinished arm, lightly glazed," or "sharp mussel shells,"— Bly does not overly depend upon these devices to achieve his artistic ends. In the examples above, there is some intricate use of alliteration, particularly in "lightly glazed," where the *l* sounds in "lightly" alliterate with the internal *l* in "glazed," and even more notably in "sharp mussel shells," in which the *s* sounds alliterate in four instances while the *l* sound in "mussel" also alliterates with a similar sound in "shells." Assonance plays less of a role in this poem than alliteration.

Bly's use of metaphors is striking. He compares the dying seal to a brown log, the seal's cry to cries from Christmas toys, the seal's skin to an old overcoat, the seal itself to "an old lady who has lost her hair," and, most strikingly toward the end of the poem and the end of the seal's life, the crown of the seal's head to "a boy's leather jacket bending over some bicycle bars." These metaphors serve Bly well poetically because they are both visual and commonplace.

The major literary device Bly employs in "The Dead Seal near McClure's Beach" is imagery, most of which is visual. Bly makes his readers feel the textures of the seal's skin, the grittiness of the sand, the sting of grains of sand as they blow across the beach toward the sea. He describes the dying seal in considerable detail despite the brevity of the poem. Bly's readers know where the seal's flippers are and what they look like. They can visualize the seal's small eyes, first closed, then slanted. They observe its ribs, the vertebrae of its back, the whiskers "as white as porcupine quills," the sloping forehead.

All of this is overt observation. Bly does not presume to penetrate the seal's mind, which poetically would constitute an invasion of the subject's privacy and dignity. This would result in a maudlin, sickeningly sentimental poem, which this is not. The author depends upon the narrator to state the facts objectively, allowing readers to draw their own conclusions.

Themes and Meanings

As the title of this prose poem suggests, its prevailing theme is death, specifically the impending death of a beached seal, a victim of an oil spill. Its body, sleek with oil, rests on the beach resembling something inanimate, in Bly's words, "a brown log." There is still life in the seal. Despite its hopeless situation, it struggles to stay alive, clings to the small flicker of life that remains within it.

The seal becomes a metaphor for something larger. Through implication and subtle references, Bly suggests that the industrial-technological complex that has landed the seal in its present plight may indeed be threatening human life as well. Bly uses the last lines of this stirring prose poem to suggest this possibility. He implies that the seal, in death, will have a new life, one in which it will again swim "in long loops through the pure death, ducking under as assassinations break above you."

Bly uses two of his ten Point Reyes poems to comment on contemporary issues. "Finding a Salamander on Inverness Ridge," in which Bly decries the U.S. involvement in the Vietnam War, is a political poem that does not work fully because it fails to sustain a dialectical tension. "The Dead Seal near McClure's Beach," however, is a more subtle poem and lends itself better to poetic prose than the earlier poem does.

In this poem, Bly sketches a vivid word picture, invoking his readers' sympathy with the beached seal but never sentimentalizing his portrait of the dying animal. His approach is matter-of-fact: He casts the narrator as an intruder; the seal wants him to go; he goes. There is a sense here of the unity of all living things as well as the separateness of each living thing, the ying and the yang found in much of Bly's poetry. In the end, like the seal, all living things are alone. Also, all living things face overwhelming threats from events such as the oil spill that has beached the proud seal, now dying alone and with dignity on the deserted Northern California beach.

Bly makes his point in this prose poem through restraint and understatement. He tells nothing in detail about the oil spill, although at the time the poem was written, numerous oil spills had threatened the environments of many pristine areas. The public was sufficiently aware of the possibility and danger of such catastrophes that Bly could safely leave his readers to construct their own details once he had planted in their minds the hint of the points he was trying to make.

R. Baird Shuman

DEAD SOLDIERS

Author: James Fenton (1949-   )
Type of poem: Narrative
First published: 1981; collected in *The Memory of War: Poems, 1968-1982*, 1982

The Poem

"Dead Soldiers" is James Fenton's narrative of his memory of a luncheon engagement in 1973 on the edge of a jungle battlefield with a member of the Cambodian royal family—Prince Norodom Chantaraingsey—during that country's long-running civil war. The poem's ten stanzas contain varying numbers of lines of free verse that are deliberately conversational, straightforward, and nonpoetic in the traditional sense. This is poetry as news report, a deceptively simple account that gains power from the total impact of the poem rather than from the individual lines or words.

In the first five stanzas, the poem simply recounts the events of the lunch: It was hot and the poet was "glad of [his] white suit for the first time that day." The meal was an elaborate one: Dishes of frogs' legs, pregnant turtles and their eggs, marsh irises in fish sauce, and banana salad were served on the "dazzling tablecloth" and were accompanied by crates of brandy and soda, which were brought in by bicycles. During the lunch, armored personnel carriers (APCs—military vehicles similar to tanks) were spread out along the roadside to fire into the jungle at the unseen and perhaps absent enemy. Despite the elaborate menu, the meal was largely a liquid one during which many bottles of Napoleon brandy were steadily consumed. These empty bottles, known in slang as "dead soldiers," give the poem its title. While drinking and dining, the poet talked with the prince. Now, years later, the poet wishes instead he had spoken with the prince's drunken aide, a man who was the brother of Saloth Sar, better known as Pol Pot, leader of the violently revolutionary Khmer Rouge faction against whom the prince was fighting.

In the second five stanzas of the poem, the poet recalls that he did speak later with the prince's aide, who was nicknamed "the Jockey Cap," and that he was convinced that when the ruling elite was ousted from power, both the prince and the Jockey Cap would end up in comfortable exile in the south of France far from any war. In that setting, the only conflicts they would face would be "cafe warfare," and, if they had to be "reduced in circumstances" (a tellingly ironic phrase), they would continue to enjoy the good life that they had managed to import even into the midst of jungle fighting. Now, however, the poet realizes he was wrong because the conflict was a family quarrel as much as a revolution or a civil war: The prince was fighting his nephew Prince Norodom Sihanouk while the Jockey Cap was pitted against his brother Pol Pot. In such a struggle, the conflict is so vicious that the combatants are less concerned about victory for themselves than in simply keeping their relatives from tasting even the faintest fruits of victory. The poem concludes with the observations that while the two princes and Pol Pot are still fighting, the Jockey Cap probably has not "survived his good/ connections."

Forms and Devices

In form and presentation, "Dead Soldiers" is often closer to a prose news story than a traditional poem. Fenton has chosen to use irregular free verse without rhyme or other familiar devices, most likely because these obvious devices might come between his story and the reader. The purpose seems clear: to present the incidents of the poem and their meaning without any interpretation (except that of irony). The major poetic devices Fenton employs in "Dead Soldiers" are deceptively straightforward narrative coupled with a devastatingly dry use of irony. The narrative allows him to load the poem with a number of details that, innocent enough in themselves, coalesce to present the image of a murderous civil war waged with the incongruous juxtaposition of brutal savagery and elaborate luxury. The irony permits Fenton to comment upon people and events without overtly taking a moral position, a most useful device when writing about a situation so stained with confusion and ambiguity. Perhaps only deadpan narrative such as that employed in "Dead Soldiers" could successfully present the surreal scene of the poem: an elaborate luncheon, held on the edge of a jungle battlefield, complete with ice, brandy, soda, and almost decadent dishes. While the diners ate frogs' legs and the eggs of pregnant turtles ("boiled in the carapace"), troops and military vehicles advanced around them, firing into the sugar palms.

The narrative of the poem dissolves into irony. The site was not a true battlefield at all. The APCs fired into the jungle but "met no resistance." This supposedly military event was actually nothing but a drunken picnic, and the only "dead soldiers" it brought were the empty bottles of Napoleon brandy that piled up at the feet of the diners. Fenton inserts another sharp and typically understated irony when he notes that "On every bottle, Napoleon Bonaparte/ Pleaded for the authenticity of the spirit." On the surface, the narrative is blandly truthful: The image of the French emperor without validates the spirit within; in other words, a picture of Napoleon on the label means there is indeed brandy ("spirits" in the literal but also metaphorical sense) inside the bottle. Fenton's underlying meaning is much more corrosive: Napoleon was summoned up to validate this futile alcoholic exercise in the tropics as a real battle, something to equal the epic events of Napoleon's greatest victories and defeats at Austerlitz and Waterloo, respectively. Few comparisons could be more ironic or more devastating.

This devastating irony is underscored by the poem's next shift, which is a forecast of the prince and the Jockey Cap in the future, living in France "after the game was up," as if the civil war in Cambodia, perhaps all Indochina, was only a contest from which the lucky few could escape into comfortable exile. That setting replicates, in ironic reversal, the scene of the poem. In the future, the elegant life of dining and drinking will indeed be the only real thing; actual battle will be reduced to nothing but "cafe warfare" and matchboxes will easily substitute for APCs—perhaps because back in Cambodia, real APCs were as useless as matchboxes. In a sense, the phony yet deadly war that the prince played with real lives in Cambodia is reduced to its essence of make-believe: Nothing is real now, and nothing will be real then, except for the death and suffering of the "dead soldiers" (not the bottles, but human beings) who are invoked but never mentioned throughout the poem.

In "Dead Soldiers," Fenton switches constantly, almost casually, between these two levels of pretense and reality. On one hand, there is the battlefield that is actually the setting for an alcoholic revelry, but on the other hand, somewhere in the jungle, men and women are really suffering and dying. In one sense, there are figures who posture as leaders of countries and revolutions, but, in another sense, they are actually locked in an intense family conflict that involves only themselves, no matter how many thousands it kills, maims, and destroys. These contradictions are made stronger by the poem's indirect, matter-of-fact presentation of them.

Themes and Meanings

During his career, Fenton was a freelance reporter in Indochina, and a number of his poems deal with the violent revolutionary and civil wars in that region that he witnessed firsthand. The central theme of "Dead Soldiers" focuses on two primary aspects of those conflicts: first, the manner in which the brutality of war can coexist with a superficial "cultured" life; and second, the tendency for interfamily conflicts to be the most vicious and unforgiving of all. The first theme is announced boldly in the second line of the poem when Fenton notes that the prince had "Invited [him] to lunch on the battlefield," an invitation that would make sense perhaps only in such a surreal atmosphere as that of the Cambodian civil war. Yet the invitation is consistent with the situation because, as the poem notes with characteristic irony, "They lived well, the mad Norodoms, they had style." While this luncheon was unfolding, troops and armored personnel carriers were pushing into the jungle, seeking rebel soldiers to fight and kill, but none was there. However, just because there were no casualties on this particular battlefield does not mean there was none elsewhere or that the war was without victims. Those casualties and that violence were real and the luxurious lunch only underscored their true horror. The second theme, that of internecine family conflict, is more casually introduced and embroidered upon. In the fifth stanza, the poem casually notes that the prince's drunken aide, the Jockey Cap, was Saloth Sar's brother and reveals, a few lines later, that "Saloth Sar, for instance,/ Was Pol Pot's real name." In such a casual fashion is the identity of one of the twentieth century's most infamous mass murderers uncovered and linked to this seemingly minor incident in a distant jungle.

"Dead Soldiers" is a deceptively simple poem, a story that seems to have no meaning beyond the events it relates. However, once its narrative is opened to reveal its ironies and deeper references, it is clear that Fenton is writing a modern variant of Joseph Conrad's *Heart of Darkness* (1902), where the slim veneer of "civilization" is all too ready to crack, and the dead soldiers of his title are not only so many empty bottles but also too many fallen bodies.

Michael Witkoski

DEAR AUNT CHOFI

Author: Daisy Zamora (1950-   )
Type of poem: Epistle/letter in verse
First published: 1988, as "Querida tía Chofi," in *En limpio se escribe la vida*, 1988; English translation collected in *Clean Slate*, 1993

The Poem

"Dear Aunt Chofi" is a long poem in free verse with thirteen stanzas containing more than ninety-five lines in the English version. The title clearly suggests a letter from a niece to her aunt and serves to underscore the monologic nature of the poem, which is a one-sided conversation between the niece and her deceased Aunt Sofía. The narrator, "I," addresses herself to "you," the aunt, thus making the reader an outside observer, an eavesdropper on a conversation in print. Chofi is a fond nickname for Sofía, which means "wisdom." As she eulogizes her aunt, the narrator reviews the aunt's life.

The first stanza takes Aunt Chofi from birth to widowhood. She was "A rebel from birth" who insisted on marrying the man she loved despite her family's disapproval. The family's judgment was better than Sofía's, but that "purgatory" chapter of her life ended when her husband broke his neck in a drunken fall. "And I listened to you tell it," says the narrator, who heard Aunt Chofi's stories while witnessing her activities, described in the second stanza, as a baker, a creator of popular and religious images for ritualistic consumption at weddings and baptisms.

The third and fourth stanzas reveal that Chofi was an artist who smoked incessantly and painted vigorously, ignoring, or perhaps requiring, the chaos around her. As she painted, she was "Always talking, conversing" while her room became an ashtray for innumerable cigarette butts.

In the fifth, sixth, and seventh stanzas, the reader learns that Chofi was a sort of *curandera*, or folk healer, who served as "midwife, nurse" and who "laid out corpses, attended drunks,/ defended all lost causes//... even fought with the Guard/ and ended up exiled in Mexico." "The Guard" refers to the National Guard of Nicaragua, an American-trained army that supported the Somoza family dictatorship of thirty years that led to the Sandinista revolution in the late 1970's.

The eighth and ninth stanzas portray an older Aunt Chofi with "graying hair." A mother herself, Aunt Chofi "slaved" so her daughter could study in Mexico and the United States, but the daughter distanced herself ever further from her mother. Indeed, Aunt Chofi dies without her only daughter present. Though the daughter received the news of her mother's death in distant Buenos Aires, Argentina, the niece was with her aunt, as the tenth stanza indicates: "The morning before your death/ you were the same as ever,/ vociferous and loud-mouthed/ only complaining of great pain."

The last three stanzas bring Aunt Chofi full circle, from her birth as a rebel to her posthumous condition, where she will "answer only to bones," not to parents, husbands, daughters, or societal expectations. Aunt Chofi believed she had had many lives, many incarnations: in one "a little girl who died/ at birth, in another an adventurous male." The poet implies that "Dear Aunt Chofi" is another reincarnation of her beloved Sofía: "Now that you no longer exist, exist no longer/ perhaps you recognize yourself/ in this mirror." If the eyes are the mirror of the soul, this poem is surely the mirror of a life as well as a celebration of it.

Forms and Devices

The most obvious and most important device in this poem is the form itself. As the title indicates, the poem is a letter to Aunt Chofi. Unlike most letters, however, this one anticipates no reply, for it asks no questions, and it engages in no dialogue. The poet mentions herself only twice, and then only as Chofi's audience, demonstrating the importance of storytelling and the oral tradition: "I listened to you tell it" and "You, who told me about your perils." The remainder of the poem is addressed directly to Aunt Chofi, using the familiar *tú* form in the Spanish to indicate the intimacy of the relationship between the niece and her aunt. The poem recounts the aunt's life in a past tense that suggests repeated or ongoing activity rather than completed, finalized activity. Unfortunately, the use of the imperfect in Spanish, like the use of the *tú* form, is difficult to capture in translation to English.

The poem depends primarily on the list technique to build an image of Aunt Chofi by accretion of detail and to suggest the rich chaos that was her life: "Your habitat filled with brushes,/ oil paints, plaster molds, easels,/ canvases, canvas stretchers, statues of saints." The poet uses several metaphors as well. Aunt Chofi was an "Admirable Amazon in [her] fantastic feats." She was a "Witch doctor" who mixed medicines and potions to cure and prevent disease. Her life with her drunken husband was "a purgatory, a living hell."

Such metaphors create a vivid image of Chofi's personality, but perhaps the most important symbol in the poem is the mirror. Aunt Chofi has told her niece about her "perils in the mirror"—perhaps a reference to aging—and the niece has responded with "this mirror," the poem itself, which is meant to mirror the sheer energy and vivacity of Aunt Chofi's life. As Chofi, the "artisan" of paint brush and cake decorating, rendered her saints and Cinderellas, so too has the poet rendered a likeness of her aunt.

Themes and Meanings

"Dear Aunt Chofi" is about the life of a particular woman, but it is also about the artist as woman and rebel and about a woman's life in Nicaragua during a particular historical period. Doubly an artist (both painter and baker), Chofi's art was in her cakes, which she baked and decorated with such popular images as Snow White and the Seven Dwarfs and Cinderella for such conventional occasions as baptisms, first communions, adolescent coming out parties, and weddings. Yet Chofi was a woman who resisted societal expectations. She married against her family's wishes, she smoked when women were not allowed to smoke, and she ignored her housekeeping responsibilities, leaving her bed unmade while she painted canvases. Drawn to the mysterious, she "fell in love/ with the first legitimate guru from India/ to pass through Managua" and invented drinks to prevent "all possible diseases." Unlike most women, she never settled down but was "Always in transit," living in various rented rooms. Yet she was a beautiful young woman and later a dedicated mother to her only daughter.

Daisy Zamora grew up in a Nicaragua under the dictatorship of the Somoza family. When she was only four years old, her father was one of a group of insurgents imprisoned for attempting to overthrow the tyrannical government of Anastasio Somoza García, the father of the Anastasio Somoza Debayle who was overthrown by Zamora and her fellow revolutionaries in 1979. The Somoza dictatorship's power was maintained by the U.S.-trained and backed National Guard. As the poem informs the reader, Aunt Chofi's resistance to the Guard forced her into exile in Mexico. In fact, many Nicaraguans lived in exile during the Somoza dictatorship.

This poem, like many of her others in *Clean Slate*, focuses on a woman who manages to break through the limitations that her family and society try to impose. Though the consequences of self-motivation and striving to achieve her dreams may be as serious as the "living hell" of her marriage to Guillermo, the resultant freedom portrayed here seems well worth the difficulties. Another of Zamora's themes, motherhood, also arises in "Dear Aunt Chofi." Sadly, despite Chofi's dedication to her daughter, her daughter travels farther and farther away in an apparent attempt to create a physical distance to replicate the personal distance that she desires.

"Dear Aunt Chofi" is a "web of intimate sensibilities, founded in the concrete and even the mundane," as Barbara Paschke points out in her introduction to Zamora's *Riverbed of Memory* (1992). In "Dear Aunt Chofi," Daisy Zamora chronicles her aunt's life while witnessing to the time, place, and conditions for women evoked in the poem.

Linda Ledford-Miller

DEAR JOHN, DEAR COLTRANE

Author: Michael S. Harper (1938-   )
Type of poem: Elegy
First published: 1970, in *Dear John, Dear Coltrane*

The Poem

"Dear John, Dear Coltrane" is about love and concerns how pain and suffering can be transcended through "a love supreme." Divided into two different but unified voices, the poem reflects solemnly and antiphonally on an acceptance of physical decay, spiritual malaise, and fragmentation. Throughout the poem, decay and disease are regarded as a part of a natural cycle that can lead to an expression of love. Pain is regarded as necessary—"there is no substitute for pain"—and vital to the creative act, as suggested by images of planting and harvest (seed, fallow, roots) or escape and revitalization: "move by river . . . singing." Singing or creating music (or poetry) becomes the manner in which love of life is expressed.

The italicized lines are directly related to the voice and music of John Coltrane, a tenor and soprano saxophone player, who was born in Hamlet, North Carolina, in 1926 and died in Huntington, New York, near "the electric city," New York City, in 1967. Coltrane introduced a vibrant singing sound to the upper registers of the tenor sax and had a revolutionary effect on the use of the saxophone in jazz. His masterpiece, "A Love Supreme," is a four-part inspirational work produced in 1964 on which he literally sings, "a love supreme, a love supreme." In that composition, the last movement is improvised entirely from the syllabic content of a poem Coltrane had written; thus, Coltrane's musical composition was inspired by poetry as this poem is inspired by a musical composition.

The poetic voice describes the physical deterioration of Coltrane and in so doing bears "witness to this love" expressed by Coltrane and his music. The voice also continues the tradition of paying homage to heroes who have maintained a courage and will to struggle on despite personal suffering and pain. The poet's eulogy is both secular and religious as it describes the symptoms of illness—"impotence," "diseased liver" and spiritual malaise—which lead, paradoxically, to a "purity" in Coltrane's music. Disease and decay do not conquer the will, as Coltrane still "pumps out, the tenor kiss, tenor love."

Images related to Coltrane provide a counterpoint to the larger musical tradition among African Americans: spirituals, urban blues, and jazz. The creative act—musical composition—is a testament to one's being: To sing or shout of one's agony gives acknowledgment to one's existence. The poet testifies to the endurance of Coltrane by invoking images of escape, of "rivers and swamps" used by African Americans to flee physical and spiritual slavery, "singing: a love supreme."

This reference to spirituals and their evolution is followed by descriptions of plodding into the electric city and Coltrane's fragility and suffering. Significantly, spirituals and blues are direct influences on the evolution of jazz. The pattern of interlocking the African American musical tradition with Coltrane's individual life experiences illustrates the redemptive nature of music. The intensity of Coltrane's love also resonates with religious traditions that acknowledge humans as heroes when they maintain an embracing love of others despite private pain and suffering. Thus the universality of transcending personal pain and loss through love is linked to a jazz artist whose secular music is an expression of his love.

The poem, as elegies often are, is also a melancholy reflection upon life's transience. The question "what does it all mean?" has no definitive answer; there can ultimately be no answer except in how one responds to life. Paradoxically, the answer is to assert oneself: "cause I am." Coltrane's response to personal pain is through his music: the tenor kiss which, metaphorically, is a kiss of love coming from a heart in all its purity.

Forms and Devices

This lyric poem can be considered a jazz elegy in which voice and idiom are central to the poem's form and content. Contained within the formal structure is the traditional lament for a friend or a public figure. The poem follows a form that Harper has called "modal," a term he borrowed from music (it refers to types of scales often used in jazz improvisation). Harper uses the term to refer both to his principle of composition and to his ethical vision; "modality" encompasses "relationships" and "energy." It is always, he says, *about unity.* The form of "Dear John, Dear Coltrane" fittingly resembles the structure of a jazz number in which improvisation is open-ended. The first half of the title ("Dear John") indicates a personal letter of love that says goodbye (the poem was written before Coltrane's death). The second half ("Dear Coltrane") represents a public or formal letter of good-bye. The double title reflects the multiple meanings of the poem—personal and communal, present and historical.

Many of the poem's images are evolved from literary and historical allusions related to African American idioms and tradition. In the formal improvisational structure of the poem—itself a seeming contradiction—Harper relies on a formal arrangement of musical notes (words) being played (read or sung) to evoke emotions. Feelings are evoked by the arrangement of the "notes" and how they are played. On the one hand, the note "Dear John" is suggestive of an ancestral voice, John the Baptist, who baptizes Christ much like John Coltrane provides a baptism for the poet and for other saxophone players. On the other hand, "Dear John" echoes Father John in Jean Toomer's *Cane* (1923), who requests that Kabnis do something about "the sin the white folks 'mitted when they made th Bible lie." This kind of multi-referent suggests an improvisation which occurs within the context of a jazz musical composition.

The images throughout are often double entendres evolving from an African American historical point of view. As an example, the images of "Sex fingers toes" suggest the birth of Coltrane in North Carolina. They also are the necessary components of playing music and are suggestive of the aura of jazz. They are also, as Harper has indicated, images of sexual trophies taken from African American men who were lynched. Historical documents reveal that African American men were often castrated (de-sexed) before being lynched or burned and that spectators often took parts of the body of the victim as souvenirs.

Further, the images contrast with, or are in musical counterpoint to, the images of sterility and impotence—"genitals gone or going/ seed burned out." These images, juxtaposed to the images of family and church which literally influenced the "birth" of Coltrane's music, resonate with private, public, racial, and historical echoes. Implicit in all these images is the concept of humans having distinctive bodies which are separate from their souls, especially in the Christian context.

The metaphor of the marketplace and the religious tradition on the personal development of Coltrane and on the African American musical tradition is developed throughout the poem. These influences led to the development of Coltrane as artist and as propagator of the faith in people. His personal plight reflects how African Americans survived the institution of slavery. Images of planting further extend this "solo" theme as if the musician were planting the seed of spiritual revitalization despite physical impotence. The land is ripe for planting as Coltrane figuratively tucks his roots in the fallow fields of the public mind. The same situation applied for many African Americans escaping a slavery of the body or of the soul. In this manner, the poet relies upon historical idiom to convey the private agonies of a loved one.

The antiphonally playful section of "Why you so funky" and the italicized sections from Coltrane's music add a slightly different focus to the poem's voice. These idioms, from African American musical slang, evolve from the African American call-response religious tradition and the ballad tradition. This call-response form gives an answer of renewal to any question raised: "cause I am." Implicit in the question "Why you so black?" is the reference to an equally unanswerable question in another famous tune: "What did I do to be so black and blue?" There is no answer other than the assertion of one's being.

Themes and Meanings

The poem's aim is to characterize the redemptive nature of the African American experience in terms of the painful and private life of an African American musician. It progresses from the incantatory to personal description back to the incantatory to reveal the suffering of African Americans. The italicized repetitive incantation of "a love supreme," taken from the musical text as John Coltrane sang it, summarizes the poet's conception of the sustaining force that leads to wholeness despite pain and agony. Significantly, the recurrent leitmotif of supreme love binds each disparate image in the poem to the others.

Love characterizes the voice and spirit of Coltrane and the voice of the poet. A supreme love is needed to hold steady in the face of losing one's physical and symbolic manhood—"genitals gone or going/ seed burned out." Both voices are testaments to the enduring ability of love to create art from the painful and private agonies of being an African American.

The poem represents a poetic attempt to resist the assault against human dignity as music has done. The nightmare of loss, literally and figuratively, establishes responsibility for the creative artist. For the poet, the responsibility is to bring harmony out of chaos and to challenge the collective amnesia related to the personal and the communal. Harper accomplishes, in "Dear John, Dear Coltrane," what Robert Frost suggested the job of a poet is: to make us remember what we have forgotten. His poem makes readers remember John Coltrane and the essence and vitality he and other African American innovators represent. It also testifies to the eternal spirit that should guide humankind: "a love supreme, a love supreme."

Norris B. Clark

DEATH & CO.

Author: Sylvia Plath (1932-1963)
Type of poem: Meditation
First published: 1963; collected in *Ariel*, 1965

The Poem

"Death & Co." is a short poem in free verse, its thirty-one lines divided into seven stanzas. The title suggests the name of a business or corporation; its function is to establish the mood of the poem, which is ironic and mocking. Death is often viewed with ambivalence, something that not only takes away life but also (sometimes mistakenly) offers comfort to those who are in pain or who believe in an afterlife; death can seem cold and officious, but also, perhaps, ironic in the form it finally takes. The poem is written in the first person in the form of a confession monologue in which the speaker mockingly describes a terrifying—and coldly businesslike—scene unfolding before her eyes. While it is often the case that poets use a persona to distinguish themselves from the poem's speaker, no such distinction is implied in this poem. The poet Sylvia Plath, like the speaker, conceives a monologue wherein one person speaks alone. Although Plath is considered by many to be a "confessional" poet, this poem seems less like a confession to someone, explicitly or implicitly, and more like a monologue to the self.

"Death & Co." begins with the idea of a duality, a form common to many of the subjects in Plath's poetry. In this case, the speaker, while being visited by two mordant and menacing figures, becomes aware that death is not singular but has two faces. It is a realization that does not surprise her ("It seems perfectly natural now"), but it terrifies her nonetheless. She graphically describes first the one face and then the other, beginning with "the one who never looks up." He is cold and distant, and his eyes are lidded to avoid contact with the speaker. He reminds her of a marble statue, a death mask "like Blake's." In the second stanza, the poet continues the litany of characteristics that distinguish the first face of death. He publicly exhibits the trademark signs of the *memento mori*, reminding the speaker how accomplished he is by the appearance of his many birthmarks. By the end of this stanza, the poet realizes that she is his next victim. Her statement "I am red meat" mocks the serious nature of her realization while revealing her inevitable fear of the moment. She steps aside as he tries to grab her: "I am not his yet." Still overtly threatening, he begins to play a psychological game with her by undermining those things in her physical world she feels are safe: her physical attractiveness and her children. The speaker of the poem notes his overarching self-confidence.

While he is a perfectionist, a kind of artist bragging about his accomplishments, his partner is oily, sociable, and fawning. The first wants to be respected and admired, the second "wants to be loved." Yet they operate together: "The frost makes a flower,/ The dew makes a star." Hoping to be noticed by neither figure, the speaker retreats into stasis. However, the lure and inevitability of the business the two contradictory figures have come for is pronounced, in the speaker's mind, by the inevitable ringing of the bells. By the last line of the poem she knows her time is up, but her sarcasm remains: "Somebody's done for."

Forms and Devices

Early criticism of Plath's poetry tended to see it as confessional in nature, an autobiography of the poet's personal neuroses. Following that line of thinking, readers who examine the imagery closely will time and again be referred back to the poet's own desperate life, which was filled with shame and psychic fragility. The early critics viewed her work as successful not because it was strictly confessional but because the self placed at the center of the poem makes "vulnerability and shame" representative of a wider civilization. The private events are universalized through the speaking voice. However, later literary critics began to focus more on her developing poetic and the achievement of her voice and tone, while admitting that much of her content was in fact drawn from her own life. Perhaps the strongest reason to believe that Plath's clever crafting of her poetry places her outside the strictly confessional school of poetry (a school that includes the poets John Berryman, Theodore Roethke, and Anne Sexton) is that she avoids sounding confessional; she lacks self-pity and an overreaction to what might seem appropriately terrifying. In other words, she constructs in her later poems dramatically staged performances that pose a tension through the face-off between life, movement, and energy on one hand and death, inertia, and passivity on the other.

This juxtaposition between life force and death force may be said to be at the heart of "Death & Co.," which reads like a bizarre juxtaposition of things public and private. Characteristic of this poem as well as several other of Plath's later poems are the self-reflexive quality of her experience, a rhythmic energy, clearly ambiguous images, and the colloquialisms of the speaking voice. All of this suggests that the poem is staged as a process of change and discovery narrated by a speaker who is both mocking and vengeful. For instance, "Death & Co." opens with a juxtaposition of the two figures of death that appear before the speaker. As the poet's discovery of their business unfolds, she carefully controls her response to their visit with a form of self-parody that helps keep in mind the exchange between the audience's reception and her own feelings. She imposes limits of rhyme and rhythm so she can measure changes within her personal situation. The rhythmical energy of the speaking voice, in fact, is a reminder of how sporting, playful, vengeful, or mocking she can be. The first two stanzas, for example, include the repetition of numbers ("Two, of course there are two"), colors ("nude/ Verdigris" and "red meat"), alliteration ("balled, like Blake's"), and slant rhyme ("birthmarks that are his trademark"). Sentence patterns are repeated again and again with interesting developments: "He tells me how badly I photograph./ He tells me how sweet." The rhymes are widely separated ("sweet" in the third stanza rhymes with "feet" in the fourth stanza). However, the self-conscious, performing, and poetic self of the speaker puts her in touch with moment-to-moment changes and forces the audience to sit rapt, to accept the form as expression and artifact. It is characteristic of Plath to end her poetry with the same ironic awareness held by the speaker throughout the poem. In the final stanza and last line of "Death & Co.," her ear for music and vernacular is right on the mark. She is still recording her speaker's shifting sensibility even to the point that the speaker, feeling personally diminished, still maintains her voice of manic buffoonery.

Themes and Meanings

"Death & Co." is a poem about life and death. How does a woman with a troubled relationship to both life and death envision the moment when death comes to visit her? How does her poetic vision of this complicated scene get articulated? References to death abound in Plath's poems (she attempted suicide three times, the last successfully), yet her differing figures of death reveal a fascination more with how the living view death itself than with what they imagine death to be like after life. One may wonder if this is a kind of madness. In her many poems that address the theme of death (especially her last poems, collected in *Ariel*), the images are frightening and surreal. Still, the poetry out of which "Death & Co." comes is not without a kind of history. Emily Dickinson wrote harrowing poems on madness and dying, while Theodore Roethke, Anne Sexton, Robert Lowell, and Hayden Carruth all have explored similar subject matter.

The common theme among Plath's "death poems" is, interestingly, the ambivalent attitude toward death they reveal. In "Death & Co.," the ambivalence takes the form of a speaker who seems part of a dramatically staged performance of being in wait for death while revealing an assertiveness, wit, ingenuity, and sheer life force in attempting to outwit death. She performs even though she is faced with the suffering and pain of personal failure (how badly she photographs and her dead babies) as well as inherited cultural myths. The speaker avoids confessional or self-pitying overreactions. In fact, the performing self suggests underlying feelings of comedy.

"Death & Co." is also about poetry as a process of discovery and reaction. As the poet reveals the speaker's fantasy (or her madness) about death as a slowly savored, dramatic show of loss, pain, and personal diminishment, readers see that the shifting sensibility offers a close-up scrutiny of just how one is shaped by and impelled to shape her material. In her occasional narrative asides ("I am red meat," "I am not his yet," "I do not stir") it is not clear whether she speaks to an audience or to herself. What is important is not to whom she addresses her monologue but that she experiences this performance as an emotionally charged process of discovery and reaction. The self-conscious performance, then, becomes a substitute for a fixed identity, suggesting that for Plath any attempted literary shaping or definition of self is inadequate and unfinished.

Holli G. Levitsky

DEATH, BE NOT PROUD

Author: John Donne (1572-1631)
Type of poem: Sonnet
First published: 1633, in *Poems, by J. D.: With Elegies on the Authors Death*

The Poem

Holy Sonnet 10 (in a series of nineteen) gets its traditional title from the first four words of the poem, in which the poet issues a challenge to death that it should not boast of its conquests of people nor take pride in their fear of it. The poet depicts death as a force that is supposed to be "mighty and dreadful" because it kills everybody, but he denies its invincibility, pitying "poor" death and declaring that it will not kill him. Assuming the voice of a preacher—John Donne was an Anglican minister—the poet attempts to convince his audience, by the power of his rhetorical attack and his faith in the afterlife, not to be afraid of death, saying that people actually do not die forever.

In a series of paradoxes, the poet attacks the conventional characterization of death as man's invincible conqueror. Rather than being a fearful experience, death brings greater release and pleasure than rest and sleep, which people use to restore their energy. Death not only provides "Rest of . . . bones" but also "soul's delivery," a release into a peaceful eternity. Moreover, death is not the tyrant that it imagines itself to be; rather, it is a slave to the arbitrary dictates of fate and chance and to the whims of capricious monarchs and murderers.

The poet concludes his attack with a series of lines beginning with the word "and" as a connected summary of the charges he amasses against death. Death is associated only with the most destructive elements in life—poison, war, and sickness. Moreover, opium and other drugs can put a person to sleep as easily and better than death does. Thus, as a result of its servility, weaknesses, and association with the worst human events, death should not swell with pride. The final two lines, an unrhyming couplet, sum up the poet's defeat of vainglorious death: People may die, but they do not stay dead. They awaken from death as if from a short sleep into an eternity in which "death shall be no more." Death shall die then, but humans will live eternally. In fourteen lines, Donne has carried out an effective rhetorical attack against the invincibility of death and, at the same time, has declared his faith in an eternal afterlife's joys that shall transcend the horrors of earthly life.

Forms and Devices

Donne uses his characteristic metaphysical wit in the choice of structure, poetic techniques, diction, sounds, meter, irony, and paradox. The structure of "Death, be not proud" consists of three units of four lines (quatrains) and a final unrhyming couplet. Each of the quatrains is composed of one sentence that Donne artfully extends over the four lines, thus imparting a sense of unity and development. Each quatrain presents an important link in the exposition of the argument against death, and the couplet both concludes and summarizes the attack with a ringing declaration of faith in the certainty of the afterlife and the demise of death.

In the first quatrain, the poet declares that death cannot kill its victims—that is, eliminate their existence forever. This quatrain ends with the poet's assertion of will in the face of death ("nor yet canst thou kill me") with the personal pronoun "me" representing the power of the individual to defy death. The next four lines depict the ways in which death actually is pleasurable and provides the soul's delivery into eternity. The third quatrain groups death with the baleful instruments that induce it, and it ends with the only question in the poem, which recalls the first four words of the poem— Why does death puff with pride if it is not the invincible vanquisher of men it imagines itself to be?

The ending couplet reduces death to a short sleep before the eternal awakening when "Death . . . shalt die." The use of sibilants in "short sleep" and in the future auxiliaries "shall" and "shalt" intensifies the swiftness of the movement into eternity. Finally, "eternally" in "we wake eternally"—along with "delivery" in "soul's delivery"—is the longest word syllabically in the poem, and it represents the lasting victory over transitory, monosyllabic death.

The principal poetic techniques used by Donne to diminish death are to depict it as a person and then to challenge death as if the poet is engaged in single combat with it. Death can come in so many ways at any time to anybody that it seems to have myriad forms, so Donne reduces death by personifying it as a weak person subservient to the worst elements of life and unable to counter the poet's challenge.

Another technique employed to diminish the power of death is through the alternation of regular and unconventional prosodic stress. When Donne wants to show that death is not to be feared, he orders it within the regular iambic beat ("And soonest our best men with thee do go"), but when he wants to attack death, he employs a pounding, sustained stress ("Death, be not proud," "Death, thou shalt die"). Similarly, Donne's choice of primarily monosyllabic words enhances the power of his simple declaration of defiance to death.

One of the central ironies of the poem is demonstrated by Donne's use of variants of death and words related to it to dominate a poem directed against death. Death is the first word of the sonnet, and the last line, which declares the end of death, contains "death" twice and "die" as the last word of the couplet. The poet does not run away from death; he faces it directly and finally reduces it to the isolated and unrhyming last word of the poem. Moreover, since most of the other words in the poem contain the letters *d* and *t*, which are found in "death," it is as if they are surrounding and attacking death on its own phonetic grounds—"not," "proud," "art," "but," "though," "yet," "canst," "those," "then," "thinkst," "dost," and "desperate."

Themes and Meanings

"Death, be not proud" is a sonnet concerning the ways in which one can defeat the fear of death and anticipate the happiness of an eternal afterlife. The poet creates various derogatory images of death in an effort to reduce its power as humankind's most ubiquitous enemy. Life not only ends in death, it also is dominated by the presence and potentiality of death, which can be encountered anywhere at any time. It comes in many shapes and ways, but Donne wants to show that death is not the end but only the short passage to an eternal afterlife where death will not exist. Therefore, the poem consists of a series of paradoxical images of death as powerful, yet weak and servile. Donne appears as the preacher-poet-philosopher looking on the death skull and describing the ways in which one can deny its victories.

The transcendence of death through faith in an afterlife is not the conventional theme of the Renaissance sonnet. Sonnets usually concern love problems between a plaintive lover and a hardhearted mistress whose love he is trying to win through the persuasiveness of his rhetorical suffering and wooing. William Shakespeare's sonnets deal with his rivalries with other poets and his tempestuous relationships with lovers, but they also present the conflict between time, the destroyer, and human beauty as expressed in timeless poetry. Shakespeare defiantly declares that his loved one "shall shine more bright in these contents [poem]/ Than unswept stone, besmeared with sluttish time." Donne, on the other hand, places his faith in the certainty of an afterlife as the antidote to the inevitability of death in the physical world.

Donne's themes throughout the Holy Sonnets are anguished, because his is not an easy faith. Donne petitions God for help to overcome his temptations by drawing him toward God like a magnet and by replacing the fire of lust with the fiery spiritual zeal that will heal his divided self. He uses violent physical images of imprisonment, battering, and ravishment as the means of God's releasing him from the transitory world into the eternal.

In Holy Sonnet 10, Donne wants to release humans from the horrors of death that are found in war, sickness, poison, and crime and which take the best people soonest to their graves. He consoles his audience by arguing that earthly life is not the final existence. If it were, death would win and deserve to be proud of its victories. Because of the afterlife, however, death's horrors are diminished, its power is reduced, and finally, death is dismissed as an insuperable force. Donne does not flinch from the horrors of earthly life, but he is determined to impart meaning to one's existence by describing one's final destination.

Frank Ardolino

DEATH FUGUE

Author: Paul Celan (Paul Antschel, 1920-1970)
Type of poem: Lyric
First published: 1952, as "Todesfuge," in *Mohn und Gedächtnis*; English translation
collected in *Poems of Paul Celan*, 1988

The Poem

"Death Fugue" is structured like a musical fugue, in which a main idea or phrase is
systematically repeated throughout the composition. The six irregular stanzas present
the speaker's perspective on a Nazi concentration camp; the lack of punctuation be-
tween thoughts suggests the deterioration of the speaker's consciousness as he ex-
poses the atrocities which the crematorium has wreaked upon those condemned to
die. He also repeats incessantly, as if to suggest an urgent need to fill the void of death.
Paul Celan's parents both were murdered in a concentration camp; Celan himself was
taken to a forced-labor camp. Throughout his life he was haunted by their deaths and,
in a sense, by his own survival.

The first stanza is an exposition of the time, space, and place of the death camp. The
poem's narrator speaks for a collective and condemned "we" who dig graves from
morning to night. The repetitiveness of time is revealed in the first two lines of the
poem: "daybreak" is followed by "sundown," which is followed respectively by
"noon," "morning," and "night" again. Time has ceased to flow with distinction for
these workers of the death factory. Meanwhile, the officer who is responsible for
keeping the gravediggers in line is seen writing letters home to Germany. That he cor-
responds nightly with the motherland indicates that the camps are outside Germany.

Each subsequent stanza reveals the cruelly civic and barbaric nature of the camps.
Every image presented is "answered" by an opposing one. The golden hair of
Margarete from Germany, for example, contrasts with the "ashen" hair of the Jew
Shulamith. Daybreak soon becomes dusk or "sundown"; the sound of the spades hit-
ting dirt is juxtaposed against the sound of Jews forced to sing and dance as they dig;
the "black milk of daybreak" which characterizes the sky under which the Jews dig is
contrasted with the starry and brilliant night under which the officer writes home.

The sharp distinctions between the condemned Jews and the Germans in the open-
ing stanzas emphasize the relationship between the victims and their oppressors. As
the poem progresses, the relationship intensifies. The officer "calls out more darkly"
and demands that the condemned "jab deeper into the earth." The swifter the com-
mands, the more quickly the condemned must act in their movements toward death. In
order to hasten their final annihilation, the officer steps out of his house and moves
closer to the condemned; he stops and gives himself the necessary distance to fire his
"leaden bullets" at any who disobey him. The rest will be gassed to death in the crema-
torium.

In the last stanza, the separation between the dead and those responsible for death is expressed in the even number of lines describing each. The first half of the stanza reiterates the scene of the gravediggers, while the second half cruelly crowns death as "a master from Germany." This phrase is repeated as the speaker faces the point of death (signified by the point of the gun). The last lines shift back to contrasting the hair of Margarete with that of Shulamith; with the striking contrast of each with regard to life and death, this image expresses the final tendrils of death.

Forms and Devices

The musical structure, as well as the allusion to music within the poem, belies the anguish of death, particularly the mass deaths in the concentration camps. Some have objected to the poet's "aestheticizing" the death camps, particularly charging Celan with the audacity to write lyric poetry after the Holocaust. Others perceive that the death of Celan's parents in Transnistria compelled the poet to transpose personal anguish into art, as this early poem suggests.

In fact, the systematic repetition and the musical aspects of the poem indicate that the condemned are no longer in control of life. Their activities are as mindless as their forced and mechanized behavior is soulless. They "speak" and "think" in run-on phrases, and the poem literally reflects their mental and physical deterioration. They dig graves and are forced to sing and dance even as they prepare for death; in the final coup de grâce, they beg for death so they can disappear into nothingness. Ironically, they sing for death in order to escape from death.

With the exception of stanzas 3 and 5 (which serve as the "counterpoint" in the musical fugue structure), the second half of each stanza shifts from the viewpoint of the condemned to the officer and what he represents—Nazi Germany. These sections reinforce the oppressiveness of the concentration camp. Each is as repetitive as the first section, but with a difference, since here, the officer acts as an agent of death. His power over the condemned can be seen in the variety of terrors he is capable of causing: "whistles his Jews," "commands us strike up for the dance," "grabs his iron," "plays with the serpents," "strikes you with leaden bullets," and "sets his pack on us." If the condemned have only one course available to them, it is the task of the officer to both hasten and torment them toward this end.

The poem's effect derives as much from the irony of the musical aspects as it does from the juxtaposition of extreme opposites. The first image, "black milk," is already suggestive of the deep taint of death. If the infant drinks of the mother's nourishment in its whiteness and purity, the condemned victims drink endlessly the dregs of their graves. They are doomed to the black smoke of the crematorium. Shulamith's "ashen hair" reinforces the results of cremation, while it contrasts with the "golden hair" of Margarete. The blond hair, as well as the officer's blue eyes, contrasts with the dark and black of the victims.

The shifts in opposing images, besides indicating the difference between the Germans and the Jews, also create the effect of heightened emotion and a sense of growing despair. The officer's perfunctory commands (reporting to Germany and keeping the prisoners in line) give way to increasingly cruel treatment and attitude.

In stanza 3, the speaker observes that the officer is noticeably more excited and animated. In stanza 5, "He calls out more sweetly play death death is a master from Germany," and he promises the condemned a space in the crematorium, "a grave you will have in the clouds."

In the next stanza, "he grants us a grave in the air" is a remark that expresses a twisted gratitude. These images serve as a counterpoint, an answer to the main theme of the men digging their own graves. As the condemned grow more mechanical and hopeless, the officer expresses a malicious glee at the pain he inflicts. In the end, it is death—as signified by the Nazis—which reigns supreme.

Themes and Meanings

"Death Fugue" exposes the savage cruelty of the concentration camps by plainly describing the conditions. Everything that is human and active (working, singing, dancing, writing) is directed toward death. Without being didactic, the poet expresses the unforgettable conditions of the camps. The very vividness of the poem's first-person narration, however, also points to an incongruity within the poem: The poem's speaker, along with the other people in the camp, may be assumed to have been killed. Celan uses this incongruity to remind readers how far they will always be from knowing the full truth of the death camps.

The musical structure distances the reader from the events as they are presented in the poem. Rather than elicit an aesthetically pleased response from the reader, the poem achieves an opposite effect by making each episode tell what happened as directly as possible, but in language that also reflects the progression toward death. The poet drives each point home with the repetition of images, especially the ones that lead from digging the graves to the final end, represented by the rising smoke.

In addition to the musical association of the word "fugue" (which comes from the Latin word meaning "to flee"), there is a psychological meaning, a state in which a patient suffers from a pathological amnesiac condition and has no recollection of incidents that occurred during the illness. Viewed from this perspective, the poem could also express the devastating historical fact of the Holocaust. It is impossible to forget the millions who were condemned to die by the Nazis, even though the full extent of what happened may never be known. Those involved have tried to flee from taking responsibility for their crimes. At the Nuremberg trials, for example, the Nazis frequently claimed that what happened at the death camps was the result of their merely following orders.

Cynthia Wong

DEATH IN THE DAWN

Author: Wole Soyinka (1934-   )
Type of poem: Lyric
First published: 1967, in *Idanre and Other Poems*

The Poem

"Death in the Dawn" is a free-verse poem in seven stanzas and thirty-five lines of variable length. While it is in a sense a monologue, an address to the reader as a "traveller," and a narrative account of life as a journey, its introspective conclusion about the self may best identify it as a lyric. The paradoxical title (death might be expected to take place in the evening) announces the contradictory concepts the poem will explore. Any concept implies its opposite, but in fact two deaths do occur during this dawn.

Wole Soyinka provides a prose headnote describing the occasion that apparently gave rise to the composition, the actual setting on a road into Lagos, Nigeria, and a summary of the two accidents causing the deaths of a white cockerel and a human being. These accidents provide the two climactic moments in the poem, the first in stanza 4 and the second in stanza 7.

Stanza 1 makes two demands on the reader. All readers are travelers who have no choice but to begin life's journey at birth, in a state of innocence: "Traveller, you must set out/ At dawn." They must also experience reality and the fundamental fact of life, a dependence on water and air: "The dog-nose wetness of earth."

In stanza 2, as the headnote explained, the traveler is the driver of an automobile who can now turn off the headlights because the sun is rising. The natural and human events of morning become slowly visible: the coloring of the sky, farmers heading for fields, the gradually "receding" shadows of trees, market people in "swift, mute/ Processions" making their way to towns. A mist that has not yet lifted partially covers the scene when, in stanza 4, the first accident occurs.

The headnote suggests that the cockerel had some responsibility for its own death, as it "flew out of the dusk and smashed itself against my windscreen." The cockerel in the poem becomes a sacrifice in a propitiation rite, with no hint of who is performing the ceremony—the driver, the cockerel, or some unknown power. In any case, the poet announces the death as a significant but "futile rite." The act has suddenly turned the current season into winter: The cockerel's feathers become snowflakes; the symbol of dawn is dead. The driver does not seem to take the death seriously, despite the obvious signs that he should exercise caution.

The second part of the poem begins in an indented stanza 5, with a voice from the past ("the mother") warning a child to beware of danger on the road of life.

The narrator then resumes with an interpretation for the traveler of the cockerel's death. It is one of many "presages" of human achievement. Anyone who gets in the way of "man's Progression" will experience such a "Perverse impalement."

Then, in the final stanza, the warning of stanza 4 and the prayer of stanza 5 materialize in the death of a human being in an automobile accident. The narrator sees "another Wraith," not the cockerel's this time but a fellow creature's, a "Brother" killed in and by his own "invention." Not only does the narrator now question the presumed rightness of human progress in science and technology, but also he indicts and mocks himself as both killer and victim.

Forms and Devices

Soyinka is a Nigerian, a Yoruba, writing in English. His anticipated audience thus extends far beyond his own country and his own culture. The imagery he uses in "Death in the Dawn" is easily recognizable to a Western reader in its descriptive function and its significance. It is, at least on the surface, conventional—even, one might be tempted to say, universal. Dawn and spring represent the beginning of life, evening and winter the end of it. Light is life; darkness and shadows are death. Life is a journey. The strangeness and novelty of twilight seem to be privileged over the "naked" day, as is the natural over the artificial. Even the notion of sacrifice has a positive force; one ignores its rites at one's peril. Such imagery uses language that is accessible to, for example, an American audience as well as, one assumes, a Yoruba audience.

A dominant allusion in the poem is distinctively Western, although not American but French. Stanzas 2 and 3 paint a picture of the dawn the driver sees, a painting in the style and technique of certain French Impressionists: pointillism. The narrator announces nature's artistry with the "Faint brush pricklings" that color the sky and light the earth below. The resulting scene is a characteristically luminous, subjective impression of nature: the "Cottoned feet" of the farmers, the "soft kindling, soft receding" of the shadows, "the mist," the "faceless throng," and the "grey byways." The narrator then closes the description by calling it a "counterpane," literally a "pricked" quilt. This making of impressions with points translates in the real world into a "Perverse impalement" of the cockerel in stanza 6. Something significant has happened to this innocent image.

Another characteristically Western feature in the imagery is the habit of pairing off concepts as opposites. Every image, conventional or otherwise, has its stated or implied contrary, beginning with the title's juxtaposition of dawn and death. The cockerel is both a harbinger of morning and the apocalyptic messenger of death. Dawn as twilight resembles evening, its opposite. The automobile, symbol of human progress, destroys its symbolic inventor. The mother in stanza 5 designates "The right foot for joy, the left, dread." The farmer in stanza 2 must kill the earthworm to cultivate the soil. Not at all averse to using puns, Soyinka chooses the words "counter" (opposite) and "pane" (pain, pane of glass, point)—in a form commonly used to name a soft cover for a bed—to describe the scene and the instrument (the windshield) that kills the cockerel. Further, the poet uses the Impressionist technique pointillism ("pricklings") to create a soft painting.

Like its imagery, the form of the poem moves in opposites, from the tranquil, cushioned setting of stanzas 2 and 3 to the grim death of stanza 4 and from the vain optimism of stanza 6 to the shocked doubt of stanza 7. It would seem that Soyinka is consciously using, rather than being used by, these conventional images, these binary oppositions.

Themes and Meanings

One central fact about the poem seems clear enough: It begins as a lesson for someone else and ends as a question about the self. It is "a word to the wise" that turns back on itself. It is a discourse that demystifies but that then undercuts itself to demystify again.

The advice offered in stanza 1 seems reasonable enough, close as it is to being a set of truisms. Perhaps the obviousness of the direction and its generality are the problem. In any case, what the speaker goes on to advise, in stanzas 2 and 3, offers inadequate means to experience reality. The direct contact of feet on "The dog-nose wetness of earth" translates not into doing and living but into observing the sensuousness and beauty of the earth, its "joys and apprehensions," from inside an automobile. The windshield becomes a barrier and nature a scene or a painting—a work of art. Art, it would seem, at least this kind of art, is an escape from reality. The death of the cockerel explodes the myth, as another voice, in stanza 4, declares: subjective impressions deceive.

Yet they persist; neither the warning of the smashed cockerel nor the mother's reasonable advice in stanza 5, in the form of a prayer that hopes futilely to protect, can divert the willful narrator-prophet. In stanza 6, the original voice, turned defiant, abandons art for the more aggressive (perhaps masculine) "marvels" of technology. The second voice returns in the final stanza to suggest the failure of both technology and the ego that glorifies it. Perhaps at this point the two voices merge. The human death may shake the cocksureness of the innocent and wake him out of his dream.

The form of the poem, then, as with the imagery, seems to rely on a conventional narrative device that identifies meaning with discovery, the initiation theme according to which the innocent achieve maturity. The poem seems to be a melange of at least two voices or narrators, one naive, the other skeptical—perhaps two attitudes within one persona playing against one another in point-counterpoint. The reader discovers that the would-be prophet is not reliable, that art is not a sure guide to experience, and that technology and human inventiveness are not immune from repercussions. The other voice can only warn (in stanza 4) that rites may prove futile and, at the end, question its own assumptions, its creativity, and its social and personal identity.

If the poem is about itself as well as about human experience, it warns that it is not a source of truth. It is largely bound by its own language. A Yoruba uses English words (including the concept of "winter") for a Nigerian setting, a Western concept of art (pointillism), and a product of Western technology (the automobile) to define life and the self. Yet the poem is probably not a condemnation of the West, which is viewed sometimes as having stepped in between the self and the world. It does not finally or necessarily privilege one culture over another, nor, more generally, does it privilege one value over its opposite. It does not blame a culture but tries to name a situation. It suggests the unpredictability of life and the difficulty (or impossibility) of knowing the "dog-nose wetness of earth," of controlling anything—one's fate, one's products, one's words, or the self.

Yoruba mythology offers its own commentary in the naming: The god Ogun is a blacksmith who creates bridges across the voids of human thought and a warrior who annihilates even his own army. Dual, contradictory roles are not the sacred preserves of Western thought. Ogun, Soyinka's favorite divinity, is the inventor of the automobile, the symbol of human progress; he is the creator and the destroyer. The poem does not condemn; it faces the riddle of reality. Its final question about the identity of the self is at the same time compassionate, self-effacing, and egocentric.

Thomas Banks

THE DEATH OF A TOAD

Author: Richard Wilbur (1921-   )
Type of poem: Elegy
First published: 1950, in *Ceremony and Other Poems*

The Poem

Richard Wilbur's "The Death of a Toad" hauntingly depicts the demise of a toad "caught" and "clipped" by a power mower in a garden accident. The incident was apparently witnessed by Wilbur, who responded in verse—enlarging the event to metaphoric and symbolic proportions reflecting the poet's concerns with a metaphysical reality beyond material existence; with the nature and meaning of death; and with the extinction of primal forces by an inevitable, unstoppable, and impersonal technology. The poem is composed of three stanzas, each with six lines of varying lengths, visually and metrically balanced to one another. The form and balance of the stanzas create a visual and formal precision, a sort of metrical "cage" in ironic counterpoint to the disturbing portrayal of the toad's last moments on earth.

The first stanza of the poem relates the mutilating event and the subsequent "hobbling hop" that the toad manages in an attempt to find a suitable and serene place to die. Wilbur utilizes inverted word order in the opening line ("A toad the power mower caught") and a series of directional prepositional phrases so that the reader visually and emotionally follows the toad to "a final glade." The second and pivotal stanza focuses on the actual death of the creature and frighteningly mirrors it (an image repeated in the last stanza) in the toad's "banked and staring" eyes. This stanza underscores the absolute finality and impersonality of death.

Stanza 2 also ends in an uncompleted thought, a prepositional phrase punctuated with a comma—joining it irrevocably with the last stanza, which portrays the dead toad and its "attending" to something beyond itself. The repetition of the preposition "toward" in both the second and the last stanzas arrests the reader's attention, forcing the reader to consider various possibilities or realities beyond the material—and now lifeless—form of the "antique" toad.

The final stanza then couples these possibilities with a depressing and ironic image of the dying day reflected in the toad's still reflecting—but unperceiving—eyes. It is in the final stanza that the image of a cold, relentless, impersonal technology (the "power mower" of the poem's first line) is reiterated and juxtaposed with an irrelevant nature that has become "castrate" and "haggard" as reflected in the toad's eyes, "which still appear to watch." This last clause is an indication of the powerful wordplay Wilbur customarily includes in his poems: The word "still" means both "continually" and "silent," which also underscores the dual meaning of "appear"—a word appealing to one's sense of sight, which also means "seems." The double entendre prevails with the final word of line 17: "watch." The toad looks or seems to "watch." The question is implied: What is he watching?

This quietly terrifying poem not only examines death but also questions one's presumptions about its meaning. Lost is the grandeur, even the pathos, of this creature's death because the event is bathed in the irony of accident and of bearing witness to a life force it can no longer perceive or enjoy. In addition, its future is almost trivialized—and along with it humankind's future—because of a machine's barbaric indiscretion.

Forms and Devices

Wilbur's poetry is universally recognized and honored for its skill, sophistication, wit, formality, elegance, control, expertise, and impersonal and artful style. Wilbur is viewed as a poet who eschews social and political commentary, choosing to remain impersonal, refusing to put self-confession at the center of his poems and instead emphasizing skilled craftmanship and formal patterns of verse. In an interview, Wilbur registered his doubts about free verse as a stylistic form, claiming it "loses all sorts of opportunities for power, emphasis, and precision—especially rhythmic precision" and that "forms and meters" are not limiting (as modernist poets might argue) but challenging to the "good poet" and clearly "undated and indeed timeless."

"The Death of a Toad" is highly stylized and visually precise, with symmetrical stanzas that employ such elegant constructions as inverted word order and a preponderance of prepositional phrases that create an intensity and complexity of visual and emotional effect:

> To the garden verge, and sanctuaried him
> Under the cineraria leaves, in the shade
>   Of the ashen heartshaped leaves, in a dim,
>   Low, and a final glade.

The effects of these prepositional phrases are varied, creating linguistic and thematic emphases while also providing a rhythmic reinforcement. This sound and thematic complexity is also complemented by the use of the present tense for the toad ("He lies . . . dies"; "the heartsblood goes . . . flows"), which creates an intense immediacy. The reader not only experiences the death of the toad but also watches it watching its own death: "In the wide and antique eyes, which still appear/ To watch." The ultimate power of the final stanza is that all this watching suggests a universal significance for the human poet left behind. The toad reflects a paradoxical "unseeing," a representative of a seemingly sighted but in reality "blind" human population that has lost the ability to truly see nature, its primal energy, and humankind's own connection to it.

The poem also utilizes powerful sound devices, such as alliteration, in "caught,/ Chewed and clipped," "hobbling hop," "still . . . stone,/ And soundlessly," and in the powerful concluding stanza's "Day dwindles, drowning." The rhyme scheme employed is *aabcbc* throughout, and an intricate combination of iambic, trochaic, and anapestic metrical construction echoes the visual symmetry of each stanza.

The poet's diction underscores the poem's careful and masterful planning—words such as "cineraria," "heartsblood," and "Amphibia's emperies" elevate the toad's predicament. Two examples of disturbing diction occur in the second and third stanzas and highlight the perplexing and paradoxical nature of the poem, which plunges the reader into—as has been described as a quality of Wilbur's poems—"a sort of paralyzing terror just below the surface." As the blood flows into the "folds and wizenings . . . In the gutters of the banked and staring eyes," the raw nature of the toad is evoked, and his life force and simultaneous antiquity, linking him to primordial nature and earth, are strikingly perceived. And in the final stanza, nature mutates (as reflected in the toad's eyes) into a terrible opposite of itself with the peculiar adjectival choices of "castrate" (describing the lawn) and "haggard" (describing the daylight).

This sampling of the forms and devices of "The Death of a Toad" are indicative of its complexity and high artistry. Another device, Wilbur's use of metaphor, is inextricably tied to theme.

Themes and Meanings

If the plight of humankind is equated with the toad's, then the picture painted by the poem's episode is that human beings are mere victims of a machinery of their own making, symbolically enlarged to all of human technology in the image of the power mower. This is coupled with the idea that the human spirit hopes for a spiritual existence beyond the physical world that assumes various and ambiguous forms—in the poem as a nothingness ("some deep monotone"), a perfect heaven ("ebullient seas/ And cooling shores"), or a grand and opulent reward ("emperies").

Yet, unfortunately, these forms are undermined by a depressing and bereft world— bereft, perhaps, of certain knowledges, such as the watching of the toad, that one has lost or looks upon without seeing. The toad is also emblematic of all of nature—from the beginning of time—because it is described as "antique" and "original" and having an "earthen hide." The loss of humans' sense of primal energy and their connection to nature is reflected not only in the toad's eyes but also in the poet's awareness that they merely "appear to watch." Thus, the toad is at once a metaphor for humankind and nature, irrevocably linking the two. Representative of vibrant, vital, and primal nature, the toad also stands for humankind unwaryingly mowed down by its own technology. It is this very dichotomy and ambiguity—toad as human and toad as nonhuman—that reverberates such a richness of meaning in the poem. If this symbolic and paradoxical connection is made, the poem can be viewed as commenting not only on distanced, impersonal, abstracted death but also on one's own death or distancing from humanity's primal roots and perceived "mastery" of nature through destructive and alienating technological advances.

The poem is sad, haunting, and multifarious in meaning. It raises complicated questions, provides no answers, and seems to comment disconsolately on this melancholic state of things in which humans and the toad are unseeing. The perspective of the poet who records and ultimately "sees" is not a hopeful one but is, on the contrary, despairingly morose, with the poem punctuating its finality with the vision of a "castrate" nature and the death-dealing scene of day "drowning." The toad, it seems, mirrors humankind's demise, from its own powerful and "rare" nature.

Sherry Morton-Mollo

THE DEATH OF MARILYN MONROE

Author: Sharon Olds (1942-   )
Type of poem: Elegy
First published: 1984, in *The Dead and the Living*

The Poem

Sharon Olds's "The Death of Marilyn Monroe" is a brief free-verse poem consisting of five grammatical sentences arranged into twenty-six lines and divided into four verse paragraphs. Only the title identifies the deceased of the poem as famous actress Marilyn Monroe. The poem concentrates on "the ambulance men" who transported her corpse. The second sentence indicates the focus of the poem: "These men were never the same." The remainder of the poem describes how the lives of the three paramedics were altered by their encounter with the dead celebrity: One becomes depressed and impotent; one grows alienated from his job and changes his thoughts on mortality; one finds his attitude toward his wife subtly altered.

The poem works by implication, developing a tension between the fame of the ostensible titular subject and the effects on ordinary people who encountered her shortly after death. The poem is not an elegy in the formal sense of a sustained meditation on grave subjects occasioned by a death, nor is it in elegiac meter or in the form of the English pastoral elegy. Nevertheless, the poem is a brief meditation on mortality, sexuality, and celebrity, and it draws its inspiration from an encounter with death. Thus, the term elegy seems justified in categorizing the poem, as long as one qualifies it as a contemporary, free-verse elegy.

Forms and Devices

The language of "The Death of Marilyn Monroe" is deliberately plain and straightforward. Figurative language is rare (her body is described with the simile "heavy as iron"), the diction is familiar, everyday spoken English, and the sentences are frankly prosaic. While some of these elements are typical of Olds, others are not. Indeed, Olds's poetry is known for its vivid figurative language and powerful, even sometimes gaudy, imagery. Here she intentionally strives for an "ordinary" register, to use a word important to the poem. This ordinariness forms a deliberate contrast with the sensationalism that characterized press coverage of Marilyn Monroe's death and that has indeed characterized the growth of her posthumous legend. Olds has a different story to tell.

The first verse paragraph is essentially descriptive. It uses tactile and visual imagery to depict the physical interaction of the ambulance men and Monroe's body. The inertness of her body is conveyed by the ways in which the men manipulate her, closing her eyes and tying her arms down on a stretcher. Yet two subjunctive or conditional phrases complicate the apparently straightforward description. The men free a caught piece of hair "as if it mattered," and they carry her body "as if it were she." This phrasing calls attention to the transformation of death: She can no longer feel; she is no longer the person associated with her famous name.

Similar spare diction characterizes the enumeration of the fates of the ambulance men. In just a few phrases each, Olds identifies the melancholy transformations the dead celebrity works on the men who encounter her. Here, as in all free verse, line breaks are important. Some lines end with a natural pause created by the end of a grammatical phrase: "and one found himself standing at night/ in the doorway to a room of sleep." Most of the line breaks interrupt grammatical phrases, making the poem slower and more somber. The line breaks in the third verse paragraph seem especially unusual. The first break emphasizes with the literal arrangement of the words on the page the "turning" or conversion the men experience: "Their lives took/ a turn." The breaks between "not" and "like" and "looked" and "different" emphasize the strangeness of the feelings with which the men are left.

The final lines of the poem provide a wonderful illustration of how repetition and line breaks can communicate emotion. The descriptive image is simple: One of the men finds himself awake at night looking in on his sleeping wife breathing. However, the repetition and line breaks charge this simple act with feeling: "listening to a/ woman breathing, just an ordinary/ woman/ breathing." Repeating both "woman" and "breathing," and giving each word a line to itself, calls attention to the issues of gender and mortality in the poem. The man's wife is breathing in an ordinary way, unlike the body of Marilyn Monroe, which was not sentient or, indeed, ordinary. And yet, literally stripped of her glamour, Monroe in death reaches toward an ordinariness that perhaps her troubled and famous life led her to crave. As was the case throughout her career, Monroe was a figure watched and observed by men.

Themes and Meanings

The collection in which this poem appears is divided into two sections: "Poems for the Dead" and "Poems for the Living." "Poems for the Dead," in turn, is divided into the sections "Public" and "Private." Of the nine "Public" poems, the piece about Marilyn Monroe depends the most on understanding her iconic significance in American culture. Monroe's fame came from a series of motion pictures in the 1950's, films that made her the most famous actress of her era. Her film roles and her modeling presented her very explicitly as a sex symbol, and her image became immediately recognizable to an enormous public. Her fame was further magnified by her marriage to baseball star Joe DiMaggio, a later marriage to playwright Arthur Miller, and rumored affairs with President John F. Kennedy and Attorney General Robert Kennedy. Her suicide by drug overdose at age thirty-six sealed her legendary status, preserving her life story as a myth combining innocence and sexuality with the tragedy of premature death.

Like Elvis Presley, Monroe has grown in legendary status since her death. More than two hundred books about her are in print, and her legend has attracted treatments from authors Gloria Steinem and Joyce Carol Oates and artist Andy Warhol, whose lithograph of Monroe is as famous as those of Campbell's soup cans. It is against this legendary or iconic status that Olds's simple poem needs to be read.

"The Death of Marilyn Monroe" seems to echo the well-known song "Candle in the Wind," by Elton John and Bernie Taupin. Both works emphasize the difference between legend and human being, made more pronounced and poignant by the physical realities of her death. While John's song laments that the sensationalizing newspapers seized upon the fact that Monroe's body was discovered "in the nude," Olds's poem describes her famous breasts "flattened by gravity," a phrase that suggests how her mortality literally brings her down to earth.

While the quiet simplicity of the poem contrasts with the shrill cultural industries that market and exploit Monroe's image, Olds subtly continues Monroe's role as a woman looked at by men, a woman whose body has the power to change those who gaze upon it. The poem restores her dignity, but it does not free her from the gendered context of woman as body and woman as object to be viewed by the male gaze. This is not to say that the ambulance men are represented as lascivious or leering; they are not. Yet just as the living Monroe suffered from being turned into a visual image, being nothing more than her body, so too does the dead Monroe become literally all body, divorced from spirit.

On the night of her death, the men go for their after-work drink, but, significantly, "they could not meet/ each other's eyes." Their sense of shame is concentrated in the eyes, concentrated on what they have seen. For one of the men, the sight of the dead Monroe transforms how his wife looks and turns death into a place where Marilyn Monroe awaits him. Another experiences pains, nightmare, depression, and impotence. That the sight of the dead Monroe unmans him, so to speak, suggests the larger theme of how individual sexuality is shaped by cultural myths. The death of the legendary figure makes the ordinary world seem strange and insubstantial. At least two of the men seem alienated from their familiar world by their contact with Monroe's body: Some of the vitality that has flowed from her seems drained from them as well.

The third man, who is listening to an ordinary woman breathing, is more complex. Like the other two, he seems alienated from the real world by seeing a legendary figure revealed as all too human. However, the language suggests that the public death may have led him to appreciate the miracle of his (and his wife's) private, ordinary life. From the icon who is transformed by cultural myth to a complex of images and significations to the life breath of an ordinary woman is a long passage. Yet this poem attempts to navigate that passage, showing, as elegies generally do, how the encounter with death intensifies the poignancy of life by reminding the reader of its preciousness and its fleeting quality.

Christopher Ames

THE DEATH OF THE BALL TURRET GUNNER

Author: Randall Jarrell (1914-1965)
Type of poem: Narrative
First published: 1945, in *Little Friend, Little Friend*

The Poem

A gem of a small poem, Randall Jarrell's "The Death of the Ball Turret Gunner" is often used in classrooms to exemplify the sustained metaphor. One of the poems based on Jarrell's own experience in World War II, this tiny poem presents a layered message about the waste of war. The five-line highly compressed poem is as deliberately claustrophobic as the setting, the ball turret of a war plane. The brief first-person narrative describes how the young man fell "from [his] mother's sleep" into the state, which confined him to the ball turret, another womb, another sleep: "I hunched in its belly till my wet fur froze." He awakened from the successive wombs, mother's and state's, only to die: "Six miles from earth, loosed from its dream of life,/ I woke to black flak and the nightmare fighters." The last line provides a chill postmortem observation: "When I died they washed me out of the turret with a hose."

Jarrell provided a note to the poem for those not familiar with the plane he described. A ball turret was a plexiglass sphere recessed into a B-17 or a B-24. Two machine guns and a small man were fitted inside. When the gunner tracked with his machine guns a fighter attacking from below, he revolved with the turret. "The hose was a steam hose." Contemporary readers may be familiar with the architecture of the ball turret from such films as *Memphis Belle* (1990), which shows the small enclosure where the ball turret gunner is confined. The space is hardly larger than his body and allows room only for necessary movement.

This is one of the many poems Jarrell wrote about his war experience. He intended to be a pilot but was unsuccessful in completing the program; he then became a trainer and control tower operator. "The Death of the Ball Turret Gunner" was published in 1945 to a readership war-stunned and war-weary. In it and in his other poems of this 1945 collection, Jarrell stresses the ironic contrast between the tough, hard war machines of the state and the vulnerable, often very young individuals who are at their mercy. Thus the villains were not the Germans nor the Japanese but rather the war situation itself—a message not always well received at the time.

The blunt concluding image underscores the theme that the young man's birth was his death. He never got to awaken to life; his only awakening was to "black flak and the nightmare fighters," his own victimhood and sacrifice. The abortion image at the end, when the steam hose washes the body out of the turret shell, leads some to think that the poem is about abortion. Yet here the abortion is the vehicle, not the tenor, of the metaphor: The poem is about how war aborts lives.

Forms and Devices

"The Death of the Ball Turret Gunner" is a conceit, or extended metaphor. It was characteristic of Jarrell to see the soldier as a sacrificed child, and he relates this to maximum effect in the poem. The gunner is compared with a fetus, a baby animal in the womb: "my wet fur froze." The jackets the gunners wore had fur inside, and thus the double image is created of the young man in the jacket and the infant animal. The equation of birth with death is continued throughout the poem, ending with the flat final statement of a life aborted. The machine survives while the flesh dies.

The rhythms of the poem enhance its message. Its first line appears to set up a relaxed, iambic pentameter pace, but this is not sustained. The second line picks up the rhythm, using anapests and other metrical feet; the rest of the poem continues to play with the meter, though the third line too may be read as a flexible iambic pentameter, and the second and fourth lines may be read as containing four stresses each. The last line is longer than the rest, and its blunt horror seems to leap out at the reader.

Another dimension to the metaphor is its sequence of circles and centers: the airman first in his mother's womb; then in the belly of the plane; then in the air above the earth, "loosed from its dream of life" where he wakens to his own death, "the nightmare fighters." He is never centered on the earth, autonomous. The dreaming, sleeping, and waking cycle is fused with the life and death sequence. He awakens from dream only to nightmare, never to life.

Every word contributes to the whole in this economical poem. Unlike longer, more discursive war poems, "The Death of the Ball Turret Gunner" gives only a flash into the mind of this soldier victim, just as his consciousness had only the briefest of chances to observe and reflect.

Themes and Meanings

Jarrell's war poems show the cost of war in terms of losses; one of his poetry books is even entitled *Losses* (1948). Critics have complained that Jarrell's World War II poems diminish heroic participants to a metaphor of lambs to slaughter—"killable puppets," as author James Dickey put it. However, Jarrell saw the soldiers as victims indeed, children to become blood sacrifices. In other poems Jarrell juxtaposes the open-hearted expectations of children with the grim reality of war in a variety of ways; sometimes the children are not soldiers but simply real children who believe in the goodness of adults, and whose innocence will be destroyed by the exigencies of war.

However, the innocents are frequently the soldiers themselves who seem randomly chosen to kill or be killed, without their having a voice. Jarrell never lets the reader forget that these are people, individuals with their own potentials, who are being sacrificed to the machine of war. Often his method is to focus on the clear, childlike perceptions of the speaker and his ignorance of the machine that has him in its grip. There is certainly something of a child's voice in this speaker, who from beyond the grave describes the mechanics of removing his body from the turret. He never does understand what controlled his fate; he never does truly awaken to anything but the fact that he was born to be a victim. The device of having the dead soldier speak owes something to Wilfred Owen, Thomas Hardy, and others; it provides a way of allowing the poet to present his own perspective on the situation as well as the gunner's.

The poem sums up Jarrell's reflections on war's destructiveness. Unlike some of his longer war poems, it does not meditate on or reflect about the issues it raises but merely reports, in concentrated form, a single event that would be one of many such events experienced by all sides in the conflict. Jarrell's war poems are not satisfying to all, because they do not answer the question of whether the waste of war is necessary—he does not resolve whether war is an outrageous abuse of human capabilities or whether it is something like an act of God.

Jarrell was a participant in the war and served as an instructor-trainer for navigators. So he would have felt great sorrow and pity for those he carefully trained and sent off who did not come back. However, the necessity of sending them off is not fully explored. As a result, the more didactic among the poems may seem either sentimental or morally empty: "What is demanded in the trade of states/ But lives, your lives?—the one commodity," the speaker asks in "The Sick Naught," but the poem does little but wonder heavily about this irony. However, in "The Death of the Ball Turret Gunner," the tight construction, the compact conceit, and the startling postmortem voice come together in a poem that encapsulates the waste and the pity of war. This poem, considered by many one of the best poems of World War II, deservedly appears in hundreds of texts and anthologies.

Janet McCann

DEATH'S BLUE-EYED GIRL

Author: Linda Pastan (1932-   )
Type of poem: Lyric
First published: 1970; collected in *Aspects of Eve*, 1975

The Poem

"Death's Blue-Eyed Girl" is a short poem in accentual-syllabic meter. Its fourteen lines are divided into two stanzas. The first four-line stanza introduces the thematic question of the poem by way of two related similes; it also identifies the poem's intended audience and establishes a meditative mood. The second stanza attempts to answer the question posed at the beginning of the poem: When does death become a real presence in life? This stanza is a meditation on death and one's shifting perceptions of death and loss. The ideas in the poem are developed almost entirely through the use of metaphor.

The title of the poem recalls a line from E. E. Cummings's poem "Buffalo Bill 's." That poem, which was published in 1923, is about the death of the speaker's childhood hero (Buffalo Bill). In the final lines, the speaker personifies death in order to make sense of the loss of someone who seemed immortal. He asks, "and what i want to know is/ how do you like your blueeyed boy/ Mister Death." In Linda Pastan's poem, the blue-eyed girl refers to Elaine, someone close to the speaker, who has died. Pastan also personifies death at the end of the poem, turning it into a magician. The debt to E. E. Cummings is clear in both the specific language and the thematic concerns of Pastan's poem.

The speaker in the poem is not a persona distinct from the poet, and the "you" addressed is a relative, spouse, or close friend. Yet the "you" addressed in the poem also extends to include the readers, who, as they read the poem, begin to feel as if they are overhearing an intimate conversation between two people. This sense of intimacy provides an important cue for the readers; it is as if the speaker is conscious of them listening in and wants them to consider the question she is asking. In this way, the poem is both meditative and inclusive, and, consequently, more compelling.

The poem begins with two similes that suggest the complexity of the questions being asked. The first, and most obvious, is, When does death become a common, even comfortable, presence in people's lives? The second question is, How does one move from the child's sense of invulnerability in the natural world to the adult's understanding that death is everywhere in nature?

The second stanza tries to answer these questions. The speaker begins by recalling her childhood response to death. Then she felt invulnerable, immortal, untouchable; death remained a distant abstraction and, ironically, a kind of last hope if she should "fall too far." Then the memory of Elaine enters the poem. The speaker describes her as she last remembers her: alive, vital, and creative. As quickly as the memory of Elaine appears, it vanishes. The poet ends the poem by personifying death as a magician who simply whisked Elaine away. The reader has been carried deep into the poem, and suddenly it is over. In this way, the poem mimics the very event it describes: Death is often a sudden loss, a kind of sleight of hand that shocks and surprises.

Forms and Devices

At first glance, the poem may seem formless, but closer inspection reveals that it is written in accentual-syllabic meter. Each line has nine, ten, or eleven syllables, and four or five of the syllables are accented in every line. The meter is roughly dactylic tetrameter; variations in the pattern are frequent. Two of the variations are worth noting.

The first occurs in line 9 and is repeated in line 12. These lines are the two longest in the poem, each having eleven syllables. The thematic connection between the lines is emphasized by their shared syllable count. Line 9 states that death is, to the child, "a safety net." Line 12 mentions that although Elaine seemed anchored to this life by the child on her hip who served as a kind of "ballast," she was also "distracted with poems." Although the connection is subtle, perhaps the reader is encouraged to see that poems are also a kind of safety net, a way that one might begin to understand death. Yet there is irony in this connection; death is not a safety net, and it is Elaine's death that teaches the speaker this fact.

The second variation that is thematically important occurs in the last line. This line has only seven syllables. As the shortest line in the poem, it serves two purposes: It helps end the poem cleanly and decisively, and it reflects the idea of the poem. Death is also quick, decisive, and final. It is important to note that this is one of the few lines in the poem that are not metaphors; "She was gone" is the most direct statement in the poem. By using this device, the speaker seems to be undermining her own attempt to put death into a poem. Ultimately, one realizes, death is a fact; even poetry cannot save one.

The most common poetic device used in the poem is metaphor. There are four sets of metaphors at work. The first set, found in the first four lines of the poem, introduces the theme of transition. The flowers in the garden begin to smell "like a funeral chapel" and the breeze like a "nurse's hand" on the forehead.

The second set of metaphors, in lines 7 through 9, explains the child's response to death. Children feel invulnerable and challenge death by "sending . . . kites up for the lightening" and swimming naked at night. In line 9, death, the "safety net," is clearly the invention of the child who does not or cannot understand its finality.

In lines 11 and 12, the metaphor of the child as ballast helps the reader understand both Elaine's fragile connection to this life and the speaker's developing perception of life's transience. Each person, it seems, is temporarily stabilized in this life by various kinds of ballast that may slip at any time.

Realizing this, the reader is prepared for the final metaphor in the last two lines of the poem. Death is real, no doubt, but it still retains its "magic." The image of death as a magician who waves and bows and shows his empty sleeves belongs in the world of the child. Yet it is the adult who invents the metaphor in the poem in order to come to terms with death. In this way, Pastan is able to indulge the child's fascination with the magic of the world despite the reality of death.

Themes and Meanings

"Death's Blue-Eyed Girl" is a poem about loss, and death in the poem is emblematic of all loss. Yet the poem is more than simply another meditation on death. It is also about not losing, about saving what can be saved in this life: the affable indifference of childhood, the pleasure of making, the memory of a defining gesture. The means to this end for the speaker is her art, her poetry.

In this way, "death's blue-eyed girl" is not only Elaine but the speaker/poet as well. Throughout her life she has moved from one set of images defining death to another and then to yet another. In the end, as an adult in full view of the reality of death, she still refuses to give up, to be defeated by death. Instead, she uses it as a means to create, thus denying its power over her.

The final image of death as a magician serves this purpose well. As long as the poet is able to describe death as she sees fit, she is in control. The playful image of the magician underscores Pastan's refusal to give in to death's power. Instead, she reminds the reader again of the child's ability to invent, and while the poem does not ignore the reality of death (the last line clearly admits this), neither does it deny the importance of invention.

The theme of the poem is echoed in the epigraph to *Aspects of Eve*, the collection in which it appears. Taken from "Eve's Exile" by Archibald MacLeish, the epigraph reads: "Space within its time revolves/ But Eve must spin as Adam delves/ Because our exile is ourselves." Locked in one's own existence, without hope of paradise, one must labor to make sense of the world. That is exactly what the speaker in "Death's Blue-Eyed Girl" is doing.

The final message of the poem is that the creative urge, however it reveals itself, is one's best "safety net" against the fearful reality of one's own mortality. By employing one's creative faculties in ways that confirm life, one also becomes a magician; there is little else one can hope to have to offer comfort.

Judith Kleck

DEER DANCE/FOR YOUR RETURN

Author: Leslie Marmon Silko (1948-   )
Type of poem: Lyric
First published: 1981, in *Storyteller*

The Poem

Written in free verse in seventy-two lines with an additional short paragraph of explanation following, Leslie Marmon Silko's poem "Deer Dance/For Your Return" is a lyrical appeal for a return. It is a plea that re-creates and gives life to the very thing whose loss is dreaded. Subtitled "for Denny," Silko's poem invites the reader to link the absence of "Denny" (the man for whom the poem is written) to the ceremonial deer dance of the Laguna people to whom the poet belongs.

The reader is advised to go directly to the final paragraph of prose, which explains the function and meaning of the deer dance from which the significance of the poem is derived. The dance is performed "to honor and pay thanks to the deer spirits," and the poem is a performance that embodies the values and culture of the pueblo (or people) from which it comes.

The Laguna are thankful to the deer spirits, since the deer each year have allowed themselves to be killed by hunters in the fall. Their flesh sustains the Laguna Pueblo throughout the winter. The Laguna understand that such a gift requires an appropriate reciprocal expression. The proper performance of this ceremony is important, since it invites and enables the deer spirits to return to the mountains to be "reborn into more deer." As Silko explains, the deer "will, remembering the reverence and appreciation of the people, once more come home with the hunters."

Returning from the explanatory final paragraph to the lyrical part of the poem, one sees that Silko is performing a lyrical ceremony in words that is intended to be a verbal evocation of the dance ceremony of her Pueblo. Hers are words of honoring and thanksgiving. The deer are addressed as tenderly as a beloved friend, and the deer themselves are a part of the culture that their lives sustain.

From the point of view of the speaker, the poet promises in the opening stanza that if "this/ will hasten your return," she will blow "down-feathered" clouds that gather above the pine forest and darken the vision as the deer is "born back/ to the mountain."

In the second stanza, Silko moves back to a time years ago when she saw "through the yellow oak leaves/ antlers polished like stones." She sees a deer in the canyon stream. Seeing the animal is a moment of vision and desire: There is a palpable shift in the experience of time, and the poet is filled with longing. "Morning," Silko writes, "turned in the sky/ I wanted the gift/ You carry on moon-color shoulders." On the one hand, she desires the wonderful head and antlers and body of the deer living and free, but on the other hand, she recognizes that the entire body "holds the long winter" in the sense that without the sacrifice of that body, the Pueblo would not be able to survive the winter.

In the next section of the poem, Silko emphasizes the cyclical pattern of the deer's presence in the life of the Laguna people. "You have," she writes, "come home with me before." Here, speaking for her community, she reminds the deer that "The people welcome you." In remembering the past gifts she has offered the deer—a red blanket, turquoise, silver rings—the poet renews her gratitude and reverence for the animal. The offering of ancient and unique treasures suggests the strange and exotic nature of the deer, but he is also intimately familiar and is given "blue corn meal saved special."

The poet practices her ceremonial ritual of gift giving and gratitude "while others are sleeping," and ties feathers onto the deer's antlers. She whispers close to the animal, "we have missed you/ I have longed for you." In these two lines, the communal "we" is linked to the subjective "I," and the poet suggests the intermediary between the private and the public that is the traditional one for the lyrical priest-poet.

In asking for the deer's return, the poet is also accepting that the deer will depart: "Losses are certain/ in the pattern of this dance." If losses are certain, however, so is the pattern of the dance or of the hunt, and the dance and the hunt mirror each other. Without the hunt there could be no dance; without the dance there could be no hunt. The poem puts the reader in the place of a hunter in the process of desiring and seeking, and in the place of the dancer in the process of recovering from loss. The hunter approaches "blind curves in the trail," places where the turns in the road obscure the near distance. The deer might be there, but even its image "leaps away/ loose again to run the hills." The final two words of the stanza, "Go quickly," suggest that the poet both desires the deer (and so wishes it to go quickly back to the mountains where it will be reborn) and wishes it to escape entirely (so that it will never die).

In the seventh stanza, Silko moves even more deeply into the language of ceremony. The ceremonial language she adopts actualizes the poetic world toward which ordinary language merely points. "How beautiful," she writes, "this last time/ I touch you/ to believe/ and hasten the return/ of lava-slope hills and your next-year heart." The hills on which the deer runs, the land on which the Laguna live, and the living spirit of the deer are connected and interdependent.

The heart of the deer, imaginatively poised in life between death and rebirth, is echoed in the beating of the heart of the poet, whose "heart still beats/ in the tall grass/ where you stopped." Again Silko must implore, "Go quickly." The deer must go so that it can return.

In the next two stanzas, the poet makes possible a future by imagining it: "I will walk these hills and/ pray you will come again." The heart that had beat in an echo of the deer is now "full for you/ to wait your return." As the sun sets, as the heat of the rocks dissipates, as the shapes of things change and grow unfamiliar, the poet hears the hooves of the deer "scatter rocks/ down the hillside." The longed-for return has occurred; the poet turns to the animal and recognizes that "The run/ for the length of the mountain/ is only beginning."

Forms and Devices

"Deer Dance/For Your Return" fulfills virtually all the classical requirements for the lyric form. It displays qualities of metrical coherence, it is securely subjective, expressing passion and sensuality, and it is constructed out of a keen appreciation for the particularity of image. More striking than any of these specific lyrical elements, however, is that Silko's poem arises out of and powerfully evokes its musical and choreic roots in the dances, chants, narratives, and songs of the Laguna peoples of the American Southwest.

One of the ideals of lyric poetry is to achieve a virtual transparency of language. The lyric poet wants to seem to be spontaneously expressing and evoking a spiritual dimension that is available to anyone. Silko links the goal of naturalness and spontaneity to the poetic dance performance of her people.

Themes and Meanings

"Deer Dance/For Your Return" traces a loss and at the same time performs a ritual or ceremony that achieves recovery from that loss. While the language and allusions of the poem are all directed toward the communal deer dance, the contemporary reader understands the imaginative connection between the deer and the Pueblo and any relationship of love and need. In her correspondence with the American poet James Wright, Silko mentions her reading of the seventeenth century Dutch philosopher Baruch Spinoza, who thought that the most significant human capacity was that of being able to love—virtually anything—and to love without the expectation that the loved object or person would love in return. She achieves a dimension of selfless love of the deer in "Deer Dance/For Your Return." At the same time, it is clear that the deer is either literally (for the people of the Pueblo) or metaphorically (for the contemporary lover) a matter of life and death.

The poem begins in a conditional, uncertain state ("If this will hasten your return") and concludes with a certainty that "The run/ for the length of the mountains/ is only the beginning." The movement from speculation to certainty, from loss to restoration, is the most significant theme of the poem. Without diminishing in any way the reservations one must have in an uncertain world, the poem affirms the possibility of reciprocity between human beings (both alone and in community) and the natural world.

Sharon Bassett

DEFENESTRATION OF PRAGUE

Author: Susan Howe (1937-   )
Type of poem: Poetic sequence
First published: 1983

The Poem

Defenestration of Prague is a complex interweaving of various perspectives and commentaries on the nature of being female in a world of patriarchal institutions. Primarily the poem is about the life and times of Hester (or Esther) Johnson (1680-1728), an Englishwoman who became the mistress of Jonathan Swift (1668-1745), the Irish satirical poet and Anglican bishop. Hester, or Stella, as she was known to Swift, remained Swift's mistress and housekeeper throughout her adult life. Their relationship was kept a careful secret over the years, which is part of what the poem explores.

The poem is divided into many separate units of discourse, each varying its mode of articulation as the subjects of women and gender oppression are scrutinized. The poem has a wide range of formal strategies, from loose-knit fragments of memory and historic allusion to the fully fleshed lyrics of "Speeches at the Barriers," which develop certain of the basic themes of the poem, to the dramatic episodes of the second part of the poem, "The Liberties."

Though a narrative in the general sense of a story, the poem also experiments in telling a tale from multiple points of view anchored in the poet's own personal examination of female suppression. Hence, the story is told by a narrator who is herself anxiously engaged in the process by which even the terms to be used are sifted for their meanings, their historical and etymological content. What serves as evidence is a composite of widely scattered forms of personal testimony—not only from the bits and scraps of Hester Johnson's few lyrics and comments but also from other writers, male and female, who have versions of the story or parallel situations to report.

Susan Howe's finished version achieves two goals simultaneously: to study the life of one woman whose existence is utterly eclipsed by the fame and influence of her male lover, and to argue that such a case is not unique to one century or culture but unfolds a principle underlying much of Western existence. There is a third, more tentative purpose in telling this story: to indicate in hazy outline something of the battle that rages between self and soul, as encoded in these images of men and women participating in a relationship fraught with tension, conflict, and unequal privilege. Howe's concern is how such lives turn out to be keys to understanding the lopsidedness of cultural life and the chaos that rages behind conventional historical assumptions.

The work is divided into two main parts. The first, entitled "Defenestration of Prague," has mainly to do with Hester Johnson's voyage to Ireland to join Swift and to look after her inherited properties there. The experience of the voyage and arrival in Ireland, a kind of wilderness, is equated in the narrative with other women's adventures trekking to frontiers in colonial America. The second part, "The Liberties," is concerned with the nature of Johnson's relationship to Swift and with analogous relations between powerful patriarchs and their mistresses, wives, or daughters. In particular, Howe comments on the situation of Emily Dickinson, who remained housebound much of her adult life while writing brilliant but unpublished poems. Lines and phrases of Dickinson's poems come into the text at various moments. In the "Book of Cordelia," a dramatic masque compares the crises of Cordelia, Lear's daughter, and Stella as they confront the emptiness of their lives as victims of sexual inequality. Like other of William Shakespeare's victims, Cordelia achieves liberation only through death, as does Stella. Hence the title of the second part is "The Liberties": It recounts the women's final moments of life as they escape from the bondage of being female.

Forms and Devices

Form is the principal achievement of this work; its use of quotation, echoed paraphrase, fragmentary allusion, song, balladlike narrative, prose introduction and critical commentary, and scholarly apparatus constitute a new texture and structural diversity for the long poem. Through these varying modes of telling a story, the life of one woman is elevated to an archetype of the plight of female nature in Western life. The flow of discourse is disrupted internally by the ever-changing locus of a voice, which appears to emanate from different sources of information provided by the poem. The reader is at once in the thoughts of the poet herself, in the character's mind, seeing through the perspective of invisible witnesses, or reliving aspects of Hester Johnson's experience through analogous situations stated in poems, letters, and historical data. This kaleidoscopic array of media for telling the life of one person opens the narrative to epic universality without heroizing the subject. The poem tackles one of the essential debates of modern time, the revisioning of history through examination of so-called peripheral evidence. Here is a rare instance of a poem taking up a leading issue of academic debate, the reconceiving of the past through a nexus of contending viewpoints and unused facts in what has been called "new historicism." The poem shoulders part of the burden of such revisionism without proposing a full-scale argument of its own. It is a poem foremost, an argument secondarily.

Howe's narrative method is derived from other long poems, chiefly from the work of the poet Charles Olson, whose open poetry specialized in discontinuous narrative using myth, association, and line fragments to establish a "field" of reference informing an event or situation in his verse. Such openness dissolved formal boundaries between poetic language and the surrounding world of prose reality. The new poem was porous and subject to the influences of other texts and realities, which it incorporated into its flexible structure. Such are Howe's working principles as well.

Howe has been grouped with certain other poets in a movement called "language" poetry, which emphasizes composition as a process and human expression as ambiguous and chaotic. Though she draws attention to the accretive and aleatory patterns of writing poetry, she will not stray beyond a certain "meaning" boundary in breaking down language to its nonsemantic detritus of syllables and punctuation, as have other "language" poets. Also evident is the dense verbal conciseness of Emily Dickinson, whom Howe reveres here and elsewhere in her work, and the wordplay of Gertrude Stein, who not only punned on the associative relations among words but also exploded conventional syntactical relations. Both Dickinson and Stein helped to establish a feminine poetics and literary tradition from which Howe derives her own mode of composition.

Howe is not, however, a militant or doctrinaire feminist in this poem. Her views on the life of Hester Johnson are too complex to comply with any orthodoxy on either side of the gender debate. Instead, she assimilates into her historical views the attitudes of Jonathan Swift (from whom she quotes liberally) and of Shakespeare, with whom she is evidently in sympathy for part of her argument. Howe's method of telling one woman's story is both to establish the principle of sexual inequality and its damage to women and to note the ambiguous forces that perpetuate the oppression of females in patriarchal societies. Men are not lumped together as villains; social institutions and cultural habits are criticized more emphatically than are particular figures or social groups.

Howe's phrase for describing the terms in which people live their lives is "endless PROTEANL inkages," where the social ambiguity of evil and oppression is pointed up. The social rules constitute a heritage without firm beginning or end; they change according to the vagaries of social evolution. Thus the limits placed on behavior and access to privilege form an endlessly changeful framework of linked causes, the linkages of her ambivalent phrase. It is this protean state of things that Howe strives to reproduce through her intertextual narrative, which affirms and distorts the causality of the poem's events as a way of mimicking social history itself.

Defenestration of Prague uses a large rectangular page that gives the poetry ample room to explore open structures. Some of the poems are composed of loosely suspended lines featuring large gaps to underscore textualized silences, pauses, abruptly severed lines of thought, or the fragmentation of words themselves. Howe thus reminds the reader that her thinking is a process of digging down through history to learn the experience of a woman whose silence and obscurity make her largely inaccessible to the author.

Themes and Meanings

The oblique narrative development of the poem yields few clues to the structure of the work. The aim of the poem is not to tell a story but to reenact the process of thinking about one woman's experience of being kept by a man. The passive role of Stella suggests analogous situations of other oppressed or denied women, including the American poet Emily Dickinson, who remained a recluse in her father's house in Amherst, Massachusetts, and Cordelia, Lear's daughter, who remained faithful to a father who disowned and condemned her. Other women enter the discourse as memory sifts through the pattern of the abused or persecuted female across Western history.

The title of the work is never directly engaged by the text but signifies a historic principle of oppressive authority from which one is to infer the situation of the Western female. The "Defenestration of Prague" refers to an incident in 1618 when Protestant Czechs hurled two Catholic representatives of the Hapsburg empire to their death, thus beginning the Thirty Years' War in which Protestant and Catholic forces across Europe fought for religious and political supremacy. The Catholics won under the combined banners of France and Austria, and the Hapsburgs crushed Czech culture and language and imposed Catholicism as the state religion. The incident marks the beginnings of modern warfare and the spread of imperial aggression across Europe, forces that continue to shape Western life today. From another perspective, the incident illustrates the aggressions of raw power and the desperate plight of subjugated people. When this is translated into sexual history, one sees the parallel in the bright and public career of Jonathan Swift and the shadowy existence of Hester Johnson in their long but inconclusive relationship.

Howe's interest in taking up this story of a love affair outside of marriage is manifold. On the one hand, it is a study of the female's sacrifice of independence and autonomy for love. It is made clear to the reader that Hester Johnson inherited property and a small trust that would have enabled her to live a sufficient life on her own. Instead, she chose to live for Jonathan Swift, as his lover and housekeeper, and to abide by his rules of secrecy in their relationship, thereby suffering the silent rebuke of other women who disapproved of the arrangement. Howe explores throughout the sequence Johnson's possible motives for enduring these hardships of a romance without benefit of matrimony or social status.

The most compelling explanation is for the adventure itself; the trip to Ireland is reenacted lovingly through Howe's fragmentary, multilayered narrative. Howe's contention is that an era of female exploration of the world was opening on both sides of the Atlantic, and women accommodated to oppressive circumstances in order to expand their knowledge and horizons. Historical complexity is preserved in another contention that while women roamed into wilderness country their oppression by men was uppermost; in the same era, women were both shackled to antiquated social roles and driven to the frontiers of society and self-knowledge by wanderlust. That explains as well Howe's interest in Dickinson's life and art, where this same paradox is evident. Dickinson, as Howe remarks emphatically in her study of the poet, *My Emily Dickinson* (1985), so engaged poetry that it led her "self to a transfiguration of gender," while remaining the prisoner of her bedroom and family house.

Indeed, the hidden text behind *Defenestration of Prague* lies in this subsequent critical study of another woman in captivity. Both Johnson and Dickinson were forced into reclusive and passive lives to escape from the exigencies of marriage and child rearing, which would have sapped their intellectual energies and dulled their spirits. The worse hardship for both was the fate of marriage itself. That explains at bottom why these women endured such paltry circumstances for their lives; they were avoiding a worse fate as wives and mothers in an age that sorely abused these functions.

The taunting argument of *Defenestration of Prague* is that Howe cannot locate the real vein of sense in her subject because Johnson did not record it in any usable form.

She had lived her life in patient solicitude of her successful male lover, and what she confided in her letters has vanished from the archives of her correspondents. In a way, the sequence served as preparation for studying another life that was recorded (and brilliantly) two centuries later than Johnson's—that of Dickinson. Between these two women, Howe seems to say, one has a sliver of evolutionary evidence of the rebirth of the female in modern Western history. The nineteenth century saw the rise of female literary genius in the work of George Eliot (Mary Ann Evans) and Emily Brontë, both featured in *My Emily Dickinson*, as well that of Mary Rowlandson, whose captivity among the Indians was recorded in her *Narrative of the Captivity of Mrs. Mary Rowlandson*, published in Cambridge, Massachusetts, in 1682. Each of these women, according to Howe, explored the frontiers of the human psyche from the female point of view. Howe herself must be counted among them as a formidable explorer of this territory.

Paul Christensen

THE DEFINITION OF LOVE

Author: Andrew Marvell (1621-1678)
Type of poem: Lyric
First published: 1681, in *Miscellaneous Poems*

The Poem

Andrew Marvell is classified as a Metaphysical poet. The Metaphysical poets flourished in the first half of the seventeenth century; their love poetry deals with the philosophical, not the romantic, aspects of being in love. The title suggests such an approach. The eight quatrains of the poem appear as an argument leading to the "therefore" of the final stanza, which has the terseness and compactness normally associated with definitions. It must be realized, however, that much Metaphysical poetry utilizes ambiguity, double meanings, and ironies. Here the term "definition" has its original Latin meaning of "restriction" as a double meaning. Marvell's aim is to link the two meanings.

The poet speaks in the first person about "my love." It soon becomes clear that "love" refers to the state, not the person, who is never described. The love poetry of the most famous Metaphysical poet, John Donne, works similarly; the object of love remains almost a fiction or cipher. Only in the first stanza is the object of love mentioned, in an enigmatic statement that "it" is "strange and high." This suggests, perhaps, the aristocratic origins and uniqueness of the lady, as well as the quality of the poet's love: It is elevated and outrageous that he should dare to love someone so nobly born.

He does not trace the birth of his love in terms of time and place but by abstractions, here personified as "Despair" and "Impossibility." In the second stanza, "magnanimous Despair" is contrasted with "feeble Hope." The oxymoron is at the heart of the poem—it could mean that, because of the lady's nobility, he could never win her, but since his is a noble love, he has become greathearted (the literal meaning of magnanimous), the highest Aristotelian virtue. If he had merely hoped for a suitable partner, he would never have allowed himself to fall in love with the lady. All this gives the poem a definite locus. Other interpretations might suggest, more abstractly, that only despair can provide the strength and integrity of emotion that are necessary to break the lover out of a second-rate love. Idealism both elevates the love and proclaims its unattainability.

The third stanza introduces a third term—Fate. If it were up to love alone, the poet would soon consummate his love, but Fate will not allow this. The next stanza expands on this: Fate, like a jealous lover, wants to guard her own power. True fulfilled love not only has great power but also is self-determining—a theme John Donne explored in "The Ecstasy." Donne believed that such a state was possible; Marvell does not.

The poem then sets up a series of extended images to explore this: In stanzas 5 and

6, the image is of the two lovers as two poles, on which "Love's whole world" turns. They are never able to touch, because to do so would be to collapse that very world, to cause it to lose its dimensions. In stanza 7, the image becomes geometrical: Lesser loves may touch, as oblique lines will; perfect loves run as do parallel lines (perhaps as parallel circles, the typical symbol of perfection), and never join.

The final stanza does not continue these images but returns to the triad of love, Fate, and the lovers. Their fate is, paradoxically, always to be separated, yet to be in true "conjunction of the Mind."

Forms and Devices

The tone of the poem is humorous and ironic, only occasionally jarring the reader with the passion behind such words as "iron wedges," "crowds," "giddy heaven," or "some new convulsion." Marvell's control here is similar to that in his "To His Coy Mistress"; there is less violence here, however, and the humor is therefore greater.

The tone is established in two main ways: first, through the very tight, economic verse form that Marvell learned from the classical poets (Marvell was an excellent Latinist). The meter is a very regular iambic tetrameter, with accentuated alternating rhymes. The feel is of couplet form, with heavy punctuation at the end of every second line. Each stanza is a complete sentence. The effect is of tight control, an economy that belongs to the enigmatic and the paradoxical. The meter is able to pass from simple monosyllables to technical and abstract polysyllables with fluency and sharpness. The form is so "defined," so "restricted," that it invites the ironic awareness of the tension between formal control and the situational powerlessness of the poet. The words are mathematically placed in terms of balance and closure, yet the sense is of inconclusiveness, even failure. The tone is thus delicately balanced, tongue-in-cheek. Marvell's sheer dexterity can be seen when one compares this poem to one by another Metaphysical poet, Abraham Cowley. Cowley's "Impossibilities" plays on the same ideas, but it does so clumsily and obviously. The most marked comparison, however, is with Donne's "The Ecstasy": Donne uses a similar verse form, but his poem is committed, flexible in its energies and celebration of union, while Marvell's is ironically controlled, ambiguous, refusing to acknowledge passion.

The second way in which tone is established is by means of wit. Much has been written on the Metaphysical concept of wit. It has to do with the quick play of the mind, the ability to be intelligent and poetic at the same time and, above all, to achieve new insight by means of joining the most unlikely concepts. The imagery that is the expression of this "conjunction of the Mind" is termed a conceit. Marvell's conceits are geometrical and astronomical. While the latter may be associated in readers' minds with love, the former certainly is not. Marvell, who draws upon neo-Platonic symbolism and correspondences of geometrical forms and types of love, uses them so easily that one is unaware of his erudition. His use of astronomy to suggest "star-crossed lovers" provides a new dimension in its conflation of astrological and astronomical elements into a modern cosmology of poles, axes, and "planispheres."

His contrast of Hope's "tinsel wing" with Fate's "iron wedges" is also striking, as is the personification of Fate jealously squeezing itself between the lovers, suggesting something claustrophobic. Sometimes the conceits do not logically fit together—there are parallel lines and conjunctions; Fate comes between the lovers, yet "Love's whole world" also occupies the same space. The humorous tone allows such discrepancies—indeed, they become part of the joke.

Themes and Meanings

Marvell's ironic tone and paradoxical discourse have led to a variety of interpretations, ranging from seeing the poem as a courtly, exaggerated compliment to an aristocratic lady (as were some of Donne's poems) to seeing it as an allegorical expression of the Platonic concept of divine love. The most obvious way to view the poem, however, is as a witty but nevertheless committed exploration of the ontology of love. The poem does this in two ways; first, by setting out the matrices of love and destiny in order to find the impossibility of arriving at an equation that will balance desire and fulfillment; and second, by examining the inner contradictions of the notion of pure love.

John Donne's poetry speaks of lovers who are able to create their own destiny. Even when external forces create a separation, the ontology of union is not affected—as in "A Valediction: Forbidding Mourning." By contrast, Marvell suggests that it is not only external forces (perhaps of degree or rank) that prevent union but also the nature of the human condition. Ultimately, destiny is "how things are." In other poems, Marvell holds a Christian Platonistic view that sees man as fallen and separated from perfection. Fate is thus God's punishment, the refusal to allow Edenic perfection for the lovers and the fact that nature is now structured for imperfection. To attain perfection would be "unnatural," destructive; Earth might "some new convulsion tear" (the first convulsion was the Edenic fall).

This leads to the poem's use of inner contradiction. The conceit of parallelism highlights this: Perfect parallels, by their very nature, cannot join. This is not some arbitrary external force; it is at the heart of the logical structure of things. These must exist in tension, the unresolvability of which produces, paradoxically, both despair and magnanimity. If the minds are perfectly in tune, Platonically, the bodies must stay apart—this sentiment is also expressed in Marvell's "Young Love." This is Marvell's choice. If bodies come together, perfection is lost, and their love ceases to be pure. One cannot have it both ways. This is the human restriction.

David Barratt

DEJECTION: AN ODE

Author: Samuel Taylor Coleridge (1772-1834)
Type of poem: Ode
First published: 1802; collected in *Sibylline Leaves*, 1817

The Poem

"Dejection: An Ode" is an ode in eight stanzas that vary greatly in the number of lines, the length of line, and in thought and imagery. The title announces the subject of the poem, which becomes apparent in the first stanza. The poet is surveying the tranquil night sky in which the new moon can be seen. He recalls an old ballad, which predicted that when the new moon can be seen with the old moon "in its arms," a storm may be brewing. He hopes this is true, because he is sunk in depression and remembers past occasions when the driving energy of a storm has enlivened his creative spirit.

In stanza 2, the poet elaborates on his dejected state of mind, which is deep and pervasive. Nothing seems able to lift it. Addressing a "Lady" (who is Coleridge's friend Sara Hutchinson), he says that in this mood he has been gazing at the western sky all evening. Although he can see how beautiful the scene is, he cannot feel this beauty in his inner being.

This observation leads him, in the short stanza 3, to reflect philosophically on his situation. The source of his poetic power is failing him, and the knowledge of this weighs him down. He realizes that he could gaze out forever on the external scene but that it would be no use to him. The "passion and the life" that he seeks is not to be found outside the human mind, but within it.

In stanzas 4 and 5, the poet again addresses Sara directly, elaborating on his philosophy of imaginative perception. He states that if one is to see anything of higher value in nature, one must supply it oneself. For nature to be clothed in light and glory, light and glory must emanate from the soul itself. These qualities cannot be found in outer things, which of themselves are merely cold and dead. The poet calls this power joy. It permits a marriage between man and nature, which creates "a new heaven and a new earth." The reference is to the Christian Millennium, foretold in the New Testament Book of Revelation. Such perception is available only to the pure.

In stanza 6, the poet looks back at a time when he possessed this joy, which could even withstand personal misfortune. Then he was full of hope, but now he feels that his imaginative and poetic power, which nature gave him at birth, has vanished.

In stanza 7, the poet turns from these dismal thoughts and listens to the wind, which has gathered strength in the time he has been contemplating. In an apostrophe to the wind, he compares it first to a "mad Lutanist," then to an actor, perfectly enunciating a variety of sounds, and then to a poet, moved to the frenzy of inspiration. He wonders what story the wind is telling. First he thinks of the headlong retreat of a defeated army, groaning in pain. Then, with a sudden lessening of the noise, he thinks that it tells another tale, of a lost child screaming for her mother.

In the final stanza, the poet's thoughts turn to Sara. He hopes that sleep may visit her, since it is denied to him. Invoking the joy to which he had given so much importance in stanza 5, he expresses the wish that Sara may rise in the morning with an uplifted spirit, and that her life may always be full of rejoicing.

Forms and Devices

"Dejection: An Ode" is sometimes classified as one of Coleridge's "conversation" poems, a group which includes "The Eolian Harp" (1796), "Frost at Midnight" (1798), and others. The opening line of the ode ("Well! if the bard was weather-wise") strikes the informal tone of the speaking voice. As in the other conversation poems, the poet addresses an absent auditor, in this case Sara. Also like the other conversation poems, the ode possesses a tripartite, rondo structure. It starts with a description of a tranquil natural scene (as in "The Eolian Harp," for example), juxtaposed and contrasted with the poet's own mood (as in "Frost at Midnight"). A meditation follows, in which the poet grapples with emotional and intellectual questions, before the poem returns to the outer scene. The rhythm of the poem, at both inner and outer level, is one of calm, followed by storm, followed by calm.

There are also, however, many differences between the ode and the conversation poems. The informal tone of the ode's first line is not maintained throughout, but gives way to the more lofty and dignified manner that traditionally characterizes the ode. Also, the poem is in rhymed verse, as opposed to the blank verse of the conversation poems. The incantatory power contained in the tetrameter and trimeter rhyming couplets in stanzas 1 and 7, for example, bear a greater resemblance to Coleridge's *The Rime of the Ancient Mariner* (1798) and *Christabel* (1816) than to the conversation poems. Another difference is in how the theme of the poem emerges. In "Dejection: An Ode," the theme emerges quickly and deliberately, rather than slipping in apparently by accident, an effect Coleridge cultivated so carefully in the conversation poems. Also dissimilar are the rapid shifts of thought, feeling, and subject that characterize "Dejection: An Ode," unlike the associative links that make the conversation poems flow so smoothly from one idea to the next.

Imagery of the weather—wind, rain, and storm—dominates stanzas 1 and 7. In stanza 7, the noise of the storm is described in a stream of metaphors: as an aeolian harp—a stringed instrument that produces music when the wind sweeps over it—an actor, a poet, a retreating army, and a little child. The imaginative activity shown by the poet at the height of the storm is an implicit denial of his statement that he has completely lost his imaginative power.

Two other images, of serpent and bird, are worthy of note. The first lines of stanza 7, "Hence, viper thoughts, that coil around my mind/ Reality's dark dream!" expresses the enclosing, suffocating feeling the poet is experiencing. In the following stanza, the image of serpent is contrasted with the image of sleep visiting the Lady "with wings of healing," a birdlike image suggesting freedom, flight, and expansion. Taken together, the two make up one way in which the opposites which Coleridge saw at work everywhere in existence, and which he once called the "Confining Form" and the "Free Life," can be experienced.

Themes and Meanings

Coleridge composed "Dejection: An Ode" as a direct response to the first four stanzas of William Wordsworth's "Ode: Intimations of Immortality" (1807), in which Wordsworth lamented the loss of his childhood ability to see nature clothed in celestial light. Some of the phrases in Coleridge's ode are clearly intended as allusions to Wordsworth's poem. Compare, for example, Coleridge's "I see, not feel, how beautiful they are" with Wordsworth's "The fullness of your bliss, I feel—I feel it all."

In its theory of perception, the ode marks a sharp break with Wordsworth's views, which Coleridge had previously shared. Wordsworth thought that a higher vision of life could be obtained through an "ennobling interchange," or marriage, between the human mind and nature. Coleridge had himself placed a very high value on the role that nature should play in the education of the human mind, especially in poems such as "Frost at Midnight" and "The Dungeon" (1798). In "Dejection: An Ode," he repudiates this view. He gazes out on a beautiful scene, but this does nothing to lift his spirits or rekindle his imaginative power. He concludes that "outward forms" are of no use unless the inner mind is vibrant: "we receive but what we give,/ And in our life alone does Nature live." Only if the mind is full of joy will it be able to perceive the unifying spirit that runs through all things, and so overcome the split between subject and object. Only then can Wordsworth's marriage metaphor, which Coleridge also employs in this poem, have any meaning.

Interpreters have differed over the question of whether the poet (as speaker) shows any imaginative growth during the course of the poem. The general view is that he does not and that the final stanza, even though it brings the poem to a peaceful conclusion, is a defeat for the poet, since he can contemplate the possibility of joy only for his friend, not for himself. Unlike Wordsworth in the "Ode: Intimations of Immortality," Coleridge can find no consoling thoughts to live by or convince himself that he has gained more than he has lost. A minority view sees evidence in stanza 7 that the poet has rekindled an imaginative spark and that as a result, in the calm final stanza, he is able to transcend his sense of separateness and feel compassion for another human being.

Bryan Aubrey

DELIGHT IN DISORDER

Author: Robert Herrick (1591-1674)
Type of poem: Lyric
First published: 1648, in *Hesperides: Or, The Works Both Humane and Divine of Robert Herrick, Esq.*

The Poem

Much poetry of the late sixteenth and early seventeenth centuries incorporates the idea of a "slight disorder in the dress" as well as in the hair of its female subjects. Ben Jonson notes that there is something suspicious about a woman who is always neatly dressed: What is she hiding? He calls for the "sweet neglect" of "robes loosely flowing, hair as free" in the woman who would capture his heart. Similarly, Richard Lovelace bids Amarantha to "dishevel Her Hair," letting it fly "as unconfined/ As its calm ravisher, the wind," that she might "shake [her] head and scatter day." Probably the best known of all poems with this bent is Robert Herrick's "Delight in Disorder."

Herrick first praises a wantonness, or playfulness, which he discovers in clothes arrayed in "sweet disorder." He proceeds to describe that disorder, beginning with a scarf thrown about the shoulders. It is a scarf of "lawn," a linen cloth woven so fine that it has a diaphanous quality. (Herrick found this quality engaging in one of his many Julia poems, "To Julia in Lawn at Dawn.") Herrick then takes note of the lace embroidery that decorates the lady's stomacher, a garment worn beneath the bodice. It is not the quality or the design of the lace that he notes, or how well it complements the garment to which it is sewn, but simply the fact that it is not quite perfect in its placement; it is indeed an "erring lace." The next element of the lady's dress that catches Herrick's eye is a cuff decorated with ribbons. He tells nothing of the design of the blouse or the color of the ribbons. All that catches his wayward eye is the suggestion of neglect in the cuff, and that the ribbons are not fixed carefully in place, but rather "flow confusedly." He then proceeds to the petticoat, noting that its smooth spread is broken by a wave. In Herrick's susceptible perception, this is no calm wave quietly wending its way to shore, but a veritable whitecap in a tempest. Finally, Herrick ends his catalog by arriving at the shoestring. Even in this trivial item of dress his responsive heart finds a "wild civility."

The denouement of all this is simple: Herrick finds such disorder far more bewitching than when "art/ Is too precise in every part." His taste runs to the free and unconfined rather than to the carefully tailored garment. However uncomfortable it might make his ladyfriend, Herrick would object not in the slightest should a strong wind move each bit of clothing into a wonder of disarray; he would rejoice in the dishevelment.

Forms and Devices

This poem is little more than a long synecdoche or metonymy. While describing the clothes, Herrick is really hoping for some "sweet disorder" or even a touch of wantonness in the lady associated with them. An "erring lace" is a much-desired corrective to a straight-laced woman, and a neglectful cuff might indicate a touch of neglect in adhering to the strict moral precepts inculcated by cautious elders. A mind that sometimes thinks confusedly and a heart with a touch of the tempestuous are certainly elements to be desired. Even so, all caution is not to be thrown to the winds—a touch of civility remains amid the wildness, though it is certainly not the major attribute: It is confined to the shoestring—hardly a major restraint.

The civility of the poem is also retained in its carefully constructed series of couplets in iambic tetrameter ("distraction" was a four-syllable word in the seventeenth century). The only breaks in the sweet falling of the iambs are in the second line, which begins with the trochaic "Kindles," emphasizing the wilder rhythm of fire, and the eighth line, which begins with "Ribbons," also a trochee, endowing the streamers with a strong, independent flow. "Into," beginning the fourth line, could also be read as a trochee, and in each case the strong opening beat of the word is made more emphatic because it follows an enjambment.

Much of the power of this poem comes in the connotative suggestions of the words. "Kindles" suggests the beginning of an inner fire, and "wantonness," though its primary meaning in the seventeenth century was merely playfulness, did also have its modern suggestion of lighthearted sexual play. "Distraction" suggests that one's mind can wander from the mundane to the exciting, and, as was mentioned earlier, an "erring" lace hints that the lady herself might be willing to wander. The word "enthralls" instead of the more straightforward "encircles" suggests that it is more than the lady's waist that is captured by the lace embroidery. A "winning" wave in the petticoat surely gathers a prize of hearts, a "careless" shoestring indicates one who does not care overmuch for restrictions, and a "wild" civility connotes freedom from the restrictions of a watchful society. Since love is a witch, it is not absolutely clear that "bewitch" is not strictly denotative in its effect on the poem. The oxymorons "sweet disorder" and "wild civility" (and perhaps "fine distraction") serve to create a tension that keeps the reader aware that the poet is speaking of a woman as well as the clothes she is wearing.

The syntax of the poem also increases its tension. After the declarative statement of the first couplet, the poem continues in one long sentence with six extensively developed subjects (lawn, lace, cuff, ribbons, wave, and shoestring) all holding the verb in abeyance, endowing the poem with the power of suspense.

Themes and Meanings

Robert Herrick is primarily a poet of celebration. The opening poem of *Hesperides* is a catalog of the myriad pleasures of nature, society, and folklore that inspire his poetry, and not the least among these is love: "I write of youth, of love, and have accesse/ By these, to sing of cleanly-wantonnesse." "Delight in Disorder" is a poem celebrating cleanly wantonness. Its theme cannot be more accurately and concisely stated than this.

In the poems of John Donne, another cleric of the seventeenth century, one is sure of the wantonness, but not entirely convinced of the cleanliness. In George Herbert's love poems, all addressed to God, one is sure of their intense cleanliness, but something of the wantonness is (appropriately) lacking. Herrick manages to bring these two somewhat contradictory qualities into perfect union.

It is interesting to remember that Herrick was the son of a goldsmith and was himself apprenticed to a goldsmith for several years. It is likely that some of this training carried over into his poems, for they have all the perfection, balance, and delicacy produced by exquisite craftsmanship. They are well-wrought ornaments, fit for the dragon-guarded tree in the garden of the Hesperides. This makes them difficult to dissect and analyze in books of literary criticism. Virgil Heltzel used to tell his classes of the professor who wrestled for years with the problem of how to teach Herrick. His solution was this: to read the poem as intelligently and musically as he could, to wait a moment for the experience to be appreciated, and then to remark, "Gentlemen, a gem!"

Howard C. Adams

DEPRESSION DAYS

Author: Pat Mora (1942-   )
Type of poem: Lyric
First published: 1995, in *Agua Santa/Holy Water*

The Poem

"Depression Days" is a short poem in free verse, consisting of thirty-five lines divided into seven stanzas. The title suggests not only a mood but also a specific historical period, 1929-1939. The Depression evokes a time of hardship and suffering because of a shortage of provisions and work. The poem, dedicated to Eduardo Delgado, focuses on the challenges presented to the main character by economic misery and racial discrimination. Pat Mora refers to him in the third person and does not specifically identify him by name until the fifth stanza, when she calls him her "uncle."

The historical context is important to an understanding of "Depression Days." The poem emphasizes the economic impact of the Great Depression and the involvement of Mora's uncle with the Civilian Conservation Corps (CCC), mentioned in line 8. The CCC, one of the most popular relief agencies of the New Deal, provided outdoor employment for numerous young men from 1933 to 1942. Many of the jobs were in conservation, usually in the nation's parks and forests. The enrollees lived in campsites set up in different states participating in the relief program. One of those work camps is the specific setting for the poem.

The poem begins by projecting the character into darkness as he spends "his last fifteen cents" to purchase a movie ticket. With the last coins in his pocket, he buys a ticket to forget the harsh realities of his personal life. Literally and figuratively, "He buys the dark." He escapes the light and reality by hiding in the darkness of a theater. As the film begins, he joins its seafaring men on the deck of the ship as their voices sing out, "Red Sails in the Sunset," a popular English song of the mid 1930's. Once on board the ship, the character embarks on a metaphoric voyage of self-discovery.

The next five stanzas begin exactly the same, with "He tries not to think," and then catalog life's harsh realities, which the man tries to obliterate from his mind as he adventures in the films. His first memory focuses on the previous night, presumably in the campsite, as he lay on his cot. This frame begins another movie, starring himself in the private role of "border kid playing CCC lumberjack." The dark continues in the second stanza, but here it is a darkness left by the death of his father. The death has obligated the young man to work with the CCC, a work program established by President Franklin D. Roosevelt to provide financial assistance to needy families.

The poem then describes the natural elements with which the workers must contend. The character tries not to think of the other Mexican workers who joined him in the truck in the cold morning as they rode to work. The only Spanish line in the poem is their own comment to each other regarding the weather: "¡Caramba, qué frío!" The workers' growling stomachs, which sound like the grinding gears in a truck, reveal their need to earn paychecks to buy food. Later, the "desert wind" makes its way into "the barracks" where the young workers reside, "herding" them like animals to gather near the warm stove. Delgado jokingly questions the reality of his own life as he asks, "Am I alive, doc?"

The fifth stanza introduces a disturbing conflict involving the sergeant. Because the Army directed the CCC work camps, a sergeant supervises this group. The young man, now identified as Delgado, tries to forget the sergeant's voice "spitting" out his name and his own voice confirming that he indeed is Delgado. The stern frown and twitch of lips describe the sergeant's attitude. The sixth stanza continues with Delgado trying to forget the sergeant's words: "You don't look Mexican, Delgado. Just change your name . . ./ . . . and you've got a job." Having the power to select those who get jobs, the sergeant offers Delgado an opportunity and a solution if only the latter will abandon his name and identity.

The seventh stanza concludes the poem by repeating the opening line: Delgado "buys the dark/ with his last fifteen cents" and returns to the darkness, where he began. The stanza indirectly reveals Delgado's rejection of the sergeant's proposition and recalls those affected by his decision.

Forms and Devices

Cinematic images structure "Depression Days." Mora effectively contrasts the fantasy of films with the reality of Delgado's life. They provide a means to escape and a chance to assume romanticized roles in several different films. The poem begins with the character watching "Reel after reel," but the second stanza intrudes with a very personal projection of scenes that Delgado "tries not to think of." The following five stanzas list experiences that he would prefer to forget but cannot. Those scenes are private, but they also apply to many others who found themselves in the same predicament during the Great Depression. The darkness of the theater functions as a framing device for the poem. Within the frame, Mora unravels a very disturbing experience.

The imagery of money and hunger in the poem is particularly relevant to the Great Depression. In both the first and last stanzas Delgado "buys the dark" with fifteen cents. References to "hungry for paychecks," the offer of a job, "the bare icebox," and "the price of eggs and names and skin" remind readers of Delgado's hunger and desperate need for a job. The young men's extreme hunger becomes more evident through their growling stomachs, "screechy as gears." Their hunger is further emphasized by references to "bare flesh" and the question involving being alive. In the last line Mora juxtaposes "the price of eggs" with the price of the last two items, "names and skin"—the price to be paid for having a Mexican name or dark-complected skin.

Mora uses repetition as a technique to remind the readers of the reason Delgado seeks the darkness. The first two lines in stanza 1 are repeated in stanza 7: "He buys the dark/ with his last fifteen cents." Enclosed within these two stanzas, the other five stanzas begin by repeating the refrain: "He tries not to think," followed by those scenes Delgado wishes to forget. The repetition reinforces the fact that he does think about them.

Themes and Meanings

Two closely related themes appear in "Depression Days," a powerful political poem about a significant historical decade and its effect on Mexican Americans. One of the themes is the horror of racial discrimination. Delgado, victimized because of his Mexican name, vividly exemplifies the object of racial discrimination. Discrimination threatens to deprive the "border kid" of a job. Although he is of Mexican ancestry, Delgado does not appear to be Mexican and could easily pass for Anglo, so he faces a terrible dilemma: Forsaking his cultural heritage and his identity would assure him of a job and thus end his economic misery.

The issue of identity is another prevalent theme in this poem, as it is in several of Mora's other works. The sergeant's order to Delgado to change his name so that he can get a job is a very tempting offer, given the time period and the economic crisis. Delgado remembers at this decisive point "his father who never understood/ this country." His family name, which comes from his father, provides him with a sense of who he is. Delgado has to consider whether changing his name would solve his problems and would allow him to fit in any better. An image of his mother comes to mind as he considers what his decision will mean. If Delgado changes his name he will gain a job, but he will also lose his identity. Names provide a sense of cultural heritage, of where one comes from. They identify people as individuals. In the poem "Legal Alien," Mora writes about the feeling of discomfort caused by living in two cultures, "sliding back and forth/ between the fringes of both worlds." Frequently, people who are bilingual and bicultural have no definite place in either world and can claim membership in neither. Mora does not provide a solution to the problems of discrimination and identity, nor does she philosophize. Instead, she poses a challenge for readers to consider what they would do in Delgado's situation.

Gloria Duarte-Valverde

THE DESCENT

Author: William Carlos Williams (1883-1963)
Type of poem: Meditation
First published: 1948; collected in *Paterson (Book Two)*, 1948

The Poem

"The Descent" is a brief lyric of forty-four lines, most of which contain five or six syllables. It is noteworthy, in part, because it is William Carlos Williams's first use of the forms that became a pattern for much of his later verse, the triadic line and the variable foot. This pattern provided Williams with a style that was flexible enough to allow him to avoid what he regarded as the straitjacket of strict meter.

This poem was written in Williams's later years and is concerned with the limitations and the consolations of growing old. Memory provides some relief from the cares of age, he says, ". . . a kind/ of accomplishment,/ a sort of renewal," since it presents the past in a new light and therefore opens the way to formerly unexplored territory.

Aging is a kind of defeat, he acknowledges. Yet even defeat is never total, since it, too, introduces the individual to "a world unsuspected." More important, "With evening, love wakens," and it is somehow new, because it is no longer attached as closely to physical desire. Instead, it takes on a new character: It becomes "Love without shadows."

In the concluding section, he recognizes again "The descent/ made up of despairs/ and without accomplishment." Still, it brings "a new awakening" that cannot be destroyed. Accomplishment, some kinds of love, and the eager hope for the future may all be gone, but the rewards of the descent itself are "indestructible."

Forms and Devices

Almost from the beginning of his career as a poet (he was also a physician), Williams avoided the traditional forms. His verse was consequently called "free verse," but he disliked the name and its implications and tried for many years to find a form that would provide a general pattern without unduly restricting the writer.

Williams believed that he had found such a form, and it saw its first extended use in "The Descent," which appeared first in the second installment (*Book Two*) of his long poem *Paterson* and which was later printed separately. The terms Williams used to describe this new "measure" were the "variable foot" and the "triadic line," terms that referred to the way in which the poem should be read and the way in which it appeared on the printed page. The variable foot was the unit of the line or measure, and most lines (though by no means all) contained three such feet and could thus be called triadic. The first section of "The Descent" neatly illustrates the form:

```
            the descent beckons
                    as the ascent beckoned.
                            Memory is a kind
        of accomplishment,
                    a sort of renewal
                            even
        an initiation, since the spaces it opens are new places
                    inhabited by hordes
                            heretofore unrealized.
```

In Williams's view, each short grouping constituted a measure, and the three taken together constituted a longer measure, or a line. He made much use of the form throughout the rest of his poetic career, not only in short lyric poems but also in such later long poems as "Asphodel, That Greeny Flower" and "The Desert Music."

Apart from the introduction of the new form, "The Descent" is unusual in Williams's work for the general quality of its imagery. In most of his verse, Williams used concrete and detailed images (he was frequently referred to as an Imagist poet), whether drawn from the natural world or from precise observation of human beings and their behavior. In "The Descent," however, the imagery is general and lacking in detail; many of the nouns used refer to groups or general qualities. Williams refers to "hordes" and "movements," and he repeats the word "world" several times. One near approach to specific imagery is his use of "white" and "whiteness," but it could be argued that white is the least evocative of colors—in fact, the word is often used to indicate something free from color. The image of night advancing is suggestive but also general.

The reason for this generality is that "The Descent" is meditative, a style in which Williams was not accustomed to writing, and in the poem he was less concerned with evoking the reader's response to specific images than he was in conveying the idea of what it is to age and the consolations of aging. When he returned to these subjects later in his writing career (for example, in "Asphodel, That Greeny Flower"), he presented his ideas more often through specific sensory imagery.

In "The Descent," the overriding image is the general one of descending, used as a metaphor for the aging process. Because Williams distrusted metaphor, this general one is the only figure of speech (other than personification) used in the poem. Williams immediately rejects the notion that descending into age is repugnant by insisting that it "beckons" and that memory can open the way to new places, not arid and sparse but inhabited by "hordes." Even if the descent consists of "despairs," it also implies "a new awakening:/ which is a reversal/ of despair."

Themes and Meanings

By the time Williams wrote *Paterson (Book Two)*, containing the lines which eventually were entitled "The Descent," he was in his early sixties. The series of strokes that would eventually lead him to turn his medical practice over to his son was still in the future, but he had begun to devote more attention in his poetry to the approach of old age and death. Part 3 of *Paterson (Book Two)* opens with a brief lyric advising poets to look for "the nul," which is the final end, "the death of all. . . . " Yet, that lyric ends with the amused, resigned lines, "But Spring shall come and flowers will bloom/ and man must chatter of his doom. . . . " The lines of "The Descent" follow immediately, an example of humankind's "chatter" but also a response to nonsense about doom.

In a real sense, "The Descent" is a general comment on Williams's new concern with aging and approaching death. Almost at once, he began to present the general in more specific terms; the poem in *Paterson (Book Two)* is followed immediately by a short lyric, enjoining the reader to listen to "the pouring water!/ The dogs and trees/ [which] conspire to invent/ a world—gone!" Every world is invented—and will disappear—but this one is to be enjoyed as long as it lasts. When the poem appeared in *The Desert Music and Other Poems*, it was placed first in the volume, followed by "To Daphne and Virginia," a poem about his daughters-in-law that associates them with love and with the particularly sensuous odor of boxwood.

"The Descent," then, is the introduction to a theme that would preoccupy Williams during his later years and that would become the subject of his later long poems, "Asphodel, That Greeny Flower" and "The Desert Music." He would go on to elaborate the themes of the blessings of memory and the rewards of a love in which passion plays a lesser role, and he would introduce new themes, refinements and extensions of the ideas introduced in "The Descent." Ultimately, however, "The Descent" is the necessary first statement of that abiding concern.

John M. Muste

A DESCRIPTION OF A CITY SHOWER

Author: Jonathan Swift (1667-1745)
Type of poem: Mock pastoral
First published: 1710; collected in *Miscellanies in Prose and Verse*, 1711

The Poem

Jonathan Swift's "A Description of a City Shower" is a sixty-three-line poem written in thirty-one of the end-rhymed iambic pentameter couplets still known as "heroic couplets," with the final line of iambic hexameter creating a closing triplet. (The heroic couplet was the most popular verse form of Swift's day and takes its name from its frequent use in English translations of classical epic—or, as it was then termed, "heroic"—poetry.) Swift's title is somewhat ironically misleading: Although he certainly provides a vivid enough description of a turbulent rain shower rolling through the streets of early eighteenth century London, the poem's central concern is with the city's inhabitants who are caught by Swift in a series of comic vignettes as they scurry to avoid the impending "flood."

At the time of the poem's initial publication, London was the center of English commerce and culture as well as Europe's leading trade center—a bustling, rapidly expanding metropolis that progressive Englishmen could regard with great pride. ("When a man is tired of London," wrote Samuel Johnson, a leading eighteenth century man of letters, "he is tired of life; for there is in London all that life can afford.") The Great Fire of 1666 had destroyed huge stretches of the city, and much of the newly rebuilt London, including the Christopher Wren-designed St. Paul's Cathedral, struck resident Londoners and visitors alike as a dazzling achievement.

However, if the lofty prospect of Wren's cathedral could dazzle a viewer, only a slight shift in perspective—downward, to eye or ground level—was likely to elicit an entirely different set of responses. Swift's London, like any great city, was a place of dramatic contrasts. Much of the landscape was admittedly new, but parts of the old city remained, replete with dark, claustrophobic streets and badly overcrowded tenements in which poverty and disease were the rule. Plumbing was primitive if not nonexistent, making waste disposal an enormous and constant problem. (The poem's final three lines, which might strike a modern reader as purposefully disgusting, are exaggerated only in a technical sense; many a Londoner no doubt witnessed worse.) Even in London's better areas, open drains ("Kennels") ran down the sides of dirt streets; in the early morning, when the contents of morning chamber pots were routinely tossed out of second-floor windows, pedestrians were well-advised to keep to the inside of the sidewalks. This London—the London seen by the "needy Poet" caught in the "Dust and Rain" of the street—is the London of Swift's poem. It is a city packed with perfectly ordinary people, all of them—like Susan taking down her clothes from the clothesline and the foppish young law student (the "Templer spruce") waiting for a break in the rain—doing perfectly ordinary things. Yet the poem's language—ornate, elevated, and rich with classical allusions—suggests that this seemingly everyday event is anything but ordinary.

Forms and Devices

The time during which Swift lived and wrote has often been termed the neoclassical age because the period witnessed a sweeping revival of classical literature. The works of Greek and Roman writers were studied, praised, and frequently imitated, and most educated English readers of Swift's day would have been familiar with the poetic genres of the ancient world. One very popular and often imitated classical genre was pastoral poetry (from *pastor,* the Latin word for shepherd), which celebrated rural life and often contrasted the (supposedly) simple, unspoiled life of herdsmen and farmers with the hectic, corrupt, and overly civilized life of city dwellers.

While Swift had no objections to the pastoral poems of such classical writers as the great Roman poet Vergil, he had little patience with the shallowness and artificiality of much eighteenth century pastoral poetry, which used highly ornate language to describe the lives of its rural subjects in lavish, unrealistic detail. For Swift, this not only made for bad poetry but also made for poetry that was aesthetically dishonest and morally irresponsible. (The primary purpose of art, according to neoclassical literary theory, was to provide moral instruction, and moral instruction could hardly proceed from what was essentially a lie.) To demonstrate how empty pastoral poetry had become as a form in the hands of most eighteenth century imitators, Swift and several of his contemporaries wrote a number of poems such as "A Description of a City Shower" that employ the elevated language and classical allusions of pastoral poetry to describe seemingly ordinary scenes of urban life. This form (of which John Gay's 1714 *The Shepherd's Week* is an outstanding example) lies somewhere between satire and parody and is known as "mock pastoral." The results of such compoundings of realism with romance vary in complexity, but the most obvious common effect is an ironic—and intentionally comic, if dark—sense of incongruity created by the discrepancy between the poem's "high" language and its "low" subject matter.

In "A Description of a City Shower," the incongruity first arises from the degree of seriousness assigned to an event as commonplace as a rain shower. In addition to the grandiose language found in the poem's first twelve lines, the scene seems charged with a nearly epic sense of anticipation. Prophecies and oracles often play important roles in both classical epics and tragedies, and here Swift provides a bevy of signs and omens ("Prognosticks")—from the behavior of the "pensive Cat" to various physical aches and pains—that seem to portend something much grander and more ominous than a simple shower. It is in the poem's second verse paragraph, however, that Swift's design becomes strikingly clear. Word choice, allusion, and imagery combine to create the comic incongruity characteristic of the mock pastoral form. The personified south wind rises in the sky ("the Welkin") on "dabbled [dirty] Wings" and brings with it a dark cloud heavy with rain. While Swift's comparison of the rain cloud to a "Drunkard" that, having "swill'd more Liquor than it could contain," is preparing to give "it up again" may strike modern readers as rather crude, it would hardly have offended the eighteenth century sensibility, which would have delighted in Swift's clever spin on the extended simile so typical of epic poetry.

As the rain begins in earnest, the language of the third and fourth verse paragraphs continues to stress the ironic gap between classical literature and everyday behavior, even going so far as to suggest that the coming "deluge" will rival the biblical flood of Noah. As Londoners dart about in search of shelter, old enmities are forgotten. "Triumphant Tories, and desponding Whigs" (members of opposing political parties) put aside their differences "and join to save their Wigs." In the poem's most elaborate "epic" simile, a "Beau" (a young man-about-town) who is nervously waiting out the rain within a sedan chair is compared to the Greeks hiding within the Trojan Horse, bringing to mind Aeneas's account of the fall of Troy in book 2 of Vergil's *Aeneid* (c. 29-19 B.C.E.; English translation, 1553). The final image of the "huge Confluent" coursing uncontrollably through London seems nearly apocalyptic, threatening to engulf the entire city—until one realizes that the distance between Smithfield market and Holborn bridge is little more than a stone's throw.

Themes and Meanings

Swift remains the premier satirist in the English language. (His 1726 prose satire *Gulliver's Travels* is arguably the finest satire in any language.) Besides a powerful intelligence and an essential dissatisfaction with the human condition, the satirist must possess an eye keen enough to discern the follies that so often arise from confusing appearance and reality—which is precisely what eighteenth century pastoral poetry routinely did. The facts of eighteenth century rural life were cold and hard. Farmers and rural workers lived lives at the other end of the spectrum from the hazily romantic imaginings of pastoral poetry. Like their lower-class counterparts in the city, they worked long, back-breaking hours, usually for little more than a subsistence wage. No amount of flowery language or elaborate, classical imagery could improve their lot or effectively substitute fantasy for reality.

It would be wrong, however, to imagine a savagely indignant Swift behind "A Description of a City Shower." The tone, in fact, is much more one of wry amusement than anger, and even the poem's array of frankly repellent images—from the poet's filthy coat to the "Drowned Puppies," decaying fish, and "Dead Cats" of the concluding lines—in the end seem more comically grotesque than offensive.

Michael Stuprich

A DESCRIPTION OF THE MORNING

Author: Jonathan Swift (1667-1745)
Type of poem: Satire
First published: 1709; collected in *Miscellanies in Prose and Verse*, 1711

The Poem

Jonathan Swift was much involved in the launching of his friend Sir Richard Steele's new literary enterprise, a thrice-weekly paper of familiar essays and news called *The Tatler*. One of Swift's contributions was the eighteen-line poem called "A Description of the Morning," which appeared in the ninth paper on April 30, 1709, only two weeks after the publication debuted. The poem gives a series of photographic impressions of London life, specifically, as Steele remarked, of life in the West End of London.

The poem opens at daybreak, with only a few coaches yet on the scene to carry about their passengers. The first scene is of Betty, a stock name for a female servant, leaving her master's bed. In an effort to cover up her deed, she goes to her room and ruffles the covers of her own unused bed. Next, three cleaners take the stage for their brief appearances. An apprentice cleans with a half-hearted effort, while Moll skillfully whirls her mop as a prelude to scrubbing the entry stairs. A youth sweeps the "kennel," or gutter, with a stubby broom (in search of used nails, as a note by Swift explains).

Two workers next demand the reader's attention, one selling coal—then widely used domestically for cooking and warmth or for cottage industries requiring fire—the other announcing his availability to sweep chimneys. The "shriller notes" of the sweep imply the grim reality that children were forced into this dangerous and debilitating job, often working from dawn to dusk. While bill collectors ("duns") gather before an aristocrat's house, another loud voice intrudes. It belongs to another "Moll": This one may be selling brick dust, used as a scouring powder, or (since Swift calls her "Brickdust Moll") Swift may have in mind her working-class complexion, scorched by the sun. The name "Moll" has seedy associations. Cutpurse Moll was the name of an infamous seventeenth century pickpocket, and the name in Swift's day was associated with prostitution.

While the above are all starting their day, another group has just finished their night's work. Thieves are welcomed back to jail by the "turnkey," or jail keeper, who has let them out to steal—for his sizable cut of the take. Next, ironically, "watchful bailiffs" assume their posts. The poems closes with schoolboys reluctantly finding their way to school.

Forms and Devices

The poem, satiric in manner, has models in the classical satires of Horace and Juvenal and contains echoes of William Shakespeare's *As You Like It*. Swift's satires tend to be Juvenalian, or biting, but here he tends more to the Horatian, or urbane and gentle, mode. As with all true satires, the poem points to human failings with an eye to correction. The poem was also one of the first English examples of what is variously called the town eclogue, urban pastoral, or ironic pastoral—all designating a poem about the city. In "A Description of the Morning" and its companion piece, "A Description of a City Shower," which also appeared in *The Tatler*, Swift introduced something quite out of the norm for Augustan poetry. Steele avowed that Swift "has run into a Way perfectly New" of presenting "the Incidents just as they really appear." This puts Swift toward the head of a long line of realistic writers.

The poem takes the simple form of a list or series of snapshots. Several deftly drawn characters make cameo appearances, and each actively engages in work which defines both their individual lives and, collectively, the life of the city as seen from the working-class perspective. The upper classes would not even be awake yet in eighteenth century England. C. N. Manlove has noticed that the series of scenes has a general movement from the inside to the outside: from the master's bedroom to the entry way to the street and finally to the lord's front gate. Similarly, as the morning broadens into day, the verbs move from the past tense to the present.

Themes and Meanings

"A Description of the Morning" has much in common with Swift's other work in both prose and poetry. Swift loves detail, especially detail that exposes human weakness and gives no quarter to vanity, as in his descriptions of the human body and bodily functions in *Gulliver's Travels*. No direct commentary is needed; the facts are made to speak for themselves. Similarly, Swift here makes no explicit comment on the morality or quality of working-class London. Yet taken together, the scenes give the impression of a city that is a noisy, dirty place. It is populated by people who at best are reluctant to work or learn and at worst are deceptive, manipulative, and immoral.

Swift, the dean of St. Patrick's Cathedral in Dublin, is ever fulfilling the preacher's role in pointing up the weakness in human nature and the resultant failings in human behavior. Master and servant alike are involved in sexual sin, which they take pains to keep hidden, while further immorality is suggested by the twice-used stock name for a prostitute, Moll. The moral and social order is shown to be in an advanced state of decay, as those charged with maintaining law and order use their power to rob the very people they are charged with protecting—all for personal gain.

Lesser lapses fill in the gaps. The young apprentice scrimps by with the mere appearance of cleanliness, and schoolboys dawdle, reluctant to take advantage of their educational privilege. Even more subtle is the suggestion of class distinction and the gap between rich and poor. The conveyances out at daybreak are "hackney" coaches, which means they are for hire or rent. The rich would have their own. The bill collectors gathering before the gate are dependent on "his Lordship," and men and women ignominiously bawl through the streets in search of customers. Such detail as the "broomy stumps," suggesting worn-out equipment, points to the Spartan condition of the youth's life as he looks for recyclable nails.

Swift does not force this kind of judgment from his readers; the narrative voice never obtrudes. He also makes no effort to tie the descriptions together by a narrative thread or any other device. The images bump against one another with all the randomness typical of the street. Yet, with all its apparent indirection, the poem gives a subtle critique of human nature. With its realism so concretely realized, the pettiness, nastiness, and seaminess of urban London become undeniable. The satiric touch is lighter than usual for Swift, who often pushes the filth under readers' noses. For example, he spares them images of the chamber pot, routinely dumped into the street in his day. Such understatement allows the reader to draw conclusions personally, but they are made nearly inevitable: Such pervasive shortcomings must point to elemental flaws in human character, which, as Swift is always suggesting, need radical moral solutions.

Wayne Martindale

THE DESERT MUSIC

Author: William Carlos Williams (1883-1963)
Type of poem: Lyric
First published: 1951; collected in *The Desert Music and Other Poems*, 1954

The Poem

"The Desert Music" is a relatively lengthy open-form poem. The title refers to the topic of the poem, a desert journey, as well as to the musical imagery present throughout the work. The poem is written primarily in the first person and appears to be drawn from the personal experiences of the author. The poet functions as a speaker of the poem as well as an observer within the poem. In describing his purpose, the speaker states that his goal is, when describing his desert journey, "—to tell/ what subsequently I saw and what heard." When functioning as an observer, the speaker identifies himself by name (William Carlos Williams). He also mentions that the group with which he is traveling includes a total of seven members, and he specifically describes an incident involving one of his friends in particular (identified by the initial H.). In addition, as speaker, Williams refers to the actions of his wife, giving her name as Floss.

The journey described in the poem is likened to a dance that begins and ends with the speaker's observation of a figure located on the international bridge between the United States and Mexico:

> —the dance begins: to end about
> a form propped motionless—on the bridge
> between Juarez and El Paso—unrecognizable
> in the semi-dark.

Here the speaker establishes a specific setting for the events outlined in the poem. He describes a journey, taken with several friends, from California, through El Paso, Texas, to Juarez, Mexico.

The events in the poem are generally presented chronologically as the speaker travels from one location to the next. There are numerous references to the characteristics of the people that the speaker encounters while in each specific location. First he describes the figure on the bridge, then he describes the attributes of the Texans he meets throughout his travels. He asks, "What makes Texans so tall?" Later he describes the children who beg for pennies (expressing annoyance at their grasping fingers), the Indians at the market booths (who seem to be asleep but are actually alert), and a woman he observes while at a nightclub. Williams expresses his admiration for this woman, a striptease dancer, because she does not let her worn-out form prevent her from practicing the art of dancing. In general, the speaker's descriptions are brief but vivid, and they focus on what is observable to the human eye. However, the speaker interjects his concerns as a poet regarding the best way to create a poem that will reflect the experiences of his journey without copying nature.

The closing of the poem is similar to its opening in that the speaker again refers to the figure by the side of the bridge. The events presented seem to have taken place over a period of several days, with much of the description focusing on incidents occurring during the evening hours. The return to a description of the unknown figure near the international boundary seems to mark, for the speaker, the beginning and end of his journey.

Forms and Devices

Although a number of poetic devices, such as repetition and imagery, are present within the poem, in general, one of the interesting features associated with "The Desert Music" (as well as with many of Williams's other poems) is the absence of conventional form and content. As previously noted, the poem is open in its form and therefore does not include the use of a specific rhyming pattern or a specific metrical construction. To establish a coherence and a cadence, Williams uses punctuation such as dashes, commas, and end marks to signify the ways in which the lines should be read. Williams was often recognized as a poet who experimented with various forms and techniques in his effort to imitate the sounds and scenes of life.

Williams is also noted for using language that is direct and succinct rather than language that ornaments or embellishes. "The Desert Music" uses the common vernacular, and Williams presents images in an economical fashion. As a result, some of the scenes depicted have almost a photographic quality. The market scene is particularly vivid in its presentation. Williams identifies the items sold in the market booths in a way that renders the "baked red-clay utensils, daubed/ with blue, silverware,/ dried peppers, onions, print goods, children's/ clothing" visible and concrete.

While "The Desert Music" presents many vivid images and is somewhat reminiscent of Williams's earlier poems that have been closely associated with the Imagist movement, this poem illustrates his move toward Objectivism. In this latter approach to poetry, the poem becomes an object, and in "The Desert Music" the poet struggles with the question, "How shall we get said what must be said?" To answer this question within the framework of "The Desert Music," Williams repeatedly refers to music and dance.

The speaker first mentions music when he describes the figure on the bridge. In referring to the music of the desert in relationship to the figure, the speaker says, "A music/ supersedes his composure, hallooing to us/ across a great distance" Later, the speaker notes the presence of music as he and his friends drive through the desert. He describes the music as being the "music of survival, subdued, distant, half/ heard." When describing the erotic dancer, he notes that "She fits/ the music," suggesting that as a result she is able to transcend her audience and become virtuous through her art.

In addition to repeatedly referring to music and dance, the speaker repeats his concerns about producing a poem that does not copy nature but rather imitates it in a unique way. He also questions the purpose of writing poetry. In an implied conversation, the speaker responds to the question, "Why/ does one want to write a poem?" His response is direct and simple: "Because it is there to be written." This question-and-response pattern is evident throughout the poem in a way that resembles a refrain in a musical composition, and Williams's thoughts are interspersed with the descriptions of the desert journey.

Themes and Meanings

"The Desert Music" is a poem about imitating life through the creation of poetry. The speaker continually raises questions relating to the nature and significance of poetry. He responds to the questions in the form of an open dialogue and defines himself as a poet in an insistent and repetitive manner. The form of the poem serves as a challenge to the conventions of the Romantics and the Georgians, who Williams felt were restricted in their approach to poetry by their use of traditional patterns of organization. The poem also expresses a resistance to the use of elevated language and traditional subject matter. The poem is seen as an enduring object connected to the reality of human experience through the use of precise and rhythmic language.

"The Desert Music" is also a poem about a journey taken as a way of finding "relief from that changeless, endless/ inescapable and insistent music." During the journey from California to Mexico, Williams appears to be searching for companionship and for experiences that will help him make connections with the people he meets. The photographic images he presents seem to reflect his interest in the particular, rather than the general, aspects of life. The cyclical nature ("Egg-shaped!") of the journey isolates the events described in the poem within a specific time frame and presents the journey as being complete.

The common subject matter of the poem links the everyday experiences of the individual to the poetic structure, and even though the speaker continually interrupts the description of the journey, it is possible to trace the travels of Williams and his companions. The figure on the bridge is present at both the beginning and the ending of the poem, and his location at the international boundary is significant because it is there that he will not be disturbed.

"The Desert Music" incorporates within its structure the theme of the significance of poetry as well as the theme of the importance of shared experiences and objects. While these themes are often addressed in modern poetry, the uniqueness of Williams's method of presentation sets this poem apart. The absence of a prescribed form as well as the absence of ornamental language lend a somewhat raw quality to the work that many readers have found refreshing and provocative. In addition, the presence of the two themes in juxtaposition to each other creates a tension between the experience of the poet and the experience of the reader.

Julie Sherrick

THE DESERTED VILLAGE

Author: Oliver Goldsmith (1728 or 1730-1774)
Type of poem: Meditation
First published: 1770

The Poem

The Deserted Village is a long poem, its 430 lines distributed among twenty-five verse paragraphs of varying length. All the lines are given in heroic couplets. It is clear that Oliver Goldsmith as poet is the persona of the poem. The first-person narration is used to express a lamentation, as it were, for the passing of a way of life.

The meaning of the title is readily evident; it not only lists the poem's subject, but suggests its theme as well. Roughly, the poem can be divided into three main sections: a description of the village as it used to be at the time of the poet's youth; a description of the village "today," in the poet's maturity; and the concluding section that somewhat details life in America, where the occupants of Auburn have gone.

"Sweet Auburn" has been identified as Lissoy, Ireland, the poet's hometown. In the first paragraphs of the poem, Auburn is, strangely enough, described as if it were an English town—a fact that makes for what often has been called the only genuine weakness of the work. The details and images of life in this rustic village are consistently English: Indeed, the poet directly refers to England at the beginning of the fourth paragraph. He creates a picture of rustic life in England when times were simpler; land was owned and used commonly by farmers; the people were good and united by common purpose, integrity, and society; and all lived in accord with nature.

All of this is gone now. The poet explains that he had intended to retire in Auburn, where he had fantasized that nightly around a fire on the village common he would tell tales and share with villagers his book-learning and other experiences. He has returned to find the village deserted, in a state of disuse and decay. As he surveys the empty village, images and memories abound; in particular, he recalls the village preacher, a goodly sort who had fed beggars and earned the respect of the villagers: "Truth from his lips prevailed with double sway/ And fools, who came to scoff, remained to pray." Similarly, the village schoolmaster, though a tyrant in the classroom, was given a special place of honor in the community because of his singular knowledge. Goldsmith's intention to return to the home of his youth and be held in similar regard has been thwarted.

The village is deserted because its occupants have been forced to leave. The government had put an end to the common land that gave rise to the social order and livelihood of the villagers, who were left either to move to a city or migrate to America. Goldsmith recognizes in this the passing of a way of life, which he truly laments. The poet describes America as overrun with fierce and hideous animals as well as "savage men," and he paints a stark contrast between their idyllic life here and the murderous savagery there. The poem ends with an expression that the poor may be "blest" and that those who have caused these social and economic changes would see the error of their ways.

Forms and Devices

The Deserted Village is written in heroic verse. As such, it contains many elements of both lyrical and pastoral poetry in terms of its subject matter and expression. Goldsmith's superbly written lines at times have lyrical qualities; his depiction of rustic characters and life—particularly repeated references to the swain (a somewhat mildly disguised allusion to his own childhood) and milkmaid—loosely qualify the poem as a pastoral in terms of its subject. Nevertheless, the poem is heroic because of its rhyme scheme and meter as well as other poetic conventions of the form.

The couplets display near-perfect end rhyme in most cases (an exception occurs in lines 205 and 206 wherein "aught" is rhymed with "fault"). Many lines contain alliteration, such as in the phrases "The whitewashed wall," the "clock that clicked," and "double debt." The poet frequently employs assonance ("Amazed the gazing rustics" and "importance to the poor man's heart"). The poem is written in iambic pentameter.

Perhaps Goldsmith's second most important poetic device is his use of metaphor. Central to an understanding of the poem itself is the realization that "Auburn" is representative of all such small villages of the time of which the poet writes. That the town is idyllically and fictionally described in the first section (England) while realistically and autobiographically, though romantically, described in the second (Ireland) is of no genuine significance to the poem's overall theme. The town itself is a metaphor for a departed way of life.

Similarly, the town is given a metaphorical embodiment as a woman starting in line 287 and continuing for several paragraphs. Auburn is likened to "some fair female, unadorned and plain," one who is "In nature's simplest charms at first arrayed." This woman, so pure and rustic in her roots and previous life, is now poverty stricken, demoralized, and gone. The poet records that "her friends, her virtue, fled." Auburn has metaphorically been forced into prostitution, then to flee her spinning "wheel, and robes of country brown."

America exists imagistically and metaphorically in the poem. It is called a "horrid shore," a place full of wild animals and savage men given to murder. "Rural virtues" have left the land to be not so much relocated as dislocated in a land where barbarity abounds because of the absence of civilization. America is seen as a place filled with hardship and immorality.

The poet makes his own role metaphorical by comparing his function to that of a solitary bird singing its way through this present existence. When the poet returns to survey the village and study the meanings of its deserted state, he becomes like this bird; The Deserted Village becomes his song.

Themes and Meanings

Goldsmith's main purpose in writing The Deserted Village was to mourn the passing of a way of life. Undoubtedly, he too much romanticizes and idealizes the beauty and simplicity of the village; the purity, innocence, and honesty of its people; and the genuine goodness of their lives. The poet captures the essence of all things good about an agrarian village with common lands, trusting people, and social order and stability;

he totally ignores any negative aspects of such an existence, particularly those of pervasive ignorance and incessant hard work—in short, of peasantry. At the same time, he overdramatizes the barbarity and hardship of America and those who went there from such places as England and Ireland.

The poem also can be interpreted as a series of futile indictments. Primarily, the English government is castigated for systematically destroying a way of life that, as Goldsmith recalls from his own youth, was faultlessly good. Developments in agriculture required an end to commonly used land for grazing and farming; in its place, a more productive system required individual ownership and control of small farms. The government had enacted such changes without regard for those whose livelihood and way of living it was uprooting. In his metaphor of Auburn as woman-become-prostitute, it is the English government to which Goldsmith refers when he uses the word "betrayer."

At the same time, America is held up with contempt for the worst of its faults, and this is done with a complete absence of recognition of its good points. Not only have the English government and the "rich" victimized these villagers by driving them away from hearth and home, but also America will continue the persecution with the "various terrors of that horrid shore." America is a place where the sun is too hot and the "birds forget to sing." It is overrun with wild animals (bats, scorpions, rattlesnakes) that will traumatize the harmless and simplistic newcomers. Even nature is participatory; Goldsmith mentions the "mad tornado" and "ravaged landscape," which are unfairly contrasted with "The cooling brook, the grassy-vested green,/ The breezy covert of the warbling grove,/ That only sheltered thefts of harmless love."

The theme of *The Deserted Village* transcends the cliché "you can't go home again." The poet accepts this fact and focuses on the loss of rustic goodness and the inevitable effort of progress to displace such goodness in the name of callous wealth. Toward the end of the poem, he does manage to utter his eternal "Farewell." He is content to hope only that goodness and simplicity in a way of life will not be forgotten as part of cultural heritage and history. He addresses himself with:

> Still let thy voice, prevailing over time,
> Redress the rigors of this inclement clime;
> Aid slighted truth with thy persuasive strain;
> Teaching erring man to spurn the rage of gain;
> Teach him that states, of native strength possessed,
> Though very poor, may still be very blest;

Goldsmith's recognition is that "erring man" possibly can be taught, if not to undo such actions, at least to understand and appreciate them.

The last four lines were added by Samuel Johnson, with Goldsmith's approval. They enhance the indictment of business and wealth that result in a denigration and diminishing of rustic goodness. In the last two lines, it is seen that individuals can resist such changes through perseverance "As rocks resist the billows and the sky."

Carl Singleton

DESIGN

Author: Robert Frost (1874-1963)
Type of poem: Sonnet
First published: 1922; collected in *A Further Range*, 1936

The Poem

"Design" is an atypical Petrarchan (or Italian) sonnet, because though its octave (the first eight lines) sets forth a situation, and the sestet (the final six lines) reacts to it, Robert Frost's theme is not love, and his sestet concludes with a couplet—more common to the Shakespearean (Elizabethan) sonnet. Further, though the octave rhyme scheme is the Petrarchan *abbaabba*, the sestet is a rare *acaacc*, a three-rhyme pattern that is unusually restrictive for a poem in English, which is a difficult rhyming language. Since the structure of the poem departs from tradition, the reader may wonder about the appropriateness of "Design" as its title; perhaps Frost is mocking, or at least questioning, the very notion of order.

The literal content of the sonnet seems straightforward. While wandering about the countryside, the first-person narrator, apparently Frost himself, is on a hill and happens to see a flower—a "heal-all"—on which a spider sits with a dead moth. The spider is fat (probably from having consumed a previous victim), dimpled, and white. The flower, also white, is "like a froth," and the moth is said to be similar to "a white piece of rigid satin cloth." The three objects presumably are dead, like "the ingredients of a witches' broth." The lilting rhythm of the opening five words and the description of the spider as dimpled are deceptive, for the lightness of touch they convey is quickly overtaken by the subsequent details and their pervasive focus upon death. The octave, therefore, does not merely develop the sonnet's substantive base; by toying with the reader, it also establishes a mood of uncertainty, even foreboding, and raises questions about what is to come in the second part.

The reader of a sonnet normally can expect commentary, perhaps even resolution, in a sestet. Such is not the case in the last six lines of Frost's poem, which consist of three questions and a closing speculative statement. In the first four lines, a perplexed narrator articulates the same matters that bother the reader, whose surrogate he is. He wonders, for instance, about the incongruous scene, asking how its components—flower, spider, moth—happened to come together at that particular place and time. What "steered" them there, he asks—and for what purpose or "design"? In the closing couplet, the speaker reiterates his concern: Did chance bring about the meeting, or did some power orchestrate the event? Indeed, would a supreme being even bother with such matters?

By raising unanswered questions in the sestet, Frost leaves the reader with a sense of unease, incompleteness. The incongruity between the confident clarity of the title and subsequent descriptions and questions is heightened by Frost's emphatic use of the word "design" twice in the last two lines. So whereas the title initially exudes a forthright assertiveness suggestive of order, once one reads through the poem, the title

"Design" takes on ironic, maybe even skeptical overtones. Like so much else in the Frost canon, this is a linguistically simple poem—75 percent of the words are monosyllabic—that plumbs the depths of the human condition.

Forms and Devices

Frost begins "Design" deceptively in that he describes the dead spider as dimpled, for the term more often is used about a baby and usually has pleasant connotations. A dimple, though, is simply an indentation, so Frost may be literal in his description of a fat, shriveled creature whose color has faded.

The heal-all, more commonly known as self-heal, is a violet-blue flower reputed to have medicinal powers, but here it is white, similarly drained of its color in death. The third object in the poem is a moth, also white, like the rigid satin cloth that typically lines a coffin. Further, to emphasize death, Frost surely chose the adjective "rigid" to suggest rigor mortis. The narrator also links the three things with blight, a condition of destructive decay. In the light of all this, how can the objects be said to be ready to begin the morning "right," or correctly? Maybe Frost is punning, leading the reader astray, as he does at the start of the sonnet. (Perhaps he intends "rite," as in a ritual.) The next line, with its allusion to a witches' broth, an essential component of an unholy ceremony, suggests this possibility.

The octave concludes with a variation on its opening, a list of the three objects, now joined as ingredients of an unsavory stew. Frost first calls attention to the spider's whiteness by describing it as a snow drop, an early-blooming flower. The next part of the series—"a flower like a froth"—could provide a link either to the snow-drop or to the white heal-all, but why does Frost say "froth"? Simply because the white flowers resemble foam? His choice of language may be more purposeful, with "froth" referring to a salivary foam indicative of disease. Similarly evoking various interpretations is the comparison of the dead moth's wings to a paper kite. In addition to denoting a toy that wafts in a breeze, the word "kite" refers to a bird of prey, and white kites are used in Asian funeral rites. In sum, Frost's octave incrementally develops an unmistakable image pattern of death, destruction, disease, and decay.

In the first few lines of the sestet, there is a temporary shift in style and tone, attributable to such words as "wayside," "innocent," and "kindred," all of which have positive connotations. Having moved toward serenity with his first two questions, Frost attempts his answer by raising a third one: "What but design of darkness to appall?" In a poem dominated by an albino death scene, the word "darkness" is jarring and signals an abrupt shift in tone. This shift is reinforced by the last word, which is the most heavily accented of the seven words in the line. "Appall" means to dismay or to fill with consternation, either of which sense fits the context, and it derives from Latin and Middle English words which refer to growing pale or faint, both of which meanings are relevant. They suggest that the startled narrator and reader might become as white as the dead trio. Immediately upon raising the dreadful possibility of some malevolent force having been responsible for the albino tableau, Frost ends the poem inconclusively. "If," the first word of his last line, warrants the most emphasis.

Themes and Meanings

Since he alludes to the New Testament book of Matthew elsewhere in his poetry, Frost certainly had read Matthew 10:29: "Are not two sparrows sold for a farthing? And one of them shall not fall on the ground without your Father." He was familiar, therefore, with the tradition of an omniscient and omnipotent God. He surely had read Job's impassioned questioning of God's purpose. In addition, Frost taught the philosophy of William James to students at Plymouth Normal School in New Hampshire, and in James's *Pragmatism* is the statement: "Let me pass to a very cognate philosophic problem, the question of design in nature." This text may or may not have served as Frost's source for the poem. In any event, Frost, like poets that preceded and followed him, was skeptical about the extent to which the Creator was benign, and he wondered about the degree of his involvement with his creations.

For example, William Blake in "The Tyger" (1794) wonders whether the same God could create both the fierce and the gentle; he asks the tiger, "Did he who made the lamb make thee?" In Thomas Hardy's "An August Midnight" (1899), a spider symbolizes evil in God's design. In Robert Lowell's "Mr. Edwards and the Spider" (1946), the black widow represents the damned soul. On the other hand, in Walt Whitman's "A Noiseless Patient Spider" (1891), the creature is benign.

Frost is expressing a sense of bewilderment felt by many religious people at one time or another: How does one reconcile death and evil with a benevolent deity? Fundamental to this problem is the extent to which God assumes a monitoring role—whether God watches over the details of the world or is concerned only with the grand design. Does Frost's bleak scene of death in "Design" call Matthew into question? Moreover, Genesis 1:31 says, "God saw everything that he had made, and, behold, it was very good." Does Frost intend the sonnet "Design," a meditation upon a dark reality, to refute this judgment? More likely, given the prevalence of questions in the sestet and the "If" at the start of the last line, he is unready to reach definitive conclusions. The questions alone are unsettling enough.

"Design" is one of Robert Frost's greatest poems, a structural and substantive masterpiece. His deliberate departures from sonnet traditions, his richly allusive language, and the sly ironic touches complement one another, and they demonstrate that an artist sometimes attains a degree of perfection that is lacking in nature.

Gerald H. Strauss

THE DESTRUCTION OF SENNACHERIB

Author: George Gordon, Lord Byron (1788-1824)
Type of poem: Lyric
First published: 1815, in *Hebrew Melodies Ancient and Modern*

The Poem

In 1815 George Gordon, Lord Byron wrote a poem about the biblical story of Sennacherib, whose destruction is related in the nineteenth chapter of the Second Book of Kings. Sennacherib was the emperor of Assyria from 705 to 681 B.C.E. In 701 B.C.E., his forces laid siege to Jerusalem.

The Assyrians had conquered the entire Near East except for tiny Judah, the last remaining Israelite kingdom, which was militarily weak. Few thought it possible that their walled capital city, Jerusalem, could hold out long against such forceful Assyrian military might. The Assyrians were a regimented and militaristic society, and aggressiveness was their trademark. Byron's comparison of them to "wol[ves] on the fold" grasps the animal intensity characteristic of their assaults. "Fold" means sheepfold, or pen of sheep; "wolf on the fold," an image itself derived from the Bible, refers to an evil predator among the innocent.

In Byron's poem, the Assyrians are arrayed with fine clothing and mighty weaponry. Yet in the second stanza readers are told that all these material goods have not availed them. The division between the two couplets in this stanza is abrupt. At one moment, the Assyrians resemble the green of the summer: beautiful, prosperous, with nature itself on their side. At the next moment, they are like the withered leaves of autumn, drained of life and blown in many ways. The mighty Assyrians have been defeated, but Byron asks by whom and how. After all, no other nation could come close to the Assyrians' military power.

The third stanza gives the answer: It is not a human, but rather a supernatural force. The "Angel of Death" has wished a fatal sleep on the Assyrians. His breath has deadened their eyes, stopped their breathing, and reduced their hearts to one final beat. Even the horses are not spared. The pride of the Assyrian army, accustomed to carrying their riders to victory, the great steeds foam at the mouth, diseased and maddened. As great as both horse and rider appeared but a moment before, they are now humbled and indeed reduced to utter destruction.

The horses' riders—Byron uses the singular for poetic effect, but in fact he is talking about groups of dead soldiers—who were ready to attack an instant ago, now lie as if they were never alive at all, their skin and armor disintegrating. The lances with which they were going to fight and the trumpet that was going to hail their victory are both stilled. Jerusalem, the city of God's people, has been spared.

In Ashur (the original capital of the Assyrian kingdom, also another name for Assyria as a whole) the wives of the soldiers sit waiting. When they realize their husbands will not return, they are desolate. Unlike the people of Jerusalem, the Assyrians worship idols, not the Judeo-Christian God. The supernatural force shown by the God of the Bible therefore prevails over the material gods worshipped by the attacking armies.

Forms and Devices

"The Destruction of Sennacherib" is written in six stanzas of four lines each. Each line has twelve syllables and is subdivided into four groups of three, with the emphasis on the final syllable of that group, for instance, "like a wolf" in line 1. This is called anapestic tetrameter: An anapest is a foot in which the third syllable is accented, whereas the first and second are not, and tetrameter refers to the four of these feet that make up the line. Anapestic tetrameter is often found in poems with strong aural effects, story-driven poems that use sound and rhythm to give their tales impact.

Knowing the metrical scheme helps the reader determine how the various lines are sounded out. "Assyrian" in the first line, a word which in contemporary spoken English is four syllables (as-SYR-ee-an), is elided to three (a-SYR-yan). Part of Byron's metrical task is to intertwine the proper names pertaining to the story he is telling with the rolling, melodious rhythm of his general diction. Byron deftly integrates these names of remote antiquity with words that were standard elements in the poetic diction of his own day.

The poem's rhyme scheme reinforces this combination of might and mellifluousness. The first two lines of each stanza rhyme which each other, as do the second two, making the scheme *aabb*. This apposition of sounds is forceful. Byron uses other poetic effects to reinforce this power, such as alliteration in line 3, "sheen of their spears was like stars on the sea." In this line, a series of disparate images is threaded together, linked as much by their alliteration as by any thematic association.

The seasonal similes in the second stanza are notable in that their imagery almost covers up their meaning. The reader begins to think about the leafiness of summer and the barrenness of autumn and only reluctantly comes back to the sudden change in the Assyrians' fortunes that the similes are meant to exemplify. A simile is also used in the fourth stanza, when the foam produced by the horse's death throes is compared, slightly incongruously, to the froth on top of ocean waves.

Byron also organizes the poem by his patterning of the words at the beginning of each line. "Like" and "That" are alternated in the second stanza. In four of the six stanzas, "And" begins consecutive lines (in another, it is at the start of alternate lines). This poetic device is called anaphora, the reiteration of an initial word. The fact that "and" is a conjunctive word not often found at the beginning of sentences gives the lines a striking urgency and adds a sense of crisis to the declarative thump of the lines' verbal repetition.

The critic Northrop Frye commented that the poem is characterized by a kind of "poetic jazz" that leads to the sheer sound effects mattering as much as the meaning. Other critics have seen in the abrupt ending of the poem, the way God is introduced only at the last minute, a kind of resistance to closure, a reluctance to neaten matters.

Themes and Meanings

"The Destruction of Sennacherib" was part of a collection of poems called *Hebrew Melodies Ancient and Modern*, published in 1815. The collection was commissioned by the composer Isaac Nathan, who had compiled a set of old (though post-biblical) tunes from Jewish musical tradition. Byron then wrote poems to parallel the tunes, though evidently he did not attempt to match a poem to a specific piece of music. *Hebrew Melodies Ancient and Modern* was an atypical collection for Byron in that the poems were short, often deeply felt lyrics, not mock epics or satiric narratives. "The Destruction of Sennacherib" has found considerable fame as an anthology piece and a poem for recital. It is, however, only the second most famous poem in *Hebrew Melodies Ancient and Modern*, though the most famous, "She Walks in Beauty," does not deal with the biblical subjects that are characteristic of the volume.

Interestingly, Byron is usually considered a wholly secular poet. For Byron, largely interested in adventure, satire, and *vers de societé* (verse chronicling the doings of high society), this Old Testament subject seems an unlikely one. "The Destruction of Sennacherib," however, is the most famous poem on a biblical subject to come out of the English Romantic movement. Although Byron's fellow poets William Wordsworth and Samuel Taylor Coleridge both became professed Christians in the later portions of their careers, neither wrote a biblical poem as famous or as memorable as that written by Byron, so often castigated in conservative quarters as an unreliable freethinker.

Byron's poem takes completely the position found in the Old Testament. Sennacherib is an evil tyrant, and Judah's delivery from him was a result of miraculous divine intervention. If anything, Byron's poem could be criticized for taking an overly Christian view of what was originally a Jewish subject. This Christianizing is also seen in the final line of the first stanza, where the mention of Galilee alludes to Jesus Christ. As a geographical term for the lake near the head of the Jordan River, the word "Galilee" was not in use until the third or second century B.C.E., so its presence here is anachronistic. However, its strong Christian associations—Galilee being the region where Jesus Christ grew up and began his ministry—were clearly important to Byron, even though his musical collaborator, Isaac Nathan, was a Jew.

To an Englishman writing in 1815, the threat posed to Jerusalem by the tyrant Sennacherib would have had its natural analogue in the threat posed to peace and order by the French emperor Napoleon. Byron referred to Napoleon as "a wolf" in other poems. The Napoleonic allusion is not the predominant theme of the poem, however; "The Destruction of Sennacherib" is mainly about the Assyrian emperor, about the original biblical story of his demise.

Nicholas Birns

DETECTIVE STORY

Author: W. H. Auden (1907-1973)
type of poem: Lyric
First published: 1937, in *Letters from Iceland*

The Poem
"Detective Story" was first published in *Letters from Iceland*, a 1937 account by W. H. Auden and Louis MacNeice of their 1936 trip to Iceland. The book is presented in the form of prose and verse letters to their friends and relatives and to Lord Byron, who was famous for his travels as well as for his poetry. Far from a conventional travel book, *Letters from Iceland* offers Auden the opportunity to comment on important and trivial matters concerning the world at large.

"Detective Story" appears in a letter to his wife, Erika Mann Auden, as an explanation of "why people read detective stories." The twenty-seven-line free-verse poem, presented in five verse paragraphs, follows the pattern of the traditional English detective story. The opening paragraph describes a typical setting, either a quiet village or an urban flat, where the "three or four things/ that happen to a man do happen." The setting or "landscape" in which a person finds himself also defines him, creates the "map of his life," and marks the spot where he first discovers happiness.

In the second paragraph, the narrator begins wondering about this anonymous man trapped in a slowly unraveling mystery. Whether an "unknown tramp" or a "rich man," he is an "enigma . . . with a buried past." Then the happiness of the first paragraph becomes "our happiness," suggesting that this apparently shared happiness owes something to "blackmail and philandering."

The third paragraph hurries through the "traditional" elements of the story, explaining how "all goes to plan," "down to the thrilling final chase, the kill." These traditional elements include the murderer's lies and inevitable confession.

The focus in the final two paragraphs shifts to the mind of the detective story reader. He wonders if the guilty verdict is just, until the execution is carried out, and he then feels relief that justice has been served. According to the narrating sensibility, the murderer has been executed to kill time for the reader. The poem ends with the ambiguous, ominous observation, "Someone must pay for/ our loss of happiness, our happiness itself."

Forms and Devices
The structure of "Detective Story" is meant to trap the reader just as a fictional detective does a murderer. Auden eases his reader into a formulaic setting with which the reader can identify and fills it with signs of life, only to reveal suddenly that a murder has taken place. Auden's reader, like the reader of a detective story, feels himself or herself above all this turmoil, only to be dragged down into confronting the morality of taking pleasure in crime and punishment.

Auden uses ambiguous pronoun references to draw the reader into his moral web. The poem opens, "for who is ever quite without his landscape." The reader clearly is meant to identify with this "who," with this typical man living an ordinary life in his ordinary dwelling. The deliberate vagueness of Auden's description also invites identification with this man's landscape: "The straggling village street, the house in trees,/ all near the church, or else the gloomy town house." The reader identifies with the happiness of Auden's anonymous man only to have it become "our happiness" as a result of being entertained by his fictional man's misery. The focus of the poem becomes not "he" and "his" but "us" and "our."

Auden's imagery describes both an everyday world and a world of sin, crime, and death. In the context of the later paragraphs, the "straggling" and "gloomy" of the opening lines assume a more ominous suggestiveness than first appears. The lines "mark the spot/ where the body of his happiness was first discovered" become not a metaphor for an ordinary location but the site of a possible murder. The metaphorical "body" becomes a literal one. Similarly, the "buried past" of the second paragraph suggests both unrevealed truths and a literal burial.

Auden employs ironic juxtaposition with "the thrilling final chase, the kill" to suggest the reader's duplicity in the death of the murderer. This idea is reinforced by "but time is always killed." In both instances, "kill" and "killed" appear to be meant metaphorically, but the literal meanings are applicable as well.

Themes and Meanings

Auden elaborated upon his feelings about mystery in his 1948 essay "The Guilty Vicarage," in which he admitted, "For me . . . the reading of detective stories is an addiction like tobacco or alcohol." He identifies five basic elements as "the milieu, the victim, the murderer, the suspects, the detectives." "Detective Story" has five paragraphs, with the first three corresponding to the first three of Auden's mystery elements, followed by the reader substituting for the suspects and detectives.

"The Guilty Vicarage" is almost an explication of "Detective Story," whose main theme, as with most of Auden's poetry of the 1930's and 1940's, is guilt. "All crimes . . . are offenses against oneself," Auden writes in his essay. His poem shows how a murderer virtually condemns himself to death by committing his crime, how he must be consumed by guilt. Auden writes that society must assume the role of punisher of the murderer. In "Detective Story," the reader, representative of society, feels momentary unease at the carrying out of the verdict.

"Execution," according to Auden, "is the act of atonement by which the murderer is forgiven by society. In real life I disapprove of capital punishment, but in a detective story the murderer must have no future." Auden's reader senses the justness of the punishment, especially since it meets the demands of the fictional formula, while being disturbed that someone (although a fictional character) has to die to fulfill his or her need for entertainment. Auden defines the murder in a detective story as "the act of disruption by which innocence is lost," and his poem forces the reader to share in this loss of innocence.

Auden ends "The Guilty Vicarage" by admitting having desires that make "me feel guilty"; in worrying about this guilt, he feels "guilty about guilt." He suspects "that the typical reader of detective stories is, like myself, a person who suffers from a sense of sin." The emphasis on the reader in "Detective Story" is therefore appropriate, since one of the purposes of mystery fiction for Auden is the expiation of the reader's guilt. Since the characters do not exist, the reader must experience their guilt for them. On another level, the "magical satisfaction" of the detective story for the reader "is the illusion of being dissociated from the murderer." The key word is "illusion" since for Auden the reader's and the murderer's guilt is a shared burden.

It is fitting that "Detective Story" ends "Someone must pay for/ Our loss of happiness, our happiness itself." To enjoy mystery fiction, the reader must have sinned, must have experienced guilt: "Our loss of happiness." The murderer in the story is vicariously punished for this loss. Such guilt and punishment are necessary for redemption—"our happiness itself." This poem about a seemingly mundane subject thus opens gradually to encompass the entire moral universe.

Michael Adams

A DICE-THROW

Author: Stéphane Mallarmé (1842-1898)
Type of poem: Meditation
First published: 1897, as *Un Coup de dés jamais n'abolira le hasard*; English translation collected in *An Anthology of French Poetry from Nerval to Valéry in English Translation with French Originals*, 1958

The Poem

The form of *A Dice-Throw* does not resemble that of other poetry. Instead of arranging words in regular verses and meter, Stéphane Mallarmé seems to have flung them in random patterns and in four different typefaces across a series of ten double (that is, verso joined to the following recto) pages. Close analysis reveals, however, that the positioning of the words is closely linked to their meaning, while the patterns they form have been recognized as schematic representations of themes of the poem.

The subject of the poem, the dice-throw, is the act of poetic creation. Mallarmé reveals this most specifically with one sentence at the end of the final page, the only sentence syntactically distinct from the body of the poem, that states, "Each thought throws the dice." Prior to this, an extremely elaborate construction spread over ten double pages has interwoven several lines of thought all syntactically connected and all related to the poetic process.

The central sentence, or main clause, of the poem is spread in four pieces on pages I, IV and VIII. (Critics have designated the double pages of the poem with roman numerals.) This sentence, entirely in large capitals, reads: "A DICE-THROW/ NEVER/ WILL ABOLISH/ FATE." If the dice-throw represents poetic creation, its inability to abolish fate, or *le hasard*, which also contains a suggestion of randomness, reflects the inability of the poet to express the absolute in his work.

This limitation tormented Mallarmé. Much of his poetry documents his attempts to transfer to the hauntingly white page before him a refined poetic vision for which language seemed an inadequate vehicle. Mallarmé dreamed of the creation of an absolute Book, a distillation of human thought, for which he sought to create a new form of poetic expression. The Book was never completed, but the poem "A Dice-Throw" is seen as Mallarmé's most evolved text created in this attempt to record the absolute.

Syntactically, the balance of the poem represents an attempt to modify the overarching negative sentence. Thus the structure mirrors the struggle of the poet attempting to modify the impossibility of poetic creation. The first modifier begins at the bottom of the first page, immediately after the principal negation, "NEVER." In smaller capitals, Mallarmé inserts: "EVEN WHEN THROWN IN ETERNAL CIRCUMSTANCES/ FROM THE DEPTH OF A SHIPWRECK."

The mention of depth in a line at the extreme bottom of the page reveals a playful aspect of Mallarmé's otherwise serious poem. Phrases often present ideas linked to their relative position on the page. As readers proceed to page II, they find the words there arranged in a pattern suggestive of a high-masted ship listing to one side in apparent shipwreck.

The shipwreck was Mallarmé's emblem of failure, reflecting the failure of his creation. Throughout the rest of the poem, images of poetry and shipwreck, of hope and despair, alternate, aptly conveying Mallarmé's renewed but doomed attempt.

Forms and Devices

Because Mallarmé's irregular placement of words on the page abandoned the poetic conventions of rhyme and meter, he must rely for unity on syntax, the interweaving of related images, and visualizations based on these images. If such an extended utterance is to be related to a single sentence structure, parallel or alternate possibilities may serve to unite a number of separate visions. Thus Mallarmé introduces a number of sections with subjunctives ("SOIT que . . . ," page II), "as if" (page V), or "if" (page VII), followed by the subjunctives and conditional of page VIII. All these tentative verb forms reflect Mallarmé's own hesitation in the creation of his poem.

Despite the tenuousness of their context, Mallarmé's central images present specific pictures. Their interpretation, however, remains difficult when multiple images intertwine on the same page. Page II, for example, combines images of ship and sea with those of flight and bird. In selecting these particular images, Mallarmé continues to draw on the example of Charles Baudelaire, who had strongly influenced Mallarmé's early work. The "Abyss" reflects the vastness of Baudelaire's sea, but when Mallarmé adds "the Abyss/ whitened spreads furious . . . ," the suggestion of storm-whitened waves ties in with his concept of shipwreck.

The phrases following the image of the Abyss, however, do not seem to relate to the sea: "under an incline/ soar desperately/ a wing/ its own." The "incline" seems to refer to the positioning of these phrases on the page. They form a part of what may be the tilting of the mast of the ship. In the larger context of the poem, however, where phrases consistently traverse each page from upper left to lower right, the slanting motion may also follow that of the thrown dice.

Meanwhile the motif of the bird, introduced with "soar" and "wing," suggests the flight that for both Baudelaire and Mallarmé could be that of the poet's inspiration. This flight advances, with Mallarmé again playing with his words as "par/ avance" leaps across the barrier of the book's spine to enter the previously blank recto page, but immediately encounters "a difficulty in bringing up the flight." The frustrated flight falls back in a way that parallels the shipwreck to be "hidden in the depth" as images of the wreck "like the hull/ of a ship" sink literally to the bottom of the page.

The similar visualization of sloping lines as the basic form of the dice-throw, the listing ship, and the bird's flight implies a common thread linking these elements. All become for Mallarmé emblems of the poetic process, a creativity he cannot describe directly but can suggest through multiple images that convey an idea of it through their common elements.

As the bird attempted to take flight and failed, following pages convey similar poetic attempts. The enigmatic figure of "THE MASTER" seems ready "to throw it" but "hesitates" (page III), and amid a lengthy italicized section floats *"the lost solitary feather"* (page VI) of the poet's pen. Solitude and loss are never total, however, as a single "except" breaks into this otherwise blank verso page leading to a continuing of the text and of the poet's hope.

Themes and Meanings

If Mallarmé could never directly state the meaning of his poem except through oblique analogies, must poetry remain incapable of expressing a transcendent vision? Mallarmé remained optimistically dedicated to the creation of his Book and saw the blank paper in front of him as a kind of stage on which the drama of poetry would ultimately unfold. Immediately after "LE HASARD" closes the principal element of the poem on page VIII, the final passage in italics states, *"Falls/ the pen/ rhythmic suspending of the sinister/ to bury itself."* As the text has reached again the bottom of a page, the fall of the dice seems preempted by that of the pen, denoting a cessation of composition.

As the reader turns to the next page, however, the text naturally begins again at the upper left. The turn of the page brings a return to hope. Here a final segment in large capitals spread across pages IX and X concludes that "NOTHING/ WILL HAVE TAKEN PLACE/ BUT THE PLACE/ EXCEPT/ PERHAPS/ A CONSTELLATION." The linking of place with nothingness evokes the empty page on which the poem has not yet been written, but "PERHAPS," the first word to appear on the upper left of the final page, marks the last resurgence of hope that something will fill the emptiness.

The last image Mallarmé offers the reader, the enigmatic CONSTELLATION, must then represent the long-awaited poetic utterance. The CONSTELLATION contains, however, an essential ambiguity. There are many constellations in the heavens, each with a distinct form. Just before the CONSTELLATION, however, Mallarmé has provided the hint of "towards/ it must be/ the Septentrion so North." A northern constellation might prove to be the Big Dipper, and indeed the words on page X, with a handle of four phrases extending to the upper left, form a pattern suggesting that constellation.

Why did Mallarmé choose the constellation, however, as his emblem of poetry? Furthermore, why did he choose this one? The constellation provides an apt image in that, like the poem, it is composed of a number of separate elements, its stars, drawn together to form a recognizable pattern. Yet this pattern is not inherent in the stars themselves. The perception of human observers posits the pattern, as the poet posits the form of his poem. This essentially subjective process seems out of harmony with the absolute Mallarmé sought to express.

Here the choice of the Big Dipper comes into play. This is the star pattern that helps human beings locate the fixed point, the North Star. Thus, through recognition of the patterns fusing either stars or poetic images, one can after all find an immutable element. Mallarmé seems to have vindicated his poetry as a progression to the absolute, but one further element remains: If the words of page X represent the Big Dipper, the North Star to which they point would exist beyond the confines of the page. The poem has portrayed the progression toward the absolute but not the absolute itself.

Dorothy M. Betz

DIEN CAI DAU

Author: Yusef Komunyakaa (1947-   )
Type of poem: Poetic sequence
First published: 1988

The Poems

The forty-three poems of *Dien Cai Dau* focus powerfully on familiar Vietnam War-era images, nightmares, and moral dilemmas that the United States at large still mulls over. Yusef Komunyakaa's subtle lyrical poems also provoke larger questions: When is killing right or wrong in wartime? How does one define a moral act in such chaos? How do "loving" relations (between men and women, between comrades in arms, between combatants) mutate in such conditions? What is the lasting effect on the survivors, the culture, and the land?

Komunyakaa, as a former combatant, chooses not to moralize. Though haunted by his Vietnam experience, he is not brutalized or desensitized. The poems (many of which reappear in the Pulitzer Prize-winning *Neon Vernacular*, 1993) show the poet remembering past battle scenes and grappling with unresolved moral questions that filter the present with ghostlike intensity. The phrase *dien cai dau* (loosely translatable as "crazy head") refers to the dizzying effects of war on all participants. Komunyakaa shows soldiers as "crazy heads" reacting "logically" to the illogical chaos of war. The war between cultures (black and white, Asian and American, men and women) is mediated by the observing poet, himself one of those struggling to make sense of the strangely beautiful but horrifying events of a very peculiar war.

Komunyakaa avoids abstractions. Poem after poem provides the voice of the simple soldier, fearful yet fascinated amid killing and destruction. "You and I Are Disappearing" presents a recurring memory of a girl burning to death in a linked series of metaphorical images: "She burns like a cattail torch/ dipped in gasoline./ She glows like the fat tip/ of a banker's cigar,/ silent as quicksilver./ A tiger under a rainbow/ at nightfall." The end of the poem carries Komunyakaa's emotional response: "She burns like a burning bush/ driven by a godawful wind." The "godawful wind" is the war itself, fueled by ill-defined, largely out-of-control forces.

The poems illustrate the ironies of this confused war. As soldiers view a Bob Hope United Service Organizations (USO) show in "Communiqué," inflamed lust contrasts with the horrifying "show" of war the soldiers cannot forget. "[W]e want the Gold Diggers,/ want a flash of legs/ through the hemorrhage of vermilion, giving us/ something to kill for." When the show ends and the music of desire has dissipated, the sitting soldiers hold their helmets "like rain-polished skulls."

Despite the carnage and destruction, all is not despair—for there are survivors. Those fated to live, even for the moment, cultivate a mystical, eclectic religiosity that borders on superstition. Belief in ghosts and higher beings helps to explain the shocking present. In "Thanks," the soldier wonders about this ill-defined presence, possibly a god, that has kept him alive: "What made me spot the monarch/ writhing on a single thread/ tied to a farmer's gate,/ holding the day together/ like an unfingered guitar string,/ is beyond me." Though he refuses to codify the force into a recognizable theology, he believes fully that "something" protects him while allowing others to die. Intuitively connecting the seen with the unseen is a means of staying alive, of "living right." When all rules are suspended, new connections freely combine in patterns of thought that do not necessarily disappear when veterans return home. In "Report from the Skull's Diorama," the soldier, now at home, relives a battle scene when he sees a photograph used by the enemy as propaganda (*"VC didn't kill/ Dr. Martin Luther King"*). He sees again the chopper leaving the battle zone, strewn with bodies and propaganda "leaflets/ clinging to the men & stumps,/ waving to me across the years." The meaning of the scene and the rightness and wrongness of actions are still somehow superfluous, overwhelmed in the present, at home, by haunting images.

Many poems in *Dien Cai Dau* depict the hyperalert fear emanating from life-threatening experiences. With lives on the line, the soldiers are open, their pores aware. "Red Pagoda" illustrates how the seemingly indefensible brutality of war can become inherently sane when placed in context. When the soldiers, fresh from a firefight, find they are unscathed, they destroy a pagoda in a real and symbolic frenzy in order to kill the fear and sense of frustration imposed by the war: "in our joy, we kick/ & smash the pagoda/ till it's dried blood/ covering the ground."

To stay alive, the soldier must be aware of the environment and all that lives there. Amid snakes, monkeys, and exotic plants live the Vietcong, who are there to kill Americans. In this natural world, insights are needed that cannot be found on linear military maps. In "A Greenness Taller Than Gods," Komunyakaa asks, "When will we learn/ to move like trees move?" Each plant, each shadow is ominous and fascinating. Even the grass they walk on aims "for the family jewels." A soldier cries over the death of a boy: "He won't stay dead, dammit!" Because this intense world produces memories that "won't stay down," all of life, both past and present, remains alive.

Forms and Devices

Komunyakaa, a master of the free-verse form and the editor of several volumes of jazz poetry, follows the internal rhythm of the line, "hearing" the power of the image and tailoring the meaning for effect, in terms of both style and tone. In "Please," a poem from *Toys in a Field* (1986), he displays the sense of the dance as he describes a fellow soldier running to his death: "You were a greenhorn, so fearless,/ even foolish,/ & when I said *go*, Henry,/ you went dancing on a red string/ of bullets from that tree line/ as it moved from a low cloud."

In *Dien Cai Dau*, Komunyakaa focuses on narratives composed of imagery-rich scenes filled with color and sensory detail. He is not afraid to intersperse action with matter-of-fact dialogue. In "Fragging," as five men "pull straws/ under a tree on a hillside," one says, "Hell,/ the truth is the truth." The statement is specific to the moment at hand, yet it provokes larger questions that linger through the poem. What is the truth in war? Who counts and who does not? What acts are justifiable? When the fifth soldier "a finger/ into a metal ring, he's married/ to his devil." That juxtaposition of "married" to the "devil" is Komunyakaa's comment on the scene. When the grenade explodes, "Everything/ breaks for green cover,/ like a hundred red birds/ released from a wooden box." The colorful freshness of the metaphor contrasts with the messiness of the moral dilemmas. The metaphorical phrases function as action photographs, the moment frozen at its most significant stage. The color and beauty mesmerize, the very transparency of the language making the horror of the actions, as well as its peculiar logic, all too clear.

The metaphorical language captures the surreal immediacy of action while also suggesting that larger themes are at work. When Komunyakaa tells the reader, in "Ambush," that "A tiger circles us, in his broken cage/ between sky & what's human," he describes a real creature stalking soldiers in the jungle. On another level, the broken cage functions as a metaphor for the jungled chaos itself, and the tiger stands in as the looming violence the soldiers fight against, both within themselves and without. When Komunyakaa remembers "the cough of a mortar tube," the weapon is specific and real, and yet it is also a metaphor for the technological horror that threatens to obliterate all semblance of humanity.

Like a jazz composer, Komunyakaa routinely juxtaposes the seemingly incongruous. This coming together of unusual images (of beauty and horror, of nature's serenity and war's destruction) forces the reader to make surprising connections and gives the poems a surreal immediacy that reverberates. In "2527th Birthday of the Buddha," a monk leaps from a motorcycle, very much alive. Within moments, "he burned like a bundle of black joss sticks." The final line, "Waves of saffron robes bowed to the gasoline can," links the modern motorcycle and the gasoline can with the "ancient" Buddhist robes, showing, without explication, the crash of cultures as the crass modern world bangs against ancient dignity in an absurd struggle. The strange beauty of the saffron robes combines with a horror beyond words.

Succinct detail shows the soldier's intimacy with the natural world and past actions. In "Camouflaging the Chimera," the dreamy peace between actions is illustrated with quiet, fluid pacing. "We hugged bamboo & and leaned/ against a breeze off the river,/ slow-dragging with ghosts." The originality of the figurative language and the stacking of image upon image carries the meaning of the poem.

The brevity of the lines also conveys movement. Because few lines contain more than five words, imagery is highlighted and never strays far from the moment or strains for effect. Imagery is exact to the moment and yet reveals more beyond the immediate moment, such as the scene of rape in "Re-creating the Scene": "They hold her down/ with their eyes,/ taking turns, piling stones/ on her father's grave." The pacing is immediate, phrased in active verbs and everyday language yet conveying the sacrilege, the desecration of more than simple flesh. Verb acting upon verb produces the compounding image symbolizing the larger rape the war is committing on the soldiers, the Vietnamese people, and the land itself.

Isolating a single scene with photographic clarity reveals the contradictions soldiers faced daily. In "A Break from the Bush," the linked, dancing fragments of meaning build and confuse even while they demonstrate the irony of a soldier's fate: "CI, who in three days will trip/ a fragmentation mine, runs after the ball/ into the white-caps,/ laughing." Komunyakaa mixes a memory that captures the laughter and the beauty of the ocean waves with the ominous reality of death and war.

A sense of the fantastic pervades the imagery. In "Prisoners," the captured Vietcong look "like/ marionettes hooked to strings of light." Those puppets, propped up by an unreal light, at first merely fascinate. Further reflection reveals their real significance, for all the soldiers are mere puppets fighting for autonomy against larger forces. The rhythm of movement at the end of "Jungle Surrender" links a series of images from the story of the moment that ache for later reflection: "Moving toward what waits be-hind the trees./ the prisoner goes deeper into himself, away/ from how a man's heart divides him, deeper/ into the jungle's indigo mystery & beauty." This later reflection is the reason for the writing of these poems.

Themes and Meanings

For the American soldier fighting to survive in an alien jungle, even the familiar could be turned on its head. In "Hanoi Hannah," even Ray Charles's voice echoing in the darkness becomes a tool of propaganda for the Vietcong, reminding the soldier that nothing exists in isolation. Even in remote Southeast Asia, the realities of Ameri-can racial and cultural history intervene. When the death of Martin Luther King, Jr., is also used as a propaganda weapon, it is directly linked for the black soldier with the deaths of comrades in arms.

Komunyakaa portrays the absurd sense of chaos in a world that nothing can be pinned to, a world where those in control remake the rules daily for their own good, where even the leaders are adrift in currents they cannot understand, where the results of actions can only be seen in retrospect. In "Re-creating the Scene," when a Vietnam-ese woman is raped by three soldiers, "she floats on their rage/ like a torn water flower,/ defining night inside a machine/ where men are gods." When authorities in-tervene, the woman is killed, the story is confused by counterstories, and nothing is settled; as for the baby that survives, its future is as uncertain as the men, the country, and the war itself.

When chaos dispenses with civilized "rules," when fear overwhelms love, present desires take precedence over long-term goals. In "One More Loss to Count," an Ameri-can soldier and a Vietnamese woman, each with lovers elsewhere, slide into the arms of the moment. Even as he acts, the soldier recognizes that a line has been crossed and that there is no pretending that anything of worth can be preserved. Vietnam itself, the poems suggest, has crossed the line, both for soldiers and for those left at home, and thus has tainted the delicate balance of "civilized" morality for some time to come.

Even when the soldiers are "safe" at home they struggle to digest the past and un-derstand what was lost and gained. Haunted by ghosts, the soldier knows, in "Missing in Action," that "we can't make one man/ walk the earth again." Something irretriev-able has been lost, Komunyakaa suggests, and the men, the culture, and the earth itself must remake themselves in new forms.

Classifications of race, nationality, and gender are also changed when normal contexts are destroyed. In "Tu Do Street," the familiar segregated worlds the black soldier knew in America lose their boundaries as black and white soldiers sleep with the same women—whose brothers fight them in the bush. All of them are more interconnected than any can realize: "these rooms/ run into each other like tunnels/ leading to the underworld." Above all, they are connected by a heightened knowledge of death. In "Donut Dollies," when battle-weary soldiers with "the names of dead men/ caught in their throats" fail to notice the perky "dollies" who greet them, both the numb infantrymen and the women must learn new roles.

Those experiencing the extremes are linked to those who have shared similar moments, all holders of "insider knowledge." Komunyakaa seeks understanding, even kinship, with those he fought against. "Prisoners" describes his fascination with Vietcong prisoners of war who fail to crack under interrogation: "I remember how one day/ I almost bowed to such figures." In "Sappers," a soldier marvels at the enemy's determination, even as they push forward to kill him: "Opium, horse, nothing/ sends anybody through concertina/ this way." As the Vietcong "try to fling themselves/ into our arms," he marvels at the intimacy he feels for those who share similar visions of death, passion, and hate.

Haunted by ghosts, Komunyakaa vividly describes the soldier reliving scenes that he still milks for meaning. For those who have lived intensely, memories are the haunting heartbeat of the present. In a literal sense, the soldier, well trained to avoid danger, has trouble adjusting to a world of "safety." In "Losses," the soldier, back home, "scouts the edge of town,/ always with one ear/ cocked & ready to retreat." In a metaphorical sense, he replays endless scenes, working to find meaning for past moments he had no time to ponder in the heat of battle. The lessons learned—the intimacy of man with nature, the link between killing and lust, the new definitions of race and culture, the raw excitement of extreme behavior and its accompanying emotional explosiveness—must be linked with those irretrievable moments before the present can proceed. Until these ghosts are exorcised, more "crazy heads" will rule the day.

Mark Vogel

DIFFICULT TIMES

Author: Bertolt Brecht (1898-1956)
Type of poem: Meditation
First published: 1964, as "Schwierige Zeiten," in *Gedichte, vol. 7: 1948-1956*; English translation collected in *Bertolt Brecht: Poems, 1913-1956*, 1976

The Poem

"Difficult Times" is a short (nine lines), unrhymed poem, written in free verse with an irregular rhythmic pattern. Using the first person, Brecht makes it clear that it is he who is speaking directly to the reader.

The first image is of the speaker standing at his desk and looking out the window, presumably ruminating during a lull in his work. There is a hint of restlessness implied in this action. As he looks into the garden, he vaguely discerns an elderberry bush ("elder tree"). He sees red and black shapes that remind him of such a bush that existed in his childhood home in Augsburg. The poem's last four lines concern indecision and the fact that he would need to put on his glasses in order to see the tree clearly. He "quite seriously" debates with himself whether to go from the desk to the table to get his spectacles, thus enabling him to see "Those black berries again." The poem ends without stating whether he decides to get his glasses, but the fact that it does not say that he does implies inaction.

The reason or reasons why the speaker is living in "Difficult Times" are not explicitly stated in the poem. However, the poem was written very late in Brecht's life, and the indecision, inability to see well, and perhaps even the physical difficulty of going from one part of the room to another obviously reflect the difficulties of advancing age. (In another late poem, "Things Change," Brecht refers to himself as both a young man and "an old man forgetting his name.") In addition, Brecht may be implying that both personal regrets and the political situation in Europe have made the times difficult. As an exile from his native land, Brecht had moved from place to place, changing countries of residence, as he once put it, "more often than I changed shirts." He had had several wives and numerous mistresses (sometimes simultaneously), so that difficult memories and personal regrets would seem inevitable.

Forms and Devices

In his many essays about the style and function of poetry, Brecht spoke of writing in "Basic German" and of using what he calls the *gestich* form. In Brecht's *Selected Poems* (1947), edited by R. H. Hays, this is explained as "slightly formalized speech rhythms with certain forced pauses produced by arbitrary line divisions to preserve a calculated emphasis." The *gestich* form is evident here. This form includes the notion that the poem when read aloud should follow the "gesture" of the reader—as an actor would deliver lines of dialogue in a play. Brecht also cited his desire to avoid traditional poetic forms with many layers of hidden meanings which would make them less intelligible to the "folk" for whom he is writing. As Hays notes, Brecht's work, including this poem, "lacks sensuous decoration and uses images with economy in the service of the idea."

Despite Brecht's stated intentions not to employ layers of hidden meanings, traditional poetic devices, and symbols in his poetry, the very nature of the genre makes such a course difficult. Poetry is a form in which "shorthand" language is used to express ideas and meanings which would require in prose more length, more detail, and more explication. Brecht uses symbolism in "Difficult Times." The desk indicates the work of writing, and the eyeglasses a potential aid in seeing one's situation and life more clearly. The elderberry bush (also known as the tamarind) also has symbolic biblical and folkloric connotations. In *The Magic Garden* (1976), by Anthony S. Mercante, two entries are notable, and both are tragic. First, it is said that the wood from the elder was used to construct the cross on which Christ was crucified. Second, as the legend goes, Judas Iscariot, although he had been forgiven by Jesus, was so distraught over his act of betrayal that "he saw a tamarind tree, tall and beautiful. Then the Devil entered his mind and he took a rope, made a noose, and hanged himself from the tree, which became short and twisted."

These negative images connect in an ironic way to the poet's childhood memory of the elder tree. As a child, Brecht was presumably innocent, trusting, and relatively happy. Then, as a young man, by his own account, his experience as a medical corpsman in the German army reinforced what he had decided in 1916 about patriotism and armed service: "[T]he statement that it is sweet and an honor to die for the Fatherland can only be rated as propaganda." By the end of World War I he had joined the many young men of his generation in their disillusionment, distrust of government, and hatred of armed conflict. Now, forty years later, the world had endured an even bloodier war; still the prospect of permanent peace was as distant as ever.

Themes and Meanings

The poem's primary level of meaning concerns the difficulties of growing older— the physical difficulties (failing senses), the mental difficulties (failing concentration and difficulties in making decisions), and the fact that one remembers one's youth, when one was healthier and happier. Beyond these meanings, however, if one looks at Brecht's life, one can also theorize that he may be brooding over particular memories, regrets, and dissatisfactions. As most people do, Brecht probably had regrets about the life he had led, goals he had not reached, and people he had hurt.

It is conceivable, for example, that Brecht suffered some remorse over his use of "collaborators" to compose the plays which brought him acclaim. Bruce Cook, in *Brecht in Exile* (1982), explains that Brecht rationalized this practice by stating that "the work profits if many take part in it." (Brecht did credit those who worked with him, although credit was given in very small type on the reverse side of the title page, tucked into the copyright material.) John Fuegi, in *Brecht & Company* (1994), argues that great as he had been as a theatrical innovator and director, Brecht had not in fact been the playwright he had pretended to be. Those who had actually created the works never received the money nor the acclaim they deserved.

Perhaps more than personal concerns, political and social concerns could also have made Brecht's last years "Difficult Times." In all Brecht's work the most consistently recognizable element is social content. All the plays (the genre for which he is best known) were meant to "teach" audiences, to make them aware of universal problems, particularly the absence of peace and the horrors of war. Now, back in his homeland in the 1950's, after living many years abroad, he was undoubtedly disturbed by the fact of the Cold War.

After the rise of Adolf Hitler in the 1930's, Brecht had become active in the fight against fascism, which in Europe at the time widely meant favoring communism. He fled Hitler's Germany to live in various Scandinavian countries, including Finland (until that government formed an alliance with the Third Reich), finally settling in Santa Monica, California, in 1941. He left there in October, 1947, and ultimately accepted the invitation of the East German government to head a theater—the Berlin Ensemble—in the communist sector of Berlin. However, between the time of his leaving Europe and his return, a number of disquieting events had taken place.

Although before World War II Brecht has publicly affirmed that the Soviet Union represented the "most progressive social system of our age," he had to admit after the purges under Soviet dictator Josef Stalin and the subsequent revelations about life in the Soviet Union that there was not too much difference between various types of totalitarian regimes. Neither fascism nor communism had provided much benefit for the "folk," and now the former allies against Hitler seemed determined to avoid permanent peace. All was not well in a world divided, a city divided, and people in conflict.

In his introduction to Klaus Volker's book *Brecht Chronicle* (1975), Carl Weber writes that "the refugee and persecuted are becoming the archetypes of the century," and assuredly Brecht fits this profile, notwithstanding the fact that much of that characterization was carefully created by the man himself. Although at the time this poem was written Brecht was no longer a persecuted refugee, the times remained difficult for him, probably largely because of his reflections. An aura of discontent permeates the poem. It suggests regret about the past and uneasiness about the present with no suggestion of future improvement, as after old age comes death.

Edythe M. McGovern

DIGGING

Author: Seamus Heaney (1939-   )
Type of poem: Lyric
First published: 1966, in *Death of a Naturalist*

The Poem

"Digging" is a relatively short poem (thirty-one lines) in free verse. While it has no set pattern of doing so, it breaks up into stanzas of two to five lines. The presence in the poem of the first person "I" who wields a pen, and the family reminiscences, identify the speaker as Seamus Heaney himself and the poem as autobiographical. The poem is filled with the terminology of Heaney's native Ireland.

Heaney begins the poem with an image of himself, pen in hand. He hears or is remembering the sound of digging under his window. It is his "father, digging"; however, the reader is told in line 7 that it is an echo from the past. Knowing that, "to 'look down' " can be understood to refer both to the memory of his father's presence below the window and to looking back through time to it. The image of his father as he "Bends low" can also mean two things: the bending that accompanies digging and the stooping of age.

Because his father is dead, "twenty years away," the sound can also echo the digging of graves, an image that is further reinforced by the evocations of the smell and feel of the soil. The father who is dead was a laborer, a potato farmer, as his father before him was a digger of "turf," or peat.

The middle stanzas paint a picture of the activity of digging, as it was part of Heaney's childhood: The father stoops "in rhythm," and the spade is held "firmly." The separate parts of the father's body and the spade are described as if they are entwined: The father's boot is on the "lug" (the flat top of the metal scoop of the shovel), the "shaft" (wooden handle) is aligned with his knee. The potatoes themselves are loved for their "cool hardness," and digging them is regarded as an art that is boasted of generations later.

The memory of his father's work leads Heaney to the vivid recollection of bringing a bottle of milk, "Corked sloppily with paper," to his grandfather on "Toner's bog." There, he dug up the dense, wet soil, which was made up of decayed moss and other vegetable matter and blocks of which were cut out, dried, and burned for fuel. Heaney recalls the brief pause his grandfather took to drink the whole bottle and the style with which he "fell to" work again. The double meaning of the father's "Stooping" echoes in the "going down and down" of the grandfather: It can mean both the labor he was engaged in and the lowering of his body into the grave.

In the second to the last stanza, Heaney's recollection becomes purely sensory: memories of his father in "The cold smell of potato mould" and his grandfather in "the squelch and slap/ Of soggy peat." What these memories have "awaken[ed]" are the "living roots" in Heaney's head. The labor of his forefathers is his legacy, for better and for worse, but he lacks something they had: He has "no spade to follow men like them." In the final stanza, he states again that what he does have is his pen; he will do with his instrument what they did with theirs.

Forms and Devices

Heaney's precise description of the way he holds his instrument is the first of many. It is echoed in the description of the way his father holds his. Such a technique has two effects. First, the reader's sensory experience of the poem is very strong: He or she sees, feels, smells, and hears all that Heaney is remembering. Second, such precision requires great control, and the implied power behind such control carries with it a further implication of the violence that might be unleashed were it not controlled.

Heaney manages to reinforce this undercurrent of implied violence with the way he uses and does not use rhyme and meter. The first two lines of the poem are a rhymed iambic tetrameter couplet. The first line has four strong or stressed syllables, alternating with unstressed syllables. Each unstressed/stressed pair is a foot, called an iamb, and a four-foot line is a tetrameter; a two-line stanza is a couplet. The meter in Heaney's poem is so neat as to be almost singsong in rhythm. The second line is not as exact, but it still holds to the metrical pattern established by the first; most important, in both lines, the final syllable is strong and rhymes.

The second stanza shifts to a loose iambic pentameter (five unstressed/stressed beats) and also continues to rhyme loosely. After this, however, the poem takes a completely unrhymed, unmetrical form until the final three lines. The first of those final lines repeats the first, which is also the most perfectly metrical, line of the poem. In its first appearance, the strength of the pattern within this line raised an expectation of a continuation of the pattern, an expectation that was met.

When that first line appears again, the same expectation is raised. The first half of the second line also appears again, increasing that sense of expectation. The final four words, however, do not appear. Instead, the anticipated second line is cut into two blunt lines ("squat" as the pen), and there is no rhyme at all.

The poetic forms the first five lines take are those established by English poets. When Heaney begins to recount his uniquely Irish memories, he shifts out of English poetic style. By returning to the metrical line in the last stanza but then severing it and rejecting the rhyme, Heaney communicates with this product of his pen exactly what it is he intends to do by wielding that pen.

Themes and Meanings

The repeated association of instrument and weapon gives the reader a hint as to the predominant theme of the poem. As the pen is overtly named a weapon, so the spade can by implication also be understood as a weapon. Many of the images then take on a double meaning: Rooting "out tall tops" could be mowing down men, and burying "the bright edge deep" could connote a blade cutting into flesh. "Lug," "shaft," and "levered" are all words that could be associated with weapons, and even the beloved "cool hardness in our hands" could mean grenades, not merely potatoes. "By God, the old man could handle a spade" might be said as admiringly by one rebel of another as by farmers of one another: "Nicking and slicing neatly" could apply to blade work as well as to spade work, and "heaving sods," in slang, could refer to bodies as well as dirt.

This very wordplay on bodies and dirt, sods and clods, also maintains the association of living and dead that the mixed images of the poem have produced. Not only did the sound of digging begin a recollection of the father's life, but it also was a reminder of his death as well. The potato crop grows in "mould," in decomposition, and turf is itself concentrated decomposition. All digging, then, is in among dead things, graves, "mould," "turf."

The mention of these two products and the hard labor necessary to obtain them establishes the context in which Heaney is writing: He comes from a family—and, on a larger scale, a culture—that has struggled for survival. That the bog on which his grandfather cut turf was "Toner's" implies further that the fruits of their labor may not even have been their own.

These were necessary commodities—potatoes were the staple crop, and turf was the primary source of fuel—so necessary that their failure meant the end of the community. Yet, while the father's and the grandfather's digging was for the purpose of providing sustenance, it has resulted in their deaths. Understanding that, the play between words that mean both men and dirt also gives further impetus to the implications of violence: These laboring men are "like dirt."

Yet, while the implication of violence is very strong, embedded in the poem is the image of Heaney's spade-wielding grandfather drinking milk. In sixteenth century English accounts of the Irish, one cultural characteristic regarded as strange is an Irish preference of milk to meat. Such a preference is one that speaks against blood-thirstiness. By raising this image, with its unavoidable association with the "milk of human kindness," Heaney identifies the tendency to violence that the poem displays as an imposition by others.

Thus, in the same way as the poem cuts through the constraints of English versification, it digs up "living roots." By taking to the pen, Heaney participates in the process of reclaiming an Irish memory and identity that has been long buried and that will provide sustenance and fuel in its own way.

Laurie Glover

DIRECTIVE

Author: Robert Frost (1874-1963)
Type of poem: Meditation
First published: 1946; collected in *Steeple Bush*, 1947

The Poem

"Directive" is a sixty-two-line poem in blank verse. Because it contains elements of the lyric, the dramatic monologue, the narrative poem, the parody, and the meditation, it is difficult to classify. Its ambiguous form complements the unsettled, willfully contradictory quality that infuses the whole poem. The title, suggesting an important instruction or edict, is also ambiguous, since the various instructions given in the poem are neither clear nor easily followed; the poem is as much anti-directive as directive.

Addressing an unspecified "you," with whom the reader may identify, the poem contains a series of imperative (or command) sentences. In line 38, however, two-thirds of the way through the poem, the narrator reveals a first-person identity. From that point on, the poem evolves into a confrontation between narrator and implied reader. The poem begins by creating the illusion of a particular time and place: "Back out of all this now too much for us,/ Back in a time made simple by the loss/ Of detail, burned, dissolved, and broken off/ Like graveyard marble sculpture in the weather." These slippery lines do not, in fact, specify a time or place; they start in nostalgia and end in an ominous reference to the human inability to fathom the past.

The contradictions continue in the lines that complete the opening statement: "There is a house that is no more a house/ Upon a farm that is no more a farm/ And in a town that is no more a town." The poem thus propels the reader both backward and forward in time. The reader is asked to acknowledge presences in absences, to accept the coexistence of the two.

Although it is unclear at first whether the narrator is the guide he mentions "Who only has at heart your getting lost," he assumes that role later in the poem as his own desire to perplex becomes obvious. He describes a road into the past—one that evokes his own paranoid awareness of history—and pretends to soothe the reader's fears "Of being watched from forty cellar holes" by explicitly pointing out that such perils exist. Skewering the reader with his dark humor throughout the poem, he is the personification of an unreliable narrator, someone whose word must be questioned at every turn.

In the last third of the poem, the narrator compares "the playhouse of the children" with the remains of a house, "a belilaced cellar hole." He ironically eulogizes the latter, a decaying indentation rather than a sturdy, upright structure. Ultimately, however, the "house of make-believe" and the vanished "house in earnest" seem more alike than different. Is a "house in earnest" that no longer exists any more real than a make-believe one that still does? Regardless of the answer, the poem suggests a poignancy in both of them.

"Directive" seems to end on a note of spiritual renewal, but the "broken drinking goblet like the Grail" comes from the children's playhouse; it is a parody of the legendary relic of biblical times. Because it is broken, this flawed vessel offers little in the way of lasting grace. If one is to "Drink and be whole again beyond confusion," the experience of salvation promises to be as disturbing and unsatisfactory as the awkward journey toward the healing drink.

Forms and Devices

Robert Frost is a master of paradox—that is, the formulation of contradictory statements that contain surprising truths. "Directive" as a whole is grounded in paradox. As a result, one may come away from it questioning not merely the reliability of its narrator but the reliability of all narrators as well, whether they are poets, prophets, or signs along the road. The poem's paradoxical nature is quickly established in the contradictory representations of house, farm, and town. The "guide" is also a paradoxical figure, since his directions are intended to confuse. And the narrator who pretends to assuage the reader's anxieties seems to be a malevolent puppeteer. The effect of all this is to undermine one's confidence in him—and in one's own ability to interpret fact, doctrine, and truth.

Certain capitalized words add to the poem's disconcerting quality. The "enormous Glacier" evokes a past that is both powerful and frightening. "Panther Mountain," the remains of prehistoric shifts in land and ice, suggests wildness and danger lurking in the present. The capitalized "Grail," along with "Saint Mark," reminds the reader how much importance has been placed in myth and doctrine grounded in faith; the sign reading "CLOSED to all but me" is an unsettling reminder of how limited human perceptions often are.

Frost's use of a single rhetorical question also deserves attention. After describing the startling rustling sounds of trees, the narrator declares: "Charge that to upstart inexperience./ Where were they all not twenty years ago?" While he seems to be referring, oddly, to the "inexperience" of the trees, the ironic comment may also apply to the "inexperience" of even the most seasoned traveler, reader, or self-proclaimed authority of any kind.

He obliquely answers his own question: "They think too much of having shaded out/ a few old pecker-fretted apple trees." These lines imply that those who have overtaken and overshadowed their predecessors are not necessarily as grand as they think they are. The rhetorical question and its implied answer cause one further to doubt one's own convictions. There is no solid ground, figurative or otherwise, in this particular journey.

The two parenthetical statements near the end of the poem further undermine the reader's confidence in his or her own perceptions. The first one pretends to present knowledge that everyone already possesses: "(We know the valley streams that when aroused/ Will leave their tatters hung on barb and thorn.)" There is, however, nothing self-evident in the statement; the revelation is violent, conjuring up images of a biblical deluge or, at the very least, an overwhelming force lurking within a gentle current. The presumption that the reader would share this insight is disturbing in itself.

Frost's second parenthetical insertion may seem to be a whimsical afterthought, but it serves to parody medieval legends about the Holy Grail, Christ's cup at the Last Supper. In Frost's ironic revision of the legends, "(I stole the goblet from the children's playhouse.)" Thus the Grail is reduced to a stolen toy. It is one more of those "playthings" to which the narrator refers when he says: "Weep for what little things could make them glad."

The paradoxes in "Directive" are reinforced by the perplexing landscape the narrator describes. Nothing is quite what it seems or what the reader might expect it to be—not house, farm, town, guide, or Holy Grail. Even the road "May seem as if it should have been a quarry." The whole poem is akin to a difficult landscape in which one cannot move forward without constantly casting worried glances over one's shoulder.

Themes and Meanings

In "Birches," first published in 1915, Frost writes that sometimes "life is too much like a pathless wood/ Where your face burns and tickles with the cobwebs/ Broken across it, and one eye is weeping/ From a twig's having lashed across it open." In that famous early poem, the narrator's ingenuous desire to "get away from earth awhile/ And then come back" by swinging on birch limbs is easily appreciated. A trustworthy person who believes in the restorative powers of both heaven and earth, he stands in contrast to the more cynical narrator of "Directive." The later poem develops the anxieties that are only touched upon in "Birches."

The role of the narrator is central to the meaning of "Directive." At every step of the journey, one must confront his unreliability, his willful perversity. He is determined to confound the reader, and in the end this antagonistic stance tells much about him.

A guide who speaks in knotty paradoxes, who demands undivided attention, who plans to get the reader lost, is someone fighting a significant battle with himself. His is a mind obsessed with the past, painfully aware of the forces in nature that can wipe out a detail on a tombstone, an apple tree, a whole village. He cannot comment on a deserted children's playhouse without insinuating that the remains of an adult dwelling are equally pathetic. He equates a broken cup with the Holy Grail and then concludes: "Drink and be whole again beyond confusion"—a command that dares the reader to believe in him at the last.

In "Directive," Frost examines that dare and its pitfalls: Can one trust any narrator, real or fictive? (One might argue that to read a poem is to take the dare, to seek understanding beyond confusion.) The reader comes away with other questions as well. Does one achieve any wholeness upon completing the journey that the poem sets forth? What are the ramifications of acknowledging that many of one's actions are based on a combination of misinformation and blind trust? Three decades after the gentle complicity of "Birches," Frost creates a persona who is as hard to dismiss as he is to trust. Instead of nodding and smiling at the fellow who would swing boyishly on a birch limb, readers now draw back, puzzled and amazed by the guide who has turned against them.

More to the point, however, the narrator of "Directive" seems to have turned against himself. He is so aware of change and loss, so paranoid about the present, that he cannot offer solace to anyone. His paradoxical instructions may belie his own need for order, permanence, and solid ground. He himself may long for the purifying drink he mockingly offers to the reader in the end.

Hilary Holladay

DIRGE

Author: Kenneth Fearing (1902-1961)
Type of poem: Satire
First published: 1935, in *Poems*

The Poem

A dirge usually is a poem marked by the heavy melody of death—a poem serving to remind the reader of his or her own mortality as it commemorates the passing of another. Kenneth Fearing's "Dirge" has this characteristic, but it is carefully calculated to shock the reader by its clash in tone, substituting the harsh clang of slang for the usual and expected solemnity of the traditional dirge.

The poem begins with the description of a bad day at the height of the Depression. The numbers are backward, the stocks are falling, and the conditions at the racetrack belie the bettor's expectations. The next stanza, or verse paragraph, introduces the stereotyped sense of values of the "executive type": Success is marked by the latest advertised virtues of the most up-to-date automobile, by marriage to a celebrity, by low golf scores and luck at the gambling table. All this success, however, is clouded in an ominous warning in terms of superstition, astrology, and commerce: "beware of liquidated rails."

The next verse paragraph announces the ephemeral nature of a man's certainty, even that built up over a lifetime of established habits. No matter how many times bills have been paid promptly, no amount of past financial virtue can keep the gas from being shut off, the bank from foreclosing, the landlord from evicting, or the radio from breaking when there is no money to pay the bills. The hour comes when the thin-spun life is slit, or, in Fearing's terms, when "twelve o'clock arrived just once too often."

The eulogy that follows is like none ever heard at a funeral.

> And wow he died as wow he lived,
> Going whop to the office and blooie home to sleep and biff got
> married and bam had children and oof got fired,
> Zowie did he live and zowie did he die.

The names of the pallbearers taking the casket to the grave are if anything even more effective in emphasizing the depersonalization of a life that had disintegrated from commercialism into nothing at all: One is called "who the hell are you," another "where the hell're we going," and the third "who the hell cares." All are plodding next to the wreath caringly contributed by a gentleman named "why the hell not." Who will miss this wayward minion of Wall Street, one may wonder? The circulation department of his favorite newspaper and the New York City subway system—fitting mourners for the person whose total value system was composed of the latest in automotive pizzazz and the glitz associated with financial success.

Forms and Devices

"Dirge" is written in free verse with stanzas of varying length, containing varying line lengths within those stanzas. Much of the power of the poetry comes from Fearing's use of balance, antithesis, and especially repetition within the lines of the poem. It is also a poem of marked rhythm and calculated sounds; it demands to be read aloud.

The opening stanza makes careful use of parallel construction to emphasize three instances of failure piling up, pressing on the victim: The numbers come up backward, the stocks drop, and the track is unfavorable. The second stanza continues the pattern of repetition with three effective uses of apostrophe, which evoke a sense of urgency: "O executive type, . . ./ O fellow with a will, . . ./ O democratic voter." In the third stanza, the repetition moves to words ("Denouement to denouement, . . . the certain, certain way") and the forceful use of anaphora (each phrase ringing in with a powerful "nevertheless").

The repetition in the fifth stanza introduces a sudden and dramatic shift in diction to emphasize the shallowness and the "hype" that characterized the life of the deceased. The choice of words comes right out of the comic-strip dictionary of the Dynamic Duo. The events of the subject's life are punctuated rhythmically with "wow," "whop," "blooie," "biff," "bam," "oof," and "zowie." The poem's final line moves into the final repetitious tolling of the funeral knell, which sounds, perhaps, a bit more like a gong than the mournful tolling of the steeple bell: "Bong, Mr., bong, Mr., bong, Mr., bong."

"Dirge" is not without its calculated use of alliteration, probably the smallest form of repetition. The repeated words give automatic alliteration, but in addition to this the poet gains rhythmic emphasis in the second stanza by referring to the "fellow with a will who won't take no" and must "watch out for three cigarettes on the same single match." Fearing risks redundancy to achieve the alliterated sibilants in the last phrase, but gains an onomatopoeic reverberance of the match striking and hissing into flame. In the succeeding stanza, the alliterated plosives in "a personal pride in . . ./ his own, private life" suggest something of the bluster with which the deceased developed even his interpersonal relationships.

Although not rich in metaphor, the poem certainly contains metaphorical overtones in the names of the pallbearers, in the use of "denouement" to describe the series of closures in the daily life, and in the "finis" marking the final cadence of the late lamented. It is an ironic comparison: There certainly was little to suggest artistic composition in the closure of this failed businessman. The means of his death remains a mystery, although the number of suicides brought on by bank failures in the early Depression certainly leaves the reader with some suspicion. There is also metaphoric ambiguity in the doubly ominous term "liquidated rails," which, in addition to its literal meaning of a failed stock, suggests the train that no longer has any destination, any sense of direction.

The ambiguity of the final line surely is calculated by the poet. The series of "bongs" trivialize the tolling of the death knell so poignantly personalized by John

Donne, but why does Fearing here sandwich a "Mr." between each nonresonant stroke? Is it a vocative, "Bong, Mr."? Is it an appellation, "Mr. Bong"? The deceased is unnamed throughout the poem, and it certainly could be intended that Mr. "who the hell cares" is bearing the casket of Mr. Bong, full of sound, if not fury, and signifying nothing.

Themes and Meanings

"Dirge" is a satire exposing the emptiness of the value system of the upwardly mobile executive of the early years of the Great Depression. It begins with the lack of any meaning in the concept of work, which turns out to be nothing more than a huge gambling game. Whether one is betting on the numbers, on the fifth race, or on the stock market, it is all the same: There is no value beyond the bet—the winning or losing.

It is winning, however, that pays off, and what are the stakes? One finds them in the adman's contributions to the daily newspaper or the magazine section. One gets to drive a car with floating power (making the latest in engine mounts sound like a miracle from another world) and with knee action (making the latest technology in wheel suspension sound almost personal); a body can slide into the vehicle on the smoothness of silk, and beneath the foot is the super power of an advanced six-cylinder engine. Success at the altar is not to wed a compatible real-life woman, but to latch onto a movie star. Success at the gaming table is to companion with lady luck.

The values of daily living that give the "hero" of this poem his personal pride in his private life are the values of routine living. Paying bills on time gives the ultimate in satisfaction. There is pleasure in the security of knowing one is acceptable, choosing a gray tweed suit from the tailor, a fashionable straw hat from the milliner, and straight Scotch from the bartender. The dimensions of life are full with a short step, a long look, and a deep breath.

If there is little meaning in this, at least one can endow it with a little excitement by injecting some Dreiser-like slang. "Wow he died as wow he lived" endows life with all the swinging, zesty virtues of a cheerleader at his or her invigorating best. The content of the days between birth and death can be charged equally with excitement: "whop to the office and blooie home to sleep and biff got/ married and bam had children and oof got fired." Lest the reader forget how splendid all this is, the final line of the fifth stanza gets back into the great, empty swing of things: "Zowie did he live and zowie did he die." Along with politics ("Wham, Mr. Roosevelt") and consumerism ("Pow, Sears Roebuck"), there is a slight nod to nature ("awk, big dipper;/ bop summer rain"), but it is too little too late and irreparably flawed with an awk and a bop. Something, suggests Fearing, is missing in the values evoked by this man.

The satirical tone of "Dirge" leaves readers with a dehumanized person. The poem may depict a funeral, but there are no tears shed over the values that have died.

Howard C. Adams

THE DISABLED DEBAUCHEE

Author: John Wilmot, earl of Rochester (1647-1680)
Type of poem: Mock epic
First published: 1680, in *Poems on Several Occasions*

The Poem

"The Disabled Debauchee," called in some texts "The Maim'd Debauchee" or "The Maim'd Drunkard," is written in a form known as the heroic stanza. The heroic stanza was used by poets of John Wilmot, earl of Rochester's day for epic verse; some notable examples include John Dryden's *Heroic Stanzas* (1659) and *Annus Mirabilis* (1667) and Sir William Davenant's *Gondibert* (1651).

The speaker in "The Disabled Debauchee" cannot necessarily be identified with Rochester himself. Though part of the poem's intent is to mock the speaker, it is possible that Rochester is offering his audience amusement at his own expense. It seems more likely, however, that the speaker is a fictitious character whom Rochester sets up as a target for derision.

The speaker gives a tongue-in-cheek description of the way in which, when he is "disabled" sometime in the future by drink and debauchery, he will exhort others to the debauchery that he had practiced himself when he was able. He compares himself to a retired "brave admiral" from a long-past war who takes vicarious pleasure in watching battles (from a safe distance!) and reliving his days of glory.

He describes the social milieu in which he moves as being like a battleground, and the ladies and gentlemen of his company who drink and flirt as combatants in a war. The speaker relishes the thought that he will inspire those who are still able to "fight" in this kind of "war" to new heights of revelry and debauchery by telling them about his past exploits. He will encourage the combatants who are frightened at his battle scars by telling them that "Past joys have more than paid what I endure," and he will rouse the dull and lazy participants by telling what he used to do when he was "able to bear arms." In this way, he will spur all his fellows to "important mischief." The scenes of debauchery and mischief he conjures up grow from harmless jibes at the dinner table to all kinds of wanton and destructive acts.

In the final stanza, the speaker makes a witty assessment of his future role that seems at once both self-mocking and smug; he says that he will "safe from danger, valiantly advise," and that "Shelter'd in impotence . . ./ . . . being good for nothing else," he will "be wise."

Forms and Devices

The central device in "The Disabled Debauchee" is a conceit, or elaborate, extended metaphor. The conceit in this poem, the comparison of the speaker to an admiral and his social setting to a battleground, is maintained throughout. Metaphors are nested within metaphors as the poet embellishes his central conceit with other fanciful images. The eyes of the "brave admiral," for example, flash with fierce rage as he views the battle, like "black clouds when lightning breaks away." The poem is marked by a complex grammatical structure and rhetorical flourishes. These qualities, combined with the intricate clustering of metaphors, result in a clever, intellectual, and highly artificial poem. This type of complex and slyly humorous poem was much admired in Rochester's era, the Restoration, in which refined, well-educated gentlemen vied to be the wittiest of King Charles II's courtiers.

The imagery is an important element of the satire in "The Disabled Debauchee." The poem begins with whimsical images: "fleets of glasses sail around the board" ("board" here being a dining table), with "volleys of Wit" as their artillery. The effect is gently humorous as the scenes of the dining table and ballroom offer a comical contrast to the speaker's chosen metaphor of warfare. As the poem progresses, though, the scenes he describes become uglier and more violent, and move into line with the metaphor of the battle. He speaks of "whores attack[ing] their lords at home,/ Bawds' quarters beaten up . . ./ Windows demolished, watches overcome." The speaker gleefully describes these activities as "handsome ills by my contrivance done." The speaker is soon exhorting his companions to set fire to "some ancient church."

Even as the images take on the quality of an actual battle, however, the speaker is careful to remind his audience subtly that this "battle" is an inversion of the kind of battle usually described in a heroic stanza, in which courageous soldiers fight for a just cause. "The Disabled Debauchee" urges his fellows not to valor but to "mischief" and "lewdness." When the "ghost of [his] departed vice" urges a reluctant reveler to repent, the repentance consists of forswearing virtue for vice and joining the others in drinking.

Themes and Meanings

Framing his mocking and comical treatment of the subject of his poem in the heroic stanza form enables Rochester to give two edges to his satire. He mocks the language and attitudes of conventional heroic verse and at the same time mocks the wanton, decidedly unheroic society depicted in his poem.

The notion that the social and the amatory are essentially combative and akin to war is a common theme in Rochester's poetry, particularly in his satires, lampoons, and bawdy verses. "Insulting Beauty" describes a beautiful woman as "killing fair" ("fair" here meaning lovely rather than just), with "conquering eyes" that enslave the admiring speaker. "While on those Lovely Looks" offers a similar view of love, in which the battle between the lovers ends with the paradox that "The victor lives with empty pride,/ The vanquished die with pleasure."

This outlook is partly a romantic convention, in which the lover is struck and wounded by Cupid's arrow and whose life thenceforth is at the disposal of the beloved. Another source of Rochester's particular perspective on the combative nature of love and social relations is the cynicism common to the literary wits of Charles II's court, which can also be found in Restoration comedies such as George Etherege's *The Man of Mode* (1676) and William Congreve's *The Way of the World* (1700). This cynicism is partly a result of the intellectual climate of the times and partly a fashionable literary affectation.

Rochester's poetry, however, has a dark and ambivalent side that sets it apart from other conventionally cynical and satirical works of his day. Rochester's psyche seems to have contained an element of nihilism and a genuine hatred and contempt for humankind's flaws that show through even in his lighter satires. Paradoxically, his poems also exhibit an uncommonly exuberant relish for the very vices he deplores. In "The Disabled Debauchee," Rochester exhibits this paradoxical tendency to celebrate and condemn vice in equal measure. He clearly scorns the companions of the "brave Admiral" who can so easily be encouraged to attack people and destroy property. Yet part of Rochester is the "brave admiral"; biographical details of Rochester's life show him as a rioter and reveler of the same cloth as the ones he mocks in his poem, and within the poem itself one senses that he takes some pleasure in describing the mischief and vice. He seems to feel keenly that the mind and the emotions or senses are frequently at odds and that human nature has several conflicting sides, and many of his poems are expressions of this ambivalence. In "Absent from Thee I Languish Still," for example, the speaker upbraids himself for his infidelities, which cause heartache not only to his mistress but to himself as well, yet he acknowledges his inability to remain faithful and predicts that he will die miserably in the arms of another.

In "The Disabled Debauchee," the narrator speaks fondly of love and wine and claims that the joy of debauchery is worth the attendant "scars," but the depictions of many of the scenes are deliberately and brutally ugly. Rochester cannot wholeheartedly enjoy or condemn the society he satirizes; the scenes he describes simultaneously attract and repel him. "The Disabled Debauchee" shows Rochester as a realist who understands man's self-contradictory impulses and the complexity of human nature.

Catherine Swanson

THE DISAPPOINTMENT

Author: Aphra Behn (1640-1689)
Type of poem: Narrative
First published: 1684, in *Poems upon Several Occasions, with A Voyage to the Island of Love*

The Poem

"The Disappointment" is a narrative poem in lyric form. It consists of fourteen numbered stanzas of ten lines each, and it tells the story of a single romantic tryst. It is written from the woman's point of view, explaining her frustration or disappointment when her young "Swain" is unable to make good on his promise.

Sexual dysfunction was a subject of ridicule in erotic poetry long before it became a subject of concern in advice columns. There is a classical precedent for "The Disappointment" in the last book of Ovid's *Amores* (*Loves,* 2 B.C.E.); however, the immediate source is an anonymous French poem, "Sur une Impuissance" (on an impotence, 1661), which Aphra Behn freely translates. Her poem is frankly erotic, and the author would have been called a "libertine" even in the relatively carefree days of King Charles II, affectionately known as the Merry Monarch. Behn was called much worse in the eighteenth and nineteenth centuries, but in the twentieth century was hailed as the first English woman to earn a living as a writer. Today "The Disappointment" tends to amuse readers rather than to shock or to titillate. Behn appeals to feminists as a woman who was comfortable with her sexuality.

The lovers in the poem have Greek names; he is "the Amorous *Lysander*," and she is "fair *Cloris*." They are said to be a shepherd and a shepherdess who meet toward dusk in "a lone Thicket made for Love." Their embraces become a kind of sexual warfare in which he prepares to take the victor's "Spoils." The story is straightforward. Lysander comes upon Cloris by surprise. He uses a degree of "force," but she "permits" his advances. She does all the talking, saying no in a way that he takes, correctly, to mean yes (stanza 3):

> *My Dearer Honour ev'n to You*
> *I cannot, must not give—Retire,*
> *Or take this Life, whose chiefest part*
> *I gave you with the Conquest of my Heart.*

They kiss and touch until she is "half dead and breathless," indeed "Defenceless." She offers her virginity, but he is "Unable to perform the Sacrifice." He tries to rouse himself but fails miserably. She offers to help, but she finds that it is no use and runs away. He is left alone, cursing (stanza 9):

> He curs'd his Birth, his Fate, his Stars;
> But more the *Shepherdess*'s Charms,
> Whose soft betwitching Influence
> Had Damn'd him to the *Hell* of Impotence.

Forms and Devices

The verse stanzas divide the story into a series of moments. Each stanza is composed of two quatrains and a couplet, rhyming *abbacddcee* or occasionally *abbacdcdee*. The rhymes are sometimes partial, as with "guess" and "exprest" in stanza 12, but these half rhymes only add to the comic effect. The last line of each stanza is a stately iambic pentameter, whereas the other lines are in iambic tetrameter; the longer line stops the movement and lets the reader savor the situation. For example, when Lysander approaches the "Altar" of love, Behn calls it "That Fountain where Delight still flows,/ And gives the Universal World Repose."

The poem is thus more like a sequence of songs than a short story, more like a set of snapshots than a film. In photojournalism the trick is to capture interesting poses at the right intervals. Behn's timing is just right—and certainly better than poor Lysander's. The first seven of the fourteen stanzas are devoted to his approach, the last seven to his unhappy retreat. The first stanza stops with her eyes, the second with her speechless response to Lysander, the third with her acquiescence to his approaches, and so forth. Similarly, the last stanza ends with his curse, the penultimate with her disappearance, the third from last with her hasty departure. The poem's central line reveals that Lysander is "Unable to perform." The last line, indeed the last word, gives the diagnosis: "Impotence."

Behn uses poetic paraphrase to give the poem a comic seriousness. She says that Lysander spots Cloris as the sun is setting, or rather as "That Gilded Planet of the Day/. . . Was now descending to the Sea." She uses poetic exaggeration, or hyperbole, to make the story seem serious but not too serious. The only light available is the light from Cloris's eyes, which are brighter than the sun. She also employs mythological references to make the characters seem important, even while the reader realizes that they are mere flesh and blood. The chariot is that of Helios of Greek myth. When Cloris is still sufficiently in the dark to think that a "Potent God" awaits her, in stanza 11, Lysander's organ is called "*Priapas*"—that is, Priapus, the god of male fertility. Yet Lysander's Priapas turns out to be "Fabulous" (in the sense of being a fable, "as Poets feign," not in the modern sense of being especially good). Cloris runs away as Daphne ran away from Apollo when Apollo accosted her, or as Venus ran from the sight of her "slain" lover, Adonis. Classical elements such as these give the poem a mock-heroic quality. Aphra Behn wrote poems under the pen name Astrea, a mythological reference to the Roman goddess of justice who was said to have lived on earth in the Golden Age.

Themes and Meanings

"The Disappointment" is a poem on the sensitive and sometimes taboo subject of male impotence. Other English poets wrote on such topics before the twentieth century, none more infamously than Behn's friend John Wilmot, the second earl of Rochester, whose poem "Imperfect Enjoyment" was based on the same French original as Behn's poem and first appeared in the same volume of poetry. Rochester was thought to have written both poems until scholars established Behn's authorship from manuscript evidence. Whereas "Imperfect Enjoyment" sympathizes with the impotent man, who ends up cursing the temptress, "The Disappointment" sympathizes with the woman. In the last stanza, the narrative turns from the third person to the first as the narrator says, "The *Nymph* is Resentments none but I/ Can well Imagine or Condole." "Resentments" here is closer to the French *ressentiment*, a feeling of injury, than to the modern sense of personal grievance. The female narrator can imagine the female lover's position better than a male narrator possibly could, and so can offer condolence. The feeling of disappointment is mutual, and like other versions, Behn's narrative ends with the man's lament. When Behn's shepherd curses the shepherdess and her "Influence," he also curses the stars, and with just as much reason. "Influence" was a technical term in astrology, describing the way a heavenly body can affect humans through rays that flow into them, and Behn used the word in the old sense as well as the modern one. The man could as well blame the stars or planets as blame the equally unfortunate woman.

Behn reveals herself as a good psychologist, realizing that the real "Strife" is not so much between two lovers as between desire and fulfillment. She introduces Lysander as a man with "an impatient Passion," which bodes ill. Before he can "perform," he is "o'er-Ravished"—that is, overstimulated (stanza 7). He is "too transported," or moved, by what he sees. His pleasure becomes pain, Behn explains in stanza 8, because "too much Love destroys" the pleasure. At this point no technique or "Art" can help him. His overzealous "Rage" for sex has "debauch'd his Love." When Cloris tries to arouse him, she finds "a snake." More specifically, she finds that he is "Disarm'd of all his Awful Fires./ And Cold as Flow'rs bath'd in the Morning-Dew." The imagery suggests (but does not confirm) that he has ejaculated prematurely.

It took real spunk for a woman to write a poem like "The Disappointment" in the seventeenth century, and Aphra Behn certainly had it. She wrote plays for the stage at a time when humor was often bawdy, and she was notable for her love intrigues. The satirist Alexander Pope remarked of her stage presence that she "loosely does . . . tread [the stage]/ Who safely puts all characters to bed." She did not cater to men's fantasies; she told it as she saw it. Women who read "The Disappointment" can understand why feminists from Virginia Woolf to Germaine Greer have embraced Aphra Behn as a true predecessor.

Thomas Willard

A DISPLAY OF MACKEREL

Author: Mark Doty (1953-   )
Type of poem: Meditation
First published: 1995, in *Atlantis*

The Poem

Mark Doty's "A Display of Mackerel" is a meditation on beauty and on beauty's ability to triumph over death. This free-verse poem comprises seventeen three-line stanzas and describes the poet's encounter with a display of fish. Doty skillfully explores the rich implications of this encounter. As the living poet admires the dead fish, the human soul encounters the extraordinary beauty of the display and finds within this beauty a possible antidote for the fear of death. With gradually expanding complexity, Doty infuses this encounter with associations and intimations that transcend the mere fact of mackerel on ice. Through a systematic appraisal of paradoxes, the poet leads his reader along the pathways of the poetic imagination, dismantling humanity's anxieties about life, death, and the eternity of the soul.

"A Display of Mackerel" opens with a straightforward description of the fish lying on ice in rows. Having established a foundation of mundane description, Doty quickly departs from factuality and starts to explore the associations the mackerel inspire in him. Shortly after the first stanza, the first images of the extraordinary, the beautiful, and the precious begin to intrude upon the everyday: Not only are the fish dark and cold, but also "each [is] a foot of luminosity." By the third stanza, the fish have become a lens through which Doty will consider important issues of existence: "radiant sections/ like seams of lead/ in a Tiffany window." Despite the fact that they are dead, cold, and nonhuman, the mackerel represent a precious, shimmering realm of existence far removed from unpleasant and unsettling conceptions of death.

In the next few stanzas, Doty extends his meditations on life and death and draws the reader into this process by way of direct address. The poet instructs the readers to expand their consideration of the fish: "think abalone" and "think sun on gasoline." In the tradition of Romantic poets such as William Wordsworth—who viewed nature as a primary source of the highest poetic and spiritual revelation—Doty perceives divine significance in the universe of beauty and selflessness the mackerel inhabit: "Splendor, and splendor,/ and not a one in any way/ distinguished from the other."

Midway through the poem, the poetic transformation of the mackerel into exemplars of life, death, and the unity of existence is complete. As the momentum of poetic imagery and paradox increases, "A Display of Mackerel" accumulates terms and phrases that suggest spiritual and existential complexity: "they're *all* exact expressions/ of the one soul,/ each a perfect fulfillment/ of heaven's template." Once the connection between the mackerel and spirituality has been consummated, Doty consolidates the poem's personification of and identification with the fish by considering an existential trade. Would humanity exchange its troubled, individualistic ideas of life for the serenity and beauty of a mackerel's existence?

> Suppose we could iridesce,
>
> like these, and lose ourselves
> entirely in the universe
> of shimmer—would you want
>
> to be yourself only,
> unduplicatable, doomed
> to be lost?

Having extracted beauty and this question from his encounter with the display of mackerel, Doty completes the arc of the poem by returning to the fish. While they were an objective "they" in the poem's opening description, the fish are personified by Doty at the end of the poem; they are no longer alien but intimate. He knows that they prefer to be as they are, "flashing" and "multitudinous." He knows that they do not care that they are dead. He can imagine their happiness "even on ice, to be together, selfless,/ which is the price of gleaming."

Forms and Devices

"A Display of Mackerel" and the collection to which it belongs, *Atlantis*, mark an important transition in Doty's work. While *My Alexandria* (1993) is praised for its explorations of the theme of loss, the poems in that collection articulate a conflicted and skeptical attitude about poetry's transcendent powers. In contrast, "A Display of Mackerel" insists upon hope in the face of loss and revels in the ability of poetry to redeem and transform reality. In this poem and throughout *Atlantis*, Doty constructs numerous paradoxical linkages between the natural and the human-made ("sun on gasoline"), between the dead and the living ("bolting forward, heedless of stasis"), and between individuality and collectivity ("the rainbowed school// in which no verb is singular,/ or every one is"). These paradoxical juxtapositions produce an atmosphere in which impossibilities become possible, connections between disparate elements flourish, and the poetic imagination transforms everyday reality.

The poem mixes several levels of poetic language to create this magical, transformative effect. The language of precise description ("parallel rows") combines with spiritual terms ("each a perfect fulfillment/ of heaven's template"), blends with language relating to natural beauty ("luminosity," "radiant," "shimmer," "gleaming"), and mixes with worldly value ("Tiffany window," and "this enameling the jeweler's/ made"). This combination of linguistic levels produces a fluid, multiple context in which Doty reveals his meditations on life and death. When taken as a whole, this mixture of levels of beauty and value suggests one of the important meanings of the poem: There is spiritual awakening in the most ordinary moments, and there is significance in the most accidental encounters. By combining this multiplicity of types of language into one poem, Doty replicates the spiritual oneness the poem proposes.

The juxtaposition of paradoxical ideas and this mixture of levels of language support a third poetic technique contributing to the poem's meditative atmosphere: Imagery, that very basic element of poetic expression, is amplified in "A Display of Mackerel." Doty's quickly shifting use of poetic imagery feeds the paradoxical and combinative logic of the poem. In the course of the poem, the fish are related to images of light, windows, rainbows, soapbubbles, jewelry, and a classroom. The speed at which Doty introduces and then alters these images contributes to the wonder and magic that lies behind the poem's expression. In general, Doty's imagery falls into two categories that, taken together, point to the two realms of existence the poem's meditations are bridging. On one hand, the poem is filled with images of external beauty; on the other hand, there are many images of internal spirituality and intellect. Together, the two categories form an equation between beauty and spirit that Doty extends to all of creation. Living or dead, fish or human, individual or collective, life is beautiful; the end of life need not be tragic.

Themes and Meanings

"A Display of Mackerel" is an excellent example of poetry's ability to link complex realizations about self and existence to that which is generally considered mundane and even unpleasant. In Doty's hands, a display of dead fish becomes a window into the nature of the soul and a measure of human anxiety about death. In the course of the poem he asks and alludes to several important questions: What are the boundaries of life and death? Is death final and annihilating? Or may death be eclipsed by something else? By applying imagination to the observed world, Doty harmonizes levels of expression and orders of existence. The "price of gleaming" indicated in the poem's final line is a happiness, a selflessness, and a togetherness that confounds even death. Persisting beyond the boundaries of individual existence and physiological function, this greater form of existence, predicated on total investment in the gleaming accident of the spirit, is a refuge for the poet and an antidote to the tragedy of death. It is not a solution to death per se but rather an awareness of beauty's relentlessness that is at least partially realized by the poem itself.

Yet in these meditations on life and death, the reader can sense a tragedy behind the poem. The collection to which this poem belongs is dedicated to Wally Roberts, Doty's lover who died a year before the publication of *Atlantis* of complications due to acquired immunodeficiency syndrome (AIDS). In the light of this death—which is chronicled in Doty's memoir *Heaven's Coast* (1996)—one may read this poem and a large part of Doty's work as engaged in a dialogue with loss and the redemption of love in spite of death. By considering how love and death influence the meaning of "A Display of Mackerel," one may read Doty's poetry as an important late twentieth century expression of themes that run throughout the history of Western literature (the elegy, Romanticism, modernism). The intimation that in the end life triumphs over death—that there is a possible antidote to the losses of death—is crucial to reading this poem as an antielegy, a celebration of the beauty of the spirit in spite of death.

Finally, "A Display of Mackerel" is firmly grounded in an impressive poetic tradition. Echoing the spiritual luminosity of Wordsworth, the poem also invites comparisons with the transcendental poetry of Emily Dickinson and the meditations of Wallace Stevens. "A Display of Mackerel" is an excellent example of the vitality of the poetic imagination in American literature. It is a meditation on the power poetry holds to strip reality of its familiarity and to address the complexities of the soul.

Daniel M. Scott III

THE DISTANCES

Author: Charles Olson (1910-1970)
Type of poem: Meditation
First published: 1960, in *The Distances*

The Poem

"The Distances" is a meditation on love and human alienation, but the poem does not present its argument or define its terms in a straightforward way. The poem begins, "So the distances are Galatea," with the conjunction "so" suggesting that the reader has walked into the middle of a conversation. Something has been left out, and this is typical of Olson's poetry—he often juxtaposes fragments so that the reader must draw the connections or attempt to fill in the blanks. The reader may wonder what kind of "distances" the speaker has in mind and how such distances are connected to the mythological Galatea. The poem is a sometimes cryptic, sometimes disturbing, but finally profoundly moving meditation on the "distances" that human beings put between themselves and others, and the powerful force that "knows no distance," love. The philosophical discussion is illustrated by references to a Greek myth, a newspaper story from Florida, Olson's book *Call Me Ishmael*, the Greek god Zeus, and the Roman leaders Julius Caesar and his adopted son, Caesar Augustus.

The poem opens and closes with references to the myth of Pygmalion and Galatea. In the myth, Pygmalion, the King of Cyprus, falls in love with the unattainable Aphrodite, goddess of love. He sculpts an ivory image of her, places it in his bed, and then prays to Aphrodite for compassion. The goddess brings the statue to life as Galatea, an actual woman who becomes Pygmalion's wife. Following these brief references to the Pygmalion myth are references to "a German inventor in Key West/ who had a Cuban girl, and kept her, after her death/ in his bed." These lines allude to an incident reported in the Key West newspapers in 1952, in which police arrested an eighty-three-year-old man, Karl Tanzler, who had fallen in love with an ill Cuban girl, removed her body from its grave, preserved it, and kept it for eight years in his house. The police found the corpse dressed for bed, with fresh flowers in its hair.

From this bizarre modern version of the Pygmalion story, the poem moves to its most obscure section, in which "sons" go "down La Cluny's steps to the old man sitting/ a god throned on torsoes" in search of "a secret" that can perhaps "undo distance." "La Cluny" may refer to the Musée de Cluny in Paris or to the Abbaye de Cluny in Mâcon, France, but the geographical referent is less important than the psychological theme. In *Call Me Ishmael*, Olson traces the theme of the rebellious or exiled son, separated from the father, through various ancient myths and connects this theme with the idea that the "deeper part" of the human self is obscure and buried. To discover this deeper self one needs to "go down" into the depths of the psyche, where one will find, "throned on torsos," the father, "your own grim sire, who did beget ye, exiled sons." The separation of father from son, suggests Olson, is psychologically entangled with the distance between the superficial self and the deep self.

Threaded throughout the poem are repeated references to "old Zeus" and "young Augustus," and just before the poem's end the speaker imagines "[Julius] Caesar" stroking the cheek of his adopted son, "young Augustus [Octavian]." At this point all of the stories are conflated: "old Zeus" hides "young/ Galatea"; "the girl who makes you weep" is both Galatea and "the corpse [kept] alive by all/ your arts"; and Julius strokes the "stone face" of "young Augustus." The poem ends with a kind of prayer that love will "yield/ to this man/ that the impossible distance/ be healed." The prayer is answered with Aphrodite's words: "I wake you,/ stone. Love this man."

Forms and Devices

Although "The Distances" is rich in imagery and allusion, most of the forms and devices of traditional poetry are absent. Olson uses no rhyme, no meter, and no stanza breaks, and he violates conventions of syntax, spelling ("torsoes" instead of "torsos"), capitalization, and punctuation. His lines are unpredictable in length, in spacing, and in their left margins, which may begin at any of four different tab settings. In some ways the poem has the look of the American poet William Carlos Williams's well-known "triadic stanza," in which the left margin of each line is indented farther than the previous line's, so that each three-line stanza looks like a descending set of steps. Olson, however, is not as regular as Williams in his use of the pattern; his margins move in an entirely unpredictable manner. The lines are heavily enjambed, and punctuation is sparse. In fact, no periods appear until the poem's final line. In addition, none of the stories is fully told. Instead readers are given bits and pieces of narrative. All of this forces the reader to read slowly and to reread. The unpredictable line breaks and irregular spacings suggest a hesitating, uncertain voice groping toward meaning. This uncertainty is further stressed when, at two points, sentences with the syntax of statements conclude with question marks.

The jagged, broken quality of the poem's form is offset, however, by several patterns of repetition and contrast. The most obvious of these is the pair of names "old Zeus" and "young Augustus," which are repeated together or singly six times in the poem. The paired names stress the "distance" between both old-young and human-divine, but they also personify the kinds of desire—for "mastery" and "control"—that people mistake or substitute for love and that end up creating "the distances." The different stories referred to in the poem repeat a similar theme, which Olson stresses by blending details of the Pygmalion, the Key West, and the La Cluny stories into one another.

Pygmalion and the German inventor believe that they can create an object for their love, while the "sons" in La Cluny learn nothing and "go away" disappointed because they expected to find, and hence to possess or control, the "secret" that can "undo distance." One final structural contrast in the poem is the juxtaposition of abstract, metaphysical language, as in "Death is a loving matter, then, a horror/ we cannot bide," with vivid, concrete images, such as the German inventor with the dead Cuban girl in his bed. Olson's is an erudite, intellectually demanding poetry.

Themes and Meanings

The poem's title states its topic: the "distances" that human beings create that isolate them from one another and from the world in which they live. Distances separate men from women, fathers from sons, the old from the young, the divine from the human, and the superficial self from the deep self. The poem suggests that such distances arise because people misunderstand the nature of love; instead of recognizing love as a universal force of nature that "places all where each is, as they are, for every moment," they understand love to mean their own "mastery" or "control" over whatever persons or objects they find most precious. Love then becomes perverted into little more than a form of greed. Like the German inventor, people convince themselves that they can turn death into life, or they search for the "secret" that will "undo distance" and give them the mastery they desire.

The poem suggests that human beings, having created these "distances" by seeing human relationships in terms of "mastery" or "control," cannot hope to "undo distance" by means of mastery or control. Instead they must yield to the power of love, a divine force of nature personified by Aphrodite, which alone can heal "the impossible distance" between man and woman, father and son, the old and the young, the divine and the human, the superficial self and the deep self.

Pygmalion is mistaken when he believes that he can somehow compel or possess Aphrodite's love by producing a stone image of her and setting it in his bed—that is precisely the kind of misunderstanding of love that creates "the distances." However, unlike the German inventor, Pygmalion corrects his mistake when, instead of seeking to control the goddess, he yields to her power and adopts a reverent attitude of prayer. It is this new attitude, this change of heart, that leads the goddess to bring the stone to life—not as Aphrodite, which was Pygmalion's original greedy desire, but as Galatea, an actual woman who is capable of giving to Pygmalion what each human, according to this poem, needs most vitally: love.

Gary Grieve-Carlson

THE DISTANT FOOTSTEPS

Author: César Vallejo (1892-1938)
Type of poem: Lyric
First published: 1918, as "Los pasos lejanos," in *Los heraldos negros*; English translation collected in *The Black Heralds*, 1990

The Poem

"The Distant Footsteps" is a short poem of twenty lines divided into four stanzas. The first and third stanzas are quatrains; the second and fourth stanzas are sestets. The poem is in free verse, a fact of some significance since many of the poems in César Vallejo's first volume (in which this poem appears) are written in traditional, rhymed forms. By the end of the volume, Vallejo was working in free verse and moving toward the revolutionary techniques of his later poetry (see, for example, *Trilce*, 1922).

The title establishes the themes of departure and separation that are so important to this poem and Vallejo's early work. A central obsession for Vallejo was the anguish associated with the trauma of leaving home for the capital, Lima, when he was a young man. Lost in the city, he longs for the home he has left behind. He also experiences some guilt at having abandoned that home.

Vallejo, a poet of personal experience and intense self-reflection, frequently uses the first person, as in this poem. The emphasis, then, is on giving voice to personal reflections about family relationships. The poet begins by observing his father, who is sleeping peacefully and gently. It is afternoon. The poet can find no bitterness in his father's appearance, but he does not discount the possibility that somewhere inside the father may harbor some bitterness. Curiously, and significantly, the poet believes that the father's bitterness, if it does in fact exist, is the poet's own fault.

In the second stanza, the poet identifies a general loneliness in this home. This loneliness is associated, by juxtaposition, with prayer, although who is doing the praying—and why—is not revealed. One might ask whether this is a prayer of praise, supplication, mourning, or something else. For the moment, this information is withheld. The loneliness, however, seems to have something to do with missing children, for there is "no news of the children today." This sixth line raises a question: Is the poet actually on the scene? Since the children are gone, and since the poet is one of those children, it seems that he, too, is missing from the scene. This would mean that the observations he is making concerning the activities of his parents are products of his imagination. Regardless, the poet's reflections involve much speculation. In imagining his father awakening, for example, he believes his father thinks of the Holy Family's flight into Egypt to escape Herod's decree.

The poet's mother is introduced in the third stanza. He imagines her walking in an orchard recalling the distant past. Like the father, the mother is gentle. The poet does not, however, hint at any adversarial relationship with her, as he had in his father's case.

The final stanza repeats the sense of loneliness and vacancy, and it associates this sense with the image of "two, old, white curving roads." These roads provide the poet's means of departure, but the nature of this departure is uncertain. Was it necessary? Did he leave reluctantly, or was he escaping, and does he now feel guilty for doing so? The final emotion is ambiguous.

Forms and Devices

"The Distant Footsteps" presents a series of images that provide the poet with an opportunity for reflection on loss and departure. The poet offers simple statements of observation, and uses these statements as springboards for more speculative ruminations on the emotional state of both those whom he is observing and of himself. There are three such observations: the father sleeping; the father waking; the mother walking. These three main observations lead in turn to three main speculations, each beginning with the same phrase, "if there's. . . . " Thus, the poet concludes that any bitterness or distance in his father must be the poet's own fault. Similarly, the poet decides that the two curving roads are the source of the brokenness that he interprets as part of the domestic scene that he is observing.

There is, however, nothing neat and tidy—and certainly nothing predictable—in the poet's use of this pattern of observation or speculation. Any sense in this pattern is, in fact, undermined by the poet's reluctance to settle for obvious or trite responses to his observations. Vallejo was a poet of stunning juxtaposition, of what the American poet (and translator of Vallejo) Robert Bly called "swift associations." This early poem is a good illustration. The leaps are dramatic and bold: The poet connects a man waking in a lonely house with the flight of the Holy Family, and then somehow associates this flight with a departure that heals a wound or at least dresses it. One of the difficulties for the reader is that the ambiguity of this technique tends to raise more questions than it answers. The father here might identify with Joseph, Jesus, or even Herod. Perhaps it is the general notion of fleeing tyranny that is suggested. The "goodbye" mentioned in line 8 may be the father's goodbye or one of his children's.

The open-endedness of Vallejo's juxtaposition is intentional: Vallejo is trying to introduce as many levels of meaning as possible. A favorite Vallejo device is using words with multiple meanings in Spanish, a poetic device that does not easily translate. Certain parallel constructions also emphasize opposition. In lines 13 and 14, the mother is described as "so soft,/ so much wing, so much outgoing, so much love." These four "so" constructions, which detail the positive qualities of the mother, are negated by four "no" constructions in lines 15 and 16: "no bustling,/ no news, no green, no childhood." Opposition is thus one of Vallejo's techniques.

Themes and Meanings

"The Distant Footsteps" is included in a section of *The Black Heralds* called "Canciones de Hogar" ("Songs of Home"). The notion of home for Vallejo, however, proves as elusive as it does for the American poet Robert Frost. Many of Vallejo's poems view the home, and the world at large, from the point of view of the orphan.

Vallejo considered orphanhood, literal or figurative, the general condition of all human beings. This poem captures the profound ambiguity of that condition.

While the section is called "Songs of Home," "The Distant Footsteps" might more accurately be read as a poem about the loss of home. The poet's status is uncertain; he seems to be on uncertain ground despite the familiarity of the setting. Indeed, it is not entirely clear that the poet is actually on the scene. Perhaps he is only imagining everything; perhaps the poem is his vision of home after he has gone. The ambiguity of this status is not at all unusual in Vallejo's work. He is a poet dedicated to the exploration of absurdity and senselessness in the world—even the world of the home. It is as if the things once familiar to him had taken on new meaning, but a meaning that now escapes him.

Thus the father's peacefulness may conceal bitterness, and his nearness may conceal distance. Similarly, the road might initially seem a means of escape, but it must also be seen as the route of banishment and hence of orphanhood. The poet therefore speaks of two roads, roads that are the source of the brokenness and weakness he feels this lonely afternoon. One does not know whether the roads are parallel, whether they lead in opposite directions, or whether they branch apart. Perhaps it does not matter. The point is that the poet leaves by both of them: "Down them my heart goes on foot." This disturbing image—so jarring linguistically—suggests the poet's reluctance in departing.

The central question about this departure, both for the reader and for the poet himself, is whether it is willed or forced—that is, does the poet leave by choice or is he forced to leave? The poet himself is not sure; in the same way that birth is not chosen and yet is necessary for life, the child must leave the home, becoming in essence an orphan. This is the tragic destiny of human beings: One must abandon and be abandoned. So in this case, the ambiguity of the situation leaves the poet saddened and helpless. Vallejo seems to turn around Robert Frost's line that "Home is the place where, when you have to go there,/ they have to take you in." For Vallejo, home is the place one must leave, however reluctantly. It is a place where one cannot stay. One is missed, and yet there is no place for him or her. Nearness is distance.

This is not a poem that pretends to present to the reader a neatly packaged truth, nor is it a poem that expresses a simple emotion. For Vallejo, truth is elusive, and emotions are complex, even contradictory. "The Distant Footsteps" is best read as a poem that gives voice to those contradictory emotions.

Stephen Benz

DIVERS DOTH USE

Author: Sir Thomas Wyatt (1503-1542)
Type of poem: Sonnet
First published: wr.c. 1530's, in Devonshire Manuscript #17492; collected in *Collected Poems*, 1969

The Poem

"Divers Doth Use" is a sonnet in the Italian, or Petrarchan, form, rhymed *abbaabba*, *cddcee*, and thus structured as an octave and a sestet, rather than in the four quatrains of the English, or Shakespearean, sonnet. As in many of Sir Thomas Wyatt's shorter lyrics, the subject here is the ending of romantic relationships in the context of a sophisticated Renaissance court whose sexual mores are promiscuous and whose social manners are often modeled after those found in poetry. The first-person voice in the poem, whether Wyatt's or that of an imaginary persona, speaks of typical male responses to female infidelity and offers, in contrast to those responses, his own attitude, which, he claims, is stalwart and stoic.

The octave opens with the speaker deriding diverse men whom he either knows firsthand or has heard about who behave childishly and poetically in the face of their beloveds' unfaithfulness: men who weep and moan endlessly—"never for to lin [cease]" (line 3)—not in order to effect any change in their situations but, paradoxically, in order to alleviate their woe. In other words, they weep to appease their weeping: not a particularly mature or effective response. Such ostentatious expressions of woe are mere affectations.

There are other men, the poem continues, who behave viciously, by insulting their former lovers as false (that is, as promiscuous), but then quickly redirect their passions and love poems to other women. Men who react in this way simply testify to the inconstancy of their own affections and prove themselves to be "false."

At line 9, the formal turn—the point in a sonnet that marks the beginning of an antithesis or redirection of the poem's focus—the speaker turns attention from the men described above to himself and his own reaction to the infidelity of his beloved. Although he too has fallen out of favor with his woman, he will not, he says, weep unduly over her infidelity or insult her as false, though false she was. Rather, he refuses to take it personally and attributes the situation to the impersonal forces of chance and change.

Finally, he accepts the woman's infidelity as natural ("of kind," line 13) and neither faults the individual woman nor loses his own composure. The failure of the relationship stems from nothing less than female psychology in general; often, he says, the only thing that pleases women is change itself.

Forms and Devices

The language of the poem is strikingly straightforward. The meter, while fairly regular iambic pentameter, creates a rhythm that seems conversational and familiar rather than formal. The speaker seems to talk to his audience directly, as if to an intimate acquaintance. This sense of familiarity, of ordinary talk, comes also from the poem's relative lack of metaphoric imagery.

The only suggestion of metaphor in the poem comes in line 12, with the word "feed": "Nor call her false that falsely did me feed." Wyatt here suggests a conceit (the Elizabethan term for metaphoric imagery) that is prevalent elsewhere in his poetry: the comparison of a romantic affair to the relationship between a wild deer and one who feeds, and thus domesticates, the animal. Except for this one metaphor, the language of the poem is remarkably prosaic and direct. This serves to make the single metaphor stand out, and calls attention to the fact that this speaker, too, despite his denials, is thinking of his romantic involvements in a literary or poetic way. This literary approach to experience is clearest in the final couplet.

The chief literary device of the last two lines is the proverb, a device that reduces human behavior and experience to a witty, often memorable sententious saying. Poets often use such sayings in juxtaposition to their own perceptions of experience, sometimes simply to revivify the wisdom of popular aphorisms, sometimes to suggest their insufficiency or the banality of their wisdom. Wyatt's last line, "Often change doth please a woman's mind," derives from a popular misogynistic proverb: "Winter winds and women's minds change oft." Wyatt's paraphrase creates an equally memorable and sententious expression of this idea. The question this device invites at the end of the poem is whether this reaction to infidelity is more valid or more positive than those the speaker derides.

Themes and Meanings

As much as Wyatt's personae complain about female behavior, his poems often reflect more poignantly on male attitudes and actions. In a promiscuous court such as Henry VIII's, in which the men and women all seem to indulge in rather loose expression of sexual desires, why is it that men react so vehemently and emotionally, so irrationally, to infidelity, especially given their own participation in and enjoyment of this state of affairs?

In writing about love, a great many poets suggest that behavior in romantic situations has much to do with who lovers imagine their beloveds to be. Such a powerful emotion as love often leads people to create elaborate, imaginative conceptions of others, conceptions that are not usually very truthful or accurate. When a lover discovers that his beloved is not the person he imagined her to be, the consequent disillusionment can lead to bitter reactions. Witness, for example, the disillusionment of the speaker in William Shakespeare's Sonnet 147 ("My love is as a fever, longing still"): "For I have sworn thee fair and thought thee bright,/ Who art as black as hell, as dark as night." This bitter derision of the beloved seems an echo of the kind of responses of which Wyatt's speaker complains.

Yet one might ask whether the attitude of Wyatt's persona is any better. In subtle ways, Wyatt suggests that this man's manner of dealing with infidelity is also literary—that is, that his manner mimics a popular poetic or proverbial expression that may not accurately reflect the real experience, the actual situation. Although he says he will not call the woman false, he goes on to do just that, and the proverb he picks up to support his own stoic attitude does worse than simply insult the individual woman: It insults all women as innately false.

Reading poetry from a different age and culture presents two fundamental questions: To what extent does the poet's thinking differ from present-day thinking? To what extent does it differ from that of his contemporaries? Viewing this poem as is done here implies that Wyatt was able to distance himself from the conventional misogyny of his age enough to see male attitudes toward women as the creation of their own false expectations and double standards. The whole body of Wyatt's love poetry substantiates this conclusion; Wyatt shows himself again and again to be a keen observer of sexual politics among sophisticated courtiers, and of the literary conventions that misled those literate men and women about the identities of others and of themselves.

James Hale

DIVING INTO THE WRECK

Author: Adrienne Rich (1929-   )
Type of poem: Narrative
First published: 1973, in *Diving into the Wreck*

The Poem

"Diving into the Wreck" is a poem of ten stanzas in free verse. The poem is written in the first person. Sometimes poets use the first-person device to create a character who may have different values or beliefs from the author. In this case, however, no distinction between speaker and poet is suggested. The first-person voice allows the poet to address the reader directly, as if recounting her own experience.

The poem narrates the speaker's quest as she explores a sunken ship to discover the cause of the disaster and to salvage whatever treasures remain. The sea is a traditional literary symbol of the unconscious. To dive is to probe beneath the surface for hidden meanings, to learn about one's submerged desires and emotions. In this poem, the diver is exploring a wreck—a ship that has failed.

Preparing to dive, she reads the "book of myths" for guidance, but she must leave the book behind in order to gain direct knowledge without the intermediaries of history and language:

> the thing I came for:
> the wreck and not the story of the wreck
> the thing itself and not the myth.

She is alone in her journey. Unlike the French underwater explorer Jacques Cousteau with his many helpers, she must be alone, for the scientist may work with a team, but the quest requires isolation.

The poem is the story of a descent into the ocean to discover important knowledge of the past, to examine a wreck and to salvage the cargo. The poet describes the tools that are needed for the dive and the diver's transformation as she descends. By the time she reaches the wreck, she has become a new kind of creature, a "she/he." As the diver learns, the myth that was the starting point of her journey is incomplete and inadequate: It does not tell her story. She must, therefore, return to tell her own tale.

Forms and Devices

The poem is an extended metaphor in which the dive comes to signify the diver's quest for knowledge and power. Her descent into the primal depths of the sea of life, of consciousness, transforms her: She becomes a creature of a different world. Her discussion of the equipment she uses suggests her transformation. The "awkward mask" and crippling flippers are inappropriate for the land-based world but essential for the underwater journey. Human when she starts, she becomes "like an insect" as she crawls down the ladder. It is as if she is reversing the process of evolution as she reenters the ocean, the original source of life on earth. Once underwater, she notes that "you breathe differently down here." When she reaches the drowned vessel, she learns her true identity; she is both mermaid and merman, man and woman. There is a ritualistic quality to this stanza, as the speaker remarks, "We circle silently/ about the wreck." No longer the single diver, she has become a "we," both male and female: "I am she: I am he." She apparently has become the drowned vessel as well, the boat and its figurehead:

> whose drowned face sleeps with open eyes
> whose breasts still bear the stress
> whose silver, copper, vermeil cargo lies
> obscurely inside barrels.

By delving into the mystery, looking beneath the surface, the diver learns the secret of her own submerged power. She/he is thus restored to a complete, multifaceted identity. The diver is not only the boat and its cargo, a figurehead, an observer, an explorer. She/he is also a participant in the disaster: "we are the half-destroyed instruments/ that once held to a course." The implicit question is, can the diver carry out a salvage operation? Can the treasures she finds, "the silver, copper, vermeil cargo" be saved? The poem does not answer the question, but ends as the diver recapitulates the story of her arrival at this point, explaining how she/he found her way here carrying a book of myths "in which/ our names do not appear."

Themes and Meanings

The theme of descent and return is a traditional one in Western literature. In Homer's great epic, The Odyssey (c. 800 B.C.E.), the hero Odysseus descends to the underworld to consult with dead prophets and heroes. Because of their great wisdom, they tell him how to return safely, and he learns how to return home from his expedition. Adrienne Rich has written a modern version of this descent theme.

The implications of this wreck must be examined. What exactly has failed? Perhaps the "wreck" is the covering up of subconscious desires and knowledge as one grows up. Perhaps the diver represents all humans, submerging into the depths of personal histories to find out who they really are. This is certainly one possibility; however, if one examines the context in which this poem was written, one may learn more about Rich's intentions.

One of the clues to the meaning of the wreck and the diver is the last statement about the "book of myths/ in which/ our names do not appear." At the time she wrote this poem, Rich was learning and writing about women's experiences. Much of this material was unavailable before the women's movement began in the late 1960's. Rich was one of the pioneers in the rediscovery of women's history and women's literature. In 1971, she wrote an essay entitled "When We Dead Awaken: Writing as Re-Vision." In the article, she wrote about an awakening of women's consciousness, their "drive to self-knowledge." She wrote, "language has trapped as well as liberated us." She urged women to reexamine their history, to learn "to see—and therefore live—afresh."

Thus, the "book of myths" may be a metaphorical equivalent for the language which has trapped and liberated women. The book of myths may be Western history—the story of men's lives and experiences—that does not speak about women. If the history books do not tell women's stories, they must search the past (dive into the ocean) and find the evidence so that they can retell the old stories. Perhaps the wreck is meant to suggest the lost treasures of women's lives and ancient stories; perhaps it suggests the failure of Western history and civilization as they became rigidly patriarchal and denied the value of women. In order to solve this problem, then, to salvage the treasure, it is implied that the book of myths will need to be rewritten to include the stories of women. That is, Western civilization will need to accommodate the vision and insights of women.

To accomplish this new vision, Rich imagined a new kind of creature—the mermaid/merman, the she/he of the poem. This figure, by using the necessary tools—the knife, the camera, the flippers, the ladder, the book of myths—might return to the surface with some of the treasure from the wreck. She/he might be able to tell new stories, write a new book of myths about a new kind of person. Yet this poem does not show the diver returning to the surface. Instead, in subsequent poems, Rich continued the work of retelling the stories of women and salvaging the treasures of women's lost histories.

Karen F. Stein

DIWAN TRILOGY

Author: Gunnar Ekelöf (1907-1968)
Type of poem: Poetic sequence
First published: Dīwān över fursten av Emgión, 1965; *Sagan om Fatumeh*, 1966; English translation collected in *Selected Poems*, 1971, as *Diwan over the Prince of Emgión* and *The Tale of Fatumeh*; *Vägvisare till unterjorden*, 1967; English translation collected in *Guide to the Underworld*, 1980

The Poem

The *Diwan over the Prince of Emgión*, *The Tale of Fatumeh*, and *Guide to the Underworld*, referred to as the Diwan Trilogy, are centered on Byzantine and Middle Eastern themes, reflecting Gunnar Ekelöf's lifelong interest in Asian cultures and languages. "Diwan" or, more commonly in English, "divan," is the Arabic-Persian term for a poetic sequence or collection of single authorship, such as the fourteenth century *Divan* of Hafiz, which, like the "Diwan Trilogy," links the language of earthly and spiritual love.

The three sections of the trilogy are connected more by their ethos or personal philosophy than by any common narrative. In each of the three component parts, Ekelöf uses different narrative materials to create a personal mythology. In *The Diwan over the Prince of Emgión* and *The Tale of Fatumeh*, the element of "story" or narrative is more pronounced than in *Guide to the Underworld*. Both of the earlier works deal with close relationships: in the former, between the prince and a mystic madonna-goddess figure, as well as an unnamed woman who serves as his guide and companion upon his release from prison; in the latter, between the prostitute Fatumeh and her lover. Although *Guide to the Underworld* explores the relationship between the Devil and a young novice, it incorporates a far greater range of spokespersons and mythologies than either of the earlier sequences.

The Prince of Emgión, who revealed himself to Ekelöf in a seance as his spiritual double, serves as the poetic persona or "I" narrator throughout most of the sequence. *The Diwan over the Prince of Emgión* may be separated into several major movements: the preface, comprising the opening epigraph and the first lyric; the invocation and songs of praise to the madonna-goddess in the next fifteen poems; the following group of twenty-one lyrics, which intersperse the story of the prince's torture, blinding, and imprisonment with addresses to the divine lady and to Digenís, a soulmate and fellow prisoner of bygone days; and the concluding fifteen lyrics, which detail the prince's journey homeward with a female guide and include further praises sung to the madonna-goddess.

The opening epigraph from the *Tarjúman el-Ashwáq*, a work of the mystic Sufi tradition in classical Persian and Arabic poetry, presents the major aim of the spokesperson in *The Diwan over the Prince of Emgión*: "The word 'Her' is my aim," it states; and in "Her" name, any bartering will be with "give" and "take." To the mutilated, blinded Emgión in his dungeon, "Her" figure is indeed a focus that takes him out of his suffering and gives him the strength to rise above physical reality. The prefatory poem further states the poetic persona's aim or quest. A dream vision poses "the question of [his] life": "Did I prefer the part to the whole/ Or the whole to the part[?]" Uncompromisingly, the prince replies that he wants both and, moreover, that between fragment and totality there should be "no contradiction."

In the madonna-goddess, the prisoner finds his symbol of totality, transcendence, and survival. The opening set of lyrics addresses the prisoner's ideal in the language of erotic and spiritual love. Although the lady presides, at least metaphorically, over the night sky, the need or "oar" that propels him toward her comes "from deep within myself." She is an "invisible but present" force who, in spite of her nurturing actions, as when in a dream vision she wraps the speaker in a white garment and allows him to kiss her breasts, is yet aloof and unattainable. No material gifts come from her: Her true gift is that of "Distance," given only to those "who are strong in love." Her main effect is that of transporting the prisoner from misery to the experience of love and beauty. As the final poem of the first movement states, "beauty is a weapon/ Which fells princes to the ground." The power of tyrants is nothing in the face of the ideal of love and beauty incorporated in the Lady.

An *ayíasma*, or song in praise of the holy purifying qualities of water, begins the second movement, which deals with Emgión's imprisonment. The story of the Prince of Emgión explains this need for purification. He has beheld, he says, slaughter, treachery, and "filthy lust after power." Now, in the dungeon, he is bloodstained and tortured. His eyes have been put out by red-hot needles so that, like Sophocles' Oedipus, he is "a blinded man who sees." One of the few poems with a title, "The Logothete's Annotation," continues his biography. In a dryly bureaucratic tone, the Logothete—that is, the emperor's chief councillor—states that the prince was "Lord of the Marches." He was regarded as untrustworthy, suspected of disreputable political alliances and adherence to the Manichaean heresy, a splinter movement in the medieval Christian church that claimed that two antagonistic forces, God and the Devil, control the universe.

Yet, although he salutes both God and the Devil as prophets waging an unending war, he rejects both as tyrants. Love, represented by the lady who stands above all combat, is "a chink/ Of light between their bloody lips/ The gap through which the chosen can enter." The second movement gives way to the third, marked by yet another *ayíasma*. Water now cleanses the newly released prisoner of his worms and boils, and the barber's blade cuts the pus from his eyes. More important than the water that cleanses the body, however, is that which cleanses the spirit. The prince has now achieved the true vision, an inward one.

With the final movement, a new female figure, referred to at various times as daughter, princess, wife, and sister, enters the narrative. With this companion, who may well be an earthly manifestation of the divine goddess's love, the prince makes his way across the Fertile Crescent to his native land.

Like the *Diwan*, *The Tale of Fatumeh* is a complex poetic sequence with shifting poetic voices and a fragmented narrative that follows no linear chronological order. The general pattern consists of a framework, comprising the two first and last lyrics; a cycle of twenty-seven poems that focus on the episodes and insights preceding Fatumeh's separation from her lover; and the final set of twenty-seven poems, whose theme is loss.

The "preloss" cycle begins where the "loss" cycle ends, at the first meeting of the prostitute Fatumeh with her lover, who is here the poetic voice. A lyric celebrating the physical union of the newfound lovers follows. The sequence then shifts to give fragmentary details of Fatumeh's early life. She has been born into a "world of mirrors" and sold "to the High Gate/ Which is called Death." The daughter of a line of prostitutes, she is, at an early age, held at knifepoint and violated by a man she has spurned. Despite the sordid world in which she moves, she preserves a certain purity.

Fatumeh's relationship with her lover is not only a union of souls, but also a finding of self, symbolized by shadows, mirrors, and eyes. The lover proclaims to Fatumeh, "You gave/ My soul a shadow/ A silver lamp you gave me." The reasons for her abandonment remain obscure. One of the few titled poems of the sequence, "The Harem at Erechtheion," marks the end of the love relationship and suggests that Fatumeh has been sent to a harem. Driven out of the harem, she spends the remainder of her life as one of the "roofless people," selling her body indiscriminately until her miserable death.

Paradoxically, however, the sequence ends in a celebration of the love relationship. As Fatumeh says in a brief lyric, her lover once "washed off me/ My memories of me"; someday, when she washes his memories of her away from him, all obstacles between them will have been removed.

With *Guide to the Underworld*, the focus of the trilogy expands across centuries and cultures to include Greek and Roman as well as Asian motifs. As Ekelöf states in his notes to the Swedish edition, he conceived the third sequence in his trilogy as "the central arch of the ruin Diwan." This work deals with an underworld of visions and dreams, although the true underworld is not in Hades but in the so-called world of reality.

Ekelöf prefaced *Guide to the Underworld* with a complex diagram of the structure of the work. The poems are arranged in a complex numerical order under the headings "Water Earth," "Snakehead," "The Novice in Spálato," "Snakehead," and "Earth Water." The first section includes dramatic monologues and dialogues with such diverse poetic voices as those of Leonardo da Vinci, Odysseus, and the Arabian poet Khalaf-al-Akhmar. Gods from Greek mythology converse with their Egyptian counterparts in the guise of streetsweepers in Alexandria.

Like *The Diwan over the Prince of Emgión*, the first "Snakehead" voices the Manichaean concept that the Devil is not banished from Earth, for "a god who is always absent" has no power to abolish him. God and the Devil are thus active forces. In the major narrative segment of the sequence, "The Novice in Spálato," the Devil plays the part of an "angel," a term used here in the sense of prophet. He and a novice who sweeps the floor of a church become lovers. When the Devil tells the novice that light and shadow can exist only in conjunction, that good and evil are interdependent, the woman goes one step further in her reply: The world, she claims, is a "sterile realm/ of two males locked in combat." Like the Prince of Emgión, she has directed her vision toward a madonna-goddess who "lies outside this realm of lust and suffering." The experience of love has so transformed the Devil's perceptions that he realizes his wisdom cannot offer light to his beloved. The lovers become, like Fatumeh and her prince, each other's mirror and shadow. They separate, for the Devil has determined that their love shall be one of longing. This will in turn breed thirst, to be slaked by purifying water.

As the sequence moves from "The Novice in Spálato" to its final movement, "Earth Water," the kaleidoscopic screen mirrors in reverse the "peep-show of darkness" presented in the first half.

Forms and Devices

Most of the poems in the trilogy are written in free verse with sporadic rhymes, assonances, and repetitions. A peculiarity of Ekelöf's work is the absence of most stops between verses. Although exclamation marks and colons may occur, periods and commas are virtually absent. As a result, the verses tend to hang in suspension rather than to flow into larger syntactic structures. Within and among the verses is a constant play with verbal echoes and paradox, as in "Let us sleep/ Each alone/ Close to each other."

Ekelöf is fond of the surprise twist, and many of his poems are poised between contradictions. The final verses of the prefatory poem to *The Tale of Fatumeh*, for example, speak of how the lover's "disappearance remains." Similarly, a later poem in the same work begins by comparing love to a scalpel blade that cuts into the flesh. Paradoxically, the poem closes by stating, "For love there is no remedy/ Except the surgeon's scalpel." Ailment and cure are thus synonymous.

The Byzantine and Arabic-Persian content of the trilogy is reflected in its poetic forms. Throughout the first part of the trilogy, the song in praise of water subdivides the movements of the sequence. *The Tale of Fatumeh* acquires a thematic and formal division through the use of the *nazm*, a string of pearl beads, and the *tesbih*, a set of prayer beads. The final poem further elaborates this structure by incorporating a "snakehead" or dividing bead between the two series. The Arabic and Persian form of the *ghazal*, a short ode implementing monorhymed couplets, is used in poem 12 of the "Earth Water" segment of *Guide to the Underworld*. Because of the sparsity of rhymes in Swedish, Ekelöf adapts this form by ending the first verse of each couplet in *ingen*—that is, "no one"—leaving the alternate lines unrhymed. This is skillfully transposed in Rika Lesser's translation.

The Tale of Fatumeh and *Guide to the Underworld* reinforce structurally the central theme of mirroring. The former is encircled by a "framework" consisting of the two first and two last poems. Each set echoes the other verbally and thematically. A complex mirroring structure encases *Guide to the Underworld*—the titles of the segments before and after the climax, "The Novice in Spálato," are mirrored. Even in the numbers assigned to the poems this mirror reversal prevails; for example, the poems in the "Water Earth" segment move from one to thirteen, while those in "Earth Water" move from thirteen to one. The two halves, as Lesser notes in her introduction, also echo each other in poetic form. Both "Water Earth" and "Earth Water" contain two sets of narrative and dramatic poems.

Themes and Meanings

Vision is a central theme of all three parts of the Diwan Trilogy. In the first book, the "vision" of blindness leads the Prince of Emgión to "see" his ideal, the "All-Holy One," or the madonna-goddess. To "gaze inwardly," he contends, will reveal the truth of "what you saw" but which "you never saw" in the days of outward seeing. In *The Tale of Fatumeh*, love imparts vision. Seeing does not, however, imply outwardly visible reality; rather, it denotes a reality of the soul and of being as opposed to appearance. As Fatumeh's lover meditates, "And only Your shadow gave my soul/ Substance and Presence." In a reversal of the traditional roles of being and shadow, the vision of darkness becomes the vision of reality. This is once again explicitly voiced in *Guide to the Underworld*. The "real" consists of mirror images, shadows and dreams: As the opening poem of the sequence claims, the day is deceptive, while the darkness of night and dreams convey the truth of "your mirror image/ in a mirror-world." What one sees, the first cycle goes on to suggest, is "unreal in time," and "external distance" cannot be measured against the inner distance of the eye. The shadow world of dreams allows one to transcend the cruelty of life, to perceive that "love is the dream of beauty."

The symbol of this vision, which endows substance and presence to the soul, is the madonna-goddess. Her role is not that of the Christian virgin, for God is her subordinate in the mythology of the Diwan Trilogy. As the Prince of Emgión states, "The devil is god/ God is the devil"; each is a tyrant waging war on the other. Above them, viewed through the "narrow chink" between good and evil, stands the ideal, and the oar that rows one toward her is that of one's own longing. Nevertheless, she is unattainable. "Beauty and Love are there," says the Devil in his sermon, "but as expectation." The final poem of the trilogy asks: "How to release life? How to reach ecstasy of life?" The reply is as ephemeral as the vision of the divine lady. "The absurd belief in a grace is born, a flash/ Outside of life's actual conditions."

Anna M. Wittmann

DO NOT GO GENTLE INTO THAT GOOD NIGHT

Author: Dylan Thomas (1914-1953)
Type of poem: Lyric
First published: 1951; collected in *Collected Poems, 1934-1952*, 1952

The Poem

This nineteen-line lyric consists of five tercets (groupings of three lines) and a concluding quatrain (a four-line stanza). Addressed to the poet's father, it gives him advice about how he ought to die.

In the first tercet, Dylan Thomas tells his father to defy death. After the first line, however, he generalizes about old age, declaring that it should "burn and rave" against dying. This message is contrary to the usual association of a peaceful dying with good character and a virtuous life. Such an association, for example is found in John Donne's "A Valediction: Forbidding Mourning" (1633), or in Leo Tolstoy's *The Death of Ivan Ilyich* (1886).

In the second tercet, the poet begins a series of characterizations of the types of men who rage against death. Here it is wise men who defy death. Their defiance assumes a somewhat ambiguous character: They know that death must come, that indeed, according to the poet, it "is right," but they have not, in their lives, caused any great stir among humankind ("their words had forked no lightning"). Consequently they must now express that defiance which they previously withheld.

The third tercet deals with good men who cry that their small accomplishments might have shown brilliantly in a more dynamic setting. The poet asserts that they too should rage against death. The last opportunity for finding that setting has passed. The goodness of these men might have shown much more to advantage had they been able to live among responsive and appreciative neighbors.

The fourth tercet advises those who perceived and gloried in the light of inspiration and the development of genius in others and in themselves, but whose actions impeded its progress, to defy death. The poet calls them "wild men" because they comprehended the wildness that has long been associated with poets.

Thomas's last category, grave men who, near death, perceive again too late that they have not expressed their capacity for brightness and lightheartedness in life, must also rage against dying. Even blind eyes, he says, can "blaze like meteors." In a concluding quatrain, the poet asks his father to reward him and acknowledge his petition by showing the fierce tears of his rage against dying.

Forms and Devices

This poem is a villanelle, a type of French pastoral lyric not often found in English poetry until the late nineteenth century. It derives from peasant life, originally being a type of round sung on farms, then developed by French poets of the sixteenth and seventeenth century into its present form. For Dylan Thomas, its strictly disciplined rhyme scheme and verse format provided the framework through which he could express both a brilliant character analysis of his father and an ambivalent expression of his love toward him.

In its standardized format, the poem consists of five tercets and a quatrain, rhymed *aba, aba, aba, aba, aba, abaa*. In addition, the first and third lines of the opening tercet alternate as a refrain to the four following verses and become the last two lines of the concluding quatrain. Such a demanding restriction requires poetic ingenuity to maintain a meaningful expression. Here the form provides the poet with a suitable framework for his four characteristic types—wise, good, wild, and grave men—and enables him to equate these types with his father's character.

Dylan Thomas's poetry is consistently rich in imagery and metaphorical language. He seems almost to be an apotheosis of Welsh poetic creativity. The poetic spirit pervades his grammatical and figurative speech. The opening line, which also serves as the title of the work, contains the euphemistic metonymy for death, "that good night"—that is, a word associated with death ("night"), but termed "good" in order to overcome its negative connotations. The line also uses the adjective "gentle" instead of the adverb "gently," as would be customary. As a result, one finds the poet describing the man rather than the manner in which he must move, providing a tighter relationship to the poem as a whole.

The phrase "old age" may be thought of as personification, but it may also be interpreted as a metonymy (substitution) for his father. "Burn and rave" are intense expressions of the defiant stand the poet advocates against "the close of day," here a metaphor for death, as is "dying of the light" in the next line. "Dark is right" in the second stanza represents a terse acknowledgment of the intellectual recognition of death's inevitability, but the awareness that his father's words had "forked no lightning" is a rich metaphor for failure to influence the powerful but brilliant forces within society.

In the next stanza, the poet turns to imagery of the sea: The "frail deeds" dancing in a green bay present numerous levels of interpretation. On the level of the imagery itself, one glimpses a happy dance taking place in a surrealistic body of green water. On another level, the green bay seems to be a metaphorical representation of life itself, green frequently representing the vital and fertile elements of human existence. That frail deeds have failed to enter into the vital life stream seems to be the poet's judgment that his father, although a good man, had never experienced fully the joys that human life offers.

In the next tercet, singing "the sun in flight" returns one to metonymy, where Thomas conceives his father as recognizing the creative genius capable of some glorious poetic vision but stifling it, "grieving it." Such wild men must acknowledge the need to defy death. "Blind eyes" blazing "like meteors" in the fifth stanza introduces the first simile of the poem and maintains the celestial vision of the tercet before it.

In the concluding quatrain, the reader comes at last to the apostrophe directly addressing the poet's absent father, which confirms that he is the individual toward whom the poem is directed. The ambiguity of the poet's feelings toward his father is emphasized by the paradoxical second line of the stanza, "Curse, bless, me now," as well as by the "sad height" from which his father can view the poet. The height is metaphorical, implying the closeness to death and to vision of the elderly man; the sadness in the lines derives from his father's personal failure to fulfill his own high goals.

Themes and Meanings

"Do Not Go Gentle into That Good Night" is a poem reflecting Dylan Thomas's complex attitude toward his father, David John Thomas. The elder Thomas had been a schoolmaster in the grammar school that his son attended and had instilled in the young poet a love for the English of William Shakespeare and the Bible. He had himself written poems in his childhood and seemed to desire to create in his son the poet he had never succeeded in becoming. He had also become the model for the oracular reading voice that Thomas adopted for his own poetry.

That the younger Thomas held his father in high esteem appears clearly in the poem. The adjectives that the poet uses to characterize him are "wise," "good," "wild," and "grave." The first two are clearly laudatory, although in each case the virtue is mixed with disappointment that it had no wider effect on society. The wildness, however, adds a dimension unseen in the first two qualities: Its influence has somehow interfered with the poetic inspiration that it clearly comprehends. "Wild men" discover they "grieved" the "sun in flight." This statement is ambiguous; it could mean that the father interfered with the flights of genius in himself or in others, including Dylan. It could also refer to the poet himself, whose wildness led to dissipation responsible for his own manifold problems—by psychological transfer, he may be applying this to his father.

His father's gravity, however, is hardly characteristic of the son. Although the term suggests dignity worthy of respect, it connotes here a somberness that has been blind to human joy, something the poet had clearly experienced, as many of his poems indicate.

In the final stanza, the poet wants to wring from his father on his "sad height" a curse-blessing, somewhat in the mode of the biblical Jacob as he stole his birthright from Esau. In this case, the curse is the suffering rage the father must experience as he glimpses the glory of what might have been had he fulfilled his own promise; to some degree, he has transferred the rage to his son in the form of insecurity about his own achievement. The blessing is the genius he provided to his son—genius which he had himself fulfilled only vicariously—and supported with his strong sense of language and its power.

Russell Lord

DO NOT WEEP, MAIDEN, FOR WAR IS KIND

Author: Stephen Crane (1871-1900)
Type of poem: Meditation
First published: 1899, in *War Is Kind*

The Poem

"Do not weep, maiden, for war is kind" is Stephen Crane's poem about war and its aftermath. In twenty-six lines, the persona of the poem addresses the loved ones of the soldiers who died on the battlefield amid mayhem and chaos. Crane's use of blank verse is well suited for the subject of war because it lacks the harmonious patterns of rhyme and meter. The poem is composed of five stanzas, and the indented beginning of the second and fourth stanzas characterize a change in setting. While the first, third, and fifth stanzas focus on the survivors of dead soldiers, the indented stanzas graphically depict scenes of the battlefield. The refrain gives a structural unity to the entire poem as it consistently appears before and after each stanza: "Do not weep./ War is kind." This chorus of two lines helps to connect the emotional experience with the actual experience of war.

The poem begins with the pain of separation between a maiden and her lover who died on the battlefield. To heighten the tragic effect, the persona describes the last moment of the dying lover who "threw wild hands toward the sky" in a frantic state as he fell from his horse while "the affrighted steed ran on alone." A perceptive reader will note the ambivalent tone of the persona: On one hand, there is sympathy for the maiden's unfulfilled love; on the other hand, there is sympathy for the soldier's agony whose death marks a moment of escape from the painful state of psychological terror and physical injury.

In the third stanza, after the refrain, the poet presents another scene of tragic separation with the regiment's drums in the backdrop to cue the reader about a battle scene. Intensifying the emotional effect of the tragic separation, the speaker addresses the fatherless "babe." Again, the graphic description of the dying soldier as he tumbles "in the yellow trenches" suggests an ambivalent attitude on the part of the speaker. His fall in death makes a mockery of the glorious display of the regiment's flag with its eagle and flashing colors of red and gold. Marching behind this flag, the dying soldiers cannot rise to heroic heights because they are like wounded animals who are guided by instincts of rage and fear. Furthermore, the persona ridicules "the virtue of slaughter" that is exalted by the regiment as it trains soldiers to "drill and die." The ambivalence between tragic separation and a sense of relief amid a setting of death and destruction is also evoked through the contrasting images of the sunshine in the "yellow trench" of the fallen soldier's grave site and "slaughter" on the battlefield that creates a field "where a thousand corpses lie."

In the last stanza, the speaker addresses the mother of a dead soldier who is being honored as a hero by his regiment. Unlike stanzas 1 and 3, this stanza is not followed by a graphic depiction of her son's dying moment. In this instance, the refrain echoes a reminder to the reader that the last moment of this soldier must have been marked with the same tragic moment of pain and panic that is the lot of the regiment's men "who drill and die." The "splendid shroud" of the regiment evokes the contrast between the brutality of the battlefield and the relief that comes to the embattled and wounded soldiers in the form of death.

Forms and Devices

The title of the poem resonates with irony as it juxtaposes tears with kindness and invites the reader to connect the brutal image of war to a kind reality despite the brutal setting of a battlefield. Although the poet does not address the readers directly, he allows them to witness scenes of tragic separation between the maiden and her lover, between the child and the father, and between the mother and her son to enhance the ironic effect. The irony of the poem contrasts the expected reaction of the mourners who suffer the pangs of separation with the unexpected outcome for the fallen soldiers who are freed from their emotional and physical trauma by death. The pervasive sense of loss for a loved one makes the title sound like an understatement, thus announcing the ironic intent of the author. At the same time, the psychological and physical condition of the falling soldiers ridicules the notion of romantic heroism that disregards the realism of the battlefield where the presence of death can promise relief.

In addition to the contrasting images, which contribute to the ironic effect, Crane makes powerful use of symbol and simile to enhance the realism of the tragic outcome of war. Images such as the "wild hands" of the soldier mounted on "the affrighted steed" and "booming drums" symbolize the emotional state of men who are in a state of panic, anger, and fear. In the last stanza, the mourning mother's "heart hung humble as a button" is a simile reiterating the sorrow and helpless condition of a woman whose son has been snatched from her. The juxtaposition of the mourning mother's pain with the heroic farewell and "the splendid shroud" of her son frames the question of the "unexplained glory" claimed by the military's regiment. The contrast between romantic glory and the reality of war is also reinforced by a sarcastic tone as the poet personifies the great "Battle-God" with his "Kingdom" that consists of corpses.

The ambivalent attitude of the persona toward the tragic theme of separation confirms Crane's naturalist trend in portraying the changing phases and faces of natural forces. However, for Crane the natural cycle of events encompasses both benign and malignant forces that contribute to the complexity of the human condition. Because Crane incorporates nature's role in an ambivalent manner, it is difficult to blame nature as the source of tragedy in human life. In fact, the alternating shift from dialogue to description in the poem allows the poet to emphasize the ambivalence of the persona's attitude toward war. Ultimately, death appears as a tragic experience for the bereaved, yet it marks a moment of relief from pain.

Themes and Meanings

"Do not weep, maiden, for war is kind" is a poem in Crane's collection of poems titled *War Is Kind*. In this poem, Crane attempts to depict the theme of war in the emerging tradition of realism that questions the honor and glory of war heroes. Crane is a naturalist as well as a realist who repudiates the heroic tradition of Romanticism without compromising the complexity of human reality. The poem portrays the pain of separation caused by the brutality of war; therefore, Crane's criticism is directed toward warmongers and not strictly toward the overpowering forces of nature. Furthermore, most naturalists at this time depicted natural forces in biological terms, but Crane does not discount the psychological forces that connect human reality to one's physical surroundings and environment. Both the mourners and the dead soldiers must succumb to the supremacy of natural forces, yet the horror of the soldiers and the sorrow of the mourners are two different conditions resulting from war. In this short poem, Crane links sensory images and psychological realism to capture both the mental pain of the bereaved and the physical pain of the falling soldiers. The irony implicit in the title also illustrates the ironies latent in human reality. In this case, the irony exposes the hypocrisy of the mythic glory attributed to warring soldiers as well as the nonheroic demeanor of soldiers on the battlefield.

Although Crane uses the setting of war in many of his works, including his famous Civil War novel *The Red Badge of Courage* (1895), it was only a year before the publication of this poem that he personally observed war scenes. He was so strongly drawn to the setting of war that he attempted to join the United States Navy for active service in the Spanish-American War, but he was rejected. Consequently, in 1898 he became a war correspondent. In his war memoirs Crane writes, "It is because war is neither magnificent nor squalid; it is simply life, and an expression of life can always evade us. We can never tell life, one to another, although sometimes we think we can." In this poem, Crane attempts to capture the complexity of human life as he illustrates that in the face of adversity and pain neither the magnificent flag nor the squalid dust of the trenches can eliminate the tragic pain of separation experienced by those who have lost their loved ones on the battlefield. Crane acknowledges the controlling presence of natural forces, but, as a realist, his descriptions are not restricted to external objects and sensory images; instead, he strives to include human relationships and attitudes as an integral part of human reality.

Mabel M. Khawaja

DOCKERY AND SON

Author: Philip Larkin (1922-1985)
Type of poem: Lyric
First published: 1964, in *The Whitsun Weddings*

The Poem

"Dockery and Son" is a poem not really about either Dockery or his son; it is about the speaker, who is a typical persona of Philip Larkin. Larkin's stock persona is someone unsuccessful in love, someone whom life has passed by. It is frequently a mistake to confuse the persona with the poet, but with Larkin one usually senses there is no great gulf between the two.

The poem begins with a conversation between the Dean and the speaker, who is revisiting his college. Typically, only the Dean is directly quoted, not the speaker of the poem. The Dean happens to mention Dockery, who is younger than the speaker and whose son is now a student at this same college. The quoted conversation fades as the speaker remembers how he once had to explain his " 'version' of 'these incidents last night,' "—had to explain, as a student, disruptive behavior to the very man with whom he is now reminiscing. Time has passed; the speaker finds his old room, but the door is locked. He departs unnoticed on a train.

On the train, he starts to think about Dockery. He estimates that Dockery must have had a son when he was about the age of twenty. Then he tries to remember exactly who Dockery was. When he is about to reach a conclusion which threatens to be a commonplace—"Well it just shows/ How much . . . How little . . . "—he falls asleep. Even contemplating how time has passed unheeded, a life slept through, causes him to sleep through more time.

He is awakened by the "fumes/ And furnace-glares of Sheffield." Waiting to change trains, he examines his life to this point. His complacency has been jarred through the mention of Dockery and his son. He mentions that not to be married, have a son, or own property "still seemed quite natural." When he compares what he has not accomplished with what Dockery must have done, however, "a numbness registered the shock/ Of finding out how much had gone of life," of finding how different the speaker was from the others. The speaker notes that Dockery must have thought "adding [having a child, among other things] meant increase" and remarks that to himself "it was dilution."

He realizes that a life is ruled by "Innate assumptions." These are not ideals or ethical truths; rather, they are "more a style/ Our lives bring with them: habit for a while,/ Suddenly they harden into all we've got." He realizes that life is passing them all by, whether they make use of it or not, and "leaves what something hidden from us chose"; one is left with the sum of one's days, though the motivation for one's actions may be hidden even from oneself. After that, all that is left is "age, and then the only end of age," death.

Forms and Devices

Larkin is a great master of understatement, and "Dockery and Son" is a typical example of his muted mastery. Almost all of Larkin's poems make use of traditional forms, but rarely do those forms call attention to themselves. "Dockery and Son" is written as a series of six octaves, or eight-line stanzas, but only the final one ends with a period. The stanza is the ordering element on the page, but it does not structure the movement of the poem. Similarly, each stanza consists of four rhymes, yet the arrangement of the rhymes varies from stanza to stanza. The structure seems a random one, the reader being thrown from one stanza ahead into the next almost without knowing it—much like the speaker, who moves through stages in his life with little recognition except that time is passing.

One sees Larkin's real genius in the poem's pacing. For example, stanza 1 ends: "I try the door of where I used to live:"; the colon leads one to anticipate some discovery, something important enough to carry over the stanza break. Instead, the next stanza begins simply, "Locked." This one word, so strategically placed, undercuts all expectation and reinforces the non-event of the speaker's life.

Another example is when the speaker falls asleep: "Yawning, I suppose/ I fell asleep, waking at the fumes/ And furnace-glares of Sheffield, where I changed." The selection of the word "suppose" makes even his sleep seem questionable, certainly as unintended as most of his life. The reader would like some firm realization, some course of action decided upon; the words "where I changed" heighten the irony, making it obvious that only trains and not a course of life have been changed. This is driven further by the inclusion of the homely detail of eating an "awful pie." Yet just when the reader is resigned to the trivial, the speaker sees "the ranged/ Joining and parting lines reflect a strong// Unhindered moon." The railroad tracks here are certainly reflective of the lines that lives take, but the moon is something beyond. It is both strong and unhindered; it is beyond the petty facts of human lives. This sudden opening out into an image that can never be precisely defined is a notable aspect of Larkin's work, and it expresses a sense of the numinous that exists yet is denied to the certain knowledge of men. It offers less a glimmer of hope than a sense of a greater frustration.

Larkin's use of language is correspondingly subtle. When the speaker wonders about how Dockery "must have taken stock," he remarks: "how// Convinced he was he should be added to!/ Why did he think adding meant increase?/ To me it was dilution." The choice of having children, of commitment, is presented in the language of business. But, then, the title of the poem itself, "Dockery and Son," sounds much like a business. Within its seemingly prosaic surface, the language is the subtlest of poetry. The business of his life is a failed one; he has nothing, but it is a nothing with "all a son's harsh patronage."

Themes and Meanings

"Dockery and Son" is a portrait of how a chance remark brings about an awareness in the hearer of the emptiness of his life. A simple comment from the Dean about a schoolmate of the persona's having a son now at their college spurs a meditation about how unlived the persona's own life has been.

It is usually the chance remark or observation that elicits such a contemplation. The speaker was adventurous as a student; then called before the Dean, still "half-tight" in the morning after the previous night's exploits, he now stands before himself, trying to explain not what he did but what he did not do. Dockery himself is an abstraction, even to the speaker: "Was he that withdrawn// High-collared public-schoolboy, sharing rooms/ With Cartwright who was killed?" He remembers the dead but is unclear as to the living.

The speaker does say that to have "no son, no wife,/ No house or land still seemed quite natural," but the fact that others who were his juniors do have these things makes him realize the emptiness of time. In other words, it is only when comparing himself with others that the speaker realizes how little he has done. It is important to realize that this is not envy; the speaker does not desire Dockery's son, but he does see nothing in his own life that could be the envy of others. He has diverged "widely from the others."

At first he thinks that Dockery must have planned his life, must have seen "what he wanted, and been capable," but then dismisses this from his mind. There are certain "Innate assumptions" by which one acts, he decides; they go unquestioned at the time, and when "looked back on, they rear/ Like sand-clouds, thick and close, embodying/ For Dockery a son, for me nothing." There is a fatalism at work that seems as pronounced as that which can be found in some of the work of Thomas Hardy, to whom Larkin has admitted an indebtedness. As to what this force, this "something hidden from us," is, one should be loath to form too strict a definition; indeed, Larkin never does. It could perhaps even be an excuse for inaction. The poet does state, "Life is first boredom, then fear," but the next line asserts, "Whether or not we use it, it goes,/ And leaves what something hidden from us chose." Whether this vague something is a thing destined or simple biology, it is unknown, a life force that may not be life-affirming. Still, one does come back to that "strong// Unhindered moon" reflected by the "Joining and parting lines." This gives a shape to the speaker's meditation but is itself unknowable.

Robert Darling

DOCUMENTARY

Author: Claribel Alegria (1924-   )
Type of poem: Lyric
First published: 1989, simultaneously as "Documental" and "Documentary," in *Woman of the River*

The Poem

Claribel Alegria's "Documentary" is a nonstanzaic, 112-line poem about the poet's homeland, El Salvador. The poem begins by inviting the reader to become a camera in the hands of the poem's narrator, who speaks as a documentary film director. Together reader and narrator explore El Salvador, from the anthills to the harvest of coffee beans. The poem presents quick, vivid images of the El Salvadoran people, social problems, climate, food, and animal life in the same way a film or television crew might. After cataloging the characteristics of El Salvador, the poem's narrator laments the country's innocence and its inability to prosper.

"Documentary" opens by calling El Salvador a "queen ant/ extruding sacks of coffee," the country's primary export. The poem's next image is of a family asleep in a ditch, presumably exhausted from working the harvest on a coffee plantation. As a camera might, the poem shifts to another image "among trees" of "rapid,/ dark-skinned fingers/ stained with honey." Coffee berries must be handpicked because no one has yet found a way to harvest them by machine, and they must be picked quickly, just after they change from yellow to red. The juice from the red coffee berries stains whatever it touches.

Moving from the hands of the coffee harvesters, the poet contrasts "a long shot" of workers or "ant men/ trudging down the ravine/ with sacks of coffee" with the image of "girls in colored skirts" who "laugh and chatter" while they fill "their baskets/ with berries." The two images present the idea that while harvesting coffee is undeniably hard work, it is also a time of community. El Salvador's class system is also presented by contrasting images. The reader is asked to "hard focus on the flies/ spattering" the face of a "pregnant mother/ dozing in the hammock" and then "cut" to a "terrace of polished mosaics" where "maids in white aprons/ nourish the ladies/ who play canasta." The card-playing women "feel sorry for Cuba," thus foreshadowing the poem's subsequent mention of "the feudal power/ of fourteen families," or the wealthy landowners who, with the military, control the government of the fourteen divisions of El Salvador.

The poem then shifts from specific images to general ones. The village of Izalco "sleeps" at the foot of a volcano with the same name which, with "a subterranean growl," makes the villagers "tremble." Children die early in this poverty-stricken country, a fact the poem recognizes with the words "besides coffee/ they plant angels." Poverty forces women to "wash clothing" in the river that flows alongside a highway built to carry the coffee harvest. In the southern El Salvadoran town of

Panchimalco a prisoner waits to board a plane filled with "coffee growers/ and tourists." When the coffee harvest arrives in the marketplace, the narrator lists the native products, including "piles" of native fruits and foods available there. After the coffee harvest is in the millhouse, the poem winds to a close as the narrator catalogs the reasons her country is "wounded" and why it has become her "child," her "tears," her "obsession."

Forms and Devices

Alegria opens her poem with a simple poetic conceit. The reader is told to be the poet's camera and, as such, remember what the poet sees in El Salvador as clearly as the film in a camera records images. The conceit is sustained for the first twenty-seven lines of the poem and allows the poet to pun the technical terms used by photographers and film directors. For example, the reader is told to "focus" on a family sleeping in a ditch. The poet's choice of this word influences the reader to consider how, in spite of exhausting labor, it is not unusual for an El Salvadoran family to have inadequate shelter. Similarly, when the poem says to "shift to a long shot" so that the coffee harvesters appear to be a "file of ant men/ trudging down the ravine," the reader can understand how El Salvadoran men are like worker or soldier ants, spending their lives serving a central authority. The word "cut" ends the photographic conceit but not the series of images that continue through the middle of the poem.

"Documentary" is a didactic lyric poem, written mostly in iambic monometers, dimeters, and trimeters. The varying line lengths contribute to the drama of the poem. In several places the poet uses one-word lines to emphasize the most significant items in a long list: "blood/ illiteracy/ tuberculosis/ misery." Further, the poet is careful to incorporate into the poem Spanish names from the native El Salvadoran dialect for various fruits available at the marketplace. The poet lists each fruit ("nances," "nisperos," "zapotes," "jocotes"), honoring and respecting the language of the El Salvadoran people.

Alegria's poem uses not only concrete language but also concrete images, most of which involve the country's social and political circumstances. The poem mentions a funeral procession in which the participants "move politely aside" so the harvest can pass, and "a peasant/ with hands bound behind him" in Panchimalco, a town in southern El Salvador. Few metaphors are used in favor of the poet's concrete language, although the metaphors that are employed are vivid. El Salvador is a "queen ant," and an airplane is "a huge bee." The poem personifies several objects, including the volcano Izalco, which "sleeps" in central El Salvador, and coffee that "dances in the millhouse" where they "strip her,/ rape her, lay her out . . ./ to doze in the sun." These figures of speech convey a direct and frank impression of El Salvador.

Themes and Meanings

What is most interesting about the poetic conceit used in this poem is that it allows the reader to view El Salvador from the same perspective as the poet. Alegria has written a chronicle of images that is just as effective as a documentary film in its ability to bring the reader around to the poet's point of view, both visually and emotionally. As do most modern poets, Alegria uses the images in her poem as reinforcement for her perspective, her vision of El Salvador. She exhorts her reader, writing subjectively, as well as autobiographically, about the country in which she grew up. Alegria uses her poetry to re-create the struggle of the people of Central America.

The specific purpose of "Documentary" is to make the general reader aware of an obscure area of the world. Alegria's mother was El Salvadoran; the poet lived there and knows firsthand the way of life, economy, politics, and survival of the El Salvadoran people. Memory, exile, and abhorrence of war and violence characterize Alegria's poetry. The political content of her poems is not unusual for a writer from Central America. However, Alegria writes out of a deep love of life, rather than from a particular partisan perspective. The poet wants her readers to understand the value of freedom and to learn how people in every part of the world are connected.

The coffee harvest affects the lives of workers as well as consumers, and this fact is most noticeable at the close of the poem. The lines that catalog the negative side effects of coffee export—"malaria/ blood/ illiteracy/ tuberculosis/ misery"—introduce an image of the harvester's truck that "bellows uphill/ drowning out the lesson." The "lesson" is presented as though to a child learning the alphabet. However, instead of having the letter *A* represent an apple, as it does for most English-speaking school-children, it stands for alcoholism. Similarly, other letters of the alphabet stand for other social problems. By replacing the customary mnemonic devices for letters of the alphabet with names of social problems unique to El Salvador, the poet cleverly insinuates that coffee consumers are so unaware of the conditions under which the product they purchase is produced that they literally need the situation spelled out for them. Thus, the poet who bears witness to the struggle for survival in her homeland also makes her reader a witness to those struggles.

Even if readers of "Documentary" drink morning cups of coffee that do not come from El Salvador, they must ask how a cup of coffee might be maintaining a way of life they would not accept for their own family. That is the connection between the people in "Documentary" and the readers of the poem.

Ginger Jones

DOG

Author: Lawrence Ferlinghetti (1919-   )
Type of poem: Satire
First published: 1958, in *A Coney Island of the Mind*

The Poem

"Dog" is composed in free verse, a style that can preserve the blunt effect of common speech. Without either "a" or "the" preceding it, the word "dog" has a linguistically rudimentary quality that is in keeping with the poem's subject. "Dog" also spells "god" backward and thus anticipates one of the central concerns of the poem.

The poem begins with the dog of its title demonstrating that the canine is the measure of all things in its world. The first eighteen lines catalog the drunks, moons, fish, ants, and chickens that are the large and small of "his reality." They show too the delightful naïveté of the dog's view: Streetlights are "moons on trees"; fish lie on newsprint for no apparent reason; ants emerge mysteriously from holes; chickens' bodies are for sale in one place, and their strangely dislocated heads appear elsewhere, consigned, presumably, to the garbage. The dog's own qualities permeate all of his experience, measure it all, so that "the things he smells/ smell something like himself."

With the third occurrence of the line "The dog trots freely in the street," the catalog of perceptions continues, but the most noteworthy feature of lines 19 to 30 is the dog's standard of value. As the dog continues to trot through the urban scene, cows and policemen appear. Only the sides of beef, however, are of "use," since the dog can eat them. Policemen are inedible, but in the nonjudgmental world of the dog, they are neither loved nor hated.

San Francisco sights pass by as if the reader is being carried along by a canine tour train. The Romeo Ravioli Factory does not look or smell like its product, and therefore has little appeal to a dog whose preference runs to the immediate lure of a "tender cow." Coit's Tower, the memorial to the earthquake and fire of 1906, stands high on Telegraph Hill in San Francisco and has the appearance of an extremely large and imposing fire hydrant. Congressman Doyle, however, is not so imposing; he is "just another fire hydrant." The congressman's implied views do not impress the dog, who takes solace in his own "free world" and refuses to be muzzled and silent. One need not know anything specific about the real Congressman Doyle in order to infer that he would likely have objected to the dog's version of individualism and freedom. (A later version of "Dog," in Ferlinghetti's *Endless Life: The Selected Poems*, 1981, makes clear that Clyde Gilman Doyle was a member of the House Committee on Un-American activities.)

The last section of the poem, lines 47 to 84, begins again with "The dog trots freely in the street," but the poet no longer traces the stream of images passing before the eyes of the dog. Instead, what were implied political and philosophical issues earlier become explicit in the description of the general nature and significance of the dog's action. He is now a "real realist," a "democratic dog," an ontologist who will tell a tale with a tail. Lacking language, he will tell no lies and be no perjurer.

The final image of the dog with his ear turned toward the gramophone horn takes up the previously dramatized question of what one can know of reality and leaves it suspended.

Forms and Devices

"Dog" is one of a group of poems that were collected in the volume *A Coney Island of the Mind* under the title "Oral Messages" and were originally intended to be "spontaneously spoken" to jazz accompaniment. The repetition of words and phrases, an important source of formal patterns in "Dog," would be as evident to the ear as to the eye. Many of Lawrence Ferlinghetti's poems can be read with the syncopated swing of jazz or a shuffle blues, and "Dog" responds to such an approach. The poem's rhythm is not perfectly consistent from line to line, but four-stress lines predominate. Many of them, such as "Fish on newsprint," have few unstressed syllables, and such compression of stresses in the poem gives the impression of thoughts that are vivid and self-contained rather than complex, linked, and moving lyrically from one to the next. The simplicity of the language also helps convey the quality of the dog's perceptions and the confident matter-of-factness of a consciousness untroubled by irony and self-doubt.

The staggered lines, beginning with line 57, continue the earlier form of the free verse, but the eye tends to follow them from left to right and to make them single lines in the process. This is also the section in which the poet's presence is most obvious. The poem no longer describes what is perceived through the dog's eyes, but rather represents the dog's actions from the viewpoint of an observer. It does so first in the general terms of philosophy and politics, and then, beginning with "as if" in line 70, by means of a comparison with the Victor records mascot, which is an amusing but also powerful act of the imagination. The Victor dog shows that puzzlement in the face of the universe is common to dog and man, but the form and method of the dog's characterization creates irony, because it points up how unlike the dog's-eye view the poet's view is. The staggered long lines succeed in expressing a human mode of synthetic thought and speech, and the act of relating the San Francisco dog to the Victor dog dramatizes a human recognition of connection and similarity that is different from the dog's often fragmented experience.

Despite the seriousness of the poem's deepest themes, its use of dense stresses, simple language, and whimsical analogy gives "Dog" a light-hearted quality that is typical of many Ferlinghetti poems. "Dog" also contains examples of Ferlinghetti's fondness for wordplay: A "tough cop" isn't a tender meal; "Coit's Tower" is easily read as "coitus tower"; a "tail" tells a "tale"; the gramophone's answer is "Victorious"; and prolific use of the word "real" creates absurdity in a poem that makes the very term problematic and also punctures the ideal of "being realistic" that is so dear to the American pragmatic spirit.

Themes and Meanings

Ferlinghetti succeeds in creating a humorous yet troubling poem by considering what the measure of man is in a dog's life. The faith that "man is the measure of all things" frequently found expression in Renaissance poems such as George Herbert's "Man," which optimistically claims "He is in little all the sphere" and "Nothing we see but means our good." In "Dog," the Renaissance assumption that a felicitous correspondence exists between man and the world is set against the twentieth century conviction that life is absurd, that it is literally a dog's life. The modern worldview holds that no divinely sanctioned order exists, and that one can draw meaning from neither a divine presence within oneself nor a single knowable reality. "God" is in the dog, but only as a rearrangement of the letters of the word, and the dog's very nature colors whatever limited sense the animal makes of his world. He must always experience himself, not an independent reality.

Although pervasive anxiety or existential angst has usually been deemed the appropriate response to a universe without intrinsic meaning, the cheerful tone of Ferlinghetti's poem demonstrates that enervating despair is not his response. The dog's world is richly informed by the life of the senses "touching and tasting and testing everything," and the verse is energetic and confident. Intellect and language, however, are suspect; as Ferlinghetti says sardonically, the dog's knowledge of his world comes "without benefit of perjury," without the deceitful distortion of linguistic signs. The dog's meaning is not conveyed by language but by gesture—the "tale" is told by a "tail"—and, appropriately, the wordplay makes meaning and its expression identical, if only phonemically. At the same time, the singsong repetition of "real" seems to mock the very possibility of defining it in words.

Unconstrained by language and immersed in immediate experience, the dog is a four-footed member of the loosely defined "beat" movement and an exponent of its mysticism and anti-intellectualism. Not surprisingly, the more worldly political concerns of the beats also find expression in the poem. The dog's free enterprise, unmuzzled free speech, and self-reliance renew classic democratic virtues, yet the political establishment, in the person of Congressman Doyle, is antagonistic to such a pure expression of American values. Embodying American ideals in a dog deflates the conventional conception of them and gives the poem its clearest satirical and moral edge. The political establishment itself is satirically cut down to size by the not entirely subtle sexual meaning of the contrast between the phallic Coit's (coitus) Tower, which looms large and intimidating, and Congressman Doyle, who is not up to the comparison.

American ideals, however, are almost incidental targets in the poem. "Dog" is a dramatization of relativism and of multiple worldviews, and it warns against holding that any set of beliefs is universally true, including those held dear in America. So too, the dog's naïve worldview is attractive, but it does not hold *the* truth and cannot include the act of the human imagination in the final section of "Dog."

"Dog" asserts the value of wonder in the face of existence, acknowledges the yearning for a "Victorious answer to everything," questions whether a "hollow horn" or

Godless universe will provide it, and warns that, fixed in language, an absolute answer "to everything" would be dangerous anyway. That the poem "trots freely" under such a weight is to be wondered at, and that is the point, for laughter is a mark of knowing that there is more than one ta(i)l(e) to tell.

Peter Lapp

THE DOG

Author: Gerald Stern (1925-   )
Type of poem: Dramatic monologue
First published: 1987, in *Lovesick*

The Poem

Gerald Stern's "The Dog" is a free-verse dramatic monologue. In it, a dog speaks from the roadside where he lies dead. In the first third of the poem, the dog talks about his condition, explaining how he lay beside the road for hours before he died and how he looked after death. In the middle third of the poem the dog addresses the "lover of dead things" who will come to dispose of his body. Finally, the dog addresses the "great human heart" (which may be the same as the lover of dead things), asking it for forgiveness and love.

Stern is often compared to the nineteenth century American poet Walt Whitman for his sense of expansiveness and for his fondness for parallel series and hyperbole. All these qualities are apparent in "The Dog," as is Stern's attention to concrete detail. The dog, for example, describes his death with painful specificity, relating how he lay beside the road for two hours, whimpering and dying at last "by pulling the one leg up and stiffening." He details the particular look of death—"the hair of the chin/ curled in mid-air."

As the dog imagines the "lover of dead things" coming to dispose of his body, he expresses his fear that disgust may overtake the lover and cause him to push him perfunctorily into "that little valley" with his shoe, shutting out the memories of the dog in life and replacing those memories with "some other thing."

At last the dog makes a sort of prayer to "Great heart," asking that the human continue to love him and mourn him; asking him to "forgive the yapping, forgive/ the shitting"; and to recognize that the dog deserves his pity. After all, the dog has been "ruined" by his own love for the human, and for him the dog has given up his canine ways to do the tricks the human taught him.

Characteristically, Stern's tone changes in the last part of the poem, and the reader is led to consider that the dog's relationship to the human is not unlike a human relationship to God, who seems to have asked humans to give up their own doggishness, but who seem always to fail in their efforts to do so. The dog reminds the human that he has traded what he is by nature for traits of the parrot, the horse, and the lion, and he has done it all under the human's tutelage. Still, in the speaker's eye, the human remains "distant and brilliant and lonely."

As a Jewish poet, Stern has noted that he naturally brings a Jewish point of view to his work, but he is rarely explicitly religious in the sense of making theological pronouncements, a fact which should warn the reader from trying to turn this poem into an allegory of human/divine relationships. Nevertheless, the parallels are insistent enough not to be ignored.

Forms and Devices

Stern is not a formal poet; he uses free verse, and conventional figures of speech are rare in his poems. More typically he uses subjects that take on metaphoric significance as he explores them in detail. A good example is his well-known poem "Behaving Like a Jew," in which the speaker finds a dead opossum on the roadside. He says that he refuses to make self-satisfied comments about the creature's having rejoined the great cycle of nature; instead he intends to behave like a Jew in mourning the loss of the animal's quick spark of life. In the course of the poem, the reader recognizes a commentary on Jewish attitudes toward death and finally sees the opossum itself as a portrait of a Jew. Similarly in "The Dog," the significance of the speaker-dog grows out of the mounting detail about the dog itself and about the person (or perhaps persons) being addressed.

Stern frequently begins his work with a conversational tone, as he does here. "What I was doing with my white teeth exposed/ like that . . . I don't know," the dog begins, describing how he waited for death and the "lover of dead things" to arrive. The lover mysteriously carries a sharpened pencil and a piece of paper as if to catalogue the bodies it disposes of. As the dog describes the lover, Stern begins a series of parallel statements detailing the lover's fear of the dead animal. Beginning in line 13, eight successive clauses begin with "I know," "I think," "I want," or "I hope." The dog knows that the sight of death is terrifying to the "lover of dead things"; he wants the lover to touch him as perhaps he did in the past—"to touch my forehead once and rub my muzzle." The use of parallelism and repetition increases in the last third of the poem, particularly at the end, when the dog makes several metaphoric statements about himself, saying that his tongue is like a parrot's, the dog is a "rampant horse" and a lion.

The tone of the poem also changes in the last third, where the growing parallelism and hyperbole give a sort of prayerlike, even bardic, quality to the speaker's utterances. He addresses the "Great heart,/ great human heart," asking that it continue to love him, mourn him, pity him. He calls the human a "great loving stranger," asks him to forgive him for the things he has done—"yapping," "shitting"—which are natural parts of a dog's existence, and then reminds the human that the dog has given up his nature for "little tricks" that the human has demanded of him. He has become parrot, lion, and horse all for the sake of the cookie, the trivial reward of food, and he concludes by describing the human with three adjectives that underscore the human's distance from the dog—"oh distant and brilliant and lonely." Although sometimes Stern's hyperbole creates a comic effect, here it establishes an elevated and serious tone. The animal that began the poem speaking as a dead dog beside a ditch has risen to lyricism in his love for the "great human heart."

Themes and Meanings

Throughout "The Dog," the reader is invited to see a contrast between the responses of the dog-speaker and the humans he addresses. The dog suggests that the humans are unreliable; he fears that the lover of dead things will give in to the urge to push his body away with his shoe instead of caressing him. He feels sure that the lover of dead things will be frightened of him, or perhaps of the presence of death in him. In either case, the response stands in contradiction to the idea that this person loves dead things.

In the last third of the poem, the dog says "I have given/ my life for this, emotion has ruined me." That statement marks a transition; from this point on the dog considers what he has done out of love for the human. It was love that made him exchange his wildness for the qualities of a parrot, which says what it has been taught; for a horse, which carries humans and their burdens; and for a lion, whose strength in the dog operates on command. That is what the dog's emotion led him to do in order to woo the "distant and brilliant and lonely."

The dog's repeated yearning for the human's forgiveness, pity, and love—and the patterned way in which that yearning is expressed—is what leads the reader to consider the metaphoric possibilities of the dog-human relationship. The dog may be like a lover whose love is accepted or ignored by the capricious love object that has taught the dog tricks for the latter's convenience or amusement. Stern never defines the metaphor so specifically as to demand a particular reading. The love object may be a human lover, or God, or any passion which causes change in the lover. The reader notes the irony implicit in the ending of the poem, however, where the three adjectives—distant, brilliant, lonely—connote qualities that are not necessarily comfortable. Even in death, the dog seems to long to close the distance, to make the human lover less lonely in his brilliance even as the dog does the tricks he has learned out of love.

Ann D. Garbett

DOG FIGHT

Author: Charles Bukowski (1920-1994)
Type of poem: Narrative
First published: 1984, in *Charles Bukowski's Horses Don't Bet on People and Neither Do I*; revised as "dog fight 1990" in *what matters most is how well you walk through the fire*, 1999

The Poem

Somewhat confusingly, four different poems by Charles Bukowski in his prolific free-verse poetic oeuvre have the term "dogfight" or "dog fight" in their titles: "dogfight" in *Burning in Water, Drowning in Flame* (1974); "Dog Fight" in *Charles Bukowski's Horses Don't Bet on People and Neither Do I* (1984); "dog fight 1990" in *what matters most is how well you walk through the fire* (1999); and "dogfight over L.A." in *Open All Night: New Poems* (2000). Not surprisingly, as implied by this titular recurrence, the subjects of conflict, competition, antagonism, and aggression pervade these poems and Bukowski's poetry in general.

The 1974 "dogfight" is a twenty-four-line poem dealing with an actual fight between two dogs, the blue-collar speaker's and a white-collar professor's, emblematic of the social conflict between the owners or owners' social classes. The 1984, 1999, and 2000 poems all use the terms "dogfight" or "dog fight" metaphorically. The term for wartime combat between two opposing fighter airplanes, itself a metaphor, is applied in the 199-line 2000 poem to the speaker's long-term contention with a nauseatingly popular, social, liberal, pacifistic, and romantically successful intellectual and aesthete, and in the 41-line 1984 and 1999 poems (the latter a revision of the earlier, with several small but important changes in details) to battle with other drivers in the traffic-laden streets in the suburbs of Los Angeles.

The 1984 and 1999 versions are identical in several ways, including their vivid plot and characterization, often key elements in the poems of this author, who is also a successful short-story writer and novelist. The speaker is challenged by the tailgating of another driver, and a combination of drag racing and power-playing maneuvering ensues through the freeways and streets of Compton and Inglewood, to the outskirts of Los Angeles International Airport. During the struggle, a third driver, in a Mercedes, becomes part of the fray, and the poem's last three lines chronicle their changing position as the troupe approaches LAX, or Los Angeles International Airport:

> 1-2-3
> 2-3-1
> 3-2-1.

"1" is the speaker; "2" is probably the Mercedes; and "3" is probably the original tailgater. In transit, the poem covers the subjects of American values, skillfulness, power, freedom, and the paradoxes of antagonism or aggression.

Forms and Devices

Bukowski's changes in the 1999 version of the poem generally soften and somewhat dilute the style—the diction and punctuation—of the 1984 version, making the later version less racy in several senses, the terse raciness of the style corresponding with the vehicular dogfight and its protagonists. The tailgater's drawing "up against" (1984) the speaker's rear bumper is more vividly aggressive than "up to" (1999) the rear bumper; the speaker's "I can see his head in the rear view mirror" (1984) makes the repeated key feature of the main antagonist, his blue eyes, stand out more than "I can see his face in the rear view mirror" (1999). The speaker's formal level of usage, as in "I . . . engage myself upon/ his rear bumper," "he sucks upon a dead cigar," or "he is/ upon my bumper again" (1984), suggests a humorous, ironic overtone of a knightly joust amid the modern urban environment and situation, which is lost in the revision for stylistic consistency, "I . . . ride/ his rear bumper," "he sucks on a dead cigar," or "he is/ on my bumper again" (1999).

In both versions, the brevity and simplicity of sentence structure in many of the lines—for example, "I pull over. he passes, then slows. I don't like/ this"—contributes, along with Bukowski's refusal, like poet E. E. Cummings, to use capital letters in many conventional places, to the clipped, terse, familiar, colloquial quality appropriate to the racers' intensity and familiarity with their surroundings and equipment. However, these stylistic components are more evident in the 1984 version's "when I check the rear view," "make the green," "run the yellow into the red," and "LAX" and are weakened in the 1999 version's expansion for clarity "when I check the rear view mirror," "make the green light," "run the yellow turning into red," and "L.A. Airport."

Additionally, the 1984 version's commas in lines 1, 26, and 33—technically creating comma splices—and the enjambment in lines 20 and 35-37 help create the poem's racy flow, consonant with its intense subject, and the incessant rivalry, as well as suggesting the unity of the separate actions within the one experience of the one drawn-out competition; the 1999 version's substitution of periods in those same lines has a fragmenting effect, emphasizing the individuality of the separate actions in the race.

In the 1984 version, the metaphor of fire, appropriate to both warfare and the anger of the conflict, is continued, along with multiple puns, when the speaker shifts into the vivid present tense to "fire across 3 lanes of/ traffic, just make the off-ramp . . ./ blazing past the front of an inflammable tanker"; in the 1994 version, "cutting in front" is substituted for "blazing past the front," damping some of the humor, liveliness, and wordplay. The connotations of competitive outmaneuvering in the repeated "inner" and "inside" in the speaker's references to getting the "inner lane" and being able to "flash by inside of him" in the 1984 version are weakened in the 1999 version's substitutes "inside lane" and "flash by to the right of him."

Themes and Meanings

The poem conveys Americans' loves of the automobile, competition, skill, and freedom. The poem's inclusion and focus on the blue-eyed driver sucking "upon" the dead cigar and on the Mercedes driver suggest that the competitive instinct extends

from the middle to the upper class in American society. The strong, sometimes collo-
quial verbs—"ups it," "pull back," "pulls out," "hit the blinker," "veer down," "flash
by"—suggest the enthusiastic vigor of the rivalry, which also has overtones of com-
bat, as in the poem's title. Competition's relation to power is suggested not only by the
detailing of the jockeying for position (many of Bukowski's poems deal with horse
racing), including the poem's last three-line numerical report, but also by the actual
word "power" in the 1984 version, in the speaker's report of crossing a traffic signal,
"they make it as I power it and switch back ahead of them/ in their lane"; "power it"
and "in their lane" are deleted in the same lines of the 1999 version.

Paradoxically, the competition, because of its shared emotions and artfulness in
driving, creates a team: Three times the speaker uses the simile "we are as a team,"
and he reports near the poem's end "we are moving in perfect anger" (1984) or "we
are moving in perfect formation" (1999). In contrast to the sort of hostile, warlike de-
humanizing identification of adversaries by epithet rather than name—"blue eyes,"
"the Mercedes"—the anaphora of "we are driving with skillful nonchalance/ we are
moving in perfect anger/ we are as a team" near the poem's end reinforces the idea of
how the combatants have become unified.

Although the poem raises questions about the borderline between prose and poetry
because of its lineation, and about poets' revisions of the same poem and which ver-
sion is final or preferable, the themes of the joy of skill and the joy of freedom are un-
questionable. A relish is conveyed in the repeated technical terms of driving and in the
speaker's statement "we are driving with skillful nonchalance," the formal level of us-
age of "nonchalance" suggesting the elevation from art and emotion. The speaker's
turning on and then turning up his car radio during the fray, his revelation of the wider
and wide-open setting in "we are/ moving through a 1980 California July" (or "mov-
ing through a 1990 California July"), and that "now we are running 1-2-3, not a cop in
sight" all express the exuberance and joyous freedom often considered distinctively
American and often celebrated in the poetry of Charles Bukowski. Amid the variety in
American society, represented by the empty school bus and the parked vegetable truck
that are obstacles to the racers, the vehicular racers are moving through, in some
sense, wide open spaces, free from the intrusion of police authority or many of the
rules of the road. The speaker may have lost the dogfight, but it has been enjoyable,
and as Bukowski often explicitly indicates in his other poetry, he has gotten a good
poem out of the experience.

Norman Prinsky

DOLOR

Author: Theodore Roethke (1908-1963)
Type of poem: Lyric
First published: 1943; collected in *The Lost Son and Other Poems*, 1948

The Poem

Theodore Roethke's "Dolor" is a thirteen-line lyric poem that explores the persona's response to a life constrained in a grindingly repetitive institutional environment. The title of the poem sets the mood of sorrow, grief, and pain, which is totally unrelieved, as the accumulated details of office life bear down on the speaker of the poem.

The first eight lines of "Dolor" form a brutally graphic picture of a typical 1940's office. The persona is buried under the detritus of office life: pencils, pads, folders, paper clips. The sheer weight of inanimate objects is felt as unbearable. The proliferation of these objects—their omnipresence, their replication, their ability to smother—is both claustrophobic and quietly stultifying. Nothing breaks the sterility of this environment. No plant or family photo enlivens a desk. No untidiness testifies to the presence of messy, complicated, disorderly human beings. This is a place where the things are in control, and even the things themselves are filled with dolor.

In the final five lines, the despair of the poem deepens. The institutional environment becomes more than just boring, sad, and oppressive; it becomes a menace to life and soul. White-collar work, usually thought of as innocuous, or irritating at best, is likened to a more obviously life threatening occupation: mining. The narrator of the poem imagines the very dust on the walls of the institution burying the workers under a film as lethal as silica. The workers' passivity, their habitual inaction, allows them to be buried alive—in situ—their premature aging adding the last touch to their lack of individuation. They turn literally and figuratively gray, nondescript, lifeless, and soulless in their supposedly safe chairs.

It is hard to imagine a more critical indictment of the nine-to-five life. It is probably not surprising that Roethke, son of a greenhouse gardener, a man sheltered in the halls of academe, a lover of words and women, a drinker and a man at large, a poet with a romantic and sometimes mystical bent, would have such repugnance for the regimen and the lack of variety that he saw in the institutions around him.

What is surprising is that Roethke could skirt the imitative fallacy and manage to write about boring and mundane things in such a salient and powerful way. It is in poems such as "Dolor" that Roethke's attention to method and poetic strategies shows most clearly.

Forms and Devices

At first glance, "Dolor" appears to be an Italian sonnet, but it lacks that important fourteenth line. Although the argument of the poem begins with a descriptive octave, it finishes with only a five-line analytical resolution. Roethke has chosen to both unify and give music to this poem in ways that are distinctively his own and that suit the theme of this poem perfectly. If repetition in life is the thematic enemy in this poem, it is also Roethke's major poetic strategy. Roethke follows the famous dictum of the architect Louis Sullivan, who asserted pithily, "Form follows function," just as he takes his cue from Alexander Pope, who made clear in the eighteenth century that in poetry, "The sound must seem an echo to the sense." Repetitions of all kinds drive the poetics of "Dolor."

In the first descriptive octave, personification, the giving of human attributes to inanimate objects, is used to drive home the pervasive mood of the poem. The reader is told of the "sadness of pencils," the "dolor of pad and paper-weight," "the misery of manilla folders," and the "pathos of basin and pitcher." The repeated attribution of negative emotions to the paraphernalia of office life highlights the persona's ability to strongly empathize, to achieve John Keats's "Negative Capability," as well as to set up the irony of objects full of feeling in a place where humans are increasingly objectified. The concreteness of these first images, and the persistent use of personification, is characteristic of Roethke's early poetry, although that attention to detail was mostly trained on the organic world in famous poems such as "Root Cellar," and "Orchids." Here it is used to explore the malaise and aridity of conventional workaday life.

The repetitions in "Dolor" are also strongly auditory. Roethke uses alliteration both to hold his poem together and to give it a strikingly musical quality. Line after line, Roethke repeats initial consonant sounds: "pad and paperweight," "misery of manilla," "public places," "finer than flour." Here the form of the poem clearly echoes the sense. However, the repetition of sound elements is also more sophisticated than mere alliteration. In the opening line, "I have known the inexorable sadness of pencils," the *s* sounds fold back on each other, creating a poignant kind of beauty for the ears out of sorrow for the soul.

The sheer weight of descriptive detail in the poem is another repetitive technique. The first lines are nearly Whitmanesque in their insistent listing of objects. No detail is too insignificant to be savored. The line "Endless duplication of lives and objects" is nearly an unnecessary afterthought by the time the reader has made his or her way through all the concrete details of the opening. One of Roethke's great poetic gifts is the ability to make things, in all their specific particularity, mean something greater than themselves.

In the final section of the poem, it is metaphor that asserts the meaning of the poem most clearly. The "dust from the walls of institutions" is, after all, "more dangerous than silica." The office workers are surprisingly in no less peril in their neat, clean offices than miners are in their dirty back-breaking tunnels. There is, it seems, a black-lung disease of the soul, which is both chronic and finally fatal, the symptoms of which can clearly be seen on "the duplicate gray standard faces," sitting blissfully unaware at their desks. The dolor of the poem is unrelieved. There is no joyful resolution or even a small glimmer of hope for those toiling in conventional jobs, victims of a civilization that gives things the importance of people and treats people like things.

Themes and Meanings

Roethke, who won the Pulitzer Prize in 1954 for his 1953 book of poetry *The Waking: Poems, 1933-1953*, is universally regarded as one of the major poets of the twentieth century. His canon is rich and varied. He began his career consciously imitating such great poets as T. S. Eliot, Keats, William Wordsworth, William Blake, William Butler Yeats, and W. H. Auden. Later he acknowledged his debt to his contemporaries Louise Bogan and William Carlos Williams. At the end of his career, he was firmly in the camp of the American mystic poets such as Robert Bly and James Dickey. Yet his great achievement was the ability to synthesize all these influences and remain quintessentially Roethke, a poet of nature, love, and the omnipresent dread of death.

"Dolor" is quite an anomaly in the midst of his greenhouse poems in his second book of poetry, *The Lost Son and Other Poems*. While well-known poems such as "Root Cellar" sing the praises of fecundity and the tenaciousness of life in this volume, "Dolor" looks forward to Roethke's later concerns with the debilitating effects of aging and the inevitability of death. "Dolor" does not, however, reach the sometimes forced transcendence of his much later poetry, in which mysticism alleviates some of the pain of mortality. "Dolor" is caught somewhere between the poems like "Cuttings," inspired by Roethke's father's greenhouses, where the struggle and muck of life are crowned with the glory of new life, and one of his last cycle of poems, "Meditations of an Old Woman," which ends, with surprising optimism, "In such times, lacking a god,/ I am still happy." In "Dolor" there is only the recognition of the sadness, the uniform repetitiveness of life. It presents a locked room with no avenues of escape. It is a straightforward description of the problem of midcentury American institutional life as understood by one of its most observant and trenchant poets.

Cynthia Lee Katona

DOMINO

Author: James Merrill (1926-1995)
Type of poem: Lyric
First published: 1982; collected in *Late Settings*, 1985

The Poem

"Domino" consists of three sestets, each following a strict rhyme scheme (*abcacb*). The title of the poem presents not only the ostensible subject of the poem—Domino sugar—but also hints at other esoteric levels of meaning. In addition to representing a trade name, the title can be read as *domino*—the dative possessive case of the Latin *dominus*, meaning "lord, master," or "clergyman"—or as the name of the black game pieces marked with white dots. With this rich title, James Merrill signals the economic and theological concerns that he will explore in the poem.

On a more transparent level, the poem begins with the sugar speaking smugly of its privileged role at the table of the elite. Assuming the cool, haughty tone of its epicurean consumer, the sugar boasts that its "Delicious, white" grains are "refined" into "crystal rudiments" of a perfection that keeps them "From wholly melting in the tea."

Despite the sugar's aloofness, in the second sestet the poet reminds the reader that sugarcane is grown in a distant world in which suffering prevails: "Often a child's lament/ Filled the infested hut." The plantation owner's guilty return to check on her neglected workers ("Doña Pilar flew back for Lent/—Had she been inhumane?") does not soften the poem's harsh contrast between the worlds of the first and second stanzas.

In the third stanza, the sugar's wry voice returns to express its disdain for "History's health freak," who "appraises" society's "mess" or mealtime habits and "begs/ That such as we be given up." "The drainer of the cup," the sugar archly predicts, will "miss those sparkling dregs" when he is left with only the "Outpouring bitterness" of unsweetened tea.

This simple surface treatment of Domino sugar, however, masks Merrill's subtle treatment of at least three other subjects in "Domino": a Marxist challenge to the exploitation of workers, a presentation of the sacraments of the church (specifically, the Eucharist and penance), and a theological dispute over the renunciation of everything associated with the body.

Forms and Devices

In "Domino," Merrill creates a tight network of multiple levels of meaning, making at least three distinct readings of the poem possible beyond the poem's dialogue between the elite consumer of Domino sugar and the suffering workers who produce it. Merrill achieves this complexity by packing the texture of his lines with puns based on homophones, the recovery of root meanings, and obsolete versions of words. Merrill creates multiple meanings, each of which sustains one of the levels on which the poem can be read.

After introducing his complex title, the poet injects a pun in the poem's first line, based on the variant meanings of "refined": "reduced to a pure state" (as the sugar is), "purified or free from moral imperfection" (the result of penance), and "freed from what is coarse" but also "reduced in vigor and intensity" (both applicable to the privileged class). In the first stanza, the poet also uses "raised" to mean "cultivated" (in the case of the sugar cane), "bred" (for the privileged class), and "leavened" or "resurrected" (referring to the Eucharist wafer and the Body of Christ). Also in the first stanza, Merrill creates a pun on "word" and uses "stirred" to suggest not only the mixing of the sugar crystals in the tea but also an agitation of emotions (to which the detached privileged class remains unreceptive).

Merrill's most complex use of a pun occurs in the second sestet, when he coins the name "Pilar" in the line "Doña Pilar flew back for Lent." Most significantly, the name suggests the word "pillar" (from the Latin *pila*) with its rich array of meanings. In addition to presenting Doña Pilar as a "pillar" or "main supporter" of her capitalist society, the word suggests two other meanings: "a whipping post" (hinting at the exploitation of the sugarcane laborers but also the symbol of Christ's passion, as in Christ's "pillar of flagellation") and "a platform on which women publicly appear as penance" (connecting to the theme of Christian sacraments). Doña Pilar's name also resonates with the homophone "piller" (an obsolete form of which is "pillar") meaning "robber, despoiler, plunderer." This sense of her name is consistent with the poem's Marxist theme.

In the final stanza, Merrill introduces two more puns to sustain the poem's multiple meanings. In the first line, "mess" denotes "confusion" and a "meal" (and perhaps resonates with "messiah") but also represents an obsolete form of "mass." Thus Merrill creates a pun similar to Gerard Manley Hopkins's use of "May-mess" in "The Starlight Night" to sustain his treatment of the sacrament of the Eucharist. Finally, Merrill introduces "dregs" to suggest not only the "sediment" of sugar at the bottom of the teacup but also "the most undesirable part" (the owner class, in a Marxist's mind) and the "last remaining part" (or the body of Christ left on the cross).

Themes and Meanings

Merrill develops the Marxist theme of the conflict between laboring class and owners throughout "Domino." Merrill introduces the privileged consumer/plantation owner in the poem's first two lines: "Delicious, white, refined/ Is all that I was raised to be." These members of the elite are rational (with "crystal rudiments of mind") and detached (never "wholly melting," "however stirred").

The second stanza presents the mass of black sugarcane workers who support the few white owners (like the black background on the domino pieces). Doña Pilar, who visits the exploited laborers living in "infested" huts, represents the owner class ("Doña" comes from the same Latin source as *domino—dominus*, meaning "lord or master") and brings with her all of the meanings associated with "Pilar" (flagellation for the workers, public penance for herself, and additional plundering). In the final sestet, "History's health freak," presumably Marx, after "appraising" the "mess" of class exploitation, recommends that "such as we be given up" or overthrown. The owner/consumer concludes that the world will miss "those sparkling dregs." This final oxymoron makes Merrill's central point: To a Marxist, what sparkles most with accumulated products and refinement is "the most undesirable part" of the economic system.

Another reading of "Domino" reveals Merrill's treatment of the theme of the church's sacraments of the Eucharist and penance. The Eucharist wafer—"Delicious, white, refined"—speaks in the opening stanza. The phrase "all that I was raised to be" suggests the resurrection of the body of Christ and the unleavened state of the wafer. The wafer maintains a distinct role in the sacrament from the wine or "tea": "Still keep—however stirred—/ From wholly melting in the tea."

The second stanza focuses on the sacrament of penance. Amid the suffering of the laborers, Doña Pilar brings with her name a platform for penance and the "pillar of flagellation" (as reminder of Christ's suffering) to help her atone for her past inhumanity. The final stanza begins with an appraisal of the "mess" or Mass and ends with a reference to draining the Eucharist cup. In the final stanza, "History's health freak" (Christ, perhaps) calls for penance—"Outpouring bitterness" accompanied by certain things being "given up."

Finally, in "Domino," Merrill explores a subject closely related to the theme of sacraments—the clerical debate over the worthiness of the body. The title of the poem itself suggests the order of Dominicans. The Dominicans, in their challenge to the heretic Albigensians, insisted upon the sanctity of matter and of the ordinary people. The reminder that even Christ appeared in corporeal form is presented in the first stanza: A true "feeling for the word" keeps Christ's body ("Delicious, white" and "raised") from "wholly melting into the tea" (*t*-shaped cross). The second stanza reminds the reader that ordinary people demand the ministering that Saint Dominic prescribed and also that Christ had a human birth: "Often a child's lament/ Filled the infested hut."

In the final stanza, the heretics ("History's health freak") examine the Mass and demand that the church give up "such as we"—that is, both the common people of the second stanza and the Eucharist wafer that is transubstantiated into the Body of Christ. For the Dominicans, "the drainer of the cup"—a member of a church without the wafer as part of its Eucharist and without attention to the poor—would "miss those sparkling dregs." "Dregs" means both "most undesirable part" (the commoners or "reprobates") and "last remaining part or vestiges" (the body that is left after the departure of the spirit). Once again, the concluding oxymoron points to the tensions in the poem: What seems the "dregs" to the heretics is "sparkling" and sacred to the Dominican friars.

Janice Moore Fuller

DORDOGNE

Author: Gunnar Ekelöf (1907-1968)
Type of poem: Lyric
First published: 1951, "Dordogne," in *Om hösten*; English translation collected in
  Songs of Something Else: Selected Poems of Gunnar Ekelöf, 1982

The Poem

"Dordogne" is an unrhymed poem in free verse divided into three short stanzas. The title refers to the town situated in a mountain range in southern central France where some of the oldest remaining Paleolithic paintings were found in the nineteenth century. This was the first discovery of prehistoric European paintings, and it had a tremendous influence on art and art history. The poem's title gives the reader an unusual sense of geographic location while indicating the poem's historical content. The syllogistic, three-stanza structure of the poem suggests a technique that one often finds in Gunnar Ekelöf's poetry. First, he contrasts the past and the present, prehistorical and contemporary man, in stanzas 1 and 2. Then, in the last stanza, he draws a paradoxical truth and meaning from the juxtaposition.

Written in the third person, the poem includes no personal or subjective perspective. The tone is distanced, descriptive, and reaches an intensity only in the third stanza, in which the meaning of the poem becomes explicit. The poem begins with a brief glimpse of the present-day town that notes only one feature: an unquenchable source of water whose origin remains a mystery. This notion of something mysterious and hidden functions as a bridge to stanza 2 and the prehistorical reality of Dordogne.

In the second stanza, the poet narrator takes the reader underground and back to prehistoric times. The narrator contrasts the water, which he connects to an ice age, to the thunder and visions of the undiscovered, dead prehistoric people who still keep their secret. Ekelöf had a profound distrust of the fate of modern man and was probably sympathetic to prehistoric man. Only dead people are mentioned in this poem; undiscovered and undisturbed, they remain central to both the modern world and to the poem. Alluding to the visions of herds, Ekelöf makes the first connection between the prehistoric people and animals in stanza 2, an association he further develops in stanza 3.

The third stanza opens with an explicit thematic statement: "Their death is an Eden." The narrator explains this paradoxical belief through an allusion not to the spirits of the dead people in the cave, but to the spirits of dead and dying animals. The connection between nature and prehistoric people is a key to the poem's meaning: In a state of nature, death is paradise because death provides life. The dead become food for living organisms and ensure the continuation of life. Therefore, the narrator depicts life's circle—"to be mounted and to mount/ to hunt and be hunted, eaten and eat"—as both a positive and a negative one. Life is paradox, and only through paradox can a sense of truth be reached. In nature, both "the Lion and the Lamb" must be respected.

Forms and Devices

"Dordogne" is constructed around an opposition and an identification between life and death. The poet illustrates this paradox through a skillful use of contrasting fragments and of personification: The inanimate cave landscape seems mysteriously alive in contrast to the peaceful and dead prehistoric people who rest in the underground.

In the English translation, the use of personification begins already in the first stanza, with the reference to the mysterious source of water as "a vein of water/ that never gives out." This translation reflects the Swedish second stanza, in which Ekelöf uses the clinical phrase "blood veins of water" to describe the water source. Ekelöf's word in the first stanza is a neutral description of a source of water. This difference in the two versions is slight, however, and only serves to emphasize earlier what becomes of paramount importance later on in the poem.

The second stanza furthers the notion of the landscape being alive when it describes the caves as "the mountain's lungs of chalk and cold." This landscape is alive, a breathing, pulsating organism in which thunder "breathlessly hunts." Nature has purpose, direction, and life. The use of personification serves to create the mysterious aura that surrounds these caves and their water system. It also serves to prepare the ground for those who rest within this system, who remain a part of and apart from this living nature: the dead. The poem hinges on the contrast between their stillness and nature's violent life.

"Dordogne" is composed in a series of fragments. These fragments have an accumulative effect, which gives the poem its strange luster and vividness. As is so often the case with modernist poetry, the fragments do not necessarily add up to a comprehensive whole; rather, they function in a suggestive manner, and their meaning can only be grasped through their relation to one another. In the introduction to *Songs of Something Else*, Leonard Nathan and James Larson write that Ekelöf "once compared a good lyric poem to a bit of radioactive matter. The capacity to give off energy, he said, was less a matter of perceived content than of relations among particles making up the content, the nuances and dissonances set up between meanings which radiated lines of force."

The reader often feels the radiating quality of a lyric poem such as "Dordogne" without being able to account for it. Ekelöf's analogy of radiation in many ways illustrates how his poetry works. For example, the second and third stanzas provide a formidable contrast between the stillness of the dead, who remain undiscovered and undisturbed and who still hug their well-kept secret, and the violent agony of the great stag. To a large degree, the power of these images stems from the contrast, a contrast that also prepares the reader for the concluding paradox about the relationship between the lion and the lamb. The Edenic harmony that nature provides must be sought through the proverbial antagonism between the lion and the lamb.

Themes and Meanings

"Dordogne" is a poem about an ancient intimacy with nature, which, according to the poet, humankind has now lost. This intimacy allowed prehistoric people to participate in the natural rhythms of death and life without feelings of alienation, and it allowed them to create an art that can still astound people tens of thousands of years later. The Stone Age, to which these cave paintings belong, dates from about 750,000 years ago until about 15,000 years ago. The poem is a quest poem in which the modern poet is seeking to find not only the closeness to nature but also the creative capacity that is the well-kept secret of the ancient people. The hidden source of water becomes an image for both natural and artistic life.

The belief that ancient people had access to more wisdom and a more unified life closer to nature is common enough in modern poetry. The Romantic poets of the nineteenth century were fascinated by history and what they saw as a more genuine human experience. Great modernist works such as James Joyce's *Ulysses* (1922) and T. S. Eliot's *The Waste Land* (1922) interweave stories of contemporary people with ancient myths and tales. Ekelöf, who translated Eliot into Swedish, explored various aspects of this theme. In the poem "The Gandhara Medallion" (the Swedish original is in the collection *Färjesång*, 1941), he explores the thematics of life in death and death in life. That poem ends, "Dead you are while living/ living you are/ dead." The manner in which we die becomes for Ekelöf a crucial way to explore the difference between modern humankind and prehistoric people. Ekelöf often returned to the necessity of reaching peace and harmony through the inclusion and experience of hell and the Devil, of reaching transcendence through degradation. The Holy Spirit and human salvation, he maintained, can only be found among the poor and the sick. Yet he finds little salvation in modern death and warfare—the result, he says, of the technocratic approach to life, "The last testament of the undeveloped heart." In grotesque poems such as "Yorrick's Skull," Ekelöf depicts human bodies that are fragmented and torn apart. He describes the violent deaths of modern warfare: people without legs and arms, arms and legs without bodies. The wholeness, the intactness of the bodies resting under Dordogne indicates, in contrast, that these people conceived of a harmony in death and life that escapes modern man.

A related theme is the archetypal human desire to find salvation through a descent underground. Ekelöf pursued this theme in other poems, as well, such as "Voices from Underground" (originally in *Om hösten*, 1951) and "Thought-Poems" (originally in *Opus incertum*, 1959). "Dordogne" belongs to this group of quest poems and affirms its tradition. The poem itself bears witness to the success of the quest: Without disturbing the ancient people or ruining their secret, the poet-seeker has created a poem. Its paradoxical meaning partakes in and restores ancient human wisdom.

Gunilla Theander Kester

DOVE, THAT STAYED OUTSIDE

Author: Rainer Maria Rilke (1875-1926)
Type of poem: Lyric
First published: 1950, as "Tauben, die draussen blieb," in *Briefwechsel in Gedichten mit Erika Mitterer 1924 bis 1926*; English translation collected in *Correspondence in Verse with Erika Mitterer*, 1953

The Poem

"Dove, That Stayed Outside" (or, as translator Stephen Mitchell titles it, "Dove That Ventured Outside") is a short poem of twelve lines divided into three stanzas of four lines each. The meter of the original poem is predominantly dactylic, and the German rhymes *aabb, cdcd, eeff*. The poem is graphically striking, because it is divided vertically down its center by a break in the text, a blank space that runs through the middle of all three stanzas. This blank space reinforces the central theme of the poem, which is separation. The two parts of the poem are physically separated from one another by the blank space, but they nevertheless form the unified whole of the text.

This text is part of an exchange of letters, written in the form of poems between 1924 and 1926, between Rainer Maria Rilke and the eighteen-year-old Austrian writer Erika Mitterer (the Erika to whom the poem is addressed). This particular poem was dated August 24, 1926, only four months before Rilke died. It is in response to Mitterer's discussion of surviving a near encounter with death after a serious operation. The "festival of praising" referred to is the joy of praising life itself after a brush with death.

The first stanza describes the feeling of the dove that remains outside the dovecote and that is, therefore, united directly with the night and day. This dove that remains outside knows the mystery of the dangers and fears that threaten its flight. Stanza 2 looks at the dove that remains within the protection of the group, spared any fear and never endangered. This secure dove cannot know the tenderness of fully inhabiting a heart that one has won back from some danger. The more adventurous dove of stanza 1 gains a freedom by exploring its own abilities outside the group's protection.

Stanza 3 begins by generalizing about the condition of daring the unknown by suggesting that "everywhere" stretches itself out over "nowhere"—that is, that all of existence can only be explored by risking the encounter with nothingness or oblivion. The same sentiment is reiterated in the last image of the poem, that of the ball. The ball tossed out into space, the audacious ball, which leaves the hand as the dove leaves the dovecote in stanza 1, returns to the hand with an additional weight for having been tossed forth. Like the dove and the ball, humans gain by risking the unknown.

Forms and Devices

As in many of his poems, Rilke uses a strong central image from the natural world (the dove) to serve as a metaphor for some aspect of the human condition. In this case, the dove's activity of remaining outside the protection of the group, of daring to fly free even in a frightening and threatening world, gives the dove a sense of self-worth and a new feeling of its own capabilities. The dove who always remains in the secure position never gains this additional level of consciousness. In the same way, the human being who risks exploring terrifying parts of existence will gain a new understanding of himself or herself. The experience of being forced out over the abyss occurs unavoidably when one is ill or facing death. Although the experience may be terrifying, the person may gain a much broader understanding of existence as a whole for having dared to remain in danger.

The final image of the ball being tossed up and caught again repeats this basic metaphorical message. Just as the ball gains weight and momentum from having been thrown forth, human beings tossed into uncertainty by fate regain their stability with an added sense of comprehension and a deepened consciousness of the value of the world. A sick person who regains his or her health may well value it more than a person who has never been endangered.

The dove and the ball also share the act of flight—either voluntary (as in the case of the dove) or involuntary (as in the case of the thrown ball). Rilke often depicts flying as a risky business, full of both fear and freedom. The dove and the ball must leave the earth in order to overcome the sky; in a similar way, man must be willing to leave his familiar terrain in order to conquer new levels of consciousness and experience. All those who venture forth return enriched. Rilke reinforces this idea by rhyming *Wiederkehr* (return) and *mehr* (more, an increase) in the final two lines of the poem.

In another clever device, Rilke embodies this act of being separated by visually cleaving his own poem in two. After beginning each line, he throws the second half of the line out of its normal position by leaving a number of blank spaces between the two halves. This has the effect of tossing half of his poem out into space in the same way that the ball is tossed in the closing lines. The effect of cutting the lines in two is emphasized by the meter of the poem in German. The two syllables bordering the blank spaces are usually both stressed. This results in a breaking of the line rhythmically as well as visually into two half-lines.

The split down the center of the poem recalls the division of the dove from the dovecote and man from his normal security. It may also call to mind the threat of being cut off, sundered from life itself when one is ill. In any case, the visual effect of the ruptured poem makes one think about separation as a theme. The dove must be willing to remain separate from the dovecote, and the ball must be willing to separate from the hand in order to gain new insight and weight. A person must be willing to leave the safety of others in order to reach new levels of awareness. The frightening aspects of separation thus take on a new positive value in Rilke's poem.

Themes and Meanings

In this poem (and indeed in many of Rilke's poems), it is extremely difficult to separate poetic devices from themes. Major themes of the poem include the positive aspects of separation, the gains to be had from risking one's safety, the insights one gains from being thrown into the dangers of existence, the ways in which one achieves a fuller consciousness by looking at the abyss of nothingness. In its most trite form, one might think of Rilke's major theme as "nothing ventured, nothing gained." He expands that cliché, however, to something more like "everything ventured, all of existence gained."

Only four months before his death, Rilke was forced to contemplate these themes as he approached his final separation from life and his own confrontation with nothingness. Having survived several serious bouts of illness, he realized that human consciousness can be heightened by such an experience. He returned from each illness with a new sense of insight. The poem thus encourages its readers to face their own dangers with a sense of self-confidence and hope. Like the dove and the ball, human beings can gain from the separations they are forced to endure or bold enough to seek. This view puts a more positive light on the prospect of facing death. It gives the reader the hope that that separation too might yield as yet unimagined benefits, a hope that even this split might provide a new and unexpected wholeness as the poem creates a totality and unity despite the visual fracture that seems to break it open.

In a letter to Arthur Fischer-Colbrie eight months earlier (in December, 1925), Rilke articulated the theme of this poem in more discursive language. In a passage about the seven-year break in his poetic production that made Rilke fear that he would never write again, he happily asserts:

> "That a person who through the wretched difficulties of those years had felt himself split to the core, into a Before and an irreconcilable, dying Now: that such a person should experience the grace of perceiving how in yet more mysterious depths, *beneath* this gaping split, the continuity of his work and his soul reestablished itself, . . . seems to me more than just a private event; for with it a measure is given of the inexhaustible stratification of our nature, and how many, who, for one reason or another, believe themselves ripped apart, might draw from this example of possible continuation a special comfort."

In this passage, Rilke has the vision to perceive the wholeness that can contain the rents of existence. The poem, too, creates new unity and insight by daring to create a visual rift that helps to convey wholeness and hope.

Kathleen L. Komar

DOVER BEACH

Author: Matthew Arnold (1822-1888)
Type of poem: Dramatic monologue
First published: 1867, in *New Poems*

The Poem

"Dover Beach" is a dramatic monologue of thirty-seven lines, divided into four unequal sections or "paragraphs" of fourteen, six, eight, and nine lines. In the title, "Beach" is more significant than "Dover," for it points at the controlling image of the poem.

On a pleasant evening, the poet and his love are apparently in a room with a window affording a view of the straits of Dover on the southeast coast of England, perhaps in an inn. The poet looks out toward the French coast, some twenty-six miles away, and is attracted by the calm and serenity of the scene: the quiet sea, the moon, the blinking French lighthouse, the glimmering reflections of the famous white cliffs of Dover. He calls his love to the window to enjoy the scene and the sweet night air; there is one element out of tune with the peaceful scene, however, and the speaker strongly urges his love to "Listen!" to the rasping sound from the shingle beach as the waves, flowing in and out, drag the loose pebbles back and forth. This repetitive sound underlies the otherwise peaceful scene like background music and suggests to the speaker some unspecified, unrelenting sadness. To this point (line 14), the poem has been essentially straightforward description.

In the second section, the speaker (presumably grounded in the classics as Matthew Arnold was) is reminded that the Greek tragic dramatist Sophocles had heard the same sound in the Aegean and it had suggested to him the turbid ebb and flow of human suffering, which had been the dominant subject of his plays. (The precise passage referred to in Sophocles is obscure; several have been suggested.) The poet and his companion—or perhaps the "we" of line 18 is more generalized—are also reminded by the sound of a related but somewhat different thought.

Like the sea, Faith (principally Christianity) once girded the world, like an attractive, bright-colored scarf tightly binding all together. Now, however, the sea of faith is receding; the power of religion to give unity and meaning is waning, leaving behind only the chill wind whistling over the desolate beach. The imagery of the last four lines of this section indicates that the loss of faith is not simply unfortunate but also results in a great sense of emptiness and sterility.

In the final section, the poet turns from the troubling scene to his love, almost in desperation, seeking to find some meaning and stability in a world that is otherwise a void, and cries out for them to be true to each other, because in the vision of the poet, there is nothing else possible to give meaning to life. The world, which is apparently beautiful and new (recalling the opening six lines), is in fact not so. The world can offer none of the promises it makes: joy, love, light, certitude, peace, help for pain. What the world is really like is a battlefield at night where soldiers rush about, pursuing and firing at shadows, unable to tell friend from foe; it is a dark plain "Where ignorant armies clash by night." This famous final image of the confused battle was probably inspired by Thucydides' description of the battle of Epipolae in *Historia tou Peloponnesiacou polemou* (431-404 B.C.E.; *History of the Peloponnesian War*, 1550).

Forms and Devices

Though a dramatic monologue, "Dover Beach," Arnold's most famous poem, has notable meditative and lyric elements. The poem makes no particular attempt to follow the clipped, elliptical, semi-conversational style of the more realistic monologues of Robert Browning, but rather presents a more meditative poem, dominated by three extended images that not only carry the meaning of the poem but also provide much of the emotional and imaginative impact.

The first image mixes sight and sound and occupies the entire first section of the poem. The poet begins with a broad general view from the horizon, coming closer to that which is in the forefront of his view, the sea meeting the moon-blanched land, whence comes the disturbing sound. The deceptive calm of the opening lines is undercut by the grating surf on the beach. The deliberately plain opening, a common poetic practice in Arnold, emphasizes nouns and verbs and their emotional impact. It is only in the fourteenth line, with the mention of "an eternal note of sadness," that there is any indication that the reader will be exposed to anything more than a simple description, that in view of what follows one shall have to reorient oneself to the significance of the initial description.

The second dominant image in the poem is in lines 25 through 28, expressing the emotional impact of the loss of faith. The individual words add up—melancholy, withdrawing, retreating, vast, drear, naked—re-creating the melancholy sound of the sea withdrawing, leaving behind only a barren and rocky shore, dreary and empty. These images, emphasizing the condition after faith has left, present a void, an emptiness, almost creating a shudder in the reader; it is perhaps a more horrifying image than even the battlefield image with which the poem closes.

The last important extended image closes the poem; it is a very common practice for Arnold to supply such closing, summarizing images in an attempt to say metaphorically what he perhaps cannot express directly. (Such closings are to be clearly seen in "The Scholar-Gipsy," "Sohrab and Rustum," "Tristram and Iseult," "Rugby Chapel," and others.) The calm of the opening lines is deceptive, a dream. Underneath or behind is the reality of life—a confused struggle, no light, nothing to distinguish good from evil, friend from foe; it is the result of the thought suggested by the sound of the surf. The poem makes clear that one is not viewing this battlefield as from a distance; one is in the middle of the fight.

Arnold reinforces the impact of these images with an often subtle but evocative use of sound and syntax. The convoluted syntax of lines 7 through 14, coming as it does after the plain statements of the opening, reflects not only the actual repetitive sound of the scene but perhaps also the confusion and lack of certainty in the poet's own mind. The first fourteen lines may well also suggest a sonnet, since this gives certain appearances that it is a love poem. While the rhyme scheme and line length do not conform to the sonnet tradition, the poem is divided into octave and sestet by the turn at the first word of the ninth line, "Listen!" As if to further emphasize this line, which begins with "Listen!" and ends with "roar," it is the only line in the whole poem that does not rhyme.

Themes and Meanings

The prose work of Matthew Arnold, addressed to a more general audience, attempts to suggest to those of his day some relatively public, institutional substitute for the loss of the unifying faith that men once shared, most notably what Arnold called "Culture." Arnold's poetry, however, is more personal and ultimately less assured. Virtually all of Arnold's poetry is the record of his personal search for calm, for objectivity, for somewhere firm to stand.

As a broad generalization, the poem presents the common opposition between appearance and reality; the appearance is the opening six lines, which turn out to be a dream, while the reality of life, which the poet accepts, is the desolate beach and the confused battlefield. The poem also presents the eternal conflict between the wisdom of the heart and the wisdom of the head. The heart is attracted by the pleasant appearance of the view from the window, but the head is forced to take heed of the eternal sound of the surf, which says something entirely different. It is notable in the poem that the poet does not make a clear choice between the two; in fact, he accepts that the world is the way his reason tells him. The problem is how to reconcile these apparently irreconcilable forces. The answer given, tentatively, is that perhaps true love between two people can somehow supply meaning in a world that is still filled with confusion and struggle.

In "Dover Beach," Arnold is doing two things: chronicling and lamenting the loss of faith and seeking a substitute, here the possibility of human love for another individual. (In other poems, Arnold suggested other substitutes.) Arnold firmly believed that Christianity was dead. His reason and his knowledge and investigation of such mid-Victorian intellectual trends as the Higher Criticism of the Bible and quasi-historical concerns about the historical Jesus had convinced him that a reasonable man could no longer believe in Christianity. Yet Arnold's heart and instincts told him, not that Christianity ought to survive, but that humankind desires and indeed must have something in which to believe in order to truly live, to be truly human. Humankind wants something which can give force and meaning to life, which the modern world with its science and commercialism cannot supply. Arnold's best-known expression of this problem is in "Stanzas from the Grande Chartreuse," where he finds himself "Wandering between two worlds, one dead,/ The other powerless to be born." The dead world is Christianity, the world powerless to be born is the modern world with its deceptive attractions.

Though on one level one may call "Dover Beach" a love poem, the possibility that human love and communication can somehow make the loss of faith and certitude bearable (because it will not make the world go away) is really given short shrift. The images of sadness, melancholy, and desolation dominate the poem, while the possibility of love gets no more than two short lines. Even those two lines are overwhelmed by the emotional impact and vividness of the final image. The effect of the poem would seem to emphasize that the possibility of love is tentative at best, while the poet cannot seem to purge from his consciousness his horrifying vision of human life.

Gordon N. Bergquist

THE DOVER BITCH
A Criticism of Life

Author: Anthony Hecht (1923-   )
Type of poem: Satire
First published: 1960; collected in *The Hard Hours*, 1967

The Poem

In "Dover Beach" (1867), one of the most frequently anthologized texts in all of English literature, Matthew Arnold created a monument to Victorian angst over cosmic instability and the erosion of faith. Standing by the shore at the southern edge of England, the poet, bemoaning post-Darwinian doubt, turns to the woman beside him and proclaims that the only consolation and certainty remaining in a violent, desolate universe is their love for each other.

In "The Dover Bitch: A Criticism of Life," Anthony Hecht offers an irreverent but resonant sequel to the familiar Arnold poem. The unnamed narrator of Hecht's revision presents himself as a straight-talking acquaintance of the bombastic Arnold. Offering a dramatically different reading of the situation in "Dover Beach," he suggests that the beloved woman on whom the poet counts as the last bastion of constancy is in truth vulgar and unfaithful. He even admits to occasional casual sexual trysts with her.

In appropriating Arnold's high-minded poem to the sensibilities of a smart aleck, Hecht is offering a comic lesson in narrative perspective, a reminder that, however authoritative the proclamations in "Dover Beach" appear, there are alternatives to the way its speaker sees the world. The woman addressed in Arnold's poem is treated as part of the theatrical scenery, not as a sovereign consciousness with thoughts and feelings of her own. Hecht's speaker, however, is most intent on trying to represent her point of view. Reducing Arnold to a literary prop, he attempts to characterize her reactions to the Victorian poet's ardent rhetoric during their night at Dover Beach. Hecht's speaker claims that, far from being enamored of Arnold or inspired by his grandiose speech, she had more mundane matters on her mind, like what his whiskers might feel like against her skin. "The Dover Bitch" explains that she became angry at Arnold for ignoring her as a living, sensual woman and for using her as a mere pretext for his florid oratory.

"Dover Beach" is a monument to the "high seriousness" that, in an 1880 book called *The Study of Poetry*, Arnold extolled as a criterion for great poetry. Hecht's revision is an exercise in drollery. In contrast to the studied formality of "Dover Beach," written in four stanzas of carefully organized blank verse, "The Dover Bitch" is composed in a single twenty-nine-line stanza of free verse that simulates the nonchalance of vernacular speech. Like a casual conversation, the run-on lines seem to ramble, and instead of concluding the poem merely halts.

Forms and Devices

"So there stood Matthew Arnold and this girl," begins the anonymous speaker of "The Dover Bitch," a cheeky man who does not himself pretend to "poetry" but addresses the reader bluntly in the unadorned English of the streets, a language ostensibly so frank that it does not shy away from the tactless word "bitch." The speaker's consistent preference for colloquial over fancy language reinforces his claim to be a candid alternative to Arnold's specious magniloquence. Filled with casual utterances such as the expletives "so" and "well now" and the contractions "I'll," "it's," and "mustn't," Hecht's speaker offers the illusion of verbal spontaneity—and thus sincerity—in contrast to the evasiveness of Arnold's meticulously contrived clauses.

The speaker's apparent ability to summarize all of Arnold's elegant words in barely three lines is an implicit attack on the older poet's verbosity: "Try to be true to me,/ And I'll do the same for you, for things are bad/ All over, etc., etc." is presumably what Arnold would have said had he shared this speaker's honesty and his knack for getting directly to the point. The "etc., etc." is devastating ridicule of "Dover Beach" for being redundant, as if one need not pay much attention to exactly what Arnold is saying beyond his banal affirmation of faithful love in a treacherous world.

The subsequent account of the woman's reactions to Arnold remains colloquial and sassy, suggesting that she shares the speaker's impatience with Arnold's decorous, evasive oratory. Repetition of the sloppy, slangy intensifier "really" ("really felt sad," "really angry," "really tough") distances her further from Arnold the fastidious stylist. The line that informs readers of her resentment at being addressed "As sort of a mournful cosmic last resort"—another comic reduction of Arnold's elegant poetry—is abruptly and comically followed by the judgment that this "Is really tough on a girl, and she was pretty"—an assertion in very simple English of very simple truths that Arnold's exquisite proclamations seem to ignore. The woman deploys a vocabulary including "one or two unprintable things," obscenities that are inconceivable within Arnold's chaste and earnest poem. The speaker seems, again, to suggest that there is a greater honesty in plain, even profane English.

"She's really all right" is the speaker's final, unpretentious, and tolerant judgment. In a loose, hedonistic society where encounters are casual and occasional, he is not ashamed to admit that, neither presuming nor desiring any exclusive claim to her attention, he meets her about once a year. Arnold lamented his inability to rely on anything in this bleak universe except the woman standing beside him, and although Hecht's speaker exposes even that faith in personal love as deluded, he characterizes her as "dependable as they come." It is faint praise, since "they" evidently do not come very dependable at all, but the speaker seems willing, all in all, to settle for much less—the merely human—than Arnold is.

The final line of "The Dover Bitch" is a nonchalant non sequitur, a further affront to the tradition of the well-made poem. "And sometimes I bring her a bottle of *Nuit d'Amour*," says the speaker, in an afterthought that reinforces the image of an ordinary man speaking without premeditation. *Nuit d'Amour*, the name of what is evidently either perfume or wine, answers the woman's longing for "all the wine and enormous beds/ And blandishments in French and the perfumes," a physical longing that Arnold's metaphysical abstractions leave unsatisfied. By contrast, Hecht's speaker gives her *Nuit d'Amour*, which means "night of love" and provides an alternative, carnal version of love in answer to Arnold's abstract meditations.

Themes and Meanings

For all its mockery of Arnold, Hecht's dramatic monologue is a tribute to the power that its predecessor continues to exert. Moreover, for all its irreverence, "The Dover Bitch" is nevertheless a love poem, though it is a poem about love without illusions—as if that were not a contradiction in terms, as if love were not irreducibly itself an illusion. As an alternative to the elevated but perhaps empty sentiments that the speaker in "Dover Beach" proffers his companion, Hecht's speaker offers a kind of love that is candid and carnal, and all the more ardent for his acceptance of his beloved's imperfections. While Arnold can love the woman standing beside him on the coast at Dover evidently only by elevating her into a disembodied philosophical principle, Hecht's speaker embraces concrete love by embracing a woman who is alive in an imperfect body, one "running to fat."

In *The Study of Poetry* Arnold called poetry "a criticism of life," by which he meant not an attack on, but a disinterested examination of, the subject as it is in itself. Hecht echoes the phrase in the subtitle he attaches to "The Dover Bitch," as though the poem that follows is, in contrast to Victorian obfuscations, going to allow readers to examine life for what it is in itself. Hecht's appropriation of the phrase "a criticism of life" is perhaps also a coy play on the contemporary sense of criticism as deprecation, as though the shabby world of materialism and lust celebrated by the speaker is a sorry disappointment.

The speaker may be somewhat self-deluding when he presents himself as a clear-eyed modern man impatient with Victorian sublimation. Hecht published "The Dover Bitch" in 1960, just before a wave of feminism swept over American culture. The poem at first seems more sexually enlightened than its nineteenth century predecessor, not only in its recognition of the claims of the libido but also in its refusal to treat a woman as mere appendage to her male companion. However, just as in "Dover Beach," the woman on the strand remains unnamed and voiceless. Hecht's poem imagines what is going on in the woman's mind while she listens to Arnold on the beach, but it refuses direct access to that mind, filtering it instead through the words of the male speaker, who persistently reduces her to "this girl." Though he poses as a champion of liberation, he controls her thoughts and feelings. Hecht suggests that, though the speaker prides himself on seeing through Victorian delusions to the tangible realities of the here and now, materialism and cynicism are simply another set of illusions to which people cling as a stay against cosmic erosion.

Steven G. Kellman

A DRAFT OF SHADOWS

Author: Octavio Paz (1914-1998)
Type of poem: Narrative
First published: 1975, as *Pasado en claro*; English translation collected in *The Collected Poems of Octavio Paz: 1957-1987*, 1987

The Poem

Octavio Paz's *A Draft of Shadows* is a long poem in free verse. It contains more than three hundred lines and is divided into nineteen stanzas. The title immediately calls attention to an important motif in the poem: the movement or breath of hidden or elusive meaning. *A Draft of Shadows* is written in the first person; the narrator takes the reader on a personal and intimate journey, a journey or quest whose goal is as much to determine the nature of poetry as it is to discover the meaning of life.

Immediately, the poem concerns itself with moments of inspiration or illumination—what James Joyce has called epiphanies. Such experiences are mystical, brief, and filled with meaning. The second stanza introduces the problem of divided thought, of the opposition of culture and nature, and, by implication, natural language and experience and artificial language and experience. The narrator/poet seeks pure, natural experience to translate into life and verse. To accomplish this end, the poet explores his personal life and the lessons offered by religions.

The poem also raises immediately, in the title and in the first line, a concern with obscured light. There is a deliberate dislocation of the images of the self and of language in order to provide a new vision of truth. Therefore, linguistic and imagistic struggles occur throughout the poem. Beginning in the first stanza, there is also an attempt, which is surrealistic in nature, to restore the word, language, to an original purity. Such a concern with the restoration of language suggests a larger goal of moving beyond the temporal and spatial barriers that traditionally frame the human condition. The poem also contains a persistent interest in transcendence through subjectivity and introspection, which leads the narrator and the reader through realms of the unconscious and ultimately to truth.

Paz shifts back and forth between personal and universal experience. This shifting is intimately connected with Paz's concern with the double, since the double acts as a result of epistemological uncertainty: Behind seemingly simple appearances lie complexity and plurality. The double is also implicit in the poet's awareness of life's anguish and hopelessness. Doubt and temporal concerns, which enter *A Draft of Shadows* immediately, through both the title and the "two worlds" of the first stanza, draw the poet into a labyrinth that cannot be easily navigated. This difficulty in navigation contains, however, the possibility of revelation.

At the end of the poem, Paz reveals that the quest, the journey, of the preceding stanzas has been internal. The sights and sounds and understanding that this quest has provided are the results of a personal insight, and the narrator attains an elevated state of consciousness in which the shadows of the title of the poem envelop the words of the poem and the narrator.

Forms and Devices

The quest metaphor is latent in much of Paz's poetry, including *A Draft of Shadows*. This quest, which may be described as a search for heightened sensations, brings to the poem an element of utopianism, since it is founded on the presumption that human beings are capable of much more than they at first seem capable of doing or feeling. Furthermore, this quest or journey is primarily an inner one. It is undertaken by the active imagination and translated into poetry by means of inspiration and reflection. Therefore, in terms of Paz's theory of poetry, the poet does not see so much as invent, by using his heightened imagination. This act of invention, which is encountered in the poem in images of breath and inspiration, is also aimed at restoring language to its original purity.

A Draft of Shadows, like much of Paz's poetry, also contains a tension between conventional reality and poetic vision. This concern brings Paz into line with the Romantic William Blake. Heightened sensual experience and a return to innocence can be achieved by means of poetry, which is innocent (if its language is purified). This kind of innocence is opposed to culture and learning. Therefore, the child is the model for this natural innocence, since a child is a natural explorer. Childhood is, for Paz, usually a symbol for a lost paradise.

Perhaps the most important device the poem utilizes, however, is motion as evolution. The narrator's consciousness searches throughout the poem for answers and breakthroughs that will give life meaning. He is seeking a pattern of myths that will eternalize life and, by extension, poetry. So, throughout Paz's work, traditional mythologies are used as vehicles for specific poetic inspirations and glimpses of truth. Paz may use the symbolism, for example, of Christianity and the Nahu religion, Greco-Roman myths, Aztec myths, Brahmanism, and Buddhism. Paz retains, however, especially in *A Draft of Shadows*, a love for Mexico, for its sights and sounds and smells.

A Draft of Shadows also reflects Paz's interest in Surrealism. The poem is dedicated to two of Paz's Surrealist influences: André Breton and Benjamin Péret. *A Draft of Shadows* echoes a Surrealist exploration of the whole self by taking into account the individual, especially individual fantasies and dream worlds (which come to represent a better, more primitive experience).

Paz also makes extensive use of assonance and alliteration throughout the poem. This concern with the sounds of poetic language can be ironic, in which case the play of words not only calls to the reader's mind varieties of associative meanings, but also creates a polyvalency that in turn engenders ambiguity. Such an atmosphere fosters unusual images and verbal experimentation.

Finally, another important motif running throughout *A Draft of Shadows* is that of the imprisoning effect of time. It is the creation of myth that enables the human being to transcend time and to find meaning in life. This is why Paz is so interested in the myths of other cultures and other historical periods. There is also a sense generally in Paz's poetry—and this is very important in *A Draft of Shadows*—of the work of art, the poem, creating its own eternal moment: an awareness by the artist of a new, higher consciousness that exists apart from time. The emergence of a poem on a piece of paper, the emergence that Paz is so conscious of in *A Draft of Shadows*, is a magical act, similar to the creation of myths by a religion.

Themes and Meanings

Underlying much of Paz's poetry is a generalized myth about nature. This myth can be conceptualized as involving an opposition between good (the natural) and evil (the artificial). In many respects, Octavio Paz can be viewed as a Romantic poet, and his poetry often contains the theme of a painful separation from nature and a yearning to be reunited with nature. Such a reunification frequently involves a return to instinctive behavior, and it is often expressed in images involving a restoration of innocence.

In Paz's work, it is culture that usually forces human beings away from nature, since culture usually prizes intelligence rather than emotion. The only certainty in those of Paz's poems that reflect this theme of innocence is that which is provided by the senses. For the senses, experience is the most important criterion. In such an emphasis on sensory experience, Paz is similar to the poet Arthur Rimbaud. Rimbaud was disenchanted with the analytical, literary characteristics of the poetry of his time, and his poetics sought to recover the validity of sensual experience through sensual experience (usually excess). Both Paz and Rimbaud consider poetry to be a kind of knowledge of the self. For both, only the heightened senses can permit human beings a glimpse of truth.

The narrator, Paz, as a modern poet, is also a kind of Janus figure. He looks within himself throughout the poem and finds a disorientation that reflects the human condition. Then, looking around outside himself, the narrator sees a culture and society that are lacking in meaningful and fulfilling beliefs and myths. In a sense, the chief concern of *A Draft of Shadows* is the creation—or, rather, recreation—of myth, of the archetypal forms that primitive human beings relied upon intuitively for meaning. Such a myth is liberation through poetry, which belongs to the life-death-rebirth pattern that is basic to most religions. The myth of the return to a purified life after death formalizes the spiritual and physical aspects of life, and so formalizes the creation of a poem after difficult struggling.

Death is always present in the landscape of *A Draft of Shadows*, where light is obscured and obstructed by shadows. It is a land of rocks and scrub but most of all a land of language, of words on a page. Self-consciously, the narrator writes about the act of writing, the ways in which the words conflict and obscure the sights and feelings they are meant to reflect. *A Draft of Shadows* is very concerned with the transparency of language. So, in an important way, *A Draft of Shadows* is a kind of poetics that deals with the difficulties the poet encounters while trying to control his idiom. Words become a challenge on two levels: first, there is the imaginary, which can fill words with the spiritual and transcendent; second, there is the technical concern of poetic language, which twists and remakes language to suit specific ends. These two challenges are frequently at odds with each other, creating conflict and paradox in the poem.

Whenever *A Draft of Shadows* turns its attention to the environment, to stones and lakes and trails and goats, it reflects the narrator's interest in Mexico and a suppressed maternal tradition. The landscape in *A Draft of Shadows* contains violently antagonistic elements, a reflection of Paz's perception of Mexico. The poem reveals a suppressed violence in its opposition of passion and the fear of death.

David Lawrence Erben

DREAM HORSE

Author: Pablo Neruda (Neftalí Ricardo Reyes Basoalto, 1904-1973)
Type of poem: Lyric
First published: 1933, as "Caballo de los sueños," in *Residencia en la tierra*; English
translation collected in *Five Decades: Poems: 1925-1970*, 1974

The Poem

"Dream Horse" is a short poem in free verse; its thirty-six lines are divided into six
stanzas of varying lengths. The title suggests that the poem concerns itself with the
agency of dreams. On reading this difficult poem for the first time, the reader's im-
pression almost certainly will be that the poem incorporates dreamlike images to fur-
ther its examination of reality and the imaginative world as well as the ideas of disinte-
gration and regeneration.

The first stanza begins with the speaker referring to his own reflection, his "looking-
glass image." The speaker's narcissistic vision of himself, "with its passion for papers
and cinemas, days of the week," is an illusion, a simple reflection in a mirror. His iso-
lation is evident as he peers into this mirror to gain a sense of wholeness and self-
esteem in an otherwise hellish life. The speaker refers to his "hell's captain" and says
that he will write "the clauses, equivocally sad," that will trigger a variety of emotions.

The attention of the speaker is directed toward his daily life as he "drifts between
this point and that," searching for the words that will lend some order to his depressing
existence. He absorbs the words of the common people around him with a self-exor-
cising attentiveness, hoping to find relief from his meaningless routine. A note of sur-
prise is added when the speaker states that the advice he hears might be "glacial and
deadly." Apparently, his life allows no other choice. The speaker likens his predica-
ment and the advice he hears to "sorcery."

The third stanza marks the beginning of the speaker's dream sequence. A firm con-
nection is made between the speaker's creative powers and his ability to dream. Once
asleep, he sees a "country spread out in the sky," with "a credulous carpet of rain-
bows." The positive quality of this vision quickly gives way to "crepuscular plants"
and "a gravedigger's rubble." In order to reach this creative land, horrors must be en-
countered and overcome. The speaker is tired as he approaches the "rubble." Just be-
yond the freshly exposed soil, which is "still moist from the spade," is "a bedlam of
vegetables," where he will dream, although the nature of the dream is far from certain.

A retrospective note enters the poem as the speaker examines his reaction to the ob-
jects that he encounters on a daily basis. He seems to be suspended between two realms:
the world of systems and the world of chaos. He wants "deference," but he revolts
against certain commonly cherished items and beliefs, smashing "attractive extremes."
The speaker longs to find a place beyond the measure of time—not life or death but a
nurturing creative realm. The dream state allows him to experience this realm, but this
state is temporal, and its lack of permanence momentarily disheartens him.

Suddenly, in stanza 5, it is morning. An exclamation point signals a temporary victory. The air is colored with "a milk-heavy glow." The speaker has successfully transcended normal existence and has reached a creative dimension in which he finds himself immersed in a rejuvenating light, one that is clear and pure but tangible. He mounts one of sunrise's "red horses," invincibly soaring over churches and eluding "a dissolute army," two symbols of authority. His creative vision has brought him full circle. He has returned triumphantly; his mount's eyes "raze the darkness," and the horse carries him homeward.

The last stanza contains the speaker's thoughts about his nocturnal experience. The affirmative end to his travels in a world suspended between life and death has given him some hope. He feels that with "a spark of that perduring brightness" he will be able to claim his inheritance and pass his illumination on to the world.

Forms and Devices

The power of dreaming permeates Pablo Neruda's "Dream Horse." The very nature of the dream state connects the speaker and the reader to the world of imagination. Poetry is dependent on imagination and frequently assumes dreamlike qualities. Throughout the poem, the reader is presented with the rather ambiguous dreamworld of the speaker. The reader is likely to interpret the speaker's visions in an orderly and meaningful way, yet the imagination can be unpredictable as well as unfathomable. Night, which is typically feared, becomes an ally and offers endless possibilities. The speaker cannot harness his vision, but he attempts to present it in poetic lines for consideration. The actual structure of the poem represents a fragment of a dream vision that does not invite closure but encourages an evolving interpretation.

Imagery plays an important role in the poem. The speaker's creative self becomes his "hell's captain." The everyday advice that the speaker must patch together comes from "the nests of tailors." Rainbows become "credulous carpets," violets "drowse," and dawn is likened to "red horses." The free use of personification and metaphor, and the unusual juxtaposition of words fit nicely into the speaker's dreamworld, where the unusual becomes accepted if not ordinary.

The use of enjambment adds to the natural flow of the speaker's dream state. Dreaming resists absolutes; parameters and definition give way to flexibility. The reader is pulled from one image to the next, sometimes without break. The fluidity of the lines and their images enhances the freedom the speaker finds in his creative world.

At the conclusion of the poem, the speaker mounts his red horse and soars above the world, an allusion to Pegasus, the mythical winged horse that also represents poetic inspiration. As the speaker joyfully flies, the reader senses his momentary exaltation. The fact that the speaker has experienced something that is beyond the reach of most people is apparent as he claims that with this power he will create work that will give him his rightful inheritance. This statement ties "Dream Horse" to other poems, such as Samuel Taylor Coleridge's "Kubla Khan" and John Keats's "Ode on a Grecian Urn," that deal with the function of imagination, multiple realities, immortality, the creative vision, and the power of poetry.

Themes and Meanings

The function of time plays a key role in "Dream Horse." In his quest for creative fulfillment, the speaker finds his daily life mundane and tiresome. The reality that is founded on real time is viewed as restrictive. The speaker desires to remove himself from his reality and its measured systems and to enter a more abstract dimension, best represented by his dreamworld. His vision brings him into contact with a temporal, chaotic state that supplies the speaker with a supernatural creative energy, something that suggests an otherworldly state in which normal time does not function. Poetic knowledge is gained by his contact with the dream state, but the speaker's desire to remove himself from the confines of time is not entirely possible. One way that the speaker can reach a place unaffected by time is through the immortality of his lines. Poetry itself is the product of his contact with another realm, and poetry is the way for the speaker to transcend his mortality.

Clearly, "Dream Horse" possesses a strong oneiric, or dream-related, element. The speaker vacillates between his depressing everyday existence, a life that offers little but decay and disintegration, and the power of his dream state, an abstract realm that can be life-sustaining and regenerative as well as chaotic. The speaker's reality is not a pleasant one. He finds little with which to entertain himself except his own "looking-glass image." He listens to the solutions offered to him without much faith. His troubling life can never be rewarding, so he must reach beyond its boundaries. The speaker's quest for "a symmetrical time beyond measure" indicates that the downward spiral into disintegration might be preventable. His creative quest leads him to a place that brings a guarded hope. The poem moves from despair to elation and introspection as the speaker undergoes a subtle transformation. Regeneration is possible, especially regeneration through the creative act. At the conclusion of the poem, the speaker's pronouncement indicates that he might be able to end the cycle of decay and bring a renewal of spirit to himself and humankind.

The power of creativity is apparent in the poem. The speaker seeks a state that will free him from an unproductive life, but his desire to rid himself of his life's bonds is not an end in itself: The speaker desires a union with a state that will permit him to create. His early solipsism is not an indication that he desires only a hedonistic escape from his meaningless existence. His intent is to add to life rather than to subtract from it. His supernatural nighttime experience is the wellspring of his creative energy. He seeks to bring this force, if he can control it, to bear on his creative work.

The quest of the speaker parallels humankind's quest. He longs to find meaning in a confusing world, and although the speaker's quest is tied to the imagination and creativity, one of his goals is to achieve philosophical insight. This desire to locate a realm outside conventional reality is not unusual—ultimately, the speaker's desire to find something that will enrich his life and art reflects humankind's fundamental (and universal) desire to find meaning and illumination in a confusing modern world.

Robert Bateman

A DREAM OF A BROTHER

Author: Robert Bly (1926-   )
Type of poem: Meditation
First published: 1986, in *Selected Poems*

The Poem

"A Dream of a Brother" consists of twenty lines divided into five unrhymed quatrains written on an iambic pentameter base. That this is a dream poem, or a dreamed meditation, is made immediately clear both by the title and in the first line: "I fall asleep, and dream. . . ." This fact is important structurally and thematically. Bly has said that he began the original version of what finally became this poem by imagining his own childhood as having been made up of two individual personalities, "one of whom had betrayed the other." It is, therefore, not surprising that the poem begins with another instance of betrayal by alluding to the Old Testament story of Joseph and his brothers. In the first stanza the speaker dreams that he shows his father a "coat stained with goat's blood," a clear reference to the biblical story. In the second stanza, he says, "I sent my brother away." Having banished his brother, as Joseph's brothers did him, the speaker enfolds the biblical allusions into a quintessentially American context: "I heard he was . . . taken in by traveling Sioux."

There is a strong break after the third stanza. This is not surprising, since the two rather distinct sections of this poem come from two totally different sections in an earlier, much longer, poem entitled "The Shadow Goes Away," published in *Sleepers Joining Hands* (1973). Although in the two final stanzas Bly merges the times and places he has alluded to in the opening stanzas, these stanzas are much more personal and immediate, much more literal and specific than the first three.

The fourth stanza begins by referring to a rural high school (like the one Bly himself attended) and ends, apparently years later, in a large city (Bly lived in New York for a time). The betrayed and abandoned "brother," described as having been taken "to the other side of the river," is not missed until readers are suddenly told, "I noticed he was gone." Since the dream imagery is still in place at the end of the poem, one wonders whether this "brother" is exclusively the literal brother he seemed to be earlier or if he may now be primarily a substitute brother. He may be a "double," or an imaginary brother, buried within the speaker's own psyche and rediscovered only later in life.

In the fifth and final stanza the speaker, depressed, thinking of death, sits on the ground and weeps. "Impulses to die shoot up in the dark" near him. These impulses, like rays of light in the dark room of a dream, seem to suggest something positive, even if it is still somewhat vague or dreamlike. The poem ends with a single-line sentence that attempts to catapult the reader—as it apparently has the speaker—into a moment of insight or illumination: "In the dark the marmoset opens his eyes."

Forms and Devices

"A Dream of a Brother" had a complicated composition and publication history. In an introductory note in his *Selected Poems* (1986), Bly reports that he rewrote the poems from *Sleepers Joining Hands*, "some in minor detail, others in a larger way." "A Dream of a Brother" is one of these largely rewritten poems. Indeed, it has been culled from two separate, rather disparate, parts of the much longer and thematically quite different poem, "The Shadow Goes Away"—which itself was only the first section of a very long free-verse poem, "Sleepers Joining Hands," the title poem in Bly's book of the same name.

In addition to the fact that "A Dream of a Brother" is only one fourth as long as "The Shadow Goes Away," it is also a much more formal poem, although Bly eschews the use of a strict metrical pattern and other more formal poetic devices, perhaps for the obvious reason that such devices would seem to be inappropriate in a dream poem. Instead of such devices Bly relies on the more informal devices of juxtaposition, allusion, and imagery to organize and control his poem. The poem is also organized through the use of comparisons and contrasts. Some of these, such as the comparison between Joseph and his brothers and the speaker and his brother, are explicit, while others, such as the comparison between a literal brother and an imaginary one, are merely implied.

The poem is further built around three dominant dichotomies, each of which makes use of its own set of allusions, even though the imagery overlaps from one allusion to the next and from one stanza to another. These comparisons and contrasts, dichotomies, doubled-up allusions, and complex images bind the poem together structurally; they also come together thematically in the vivid and somewhat enigmatic reference in the final line of the poem. Allusion, startling juxtaposition, and "deep images" (Bly's own term) are devices that Bly uses in many of his poems. The deep image—which sometimes occurs as a non sequitur, at the end of a poem, or even as a kind of afterthought to the rest of the poem—is intended to connect the physical world with the spiritual world. Bly uses it to shock the reader into recognition or illumination. In the case of "A Dream of a Brother" the introduction of the marmoset (a small monkey) at the very end of the poem is important to Bly's theme; it also binds the other elements of the poem together.

Themes and Meanings

Since "A Dream of a Brother" is a dream meditation, it need not conform to the logical conventions of waking reality, and Bly exploits this possibility to the fullest by juxtaposing and drawing together disparate images and allusions. The parallel between the biblical story of Joseph and his brothers is particularly significant for the theme of the poem because Joseph was a dreamer and an interpreter of dreams. In his first stanza Bly alludes both to Joseph's "coat stained with goat's blood" and to one of his dreams, in which bundles of his brother's sheaves bow down to him. Bly counts on his readers being familiar with this biblical story and remembering that, at the end of the story, Joseph is reunited with his father and reconciled with his brothers.

To explore his subject in depth Bly draws heavily on the work of Sigmund Freud, the founder of psychoanalysis, and on Freud's student, Carl Jung, another analytical psychologist. Bly draws especially on their detailed studies of dreams and of the ways dreams affect waking life. Jung is perhaps best known for describing what he called the "collective unconscious," a substratum of the psyche in which universal, timeless, and cross-cultural elements meet and merge. Such a collective deep state of mind (itself a kind of "deep image") is most clearly evidenced in dreams or dreamlike reveries. Bly's account of his relationship with his brother—or, in terms of the Jungian trappings in the poem, his "relationship" with a separate side of his own consciousness, a "double" whom he sees as a "brother"—is therefore significant both literally and psychologically in the poem.

By drawing parallels among Jungian theory, the biblical story, early American history, and his own life, Bly stresses the universality of his theme. Further, at the end of his poem, he seems to suggest a resolution similar to that found in the biblical story. Bly's poem resolves itself with the curious and surprising reference to the marmoset ("In the dark the marmoset opens his eyes") in the final line of the poem. The suggestion seems to be that, at the end of the poem, the marmoset, although still asleep, has come to some kind of understanding. He "opens his eyes" and is awakened without literally awakening. This action is in keeping with Bly's larger theme, since he has seemed to suggest throughout the poem that people can understand things, can "see" them—even things they might not know or understand when they are awake—during sleep. In this sense "A Dream of a Brother" is both a dream journey and a dream journal describing that journey.

William V. Davis

A DREAM OF GOVERNORS

Author: Louis Simpson (1923-   )
Type of poem: Lyric
First published: 1957; collected in *A Dream of Governors*, 1959

The Poem

"A Dream of Governors" is the title poem of a five-part collection of twenty-nine poems. This lyric poem is divided into five stanzas, each composed of eight lines. An epigraph borrowed from poet Mark Van Doren provides the source for the poem's title: "The deepest dream is of mad governors." The repetitive use of "dream" in the title and the epigraph suggests a common human experience and a basic framework for the poem. Thus the events occur in a dreamworld in which deeply hidden and subjective thoughts, experiences, wishes, and inner truths surface briefly into consciousness before returning to oblivion. The poem is written in the third person from the standpoint of an objective observer who sees, hears, and feels everything the sleeper does in the dream episode. "A Dream of Governors" also uses the familiar childhood memory of reading or listening to fairy tales. Thus, the first stanza introduces characters and plot suggestive of a typical fantasy. The cast includes a knight and his lady, a dragon, a witch, and a chorus. In this scenario, the knight relives stereotypical plot actions. As a young knight, he travels from far away and accepts the supreme task of combating the city's local enemy, a dragon. After slaying the monster and routing the witch, the brave hero returns and receives his rewards. Crowned king, he marries the lady and plans to live happily ever after.

The second stanza presents emphatic contradictions. All is not well in this imaginary world. Joy has vanished. Physically, decades of idleness have transformed the vigorous hero into an aged monarch whose arduous exploits are ridiculed and recounted poetically as ancient history. The stanza's last two lines stress the ruler's self-doubts and questions. The third stanza reinforces these disturbing thoughts. The first declamatory lines recall the tedious choral platitudes in Greek tragedies. Ironically, the king apparently disregards these allusions to human folly and its ruinous consequences. His reflections parallel Jocasta's generalizations in Sophocles' *Oidipous Tyrannos* (c. 428 B.C.E.; *Oedipus Tyrannus*) that dreams should not be taken seriously. Yet the king's actions in the fourth stanza reverse Jocasta's advice as the monarch responds to the choral wisdom. In his solitary night journey, the king returns to the earlier scene of his heroism and appeals to the witch to restore "evil" and provide him with a goal. The fifth stanza completes the dream odyssey yet leaves the future open. When the queen hears the king's returning footsteps, she closes the storybook, for her husband's request has ended their make-believe, fantasy existence. Together, the royal couple watches the reality and the uncertain fate of their new world begin to unfold.

Forms and Devices

As in his other early poems, Louis Simpson follows the formal rules for regular stanzas, meters, and rhyme in "A Dream of Governors." However, he combines these conventional elements with imaginative images, metaphors, and symbols. Simpson's often-repeated poetic objective, stated in the final chapter of his book *Ships Going into the Blue: Essays and Notes on Poetry* (1994), is drawn from Joseph Conrad's preface to his novel *The Nigger of the "Narcissus"* (1897): "My task which I am trying to achieve is . . . to make you hear, to make you feel—it is, before all, to make you *see.*" Simpson uses traditional rhymed stanzas (*ababcdcd*) and iambic meters (an unaccented syllable followed by an accented syllable representing an emphatic rhythm of sound). Such a tightly controlled, conventional form provides a practical, objective base for launching imaginative, subjective, and emotional imagery or metaphors. Any unusual metaphoric or symbolic content in such a synthesis becomes much more believable and acceptable when wrapped in commonplace formulas.

The central metaphor suggests the implicit analogy between two ostensibly different things: dreams and fairy tales. In his article "Dead Horses and Live Issues" (*A Company of Poets*, 1981), Simpson, describing poetic creation, states, "The images are connected in a dream; and the deeper the dream, the stronger, the more logical, are the connections." Both dreams and fairy tales share this feature: sequences of logically related images or actions. Another parallel points to the term "governors," common to both title and epigraph, which refers to controls or restraints. However, the epigraph's qualifier, "mad," also underlines unconscious dream sensations, emotions, ideas, or even frenetic activities that lack controls or restraints. Key images that stress hearing, feeling, and seeing, combined with imaginative, associational images (mental or literary connections or relations between thoughts, feelings, or sensations arising from previous experiences), dominate the literal details supporting the basic metaphor. Visual images, along with feelings of pity, depict a frustrated and troubled sovereign who is the object of ridicule and who is absorbed with doubts about his worth. Antiphonal declamations of a Greek chorus and of Jocasta's voice echo throughout the third stanza. Moonlight visually illuminates the witch scene in stanza 4. All three imagery patterns flow together in the conclusion. The queen listens to her husband's approaching footsteps; fearful feelings of uncertainty dominate the couple's "silence," for they, recalling Metaphysical poet John Donne's lovers in "The Canonization," watch the significant event in their new world, the birth and rising flight of the winged serpent, rise in "each other's eyes."

One universal conflict, familiar throughout world legends, underscores two symbols. References to the mythic dragon signify humanity's ancient struggle against evil, while the knight represents the universal "Everyman" who battles the foe. His combat is the supreme test of power and control over this primal devil figure who symbolizes the unrestrained instincts that may surface in the deepest dream. One poem, "The Silent Generation," in the fourth section of Simpson's collection *A Dream of Governors*, provides additional thoughts on Adolf Hitler, a contemporary symbol of evil: "It was my generation/ That put the Devil down/ With great enthusiasm./ But

now our occupation/ Is gone. Our education/ Is wasted on the town." The last lines
also repeat the king's motive for restoring evil to the kingdom.

Themes and Meanings

"A Dream of Governors" is a poem about the human condition, about the gover-
nors, the rational and irrational desires and ideas that control human actions. In an-
other sense, it is also about poetic vision, about Simpson's early efforts to demonstrate
his way of seeing, feeling, understanding, and transmitting the meaning that he sees in
the actions and experiences in people's lives. By juxtaposing the literal details and in-
terrelationships of ordinary people in unusual patterns (dreams and fairy tales),
Simpson shows the outer event as well as the inner truth of the experiences, the hidden
reality behind the experiences.

One of the basic desires controlling human actions is the conscious need for feel-
ings of worth, honor, and self-validation gained from societal approval or rewards for
deeds accomplished. The young knight who wants to become a hero by slaying the
evil dragon, receiving a king's crown, and marrying his lady exemplifies this basic de-
sire, the wish fulfillment promised in a dream or fairy tale. Likewise, contemporary
people also have the same ambition to overcome their personal, competitive dragons
and become successful heroes. They, too, dream that their endeavors will merit con-
stant rewards, honor, and praise. Analogously, both fairy-tale heroes and modern peo-
ple suffer frustration, rejection, and self-doubt when their valiant efforts are only a
distant memory and not a constant presence in society's mind, and both suffer when
either of these instincts for self-worth or self-doubt become an obsession that destroys
the balance between rational and irrational thought and actions.

The basic need for keeping balances is another significant controlling force in both
the king's life and in a modern person's life. In "Dead Horses and Live Issues,"
Simpson states that "poetry represents . . . the total mind, including both reason and
unreason." He exposes the fairy-tale king to the traditional echoing maxims about the
ruinous folly of letting extreme behavior or attitudes govern his actions. Simpson
presents opposing views and does not sermonize; he lets the character decide what his
resultant actions will be. Ultimately, this objectivity is what leads the king back to the
battleground. The youthful hero has killed the dragon, but his instinctual fear of it is
buried deep within his mind. His mature self-conquest and his control of his irrational
instincts and fears allow him to balance the extremes between his rational and irratio-
nal thoughts. Therefore, both king and humanity are able to request the restoration of
"evil" to balance their lives. Contemporary humans may read the poem and think it is
only about the fairy-tale king. Some will see the analogy with human conditions.
More likely, readers will see additional levels of meaning. In an interview with Al-
berta Turner in *Fifty Contemporary Poets: The Creative Process* (1977), Simpson
states, "If a poet were sure of the exact meaning of his poem it would be a poem with a
limited meaning. But I want my poetry to open on the unknown."

Betsy P. Harfst

THE DREAM OF THE UNIFIED FIELD

Author: Jorie Graham (1951-   )
Type of poem: Lyric
First published: 1993, in *Materialism*

The Poem

"The Dream of the Unified Field" is a relatively long poem in free verse subdivided into seven sections that are further divided into twelve stanzas. It challenges conventional notions of organizational patterns of poetry while confronting the fallacy behind humankind's desire to unify experience. This fallacy is implied in its title, a reference to Albert Einstein's unsuccessful attempts to prove the theory of the unified field. The speaker (apparently Graham herself) attempts to yoke walking through a snowstorm to take a black leotard to her young daughter together with her own childhood experiences with ballet master Madame Sakaroff and finally with the initial contact of Christopher Columbus with the New World. As she weaves through the poem, she connects the immediate and personal with the distant and impersonal in ways that work naturally as well as in ways that she must force to work, thus reinforcing the impact of the title.

In the first section of the poem, as the speaker treks through the snow to carry the leotard to her daughter, she becomes caught in the "motion" of the snow—the patterns it creates in falling, the "arabesques" that it, like her daughter, performs. The transience of the snowflakes, "Gone as they hit the earth," also strikes her as she moves through their motion, finding in their symbols a clue to her own meaning, her own existence.

Upon completion of her task, she is taken by the sight and sound of a "huge flock of starlings" coursing through the snow and finally alighting in ever-shifting patterns on a bare-limbed oak tree. "Foliage of the tree of the world's waiting" she calls them, and they return her to the vision of her daughter through the window as she performs her pirouettes: "I watch the head explode, then recollect, explode, recollect."

Drawn by the screech of a single crow in the midst of the flock of starlings, the speaker feels the emptiness in her pocket which once held the balled-up leotard, and, "terrified" at that emptiness, returns to watch the unknowing child through the window. The crow draws her attention more closely, and she minutely separates the colors that make up his "blackness" as he suddenly lifts and ascends in one "blunt clean stroke" only to land to disappear again.

Crowlike, the vision of Madame Sakaroff in her studio in Stalingrad intrudes upon her consciousness. Uniting "The dream of Europe" with the New World, black crow with black dress, bird with "bird-headed knob," the vision of Madame Sakaroff brings in more explicitly the need to connect with or reject old patterns of belief. "*No one must believe in God again*," the speaker hears as, entranced, she watches Madame Sakaroff encounter herself ("her eyes eyed themselves") in the "silver film" of the mirror. That vision, however, ultimately proves unsuccessful; the speaker finds in it "no signal" and "no information" as she turns helplessly to the window of her present, seeking "what" she "should know to save" her child.

Unable to "know," she centers herself within the snowstorm, taking possession of it as well as the blizzard of her own experiences, and, through them, the "Age behind the clouds, The Great Heights." Her own desire to possess, to seek, to know becomes connected with an explorer, the "Admiral" Christopher Columbus as he, also in the midst of a snowstorm (a fiction manufactured to force the unity that may not really exist), takes harbor in Puerto de San Nicolas and places the cross signalling possession "on a conspicuous height." As the speaker had clothed her daughter in the black leotard, he clothes the young "very black Indian" woman captured by his men and returns her (apparently against her will) to her people. The final vision of the poem is the glint of gold on her nose "which was a sign there was/ gold/ on that land."

Forms and Devices

Appropriately for a poem first appearing in a collection entitled *Materialism*, "The Dream of the Unified Field" contains startlingly vivid images that seek to re-create actual experience. Not technically metaphors, the images nonetheless interconnect and react on each other, reinforcing the impact as they amass. The blackness of the leotard, the blackness of the birds, the blackness of Madame Sakaroff, even the blackness of the Indian girl all contribute to the "dream" of unity that informs the poem. Similarly, the patterning and repatterning of the dance ("I watch the head explode then recollect, explode, recollect"), the birds on the tree ("scatter, blow away, scatter, recollect"), the swirling snow ("the arabesques and runnels, gathering and loosening"), and experience ("they stick, accrue,/ grip up, connect") unite the patterning and repatterning of history, thought, and meaning both in the individual and the species. This movement reflects the building of imagery in the poem from the personal experience in the opening to the quintessential experience of burgeoning civilization at the end. Connecting these experiences is the long road, the footfall, the "white sleeping geography" often obscured by blinding snow and often directionless. It is briefly lit only by the flash of the silver mirror, the glint of the gold on the girl's nose.

The ever-changing imagery of the poem provides the perfect vehicle for the cinematic techniques that critic Helen Vendler, in *The Given and the Made* (1995), see as pervasive in Graham's poetry: "close and far focus, panning, jump-cutting, emphasis on point of view and looking." In this poem Graham employs each of these techniques, from the close-up of the crow to the panorama as it streaks into the air and lands again, from the jumps from bird to child, from child to woman, and from woman to admiral. These techniques are reinforced by the cinematic frames provided by the window that forms a frame through which she watches her daughter dance and the mirror that doubles the image of Madame Sakaroff.

The interlaced imagery in the poem also gives rise to organic patterns of lineation. Vendler notes that the use of long lines and long sentences is a distinguishing characteristic of Graham's work. In an interview with Thomas Gardner in *Denver Quarterly* 26 (Spring, 1992), Graham attributes these long lines to her need to write in lines that contain more than the typical five stresses, because they cannot be spoken or even understood "in one breath unit for the most part (and since our desire *is* to grasp them in one breath unit) [it] causes us to read the line very quickly."

Reading quickly leads, she feels, to a "rush in the line" that creates "a very different relationship with the silence: one that makes it aggressive—or at least oceanic—something that won't stay at bay. You have *fear* in the rush that can perhaps cause you to hear the *fearful* in what is rushed against." This "rush" is evident throughout "The Dream of the Unified Field" in the dashes that link images and concepts ("the century—minutes, houses going by—The Great/ Heights—") as it is in the long lines that attempt to capture and hold the essence and music of experience. An example is Madame Sakaroff's encounter with herself ("I . . ./ saw the light rippling almost shuddering where her body finally/ touched/ the image, the silver film between them like something that would have/ shed itself in nature now"). In *The Breaking of Style: Hopkins, Heaney, Graham* (1995), Vendler finds a metaphor of "Earthly desire itself" in Graham's lineation, "desire always prolonging itself further and further over a gap it nonetheless does not wish to close. In this search by desire, mind will always outrun body."

Themes and Meanings

Finding meaning in existence, finding patterns in experience, connecting in a world that has, for the most part, lost its religious and philosophical underpinning lies at the core of "The Dream of the Unified Field." Graham brings together the New World and the Old, America and Europe, innocence and experience, nature and civilization. She does so in a way that makes sense, but in a way that also seems deliberately to challenge readers to accept the connections, urges them to doubt the logic. As Graham moves from image to image, the reader must make a leap of faith, holding each in mind until, finally, at the end they coalesce into one image of desire, of longing—to possess, to protect, to comprehend, to save. Even the end is not the end, however. It is actually the beginning, with the gleam of gold luring the reader even as it lured Columbus and his followers to ever-present possibility, to the potential that is being alive. That the poem does not circle back on itself, that it does not return to the sight of the child in the black leotard but ends instead with the "very black Indian" girl with the "little piece of/ gold on her nose" brings the poem back to the title instead, to the "dream" that the unified field exists.

Jaquelyn W. Walsh

DREAM VARIATIONS

Author: Langston Hughes (1902-1967)
Type of poem: Lyric
First published: 1924, as "Dream Variation"; collected in *The Weary Blues*, 1926

The Poem

"Dream Variations" (originally "Dream Variation") consists of two stanzas, the first of nine lines, the second of eight. Its title connects it with one of Langston Hughes's major themes: dreams, especially the dreams of African Americans.

The variations referred to in the title are those that the second stanza introduces: The first eight lines of stanza 1 correspond closely, line by line, with the eight lines of stanza 2. The first lines of the two stanzas are in fact identical, but thereafter stanza 2 varies from stanza 1, sometimes by the change of but a word, sometimes by more pronounced changes. The most dramatic variation is in line 3: "To whirl and to dance" becomes "Dance! Whirl! Whirl!"

The poem is written in the first person, so it is tempting to associate the speaker with the poet himself. Yet the speaker could be either male or female (nothing in the poem is gender-specific), and Hughes's biographer, Arnold Rampersad, refers to the speaker's "childlike, perhaps androgynous persona." There is certainly a quality of innocence in the speaker's tone and therefore in the poem as a whole.

Although there is a period after the first four lines of each stanza, those lines do not constitute a complete sentence. Apparently, the period is there to make the reader pause and reflect on the opening lines before going on to complete each stanza's thought. Thematically, what divides each stanza is that the first four lines allude to daylight hours, the fifth and sixth lines to the transitional phase of evening, and the seventh and eighth lines to the coming of night. The contrast between light and dark is central to the poem.

There is a strong suggestion that the light and dark hours of the day correlate with white and black cultures and people. Thus "the white day" not only refers to the time when the sun is out but also hints at the whole workaday world in which white people (in the young Langston Hughes's experience) were mostly in charge. The poem's black speaker explicitly associates night with himself or herself: It is "Dark like me" and "Black like me."

Forms and Devices

The central contrast between light and dark, day and night, white and black, extends to the activities and the images associated with each. Daylight hours are the time of energetic exertion: Flinging arms, whirling, dancing; these exertions may be taken as representative in some degree of all daytime (and public) activities. Evening is associated with rest, night with gentleness, tenderness (and privacy). In the daytime, the self may assert itself, express itself, and expend its force; at night, there is recovery and, by implication, love.

If the most striking action of the poem is the daylight's dancing, whirling, the most striking image of the poem is the "tall tree" beneath which one may rest at evening. In the second stanza, the speaker becomes "A tall, slim tree"; the night, a personified presence, envelops and is unified with that phallic tree. That this union is implicitly sexual is reinforced by the language describing the way in which night approaches: "comes on gently," "coming tenderly."

The poem's sexual overtones are subtle; the speaker in the poem seems not to be fully conscious of them. This is part of the childlike, innocent aspect of the poem, and it is underscored by the poem's purposefully simple vocabulary. All seventy-seven words in the poem are readily accessible; none is obscure. Moreover, seventy-one of them are words of one syllable (five have two syllables, only one has three).

Each stanza begins with a succession of one-syllable words: In each case, "evening," at the end of line 5, breaks the string. All words of more than one syllable appear in lines 5 through 7. They are words that caress the ear with soft *n* and *ing* sounds (evening, Beneath, gently, evening, coming, tenderly). This reinforces the experience that these lines describe, the sense of which is conveyed overtly by words such as "gently" and "tenderly." The trisyllabic "tenderly" is climactically positioned, for effect. Then each stanza ends, as it began, with monosyllables, their clipped, staccato effect intensified by the clicking *k* sounds: "Dark like me," then "Black like me."

Evening is "cool" and "pale": The tactile and visual senses alike are muted. Rest replaces motion; the stationary tree replaces the whirling figure. Night is static, centripetal, rooted, but it is also more complex, more humane. There is something uncomfortably confrontational about flinging one's "arms wide/ In the face of the sun"—but night's confrontation is gentle, tender. At the end, the poem resolves with the blackness, not of oblivion, but a kind of fulfillment.

Themes and Meanings

Hughes wrote about dreams throughout his career, in virtually every book of poems he published. It could be argued that dreams represent the dominant theme in his poetry. "Dream Variations" is one of his earliest poems to articulate a dream, and in its enigmatic duality it is accurately representative—expressive—of its author.

The dream is dual because it embraces, or seeks to embrace, day and night, light and dark, white and black, and the other polarities associated with these: motion and rest, flux and stasis, performances both public and private. The middle line of the poem—"That is my dream!"—points to everything that comes before it, and, since the last eight lines recapitulate the first eight, it points as well to everything that follows. The duality is enigmatic, because the poem's images are ambiguous. What, if anything, apart from themselves, do the whirling and dancing stand for? How can the dream embrace both day and night and all that is associated with each? How does the poem, or how can the reader, reconcile the polarities?

Careful use of biographical materials can sometimes provide insights into a poet's work, and Rampersad's excellent two-volume *The Life of Langston Hughes* (1986) convincingly argues that Hughes was "a divided man" in his attitudes toward and feelings about race. This insight may provide one way (among many potential ways) of approaching "Dream Variations."

Hughes was of mixed ancestry, both genetically and in terms of values. He was descended from radical abolitionists, black and white, but had a father who, deep down, despised black people, including himself. Growing up, Hughes lived in both segregated and integrated neighborhoods, and he mainly attended integrated, predominantly white schools (in Kansas, Illinois, and Ohio), where he excelled. He spent an unhappy year at Columbia University, on the edge of Harlem. Part of him wanted success and recognition in the world largely controlled by whites; part of him wanted only complete solidarity with black people and black culture.

"Dream Variations" was written in Africa in 1923, during its author's first visit there (as a crew member on a freighter), and it reflects Hughes's exuberance on first leaving the Western Hemisphere, his excitement on first arriving in Africa, a certain degree of ambition, and also a measure of ambiguity. Hughes had written of Africa before he had known it firsthand: in high school, comparing a classmate with an Egyptian queen ("When Sue Wears Red"); just out of high school, tracing his heritage in waterways from the Mississippi to the Nile, the Congo, and the Euphrates ("The Negro Speaks of Rivers"). Africa was, however, much different from what he had imagined. Not only was it less glamorous and, with disease and different forms of exploitation, uglier than he had anticipated, but it was also less welcoming of him than he had hoped it would be. His copper-colored skin and nearly straight hair caused Africans to call him a white man—to his chagrin.

In "Dream Variations," Hughes expresses a desire to belong to, and hints at a fear of being rejected by, both worlds: white and black, West and East. What the poem describes is not an actuality but a dream. With the repetition in the second stanza, a wistful note creeps into the poem, and that is where one may be able to detect a hint of fear (or perhaps anxiety is a better word for the feeling). The twenty-one-year-old Hughes dreams of a grand cultural synthesis, in his own person and work. He would spend the remaining forty-four years of his life seeking to actualize the dream.

Richard Bizot

DREAMING IN DAYLIGHT

Author: Robert Penn Warren (1905-1989)
Type of poem: Meditation
First published: 1979; collected in *Being Here: Poetry, 1977-1980,* 1980

The Poem

"Dreaming in Daylight" is a poem in free verse; its forty-one lines are divided into twenty unrhymed couplets plus one final, single-line phrase. The title suggests the contradictory images of darkness and light and of nighttime dreaming (in which intuition and emotion have full play) and daydreaming (which connotes rational meditation). Written from the second-person singular point of view, the poem's only implied persona is poet Robert Penn Warren, who is also the speaker of the poem. Addressing himself as "you," he recounts to the reader personal experiences grounded in a familiar activity: a mountain climb.

In the first two stanzas, the climber energetically clambers up rocks, through thickets, and over brooks. Stopping for breath, he quotes some verse and then perceives—in the next three stanzas—that "Small eyes, or larger, with glitter in darkness, are watching" from stone crevices, leaf shadows, and hollow logs. To the climber, the eyes of nature are "like conscience . . ./ Like remorse" judging him as an outsider who does not belong. The speaker's interpretation of a watchful nature prepares the reader for the next fourteen lines. Falling into meditation about self, he complains of feeling a mysterious, internal, and physical unease that sparks a concern about his own identity: "Do you/ Know your own name?" Questioning himself as he questions the reader, the poet describes the sea below as a "heaving ocean of pastness" from which he is trying to escape. However, his flight causes him regret: "Oh, try/ To think of something your life has meant." As he seeks to contemplate his life's meaning, he admits he is more a stranger to himself than to nature.

After the twelfth couplet, there is a shift from internal to external action as the climber energetically resumes the ascent, moving higher—"For the past creeps behind you, like foam"—until he reaches the isolated peak. Now at the peak, the climber again becomes reflective and urgently admonishes himself to remember the few people he has truly loved. In the poem's last seven lines, the climber returns to his bed and wakes from his recurrent dream of being spied upon by peering, "dark-glistening" eyes. The speaker, in the last line, repeats his failure of self-discovery. The dream of the daylight has become one with the dream of night. The poet's vision is triggered by precise observation of details in nature that become metaphors for unfulfilled quests or unanswered questions. The poem concludes with the recurrent image of the alienating eyes of nature that mysteriously instill a feeling of guilt or regret in the poet for remaining a stranger to himself.

Forms and Devices

References to nature abound in Warren's poems, providing him with much of his inspiration and imagery, and "Dreaming in Daylight" is no exception. The mountain landscape seen by the climber at first presents friendly, explicit images: rocks, thickets, brooks, birches, crevices, and leaves. Yet these become implicit images of isolation and estrangement such as the "stern rock, majestic and snagged" that is a "sky-bare" peak where frost has destroyed any vegetation. They also become images of alienation: glittering, reproachful eyes peering from a "rotted-out log, from earth-aperture," metaphors for conscience or remorse that imply that the climber does not belong on the mountain. Below the mountain is a "beach of/ History" and a sea of the past from which the climber is seeking to escape by moving higher. Both serve as metaphors for the poet's concern with related issues of self-identity. Such imagery clarifies Warren's less-than-sanguine attitude toward nature. In his introduction to Joseph Conrad's novel *Nostromo* (1904), Warren observes that "man is precariously balanced in his humanity between the black inward abyss of himself and the black outward abyss of nature." Similar examples of a threatening nature can be found in Warren's later poems.

The syntax offers a variety of long and short sentences, with many phrases or sentences interrupted at the end of one stanza and completed in the next: "This/ Is the end." This structure lends a sense of ebb and flow, of activity and thought stopping and starting. The athletic and expended energy of the mountain ascent is suggested by action verbs and active images: "clamber," "crash," "leap," "past birches," "up bluff-side." However, when the climber stops and meditates the verbs become more passive and imply internal activity: "feel," "try to think," "know," "wake," and forms of the verb "to be." Sometimes action and nonaction verbs are juxtaposed to suggest that the physical activity of the climb is interrupted by periodic contemplation: "Move higher!/ For the past creeps behind you" and "You clamber up the few mossed shards that frost has ripped off./ Then stop." The poem's last five lines, as the speaker wakes from a dream, employ verbs such as "wake" and "peer" and reinforce the recurrent images of the eyes of nature "dark-glistening, like/ Conscience." The images reactivate thought of one's alienation and ignorance of self.

The continual use of the second-person singular, even though the speaker is clearly the protagonist, is significant. The poet disguises himself behind "you" and in so doing pulls the readers into his experience, compelling them to consider the same issues of identity and life's meaning that he does. At the poem's conclusion, after twenty stanzas of recurrent image patterns and self-accusatory questions, Warren characteristically concludes the work by reiterating the persona's realization that he is less a stranger to nature than to himself.

Themes and Meanings

Written when Warren was in his seventies, "Dreaming in Daylight" appears in the collection *Being Here: Poetry, 1977-1980*. In an afterword, Warren discloses that the poems are placed in thematic order "played against, or with, a shadowy narrative, a shadowy autobiography." Within the five divisions of poems moving from childhood to youth to old age, the poem at hand is listed in part 2, which finds the poet (the protagonist of all the poems) in young manhood after initially wrestling as a boy in part 1 with childhood memories and issues of life and death. Like other works in its division, the poem treats one of Warren's major themes: man's ageless drive toward self-discovery and self-determination.

Victor H. Standberg, in *The Poetic Vision of Robert Penn Warren* (1977), suggests that for Warren, individuals encounter a sense of alienation as they search for their identity in a perplexing, often corrupt or indifferent world. To overcome estrangement and pursue their intended purpose, they must undergo a period of intense self-examination that ideally can lead to further knowledge about self and the world. Although the search may not always end in success, Warren does not counsel giving up. In this piece, the poet searches for his identity within nature, a typical Warren landscape. Yet in spite of his initial joy in seeking unity with nature, the poet finds in nature no oneness but rather rejection embodied by hidden animal eyes telling him he does not belong there. The author seems to posit that the natural world is indifferent to human affairs and is neither helpful nor sympathetic as a guide in interpreting human life and in answering questions of life and death. Consequently, the climber experiences the pain of isolation and estrangement in his attempted communication with the forces of nature. He feels with dread that some mysterious internal activity "like gastritis or migraine" is going on inside himself (which may be reminiscent of the cancer or stroke that felled his parents in earlier poems). With nightmarish energy, the climber ascends ever higher to flee from the pursuing foam of the waters of the past and from history below, whose contemplation is essential to identity.

In *Knowledge and the Image of Man* (1975), Warren explains that "man's process of self-definition means that he distinguishes himself from the world and from other men. He . . . discovers separateness . . . and the pain of self-criticism and the pain of isolation." The poem's protagonist has distanced himself from the past and from history to find himself ousted by nature, abandoned by the companionship of memory, and reduced to trying desperately to recall the few people he has ever loved. Finally, the poet, waking from a nightmare ("a dream of eyes"), realizes that he has not yet achieved self-discovery. The seeker of the self has not been successful in the search. The poem may be seen as the emergence of the poet's artistic purpose or perhaps even as the final-phase efforts of a poet nearing his life's end. Yet clearly the work represents major Warren themes and demonstrates his marked accessibility to readers.

Christian H. Moe

DREAMS OF THE ANIMALS

Author: Margaret Atwood (1939-   )
Type of poem: Verse essay
First published: 1970, in *Procedures for Underground*

The Poem

Margaret Atwood's "Dreams of the Animals" consists of several verse paragraphs that explore the nature of animal "dreams" and force readers to reexamine their ideas about what distinguishes humans from animals. By assuming that animals do, in fact, dream, Atwood obliterates traditional beliefs about their mental and intellectual limitations and makes them quite human. The notion that animals "mostly . . . dream/ of other animals each according to its own kind" has a biblical ring and does seem to suggest that animal dreams lack the complexity and range of human ones. After all, moles dream of "mole smells," and frogs dream of "green and golden/ frogs."

Atwood, however, includes an indented parenthetical verse paragraph that states that some animals have "nightmares" of impending death; the ability to imagine, to anticipate what might happen, is a far cry from behavior modification, of merely reacting because of conditioning. The speaker describes the dreams of moles, frogs, fish, and birds. For the most part, the dreams are idyllic, but two dreams extend the range of animal dreams. The fish dream of "defence, attack meaningful/ patterns," and the birds dream of "territories/ enclosed by singing." The first dream connotes stratagems, and the second, acquisitions; both are usually associated with human behavior.

Halfway through the poem the dreams turn sour: "Sometimes the animals dream of evil." After repeating the first two lines about the animals dreaming "mostly" of other animals, the speaker catalogues a series of "exceptions." What distinguishes the silver fox, the armadillo, and the iguana from the mole, frog, fish, and bird is their captive state. The fox is in a roadside zoo; the armadillo is caged near a train station; and the iguana is in the window of a "petshop." In this state the fox's dreams are violent ("their necks bitten"), and the armadillo and iguana are beyond reason and sanity. In fact, the armadillo "no longer dreams/ but is insane when waking." While people can be judged insane, animals are not traditionally regarded as insane; they are more often described as "crazed," a word that is more appropriate to their appearance than to their mental state. Animals can only be insane if they were once sane—the enclosure has affected not only their bodies but also their minds.

In the case of the iguana, imprisonment has destroyed the animal's mind: The caged environment of "water-dish and sawdust" reduced the "royal-eyed" iguana to dreaming only of "sawdust," the residue after humankind has used nature for its own purposes. By removing animals from their habitats in order to exploit them financially (as pets to be sold or as objects to be exhibited for profit), humans have destroyed the minds of "dumb animals." Destruction of this magnitude can only be accomplished if the destroyers regard their victims as "less" than themselves.

Forms and Devices

In order to demonstrate the relationship between humans and animals, Atwood early on portrays humans as threatening creatures seen from the point of view of "certain mice and small rodents," whose nightmares contain "a huge pink/ shape with five claws descending." This nightmare suggests a laboratory setting complete with human investigator ("pink/ shape") and laboratory animals. From the perspective of the animals, the hand of the scientist, ostensibly conducting research for humankind's benefit, seems like "five claws." In effect, rather than personifying animals, as is often the case in literature, the speaker has robbed the scientist of his humanity and likened him to an animal, thereby raising a question about what constitutes "animal behavior."

The poem also explores the nature of the animal kingdom by comparing the "meaningful/ patterns" of the fish with the patterned "figure eights" run repeatedly by the caged armadillo, "its piglet feet pattering." The alliteration, which slows the pace and stresses the importance of the phrase, calls attention to "pattering," which, because of its likeness to the earlier "patterns," contrasts animals free in nature with those enclosed by humans. The possibility also exists that the "red and black/ striped fish" may be tropical fish enclosed within an aquarium, just as the birds, which dream of enclosing territories by singing, may be "enclosed" by netting or wire in an aviary. The ambiguity may also suggest the extent of human enclosure of animals.

Atwood also uses alliteration with the iguana—"crested, royal-eyed, ruling"—but the tone here is mock heroic because the "kingdom" that the iguana ironically rules is one of "water-dish and sawdust." The dish suggests the extent to which the animal has been made dependent upon humans, and the sawdust, with the "dust" it includes, suggests the biblical phrase "ashes to ashes and dust to dust," apocalyptic images that permeate *Procedures for Underground*. The circumscribed kingdom is not appropriate for a royal ruler with a crest.

The poem is almost equally divided between idyllic dreams and more problematic ones, and the division is visually apparent because the "exceptions" and the parenthetical verse paragraph about the laboratory animals are indented. In effect, the reader encounters reassuring material about the nature of animal dreams, but that material is undermined, subverted by evidence of how humans have exploited animals and dehumanized themselves in the process. By ending the poem with "dreams of sawdust," the only one-line verse paragraph in the poem, Atwood reiterates her notion that the potential that lies within animals has been reduced to fragments by humans who have lost their prized "humanity" in the process.

Themes and Meanings

In Atwood's fiction and poetry, animals play a significant role. Two years before *Procedures for Underground* appeared, Atwood published *The Animals in That Country*, in which she writes of anthropomorphic characters, those who are given animal characteristics. *Procedures for Underground* is saturated with poems about animals; the first poem in the volume is entitled "Eden Is a Zoo," which relates animals to memory and dream, the focus of "Dreams of the Animals." Among her writings are accounts of her visits to the zoo in Toronto, which makes her feel "nervous" because she feels that when animals are contained in an environment more suited to inanimate objects the animals go mad or die. In fact, the process of becoming inanimate is the process of dying.

"Dreams of the Animals" does describe the effects of enclosure, but it also, through the inclusion of the laboratory animals, condemns the use of animals for experimentation. The poem is certainly contemporary, for animal rights are being debated in terms of raising animals, wearing furs, and testing perfumes. What is unusual about the poem is that readers are given the animals' perspective and that humans are seen as monsters. Atwood suggests that humans and animals are interdependent and that when animals become objects, people are likewise reduced in terms of their humanity.

Procedures for Underground is also about the underworld, suggesting the existence of two worlds, one the material "real" one and one a psychic world, from which the real world can be seen differently. That is, readers see a familiar world of animals, but there is another way of regarding that world, of subverting it, and that subversive view forces readers to reevaluate assumptions they have about the nature of humans and animals. In the poem, the subversion occurs in the indented lines or the parenthetical ones, suggesting that the ideas are afterthoughts that cannot be repressed or delayed: The colon that begins line 7 would logically be placed after the end of line 4 or line 6; its position in line 7 stresses the break in thought.

The speaker, who is inseparable from Atwood, states one thing—animals dream mostly about other animals—but then undercuts that assertion. Atwood thereby deconstructs her readers' illusions and exposes them as superficial, self-serving, and egocentric. The poem itself is, as the title of the book implies, a procedure, a process necessary for an "underground," subterranean, subversive view of what readers see as their real world.

Thomas L. Erskine